AI Applications and Strategies in Teacher Education

Krista LaRue Keeley
Saskatchewan Teachers' Federation, Canada

IGI Global
Publishing Tomorrow's Research Today

Published in the United States of America by
IGI Global Scientific Publishing
701 East Chocolate Avenue
Hershey, PA, 17033, USA
Tel: 717-533-8845
Fax: 717-533-8661
E-mail: cust@igi-global.com
Website: https://www.igi-global.com

Library of Congress Cataloging-in-Publication Data

Names: Keeley, Krista LaRue, 1988- editor.
Title: AI applications and strategies in teacher education / edited by Krista LaRue Keeley.
Other titles: Artificial intelligence applications and strategies in teacher education
Description: Hershey, PA : Information Science Reference, [2025] | Includes bibliographical references and index. | Summary: "This book serves a multifaceted objective, aiming to elucidate the myriad ways in which AI can be applied in teacher education, fostering a deeper understanding of AI concepts among educators, and contributing to broader educational frameworks. By accomplishing these objectives, the book aspires to contribute significantly to the existing body of research, offering insights that are both practical and visionary"-- Provided by publisher.

Identifiers: LCCN 2024042572 (print) | LCCN 2024042573 (ebook) | ISBN 9798369354438 (h/c) | ISBN 9798369354445 (s/c) | ISBN 9798369354452 (ebook)
Subjects: LCSH: Artificial intelligence--Educational applications. | Teachers--Training of.
Classification: LCC LB1028.43 .A375 2025 (print) | LCC LB1028.43 (ebook) | DDC 370.285/63--dc23/eng/20241106
LC record available at https://lccn.loc.gov/2024042572
LC ebook record available at https://lccn.loc.gov/2024042573

Vice President of Editorial: Melissa Wagner
Managing Editor of Acquisitions: Mikaela Felty
Managing Editor of Book Development: Jocelynn Hessler
Production Manager: Mike Brehm
Cover Design: Phillip Shickler

British Cataloguing in Publication Data
A Cataloguing in Publication record for this book is available from the British Library.

Table of Contents

Detailed Table of Contents

The introduction of artificial intelligence (AI) has become a transformative force. And the integration of AI into K-12 classrooms has the potential for being a transformative force, although that has yet to be determined. Within a short amount of time, the emergence of AI programs and tools has redefined the boundaries of teaching and learning in the digital era, and thus, future educators enrolled in teacher preparation programs need to be familiar with and understand how to use and integrate AI tools within the instructional environment. Examining how and when to utilize AI with teacher preparation candidates is explored through unpacking and providing an overview of what AI looks like in K-12 education; exploring the pedagogical shifts that are needed to utilize AI; examining the inclusion of AI tools in one specific course for early childhood/elementary education majors, as well as, the themes that emerged; and providing recommendations for the reasons that AI should be incorporated into pre-service teacher preparation programs.

Recent advancements in artificial intelligence (AI) have sparked transformative possibilities in education, particularly in the realm of personalized classroom management strategies. This chapter explores the multifaceted effects of AI-powered approaches on educational settings. By leveraging AI algorithms, educators can tailor learning experiences to individual student needs, fostering a more engaging and effective educational environment. The primary objectives of this chapter are (a) to investigate the effectiveness of AI-powered personalized classroom management strategies in promoting positive student behavior, (b) to examine the impact of personalized interventions on student engagement and academic achievement, (c) To explore teachers' perceptions of AI-driven classroom management and their experiences with implementing personalized strategies, and (d) to identify best practices and recommendations for integrating AI-powered personalized classroom management strategies into educational settings.

Assessment practices in education are undergoing a significant transformation with the integration of artificial intelligence (AI) technologies. This chapter explores the evolving role of AI in revolutionizing assessment methods across educational contexts. By automating various aspects of assessment, AI offers educators and learners unprecedented opportunities for efficiency, personalization, and scalability. AI-powered assessment tools enable the automation of grading, providing educators with more time to focus on providing personalized feedback and guiding student learning. Additionally, AI can analyze vast amounts of data to identify patterns in student performance, allowing for targeted interventions and adaptive learning experiences tailored to individual needs. Furthermore, AI facilitates the development of innovative assessment formats, such as simulations and interactive scenarios, which can better assess higher-order thinking skills and real-world application of knowledge.

The interest of implementing cutting-edge technology has always been potent in education. Artificial intelligence (AI) has the potential of being a ubiquitous powerful tool that promises personalized learning, adaptive curriculum, and enhanced engagement. This chapter investigates the growing attention for integrating AI in education, with a specific focus on its application in the English as a second language (ESL) classroom. Therefore, through the lens of established ESL pedagogical principles, the authors explore the potential benefits and inherent challenges of implementing AI tools into ESL classrooms, offering practical strategies and activities that highlight AI's strengths while mitigating its limitations.

There is revolutionary potential when artificial intelligence (AI) is used into education. The use of AI in educational systems holds promise for individualized instruction and evaluation. It has, nevertheless, also made clear several serious biases and shortcomings. This chapter critically investigates the biases—such as cultural biases and socioeconomic disparities—that are ingrained in AI algorithms used in education. It looks at how inadequate AI is at meeting a range of student needs, including socioeconomic understanding and complicated emotional states. A framework is put forth to address these problems: data-driven diversity, ethical AI design, transparency and accountability, human-AI collaboration, and ongoing assessment and improvement. By putting these tactics into practice, stakeholders can minimize prejudices and fully utilize AI's promise, creating fair and productive learning environments for all students.

This chapter presents a novel GenAI tool, called PBL Support Chatbot, designed to support project-based learning (PBL) by integrating retrieval-augmented generation (RAG) and knowledge graphs (KGs). The aim is to address common challenges in PBL, such as project complexity and curriculum alignment. The tool provides students with real-time, adaptive support through a chatbot that assists in navigating PBL tasks. To illustrate its application, the authors introduce a scenario involving an introductory computer programming course where students develop a text-based adventure game. By offering personalized guidance, immediate feedback, and accurate answers to student inquiries, the tool aims to enhance critical thinking, learning outcomes, knowledge application, and student engagement in PBL environments. The initial prototype demonstrates the potential to improve the PBL learning experience. This underscores the capability of using RAG to create a dynamic, interactive learning environment that aligns with students' individual learning paths and educational goals.

The chapter examines the impact of artificial intelligence (AI) on academic integrity and human cognitive development. It highlights the potential negative effects of AI on learning experiences, such as reduced critical thinking and creativity. The chapter emphasizes the need for maintaining academic integrity in AI-driven educational systems to create an ethical learning environment. It also emphasizes the need to strike a balance between AI and human involvement to maximize benefits while mitigating drawbacks. The chapter highlights the importance of understanding AI's impact on academic integrity and cognitive development for educators, policymakers, and researchers to make informed decisions and promote healthy educational practices in the digital era.

This chapter examines the data privacy challenges posed by AI-driven education and offers strategic solutions to protect student information. The authors explore how AI systems are collecting various types of student data, from test scores to social interactions, and what this means for privacy. Through real-world examples, the authors shed light on worrying trends, like excessive surveillance and potential data breaches. The authors also tackle the legal and ethical questions that arise when AI meets education and point out how current laws often fall short in this rapidly developing field. Key findings reveal the inadequacy of current regulations and the potential for AI to exacerbate existing educational inequalities. The authors recommend implementing comprehensive data governance policies, investing in educator training on AI and privacy, and incorporating data literacy into curricula. The chapter emphasizes the need for a balanced approach that harnesses AI's benefits while protecting students' privacy through technical solutions, policy reforms, and enhanced digital literacy.

This chapter aims to compare the performances of pre-service science teachers (PSTs) and generative artificial intelligence (AI) application (ChatGPT) in answering nature of science (NoS) myths. In this study, which was designed according to a qualitative descriptive research design, the 15 most frequently encountered NoS myths were addressed to 104 PSTs and the ChatGPT. The data were analyzed using content analysis. As a result of the research, when the items related to all myths were analyzed, approximately 48% of the PSTs had myths about the NoS, while 66% of the ChatGPT answers included correct information. Therefore, ChatGPT can be effective in seeking answers to NoS myths. However, since the resources used by ChatGPT are limited to certain books, contents, or resources of certain countries, it may not be efficient enough in terms of providing information diversity. According to these results, comparison of PSTs and ChatGPT's answers are discussed.

Preface

Artificial Intelligence (AI) is reshaping the way we live, work, and learn. For educators, understanding and effectively integrating AI into the classroom is no longer a distant challenge but an essential part of preparing students for the future. This book is designed to support educators at all levels—whether they are instructors in teacher education programs, in K-12, or higher education—in not only comprehending what AI is but also applying it practically in their teaching practices.

In an age where technology is rapidly evolving, the use of AI in education has the potential to transform learning environments. From personalized learning experiences and automated grading to intelligent tutoring systems, AI offers a suite of tools that can make learning more effective, engaging, and equitable. Yet, many educators still face uncertainty or hesitation in adopting AI due to the complexity of the technology or misconceptions about its role in the classroom. This book seeks to demystify AI by providing both theoretical and practical insights into its application in educational contexts.

At its core, this book presents a holistic view on how AI can support teachers in their practice, as well as scientific, evidence-based examples and case studies that demonstrate AI's power and usefulness. These examples serve not only to highlight the vast potential of AI in improving educational outcomes but also to ground its use in research and practice. By illustrating real-world applications—such as adaptive learning platforms, data-driven decision-making, and AI-enhanced pedagogical strategies—this book offers educators a roadmap for how to incorporate AI meaningfully into their curriculum. Each chapter delves into different aspects of AI in education, from technical explanations to pedagogical benefits, providing readers with a comprehensive guide to AI's multifaceted role.

One of the key messages of this book is the importance of AI integration at every educational level. From K-12 classrooms, where AI can support differentiated instruction and enhance student engagement, to higher education and Teacher Education programs, where AI can enable more sophisticated analyses of student progress and personalized learning paths, the relevance of AI is universal. Those educators who understand and embrace AI in their teaching practices will be better equipped to not only improve their students' educational experiences but also to prepare the next generation for a future in which AI will play a significant role.

This book serves as a practical and strategic resource for educators who wish to stay at the forefront of innovation in teaching. By exploring the intersection of AI and education through in-depth analyses and case studies, it emphasizes the transformative potential of AI in creating more responsive, adaptive, and inclusive learning environments. In doing so, it empowers educators to not only utilize AI to enhance their classrooms but to also become leaders in guiding the next generation through the ever-evolving landscape of technology.

I was compelled to edit this book after developing the AI-Assisted Teacher Wellness Theory, which posits that the power of AI tools extends beyond practical applications and can positively impact teacher wellness. At a time when educator wellness is at an all-time low, AI offers potential solutions that go beyond the classroom to improve the overall well-being of teachers. This idea grew out of a personal and professional realization that while educators are continually asked to do more with less, AI can provide support that alleviates some of these burdens, allowing teachers to focus on what truly matters—connecting with and supporting their students.

When I first developed this theory, AI was still in its infancy in educational spaces. However, within just a year, AI has evolved at an extraordinary pace, and researchers, teachers, and scholars have begun to tackle some of the most pressing questions regarding its use in education: Is it ethical? Is it practical? What are its true capabilities, and how can we ensure it serves both educators and students in meaningful ways? These questions are critical, and the ongoing conversation about AI's role in education has rapidly expanded as more and more educators recognize its transformative potential.

As a former high school educator and now a Teaching and Learning Specialist at a Canadian college, I have seen firsthand the immense benefits AI can offer. From easing administrative burdens to enhancing student engagement and learning outcomes, AI provides educators with new tools that can revolutionize teaching and learning. However, before we can fully reap these benefits, we must take a thoughtful and informed approach. This means learning all that we can about how to strategically and safely incorporate AI into education in ways that benefit not only students but also educators and society as a whole.

The field of AI in education is growing rapidly, and I am proud to be part of this important conversation. As more research emerges and the technology continues to evolve, we have the opportunity to reshape the educational landscape for future generations. This book, through its collection of scientific insights, case studies, and practical examples, aims to equip educators with the knowledge they need to navigate this new frontier effectively and ethically.

AI Applications and Strategies in Teacher Education is designed not only for educators on the front lines but also for administrators who want to support their teachers in adopting AI responsibly. It speaks to educational leaders making critical decisions about the acceptance of AI in education, university professors who hold the power to teach educators how to ethically and effectively integrate AI, and policy writers who must take an informed approach to shaping AI guidelines for education. Additionally, it serves students of educational studies who are eager to take a future-focused approach to learning how to teach.

AI is for everyone in the education sphere, and it is our collective responsibility to engage with the research, embrace calculated risks, and strategically harness the transformative potential of this life-altering technology for the positive impact it promises.

I want to extend my deepest thanks to the authors who have contributed their thoughtful expertise to this book. These voices are leaders in education from around the world, and their knowledge offers invaluable insights into the evolving relationship between AI and education. This book highlights the work of educators, researchers, and innovators from diverse international contexts, emphasizing a global understanding of AI's role in transforming education. We can learn so much from their experiences and perspectives, and I am grateful for their commitment to advancing the field through their contributions.

BECOMING AI LITERATE: PREPARING FUTURE EDUCATORS FOR THE USE OF AI

This chapter is significant because it takes a "meet teachers where they are" approach to AI integration, acknowledging the varying levels of technological comfort among educators. The author highlights the fact that educators have already adapted to numerous technological shifts and encourages readers to embrace AI as a positive force for change, rather than a source of overwhelm. This chapter is highly accessible for educators at all levels of technological proficiency, as she carefully guides readers through the AI integration process while calming common fears.

EXPLORING THE EFFECTS OF AI-POWERED PERSONALIZED CLASSROOM MANAGEMENT STRATEGIES

This chapter is important to the innovation of education as it explores how Artificial Intelligence (AI) can revolutionize classroom management through personalized strategies that adapt to individual student needs, moving beyond traditional methods. By leveraging real-time data analysis, AI facilitates timely interventions, enhances learning outcomes, and streamlines administrative tasks such as attendance and grading, allowing educators to focus more on teaching. It addresses both the innovative potential of AI and the concerns about job displacement and the dehumanization of education, emphasizing the need for ethical and transparent AI practices. The chapter also highlights challenges and calls for ongoing research to maximize AI's impact on educational success and transformation.

THE ROLE OF AI IN TRANSFORMING ASSESSMENT PRACTICES IN EDUCATION

Assessment is crucial to student success, yet many classrooms have seen little meaningful advancement in this area. The comparison between traditional and AI-driven assessment practices are not only eye-opening, but extremely helpful in supporting this transition between practices. This chapter encourages educators and stakeholders across the education sector to reconsider their assessment practices and embrace the potential of AI-driven solutions to enhance and personalize learning experiences.

ESL 4.0: A PRACTICAL GUIDE TO BENEFITS, CHALLENGES, AND BEST PRACTICES FOR AI-ENHANCED LEARNING

This chapter is critical in a book about AI in teacher education because it demonstrates how AI can revolutionize ESL teaching by addressing key pedagogical challenges, such as individualized instruction, differentiated learning, and scaffolding. The integration of AI in ESL classrooms offers unprecedented opportunities for personalization, real-time adaptation, and data-driven decision-making, enhancing student engagement, motivation, and language acquisition. By exploring both the benefits and challenges of AI in this context, the chapter provides educators with practical strategies to effectively incorporate AI, making it an invaluable resource for fostering more inclusive, responsive, and effective ESL education.

NAVIGATING AI BIASES IN EDUCATION A FOUNDATION FOR EQUITABLE LEARNING

This chapter is crucial to the book as it addresses the imperative issue of AI bias, particularly in educational settings. It examines the various forms of bias that can emerge within AI platforms and the importance of educators understanding these biases when using AI in the classroom. The authors highlight current and emerging trends in AI bias, illustrating their points with case studies that show how institutions and companies have identified and addressed bias-related challenges. This chapter equips readers with the knowledge necessary to navigate AI bias responsibly and effectively.

ENHANCING PROJECT-BASED LEARNING WITH A GENAI TOOL BASED ON RETRIEVAL-AUGMENTED GENERATION AND KNOWLEDGE GRAPHS

This chapter is a fascinating example of putting AI to work in the classroom. It explores how Generative Artificial Intelligence (GenAI) can enhance Project-Based Learning (PBL) by addressing common challenges such as project complexity, curriculum alignment, and student guidance. It provides an interesting and comprehensive example of the power of AI in education, introducing a proposed GenAI tool enhanced by Retrieval-Augmented Generation (RAG) and Knowledge Graphs (KGs). This tool offers personalized support to both students and educators in PBL environments. Through case studies and practical scenarios, the chapter demonstrates how this AI tool can help overcome typical PBL obstacles, such as providing timely feedback and adaptive learning paths. By delving into the innovative potential of GenAI, this chapter inspires educators and researchers to integrate AI into their PBL frameworks while also tackling challenges like content accuracy and outdated information.

ACADEMIC INTEGRITY AND HUMAN COGNITIVE DEVELOPMENT OF LEARNERS: IS ARTIFICIAL INTELLIGENCE REPLACING HUMAN BRAIN?

This chapter is essential and highly significant, as it raises critical questions about the impact of AI on students' creativity and cognitive development. The author explores thought-provoking questions such as "Is Artificial Intelligence replacing the human brain?" and offers insights into strategies educators can adopt when integrating AI into education. It serves as an important reminder to carefully consider both the positive and negative effects of AI, encouraging educators to approach its use thoughtfully and with balance.

DATA PRIVACY IN AI-DRIVEN EDUCATION: AN IN-DEPTH EXPLORATION INTO THE DATA PRIVACY CONCERNS AND POTENTIAL SOLUTIONS

This chapter addresses one of the most pressing concerns surrounding the use of AI in education: data privacy. As AI reshapes classrooms and online learning environments, the volume of sensitive data collected grows, raising ethical and legal challenges. By exploring key privacy concerns and offering potential solutions, this chapter serves as a critical guide for educators, administrators, and policymakers in navigating the complexities of AI-driven education. Its comprehensive examination of case studies and current data privacy practices highlights the importance of creating secure, ethical, and trustworthy AI systems. This discussion is essential for ensuring that AI is implemented responsibly, safeguarding student data while unlocking AI's transformative potential in education.

USING ARTIFICIAL INTELLIGENCE TO EVALUATE THE NATURE OF SCIENCE MYTHS: A COMPARISON OF PRE-SERVICE SCIENCE TEACHERS AND CHATGPT

This chapter is noteworthy as it offers a compelling example of the intersection between science and AI technology. It demonstrates how AI can be used not only to support our understanding of the nature of science (NoS) but also to correct misconceptions that persist in public understanding. By showcasing how AI can enhance scientific literacy and debunk myths, the chapter underscores AI's potential to transform how individuals engage with and apply scientific knowledge. This exploration contributes to the book's broader theme of AI's transformative role in education and its capacity to empower learners in making informed, science-based decisions.

ARTIFICIAL INTELLIGENCE ACROSS INDUSTRIES A COMPREHENSIVE REVIEW WITH A FOCUS ON EDUCATION

This chapter is crucial not only because it delves into AI's transformative role in education, providing a comprehensive glimpse into its potential in the classroom, but also because it broadens the scope to explore how AI is revolutionizing various industries such as healthcare, finance, and entertainment. By understanding AI's impact across sectors, educators and stakeholders can better anticipate the shifts required in the classroom. The chapter offers a structured analysis of AI's evolution, its wide-ranging applications, and the lessons education can learn from other industries. It highlights both the benefits and challenges of AI integration, offering a forward-looking perspective on how AI can reshape education in the future. This broader view encourages educators to think beyond the classroom and consider what transformations may be necessary as AI becomes increasingly integrated into society.

CONSTRUCTING HUMAN SERVICE LEARNING IN THE AI DIGITAL SPHERE: CHINA'S CASE OF LIVEPBL DEEP METHOD

This chapter introduces the DEEP Method as a strategic framework for integrating Service Learning, Project-Based Learning (PBL), and AI tools to create personalized, real-world educational experiences. By demonstrating its effectiveness in real-world settings, such as digital literacy training in Beijing, the chapter showcases how the DEEP Method fosters both theoretical and practical learning. It highlights key challenges like technological accessibility and ethical considerations, such as the risk of over-reliance on AI, while emphasizing the need for a balanced approach that preserves human interaction. The chapter calls for future research to improve the DEEP Method's accessibility, adaptability, and feedback mechanisms to optimize its impact on education.

METAVERSE AND ITS UNDERLYING CHALLENGES IN HIGHER EDUCATION A CASE STUDY BASED APPROACH: BENEFITS OF METAVERSE IN HIGHER EDUCATION

This section examines the potential of the Metaverse as an evolving technology in the higher education sector. It highlights how virtual reality (VR), augmented reality (AR), and mixed reality (MR) can enhance student performance, engagement, and access to distant learners. The chapter emphasizes that while the Metaverse offers innovative ways to improve education, significant challenges—such as infrastructure deficits, financial constraints, and lack of training—must be addressed. The case studies, such as Fisk University's virtual reality tours of historical sites and New Mexico State University's plans for virtual degrees, demonstrate how early adoption of the Metaverse can shape future learning experiences.

AI Applications and Strategies in Teacher Education serves as a comprehensive resource for pre-service educators, practicing teachers, educational leaders, policy-makers, course designers, and others in the education sector eager to expand their understanding of AI. As readers progress through the book, they will deepen their AI knowledge and skills, explore detailed analyses and examples of AI's transformative power, and grapple with AI's most compelling issues. Each chapter offers a blend of practical applications and theoretical foundations, emphasizing the safe, ethical, and innovative use of AI in teacher education and beyond.

Krista LaRue Keeley
Saskatchewan Teacher's Federation, Canada

Chapter 1
Becoming AI Literate
Preparing Future Educators for the Use of AI

Christine Anne Royce
Shippensburg University, USA

ABSTRACT

The introduction of artificial intelligence (AI) has become a transformative force. And the integration of AI into K-12 classrooms has the potential for being a transformative force, although that has yet to be determined. Within a short amount of time, the emergence of AI programs and tools has redefined the boundaries of teaching and learning in the digital era, and thus, future educators enrolled in teacher preparation programs need to be familiar with and understand how to use and integrate AI tools within the instructional environment. Examining how and when to utilize AI with teacher preparation candidates is explored through unpacking and providing an overview of what AI looks like in K-12 education; exploring the pedagogical shifts that are needed to utilize AI; examining the inclusion of AI tools in one specific course for early childhood/elementary education majors, as well as, the themes that emerged; and providing recommendations for the reasons that AI should be incorporated into pre-service teacher preparation programs.

INTRODUCTION

In the field of shifting educational technology, tools, and instructional strategies, teachers made the shift to online instruction due to a necessity at the start of the pandemic. This shift to online instruction happened overnight, and thus, created an immediate need to embrace online instruction (Baidoo-Anu & Ansah, 2023). The digital tools that emerged were game changers. Artificial intelligence has the

DOI: 10.4018/979-8-3693-5443-8.ch001

potential to be even more impactful than online instruction in the field of education. While the use of AI in a person's daily life already ranges from chatbots to virtual assistants like Siri or Alexa, to facial recognition, and to algorithms that provide targeted ads, the emergence of generative AI in the education world is relatively new to a large part of the teaching population (van den Berg & du Plessis, 2023).

Over the past year and a half, the rise of AI programs and tools has redrawn the boundaries of teaching and learning in the digital age (van den Berg & du Plessis, 2023). As AI continues to gain traction, it is imperative for future educators to not only comprehend this new tool and its functionality but also to learn how to effectively integrate it into the classroom environment. This necessity for adaptation presents an exciting opportunity for educators to expand their skill set and enhance their teaching methods (Köprülü et al., 2023).

Generative AI's capabilities extend far beyond previously mentioned uses. Today, AI offers innovative approaches to designing lessons that can provide options for variations on lesson plan design and create activities that may engage students. Furthermore, AI may be used to develop prompts or questions that may serve as assessments and enhance critical thinking skills across diverse learning communities, which may broaden a student's future (Köprülü et al., 2023; World Economic Forum, 2023a). The use of the word "may" in the above narrative is intentional in that educators still need to know how to use these technological tools for a meaningful purpose.

Ready or not, the integration of artificial intelligence (AI) into K-12 classrooms has become a transformative force and will increase as the future unfolds (Staton & Murgia, 2023). As such, teacher preparation courses must evolve to include an introduction to and knowledge about AI applications, enabling future teachers to navigate and implement AI-driven pedagogies knowledgeably, purposefully, and confidently.

Being AI literate entails a technical understanding of AI tools and a pedagogical understanding of instructional design. This chapter seeks to:

- provide an overview of what AI might look like in K-12 education.
- explore how AI, pedagogical shifts that utilize AI, and the impact of AI as an educational tool can be incorporated into teacher preparation courses.
- examine a specific course example that integrated AI tools for early childhood/elementary educators.
- provide recommendations on how incorporating AI into preservice teacher preparation programs helps to prepare future educators to leverage this technology.

DEMYSTIFYING AI FOR K-12 EDUCATORS

In *The Lost Symbol* by Dan Brown, he states, "We all fear what we do not understand." Additionally, we often hear people say they fear change. In a blog post, Van Oosterom (2024) stated that people don't fear change; they fear uncertainty. In considering the speed with which AI seems to have appeared, the number of tools that have emerged for K-12 teachers, and the mixed reactions from educators at all levels on the use of AI in the classroom, this new found uncertainty is a good place to start as we begin to explore the use of AI moving forward. By starting with the need to understand and demystify artificial intelligence for educators, we can focus on providing a clear and accessible overview of what AI is, its capabilities, and its potential applications within K-12 educational settings.

UNDERSTANDING AI FUNDAMENTALS

As of the writing of this chapter, headlines, and studies have reported that ChatGPT has gone to law school and was a mediocre student (Choi et al.,2022), successfully passed a final exam in the MBA program at the Wharton School of Business (Rosenblatt, 2023b), and has likely done quite well on sliding by in essay writing at many different levels from K-college. Beyond the specific use of AI for these tasks, AI elements have been integrated into the daily landscape long before the emergence of the newest generative AI tools (Russell & Norvig, 2016). There is a difference between understanding AI and understanding the fundamentals of AI as they relate to educators, and this section will focus on the latter. For educators, understanding the foundational principles of AI is essential to harness its potential benefit and employ it within the instructional process.

To start with, a basic definition of AI is "a system's ability to interpret external data correctly, to learn from such data, and to use those learnings to achieve specific goals and tasks through flexible adaptation" (Haenlein & Kaplan, 2019, p. 5) or" the technology that builds systems to think and act like humans with the ability of achieving goals" (Akgun & Greenhow, 2021, p. 433). While the first several decades' worth of research focused on AI in a very technological approach, which included computers, robots, and other sci-fi views of what it could do, more recently, it has become part of the day-to-day experiences with limited uses such as the use of uber apps to smart home applications to predictive text in email message systems to fraud alerts with credit cards. Most recently, AIs like Gemini and ChatGPT have emerged, allowing teachers and students to pose a question and be provided with an answer. However, the answer may not be accurate or even directly answer the question. It is important to recognize that people have been using AI for multiple years and already used it in the educational space.

Ultimately, AI is a broad term encompassing the simulation of human intelligence in machines programmed to think and learn like humans. This broad field encompasses various technologies and methodologies, with machine learning (ML) being a key subset.

Machine Learning

Machine Learning (ML), at the simplest level, is a cross between computer science and statistics (Jordan & Mitchell, 2015). It is a subset of AI that focuses on developing algorithms that enable computers to learn from and make predictions or decisions based on data. ML algorithms can analyze vast amounts of student data in educational contexts to identify trends and predict outcomes. For example, adaptive learning platforms such as Khan Academy (Khan Academy, 2011) and Duolingo (Bicknell et al., 2023) utilize ML to tailor educational content to individual learners. These platforms adjust the difficulty of exercises based on a student's performance, ensuring each learner is challenged appropriately. This personalized approach helps maintain student engagement and improve learning outcomes by providing a tailored educational experience.

While more specifically discussed within the higher education level at this point, ML also powers predictive analytics tools that help colleges and universities identify students at risk of failing (Bird et al., 2023). Learning Management Systems such as PowerSchool, Schoology, and Canvas also utilize data for machine learning modeling but often note that they remove identifying information in this step (PowerSchool, 2022; Rethinam, 2014). These tools can provide early warning signs by analyzing historical data on student performance, attendance, and engagement, enabling timely interventions. This proactive approach can significantly enhance student retention and success rates. The tools that fall within this field are likely already part of the daily experience of current teachers.

Neural Networks and Deep Learning

Within machine learning, neural networks and deep learning play crucial roles. Neural networks are inspired by the human brain's structure and consist of interconnected nodes (neurons) that process data in layers, identifying patterns and making predictions. Neural networks are a subset of machine learning and are particularly effective for complex pattern recognition tasks, such as image and speech recognition. Deep learning, a more advanced form of neural networks, involves multiple layers of these nodes, allowing for the analysis of complex patterns in large datasets. This technology is the backbone of many AI applications.

In educational contexts, neural networks can analyze vast amounts of student data to identify trends and make predictions about student performance. For example, adaptive learning platforms like Coursera use neural networks to recommend courses and learning materials to users. The platform suggests the most relevant courses and resources by analyzing users' previous activities and learning preferences.

Natural Language Processing

Natural Language Processing (NLP) is a subfield of artificial intelligence (AI) that focuses on the interaction between computers and human languages. Algorithms enable computers to understand, interpret, generate, and respond to human language in a meaningful and useful way. Programs like Siri, Alexa, and Google Assistant use NLP to understand and respond to user queries.

Generative AI

Generative AI refers to a type of artificial intelligence that can create new content, such as text, images, music, or even entire virtual environments, based on patterns and examples it has learned from existing data. It works primarily through neural networks, especially deep learning models. The models contain one part that generates or creates new content and another that considers the content's authenticity. Over time, the content or output is improved based on feedback. It is the generative AI area that has created this recent recognition of AI by educators and the recognition that it can be a useful tool but can also have drawbacks.

AI'S ROLE IN EDUCATION

No Longer Hidden Tools

As stated in earlier sections, AI technologies have previously been integrated into educational settings, providing valuable tools for educators and students. The tools that utilize machine learning or deep learning aspects of AI were, to a point, "hidden" tools that teachers may have had access to but not tools that would immediately find themselves as part of the day-to-day instructional process. Then ChatGPT emerged in late 2022, Google Bard in early 2023, and many others became available for educators and students simply by opening an internet browser. Attention to and concerns about AI changed at this point, resulting in some districts and schools embracing the use of generative AI (Singer, 2023) and others cursing its existence and banning it (Rosenblatt, 2023a), placing districts, schools, teachers, and students at somewhat of a crossroads (van Rijmenam, 2023).

New Tools, Similar Crossroads

In retrospect, education has been at a similar crossroads previously. Educators in the 70s and 80s stated that we could not give students calculators as it would impact mathematics learning. In the '90s, there was pushback within the science field about using probes that would determine everything from the temperature of something to the speed of something, as using these tools would result in students not knowing how to collect data. By the early 2000s, the internet would impact students' ability to research topics and use a library (Royce, 2023). Now, it is AI. Blogs, social media groups, and other non-research-based threads and anecdotes have indicated that using AI in the classroom will potentially reduce students' ability to write an essay, develop arguments, and research topics, among other skills. However, there is a need for ongoing research in this area.

While the initial stance of integrating new technologies in prior decades was that it was a detriment to the education process (Royce, 2023), educators' practices are modified over time. AI tools can enhance learning outcomes and foster critical thinking, creativity, and problem-solving skills among students, and they can be integrated into the curriculum (Kadaruddin, 2023; Royce, 2023; van Rijmenam, 2023). When planning with these new tools, the overarching paradigm shift is to "think differently." Shippee (2019) noted that a series of questions could be asked about any new form of technology. Take, for example, the introduction of pencils into the classroom around the turn of the 20th century. Shippee (2019) notes that the series of statements and questions that likely followed: "Chalk and slate boards work just fine. Why change? The students are used to chalk. How do you expect us to introduce this new tool? How can we control appropriate pencil usage? How can we keep pencils sharpened without disrupting class? What about the safety issues with sharpened writing devices?" (p. 25). This series of questions likely occurred for every new form of technology, from pencils to the current AI situation. Moreover, with every technological innovation, you have a range from the innovators to the laggards in adoption (German et. al., 2022). Regardless of when AI is adopted, it is important to recognize that technology literacy is the third-fastest growing core skill, while curiosity and lifelong learning, resilience, flexibility, agility, motivation, and self-awareness complete the top five (World Economic Forum, 2023b). All of these skills are necessary when AI is used.

Embrace the Paradigm Shift

Beyond "think differently," Sharma (2023) indicates that rather than restricting the use of AI, educators need to reframe how AI is used in a way similar to the tools mentioned above. The integration of AI into educational practices has the potential to significantly enhance educational outcomes if used wisely, carefully, and informatively. However, this integration does require some paradigm shifts. The key paradigm shift relates to a need to change the questions asked to better align with collaborative learning in diverse environments. The questions need to focus on "how will students and teachers use this new technology?" "How does this technology help students demonstrate learning?" and "How can we balance the pros and cons of the technology?" In 2022, we entered what is being called the fifth industrial revolution, with AI entering the landscape in the fourth industrial revolution. Nosta (2023) notes that AI will continue to develop at an unprecedented rate and can be used as a tool for innovation along with humanity in this Fifth Industrial Revolution.

Connecting a Framework

One of the ways that we can shift our thinking to consider how best to incorporate AI tools into the classroom is by following Merrill's Principles of Design. Merrill's Principles of Instruction (Merrill, 2018) offer a robust framework for this integration, ensuring that AI tools are used effectively to support meaningful learning. These principles emphasize problem-centered learning, activation of prior knowledge, demonstration of skills, application of skills, and integration of skills into real-world tasks, all of which are desired skills for the future and align with the top skills identified by the World Economic Forum (2023b). Each principle is identified below, and recommendations on how AI might be used within the principle are provided.

Problem-Centered Learning: Teachers can consider what in their curriculum might be used to create immersive, problem-centered learning environments. By presenting students with real-world problems to solve or ill-defined problems, students can use AI to consider how to solve them. As there is no direct or single answer for the problem presented, students will need to develop a plan for investigation in which they might use AI tools and then evaluate the recommendations provided by generative AI programs.

Activation of Prior Knowledge: AI programs like online tutoring can assess students' understanding and activate prior knowledge. Teachers often already use this technique in benchmarking programs.

Demonstration of Skills: Rather than ask students to write an essay, you might ask them to critique two essays, both of which could be written by AI, to determine which essay better meets the criteria outlined. AI is being utilized by the teacher for a purpose that requires higher-order thinking skills on the student's part.

Application of Skills The application principle involves providing opportunities for students to practice new skills. Various AI programs can be utilized to develop a wide range of practice activities for students. An additional example of applying skills requires students to understand the outcome or goal to be achieved and then modify an initial prompt they use with AI to generate better results. This prompt engineering will help them demonstrate that they understand the parameters around the topic, including conditions and limitations.

Integration of Skills into Real-World Tasks Finally, Merrill's integration principle highlights the need for students to integrate new skills into their everyday lives. AI can facilitate this by creating opportunities for students to apply their knowledge in practical, real-world contexts. Depending on the students' age, AI simulations can be used to provide immersion experiences. For example, intermediate or middle-level students could be asked to participate in a decision-making scenario that allows them to accomplish a particular task.

Pairing Merrill's (2018) principles with the 4 C's of 21st-century skills to focus student learning is also an option for consideration. Critical thinking, communication, creativity, and collaboration are all needed when students demonstrate their understanding and apply that understanding to real-world tasks. When designing lessons, whether by hand or with the assistance of AI tools, shift from the idea of delivering content and assessing student understanding to developing dynamic and interactive lessons that may incorporate scenarios, problems, or other tasks that require students to not only learn content but apply the learning in authentic ways (Kadaruddin, 2023; van Rijmenam, 2023).

Considering this insight from Shippee (2019), "Keeping a balanced pedagogy-content experience with rapidly shifting technology is the very nature of innovativeness. .... maintaining good teaching means constantly changing. We all want a stable teacher experience, but stability cannot be defined as static or stuck. Stability includes continually shifting, learning, changing, and rebalancing. It means learning to let new tools empower you rather than overwhelm you" (p. 37).

It is important to reflect on these paradigm shifts, acknowledge that AI is already integrated into different areas within education, and recognize that the larger question for future educators is where and how they see generative AI being utilized.

AI INTEGRATION EXAMPLE IN TEACHER PREPARATION

During the Spring 2024 semester, teacher preparation candidates enrolled in a course that focuses on the use of digital tools and integration of technology into the early childhood classroom course were given one digital application project that focused on the use of AI tools. This assignment aimed to introduce students to digital tools that utilize AI features or processes that had a specific and direct connection to tasks they would do as teachers. The assignment incorporated different existing AI tools that are targeted at educators.

Overview information to the students indicated that they would be using several apps/programs during this assignment that would allow them to learn more about how AI programs can be useful in designing instructional materials. Following this introduction, students were given a set of steps that would ask them to complete a task using a particular tool. The product from one step would be used in the subsequent step.

Table 1 indicates the digital tool students were asked to use, with a synopsis of the task to be performed and, finally, the produced product. Students were asked to review the content and material at each step to check for any produced errors and highlight and fix them. Additionally, students were asked to respond to a narrative prompt about their opinion or thoughts about each tool and, finally, the use of AI in the classroom. The classification of their responses and examples follows the table.

Table 1. Digital Tools Used for Digital Application Project

Tool	Task	Product
YouTube – NatGeo Kids	• Locate a short video that could be used in a lesson.	• Identification of video and URL to the video.
TWEE	• Convert video and audio to text.	• Text narrative from the video selected.
	• Save text as a Word document and review for content and spelling.	• Word document
	• Use the tools featured in TWEE to generate warm-up discussion questions	• Potential warm-up questions for use with the video.
	• Create multiple-choice questions.	• Questions that will assess the material in the video.
Conker	• Develop and enter a prompt that is related to the topic in your video. • Submit and use the text from the video to generate grade range questions. • Share the questions and edit the content that appears to Google Forms, creating a ready-made quiz.	• Multiple choice questions that are at a particular grade level. • Quiz based on the questions created in Google Forms.

continued on following page

Table 1. Continued

Tool	Task	Product
Diffit	• Using the text from the original video, select one of the activity options that is available. • Take the text and generate a complimentary article on the topic at a lower grade level using the readability level feature.	• Word and PPT activity based on choice using this content. • Paired readings on the same topic at different grade levels based on the video.

Analysis of Student Responses

The author examined each student's response and determined the key point or points that were being explained by the student. Each point was examined for the underlying meaning that related to the question of why you would or wouldn't utilize AI in your future classroom. Reasons were identified, and then, based on those reasons, themes were identified. In examining and analyzing the student responses from this course (3 different sections with a total of n=81), themes emerged and were classified into three broad categories: In Favor of AI, Mixed Feelings About AI, and Opposed to AI. Some student responses could be classified into more than one of these broad umbrella categories. After determining a general viewpoint towards AI, the researcher looked for themes that emerged from the narratives and worked to determine an overall basis for that theme based on student narratives. The themes and summary in the researcher's terms, supported by student quotes, are shared below. Furthermore, the results are paired with information and research on emerging perspectives.

In Favor of AI

Those who expressed being in favor of AI indicated that AI could:

Assist with efficiency and help save time. The overarching reason that course participants indicated they favored AI was that AI could assist teachers and themselves as future teachers with tasks in the future. They value the time saved on routine tasks, which can be redirected towards more meaningful educational activities. One student's response clearly illustrated this perspective. "These AI tools can help cut down on planning time and give teachers more time to prepare activities and meaningful lessons when AI can create a solid backbone of a lesson."

Reasons for AI use have already promoted saving time for different tasks that an educator is responsible for completing (Akgun & Greenhow, 2021; Watson, 2023). Many online tools and blogs have touted this reason for saving teachers' time in lesson planning, grading, and creating assessments (Baidoo-Anu & Ansah, 2023; Watson, 2023). Many teachers find that AI tools allow them to focus more on student interaction and personalized teaching. By generating initial drafts of lesson plans and assessments, AI frees up valuable time for educators to engage more deeply with their students.

Enhance Personalized Learning. This theme emerged based on the preservice teacher's responses focused on differentiation. In the words of one college student, "Using AI in the classroom as a teacher is beneficial in many ways. It can enhance individualized learning by adapting to students' unique learning needs and preferences. It promotes learning outcomes by personalized pace and difficulty level for each student." The future educators recognize that AI can provide potential student engagement and indicated multiple times and ways that it was able to "personalize" learning and tailor outcomes and materials to individual students enrolled in their classes.

AI's ability to adapt to individual students' needs is seen as a significant advantage. Teachers use AI to create personalized learning experiences, adjusting the difficulty and content to suit each student's unique learning style and pace (Akgun & Greenhow, 2021; Baidoo-Anu & Ansah, 2023; Kadaruddin, 2023; Kasneci, 2023).

Support Creativity and Engagement. Similar to the personalized learning theme, course participants also indicated that they saw opportunities to use AI for creativity and engagement. Participant's responses indicated that AI tools can support creative teaching methods and, by doing so, help increase student engagement through interactive educational materials. One forward-thinking future educator indicated that "AI is a tool for learning. This tool can increase student engagement by having students construct, collaborate, and create."

Some researchers have noted that AI is also recognized for its potential to enhance creativity in teaching and learning (Kadaruddin, 2023; Kasneci, 2023). AI can also assist teachers in generating diverse and engaging content, from interactive lessons to educational games, which can make learning more enjoyable for students (Kadaruddin, 2023; Kasneci, 2023).

Mixed Reactions

Responses that included mixed reactions focused on the following:

Dependence vs. Support. Many course participants had an overarching feeling that teachers would need to find a balance between using AI as a support tool versus becoming overly dependent on it. While AI can assist significantly, it is a concern about replacing teachers' creativity and professional judgment. Several students indicated that the teacher still needed to design the lessons, and this reaction is best summarized as "AI should not be used as a creativity replacement but instead as a supporter." While AI offers substantial support, there is a concern about overreliance, which could undermine teachers' professional skills and creativity (Kasneci, 2023). The emphasis is on using AI as a supplementary tool rather than a replacement.

Fagan (2023) notes that the questions that will need to be considered are "how much," "in what ways," and "for what purposes" (n.p).

Accuracy and Customization Issues. While students were directed to review the content of the materials generated by AI, and there were a few points where a transcript was misinterpreted, students expressed concerns about the accuracy of AI-generated materials and the need for thorough review and customization. Some students indicated that the time it took to review what was generated by AI was problematic. "Sometimes going through and checking for mistakes may take longer than just creating a PowerPoint or activity yourself."

Teachers feel that AI can provide a good starting point but often requires significant modification to meet their specific needs. AI-generated content often needs careful review (Staton & Murgia, 2023) and adjustment to ensure it meets educational standards and specific classroom requirements, which can sometimes offset the time saved by using AI.

Student Use and Cheating. Not surprisingly, the misuse of AI by students to cheat or avoid learning tasks was identified in the mixed emotions response. The preservice teachers recognized the need to address cheating and brought it out in their narratives that there would need to be careful monitoring and guidance of AI use within the classroom. It should be noted that all the course participants enrolled in this course will eventually teach grades PK-4. It would be worth determining if students who would teach middle or high school would view this as a more serious concern. As this topic presented various viewpoints, two participants' quotes illustrating both the good and the bad have been selected to highlight perspectives. "... after seeing and using AI from a teacher perspective .....I won't encourage my students to use AI because there are many sites that can do your work for you, and .... that is cheating" is a glass-half-empty viewpoint, whereas "teaching children to use AI can also help them build their digital citizenship and can help them start building digital experiences that may make them more marketable in the job market in the future" helps to illustrate the glass half full viewpoint.

The potential for students at any level to misuse AI for cheating or bypassing the learning process is a significant concern. While teachers see the benefits of AI, they worry about students using AI to complete assignments dishonestly (Angwin, 2023).

Opposed to AI

This category focused less on instruction and more on interaction and skill development.

Loss of Human Touch. As noted above, the course participants enrolled in these classes will teach the youngest learners and spend much time learning to create the classroom environment. This environment includes the human element in teaching, including emotional support. A theme that emerged in opposition to AI was that the human element was seen as a significant loss when relying on AI. One preservice teacher noted, "I think if AI is being used in the right way in a classroom to enrich learning and to teach students, then there is nothing wrong with it. I don't think we should just let students solve every problem with AI and not learn anything." While the following statement may be an oversimplification, it is interesting that course participants in the classes feel that learning only happens with the teacher and not through technology.

AI's lack of emotional intelligence and personal touch is a critical drawback. Teachers believe that human interaction and the ability to understand students' emotional and social needs are irreplaceable aspects of education that AI cannot replicate, and as the use of AI unfolds, this is an area that researchers will need to examine (Baidoo-Anu & Ansah, 2023; Fagan, 2023).

Impact on Student Skills. Concern was expressed that consistent and extensive use of AI could negatively impact students' development of life skills, such as critical thinking and problem-solving. "If children start by doing this, how will they ever learn anything if they know they can just go on an AI site and have it do the work for them."

There is a strong belief that extensive use of AI could impair students' critical thinking, problem-solving, and social skills development. Teachers worry that students might rely on AI to do the work for them, which could hinder their overall development.

One caution that did not emerge in the students' reactions is the potential for biased information (Baidoo-Anu & Ansah, 2023; Staton & Murgia, 2023). Not only do educators need to utilize AI from an ethical perspective and review the content for accurate information, but they also need to be conscious of potential biases that may be produced in AI-generated responses (Akgun & Greenhow, 2021; Fagan, 2023).

Meeting the Challenges Head-on

While the last two sections outlined mixed reactions and reasons that future educators indicated that they were opposed to the use of AI, these responses could better be named problems and challenges. By positing them as problems and challenges, opportunities for reflection and discussion emerge, allowing teacher preparation programs to bring together future educators, current educators, and administrators to identify potential remedies and actions to address the problems and challenges.

As AI integration into the classroom environment is still relatively new, determining how these problems and challenges could be addressed is another avenue of inquiry related to this topic. Potential questions to investigate are based on the themes that emerged. These include:

- At the broadest level, how can teacher preparation programs bring the pros and cons and potential solutions for the identified problems and challenges to light?
- What types of education and training will assist future educators with these reservations toward a more favorable view of AI?
- Are there particular strategies that can create a paradigm shift in their thinking related to the specific challenge of cheating and plagiarism?
- Can teacher educators implement AI into their own courses to demonstrate to future educators how to implement AI in their classrooms?

While each of these questions opens another avenue of discussion and research, the one that can be addressed at this point is how do we help students become AI literate? The following sections of this chapter focus on that aspect—both the need for AI literacy and reasons why AI literacy should be integrated into teacher preparation programs.

THE NEED FOR BECOMING AI LITERATE IN EDUCATION

Regardless of one's personal feelings about AI, the reality is that AI is here to stay and will grow rapidly. Future educators must decide how and when they use AI for personal, professional, and instructional reasons. This necessity underscores the importance of AI literacy for future teachers. The author defines AI literacy as the ability to understand, use, and critically evaluate artificial intelligence technologies, which is becoming increasingly essential in the educational landscape.

Being AI literate equips educators with the knowledge to integrate AI tools effectively into their teaching practices. AI can significantly enhance instructional methods by offering personalized learning experiences, automating administrative tasks, and providing innovative ways to engage students.

Based on the existing literature, the themes that emerged in addition to the course participant's responses to what they liked or disliked about the individual tools that were part of the assignment, the following are the author's reasons as to why future educators need to learn how to utilize AI as both an instructional tool, as well as, learn how to teach students in their classrooms to use AI is essential.

TEN REASONS WHY AI SHOULD BE INTEGRATED INTO TEACHER PREPARATION PROGRAMS

The reason and a brief rationale for why all teacher preparation programs should integrate AI into teacher preparation program coursework sets the stage for future educators who will enter a classroom and world where they will be training students for a world that does not yet exist.

1. **Meeting and Using 21st-century skills**: Communication, collaboration, critical thinking, and creativity transcend any industry. No matter where someone works or what they do, they can benefit from these skills. Furthermore, while we still call these 21st-century skills, many teachers will teach well into the 21st century. AI usage and, thus, AI literacy is becoming essential in the modern workforce. Future teachers need to be equipped with the skills to prepare students for a technology-driven world, which will push the skills necessary for the 21st century. If future educators are unfamiliar with AI tools, they are entering an educational environment already missing key knowledge. As AI becomes more integrated into all aspects of life, teachers will need to update their skills to remain relevant and effective continuously. AI can also be used to support the development of 21st-century skills and those new stills that have not yet been identified.
2. **Demonstrating Technological Literacy:** Technology in education is evolving rapidly. Learning about and understanding how to make informed decisions about AI ensures that future teachers can keep up with and leverage the latest educational technologies. Future educators will have students who arrive at school aware of this technology and, therefore, need to be able to utilize it personally and integrate it into the classroom so that they can teach ethical and safe practices for the use of evolving technology. Furthermore, understanding how to utilize AI will also assist teachers in being more aware of when and how students may use (or abuse) AI.
3. **Innovating and Innovative Teaching Strategies**: While it may be slower than the workforce, AI will impact education. In today's world, students are accustomed to interactive and digital experiences in their daily lives. AI tools can replicate this interactivity in the classroom, making learning more engaging and relevant to students. AI offers new ways to enhance teaching for student learning, moving beyond traditional methods to more interactive and effective strategies. Therefore, innovation in teaching practices will be necessary to meet future students' changing needs and expectations.

4. **Differentiating Instruction:** The increasing diversity in classrooms will require teachers to be adept at using AI to provide personalized learning experiences. AI can help future teachers understand and implement differentiated instruction, adapting to the diverse needs of their students. Every student learns differently, and traditional teaching methods often fail to address these differences effectively. AI can aid the teacher in personalizing learning experiences to match individual learning preferences and paces. Providing quality one-on-one attention and feedback to all students is often a challenge with large class sizes and also depending on the level of attention each student requires. AI can support teachers by helping to give personalized instruction and feedback to their students in identified situations and with certain tasks.
5. **Making Decisions with Data:** Teachers spend significant time grading and providing feedback. AI can automate some of these tasks, freeing up time for teachers to focus on instruction and student interaction. Data-driven decision-making has become a cornerstone of effective teaching, requiring teachers to interpret and act on data insights proficiently. AI tools can be utilized to analyze data that can inform teaching practices. Future teachers need to be data literate to use these insights effectively.
6. **Demonstrating Professional Competence:** Understanding AI enhances the professional competence of future teachers, making them more competitive in the job market. As AI becomes more prevalent in education, teachers with AI skills will be in high demand. Understanding when and how to utilize AI within the classroom models for the students that there are times to use different tools and how those decisions might be made.
7. **Considering and Employing Ethical Decisions**: Making decisions about the use of and implications with use of AI in the classroom is a key reason to ensure that AI is taught. Topics ranging from how plagiarism and cheating are defined in an AI world and what exactly constitutes student cheating to recognizing biases and working to minimize misinformation presented to students all require consideration on the part of educators. Therefore, engaging future teachers in discussions on these and other ethical issues helps prepare them to address these challenges in the classroom better.
8. **Enhancing Student Support**: AI's ability to manage routines can free up time, allowing educators to spend more of their daily classroom time working with students or planning for student instruction. As noted above, teachers who utilize AI for more common or administrative tasks can utilize the available time to provide more instructional time for students.

9. **Becoming a Lifelong Learner**: Understanding AI fosters a mindset of continuous learning and adaptation, which is crucial for future teachers in a rapidly changing educational landscape. Lifelong learning and adaptability will be crucial for teachers as educational technology continues to advance.
10. **Managing Administrative Tasks**: AI can help future teachers manage classroom routines more efficiently. Generating an email to parents about upcoming events or summarizing information that can be shared in a newsletter are all examples of using AI to manage the more mundane tasks or repeatable tasks and provide the opportunity for teachers to focus on the more complex, important, and often fun tasks associated with teaching.

As AI technology evolves, it will provide even more opportunities for innovative and impactful teaching practices. AI literacy allows future educators to be knowledgeable about the topic, consider how best to address the problems and concerns that will undoubtedly arise in classrooms, and develop a plan to overcome those issues. By recognizing the above reasons and explanations for becoming AI literate, future educators can be better prepared for their future classrooms and assist their students in preparing for their futures. In conclusion, AI literacy is not just an optional skill but a necessary competency for future educators. Being AI literate enables all educators, including those currently in teacher preparation programs, to harness AI's benefits while mitigating its risks, thus ensuring that they can provide high-quality, ethical, and forward-thinking education. As AI continues to evolve, equipping teachers with AI literacy will be fundamental to the success of both educators and students in the 21st century and beyond.

REFERENCES

Akgun, S., & Greenhow, C. (2021). Artificial intelligence in education: Addressing ethical challenges in K-12 settings. *AI and Ethics*, 2(3), 431–440. DOI: 10.1007/s43681-021-00096-7 PMID: 34790956

Angwin, J. (2023, January 28). Decoding the hype about AI. *The Markup*.https://themarkup.org/hello-world/2023/01/28/decoding-the-hype-about-ai

Baidoo-Anu, D., & Ansah, L. O. (2023). Education in the era of generative artificial intelligence (AI): Understanding the potential benefits of ChatGPT in promoting teaching and learning. *Journal of AI, 7*(1), 52-62. DOI: 10.2139/ssrn.4337484

Bicknell, K., Brust, C., & Settles, B. (2023 February 5). How Duolingo's ai learns what you need to learn. https://spectrum.ieee.org/duolingo#:~:text=The%20early%20machine%2Dlearning%20work,educational%20research%20on%20spaced%20repetition)

Bird, K., Castleman, B., Mabel, Z., & Song, Y. (2021). Big data on campus: Putting predictive analytics to the test. *Education Next, 21(*4), 58-64. https://www.educationnext.org/big-data-on-campus-putting-predictive-analytics-to-the-test/

Choi, J. H., Hickman, K. E., Monahan, A. B., & Schwarcz, D. (2022). ChatGPT goes to law school. *Journal of Legal Education*, 71(3). https://jle.aals.org/home/vol71/iss3/2/

Fagan, A. (2023 May 11). Educational psychology meets generative AI. *Psychology Today*.https://www.psychologytoday.com/us/blog/psyched/202305/educational-psychology-meets-generative-ai

German, S., Royce, C. A., & DeVore-Wedding, B. R. (2022). Transforming Technology Purpose and Integration: Crossing the Technological Chasm Without Falling. In Bawa, I. P. (Ed.), *Preparing Faculty for Technology Dependency in the Post-COVID-19 Era* (pp. 153–173). IGI Global. DOI: 10.4018/978-1-7998-9235-9.ch009

Haenlein, M., & Kaplan, A. (2019). A brief history of artificial intelligence: On the past, present, and future of artificial intelligence. *California Management Review*, 61(4), 5–15. DOI: 10.1177/0008125619864925

Jordan, M. I., & Mitchell, T. M. (2015). Machine learning: Trends, perspectives, and prospects. *Science*, 349(6245), 255–260. DOI: 10.1126/science.aaa8415 PMID: 26185243

Kadaruddin, K. (2023). Empowering education through generative AI: Innovative instructional strategies for tomorrow's learners. *International Journal of Business, Law, and Education*, 4(2), 618–625. DOI: 10.56442/ijble.v4i2.215

Kasneci, E., Seßler, K., Küchemann, S., Bannert, M., Dementieva, D., Fischer, F., Gasser, U., Groh, G., Günnemann, S., Hüllermeier, E., Krusche, S., Kutyniok, G., Michaeli, T., Nerdel, C., Pfeffer, J., Poquet, O., Sailer, M., Schmidt, A., Seidel, T., & Kasneci, G. (2023). ChatGPT for good? On opportunities and challenges of large language models for education. DOI: 10.1016/j.lindif.2023.102274

Khan Academy. (2011, November 2). How Khan Academy is using machine learning to assess student mastery. https://blog.khanacademy.org/how-khan-academy-is-using-machine-learning-to/

Köprülü, F., Oyebimpe, A. O., Başarı, Ş., & Ayhan, S. B. (2023). Innovative effects of artificial intelligence on teacher education. *Conhecimento & Diversidade*, 15(40), 449–465. DOI: 10.18316/rcd.v15i40.11240

Merrill, M. D. (2018). Using the first principles of Instruction to make instruction effective, efficient, and engaging. In R. E. West (Ed.), *Foundations of Learning and Instructional Design Technology*. EdTech Books. https://press.rebus.community/practicespace/chapter/using-the-first-principles-of-instructionto- make-instruction-effective-efficient-and-engaging/

Nosta, J. (2023 October 6). The fifth industrial revolution: The dawn of the cognitive age. *Psychology Today*. https://www.psychologytoday.com/us/blog/the-digital-self/202310/the-5th-industrial-revolution-the-dawn-of-the-cognitive-age

PowerSchool. (2022, November 17). How k-12 data analytics and ai can support equitable learning. https://www.powerschool.com/blog/how-data-analytics-and-ai-support-equitable-learning/

Rethinam, V. (2014 June 12). Predictive analytics in K-12: Advantages, limitations, and implementation. *THE Journal*.https://thejournal.com/Articles/2014/06/12/Predictive-Analytics-in-K-12-Advantages-Limitations-Implementation.aspx?p=1

Rosenblatt, K. (2023, January 6). ChatGPT banned from New York City public schools' devices and networks. NBC News. https://www.nbcnews.com/tech/tech-news/new-york-city-public-schools-ban-chatgpt-devices-networks-rcna64446

Rosenblatt, K. (2023, January 24). ChatGPT passes MBA exam given by a Wharton professor. NBC News https://www.nbcnews.com/tech/tech-news/chatgpt-passes-mba-exam-wharton-professor-rcna67036

Royce, C. A. (2023, October). Looking backward to educate forward. *Interface Conference*, Missouri.

Russell, S. J., & Norvig, P. (2016). *Artificial intelligence: A modern approach* (3rd ed.). Pearson.

Sharma, S. (2023, Aug 14). Guiding students to assess the merits of artificial intelligence tools. *Edutopia.*https://www.edutopia.org/article/teaching-students-use-ai-tools/

Shippee, M. (2019). *WanderlustEDU: An educator's guide to innovation, change, and adventure.* Dave Burgess Consulting, Incorporated.

Singer, N. (2023, February 6). At this school, computer science class now includes critiquing chatbots. *The New York Times.*https://www.nytimes.com/2023/02/06/technology/chatgpt-schools-teachers-ai-ethics.html

Staton, B., & Murgia, M. (2023, May 21). The AI revolution already transforming education. *Financial Times.* https://www.ft.com/content/47fd20c6-240d-4ffa-a0de-70717712ed1c

Van den Berg, G., & du Plessis, E. (2023). ChatGPT and generative ai: Possibilities for its contribution to lesson planning, critical thinking and openness in teacher education. *Education Sciences*, 13(10), 998. DOI: 10.3390/educsci13100998

Van Oosterom, A. (2024, Feb 20). People do not fear change, we fear uncertainty and loss. Medium. https://arnevanoosterom.medium.com/people-do-not-fear-change-we-fear-uncertainty-and-loss-d48735a464a0

van Rijmenam, M. (2023 January 25). ChatGPT is a paradigm shift: Why education should embrace it. *The Digital Speaker.*https://www.thedigitalspeaker.com/chatgpt-paradigm-shift-why-education-should-embrace-it/

Watson, A. (2023). Using ChatGPT to reduce your teacher workload. *The 40 Hour Teacher Workweek.* https://usergeneratededucation.wordpress.com/wp-content/uploads/2023/06/teacher-timesavers-with-chatgpt-by-angela-watson.pdf

World Economic Forum. (2023). AI accelerates students' holistic development. https://www.weforum.org/agenda/2023/05/ai-accelerate-students-holistic-development-teaching-fulfilling/

World Economic Forum. (2023). *Future of jobs report.* https://www.weforum.org/publications/the-future-of-jobs-report-2023/

Chapter 2
Exploring the Effects of AI-Powered Personalized Classroom Management Strategies

Sushil Bhardwaj
https://orcid.org/0000-0001-5184-3866
RIMT University, India

Indu Sharma
Chandigarh University, India

ABSTRACT

Recent advancements in artificial intelligence (AI) have sparked transformative possibilities in education, particularly in the realm of personalized classroom management strategies. This chapter explores the multifaceted effects of AI-powered approaches on educational settings. By leveraging AI algorithms, educators can tailor learning experiences to individual student needs, fostering a more engaging and effective educational environment. The primary objectives of this chapter are (a) to investigate the effectiveness of AI-powered personalized classroom management strategies in promoting positive student behavior, (b) to examine the impact of personalized interventions on student engagement and academic achievement, (c) To explore teachers' perceptions of AI-driven classroom management and their experiences with implementing personalized strategies, and (d) to identify best practices and recommendations for integrating AI-powered personalized classroom management strategies into educational settings.

DOI: 10.4018/979-8-3693-5443-8.ch002

INTRODUCTION

Artificial intelligence (AI) has emerged as a promising tool in transforming traditional educational practices, particularly in the realm of personalized classroom management strategies. Personalized classroom management refers to the customization of instructional methods and classroom practices to meet the unique needs of each student. In recent years, AI has demonstrated its potential to revolutionize education by offering personalized learning experiences tailored to individual student needs. This approach contrasts with traditional one-size-fits-all methods, allowing educators to adapt content delivery, pace, and support mechanisms based on real-time data analysis (Lakshmi et al., 2022). One of the primary advantages of AI-powered personalized classroom management is its ability to continuously monitor and analyze student behavior and performance in real time. Through the use of machine learning algorithms and predictive analytics, AI systems can identify patterns and trends that may indicate a student is struggling or excelling. This allows educators to intervene promptly with targeted support or advanced challenges, thus optimizing the learning experience for each student. Such personalized strategies not only enhance student engagement and motivation but also contribute to improved learning outcomes (Madura et al., 2022). Moreover, AI can enhance the efficiency of classroom management by automating routine administrative tasks, such as attendance tracking, grading, and scheduling. This automation not only reduces the administrative burden on teachers but also allows them to focus more on instructional activities and direct interactions with students. For example, AI-driven platforms can provide real-time feedback on student assignments, identifying areas where students need improvement and suggesting resources for further study.

The chapter begins with an in-depth background on AI in education. It then delves into the significance of AI-driven classroom management, providing concrete examples to illustrate its impact. It then examines the teachers' perceptions of AI-driven classroom management and their experiences with implementing personalized strategies vary widely based on research findings. Following this, the chapter addresses the personalized interventions and its impact on student engagement and academic achievement. It also discusses the AI-Powered Personalized Classroom Management Strategies. The discussion extends to the challenges faced in implementation, followed by practical recommendations for educators and policymakers. Finally, the chapter concludes by outlining areas for future research, highlighting the need for continued exploration and innovation in this field.

Understanding teachers' perceptions of AI-driven classroom management is crucial for successful implementation. While some educators embrace AI technologies for their ability to optimize administrative tasks and provide data-driven insights (Yiping et al., 2021), others may harbor concerns about job displacement or the dehumanization of the learning process (Cui et al., 2019). Addressing these perceptions is essential for fostering teacher acceptance and effective utilization of AI tools in educational settings.

Innovative AI-powered strategies such as behavior monitoring and analysis enable educators to track student engagement and behavior patterns in real time, facilitating proactive interventions to maintain a conducive learning environment (Sana et al., 2022). Personalized learning paths leverage AI algorithms to customize educational content and learning activities based on individual student interests, strengths, and weaknesses, promoting self-paced learning and deeper engagement (Mir et al., 2022). Adaptive instructional strategies dynamically adjust teaching methods and resources in response to ongoing student performance data, ensuring optimal learning experiences (Jumming and Xu, 2019).

Predictive analytics harness AI to identify at-risk students early, allowing educators to implement timely interventions and support mechanisms (Ravi et al, 2018). AI-powered feedback and assessment systems provide immediate, personalized feedback on student work, fostering continuous improvement and mastery learning (Keqin, 2020). Moreover, data-driven decision-making frameworks enable educational leaders to utilize comprehensive analytics for curriculum planning, resource allocation, and policy formulation, optimizing educational outcomes across diverse student populations (Yuan Tiani et al., 2023). These diverse AI strategies collectively enhance the efficacy and efficiency of personalized classroom management, driving educational innovation and student success in the digital age.

Implementing personalized strategies effectively requires overcoming several challenges, including technical infrastructure readiness, data privacy concerns, and ensuring equitable access to AI resources across diverse student populations (Taoyun, 2020). The integration of AI in classroom management also brings about significant ethical and practical considerations. Issues such as data privacy, algorithmic bias, and the digital divide need to be carefully addressed to ensure that AI tools are used responsibly and equitably. Ensuring that AI systems are transparent and that their decision-making processes can be understood and scrutinized by educators, students, and parents is crucial for maintaining trust and efficacy in AI applications in education. These challenges underscore the need for comprehensive policy frameworks and professional development initiatives to support educators in leveraging AI responsibly and ethically.

SIGNIFICANCE OF EXPLORING AI-POWERED PERSONALIZED CLASSROOM MANAGEMENT

The exploration of AI-powered personalized classroom management strategies is increasingly vital in modern educational settings, offering transformative potential for both teaching and learning. These strategies leverage artificial intelligence to provide tailored educational experiences, enhancing student engagement, learning outcomes, and overall classroom dynamics.

AI-powered classroom management systems enable real-time monitoring and analysis of student behaviors and academic performance. Such systems can identify patterns and trends that may not be immediately apparent to educators, facilitating timely interventions to support students who are struggling (Jan & Nienke, 2023). For instance, AI can track student participation and alert teachers to disengagement, allowing for prompt and targeted responses to re-engage those students (Kim & Lee, 2023).

Moreover, personalized learning paths facilitated by AI ensure that educational content is customized to meet the unique needs of each student. By analyzing data on student performance, preferences, and learning styles, AI can adapt instructional materials and methods to optimize individual learning experiences (Kulkatechol & Chetneti, 2022). This tailored approach helps bridge learning gaps and promotes equity, as students receive the specific support they need to succeed.

AI also enhances the efficiency and effectiveness of classroom management. By automating routine administrative tasks such as attendance tracking, grading, and feedback provision, AI systems free up valuable time for educators to focus on instruction and personalized student support (Kamal, 2022). Additionally, AI-driven analytics provide teachers with actionable insights into student progress and classroom dynamics, enabling more informed decision-making (Ghalia et al., 2020).

Furthermore, the integration of AI in classroom management encourages a data-driven culture in education. Decisions based on empirical data rather than intuition can lead to more precise and effective educational practices. For example, AI can help identify the most effective teaching strategies and learning materials for different student groups, thereby enhancing instructional quality and outcomes (Risang, 2023). For example, a teacher with 25+ students may struggle to give individual attention to each and every student. AI can support teachers by analyzing student data, such as engagement patterns, performance metrics, and participation rates, to identify outliers. For students who are struggling, AI can flag low participation or declining grades, prompting early intervention. For those excelling, AI can suggest advanced materials or activities. Systems like IBM Watson Classroom and DreamBox Learning offer such functionalities, providing insights to help teachers tailor their instruction. These tools use machine learning algorithms to continuously monitor and assess student progress, enabling personalized attention even in large classrooms.

Exploring AI-powered personalized classroom management strategies also addresses the diverse needs of contemporary classrooms, where students come from varied backgrounds with different learning needs. AI systems can provide differentiated instruction and support, fostering an inclusive learning environment where all students have the opportunity to thrive (Setareh, 2021).

TEACHERS' PERCEPTIONS OF AI-DRIVEN CLASSROOM MANAGEMENT AND IMPLEMENTING PERSONALIZED STRATEGIES

Teachers' perceptions of AI-driven classroom management and their experiences with implementing personalized strategies vary widely based on research findings. According to recent studies, many educators view AI as a valuable tool for enhancing classroom management by providing real-time insights into student behavior and performance (Kulkatechol & Chetneti, 2022). AI-powered systems can assist in monitoring student engagement levels, identifying at-risk behaviors, and suggesting personalized interventions, which educators perceive as beneficial for maintaining a conducive learning environment (Ethan & Lilach, 2023). However, there are mixed feelings among teachers regarding the implementation of AI-driven personalized strategies. Some educators express concerns about the reliability and accuracy of AI algorithms in interpreting student data and making instructional recommendations (Yeoun & Pankaj, 2023). They emphasize the importance of maintaining human oversight and intervention to ensure that AI-generated suggestions align with pedagogical goals and student needs (Anna et al., 2023).

Teachers who have successfully integrated AI-driven personalized strategies report positive outcomes such as improved student engagement, increased academic performance, and more efficient use of instructional time (Jumming & Xu, 2019). These educators appreciate AI's ability to adapt to diverse learning needs and provide targeted support that enhances individualized learning experiences.

Moreover, research suggests that professional development plays a crucial role in shaping teachers' perceptions and competencies in using AI for classroom management. Ongoing training sessions and workshops on AI applications can help educators overcome initial skepticism and gain confidence in utilizing AI tools effectively (Bundit & Chalong, 2023). Collaborative efforts between educators and AI developers to address concerns about data privacy, algorithmic transparency, and ethical implications further contribute to enhancing teachers' acceptance and utilization of AI-driven technologies in education (Setareh & Hossien, 2023).

IMPACT OF PERSONALIZED INTERVENTIONS ON STUDENT ENGAGEMENT AND ACADEMIC ACHIEVEMENT

Personalized interventions in education have demonstrated a significant positive impact on student engagement and academic achievement. By tailoring educational strategies to individual student needs, personalized interventions address specific learning gaps, enhance motivation, and promote deeper engagement in the learning process.

Research indicates that personalized interventions, such as adaptive learning technologies and targeted tutoring programs, contribute to improved academic outcomes. For example, a study by Johnson and Williams (2022) found that students who received personalized math tutoring sessions showed greater improvement in problem-solving skills compared to their peers in traditional classroom settings.

Moreover, personalized interventions foster a sense of ownership and autonomy in students by allowing them to progress at their own pace and focus on areas where they need additional support (Suraya et al., 2022). Additionally, personalized interventions can mitigate the impact of learning disparities among students with diverse backgrounds and learning styles. By providing targeted support based on real-time data analysis, educators can ensure that every student receives the necessary resources and assistance to succeed academically (Kolchenko, 2018).

By leveraging AI algorithms to analyze student data and tailor learning experiences, these interventions provide targeted support that meets individual learning needs effectively. For instance, AI can recommend adaptive learning paths, provide real-time feedback, and offer personalized tutoring based on student performance. This approach not only improves academic outcomes but also enhances student motivation and confidence in their learning abilities, contributing to a more inclusive and effective educational environment (Mathew, 2021).

AI-POWERED PERSONALIZED CLASSROOM MANAGEMENT STRATEGIES

AI-powered personalized classroom management strategies utilize algorithms to tailor educational experiences to individual student needs. These strategies include:

Behavior Monitoring and Analysis

AI algorithms have significantly advanced behavior monitoring and analysis in educational settings by providing real-time insights into student conduct. These technologies utilize various data inputs, such as video feeds, audio recordings, and digital interactions, to identify patterns and anomalies in student behavior. For instance, systems like IBM Watson Education leverage machine learning and natural language processing to monitor student behaviors continuously, offering a nuanced understanding of classroom dynamics (Teodor et al., 2019).

Real-time behavior monitoring enables teachers to detect signs of disengagement, frustration, or disruptive actions promptly. AI can analyze facial expressions, body language, and vocal tones to assess emotional states and predict potential behavioral issues. When such behaviors are identified, the system can alert the teacher, allowing for immediate intervention before the behavior escalates. For example, an AI system might detect a student frequently looking away from the screen during an online lesson, indicating disengagement, and prompt the teacher to re-engage the student with targeted questions. AI systems can monitor student engagement through data like participation, quiz results, and interaction with learning materials. When a student shows signs of disengagement, such as reduced activity or declining performance, the AI can alert the teacher. This allows the teacher to intervene promptly with targeted strategies, such as personalized feedback, adjusted learning materials, or additional support. By identifying issues early, AI helps teachers address disengagement effectively, ensuring that students stay on track and remain actively involved in their learning. This proactive approach is more effective than traditional reactive measures, which often occur after negative behaviors have already impacted the learning environment (Feng et al., 2007).

Furthermore, AI-driven behavior analysis supports personalized interventions. By understanding individual behavior patterns, educators can tailor their strategies to address specific student needs, fostering a more positive and inclusive classroom atmosphere (Hanke et al., 2016). These AI tools also help in tracking the effectiveness of behavioral interventions over time, providing data-driven insights that can inform future teaching practices (Vera et al., 2022). AI's ability to process vast amounts of data in real-time allows for a more dynamic and responsive approach to classroom management. Additionally, the continuous monitoring of behavior ensures that any changes in student conduct are quickly noticed and addressed, which is crucial for maintaining a conducive learning environment (John et al., 2020). This leads to improved behavioral outcomes and enhances the overall learning experience (Mohammad et al., 2018).

Personalized Learning Paths Using AI

Personalized learning paths facilitated by AI are transforming education by tailoring instructional content to meet the unique needs and learning styles of each student. These AI systems leverage data from various sources, including student assessments, behavior, and engagement metrics, to create individualized learning experiences that adapt in real-time.

AI algorithms can analyze vast amounts of data to identify a student's strengths, weaknesses, and preferred learning methods. For instance, platforms like Knewton and Carnegie Learning utilize adaptive learning technologies to adjust the difficulty and style of content based on real-time performance (Wafaa et al., 2022). This ensures that students are always challenged at an appropriate level, which can enhance motivation and prevent frustration.

By providing a personalized curriculum, AI helps to keep students engaged and invested in their learning. Research shows that students who follow personalized learning paths tend to have higher engagement levels and better academic outcomes compared to those in traditional settings (Ping, 2020). These systems can recommend specific resources, activities, and pacing tailored to individual learning paces, promoting a more effective and enjoyable learning experience. One short example is an AI system that identifies a student struggling with fractions and adjusts the lesson plan to include more visual aids and interactive exercises.

Moreover, AI-powered personalized learning paths support differentiated instruction, which is essential for accommodating diverse classroom needs. Teachers can use insights generated by AI to better understand each student's progress and needs, allowing for more targeted and effective teaching strategies (Suk, 2022). This is particularly beneficial in inclusive classrooms where students have varying abilities and learning requirements.

The ability to provide immediate, personalized feedback is another significant advantage. AI systems can deliver instant feedback on assignments and assessments, helping students understand their mistakes and learn from them quickly (Fiona et al., 2023). This immediate reinforcement aids in consolidating learning and encourages continuous improvement.

Predictive Analytics for Early Intervention

Predictive analytics, a powerful application of AI, is increasingly being utilized in educational settings to identify and support at-risk students through early intervention. By analyzing vast amounts of data from various sources, predictive analytics can identify patterns and trends that may indicate future academic or behavioral issues, allowing educators to intervene before these issues escalate.

Predictive analytics systems gather data from multiple facets of a student's educational experience, including attendance records, grades, behavior logs, and engagement metrics. These systems use machine learning algorithms to process this data and generate risk profiles for individual students (Hongchao, 2019). For example, an AI system might detect a decline in a student's grades coupled with increased absenteeism and predict a higher likelihood of dropout. Early identification enables educators to provide targeted interventions such as tutoring, counseling, or parental engagement.

One example is a high school using predictive analytics to identify students at risk of failing mathematics. The system flagged a student whose homework submission rate had dropped by 40% over a month, prompting the teacher to arrange additional support sessions.

Research demonstrates that predictive analytics can significantly improve student outcomes. Schools implementing these technologies have reported higher retention rates and better academic performance (Abdolrahman, 2021). These systems provide actionable insights, helping educators tailor interventions to meet individual student needs more effectively (John et al., 2020). Moreover, predictive analytics fosters a proactive approach to education. Instead of responding to problems after they arise, schools can anticipate and address potential issues, creating a more supportive and responsive learning environment (Kulkatechol & Chetneti, 2022). This proactive stance is particularly beneficial for marginalized or underserved student populations who may be more prone to academic difficulties.

The integration of predictive analytics in educational settings represents a significant advancement in how schools support student success. By leveraging data to foresee and mitigate potential issues, educators can enhance their ability to foster positive educational outcomes and ensure that all students have the opportunity to succeed (Sana et al., 2022).

AI-Powered Feedback and Assessment

AI-powered feedback and assessment systems are revolutionizing education by providing personalized, timely, and actionable insights into student performance. These systems use machine learning algorithms and natural language processing to evaluate student work, identify strengths and weaknesses, and offer detailed feedback. This enhances the learning experience by enabling more precise and individualized guidance.

One significant advantage of AI-powered assessment is its ability to provide instant feedback. Traditional grading and feedback processes can be time-consuming, often delaying the delivery of important insights. AI systems, however, can analyze and grade assignments immediately after submission. For example, an AI-powered system can instantly evaluate a student's essay for grammar, coherence, and argument strength, offering suggestions for improvement.

AI systems can also adapt to individual learning styles and needs, offering differentiated feedback. For instance, platforms like Gradescope and Turnitin use AI to analyze written assignments, detecting plagiarism and providing originality reports

(Yiping et al., 2021). These systems can highlight specific areas where a student may need further practice or study, such as grammar or argument development, thereby promoting continuous improvement.

Moreover, AI-powered tools can assess a wide range of student outputs, from written essays to spoken language and even programming code. This versatility ensures that feedback is comprehensive and tailored to the specific type of work being evaluated. This adaptability is especially beneficial in diverse classrooms where students may have varying strengths and areas for improvement.

For example, an AI tool that evaluates student programming assignments by not only checking for correct outputs but also analyzing code efficiency and style, offering specific suggestions for optimization.

AI-driven assessment also supports teachers by reducing the administrative burden associated with grading. This allows educators to focus more on teaching and interacting with students (Alam, 2023). Additionally, AI can identify trends and patterns in student performance over time, helping teachers to adjust their instructional strategies and address common areas of difficulty (Qian et al., 2022).

Data-Driven Decision Making

Data-driven decision making (DDDM) enhanced by artificial intelligence (AI) is increasingly shaping classroom management practices by providing educators with tools to analyze, interpret, and apply data in real-time. AI algorithms enable educators to leverage various data sources such as student behavior logs, engagement metrics, and academic performance records to optimize classroom dynamics and enhance learning outcomes.

Furthermore, AI supports personalized classroom experiences by tailoring interventions and instructional strategies based on individual student needs. By analyzing historical data on student performance and behavior, AI can recommend personalized approaches to address specific challenges or strengths. For instance, an AI system can suggest differentiated assignments or adaptive learning paths for students with varying learning styles and abilities (Hanke et al., 2016).

AI-driven DDDM also enhances communication and collaboration between educators, students, and parents. By providing insights into student progress and behavior trends, AI platforms facilitate more informed discussions during parent-teacher conferences and enable collaborative problem-solving strategies (Mohammad, 2018). Moreover, AI-powered predictive analytics contribute to proactive classroom management strategies. By forecasting potential issues such as attendance trends, academic performance fluctuations, or behavioral patterns, AI enables educators to implement preventive measures and interventions before issues escalate. For example,

AI algorithms can predict student absenteeism risks based on historical attendance data, allowing teachers to implement targeted attendance improvement programs.

BENEFITS AND CHALLENGES OF AI-POWERED PERSONALIZED CLASSROOM MANAGEMENT

AI-powered personalized classroom management is transforming educational practices by offering innovative solutions to enhance learning and teaching experiences. However, its implementation presents a mix of benefits and challenges that must be carefully navigated to ensure effective and ethical use. This section delves into these aspects from a research paper perspective.

Benefits

Enhanced Individualized Learning: AI technologies enable the creation of personalized learning experiences tailored to each student's unique needs, abilities, and interests. Through machine learning algorithms, AI can analyze vast amounts of data to identify individual learning patterns and preferences, thereby facilitating the delivery of customized educational content. This individualized approach can help students engage more deeply with the material and improve their academic performance.

Real-Time Feedback and Assessment: AI systems can provide instant feedback on student assignments and activities, allowing for timely interventions. This immediate feedback helps students understand their mistakes and learn more effectively. Additionally, AI can assist teachers in identifying areas where students struggle, enabling targeted support and resources to address these challenges (Ethan & Lilach., 2023).

Efficient Administrative Support: AI-powered tools can automate routine administrative tasks such as attendance tracking, grading, and scheduling. This automation reduces the administrative burden on teachers, freeing up more time for instructional activities and direct student engagement (Yeoun et al., 2021). By streamlining these tasks, AI can help improve overall classroom efficiency and effectiveness.

Predictive Analytics for Early Intervention: AI can predict potential academic issues by analyzing trends and patterns in student performance data. Predictive analytics enable early identification of at-risk students, allowing educators to intervene with appropriate support measures before problems escalate (Ethan & Lilach., 2023). This proactive approach can significantly enhance student retention and success rates.

Improved Engagement and Motivation: Personalized learning experiences and real-time feedback can increase student engagement and motivation. AI tools can adapt content delivery based on student interests and proficiency levels, making learning more interactive and enjoyable (Yiping et al., 2019). Gamification elements, powered by AI, can further motivate students by incorporating game-like features into the learning process.

Enhanced Student-Teacher Interaction: AI-powered tools can facilitate more meaningful interactions between students and teachers by handling routine tasks. Teachers can focus on providing personalized support, addressing individual student needs, and fostering deeper, more engaging classroom discussions.

Data-Driven Insights: AI systems can aggregate and analyze vast amounts of educational data, providing teachers with valuable insights into student performance, learning trends, and potential problem areas. This data-driven approach enables more informed decision-making and the ability to tailor teaching strategies effectively.

Differentiated Instruction: AI can support differentiated instruction by identifying the diverse learning needs of students and adapting the content and pace accordingly. This ensures that all students, regardless of their learning levels, receive the appropriate challenges and support to facilitate growth.

Resource Optimization: AI can help optimize the allocation of educational resources by predicting future needs based on current trends and usage patterns. This ensures that materials, tools, and personnel are available when and where they are needed most, improving overall efficiency.

Inclusive Education: AI can play a crucial role in making education more inclusive by providing assistive technologies for students with disabilities. Tools like speech-to-text, text-to-speech, and personalized learning aids can help bridge gaps and ensure equitable access to education for all students.

Scalability: AI-powered solutions can be scaled to accommodate large numbers of students without compromising the quality of education. This is particularly beneficial in large school districts or regions with limited access to high-quality educational resources.

Continuous Improvement: AI systems can continuously learn and improve over time, becoming more effective in identifying student needs and optimizing learning processes. This ongoing refinement ensures that educational practices evolve with changing student dynamics and emerging educational challenges.

Challenges

Data Privacy and Security Concerns: The use of AI in education involves the collection and analysis of large amounts of student data, raising significant privacy and security concerns. Ensuring the confidentiality and security of this data is paramount. Schools must implement robust data protection measures and comply with relevant regulations to safeguard student information (Cui, 2019). Additionally, transparent data practices and informed consent are essential to maintaining trust among stakeholders.

Algorithmic Bias and Fairness: AI systems can perpetuate and even exacerbate existing biases if not carefully designed and monitored. Algorithmic bias can lead to unfair treatment of certain student groups, particularly those from marginalized communities. It is crucial to develop AI tools that are inclusive and equitable, taking into account diverse learning needs and backgrounds. Regular audits and adjustments are necessary to ensure that AI systems operate fairly and without discrimination.

Teacher Readiness and Professional Development: Effective integration of AI in classrooms requires teachers to be well-versed in using these technologies. However, many educators may lack the necessary skills and knowledge to utilize AI tools effectively. Comprehensive professional development programs are needed to equip teachers with the required competencies and confidence (Madura, 2022). Ongoing support and resources should also be provided to help teachers adapt to technological changes and overcome implementation challenges.

Infrastructure and Technical Support: Successful implementation of AI-powered classroom management requires adequate technological infrastructure, including reliable internet access and up-to-date hardware. Many schools, particularly those in underfunded areas, may lack the necessary resources to support AI integration. Providing the required infrastructure and technical support is essential to ensure that all students and teachers can benefit from AI technologies.

Ethical Considerations and Acceptability: The ethical implications of using AI in education must be carefully considered. Issues such as data ownership, consent, and the transparency of AI decision-making processes are critical (Jan et al., 2018). Developing ethical frameworks and guidelines for AI use in education can help address these concerns. Additionally, fostering an open dialogue with all stakeholders, including students, parents, and educators, can ensure that AI implementations are acceptable and beneficial.

Risk of Over-Reliance on Technology: There is a risk that educators may become overly reliant on AI tools, potentially neglecting traditional teaching methods and human interaction, which are crucial for holistic student development. It is important to strike a balance between leveraging AI for its benefits and maintaining the irreplaceable value of human teachers in fostering critical thinking, creativity, and social skills.

Cost and Accessibility: The cost of implementing AI technologies can be a significant barrier, especially for schools with limited budgets. Ensuring equitable access to AI tools requires investment and support from educational authorities and policymakers. Efforts should be made to make AI solutions affordable and accessible to all schools, regardless of their financial constraints.

Teacher Autonomy: The integration of AI in the classroom can sometimes undermine teacher autonomy, as reliance on AI recommendations might constrain teachers' ability to use their professional judgment and creativity. Balancing AI input with teacher expertise is essential to maintain the integrity of the teaching profession.

Training and Professional Development: Teachers and administrators require extensive training to effectively use AI tools. This includes not only technical skills but also an understanding of how to interpret AI-generated data and integrate it into their teaching practices. Continuous professional development is necessary to keep pace with technological advancements.

Resistance to Change: Some educators and stakeholders may be resistant to adopting AI technologies due to a lack of understanding, fear of job displacement, or skepticism about the effectiveness of AI in education. Addressing these concerns through clear communication and evidence-based practices is crucial for successful implementation.

Infrastructure Limitations: Many educational institutions, particularly in rural or underfunded areas, may lack the necessary infrastructure to support AI technologies. Reliable internet access, modern hardware, and technical support are prerequisites for effective AI integration.

Unintended Consequences: The use of AI in education may lead to unintended consequences, such as over-monitoring and reduced student privacy. There is also the potential for AI to inadvertently reinforce existing inequalities if not carefully managed and designed to be inclusive.

Legal Issues: The deployment of AI in education raises ethical and legal questions related to data usage, consent, and the extent to which AI should influence educational decisions. Developing robust ethical frameworks and legal guidelines is essential to address these issues responsibly.

BEST PRACTICES AND RECOMMENDATIONS FOR INTEGRATING AI-POWERED PERSONALIZED CLASSROOM MANAGEMENT STRATEGIES

Integrating AI-powered personalized classroom management strategies into educational settings requires a multifaceted approach that considers technical, pedagogical, ethical, and practical aspects. Based on recent research, here are detailed best practices and recommendations for successful implementation.

Comprehensive Professional Development: To effectively integrate AI tools, educators need extensive and ongoing professional development. Training should cover the technical aspects of using AI tools, pedagogical strategies for integrating AI into the curriculum, and ethical considerations. Research indicates that teacher readiness and confidence significantly influence the successful adoption of AI in education (Taoyun, 2022). Professional development programs should include hands-on workshops, online courses, and peer collaboration opportunities. Continuous support and resources should be available to address any challenges teachers might encounter (Risang, 2023).

Collaboration between Stakeholders: Effective integration of AI requires collaboration among educators, administrators, technologists, and policymakers. This collaboration ensures that AI tools are aligned with educational goals and practical needs. Regular meetings and feedback loops involving all stakeholders can help in refining AI tools and addressing implementation challenges (Ghaliya et al., 2020). Additionally, involving students in the feedback process can provide valuable insights into the usability and effectiveness of AI tools (Luckin et al., 2021).

Ethical Frameworks and Data Privacy: Ethical considerations are paramount in the deployment of AI technologies in education. Schools must establish robust data protection measures to safeguard student information. Transparent data practices, including informed consent from students and parents, are essential. Ethical frameworks should address data ownership, consent, algorithmic bias, and the potential for AI to reinforce existing inequalities (Junming, 2019). Regular audits and assessments of AI systems can help ensure they operate within ethical boundaries.

User-Centered Design: AI tools should be designed with the end-users—teachers and students—in mind. User-centered design involves incorporating feedback from teachers and students during the development process to ensure that the tools meet their needs and are user-friendly (Suraya et al., 2022). This approach increases the likelihood of acceptance and effective use of AI technologies in classrooms. It is essential to conduct pilot tests and iterative improvements based on user feedback.

Continuous Monitoring and Evaluation: Continuous monitoring and evaluation are crucial for assessing the effectiveness of AI tools. Implementing a feedback system where educators can report on the performance and impact of AI tools can help in making necessary adjustments (Mathew, 2021). Regular evaluations should include both qualitative and quantitative measures to understand the impact on student engagement, learning outcomes, and teacher satisfaction. This iterative process ensures that AI strategies remain relevant and effective.

Focus on Inclusivity: AI tools should cater to diverse learning needs and backgrounds. Research highlights the risk of AI exacerbating existing educational inequalities if not carefully designed (Hanke, 2016). Ensuring that AI systems are adaptable and considerate of different learning styles, abilities, and socio-economic backgrounds is crucial for equitable education. Developing AI tools that can provide personalized support to students with disabilities or those from marginalized communities can help bridge educational gaps.

Integration with Pedagogical Practices: AI should complement traditional pedagogical practices rather than replace them. Effective integration involves using AI tools to enhance teaching methods and provide additional insights into student learning. For example, AI can be used to provide real-time feedback, identify learning gaps, and suggest tailored interventions (Hongchao, 2019). Teachers should be encouraged to use AI as a supplementary tool that supports their instructional strategies and enhances student learning experiences.

Building a Supportive Infrastructure: A robust infrastructure is essential for the successful integration of AI in classrooms. This includes reliable internet access, up-to-date hardware, and technical support. Research indicates that inadequate infrastructure can hinder the effective use of AI tools. Schools should invest in the necessary technological infrastructure to ensure seamless implementation and to support both teachers and students in utilizing AI technologies effectively.

Cultivating a Culture of Innovation: Creating a culture that embraces innovation and experimentation can facilitate the successful integration of AI. Encouraging teachers to experiment with AI tools, share their experiences, and learn from each other can foster a collaborative and innovative educational environment (Ravi, 2018). Schools should recognize and reward innovative teaching practices that leverage AI to enhance learning outcomes.

Addressing Technical Challenges: Technical challenges such as software compatibility, data integration, and system reliability must be addressed proactively. Schools should work closely with AI developers to ensure that tools are compatible with existing systems and can be easily integrated into the school's technological ecosystem (Anna, 2023). Providing technical support and troubleshooting assistance can help teachers overcome any technical barriers to using AI effectively.

The integration of AI-powered personalized classroom management strategies offers significant potential to enhance educational practices. By focusing on comprehensive professional development, stakeholder collaboration, ethical frameworks, user-centered design, continuous evaluation, inclusivity, integration with pedagogical practices, supportive infrastructure, a culture of innovation, and addressing technical challenges, educators can maximize the benefits of AI in education. These best practices ensure that AI tools not only enhance teaching and learning but also address potential challenges and ethical concerns, creating more engaging, equitable, and effective learning environments.

FUTURE RESEARCH DIRECTIONS

Future research on AI-powered personalized classroom management strategies should encompass both technical aspects and psychological impacts on students and educators to comprehensively understand their effectiveness and implications. Technically, longitudinal studies are essential to evaluate the sustained effects of AI interventions on student behavior, engagement, and academic performance over extended periods. Such studies would provide valuable insights into the long-term educational trajectories influenced by AI strategies and the durability of their benefits. Furthermore, deploying AI in diverse educational settings across various age groups, socio-economic backgrounds, and cultural contexts will help assess the generalizability and adaptability of these tools, revealing how different environments might necessitate tailored AI solutions to optimize educational outcomes.

From a psychological perspective, research should delve into how AI-driven classroom management systems impact both students and educators. For students, it is crucial to examine the effects on stress levels, motivation, self-efficacy, and overall well-being. AI systems should be designed to enhance learning experiences without increasing cognitive load or inducing anxiety. For instance, personalized feedback generated by AI can significantly influence student self-perception and academic motivation, necessitating a thorough understanding of these psychological dynamics.

For educators, understanding how they adapt to and interact with AI technologies is vital. Investigating the challenges they face, the skills they need, and the professional development required to effectively integrate AI can inform the creation of support systems that facilitate smooth transitions. Educators' attitudes towards AI and their perceived efficacy of these tools can significantly impact their implementation success.

Ethical considerations, particularly concerning data privacy, consent, and algorithmic bias, must also be central to future research. Developing robust frameworks to address these issues will ensure that AI applications are used responsibly, protecting student rights and promoting fairness. Additionally, exploring the balance between AI's personalized guidance and fostering student autonomy and agency is crucial. Research should focus on how AI can empower students to take an active role in their learning while providing the necessary support to prevent dependency.

CONCLUSION

The significance of exploring AI-powered personalized classroom management strategies lies at the intersection of enhancing educational effectiveness through innovative technological applications and understanding educators' perspectives and experiences in implementing these strategies. AI technologies offer transformative opportunities in education, particularly in areas like behavior monitoring and analysis, personalized learning paths, adaptive instructional strategies, predictive analytics for early intervention, AI-powered feedback and assessment, and data-driven decision making. Teachers' perceptions and experiences with AI-driven classroom management strategies are crucial for successful implementation. Understanding their attitudes, challenges, and successes informs the development of supportive frameworks and professional development programs that facilitate effective integration into teaching practices. Educators play a pivotal role in shaping the adoption and adaptation of AI technologies in classrooms, influencing their impact on student learning and educational outcomes. Moving forward, continued research into these AI-powered strategies is essential to refine their effectiveness, address ethical considerations such as data privacy and algorithmic bias, and explore their broader implications on teaching practices and student learning experiences. By integrating insights from educational psychology, cognitive science, and human-computer interaction, educators and researchers can collaboratively leverage AI to create more engaging, equitable, and personalized learning environments that enhance educational outcomes for all students.

REFERENCES

Ashraf, A. (2023). Harnessing the Power of AI to Create Intelligent Tutoring Systems for Enhanced Classroom Experience and Improved Learning Outcomes. DOI: 10.1007/978-981-99-1767-9_42

Bundit & Chalong. (2023). Analyzing the Impact of Artificial Intelligence in Personalized Learning and Adaptive Assessment in Higher Education. International Journal of Research and Scientific Innovation. DOI: 10.51244/IJRSI.2023.10412

Ethan, M. (2023). Using AI to Implement Effective Teaching Strategies in Classrooms: Five Strategies, Including Prompts. Social Science Research Network. DOI: 10.2139/ssrn.4391243

Feng, T., Qinghua, Z., Zhiyong, G., Jin, D., & Renhou, L. (2007). Personalized Learning Strategies in an intelligent e-Learning Environment. DOI: 10.1109/CSCWD.2007.4281570

Fiona, D., Albrecht, S., Lewis, L., & Chuang. (2023). Relevance, Effort, and Perceived Quality: Language Learners' Experiences with AI-Generated Contextually Personalized Learning Material. DOI: 10.1145/3563657.3596112

Ghaliya, A. (2020). Smart Classroom Technology in Artificial Intelligence: A Review Paper. DOI: 10.5220/0010306502290235

Hanke, K. (2016, September). A Meta-Analysis of the Effects of Classroom Management Strategies and Classroom Management Programs on Students' Academic, Behavioral, Emotional, and Motivational Outcomes. *Review of Educational Research*, 86(3), 643–680. Advance online publication. DOI: 10.3102/0034654315626799

Hongchao, P. (2019). Personalized adaptive learning: an emerging pedagogical approach enabled by a smart learning environment. Smart Learning Environments, DOI: 10.1186/s40561-019-0089-y

Jan, R., & Nienke, R. (2023). Adverse effects of personalized automated feedback. DOI: 10.4995/HEAd23.2023.16195

John, N. (2020). Personalization of E-Learning Process Using AI-Powered Chatbot Integration. DOI: 10.1007/978-3-030-58124-4_20

Junming, C., & Xu, L. (2019). The Study on Students' Participation in Personalized Learning Under the Background of Artificial Intelligence. DOI: 10.1109/ITME.2019.00131

Kamal, K. (2022, January). Personalized Education Based on Hybrid Intelligent Recommendation System. *Journal of Mathematics*, 2022(1), 1313711. Advance online publication. DOI: 10.1155/2022/1313711

Keqin, L. (2020). Experimental Research of English Teaching Management Model Based on Personalized Multimedia Technology. *OAlib*, 7(4), 1–13. Advance online publication. DOI: 10.4236/oalib.1106251

Kolchenko. (2018). Can Modern AI Replace Teachers? Not so Fast! Artificial Intelligence and Adaptive Learning: Personalized Education in the AI Age. DOI: 10.21692/haps.2018.032

Kulkatechol, K. (2022). Personalized Learning Management System using a Machine Learning Technique. TEM Journal. doi: DOI: 10.18421/tem114-25

Lakshmi, G. (2022). AI-powered Digital Classroom. DOI: 10.1109/IC3I-OT53935.2022.9767944

Madura, P. (2022). AI Solution to Assist Online Education Productivity via Personalizing Learning Strategies and Analyzing the Student Performance. DOI: 10.1109/UEMCON54665.2022.9965735

Matthew, M. (2021). Personalized Learning Environments. DOI: 10.1109/ISET52350.2021.00036

Mir. (2022). AI-Based Personalized E-Learning Systems: Issues, Challenges, and Solutions. IEEE Access. DOI: 10.1109/ACCESS.2022.3193938

Mohammad, M. (2018). Identifying Classroom Management Strategies by Focusing on Diversity and Inclusion.

Ping, X. (2020). Design of Personalized Intelligent Learning Assistant System Under Artificial Intelligence Background. DOI: 10.1007/978-3-030-62743-0_27

Qian. (2022). Research on Classroom Teaching Management and Process Evaluation Based on Artificial Intelligence. DOI: 10.1109/ICENIT57306.2022.00084

Ravi, K. (2018). Augmenting Classrooms with AI for Personalized Education. DOI: 10.1109/ICASSP.2018.8461812

Risang, B. (2023). *Personalised learning with ai: implications for ignatian pedagogy.* International Journal of Educational Best Practices. DOI: 10.31258/ijebp.v7n1.p1-16

Sana, O. (2022). Applications of Artificial Intelligence in Education. doi: DOI: 10.33102/alazkiyaa.v1i1.10\

Setareh, M. (2021, May). Personalized Education in the Artificial Intelligence Era: What to Expect Next. *IEEE Signal Processing Magazine*, 38(3), 37–50. Advance online publication. DOI: 10.1109/MSP.2021.3055032

Setareh, R. (2023). Advancing Personalized and Adaptive Learning Experience in Education with Artificial Intelligence. DOI: 10.23919/EAEEIE55804.2023.10181336

Suk. (2022). Construction of Personalized Learning Model Supported by Human-computer Cooperation. DOI: 10.1145/3582580.3582588

Suraya, H. (2022). Trends on Technologies and Artificial Intelligence in Education for Personalized Learning: Systematic Literature Review. International Journal of Academic Research in Progressive Education and Development. DOI: 10.6007/IJARPED/v11-i1/12230

Taoyun, Z. (2022). An Intelligent Classroom Management System Based on AI + IOT Technology. DOI: 10.1109/ITME56794.2022.00052

Teodor. (2019). Smart classroom, internet of things and personalized teaching. DOI: 10.12955/cbup.v7.1491

Tianyi, Y. (2023). Design of Intelligent Real-Time Feedback System in Online Classroom. *Lecture Notes in Computer Science*, 14024, 326–335. Advance online publication. DOI: 10.1007/978-3-031-35946-0_27

Vera, I. (2022). Designing of personalized digital educational environment based on neural network technologies. Nucleation and Atmospheric Aerosols. DOI: 10.1063/5.0104196

Wafaa, S. (2023, January). AI-based adaptive personalized content presentation and exercises navigation for an effective and engaging E-learning platform. *Multimedia Tools and Applications*, 82(3), 3303–3333. Advance online publication. DOI: 10.1007/s11042-022-13076-8

Yeoun. (2023). AI in Classroom: Group Score Prediction System. DOI: 10.1109/ICAIIC57133.2023.10067066

Yiping, L. (2021). Research and application of personalized learning under the background of artificial intelligence. DOI: 10.1109/EIMSS53851.2021.00020

KEY TERMS AND DEFINITIONS

AI Algorithms: AI algorithms are sets of programmed rules and calculations that enable AI systems to process data, identify patterns, and make decisions or predictions. These algorithms underpin AI functionalities such as image recognition, language processing, and predictive analytics.

AI Tools: AI tools are software applications utilizing artificial intelligence to perform tasks such as data analysis, natural language processing, and predictive modeling, enhancing efficiency and decision-making capabilities.

AI-Powered Strategies: AI-powered strategies in education employ artificial intelligence technologies to optimize and enhance teaching and learning processes. These strategies include adaptive learning platforms, intelligent tutoring systems, automated grading, and data-driven decision-making tools to provide efficient, tailored educational experiences.

Artificial Intelligence (AI): Artificial Intelligence (AI) refers to the creation of computer systems capable of performing tasks that typically require human intelligence, such as learning, reasoning, problem-solving, perception, and language understanding, through techniques like machine learning and neural networks.

Data-Driven Decision Making: Data-Driven Decision Making involves using data analysis and interpretation to guide strategic business decisions, ensuring they are informed by empirical evidence rather than intuition.

Ethical Framework: An ethical framework is a structured set of guidelines and principles designed to guide behavior and decision-making, ensuring actions are ethical. In AI, it addresses issues like data privacy, fairness, transparency, and accountability in the development and application of technologies.

Personalized Classroom: A personalized classroom customizes instruction based on individual student needs, preferences, and learning styles. This approach utilizes data and technology to create adaptive learning experiences that respond to student progress, aiming to enhance engagement, motivation, and academic success.

Predictive Analysis: Predictive analysis involves using statistical techniques and AI to examine current and historical data, aiming to predict future outcomes and trends. This method helps in anticipating potential issues and making informed decisions based on data-driven insights.

Real-Time Assessment: Real-time assessment evaluates student performance instantly as they engage with tasks, providing immediate feedback. This approach helps educators make timely instructional adjustments and supports students in understanding and improving their learning outcomes as they progress.

Chapter 3
The Role of AI in Transforming Assessment Practices in Education

Vetrivel S. C.
https://orcid.org/0000-0003-3050-8211
Kongu Engineering College, India

P. Vidhyapriya
Kongu Engineering College, India

Arun V. P.
JKKN College of Engineering and Technology, India

ABSTRACT

Assessment practices in education are undergoing a significant transformation with the integration of artificial intelligence (AI) technologies. This chapter explores the evolving role of AI in revolutionizing assessment methods across educational contexts. By automating various aspects of assessment, AI offers educators and learners unprecedented opportunities for efficiency, personalization, and scalability. AI-powered assessment tools enable the automation of grading, providing educators with more time to focus on providing personalized feedback and guiding student learning. Additionally, AI can analyze vast amounts of data to identify patterns in student performance, allowing for targeted interventions and adaptive learning experiences tailored to individual needs. Furthermore, AI facilitates the development of innovative assessment formats, such as simulations and interactive scenarios, which can better assess higher-order thinking skills and real-world application of

DOI: 10.4018/979-8-3693-5443-8.ch003

knowledge.

1. INTRODUCTION

1.1 Definition and Overview of AI

Artificial Intelligence (AI) refers to the simulation of human intelligence in machines, enabling them to perform tasks that typically require human intelligence. This encompasses a wide range of capabilities, including problem-solving, perception, learning, reasoning, natural language understanding, and decision-making (Bostrum 2017). AI systems can be categorized into two main types: narrow AI and general AI. Narrow AI, also known as Weak AI, is designed for a specific task or set of tasks. Examples include virtual assistants like Siri or Alexa, recommendation systems like those used by Netflix or Amazon, and autonomous vehicles. On the other hand, General AI, also known as Strong AI or Artificial General Intelligence (AGI), refers to AI systems with human-like cognitive abilities. These systems would be capable of understanding, learning, and applying knowledge across a wide range of tasks, similar to humans. AI techniques encompass various approaches, including machine learning, neural networks, natural language processing, computer vision, and robotics. Machine learning, a subset of AI, involves training algorithms to recognize patterns and make predictions based on data without being explicitly programmed. AI has applications across numerous industries, including healthcare, finance, transportation, entertainment, education, and more (Diamandis et al., 2017). It has the potential to revolutionize how we work, live, and interact with technology. However, it also raises ethical and societal concerns, such as privacy, job displacement, bias in algorithms, and the implications of autonomous decision-making. Therefore, responsible development and deployment of AI technologies are crucial to ensuring their positive impact on society. AI technologies are revolutionizing the landscape of educational assessment by introducing a range of tools and techniques that enhance accuracy, efficiency, and personalization. At the core of these advancements are machine learning algorithms, which enable systems to analyze large datasets, identify patterns, and make predictions that can inform more nuanced and individualized assessments. For instance, natural language processing (NLP) algorithms are used to evaluate open-ended student responses, such as essays or short answers. These algorithms can understand context, assess coherence, and even detect nuances in argumentation, offering a level of evaluation that goes beyond traditional rubric-based grading. This not only saves time for educators but also reduces human bias in grading. Moreover, AI-driven adaptive learning systems are transforming formative assessment practices. These systems leverage real-time data to adjust the difficulty and content of assessments based on a student's performance. By continuously analyzing a student's responses, AI can tailor the assessment process to ensure it aligns with the student's current learning level, thus promoting mastery of concepts before progressing to more complex material. Such personalized assessments help in identifying learning gaps early on, enabling timely interventions that are crucial for student success. Another significant application of AI in educational assessment is the use of predictive analytics. By analyzing historical data, including student performance, behavioral patterns, and even socio-economic factors, AI models can predict future academic outcomes. These predictions are invaluable for educators and administrators, allowing them to proactively address potential challenges, such as identifying students at risk of falling behind or dropping out. Additionally, AI can provide insights into the effectiveness of teaching strategies and curricula, guiding educators in refining their instructional approaches. In high-stakes testing environments, AI is being employed to enhance the security and integrity of assessments. Advanced AI-powered proctoring systems use facial recognition, keystroke dynamics, and behavioral analytics to monitor test-takers, ensuring that the assessment environment remains fair and secure. These systems can detect anomalies or suspicious behavior, such as cheating attempts, in real-time, thereby safeguarding the validity of the assessment. The integration of AI in assessment practices also extends to the development of intelligent tutoring systems (ITS). These systems not only assess student performance but also offer personalized feedback and guidance, effectively acting as a virtual tutor. By analyzing student interactions and responses, ITS can provide targeted recommendations for improvement, thus supporting continuous learning and development.

1.2 Historical Context of AI in Education

The historical narrative of AI in education spans several decades, marked by pioneering research, technological advancements, and evolving pedagogical theories. In the mid-20th century, amidst the post-war technological boom, early attempts to integrate AI into education emerged as researchers and educators explored the potential of computers to augment traditional teaching methods (Ford 2018). B.F. Skinner's development of teaching machines in the 1950s exemplified one of the earliest applications of AI principles in educational practice. These machines, rooted in behaviorist theories, aimed to deliver personalized instruction by presenting learners with instructional materials and providing immediate feedback based on their responses. The emergence of expert systems and intelligent tutoring systems (ITS) in the 1970s and 1980s marked a significant milestone in the integration of AI into educational assessment. Expert systems, which mimicked the decision-making processes of human experts, offered opportunities for diagnostic assessment and adaptive learning. Meanwhile, ITS, such as the groundbreaking "SHERLOCK" system developed by Jaime Carbonell in 1970, represented a paradigm shift in personalized instruction. SHERLOCK utilized natural language processing and expert knowledge bases to provide tailored feedback and guidance to students in domains like mathematics and language learning (Garrison 2007) (Kaku 2011). Throughout the late 20th century and into the 21st century, advancements in machine learning, natural language processing, and data analytics further propelled the integration of AI into educational assessment. Automated grading systems, powered by machine learning algorithms, revolutionized the process of assessing student work, offering scalability and efficiency while maintaining reliability and validity. Adaptive learning platforms leveraged data-driven insights to personalize learning experiences, catering to individual learner needs and preferences. Predictive analytics tools analyzed vast amounts of educational data to forecast student performance and identify at-risk learners, enabling early intervention and targeted support. The historical evolution of AI in education reflects a continuous quest to leverage technology to enhance teaching and learning processes. From early experiments with teaching machines to the sophisticated AI-powered assessment tools of today, the trajectory of AI in education underscores a commitment to innovation and improvement in educational practice. As educators, researchers, and policymakers continue to explore the potential of AI technologies, the historical context serves as a foundation for understanding the opportunities and challenges that lie ahead in transforming assessment practices and improving educational outcomes for learners worldwide.

1.3 Current Trends and Innovations

Today, AI in education is characterized by several innovative trends that are reshaping how teaching and learning occur. These include the rise of personalized learning systems that adapt to individual student needs, the use of natural language processing to facilitate automated grading and feedback, and the deployment of intelligent tutoring systems that provide customized support to learners (Kelly 2017). Additionally, predictive analytics are being used to identify students at risk of falling behind, allowing for timely interventions. This section will delve into these current trends, showcasing real-world examples and case studies that illustrate the practical applications and benefits of AI technologies in educational settings.

1.4 Importance of Assessment in Education

Assessment serves as a cornerstone of the educational process, fulfilling a range of vital functions that contribute to student learning, teacher effectiveness, and educational accountability. Firstly, assessment provides educators with valuable insights into students' knowledge, skills, and understanding of academic content. By evaluating student performance through various assessment methods, such as tests, quizzes, projects, and presentations, teachers can gauge individual and collective progress, identify areas of strength and weakness, and tailor instruction to meet students' diverse learning needs (Klutka et al., 2017). Moreover, assessment serves as a diagnostic tool, helping educators identify gaps in students' understanding and address misconceptions before they become entrenched. Through formative assessment practices, such as classroom discussions, peer feedback, and self-assessment activities, teachers can monitor student learning in real-time, provide timely feedback, and scaffold instruction to support continuous improvement. Assessment also plays a pivotal role in promoting student motivation and engagement. When students receive constructive feedback on their work and see evidence of their progress over time, they are more likely to feel motivated to persist in their learning efforts and take ownership of their academic development. Additionally, assessments that incorporate authentic tasks and real-world contexts can enhance students' sense of relevance and applicability, fostering deeper learning and long-term retention of knowledge. Furthermore, assessment serves as a mechanism for accountability in education, providing stakeholders, including students, parents, policymakers, and the public, with transparent measures of educational quality and effectiveness. Standardized assessments, such as state-mandated tests and international assessments like the PISA (Programme for International Student Assessment), help policymakers evaluate the performance of educational systems, identify areas for improvement, and allocate resources strategically to support student success.

1.5 Methodology

The methodology for this chapter on "The Role of AI in Transforming Assessment Practices in Education" is structured around a comprehensive review and analysis of existing literature, case studies, and thematic insights related to the application of AI in educational assessment. The approach involves several key steps to ensure a thorough exploration of the subject matter.

1.5.1 Literature Review

The chapter begins with an extensive literature review to identify and synthesize relevant academic research, industry reports, and white papers on AI technologies in education. The literature review focuses on:

- The evolution of AI in educational assessment, tracing its development from early applications to current state-of-the-art technologies.

- The various AI algorithms and models used in assessment, including machine learning, natural language processing, and predictive analytics.
- Case studies and empirical research that demonstrate the impact of AI on assessment practices, both positive and negative.

1.5.2 Case Study Analysis

To provide practical insights into the implementation and outcomes of AI-driven assessments, the chapter includes an analysis of selected case studies from diverse educational settings. These case studies are chosen based on their relevance to the key themes of the chapter, including:

- Implementation challenges and best practices for integrating AI into assessment processes.
- Examples of AI-driven formative and summative assessments in different educational contexts, such as K-12, higher education, and vocational training.
- Outcomes and lessons learned from institutions that have adopted AI technologies for assessment.

1.5.3. Thematic Analysis

The information gathered from the literature review and case study analysis is analyzed thematically to identify recurring patterns, challenges, and emerging trends. The thematic analysis focuses on:

- The key benefits and opportunities associated with AI in assessment, such as personalization, efficiency, and scalability.
- The challenges and potential drawbacks, including issues of bias, privacy, and the digital divide.
- Future directions and emerging trends, highlighting areas of innovation and ongoing research that are likely to shape the future of AI in educational assessment.

1.5.4. Synthesis and Discussion

The final section of the chapter synthesizes the findings from the various components of the methodology to provide a comprehensive overview of the role of AI in transforming educational assessment. This synthesis includes:

- A balanced discussion of the potential and limitations of AI, drawing on the evidence and insights gathered throughout the research process.
- Recommendations for educators, policymakers, and technology developers on how to maximize the benefits of AI in assessment while mitigating risks.
- Consideration of the ethical implications of AI in education, particularly in relation to fairness, transparency, and student autonomy.

2. TRADITIONAL VS. AI-DRIVEN ASSESSMENT

2.1 Traditional Assessment Methods

Traditional assessment methods refer to the conventional approaches used to evaluate students' knowledge, skills, and understanding of academic content. These methods have been employed in education for decades and typically involve standardized formats and structured procedures. These traditional assessment methods, while widely used, are increasingly complemented by innovative approaches that leverage technology and promote deeper learning experiences (Lynch 2017) . While traditional methods provide valuable insights into students' performance, educators are continuously exploring ways to enhance assessment practices to better meet the needs of diverse learners and prepare them for success in the 21st century. Here's a detailed exploration of some common traditional assessment methods:

- **Written Examinations:** Written examinations are one of the most traditional forms of assessment, typically administered in the form of tests or quizzes. They often consist of multiple-choice questions, short-answer questions, or essay prompts designed to assess students' factual knowledge, comprehension, application, and critical thinking skills. Written examinations are widely used due to their efficiency in evaluating large groups of students and providing standardized measures of performance.
- **Homework Assignments:** Homework assignments are tasks given to students to complete outside of the classroom, such as reading assignments, problem sets, or writing exercises. While not always graded as rigorously as formal assessments, homework assignments serve as a form of practice and reinforcement of classroom learning. They allow students to apply and extend their understanding of concepts independently, providing valuable opportunities for self-directed learning and skill development.
- **Projects and Presentations**: Projects and presentations are long-term assignments that require students to research, plan, and present information on a particular topic or theme. These assessments often involve creative and

collaborative tasks, such as creating multimedia presentations, conducting experiments, or designing prototypes (Postman 1983). Projects and presentations assess students' ability to synthesize information, communicate effectively, and demonstrate mastery of complex concepts through hands-on, real-world applications.

- **Oral Examinations:** Oral examinations involve assessing students' understanding and communication skills through spoken interaction. This assessment method can take various forms, including individual interviews, group discussions, or oral presentations. Oral examinations provide opportunities for students to articulate their thoughts, demonstrate their depth of understanding, and engage in dialogue with their peers and instructors. They are particularly well-suited for assessing language proficiency, critical thinking, and interpersonal communication skills.
- **Practical Assessments**: Practical assessments evaluate students' ability to apply theoretical knowledge and skills in real-world contexts. These assessments often take place in laboratory settings, vocational workshops, or clinical placements, depending on the discipline (Tegmark 2017). Practical assessments may involve performing experiments, conducting simulations, or demonstrating technical competencies. They provide authentic measures of students' practical skills, problem-solving abilities, and professional readiness.
- **Portfolios:** Portfolios are collections of students' work samples, reflections, and self-assessments compiled over time to showcase their learning progress and achievements. Portfolios offer a holistic view of students' capabilities and growth across multiple dimensions, including academic performance, creativity, and personal development. They allow students to demonstrate their strengths and interests through diverse artifacts, such as essays, artwork, project reports, and multimedia presentations.

2.2 Limitations of Traditional Assessments

The limitations of traditional assessment methods have become increasingly apparent in the modern educational landscape. One major limitation is the lack of personalization; traditional assessments are typically designed to evaluate all students using the same criteria, failing to account for individual learning differences. Additionally, these assessments often emphasize rote memorization over critical thinking and problem-solving skills (Wheeler 2015). The feedback loop is another critical issue; it is usually delayed and generic, which can hinder timely interventions and personalized support. Moreover, the high-stakes nature of many traditional assessments can induce anxiety and stress among students, potentially affecting their performance and overall well-being. Finally, the manual grading process is time-consuming and subject to human error and bias.

2.3 Introduction to AI-Driven Assessments

AI-driven assessments represent a significant shift from traditional methods, leveraging advanced technologies to provide a more personalized, efficient, and insightful evaluation of student performance. These assessments use algorithms and machine learning models to analyze students' work, provide immediate feedback, and adapt to their learning needs. For example, adaptive testing platforms adjust the difficulty of questions based on the student's previous responses, creating a tailored testing experience that can more accurately gauge their understanding and skills (Wheeler 2019). AI-driven tools such as automated essay scoring systems can evaluate written responses in real-time, providing detailed feedback on grammar, coherence, and content quality. By harnessing the power of AI, these assessments aim to overcome the limitations of traditional methods and offer a more dynamic and supportive learning environment.

2.4 Comparative Analysis: Traditional vs. AI-Driven

1. Efficiency:
    - **Traditional Assessment:** Traditional assessment methods, such as written examinations and manual grading, can be time-consuming and labor-intensive for educators. Grading a large number of assignments or tests manually may lead to delays in providing feedback to students.
    - **AI-Driven Assessment:** AI-driven assessment tools offer significant improvements in efficiency by automating the grading process. Machine learning algorithms can quickly analyze large datasets of student responses and provide instant feedback, reducing the burden on educators and enabling timely intervention when needed.
2. Scalability:
    - **Traditional Assessment:** Traditional assessment methods may face scalability challenges, particularly in large class settings or online learning environments. Grading assignments or exams for a large number of students can be overwhelming for instructors and may compromise the quality and consistency of assessment.
    - **AI-Driven Assessment:** AI-driven assessment solutions are highly scalable, capable of handling a large volume of assessments with consistency and accuracy. Automated grading systems can process thou-

sands of student responses simultaneously, ensuring equitable treatment and standardized evaluation across all learners.

3. Personalization:
    - **Traditional Assessment:** Traditional assessment methods often lack flexibility and personalization, providing generic feedback that may not address individual learning needs. Students receive uniform scores based on predefined criteria, limiting opportunities for tailored support and differentiated instruction.
    - **AI-Driven Assessment:** AI-driven assessment tools offer personalized learning experiences by analyzing each student's performance data and providing adaptive feedback. Intelligent algorithms can identify students' strengths, weaknesses, and learning preferences, allowing for customized learning pathways and targeted interventions to support individualized learning goals.
4. Feedback Mechanisms:
    - **Traditional Assessment:** Traditional assessment methods may provide limited or delayed feedback to students, especially in large classes where instructors have limited time and resources to review and grade assignments.
    - **AI-Driven Assessment:** AI-driven assessment tools enable immediate and detailed feedback to students, enhancing the learning experience and promoting continuous improvement. Automated feedback mechanisms can identify errors, offer explanations, and suggest corrective actions in real-time, empowering students to learn from their mistakes and make progress iteratively.
5. Reliability and Consistency:
    - **Traditional Assessment:** Traditional assessment methods may be susceptible to human biases and inconsistencies in grading, leading to variations in scores and interpretations across different graders.
    - **AI-Driven Assessment:** AI-driven assessment tools offer greater reliability and consistency in scoring, as they apply standardized criteria and algorithms consistently to all student responses. By minimizing subjective judgment and human error, AI-driven assessments ensure fair and impartial evaluation of student performance.

3. TYPES OF AI TECHNOLOGIES IN EDUCATIONAL ASSESSMENT

Artificial Intelligence (AI) has significantly influenced various aspects of education, with assessment practices being one of the most impacted areas (Zuboff 2019). This chapter explores the different types of AI technologies that are currently transforming educational assessment, providing a comprehensive understanding of each technology's role, functionality, and implications for educational practices.

3.1 Machine Learning and Predictive Analytics

Machine learning and predictive analytics have emerged as transformative tools in education, revolutionizing the way educators analyze student data and make informed decisions to enhance learning outcomes. Machine learning algorithms, a subset of artificial intelligence, enable the automatic learning of patterns and trends from vast datasets, offering insights into student performance and behavior. Predictive analytics, leveraging these algorithms, forecast future trends and outcomes based on historical data, empowering educators to anticipate student needs and tailor interventions accordingly (Bahrini et al., 2023) (Baidoo-Anu et al., 2023). These technologies find applications across various educational domains, from predicting student performance and identifying at-risk learners to recommending personalized learning pathways and optimizing resource allocation. Despite their promise, challenges such as data privacy concerns and algorithmic bias require careful consideration to ensure ethical and responsible use. Nevertheless, machine learning and predictive analytics hold immense potential to revolutionize education by providing educators with data-driven insights to support student success and foster personalized learning experiences.

3.2 Natural Language Processing (NLP)

Natural Language Processing (NLP) is another pivotal AI technology used in educational assessments. NLP allows machines to understand, interpret, and generate human language, making it possible to assess students' written and spoken responses more effectively. Automated essay scoring systems, for instance, use NLP to evaluate the content, coherence, grammar, and structure of students' essays, providing instant feedback. Furthermore, NLP-based tools can analyze discussion forums, chat interactions, and other textual data to gauge students' engagement, understanding, and sentiment. This technology not only accelerates the assessment process but also offers nuanced insights into students' cognitive and linguistic abilities.

3.3 Intelligent Tutoring Systems (ITS)

Intelligent Tutoring Systems (ITS) are AI-driven platforms that provide personalized instruction and assessment. These systems simulate the one-on-one interaction between a student and a tutor, offering customized feedback and guidance based on the student's learning progress (Becker et al., 2023). ITS can diagnose students' strengths and weaknesses, adapt the learning path accordingly, and continuously assess their knowledge through interactive exercises and quizzes. The AI algorithms powering ITS ensure that the assessments are dynamically aligned with the students' learning pace and style, making education more effective and personalized (Cortiñas-Lorenzo et al., 2023) . Additionally, ITS can gather data on student interactions and learning patterns, which can be used to further refine educational strategies and interventions.

3.4 Automated Essay Scoring Systems

Automated Essay Scoring (AES) systems use AI to evaluate and grade students' written assignments. These systems employ a combination of NLP and ML to assess various aspects of writing, such as content relevance, coherence, grammar, and stylistic elements. AES systems provide instant and objective feedback, helping students to improve their writing skills through iterative learning (Crompton et al., 2023). Moreover, these systems reduce the grading burden on educators, allowing them to focus more on instructional activities rather than administrative tasks. The reliability and consistency of AES systems also ensure a fair assessment process, free from human biases and errors.

3.5 Adaptive Learning Technologies

Adaptive learning technologies leverage AI to create personalized learning experiences that adjust in real-time based on students' performance. These systems use data analytics and ML algorithms to track students' interactions, assess their knowledge levels, and adapt the instructional content accordingly. For example, if a student struggles with a particular concept, the adaptive system might provide additional resources or alternative explanations to enhance understanding. Similarly, if a student excels in a topic, the system can introduce more advanced materials to keep them challenged. Adaptive assessments embedded within these technologies ensure that students are continuously evaluated and supported according to their individual learning trajectories.

4. BENEFITS OF AI IN EDUCATIONAL ASSESSMENT

AI technologies have begun to revolutionize various sectors, and education is no exception. The application of AI in educational assessment brings numerous benefits that can significantly enhance the learning experience, provide insightful data for educators, and streamline the administrative processes within educational institutions (Denny et al., 2023). This delves into the primary advantages of AI in educational assessment, highlighting the transformative potential of these technologies.

4.1 Personalization and Adaptive Learning

One of the most compelling benefits of AI in educational assessment is the ability to personalize learning experiences. Traditional assessments often adopt a one-size-fits-all approach, which can overlook the individual needs of students. AI-driven assessments, however, utilize data to adapt to each student's learning style, pace, and level of understanding. Adaptive learning technologies can modify the difficulty of questions in real-time based on the student's performance, ensuring that each learner is challenged appropriately and supported where necessary. This personalized approach helps in identifying knowledge gaps and tailoring educational content to meet the unique needs of every student, fostering a more effective and engaging learning environment.

4.2 Timeliness and Efficiency

AI-powered assessment tools can significantly enhance the timeliness and efficiency of evaluating student performance. Traditional grading methods can be time-consuming and prone to human error, often resulting in delays in feedback that can hinder the learning process. AI algorithms can automate the grading process for various types of assessments, including multiple-choice questions, essays, and even complex problem-solving tasks (Elfaki et al., 2023). This automation not only speeds up the assessment cycle but also ensures consistent and objective grading. Immediate feedback allows students to understand their mistakes and areas for improvement promptly, promoting continuous learning and development.

4.3 Enhanced Feedback Mechanisms

Providing detailed and actionable feedback is crucial for student development, but it is often challenging to deliver in large classroom settings. AI systems can analyze student responses in-depth and generate comprehensive feedback that goes beyond simple right or wrong answers. These systems can offer insights into why a particular answer is incorrect and provide suggestions for improvement, helping students to develop a deeper understanding of the subject matter. Enhanced feedback mechanisms supported by AI can facilitate a more interactive and engaging learning experience, encouraging students to reflect on their learning process and take active steps towards improvement.

4.4 Data-Driven Insights and Decision Making

AI in educational assessment generates vast amounts of data that can be harnessed to gain valuable insights into student performance, learning patterns, and overall educational outcomes. Educators can use these data-driven insights to identify trends, predict future performance, and make informed decisions about curriculum adjustments and instructional strategies (Eager et al., 2021). For instance, if data reveals that a significant number of students are struggling with a particular concept, educators can revisit that topic and employ different teaching methods. Additionally, data analytics can help in identifying at-risk students early, allowing for timely interventions to support their academic success. The ability to make decisions based on concrete data rather than intuition or anecdotal evidence marks a significant advancement in educational practices.

4.5 Scalability and Accessibility

One of the significant challenges in education is providing quality assessment and feedback to a large number of students. AI technologies offer scalable solutions that can manage vast amounts of data and cater to large student populations without compromising the quality of assessment. This scalability is particularly beneficial in contexts such as MOOCs (Massive Open Online Courses) and other online education platforms, where traditional assessment methods may be impractical (Galdon et al., 2021). Moreover, AI-driven assessment tools can be designed to be accessible to students with disabilities, ensuring that all learners have the opportunity to benefit from personalized and efficient assessment methods. By leveraging AI, educational institutions can extend their reach and impact, making high-quality education more accessible to a broader audience. AI-driven educational assessments offer numerous benefits that enhance personalization, efficiency, feedback quality, data-driven decision-making, and scalability. These advantages collectively contribute to a more effective, engaging, and inclusive educational experience, underscoring the transformative potential of AI in education.

5. IMPLEMENTATION OF AI IN EDUCATIONAL ASSESSMENT

While the integration of AI into educational assessment offers numerous benefits, it also presents a range of challenges and potential drawbacks that must be carefully considered. One of the primary challenges is the issue of data privacy and security. AI systems rely heavily on vast amounts of student data to function effectively. This includes not only academic performance data but also personal information and behavioral analytics. Ensuring the privacy and security of this data is paramount, as any breach could have severe consequences for students' confidentiality and trust in the education system. Furthermore, the collection and storage of such sensitive information raise ethical concerns, particularly regarding the potential misuse of data or the extent to which students are aware of and consent to data collection practices. Another significant challenge is the potential for bias in AI algorithms. AI systems learn from existing data, which can sometimes reflect historical biases present in the education system or society at large. For example, if an AI model is trained on data that includes biased grading practices or reflects socio-economic disparities, the model may inadvertently perpetuate these biases in its assessments. This could lead to unfair outcomes for certain groups of students, particularly those from marginalized communities. Addressing bias in AI requires not only careful selection and preprocessing of training data but also ongoing monitoring and adjustment of AI models to ensure fairness and equity in assessments. The technical complexity of implementing AI in assessment also presents a barrier for many educational institutions, particularly those with limited resources. Developing and maintaining AI-driven assessment systems requires significant investment in technology infrastructure, skilled personnel, and ongoing training. For schools and districts with constrained budgets, the costs associated with adopting AI may be prohibitive, leading to a widening gap between well-funded and under-resourced institutions. Additionally, educators may require substantial professional development to effectively integrate AI tools into their teaching and assessment practices, which can be a time-consuming and challenging process. Moreover, the reliance on AI for assessment raises concerns about the potential loss of human judgment and the nuanced understanding that educators bring to the evaluation process. While AI can analyze data at scale and identify patterns that might be missed by human assessors, it may lack the ability to fully appreciate the context and individual circumstances that can influence student performance. For example, AI may not be able to account for factors such as a student's emotional state, personal challenges, or unique learning needs, which are often considered by teachers when making assessment decisions. This could result in assessments that, while technically accurate, lack the depth and empathy that human educators provide. Another drawback is the potential for over-reliance on AI systems, which could lead to a decrease in the development of critical assessment skills among educators. As AI takes on more of the assessment workload, there is a risk that teachers may become less engaged in the process of evaluating student work, potentially leading to a diminished understanding of student learning and progress. This could also impact the teacher-student relationship, as direct interaction and feedback are replaced by automated systems, potentially reducing the personal connection that is crucial for effective teaching and learning. Finally, there is the issue of technological dependency and the risks associated with system failures or inaccuracies. AI systems, like all technology, are not infallible and can be prone to errors or technical glitches. In high-stakes assessment scenarios, such failures could have serious consequences, such as incorrect grading, misidentification of learning gaps, or even the unfair penalization of students. Ensuring the reliability and robustness of AI systems is essential, but even with the best safeguards in place, the potential for unforeseen issues remains a concern.

5.1 Integration with Learning Management Systems (LMS)

The integration of AI-driven assessment tools with Learning Management Systems (LMS) is crucial for the seamless adoption of AI in education. LMS platforms serve as the backbone of digital learning environments, enabling the administration, documentation, tracking, reporting, and delivery of educational courses or training programs (Gmeiner et al., 2023). AI technologies can enhance these systems by automating grading processes, providing personalized learning paths, and generating real-time analytics on student performance. For successful integration, it is essential to ensure compatibility between AI tools and existing LMS infrastructure, facilitate interoperability through APIs, and provide comprehensive training for educators and administrators to effectively utilize these advanced functionalities.

5.2 Developing AI-Driven Assessment Tools

The development of AI-driven assessment tools involves a multidisciplinary approach, combining expertise in education, data science, machine learning, and user experience design. The process begins with identifying the specific educational needs and assessment goals, followed by data collection and model training. AI algorithms are trained on diverse datasets to ensure accuracy and fairness in evaluation. Additionally, these tools must be rigorously tested to validate their effectiveness and reliability in various educational contexts. Collaboration with educators and continuous feedback loops are vital to refine the tools and align them with pedagogical objectives (Hadi et al., 2023). Developing user-friendly interfaces and providing adequate support for implementation are also critical components of this process.

5.3 Training Educators and Administrators

To maximize the benefits of AI in educational assessment, comprehensive training programs for educators and administrators are imperative. These programs should cover the fundamentals of AI, its applications in education, and specific training on using AI-driven assessment tools. Training should also address ethical considerations, data privacy, and how to interpret AI-generated insights effectively. Workshops, webinars, and hands-on training sessions can help educators build confidence in integrating AI into their teaching practices (Humphry et al., 2023). Additionally, fostering a culture of continuous learning and professional development will ensure that educators remain adept at utilizing evolving AI technologies and can leverage them to enhance student outcomes.

The implementation of AI in educational assessment requires careful planning, robust tool development, and ongoing support for educators and administrators.

6. ETHICAL CONSIDERATIONS AND CHALLENGES

Ethical considerations are paramount in the integration of AI technologies into educational assessment practices. This chapter explores the multifaceted ethical challenges and considerations inherent in the adoption of AI-driven assessment systems.

6.1 Data Privacy and Security

Data privacy and security concerns arise due to the collection, storage, and utilization of vast amounts of student data in AI-driven assessment systems. Educational institutions must adhere to stringent data protection regulations, such as the General Data Protection Regulation (GDPR) and the Family Educational Rights and Privacy Act (FERPA), to safeguard student information. Moreover, ensuring encryption, access controls, and regular security audits are imperative to prevent unauthorized access or data breaches.

6.2 Bias and Fairness in AI Algorithms

The inherent biases present in AI algorithms pose a significant challenge to fair assessment practices. Biases can manifest in various forms, including gender, racial, or socioeconomic biases, which may exacerbate existing inequalities in education. It is essential to employ rigorous validation and testing procedures to identify and mitigate biases in AI algorithms. Additionally, ongoing monitoring and transparency in algorithmic decision-making processes are crucial for ensuring fairness and equity in educational assessments.

6.3 Transparency and Accountability

Transparency and accountability are essential principles for building trust in AI-driven assessment systems. Educational stakeholders, including students, teachers, and administrators, should have access to transparent explanations of how AI algorithms operate and make decisions. Clear documentation of data sources, algorithmic models, and decision-making criteria fosters accountability and allows for meaningful oversight. Moreover, establishing mechanisms for redress and recourse in cases of algorithmic errors or unjust outcomes enhances the overall transparency and accountability of AI-driven assessment systems.

6.4 Ethical Use of Student Data

The ethical use of student data encompasses responsible data collection, processing, and utilization practices. Educational institutions must obtain informed consent from students and their guardians before collecting personal data for assessment purposes. Additionally, data anonymization and minimization techniques should be employed to mitigate privacy risks and protect sensitive information (Jacques 2023). Furthermore, educators and administrators must adhere to ethical guidelines and professional standards when accessing and utilizing student data to ensure the integrity and ethical use of AI-driven assessment systems.

7. CASE STUDIES AND CURRENT EXAMPLES

- **Turnitin's Feedback Studio**: Turnitin's Feedback Studio uses AI to provide feedback on student writing assignments. It analyzes students' submissions for plagiarism, grammar errors, and writing style. Instructors can then use this feedback to guide students in improving their writing skills while ensuring academic integrity. This AI-powered tool not only streamlines the grading process but also provides personalized feedback tailored to individual students' needs.
- **Knewton Adaptive Learning Platform**: Knewton's adaptive learning platform uses AI algorithms to personalize learning materials and assessments for students. It tracks students' progress in real-time and adjusts the difficulty level of questions based on their performance. By providing targeted practice

questions and adaptive assessments, Knewton helps students master concepts at their own pace and identifies areas where they need additional support.

- **ProctorU:** ProctorU is an online proctoring service that uses AI to monitor students during exams. It employs facial recognition technology and machine learning algorithms to detect suspicious behavior, such as looking away from the screen or accessing unauthorized resources. By ensuring exam integrity in online learning environments, ProctorU enables institutions to conduct assessments remotely while maintaining academic standards.
- **Coursera's Machine Learning for Everyone**: Coursera offers a course titled "Machine Learning for Everyone," which teaches learners how to apply machine learning techniques to real-world problems, including educational assessment (Jonsson et al., 2022). The course covers topics such as predictive modeling, data preprocessing, and evaluation metrics, empowering educators to leverage AI tools for designing and analyzing assessments.
- **SMART Learning Suite**: SMART Learning Suite is an integrated set of educational tools that includes SMART Notebook, SMART Lab, and SMART Response 2. These tools leverage AI to facilitate formative assessment practices in classrooms. For example, SMART Response 2 allows teachers to create interactive quizzes and polls that automatically adapt to students' responses in real-time, providing instant feedback and insights into their understanding.
- **Duolingo English Test**: The Duolingo English Test is an AI-powered language proficiency exam used by universities and institutions worldwide for admissions purposes. It assesses students' reading, writing, speaking, and listening skills through a series of adaptive exercises. Duolingo's AI algorithms analyze students' responses and assign proficiency scores based on their performance, offering a convenient and cost-effective alternative to traditional language tests like TOEFL or IELTS.

8. IMPACT ON STAKEHOLDERS

The integration of AI in educational assessment has profound implications for various stakeholders within the education ecosystem. This chapter examines how AI-driven assessments affect students, teachers, educational institutions, and policymakers.

8.1 Impact on Students

The introduction of AI in educational assessment brings both opportunities and challenges for students. On one hand, AI enables personalized learning experiences tailored to individual needs, allowing students to progress at their own pace and receive targeted support where needed. Adaptive learning technologies powered by AI can identify students' strengths and weaknesses, offering customized learning paths to optimize their academic performance. Additionally, AI-driven assessments often provide instantaneous feedback, empowering students to reflect on their progress and make timely adjustments to their learning strategies.

However, there are concerns about the potential negative impacts of AI on students, particularly regarding data privacy and algorithmic bias (Kayalı et al., 2024). As AI systems collect vast amounts of student data, there are risks of unauthorized access, data breaches, and misuse of personal information. Moreover, algorithms used in AI-driven assessments may perpetuate biases related to race, gender, socioeconomic status, and other factors, leading to unfair outcomes for certain student groups. It is crucial for educators and policymakers to address these ethical considerations and ensure that AI technologies are deployed in a manner that safeguards students' rights and promotes equity in education.

8.2 Impact on Teachers

The integration of AI in educational assessment has significant implications for teachers, fundamentally transforming their roles in the teaching and learning process. AI-driven assessment tools can automate routine tasks such as grading assignments, analyzing student performance data, and generating personalized learning recommendations (Kazemitabaar at al., 2023) (Konecki et al., 2023). By alleviating administrative burdens, teachers can allocate more time and energy to activities that require human expertise, such as designing engaging learning experiences, providing individualized support to students, and fostering critical thinking skills. However, the adoption of AI in assessment also raises concerns about the displacement of teachers and the devaluation of their professional judgment (Kooli 2023). There is a need for educators to develop new skills and competencies to effectively leverage AI technologies in their teaching practices. Training programs and professional development initiatives should focus on helping teachers understand how AI works, how to interpret AI-generated insights, and how to integrate AI-driven assessment tools into their instructional strategies in a meaningful way. Collaboration between teachers and AI systems can enhance the quality of education and improve learning outcomes for all students.

8.3 Impact on Educational Institutions

The integration of AI in educational assessment has far-reaching implications for educational institutions, influencing their instructional practices, organizational structures, and resource allocation decisions. AI-driven assessment systems enable institutions to gather rich data insights about student learning behaviors, preferences, and performance trends. This data-driven approach can inform instructional decision-making, curriculum design, and intervention strategies to better meet the diverse needs of students (MacNeil et al., 2022) (Markel et al., 2023).Moreover, AI technologies have the potential to enhance the efficiency and scalability of assessment processes within educational institutions. Automated grading systems, predictive analytics tools, and intelligent tutoring systems can streamline administrative workflows, reduce grading time, and optimize resource allocation. However, the adoption of AI in assessment also requires investments in infrastructure, technology, and human capital. Educational institutions must carefully evaluate the costs and benefits of implementing AI-driven assessment solutions and ensure that they align with their mission, values, and educational objectives.

8.4 Impact on Policy Makers and Regulators

The integration of AI in educational assessment presents both opportunities and challenges for policymakers and regulators tasked with overseeing the education system. On one hand, AI-driven assessment technologies hold the promise of improving the efficiency, effectiveness, and equity of educational outcomes (Marquez et al., 2023). By harnessing the power of AI, policymakers can design more responsive and data-driven education policies, allocate resources more effectively, and promote innovation in teaching and learning practices (Nikolic et al., 2023). However, the widespread adoption of AI in assessment also raises complex regulatory and ethical issues that require careful consideration. Policymakers must develop clear guidelines and standards for the ethical use of AI in education, including data privacy protections, algorithmic transparency, and safeguards against bias and discrimination (Oyoo et al., 2024). Additionally, policymakers should prioritize investments in digital literacy and computational thinking skills to ensure that students are equipped to navigate an increasingly AI-driven world. Collaboration between policymakers, educators, researchers, and industry stakeholders is essential to harness the potential of AI in education while mitigating its risks and ensuring equitable access to high-quality learning opportunities for all students.

9. FUTURE DIRECTIONS AND EMERGING TRENDS IN AI FOR EDUCATIONAL ASSESSMENT

The future of AI in educational assessment is poised to be transformative, with several emerging trends and directions shaping its evolution (Parwani et al., 2024). As AI technologies continue to advance, their role in education is expected to become more sophisticated, personalized, and integral to the learning process. Below are some of the key future directions and emerging trends in this area.

- **Hyper-Personalized Learning and Assessment:** One of the most promising directions for AI in educational assessment is the move towards hyper-personalized learning experiences. By leveraging increasingly advanced AI algorithms, future systems will be able to assess not only what a student knows but also how they learn best. These systems will integrate data from various sources, including cognitive assessments, learning styles, and even emotional responses, to create a detailed profile of each student. Based on this profile, AI can deliver assessments that are perfectly tailored to the individual's needs, adjusting in real-time to provide the most effective learning pathway. This level of personalization has the potential to significantly enhance student engagement and learning outcomes.
- **AI-Driven Formative Assessment Tools:** While summative assessments provide a snapshot of student learning at the end of a course or module, formative assessments are increasingly being enhanced by AI to offer continuous feedback throughout the learning process. Future AI-driven formative assessment tools will become more adept at providing immediate, actionable insights into a student's progress (Rahman et al., 2023) . These tools will not only identify areas where a student is struggling but will also recommend specific interventions, such as targeted exercises or resources, to address these challenges. This continuous feedback loop will help students to stay on track and enable educators to make informed decisions about instruction in real-time.
- **Multi-Modal Assessment Approaches:** Another emerging trend is the development of multi-modal AI systems that assess students using a variety of inputs beyond traditional text-based responses. These systems will incorporate data from multiple sources, such as voice, facial expressions, body language, and even biometric signals, to create a more holistic understanding of a student's performance (Raji et al., 2021). For example, AI could analyze a student's tone of voice or facial expressions during an oral presentation to assess their confidence and engagement, in addition to evaluating the content

of their speech. This multi-modal approach promises to capture a broader range of student abilities and provide more comprehensive assessments.

- **Ethical AI and Fairness in Assessment:** As the adoption of AI in education grows, there will be a stronger focus on developing ethical AI systems that ensure fairness and transparency in assessments. Future research and development will likely concentrate on creating AI models that are free from bias and that provide equitable assessments for all students, regardless of their background or demographic characteristics (Vetrivel et al., 2024). Additionally, there will be an increased emphasis on explainable AI (XAI), which aims to make AI decisions more transparent and understandable to educators and students. This transparency will be critical in building trust in AI systems and ensuring that they are used responsibly in educational contexts.
- **AI and Social-Emotional Learning (SEL) Assessment:** Social-emotional learning (SEL) is becoming an integral part of education, and AI is beginning to play a role in assessing these skills. Future AI systems will be designed to evaluate and support the development of SEL competencies, such as empathy, resilience, and collaboration. By analyzing interactions in digital learning environments, AI can assess how students work together, manage stress, and respond to challenges. This information can then be used to provide feedback that helps students develop these crucial skills, which are increasingly recognized as important for success in both academic and life contexts.
- **Integration with Augmented and Virtual Reality (AR/VR):** The integration of AI with augmented and virtual reality (AR/VR) technologies is another emerging trend that will redefine educational assessments. In the future, AI-powered AR/VR environments will provide immersive assessment experiences where students can demonstrate their skills in simulated real-world scenarios. For example, a medical student could be assessed on their ability to diagnose and treat a patient in a virtual hospital setting, with AI analyzing their actions and providing feedback. This combination of AI and AR/VR will allow for more practical, skills-based assessments that are difficult to achieve in traditional classroom settings.
- **Longitudinal Data Analysis for Lifelong Learning:** As the concept of lifelong learning gains traction, AI will play a critical role in tracking and assessing an individual's learning journey over time. Future AI systems will be capable of analyzing longitudinal data, capturing a learner's progress across different stages of their education and career. This will enable more personalized learning paths that adapt as the learner's goals and circumstances change. AI-driven e-portfolios, for example, could become a standard tool for tracking skills acquisition and providing assessments that are relevant to ongoing professional development.

- **Collaborative AI Systems for Educator Support:** Looking ahead, there will be a significant focus on developing AI systems that work in collaboration with educators rather than replacing them. These systems will serve as co-assessors, offering insights and suggestions that complement the teacher's expertise (Vetrivel et al., 2024). For example, AI might provide data-driven recommendations for modifying assessments based on a student's performance trends, while the educator makes the final decision on how to apply these insights. This collaborative approach will ensure that AI enhances rather than diminishes the role of educators in the assessment process.
- **Global Standardization and Interoperability:** As AI in education continues to expand, there will be efforts to create global standards and ensure interoperability between different AI systems. This will involve developing common frameworks and protocols that allow various AI-driven assessment tools to work together seamlessly, regardless of the platform or institution. Such standardization will be crucial for enabling the widespread adoption of AI in educational assessment and ensuring that students and educators can benefit from these technologies regardless of their location or the systems they use.

10. CONCLUSION

The integration of AI into educational assessment practices offers a promising avenue for enhancing learning outcomes and streamlining assessment processes. AI technologies have the capacity to provide personalized feedback, adapt assessments to individual student needs, and automate grading, thereby saving educators valuable time and resources. However, this transformation also raises important considerations regarding data privacy, bias in algorithms, and the need for ongoing teacher training and professional development. As we navigate the evolving landscape of AI in education, it is crucial to strike a balance between leveraging the capabilities of these technologies and upholding ethical and pedagogical principles. By doing so, we can harness the full potential of AI to foster equitable, effective, and innovative assessment practices that support student learning and growth.

REFERENCES

Bahrini, A., Khamoshifar, M., Abbasimehr, H., Riggs, R. J., Esmaeili, M., Majdabadkohne, R. M., & Pasehvar, M. (2023). ChatGPT: Applications, opportunities, and threats. *Proceedings of the 2023 Systems and Information Engineering Design Symposium (SIEDS)*. DOI: 10.1109/SIEDS58326.2023.10137850

Baidoo-Anu, D., & Owusu Ansah, L. (2023). Education in the Era of Generative Artificial Intelligence (AI): Understanding the Potential Benefits of ChatGPT in Promoting Teaching and Learning. Retrieved from https://ssrn.com/abstract=4337484 DOI: 10.2139/ssrn.4337484

Becker, B. A., Denny, P., Finnie-Ansley, J., Luxton-Reilly, A., Prather, J., & Santos, E. A. (2023). Programming is hard—or at least it used to be: Educational opportunities and challenges of AI code generation. *Proceedings of the 54th ACM Technical Symposium on Computer Science Education*. DOI: 10.1145/3545945.3569759

Bostrum, N. (2017). *Superintelligence: Paths, Dangers, Strategies*. Oxford University Press.

Cortiñas-Lorenzo, K., & Lacey, G. (2023). (accepted). Toward Explainable Affective Computing: A Review. *IEEE Transactions on Neural Networks and Learning Systems*. PMID: 37220061

Crompton, H., & Burke, D. (2023). Artificial intelligence in higher education: The state of the field. *International Journal of Educational Technology in Higher Education*, 20(22), 22. DOI: 10.1186/s41239-023-00392-8

Denny, P., Kumar, V., & Giacaman, N. (2023). Conversing with Copilot: Exploring prompt engineering for solving CS1 problems using natural language. *Proceedings of the 54th ACM Technical Symposium on Computer Science Educatio*. DOI: 10.1145/3545945.3569823

Diamandis, P. H., & Kotler, S. (2020). *The Future Is Faster Than You Think: How Converging Technologies Are Transforming Business, Industries, and Our Lives*. Simon & Schuster.

Eager, B., & Brunton, R. (2023). Prompting higher education towards AI-augmented teaching and learning practice. *Journal of University Teaching & Learning Practice*, 20(02). Advance online publication. DOI: 10.53761/1.20.5.02

Elfaki, A. O., Abduljabbar, M., Ali, L., Alnajjar, F., Mehiar, D., Marei, A. M., Alhmiedat, T., & Al-Jumaily, A. (2023). Revolutionizing Social Robotics: A Cloud-Based Framework for Enhancing the Intelligence and Autonomy of Social Robots. *Robotics (Basel, Switzerland)*, 12(2), 48. DOI: 10.3390/robotics12020048

Ford, M. (2018). *Architects of Intelligence: The Truth about AI from the People Building It*. Packt Publishing Ltd.

Galdon, F., Hall, A., & Ferrarello, L. (2021). Enhancing abductive reasoning in design and engineering education via probabilistic knowledge; a case study in AI. Proceedings of the DS 110: 23rd International Conference on Engineering and Product Design Education (E&PDE 2021).

Garrison, D. R. (2007). Online community of inquiry review: Social, cognitive, and teaching presence issues. *Journal of Asynchronous Learning Networks*, 11(1), 61–72.

Gmeiner, F., Yang, H., Yao, L., Holstein, K., & Martelaro, N. (2023). Exploring challenges and opportunities to support designers in learning to co-create with AI-based manufacturing design tools. *Proceedings of the 2023 CHI Conference on Human Factors in Computing Systems*. DOI: 10.1145/3544548.3580999

Hadi, M. U., Qureshi, R., Shah, A., Irfan, M., Zafar, A., Shaikh, M. B., & Mirjalili, S. (2023). A Survey on Large Language Models: Applications, Challenges, Limitations, and Practical Usage. *TechRxiv*. DOI: 10.36227/techrxiv.23589741.v1

Humphry, T., & Fuller, A. L. (2023). Potential ChatGPT Use in Undergraduate Chemistry Laboratories. *Journal of Chemical Education*, 100(9), 1434–1436. DOI: 10.1021/acs.jchemed.3c00006

Jacques, L. (2023). Teaching CS-101 at the Dawn of ChatGPT. *ACM Inroads*, 14(2), 40–46. DOI: 10.1145/3595634

Jonsson, M., & Tholander, J. (2022). Cracking the code: Co-coding with AI in creative programming education. *Proceedings of the 14th Conference on Creativity and Cognition*. DOI: 10.1145/3527927.3532801

Kaku, M. (2011). *Physics of the Future: The Inventions That Will Transform Our Lives*. Penguin Group.

Kayalı, B., & Balat, Ş. (2024). Assessment, Evaluation, and Feedback in Online Education With Artificial Intelligence-Supported Tools. In Bansal, R., Chakir, A., Hafaz Ngah, A., Rabby, F., & Jain, A. (Eds.), *AI Algorithms and ChatGPT for Student Engagement in Online Learning* (pp. 124–135). IGI Global. DOI: 10.4018/979-8-3693-4268-8.ch008

Kazemitabaar, M., Chow, J., Ma, C. K. T., Ericson, B. J., Weintrop, D., & Grossman, T. (2023). Studying the effect of AI code generators on supporting novice learners in introductory programming. *Proceedings of the 2023 CHI Conference on Human Factors in Computing Systems*. DOI: 10.1145/3544548.3580919

Kelly, K. (2017). *The Inevitable: Understanding the 12 Technological Forces That Will Shape Our Future*. Penguin Group.

Klutka, J. (2018). *Artificial Intelligence in Higher Education: Current Uses and Future Applications*. Learning House.

Konecki, M., Konecki, M., & Biškupić, I. (2023). Using artificial intelligence in higher education. *Proceedings of the 15th International Conference on Computer Supported Education*.

Kooli, C. (2023). Chatbots in education and research: A critical examination of ethical implications and solutions. *Sustainability (Basel)*, 15(5614), 5614. DOI: 10.3390/su15075614

Lynch, J. (2017). How AI Will Destroy Education. Retrieved from https://buzzrobot.com/how-ai-will-destroy-education-20053b7b88a6

MacNeil, S., Tran, A., Mogil, D., Bernstein, S., Ross, E., & Huang, Z. (2022). Generating diverse code explanations using the GPT-3 large language model. *Proceedings of the 2022 ACM Conference on International Computing Education Research*. DOI: 10.1145/3501709.3544280

Markel, J. M., Opferman, S. G., Landay, J. A., & Piech, C. (2023). GPTeach: Interactive TA Training with GPT Based Students. In Proceedings of the Tenth ACM Conference on Learning @ Scale (L@S '23). Association for Computing Machinery.

Marquez, R., Barrios, N., Vera, R. E., Mendez, M. E., Tolosa, L., Zambrano, F., & Li, Y. (2023). A perspective on the synergistic potential of artificial intelligence and product-based learning strategies in biobased materials education. *Education for Chemical Engineers*, 44, 164–180. DOI: 10.1016/j.ece.2023.05.005

Nikolic, S., Daniel, S., Haque, R., Belkina, M., Hassan, G. M., Grundy, S., Lyden, S., Neal, P., & Sandison, C. (2023). ChatGPT versus engineering education assessment: A multidisciplinary and multi-institutional benchmarking and analysis of this generative artificial intelligence tool to investigate assessment integrity. *European Journal of Engineering Education*, 48(4), 559–614. DOI: 10.1080/03043797.2023.2213169

Oyoo, M. A. (2024). An Exploration of Mental Well-Being Among Students in Higher Learning Institutions in Western Kenya. In Aloka, P. (Ed.), *Student Well-Being in Higher Education Institutions* (pp. 1–30). IGI Global. DOI: 10.4018/979-8-3693-4417-0.ch001

Parwani, D., & Devnani, M. (2024). The Impact of Artificial Intelligence on Teacher-Learner Interaction in Virtual Education: Addressing Challenges and Embracing Opportunities. In Bansal, R., Chakir, A., Hafaz Ngah, A., Rabby, F., & Jain, A. (Eds.), *AI Algorithms and ChatGPT for Student Engagement in Online Learning* (pp. 218–241). IGI Global. DOI: 10.4018/979-8-3693-4268-8.ch015

Postman, N. (1983). *The Disappearance of Childhood*. W.H. Allen. DOI: 10.1016/S0002-7138(09)61523-5

Rahman, M. M., & Watanobe, Y. (2023). ChatGPT for education and research: Opportunities, threats, and strategies. *Applied Sciences (Basel, Switzerland)*, 13(13), 5783. DOI: 10.3390/app13095783

Raji, I. D., Scheuerman, M. K., & Amironesei, R. (2021). You can't sit with us: Exclusionary pedagogy in AI ethics education. *Proceedings of the 2021 ACM Conference on Fairness, Accountability, and Transparency, Virtual Event*. DOI: 10.1145/3442188.3445914

Tegmark, M. (2017). *Life 3.0: Being Human in the Age of Artificial Intelligence*. Penguin Group.

Vetrivel, S. C., Saravanan, T. P., Maheswari, R., & Arun, V. P. (2024). Coping Mechanisms for Stress Among Students at Universities. In Aloka, P. (Ed.), *Student Well-Being in Higher Education Institutions* (pp. 157–186). IGI Global. DOI: 10.4018/979-8-3693-4417-0.ch007

Vetrivel, S. C., Sowmiya, K. C., Gomathi, T., & Arun, V. P. (2024). Engaging Online Classes Through Gamification: Leveraging Innovative Tools and Technologies. In Bansal, R., Chakir, A., Hafaz Ngah, A., Rabby, F., & Jain, A. (Eds.), *AI Algorithms and ChatGPT for Student Engagement in Online Learning* (pp. 171–191). IGI Global. DOI: 10.4018/979-8-3693-4268-8.ch012

Wheeler, S. (2015). *Learning with 'e's: Educational Theory and Practice in the Digital Age*. Crown House.

Wheeler, S. (2019). *Digital Learning in Organizations*. Kogan Page.

Zuboff, S. (2019). *The Age of Surveillance Capitalism: The Fight for a Human Future at the New Frontier of Power*. Profile Books.

Chapter 4
ESL 4.0
A Practical Guide to Benefits, Challenges, and Best Practices for AI-Enhanced Learning

Reima Abobaker
Savannah College of Art and Design, USA

Sheena Moleta
https://orcid.org/0009-0005-2683-055X
Savannah College of Art and Design, USA

ABSTRACT

The interest of implementing cutting-edge technology has always been potent in education. Artificial intelligence (AI) has the potential of being a ubiquitous powerful tool that promises personalized learning, adaptive curriculum, and enhanced engagement. This chapter investigates the growing attention for integrating AI in education, with a specific focus on its application in the English as a second language (ESL) classroom. Therefore, through the lens of established ESL pedagogical principles, the authors explore the potential benefits and inherent challenges of implementing AI tools into ESL classrooms, offering practical strategies and activities that highlight AI's strengths while mitigating its limitations.

INTRODUCTION: AI IN THE FIELD OF EDUCATION

This paper starts with the historical development of Artificial Intelligence (AI) in the context of education and learning technologies with major milestones achieved over the years. The origins of AI in education can be dated back to the middle of

DOI: 10.4018/979-8-3693-5443-8.ch004

the twentieth century when the use of the term Artificial Intelligence was initially presented during a workshop in Dartmouth College in 1956, which may be considered as the starting point of AI in education development (Williamson & Eynon, 2020). AI's early development was concerned with emulating the ability to reason and build systems that could duplicate the procedures of human decisions, guided by an embedded knowledge base (Williamson & Eynon, 2020).

In the 1960s, a worthwhile fundamental step toward the integration of AI into education was marked by the emergence of Intelligent Tutoring Systems (ITS) as concepts for teaching that was designed to meet the individual requirements of students (Niu et al., 2022). This period also marked the use of computer-assisted instruction, that is, use of early computing technologies to support instruction (Chen et al., 2020). Nonetheless, it encountered a few problems in the past, which are called "AI winters," when its funding and popularity declined because of the unsatisfied expectations and devices' capabilities (Williamson & Eynon, 2020).

The revival of AI in education started around the year 2010 most probably due to the availability of better and more advanced machine learning models and big data. This period transitioned from simple expert systems to complex AI or artificial intelligence systems with learning capabilities and data predictive value (Williamson & Eynon, 2020). The introduction of more advanced tools such as chatbots and automated grading systems have continued to revolutionize the ways that the education procedures in tackling administrative procedures and delivering individualized learner support (Chen et al., 2020; Kamalov et al., 2023).

The current state of AI in education is filled with hope yet skepticism. Though AI is accepted by many educators as a positive force, which can foster students' learning experiences and help with the bureaucratic chores, the issues of ethics, reliability, and technology dependency are still factors to consider (Costello, 2023; Ahmad et al., 2021). For example, some studies indicate that, although AI can contribute to content design and its assessment, there is a fear among educators that it may undermine their roles or lead to a decline in teaching skills (Liu, 2023; Humble, 2023).

In addition, the integration of AI in education raises questions about equity and access, as disparities in technology availability can affect student outcomes (Ahmad et al., 2021). As AI continues to evolve, it is crucial for educators and policymakers to navigate these challenges thoughtfully, ensuring that the benefits of AI are realized while safeguarding the core values of education (Sallam, 2024).

The evolution of AI in education reflects a complex interplay of technological advancements and pedagogical innovations. Understanding this historical context is essential for framing the current discourse on AI's role in shaping the future of education.

AI and ESL Education

The field of Second Language Teaching and Learning has always been at the forefront of adopting and implementing the latest technology. There is a large body of literature exploring the effect of such technology in learners' engagement, motivation, performance, achievement, and the ultimate goal of acquisition. While technology integration in classrooms has become common, artificial intelligence (AI) has opened up a wide range of opportunities in the ESL classroom. Imagine a classroom where every student receives personalized attention, learning materials adapt in real-time to their needs, and insights from their performance guide their learning journey. This is not the future; it is today's reality in ESL education, thanks to artificial intelligence (AI).

AI offers a unique level of personalization, adaptability, and data-driven insights that promise to revolutionize the learning experience. It holds immense potential for ESL classrooms, in particular, due to its inherent alignment with core ESL pedagogical principles of individualized instruction, scaffolding and differentiated instruction, data-driven decision making, engaging and interactive learning, and learner autonomy and self-directed learning (Richards and Rodgers, 2014), which will be explored in this chapter. In addition, this chapter will also address the inherent challenges and offer practical strategies for integrating AI tools effectively.

Exploring the Advantages of AI in the ESL Classroom

Traditional technology in education has primarily been about digitizing existing teaching methodologies and administrative processes. These technologies, such as learning management systems, digital textbooks, and basic educational software, operate on pre-defined rules and cannot learn or adapt. AI, on the other hand, provides a more human-like experience since it can further process and learn from data, therefore giving an even deeper insight into learner performance and learning needs. Moreover, AI adapts content and feedback in real time, significantly improving personalized learning that goes beyond the capabilities of traditional technology.

AI's abilities go beyond personalized adaptive learning to help with the process of ESL learning and teaching at different stages of the acquisition. From the instantaneous automated grammar-correction tools to boosting engagement through lifelike immersive environments to contributing to faster curriculum development. Ultimately, AI's capabilities have the potential to significantly enhance the learning experience and outcomes by providing a more dynamic and responsive approach in comparison to ways in which traditional technology has been used. Therefore, in the following section, an overview of how AI support the fundamental pedagogical values of ESL, i.e., individualization, scaffolding and differentiation of instruction, data-driven decision-making, engagement and interactivity in learning, and learners' ability to engage in self-initiated learning and self-regulation (Richards and Rodgers, 2014), will be presented.

Individualized Instruction

Traditional ESL teaching often struggles to cater to the diverse needs and learning styles present in a single classroom. Even within one level or classroom, learners tend to have variation in their proficiency skills as they could have individual differences in their cognitive abilities, prior knowledge, and language learning ability, all of which need to be considered when designing instruction. There are other scopes of differences that need to be considered as well, such as *linguistic* backgrounds, *learning styles*, *educational backgrounds*, and *personal and cultural differences,* as age, cultural values, and learning experiences can further shape learners needs (Jahiel, 2008; Tulbure, 2011; Yassin & Almasri, 2015; Zafar & Meenakshi, 2012). These differences fuel teachers' capacity to personalize learning pathways, dynamically adjusting to each student's progress and delivering content tailored to their specific needs, boosting student engagement and motivation, which makes learning more effective.

However, putting this approach into practice can be challenging. Collecting and analyzing data on each student's needs requires significant time and effort to create individual learning plans and apply differentiated teaching techniques. In addition, customizing education to accommodate the needs of a varied group of learners may be challenging to implement on a larger scale. Consequently, the diversification of needs not addressed may tend to bring forth disengagement, frustration, and lower attainment in academics according to research. This is more so disadvantageous to the learner who may have specific learning styles or may be from a culture not catered for by the traditional approach (Slavin, 2012).

Fortunately, advancements in educational technology have made it easier to offer personalized learning experiences. AI, in particular, offers a more scalable and effective solution. Unlike conventional technology, AI systems can quickly process vast amounts of data to accurately determine individual students' language proficiency, analyze students' strengths and weaknesses, and address learners' individual needs and learning styles. Subsequently, it generates an individualized learning pathway that adjusts in real time. For example, it can adjust the difficulty level of questions or switch between different types of learning resources (videos, texts, quizzes) based on what works best for the student. Since adaptive learning offers individualized learning paths and recommendations, it consequently improves the learning process and performance (Ling & Chiang, 2022) and further boosts the use of technology that provides such personalized learning plans, enabling more customized learning opportunities (Shou et al., 2020).

AI-powered personalized adaptive learning has significantly advanced the field of ESL education, providing a tailored approach that respects and responds to each learner's needs (Xie et al., 2019). The seamless integration of diagnostics and customized pathways streamlines the personalized learning process, ensuring targeted support for specific linguistic difficulties. At the same time, adaptability ensures that the curriculum remains challenging and engaging, promoting continuous improvement and mastery of the language, ultimately enhancing language acquisition and proficiency at the learner's pace.

Differentiated Instruction and Scaffolding

The relationship between differentiated instruction and scaffolding is crucial for supporting the diverse needs of ESL learners. Differentiated instruction in ESL classrooms involves tailoring teaching methods to accommodate the varying proficiency levels and learning styles of students. This personalized approach fosters engagement, motivation, and active participation among ESL learners, leading to improved language acquisition and academic success (Reeves, 2004; Adesope et al., 2011; Ramli & Yusoff, 2020). Moreover, differentiated instruction in ESL classrooms helps address the unique challenges faced by learners, such as vocabulary acquisition and comprehension of academic content (Bhowmik & Kim, 2021). By incorporating a variety of instructional techniques, including genre-based activities, digital technology and AI integration, and adapting practices based on student needs, educators can create inclusive learning environments that cater to the linguistic and cultural diversity of ESL students (Bhowmik & Kim, 2022). This approach not only supports language development but also enhances students' critical thinking skills and cross-cultural awareness (Bhowmik & Kim, 2021). Differentiated instruction also plays a crucial role in promoting equity and inclusivity in ESL education. By recognizing and accommodating the individual strengths and needs of learners, educators can create a supportive learning environment that values linguistic diversity and fosters a sense of belonging among students (Giles, 2018). This approach is particularly important in mainstream content classrooms, where ESL students may face additional challenges in accessing academic content and demonstrating their understanding (Giles, 2018).

In the same vein, scaffolding, a key principle in ESL pedagogy, plays a significant role in ESL instruction by providing the necessary support and guidance to help ESL learners engage in challenging academic tasks (Johnson, 2018). It involves providing temporary support that gradually diminishes as learners gain confidence and competence. Scaffolding can be defined as the "process that enables a child or novice to solve a problem, carry out a task or achieve a goal which would be beyond his unassisted efforts" (Wood, Bruner & Ross, 1976, p. 90). In the context of ESL, scaffolding techniques such as teacher-student interactions, teacher modeling and peer scaffolding are commonly used to assist students in developing their language skills (Choi & Wong, 2018). Classroom-based scaffolding in which teacher-student interactions lead to the development of the targeted skill or task (Lee & Azman, 2020; Gulubba et al., 2019), and the use of teacher modeling and creative imitation as a means of scaffolding ESL skills such as writing, highlighting the practical application of scaffolding techniques in ESL contexts (Choi & Wong, 2018). Peer scaffolding, on the other hand, involves students supporting each other in language learning tasks, fostering collaboration and peer interaction to enhance language acquisition (Sari et al., 2018; Abdollahzadeh and Behroozizad, 2015; Herayati, 2019; Tinggie et al., 2023).

The integration of differentiated instruction and scaffolding in ESL classrooms is essential for creating inclusive learning environments that cater to the diverse needs of ESL learners. By differentiating instruction in material and task creation based on students' language proficiency levels and learning preferences, educators can provide targeted support to help students progress in their language development (Ndu et al., 2022). Scaffolding complements this approach by offering structured support to ESL learners as they engage in language learning activities, gradually fading support as students gain proficiency and independence (Choi & Wong, 2018; Arora et al, 2024).

One might argue, however, that there is often a gap between what teachers can offer and learners' needs, especially for those who might make similar and repetitive mistakes, which can be tiring and time consuming for teachers to provide consistent and repetitive error correction and feedback. Another issue is that some scaffolding techniques may not be as beneficial when certain skills and expertise are not present. For example, peer scaffolding can be a disadvantage to ESL learners as they have the tendency of concentrating solely on the superficial aspect of the task, overlooking the deeper discussion on the task's content. Taking writing tasks as an example, ESL learners usually focus on the local grammatical issues of sentence structure and verb tenses but face difficulty considering and assessing global issues with the writing and critiquing the rationale behind decisions related to content, semantic, and lexical competence due to their lack of expertise with such skills (Chen & Law, 2016; Wu, Petit, and Chen, 2015). The use of computer-assisted instruction, therefore, powered by AI can make learning more efficient for both sides (learners and teachers).

AI can effectively provide differentiation and scaffolding through various means. The support that AI offers entails tailored assistance with materials creation. Tools such as Diffit and Brisk assist with changing the language level of written content to accommodate learners who have different reading levels in understanding the same content. AI also is employed to provide differentiated instruction through personalized adaptive learning, adapting the educational content to meet the diverse needs of ESL learners, which would allow the possibility of creating unique paths of learning by the student's ability and performance (Taylor et al., 2021; Akavova, Temirkhanova & Lorsanova, 2023). Adaptive learning platforms, such as *MetaTutor*, can personalize the difficulty and complexity of content based on individual performance, gradually removing support as students master specific skills and help learners develop self-regulated learning skills (Azevedo et al., 2022). Similarly, AI-powered tutors can offer targeted feedback and assistance on challenging tasks, gradually withdrawing as the learner becomes more independent. These AI tools also have the potential to personalize support, emphasizing the role of the individualization of the educational process (Mindigulova, 2024).

Some researchers have explored adaptive collaborative learning support (ACLS) (Wilson & Scott, 2017), and intelligent tutoring robots (Yang & Zhang. 2019), which involve collaborative learning environments that adapt their characteristics and provide intelligent hints and feedback to improve individual learners' collaborative interactions. This demonstrates the potential of AI to offer personalized support and gradually withdraw scaffolding as learners gain mastery in specific skills. IELTS Liulishuo online platform is one of these AI-powered tools that provides language learning support and offers targeted feedback and assistance to learners who prepare for the IELTS exam (Li, 2020). This tool aligns with the elements of computer-assisted language learning (CALL) and the principles of mobile-assisted language learning (MALL). However, the author also reports some limitations with the tools, such as giving false corrections and using unfamiliar specialized lexical language when giving feedback, and further recommends that continuous examination of these tools by educators is important to evaluate its potential effects on the teaching and learning process.

Data-Driven Decision Making

Effective ESL teaching relies heavily on understanding individual student progress and identifying areas of difficulty to provide relevant and accurate feedback. Educators are consistently collecting relevant academic, behavioral, and emotional data on and about their learners through formative and summative assessments, class tasks and activities, class discussions, class observation, and exit surveys. Such data emphasizes the transformative potential of data-driven decision making in teaching and learning, highlighting the need for personalized interventions based on real-time insights (Mandinach & Jackson, 2012). Furthermore, Botvin et al. (2022) stress the importance of data-driven decision making in guiding and supporting educational decisions, which has been shown to improve teaching and promote Israeli students' learning. Other researchers also stress the significance of emotional data about learner's interest, engagement and motivation in promoting learning, especially when it is remote (Botvin et al., 2022; Usher et al., 2021). However, some traditional methods of assessment often lack the granularity and real-time insights needed for personalized interventions.

The integration of AI in ESL education represents an innovative shift away from traditional feedback and progress monitoring methods and time-consuming effort in providing accurate, consistent, and impartial evaluations. AI-powered tools such as speech recognition software and intelligent tutoring systems are at the forefront of this change. These tools enable a level of personalized learning previously unattainable, directly addressing each student's specific needs and challenges. Furthermore, AI-powered assessment tools extend the capabilities of ESL education by evaluating students' language skills through interactive exercises, speaking assessments, and writing tasks. This comprehensive evaluation provides students with clear insights into their strengths and areas for improvement, facilitating a targeted approach to language learning. The transition to AI-enhanced feedback mechanisms marks a significant evolution in ESL education, moving from generic, delayed feedback to a more engaging, effective, and responsive educational environment. This shift improves language acquisition rates and boosts students' confidence in their language skills.

Feedback

AI tools can automatically analyze and evaluate students' spoken or written English, providing instant feedback on grammar, vocabulary, pronunciation, and sentence structure. This immediate feedback allows students to see their mistakes in real time and make the necessary corrections, which can accelerate the learning process. The learning process is therefore expected to be a lot more efficient (Hwang et al., 2023). This is quite different from the traditional method, in which the feedback can come days or weeks following the assessments, hence holding up the learning process. AI's targeted approach helps learners progress faster by ensuring feedback directly applies to each learner's challenges, which traditional teaching methods may have overlooked. In addition to highlighting their errors, AI feedback helps learners understand their mistakes by explaining what they got wrong and how to improve it, allowing them to make immediate corrections. Explanations might include detailed descriptions of abstract and complex grammatical rules, a misplaced application of context, or an inaccurate pronunciation. Feedback like this often comes in step-by-step instructions, formative activities customized to the individual error pattern, and correct versus incorrect use models. Engaging with students in this way makes it easier to enact an active, hands-on approach to language learning, where corrections are not simply understood but also applied. Since AI is able to respond to every lesson, feedback can be made customized in accordance with the pace of the student's learning and the repetitive lexical and grammatical problems (Lee, Kim, & Sung, 2022). AI-based feedback helped transform language learning into an interesting, personalized, and productive experience through the provision of real-time feedback, detailed explanation, and counteractive context-specific correction addressed to the learner (Pack & Maloney, 2023; Tubino & Adachi, 2022).

In addition, these AI-powered assessment tools can provide a standardized and objective evaluation of students' language proficiency, eliminating subjective biases that may arise from human grading, ensuring that each student is graded fairly and objectively. These instruments apply to the performance of students' pre-defined criteria, and therefore, every learner is given an objective grade and fair treatment. Additionally, AI-driven assessment tools are standardized and very objective in the provision of an assessment on student language proficiency in that they eliminate subjective biases that a human grade may involve in the process (Bulut & Wongvorachan, 2022).

Progress Monitoring

Beyond the immediate provision of feedback and assessments, AI tools embody advanced capabilities for tracking and monitoring student progress. These tools offer detailed data analytics and performance tracking, allowing teachers to pinpoint specific challenges each student faces and adapt their instruction accordingly (Hashim et al., 2019; Settles et al., 2020). The insights derived from AI-driven data analysis extend beyond mere academic tracking; they empower educators to refine teaching methodologies, adjust curriculums, and optimize resource distribution, all bolstering language acquisition efforts. This continuous oversight ensures that educators can swiftly identify and address learning obstacles, adapt instructional strategies, and provide individualized support based on the student's current needs and performance (AlHarbi, 2022). AI also makes a prediction of future learning outcomes based on patterns observed to date, and that helps educators act proactively to eliminate potential challenges even before they become an obstacle to progress. For example, suggesting pre-emptive actions such as supplementary practice sessions or even targeted learning modules to avoid small problems growing to become major obstacles (Arakawa et al., 2022). In integrating AI tools for progress monitoring, educators are equipped with a powerful ally in optimizing language learning. This technology fosters a more informed, responsive, and effective educational approach, ensuring that each student's learning potential is fully realized.

Teacher Time Optimization

One of the most significant benefits of AI in ESL education is the optimization of teacher time. Teachers can utilize AI abilities to quickly and accurately evaluate essays, multiple-choice tests, and other assignments. This saves teachers a considerable amount of time on grading assignments and exams. With this freed time, educators can focus on developing interactive and engaging activities, such as cultural immersion experiences and applying complex language skills in real-life contexts, enhancing the learning experience and deepening student engagement. Additionally, educators can allocate more time to personalized student interactions, enhancing their connection with students and fostering a more prosperous, supportive learning environment (Lin, 2022). This transition towards more direct engagement improves teaching effectiveness and significantly enriches the educational journey, creating a more supportive and dynamic learning environment for students (Nazari, Shabbir, & Setiawan, 2021; Ng et al., 2023).

Integrating AI into ESL education not only enhances the learning experience for students but also elevates the teaching process. By automating certain aspects of feedback and assessment and providing immediate, detailed, and personalized feedback, pinpointing specific areas for improvement, AI enables teachers to focus on the more nuanced and complex aspects of language teaching, such as facilitating conversation practice, cultural education, and the development of critical thinking skills in a new language. This shift towards higher-level teaching tasks contributes to a more effective and enriching language learning environment. As these technologies evolve and become more integrated into language education, they promise to transform ESL education further, making it more effective, engaging, and accessible to learners worldwide (Jiang, 2022; Cantos, 2023; Hieu, 2024).

Engaging and Interactive Learning

Motivating and actively engaging students are essential aspects of promoting successful language acquisition. It has been well established in the literature that when students are engaged, they become more motivated and achieve better outcomes in language acquisition (Maru, & Pajow, 2021). In other words, for engagement to take place, educators and teachers need to provide opportunities for their learners that are carefully and thoughtfully planned by designing tasks that are doable, have potential value, do not frustrate learners, and boosts their confidence (Cambourne, 1995; Egbert, 2011). Socio-cultural theory (SCT) also provides support for the social nature of interaction in learning (Lantolf, 2006). Similarly, constructivism advocates the activity of knowledge construction (Aljohani, 2017; Huang, 2002; Simina, & Hamel, 2005). Consequently, Game-based Learning (GBL) has become an interest among educators as it entails giving a chance of learning directly through engaging in playing games, while *Gamification* involves the incorporation of game-like attributes to the activities that are not designed to be a game, thus making it fun and engaging (Gil-Aciron, 2022; James & Mayer, 2018).

AI Chatbots, AI-enhanced gamification, and virtual reality (VR) experiences powered by AI can create interactive, engaging, and immersive learning environments (Park et al., 2019). AI Chatbots can provide compelling, interactive, engaging, and immersive learning environments, reduce barriers, personalize supports, foster communication, and stimulate active engagement in any language learning activity. For example, Kohnke et al. (2023) have found that ChatGPT reduces shyness among learners as well as perceived distance between the learners and teachers, hence increasing interaction, creating an engaging learning environment through communication, and reducing barriers. AI voice chatbots, such as ELIZA, ALICE, Cleverbot, Elbot, Talk to Eve and others, may also be creatively used for language skills development with an interactive and personalized learning experience for the learners within an immersive learning environment (Duong & Suppasetseree, 2024).

AI enhances gamification by offering a more individual and adaptive experience. For example, AI provides algorithms to process data, tracking performance and personalizing elements within the game. It is a technology that dynamically adjusts difficulty levels based on the score of performance while offering personal feedback and rewards; hence, personalizing a challenge to individual interests, which can be designed in a game-like experience.

Virtual Reality (VR) and Augmented Reality (AR) enhanced with AI create immersive simulations that place learners in authentic language contexts, enhancing their curiosity and engagement. For instance, Immerse, a VR language learning platform, leverages AI technology to create realistic conversation opportunities with AI avatars. These avatars engage users in natural conversations, adapting their responses and difficulty based on the learner's level and progress. This personalized interaction provides a unique and dynamic learning experience that simulates real-world language use.

By leveraging AI abilities to enhance student engagement and motivation (Vall & Araya, 2023), educators can create dynamic and meaningful learning experiences that align with established language acquisition theories.

Learner Autonomy and Self-Directed Learning

Fostering autonomy and self-directed learning is crucial for long-term language acquisition success. When students are autonomous, it does not imply they work on a task entirely apart from their teachers; they can still be autonomous in many ways during a task while also learning from their peers and/or teachers. Many learners struggle with autonomy even if they demonstrate their ability to be autonomous; it is the responsibility of the teacher to provide the appropriate chances and learning supports to help them become more autonomous (Black & Deci, 2000). When learners participate in their own learning process, it nurtures and supports their autonomy. Strategies can include motivating learners to compile their own study materials by planning their goals, creating their own exercises to practice a grammatical or structural issue, keeping a vocabulary journal with definitions and examples sentences, and making mock exams using materials from lectures and handouts given by their teachers or created by themselves (Abobaker & Silas, 2024). However, creating such materials can be challenging of these learners as they may not have the level of expertise or the know-how to design such tasks. Therefore, AI-powered tools can support learners in generating such input to supplement their learning process as well as boost their autonomy.

AI enables learners to make informed decisions about their learning process, facilitating learner-centered education. Providing personalized learning plans, adaptive practice exercises, and instant feedback all available by a simple keystroke regardless of their language proficiency level can support learners' autonomy. AI also fosters self-regulated learning strategies, such as goal setting, self-monitoring, and self-assessment, enabling learners to become more effective and independent. AI-facilitated platforms and tools allow students to access learning resources and activities anytime and anywhere, breaking down traditional classroom barriers and supporting a more balanced integration of learning with daily life. AI assists learners with attaining lifelong learning skills critical for language acquisition and beyond.

According to research, fostering learners' autonomy in their learning process requires both learner-oriented planning of the learning contents and individualized learning tool or technology, such as an AI tool, that can empower learners in talking ownership of their learning journey (Caputo & Garrido, 2015; Garrido & Onaindia, 2013). Additionally, some studies have stressed the value of learners' ability to take control of their own learning process and become autonomous in terms of preparing, implementing, monitoring, and evaluating their own learning plans and process, especially during the COVID-19 epidemic (Hardi et al., 2022). With the support and guidance given by their teachers and AI tools, learners' autonomy in the learners can grow (Ningsih, 2019).

NAVIGATING CHALLENGES AND MITIGATING RISKS

While AI offers exciting possibilities, integrating it into the ESL classroom necessitates careful consideration of potential challenges and limitations.

Algorithmic Bias and Equity Concerns

AI algorithms are susceptible to biases present in the data they are trained on (Baker & Hawn, 2021; Wang, 2020). In other words, output generated by AI tools are as accurate as their input of data sources and content. These data sources reflect patterns and information from the real world, increasing the risk of bias if the data collection process is not monitored. Therefore, systemic bias, discrimination, inequality for marginalized groups of learners, and xenophobia (Hwang et al., 2020) could be intentionally impeded in AI tools.

The different aspects of biased data include gender, race, ethnicity, and special learning needs and abilities. This bias might manifest through stylistic elements such as dialect indicators or grammatical correctness, or through concealed structural expectations such as word counts, potentially leading to unfairly affecting learners of color and thus compromising the integrity of the scoring process. Therefore, nondiscrimination or unbiased AI algorithms and practices need to be implemented to promote equality in education (Palomares et al., 2021).

That is to say, it would be apt to say that educators should be trained in AI technically and pedagogically so that they can appropriately integrate it in different subjects (Salas-Pilco, 2020). Also, the developers ought to be careful in training the AI systems so as to minimize the systematic bias and discrimination by deploying inclusive and diverse data (Hogenhout, 2021). Moreover, the need to design and opt for tools that are equity-oriented as well as the need to monitor these on a regular basis is deemed as a critical issue to ascertain bias does not determine specific learner groups.

Overreliance on Technology and the Dehumanization of Learning

The integration of AI in education has sparked debates regarding the potential of overreliance of AI and the possibility of dehumanization of learning. The concern lies in the readiness to blindly accept technology, leading to practical problems such as misuse, overreliance, and ignorance of consequences. Learners' perceptions of AI in the classroom play a significant role in understanding the impact of technology on learning (Sumakul et al., 2022).

Language learners, specifically, may end up using AI as a crutch, hindering their overall learning. Therefore, while AI has offered many innovative ways of learning languages, it is crucial to avoid overreliance on technology and ensure that it complements rather than replaces human interaction and tailored guidance (Dignum, 2021).

AI in language teaching has limitations (Kohnke et al., 2023). Therefore, like any other sophisticated technology, AI should not replace teachers but rather serve as a tool to empower them, ensuring that it enhances the irreplaceable role of human interaction and personalized guidance in language learning (Malik & Solanki, 2021). The challenges of monitoring learner status and preferences emphasize the irreplaceable role of human teachers in providing personalized guidance (Kim & Kim, 2020). Moreover, the need to understand cultural and contextual differences in language reinforces the importance of human interaction in language learning (Vall & Araya, 2023). Therefore, it is imperative for educators to manage the use of AI as a valuable tool that empowers their significant role in the learning process.

The integration of AI in language learning has sparked significant debate regarding its potential limitations and negative impacts on student-teacher relationships and social aspects of learning. While AI offers personalized learning experiences and efficient data management, it also poses risks to interpersonal interactions that are crucial for effective education.

One of the primary concerns is that AI may diminish the quality of student-teacher relationships. The reliance on AI-driven tools can lead to a reduction in face-to-face interactions, which are essential for fostering trust and rapport between students and educators. As highlighted by Gupta (2024), the multifaceted roles of AI in education can inadvertently create a distance between students and teachers, as the human element of teaching is replaced by automated systems. This shift can undermine the emotional support and mentorship that teachers provide, which are vital for student motivation and engagement (Gupta, 2024). Furthermore, Popenici and Kerr (2017) emphasize that while AI can enhance educational outcomes, it is imperative to recognize the potential erosion of the human connection that is fundamental to effective teaching and learning.

Moreover, the social aspects of language learning are significantly impacted by AI's implementation. Language acquisition is inherently a social process, relying heavily on interaction and communication with others (Thornton, 2015). The use of AI tools, while beneficial for personalized learning, may lead to isolation as students engage more with machines than with their peers or instructors. This concern is echoed by Bai (2023), who notes that the participatory role of students in their learning process is crucial and that AI should not replace the collaborative dynamics that occur in traditional educational settings. The absence of meaningful interactions can hinder the development of critical language skills, such as speaking and listening, which thrive on social engagement (Ulfa, 2023).

Additionally, the potential for students to become overly dependent on AI tools raises concerns about their ability to think critically and engage in self-regulated learning. Jafari (2023) points out that while AI can support language learning, it should not replace the essential role of teachers in guiding students through complex linguistic concepts that require human judgment. This dependency can lead to a superficial understanding of language, as students may rely on AI for answers rather than engaging deeply with the material and their peers (Khan, 2023).

The potential of AI in support of language learning is recognized through an empirical systematic literature review (Yang & Kyun, 2022). The model of hybrid human-AI learning technologies by Molenaar (2022) suggests considering, however, that control is transferred in the interplay between the teacher and technology. Educators should be poised with an ability to manage the use of AI as a useful tool in empowering their significant role in the learning process. It is also important for educators to understand that while AI presents numerous opportunities for enhancing language learning, it is crucial to critically assess its limitations and potential negative impacts on student-teacher relationships and the social dimensions of learning. Maintaining strong interpersonal connections in educational settings is essential for fostering an environment conducive to effective learning. Therefore, educators must strive to integrate AI in ways that complement, rather than replace, the human elements of teaching.

Ethical Considerations and Data Privacy

Another concern with AI is the privacy and security of user data. AI tools collect and process large amounts of personal information about their users (Wang et al., 2019). The characteristics of the ethical AI use and data privacy guidelines include transparency and accountability. Examples of which include the General Data Protection Regulation (GDPR), which prescribes rules to guide the collection, retention, and processing of personal data; it mandates consent to use data (Milossi et al., 2021), the California Consumer Privacy Act (CCPA), which requires transparency on collection of data, among other things, and allows users to opt out. Different stakeholders, including regulators, developers, researchers, and companies, have come up with or applied several ethical guidelines meant for AI systems. These recommendations guide helpfully to the practice of ethical AI while fostering and underlining the necessary and continued collaboration concerning issues of an ethical nature connected to the development and use of AI technologies (Huriye, 2023).

In addition to general AI guidelines, ethical and privacy issues have been contextualized in the educational domain (Nguyen et al., 2022). According to Holmes et al. (2021), a well-designed framework for ethics in AI in education, combining a multidisciplinary approach and robust guidelines, is crucial for addressing complex ethical issues and ensuring student learning. Therefore, this research ensures ethical use through principles of robust protection of data, having ethical guidelines, inclusion of stakeholders, and promoting awareness of information collection and usage to ensure the right to privacy is adhered to (Klimova et al., 2023).

IMPLEMENTING AI IN THE ESL CLASSROOM: PRACTICAL STRATEGIES, ACTIVITIES, AND LESSON PLANS

This section aims to provide educators with practical approaches and exercises to help them integrate artificial intelligence tools into their classroom practices. Our goal is to make it easier for instructors to transition to an educational setting that utilizes artificial intelligence by providing systematic and detailed instructions. We will provide a step-by-step guide to introducing AI tools in the classroom, including a lesson plan to do so (see Appendix). We will also explore incorporating artificial intelligence (AI) tools into English as a Second Language (ESL) classrooms, along with activities that may be performed using these tools.

AI Implementation Guide

Creating an AI-driven learning environment in the ESL classroom can be achieved through the following steps:

Step 1: Assessment of Needs

Before choosing from the vast amount of available AI technologies, teachers should make more informed decisions by carefully assessing both the classroom environment and students' individual needs and preferences. Ensuring that the infrastructure is ready for AI tools is critical for effective integration and usage. Moreover, by identifying specific learning goals, challenges, and areas where students seek improvement, educators can choose AI tools that provide the necessary support and resources to address these areas effectively (Smith et al., 2004). This comprehensive approach ensures that technology adoption is grounded in educational objectives and maximizes the potential for AI to support and enrich the ESL learning experience.

Assessing Classroom Infrastructure:

- ***Physical Area***: Evaluate whether the classroom layout and space can support the integration of AI technologies, including necessary devices and interactive boards.
- ***Technology Access***: Consider the availability of devices such as computers, tablets, and interactive boards. Confirm that the internet connection is reliable, with adequate bandwidth to support AI tools without disruptions.
- ***Hardware Capability***: Assess if the current hardware (computers and devices) is powerful enough to run AI applications efficiently. Determine if upgrades or new hardware are needed for optimal performance.

Assessing Students' Needs:

- ***Cultural Backgrounds***. Recognize students' diverse cultural backgrounds to ensure that the chosen AI tools support inclusivity and engagement.
- ***Learning Styles and Preferences***. Identify learning preferences using direct feedback, surveys, or a learning styles questionnaire. Select an AI tool to accommodate these preferences by focusing on whether the student is a visual, audio, or kinesthetic learner or has other specific learning preferences.
- ***Learning Abilities and Digital Literacy***. Analyze students' available performance data to gather insights into their learning capabilities and digital literacy. Students have varied ways of processing information, which can significantly influence their interaction with AI-powered tools.
- ***Language Proficiency.*** Assess students' strengths and weaknesses using diagnostic methods or reviewing past performance data.

Step 2: Selection of Appropriate AI Tools

After completing the needs assessment, educators should identify and evaluate which tools are the most appropriate to enhance ESL learning in their classes. To assist educators in this, methods to identify tools and a framework to evaluate tools (Table 1) has been suggested.

Identification of Tools.

- ***Educational Technology Platforms.*** The easiest way to do this is by checking reviews, ratings, and user feedback on dedicated websites and forums specializing in educational technology. Users often provide insights into usefulness and applicability based on their experience.
- ***Review of Scholarly Articles***. Academic research and case studies can offer evidence-based evaluations of AI tools in educational settings, highlighting their impact on language teaching.
- ***Attending Educational Conferences.*** These conferences typically offer sessions about AI in education, networking opportunities with peers, and vendors who can demonstrate their products and provide specifications and details
- ***Interaction with Colleagues and Online Communities.*** Educators often share experiences and provide feedback on using particular tools.

Table 1. Evaluation framework for educational tools

Criterion	Importance	Questions for Teachers	How to Assess
Curriculum Alignment	Ensures tools align with learning goals and academic standards	Does the tool support the curriculum objectives and contribute to achieving learning goals?	Review curriculum requirements; assess how well the tool integrates with academic goals.
Learning Outcome	Evaluates the impact on ESL competencies.	What language skills does the tool target? Is there evidence of improvement in these areas?	Compare pre- and post-implementation scores.
Engagement	Measures tool's ability to maintain interest.	How does the tool keep students engaged? Are there interactive features?	Monitor usage and feedback; assess participation improvements.
Feedback Quality	Assesses relevance and helpfulness of feedback.	Is the feedback personalized and actionable? How quickly is it provided?	Review feedback samples; survey students on clarity/usefulness.
Accessibility	Guarantees access for all students, including those with disabilities.	Is the tool compatible with various devices? Does it meet accessibility standards?	Verify compliance with standards; test across devices.
Usability	Ensures tools are easily navigable for both users.	How intuitive is the interface? Can students navigate it easily?	Observe integration ease; solicit user experience feedback.
Data Privacy and Security	Ensures protection of student information.	How does the tool protect user data? Is it compliant with relevant privacy laws?	Check compliance with data protection regulations.
Cost-effectiveness	Considers benefits in relation to expenses.	Does the tool offer value for its cost? Are there free or more affordable alternatives that meet our needs?	Analyze metrics improvement against costs; consider alternatives.

Step 3: Training and Familiarization

To acquire the skills and knowledge required to incorporate AI tools into teaching practices successfully, educators should dedicate time to training and familiarization to ensure confidence and competence in utilizing AI tools in the ESL classroom (Zhao et al., 2022).

Training Programs and Resources. One way to gain training in AI tools for the ESL classroom is through formal training programs and resources. AI tool providers and educational technology organizations often offer free, comprehensive training. These sessions offer a more comprehensive overview of specific AI tools, including their features, capabilities, and best practices within educational settings. A key advantage of formal training is its direct access to experts and vendors, allowing educators to gain deeper insights, ask specific questions, and troubleshoot with AI professionals. Additionally, attending workshops and enrolling in courses offered by educational institutions, professional associations, or online platforms can be beneficial. A variety of courses and workshops that concentrate on educational technology and AI, with a strong focus on the practical use of knowledge, are available. This helps educators improve their capacity to incorporate AI tools into their teaching methods. In addition, many of these are online, like Coursera, edX, and LinkedIn Learning, which offer flexible learning, accommodating educators' schedules and learning paces. Furthermore, educators can explore online resources such as tutorials, user guides, and FAQs. Self-study encourages educators to deepen their understanding and skills independently and promotes continuous learning. By fostering a habit of self-directed, continuous learning, educators keep pace with technological advancements and enhance their ability to adapt and innovate in their educational methodologies regularly.

Hands-On Practice. Another effective method to gain proficiency in AI tools is by getting hands-on experience. This can be achieved by participating in trial periods or pilot projects. Utilizing trial periods or demo accounts allows educators to gain firsthand experience with AI tools without committing to long-term subscriptions. These trial periods allow educators to actively experiment with the tool's features and directly assess its applicability and effectiveness in their ESL classrooms. By doing so, teachers can develop a level of comfort and proficiency in using AI tools and can better identify which tools best support their educational objectives and meet the learning needs of their students. Educators can also initiate small-scale pilot projects to experiment with new AI tools in their classrooms. This hands-on method encourages practical learning and adaptation, offering teachers a real-world context to test and refine the use of AI technologies. By implementing these tools on a smaller scale, educators can gather insights into how best to employ AI to enhance ESL learning experiences, identify any challenges, and make necessary adjustments before wider implementation.

Peer Collaboration. In addition to formal education and practical experience, peer collaboration and support further enhance the learning of an unfamiliar AI tool. To gain insights from colleagues, foster a school or institution culture that promotes collaborative effort and open dialogue. Regularly engage in discussions, workshops, and projects with colleagues to explore and evaluate the use of AI tools in the classroom. By learning from the experiences of fellow educators who have already integrated AI tools, educators can gain practical insights from firsthand knowledge, significantly enhancing the understanding and application of AI. This internal collaboration is crucial for pooling collective experiences, overcoming common challenges, and identifying best practices that can be applied across different educational settings. In addition, learn from the global educator community. Cooperation boosts literacy growth in English language learners, producing benefits for both students and teachers (Fu et al., 2007). Expand and strengthen professional learning networks by connecting with educators and experts worldwide through social media platforms and online forums dedicated to educational technology. These external networks provide support and access to diverse perspectives and offer practical advice and innovative ideas on integrating AI tools in the classroom. Participating in these broader conversations keeps educators informed about emerging trends, tools, and methodologies that can be adapted to their teaching practice.

Step 4: Gradual Implementation

Moving from simpler to more complex applications allows teachers and students to become familiar with the new technology without feeling overwhelmed. By slowly introducing AI tools, teachers can address any technical or instructional challenges that may arise and provide the necessary support for students to adapt to the new learning environment. Furthermore, a gradual implementation approach allows for evaluating the effectiveness of AI tools in the ESL classroom. Teachers can assess how students respond to the new technology, identify areas for improvement, and make any necessary adjustments to ensure that the integration of AI tools aligns with the learning objectives and curriculum. This approach also provides teachers with the opportunity to receive ongoing training and professional development in using AI tools effectively. By gradually incorporating AI into the ESL classroom, teachers and students can build their confidence and competence using the tools, minimizing resistance to change and fostering a more positive attitude towards technology adoption. Table 2 outlines a phased approach to implementing AI tools in the ESL classroom, starting with simple applications and gradually introducing more complex functionalities.

Table 2. Phases of implementing AI tools in the ESL classroom

Phase	Objectives & Actions
Phase 1: Simple Applications and Functions	- Introduce AI tools with basic functionalities (e.g., vocabulary enhancement apps, simple grammar correction tools). Use these tools for homework and in-class activities to familiarize students with AI technology.
Phase 2: Complex Functions of Simple Applications	- Expand the use of basic AI tools by exploring their more advanced features (e.g., personalized quizzes, adaptive feedback). Integrate these features into regular learning activities to deepen students' engagement and understanding.
Phase 3: Simple Functions of Complex Applications	- Introduce more sophisticated AI tools, focusing on their simplest functionalities (e.g., a chatbot for conversational practice). Employ these tools in controlled settings to gradually acclimate students to more advanced AI without overwhelming them.

continued on following page

Table 2. Continued

Phase	Objectives & Actions
Phase 4: Complex Applications and Functions	- Fully integrate advanced AI applications with complex functionalities (e.g., AI-driven content creation). Use these tools for comprehensive projects and collaborative work, encouraging higher-level thinking and application of language skills.

Here are some tips for gradually implementing AI tools:

- ***Student Orientation***. Begin with structured orientations to introduce students to new AI tools. This can include interactive demonstrations, step-by-step tutorials, and guided hands-on practice sessions. The goal is to familiarize students with the technology, ensuring they understand how to use the tools effectively and confidently. Using AI with appropriate guidance has improved language teaching and learning (Al-Kaisi et. Al., 2021; Dodigovic, 2007).
- ***Ethical Considerations and Digital Literacy***. Equip students with the skills to evaluate and effectively use digital tools critically. Topics should include data privacy, bias in AI, and the ethical use of digital information. Additionally, educators should include how AI works, its limitations, and how to navigate potential challenges. This discussion will prepare students to use AI tools responsibly and be aware of their implications.
- ***Technical Support.*** Ensure that students and educators have easy access to technical support to resolve any issues that may arise during the use of AI tools. This support could be in the form of IT helpdesks, online resources, or direct assistance from the AI tool providers. Also, encourage a proactive approach to identifying and solving technical problems, ensuring minimal disruption to the learning process.

Step 5: Monitoring, Feedback, and Adjustments

The goal is to establish a continuous improvement cycle, as seen in Figure 1, that leverages monitoring and feedback to make informed adjustments to AI tool usage in the ESL classroom. Continuous improvement involves regular evaluation of the AI tools' effectiveness and collecting feedback from students to inform future teaching practices. Establish a feedback loop where adjustments are continually monitored and refined based on new feedback, ensuring the AI integration strategy remains dynamic and responsive to students' and educators' needs.

Monitoring and Feedback. Implement ongoing evaluations of AI tools' effectiveness using predefined metrics (e.g., student engagement, language proficiency improvement). Gather feedback focusing on usability, engagement, and perceived learning benefits from both students and educators on their observations and experiences through surveys, interviews, and informal discussions. Encourage educators and students to share challenges faced and suggestions for improvement. Educators should be flexible and responsive to their observations and students' and other educators' feedback and observations. Analyze the collected feedback to identify trends, successes, and opportunities for enhancing AI tool integration.

Iterative Adjustments.

1. Use insights gained from monitoring and feedback to make targeted adjustments to AI tool usage to improve effectiveness and address any identified issues.
2. Prioritize adjustments based on feedback that directly impacts learning outcomes and student engagement.
3. Based on positive outcomes and feedback, consider scaling the use of practical AI tools to other areas of the curriculum or introducing additional tools to address new learning objectives.

Figure 1. AI tools implementation improvement cycle

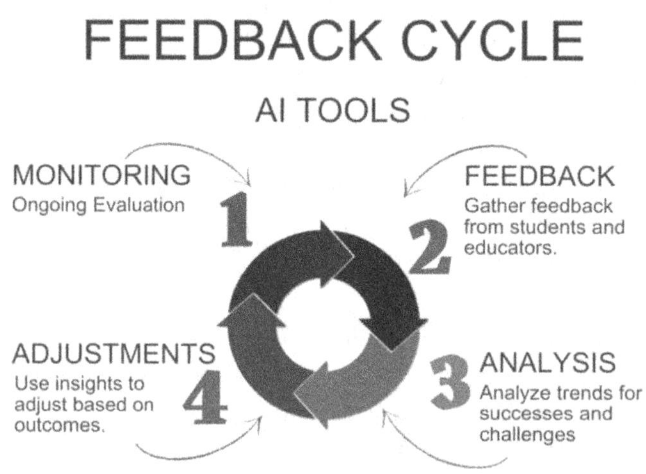

Step 6: Continuous Learning and Reflection

Artificial Intelligence (AI) has appeared in the education sector seemingly overnight, bringing with it a surge of AI tools that become more accessible each day. These tools are constantly evolving as an increasing number of organizations adopt

AI technology to improve educational experiences. The incorporation of AI in the classroom is leading to a shift in the definition of Student-Centered Learning. As a result, educational approaches must adapt to align with the evolving requirements of students (Zhai et al., 2021). To ensure the continued relevance and effectiveness of ESL teaching, instructors need to not only understand AI technology and its tools, but they should also participate in continuous professional development. A continuous learning approach entails using academic and industry resources, engaging in reflective practice, and sharing with the educational community. To stay informed about the latest AI research and trends, educators should read academic journals, attend conferences, and join professional associations dedicated to educational technology. These resources offer valuable insights into effective AI applications and future directions in education. In addition to staying current with academic and industry resources, educators should actively engage in regular reflective teaching practices to improve their use of AI in the classroom and assess the impact of AI tools on teaching effectiveness. This introspective process should entail critically analyzing experiences, identifying areas for personal growth, and setting goals for future professional development. This could include journaling, blogging, or creating digital portfolios, which provide a structured way to document progress with AI integration. Additionally, educators should share their knowledge of AI in ESL education through social media, professional forums, blogging, conference presentations, or professional publications to enrich collective knowledge and improve teaching strategies. This will help foster a community of educators dedicated to advancing AI integration in ESL education.

EFFECTIVE CLASSROOM USE OF AI AND AI-ENHANCED LEARNING TOOLS

This section explores how AI tools can be employed to optimize key areas of language education, from conducting assessments to fostering engagement. However, effective use requires more than simply adopting the technology. Using AI and AI-enhanced learning technologies in language education calls for a strategic approach to leverage AI's strengths in ways that complement traditional teaching methods. By thoughtfully integrating AI tools into classroom instruction, educators can enhance student learning experiences.

1. **Language Assessment.** Conduct initial and ongoing language assessments using AI tools to understand each student's proficiency level. These AI-powered assessments provide valuable insights through detailed analysis of students' grammar, vocabulary, pronunciation, and overall language use. Based on the results,

adapt lesson plans to address identified needs, ensuring instruction is tailored to different learning speeds and capabilities. This might involve segmenting the class based on proficiency, creating differentiated groups for instruction, or integrating specific exercises for targeted skills improvement. Additionally, AI tools can track student progress over time, identifying areas of growth or ongoing challenges, allowing educators to refine and adjust teaching strategies as needed. The continuous feedback loop provided by AI assessments ensures that both teachers and students can monitor performance and make data-driven decisions to support more personalized learning pathways.

2. **Blended Learning.** Combining AI-enhanced digital platforms with traditional classroom activities creates a rich, multidimensional educational experience. This approach supports diverse learning styles, allowing students to benefit from both the personalized pace of online tools and the classroom's interactive, communal learning environment. Utilizing technology alongside traditional resources can assist educators in addressing various challenges and enhance the students' engagement in the learning process (Kessler, 2018). It also enhances students' language skills and learner autonomy (Banditvilai, 2016). Some recent studies suggested that ChatGPT could be beneficial in a blended learning environment, supporting teachers by providing feedback while they focus on higher-order writing skills (Mizumoto et al., 2024; Teng, 2024). Another way to incorporate AI-enhanced tools with traditional classroom activities is by having VR experiences as part of the digital resources available to students. VR can transport students to environments where they can practice language skills in contexts that mimic real-world scenarios, such as navigating a city, ordering food in a restaurant, or engaging in conversations with native speakers. This immersive aspect of VR complements traditional classroom instruction by providing experiential learning that enhances comprehension and retention.
3. **Supplemental Continuous Practice.** Assign AI-enhanced tools for homework, enabling students to engage in personalized and continuous practice outside of classroom hours. These platforms can provide exercises tailored to each student's learning progress, reinforcing in-class learning and promoting mastery of language skills. For example, since chatbots are accessible anytime and anywhere, they provide a flexible option for students to practice language skills outside the classroom. Assign conversational practice with chatbots like ChatGPT as homework, allowing students to engage in personalized dialogues and practice language skills at their own pace and based on their current proficiency level. The chatbot can adapt conversations to suit individual learning needs, ensuring students receive practice relevant to their learning journey.

4. **Real-Time Feedback.** Implement tools like Grammarly for writing and PPT Presentation Coach for speaking to give students instant feedback on their language use and presentation skills. This immediate correction and guidance facilitate self-improvement and confidence in language proficiency (Chang et al., 2021). In addition, chatbots like ChatGPT can provide immediate corrections and suggestions, offering a personalized feedback loop that helps students refine their language skills in a supportive, low-pressure environment.
5. **Collaboration and Engagement.** Foster a collaborative classroom environment by leveraging AI tools that encourage interaction and teamwork, such as language learning games or peer review platforms (Terzidou et al., 2016). These activities enhance communication skills, promote critical thinking, and give students the opportunity to learn from their peers. By building a sense of community among students, AI-powered platforms make learning more engaging and enjoyable.

PRACTICAL CLASSROOM APPLICATIONS

AI tools can be integrated across various language skills and have opened new avenues for enhancing student engagement, personalization, and efficiency. These innovative technologies encompass platforms for improving reading comprehension, apps designed to aid pronunciation, vocabulary builders, and interactive chatbots that provide a comprehensive learning experience. A variety of AI language learning tools have been reviewed, and studies have shown that AI tools can significantly impact language acquisition (Kessler, 2018; Pokrivčáková, 2019).

There has been an improvement in reading comprehension (Lysenko & Abrami, 2014; Park & Kim, 2011; Xu et al., 2019). Chat functionalities and automatic speech recognition technologies have the potential to enhance the learning and teaching of foreign languages significantly (Golonka et al., 2012). Furthermore, there have been modestly positive effects on the writing quality of students as a result of computer-generated feedback on their writing (Stevenson & Phakiti, 2014). This suggests that even minimal interventions by AI can improve language skills.

The AI tools described in this section are intended to serve as examples of the technology currently enhancing ESL education. The focus is not on these particular tools but on the broader AI functionalities they represent, such as personalization, real-time feedback, and adaptive learning. While the specific tools provided may evolve or become outdated, future versions will likely build on the same foundational principles. Therefore, the examples provided illustrate the innovations educators can leverage now and in the future.

The key takeaway is AI's potential to support learning and improve outcomes. By incorporating AI into language learning, educators can more effectively meet the diverse needs of their students, creating an engaging and inclusive educational environment that supports the development of all four essential language skills. This not only makes learning more accessible and enjoyable for students but also empowers educators to deliver more personalized and impactful instruction.

Reading. *ReadTheory* employs AI to analyze students' reading levels through their interactions with texts and quiz responses. The platform automatically adjusts the complexity of subsequent reading materials to match each student's comprehension ability, ensuring that texts are neither too challenging nor too simplistic. As students work through ReadTheory, they earn knowledge points for every question they answer correctly. The more challenging the question, the more points they receive. They also earn points through quizzes, including bonus points for a perfect score.

ReadTheory's dashboard, as seen in figure 2, allows educators to see students' progress graphically. Educators can get an overview of their student's progress, see how many quizzes a student has taken, progress of grade level and Lexile level, and view the amount of knowledge points a student has received. It empowers teachers to make data-driven decisions by offering a clear, at-a-glance understanding of individual student achievements and areas needing attention. The detailed metrics and intuitive layout ensure educators can easily navigate and utilize this information to tailor instruction, support differentiated learning, and effectively track the educational growth of their students over time.

PRACTICAL APPLICATION OF READTHEORY'S AI FEATURES IN AN ESL CLASSROOM

ReadTheory can be integrated into daily or weekly reading assignments. For example, teachers could begin with a baseline evaluation week during which students spend their reading time on ReadTheory, allowing the platform to assess their initial reading levels. Following the evaluation, educators can set weekly reading goals to boost engagement and motivation. These goals should be based on knowledge points. Avoid focusing on grade levels or grades, as ReadTheory adapts to student performance: as students increase in proficiency, they encounter more challenging sections and questions, which could lead to poorer scores for stronger students. However, it also means that these students are being challenged!

There are some tips to use this tool effectively:

- To encourage confidence and motivation further, especially in those who might feel demotivated due to their reading level being lower than their peers, emphasize individual growth and praise achievements and improvements (Mueller & Dweck, 1998). An ESL instructor, or (2015), started a "Leaders" contest on her board to motivate her students. The top three leaders were awarded prizes such as mini-pops, popcorn, or free time. She noted that this simple contest encouraged her students to read more, take more quizzes, and perform well. Moreover, checking students' results for leaders was simple because ReadTheory keeps track of that for her (see Figure 2).
- Complement online reading text with traditional text (Zhao & Yang, 2021). This could be a novel for extensive reading fluency practice.
- Be consistent (Wenglinsky, 2002). Ensure ReadTheory is consistently incorporated into the teaching routine. This regularity helps build a habit among students, allows for continuous progress tracking, and reinforces the learning objectives aimed to be achieved through its use.

Figure 2. Teacher Dashboard Overview of Student Lexile Levels and Performance Metrics

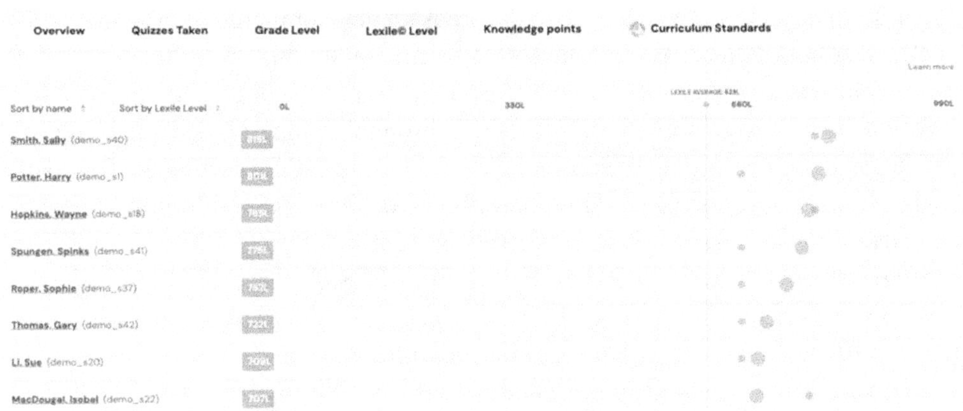

Note. This figure, used with permission from ReadTheory, displays a range of student performance data across various Lexile levels. Its purpose to illustrate the teacher's dashboard, offering a visual tool for monitoring progress in reading comprehension

Pronunciation App. *ELSA Speak* uses AI to assist learners in improving their spoken English. This application leverages speech recognition and machine learning to provide instant feedback. It analyzes the user's speech and compares it to native speaker models before providing corrective feedback on pronunciation, fluency, and intonation. After an initial assessment, it provides the learners with a personalized adaptive learning path. ELSA Speak app has gamified exercises and situational learning topics to make learning engaging and boost motivation. In addition, ELSA Speak includes a generative AI tutor and a live speech analyzer that analyzes both live and recorded speech for comprehensive speaking analysis, including grammar and vocabulary.

The ELSA Speak app has been the subject of several studies that have demonstrated its effectiveness in improving English pronunciation skills. Kholis (2021) concluded that ELSA Speak can effectively enhance students' pronunciation skills. Additionally, Darsih et al. (2021) found that the majority of students agreed that ELSA Speak App is a useful tool to improve their speaking ability, particularly in terms of pronunciation. Furthermore, Saragih et al. (2021) discussed the implementation of digital feedback on ELSA Speak for students and the benefits of digital feedback on ELSA Speak in learning English pronunciation.

PRACTICAL APPLICATION OF ELSA SPEAK'S AI FEATURES IN AN ESL CLASSROOM

Evaluation. ELSA Speak can be efficiently implemented into ESL classroom settings by first conducting an evaluation to establish each student's current pronunciation proficiency and suggesting particular areas for development. Then, using ELSA Speak's feedback, educators can develop specific, attainable speaking goals. This could entail practicing specific sounds, intonation patterns, or fluency in speaking.

Homework. Assign homework for regular pronunciation practice, enabling students to practice continuously and receive detailed, real-time feedback. To ensure consistent practice, create a reward system for achievements, highlighting progress and celebrating successes to boost motivation significantly.

Administrative Tasks. *Save* time by utilizing ELSA's dashboard to assign automated assessments, keep track of learning progress and total practice time, and interact with students and parents to report learning progress.

There are some tips to keep in mind:

- Be sure to complement ELSA Speak's lessons with human guidance and encouragement, helping students understand the nuances of pronunciation and language rhythm. ELSA Speak is better suited as an extension of in-class learning.

Writing and Vocabulary.*Quizlet* is well-known for its vocabulary-learning platform, which provides teachers with customizable study sets and learners with personalized features. Research shows that using Quizlet in the EFL classroom significantly improves L2 English vocabulary acquisition (Nguyen & Le, 2023). Quizlet's "Learn" feature uses spaced repetition algorithms to determine the optimal intervals for reviewing specific flashcards, ensuring that information is reviewed before it is likely forgotten. This method improves long-term retention of information by adapting the study sessions based on the learner's performance. In addition to this, the platform now provides a range of AI tools to enhance learning and organizational skills. Some notable ones for ESL classrooms are Magic Notes (see Figure 3), designed to assist students with note-taking; Q-Chat (see Figure 4), which is an AI-powered tutor that takes a study set and generates a quiz, demonstrates the application of the words, and also provides additional information about each word ; and Essay Starter (see Figure 5), which acts as a coach or tutor by prompting students to consider various perspectives and supporting data without directly generating outlines or papers – a unique feature compared to most AI writing tools. Several research studies have indicated that the utilization of an intelligent tutoring system led to enhanced writing quality (Weston-Sementelli et al, 2018). In addition, Quizlet leverages AI to assist in generating study materials. For example, when a user creates a new set of flashcards, Quizlet can automatically suggest definitions or answers based on the terms entered. This feature is handy for language learning, where users can quickly create vocabulary sets with accurate translations.

PRACTICAL APPLICATION OF QUIZLET'S AI FEATURES IN AN ESL CLASSROOM

Vocabulary Building. Introduce new vocabulary associated with upcoming themes or units using Quizlet's customizable study sets and AI function, which quickly produces definition suggestions. Also, encourage students to use Quizlet to create their own vocabulary sets as homework. The AI's automatic suggestion feature for definitions or translations streamlines the process, making it easier for students to focus on learning rather than setup. In addition, have students study vocabulary using the various assistance Q-chat offers; students learn faster when they actively engage with it (Miller & Metz, 2014).

Note-Taking Skills. Implement Magic Notes during listening or reading activities. After a listening exercise, for example, have students summarize the content themselves. Then, have them check using Magic Notes, which assists them in identifying key points and organizing information efficiently. In addition, Magic Notes can create flashcards and sample essay questions based on the notes.

Writing and Critical Thinking. Integrate the AI Essay Starter in writing assignments by prompting students to explore various perspectives on a topic. This fosters critical thinking and enhances their ability to construct well-rounded arguments.

Here are some tips to use Quizlet:

- While Quizlet's AI can suggest definitions and translations, it is crucial to review these for accuracy, especially in the context of language learning. Teachers should vet AI-generated content or encourage students to use multiple sources for verification, fostering critical evaluation skills.
- Incorporating competitive elements or group challenges can make learning more interactive and fun. Utilize the gamified aspects of Quizlet, such as matching games or live quizzes, to maintain student engagement and motivation (Alsawaier, 2018).

Figure 3. Quizlet's magic notes feature for enhanced study material generation

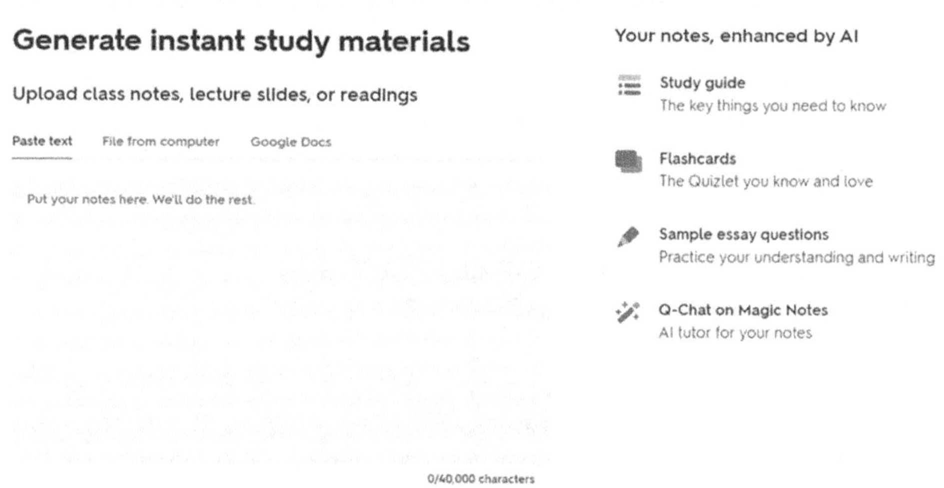

Note. This figure, adapted from Quizlet, showcases Quizlet's Magic Notes feature, which assists users in generating study materials such as study guides, flashcards, and sample essay questions, all enhanced by AI.

Figure 4. Quizlet's AI-powered tutor, Q-Chat, interface

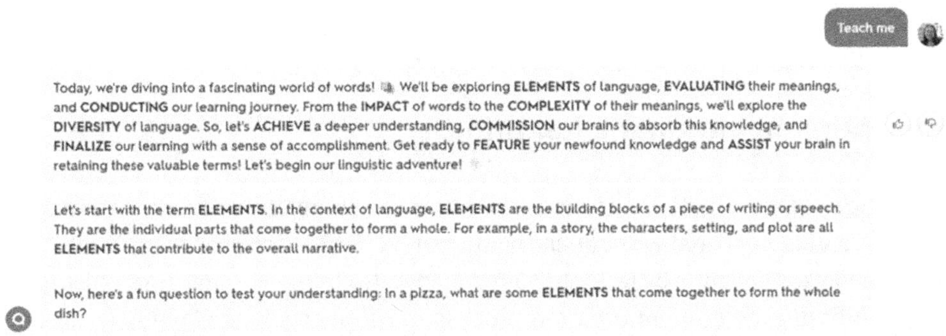

Note. This figure, adapted from Quizlet, demonstrates the Q-Chat feature, which generates quizzes and provides word applications and additional information to aid vocabulary learning. The interface showcases the tool's capability to engage students in interactive learning activities.

Figure 5. Quizlet's AI-enhanced essay starter interface

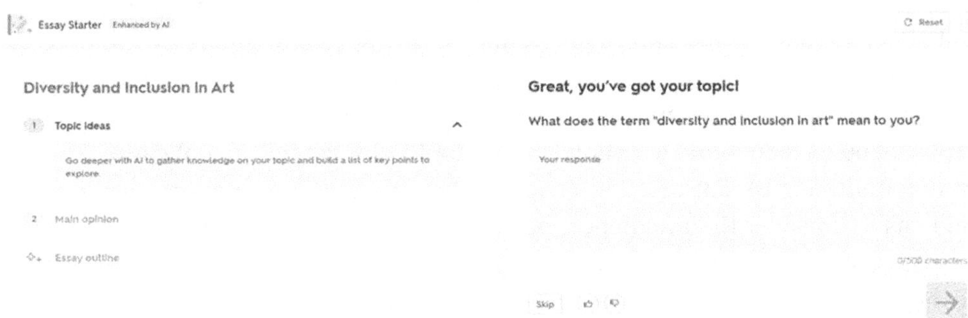

Note. This figure, adapted from Quizlet, displays Quizlet's Essay Starter feature, an AI-enhanced tool that prompts users to reflect on various aspects of a topic without generating content for them. The example in the image is encouraging students to critically engage with the term "diversity and inclusion in art," exemplifying how AI can be used to support the development of writing and critical thinking skills.

GRAMMAR AND DEEPER LANGUAGE ENGAGEMENT THROUGH HUMAN-LIKE CHATBOTS

ChatGPT is an advanced artificial intelligence (AI) system known as a generative chatbot. Unlike traditional rule-based chatbots that rely on predefined responses triggered by specific keywords or phrases, ChatGPT generates unique, unscripted responses. This capability stems from its training on vast datasets of human conversation, enabling it to discern patterns, understand language structure, and grasp context. As a result, ChatGPT is capable of producing responses that adapt to the flow of conversation, allowing for more natural, fluid, and human-like interactions.

Application in Language Learning

For Educators. ChatGPT is a versatile tool for language teachers, offering the ability to create personalized educational content. This includes worksheets, dialogues, and grading rubrics tailored to meet specific language learning objectives. By streamlining the content creation process, AI tools such as ChatGPT not only aid teachers in providing targeted support to their students, improving learning outcomes, but also reduce teachers' workload (du Boulay, 2016).

For Students. It can be used as a virtual language tutor, providing examples, explanations, and practice exercises, making it an ideal supportive companion for self-study and homework (Lin, 2023). ChatGPT allows students to practice written language in written language in contexts other than textbooks, essays, and worksheets, further enhancing their proficiency.

Using chatbots like ChatGPT for language acquisition promotes deeper engagement and understanding of the language (Kohnke et al., 2023). Students are exposed to a wide range of vocabulary, complex grammatical structures, and various forms of language use, moving beyond the constraints of conventional textbook content. This exposure helps them build a comprehensive toolkit for language application, drawn from a multitude of sources. Moreover, ChatGPT's interactive nature encourages students to consider their audience, purpose, and context in communication. This practice not only refines their conceptual understanding of communication but also advances their linguistic and discourse competence. A recent study highlighted that learners, from Macao, China, valued ChatGPT's ability to provide instant feedback and suggestions, which significantly helped them enhance their writing skills (Teng, 2024). Similarly, another study found that Iranian students who participated in a ChatGPT-based writing program experienced notable improvements in their writing abilities. These gains persisted even after the program concluded, indicating the potential for long-term benefits (Ghafoui et al., 2024).

Practical Application of ChatGPT Features in an ESL Classroom

Incorporating generative chatbots, such as ChatGPT, into ESL instruction can create a dynamic and interactive learning environment that not only improves written English grammar skills but also fosters creativity and personal expression through language (Kessler, 2018). Students can create images using one of ChatGPT's image creators, which includes a sticker maker, a coloring book creator, and Dall-E. Students also have the option to plan a party or play along in a murder mystery whodunit. Educators can tailor these activities to various proficiency levels, focusing on grammatical structures from basic to advanced.

For Younger and Lower-Level Students: Prepositional Phrases

Objective: Familiarize students with prepositional phrases to describe location and movement.

Activity 1: Teachers can present an image depicting various objects in different locations (e.g., "a cat under the table," "a book on the shelf"). Students are then tasked with describing the scene using prepositional phrases. For instance, they might write, "The cat is next to a dog", and they may see an image like Figure 6. This activity encourages accurate use of prepositions and visually reinforces the concepts.

Figure 6. Coloring book page with dog and cat created with ChatGPT

For Upper-Level Students: Advanced Descriptive Adjectives

Objective: Enhance students' ability to use descriptive adjectives and complex sentences to convey detailed and nuanced descriptions.

Activity: Provide students with a challenging image with intricate details or actions (e.g., a bustling city scene or a detailed portrait). Ask students to then attempt to recreate the image by writing complex sentences with advanced descriptive adjectives, such as "The gleaming skyscraper towers over the bustling, crowded streets below" (see Figure 7). This task encourages precision in language use and expands students' vocabulary.

Figure 7. ChatGPT created image of a futuristic cityscape

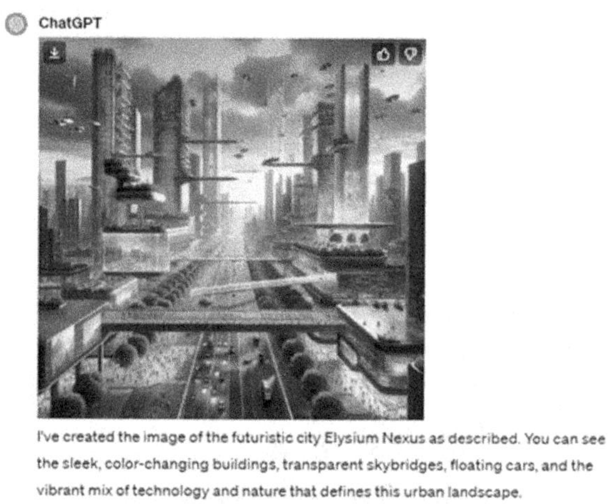

Note. This is the prompt that was used to create this image: "Describe a futuristic urban landscape that seamlessly integrates advanced technology with elements of nature, capturing the essence of a city where sleek, color-changing buildings and transparent skybridges exist in harmony with lush greenery and open parks. Include details such as floating cars, dynamic lighting, and the interplay between the city's architecture and the natural environment to convey the unique character of this metropolis."

Here are some tips to use ChatGPT:

- After students create images from the one provided, have them create their own images using the grammar they are practicing. This personalization increases engagement and motivation. Then, they share their image with the class, furthering their language learning with spoken grammar. Peer review sessions where students explain their choice of vocabulary and structure, further deepening their understanding and application of English.

- Have students save or print their images. They can put them in a digital or physical album or portfolio. This ongoing project rewards their effort and can serve as a visual progress chart of their language development, continually motivating them to add more complex and creatively designed images. Teachers can also display the images on a "Grammar Wall" in the classroom or digitally to further boost motivation and encourage peer learning.
- To differentiate instruction for various skill levels, tailor the complexity of the images and descriptions to match the students' proficiency levels. For example, use simple, clear images with straightforward actions or states for lower levels. For higher levels, choose images that require more elaborate language to describe. ChatGPT can assist teachers in generating examples and providing feedback tailored to each student's level.

TalkPal for Roleplay and Listening

TalkPal uses artificial intelligence to assist English language learners in practicing conversation skills and enhancing their speaking skills. It provides personalized and engaging sessions for learners based on their goals, pace, and language level. Learners can talk about any topic and receive messages in an authentic voice. With over 300 unique experiences, users can engage in realistic, engaging, and professional scenarios while receiving immediate personalized feedback to enhance their learning experience. Additionally, adaptive listening exercises strengthen comprehension skills.

Practical Application of TalkPal Features in an ESL Classroom

Mobile apps that utilize voice recognition technology have had a positive impact on learners' communication abilities, as well as their proficiency in grammar, reading, and writing skills (Al-Kaisi et. al., 2021). By incorporating TalkPal into the ESL curriculum, educators can give students significant opportunities to practice speaking in a supportive, interactive setting. This technique encourages active learning and helps students develop confidence in their language skills.

1. ***Introduction to TalkPal.*** Familiarize students with TalkPal's interface and features. Start by assisting students in creating their TalkPal profiles and demonstrating how to initiate talks. Then, assign a simple "Introduce Yourself" task on TalkPal, where students can practice basic greetings and self-introduction.
2. ***Thematic Conversations.*** Use TalkPal to reinforce vocabulary and phrases related to specific themes (e.g., food, hobbies, travel). Following a class lesson on a specific theme, such as food, students use TalkPal to discuss their favorite

dishes, restaurants, and culinary experiences. This can be structured using guided conversation prompts offered by the teacher.

3. ***Role-play Scenarios.*** Develop fluency and conversational skills through situational practice. Have students participate in role-play scenarios, such as ordering food in a restaurant, asking for directions, or conducting a job interview. Teachers can create these scenarios within TalkPal, and students can record their conversations for review.

Here are some tips to use TalkPal:

- While AI can provide immediate conversational practice, it may not always model perfect language use. Supplement TalkPal conversations with teacher-led reviews focusing on correcting errors and discussing more complex language rules. Encourage students to take notes on any confusing interactions for later discussion in the classroom.
- Establish clear guidelines for respectful and safe communication on TalkPal. Monitor peer interactions whenever feasible and foster an open environment where students can report uncomfortable experiences without fear of repercussions. Educate students on digital citizenship and the importance of online privacy.
- Ensure all students have access to the appropriate equipment and internet connections. Consider creating a resource pool of available devices or arranging lab time for struggling students. Offer essential tech support and tutorials for students unfamiliar with such apps.

ADDRESSING OBSTACLES IN AI IMPLEMENTATION

While integrating AI tools into education offers exciting opportunities, it is not without obstacles, and teachers play a crucial role in overcoming these challenges. Table 3 explores the challenges of implementing AI and AI-enhanced learning tools in educational settings along with proposed solutions to address these issues.

First, without proper infrastructure, AI tools cannot be effectively implemented. Limited access to necessary devices or reliable internet connectivity can restrict participation, particularly for students in low-resource areas. Moreover, high costs associated with purchasing AI tools can be prohibitive, especially for schools with limited budgets. In such cases, finding free or low-cost AI alternatives that meet educational needs may be difficult and require additional research.

In addition, even with the right tools, a lack of teacher familiarity with AI may hinder effective integration into the classroom. Teachers may struggle to use AI tools to their full potential without proper teacher training and support. Thus, ongoing professional development and support is essential although it may not always be readily available.

Furthermore, a successful implementation of AI in education requires proper alignment with the curriculum. It's imperative that educators ensure AI tools contribute to the broader educational goals. However, AI tools are often designed for general use, and as a result, they may not fully align with specific goals or standards. Additionally, personalized tools may align with student's proficiency or interest, but this can leave gaps in learning areas as well.

Equally important, ensuring that AI benefits all students equitably is crucial to fostering an inclusive learning environment. Some AI tools may not be designed to accommodate diverse learning styles, cultural backgrounds, or language levels, creating potential inequalities in learning outcomes. Moreover, certain students may find it challenging to thrive in AI-driven adaptive platforms, necessitating supplementary materials and alternative learning strategies.

Finally, one of the most significant obstacles is balancing AI with human intervention. While AI can provide immediate feedback, it may lack the depth and nuance required for complex or creative tasks, making its feedback less effective without teacher involvement to ensure students receive well-rounded and effective assessments (Mizumoto & Eguchi, 2023). Striking this balance can be time-consuming; however, the overall time saved may help to offset this. Additionally, AI-driven personalization can diminish opportunities for peer interaction and collaboration. Nevertheless, these vital learning experiences can be preserved by thoughtfully integrating group activities designed to foster collaboration and peer engagement.

Table 3. Challenges and solutions of implementing AI in education

Challenges	Solutions
Technological Infrastructure and Access	Schools can provide devices or create a technology lending program. Additionally, optimizing AI tools for low-bandwidth environments ensures more equitable access.
***Cost and Budget Constraints**	Explore various funding sources, including grants and partnerships with AI providers. Consider open-source or free AI tools as alternatives or supplements to paid options. Prioritize and phase the implementation of AI solutions based on available budget and educational impact.

continued on following page

Table 3. Continued

Challenges	Solutions
Teacher Training and Support	Leverage free training from AI tool providers: Many AI companies offer free training sessions, webinars, and support materials. Create a collaborative cloud folder where teachers can upload resources, share user manuals, and exchange ideas for implementing AI tools. This encourages collaboration and provides easy access to helpful materials. Host regular "tool share" sessions: Schedule short, informal sessions where teachers can showcase AI tools they've successfully integrated into their teaching, allowing educators to exchange practical tips and firsthand experiences.
Curriculum Alignment	Utilize AI tools as supplements, rather than replacements, to ensure all essential materials are covered in class to avoid gaps in knowledge. Tailor customizable AI tools to align with the curriculum goals and standards to reinforce the teacher's goals.
Overfitting to Student Preferences	Balance AI-driven personalization with comprehensive curriculum coverage, ensuring that students receive a well-rounded education across all necessary topics and skills.
Equity and Inclusivity	Customize AI tools to support diverse learning styles and needs, including language levels, cultural backgrounds, and abilities. Provide supplemental learning materials and activities outside the AI platform to support diverse learning styles and strategies, accommodating students who may not thrive under the adaptive platform's favored learning styles. Offer multiple formats of content (videos, texts, interactive simulations) to cater to different learning preferences.
Feedback and Assessment	Incorporate teacher feedback into the AI's feedback loop to add a human perspective, especially for more complex or creative tasks. This could involve setting aside time for one-on-one consultations, utilizing rubrics that emphasize creative and critical thinking, and encouraging self-assessment and peer feedback among students.
Loss of Social Learning Opportunities	Use AI tools that support collaborative learning environments and social interaction. Integrate group projects and discussion to enhance socialization and encourage collaboration among students, countering the de-emphasis on social learning that personalization might cause.

*Many AI tool providers offer trial versions or demonstrations, allowing educators to try the tool before making a long-term commitment.

CONCLUSION

This chapter encourages educators to embrace the shift and explore the potential of AI in ESL teaching and learning. AI offers significant possibilities for the ESL classroom, promising personalized learning, immersive experiences, and enhanced engagement. It has the potential to revolutionize ESL teaching and learning by offering tools that can adapt to individual learner needs and provide immediate feedback. It should empower educators by freeing them from administrative burdens, allowing them to focus on personalized guidance and foster human connection. Yet, integrating AI into education is not without its challenges. Its potential is coupled with concerns over ensuring equitable access to technology, maintaining the essential role of teachers, safeguarding student data privacy, and avoiding an overdependence on technological solutions. Navigating these challenges requires thoughtful consideration and strategic planning for effective implementation. As we move forward, we must approach the integration of AI with a balanced perspective.

To be able to navigate the present context and predict the future of AI in education, we need to learn from past lessons when other cutting-edge technologies were introduced.

AI in education has much potential, much like the dot com craze, but it also comes with some concerns. Just as the internet revolutionized communication and commerce, AI promises to personalize learning, automate tasks, and unlock new avenues for knowledge exploration. However, echoes of the dot com era, from inflated expectations and unsustainable models to potential job displacements, are sounding a note of caution.

The AI market is rapidly growing, with new tools and advancements being introduced regularly. However, while celebrating innovation, be cautious of hype. Not every AI solution will revolutionize education, just as not every ".com" company thrived. Long-term success in AI will depend on focusing on practical applications and building sustainable value. Therefore, when choosing AI tools, it is important to consider clear needs that will improve learning, rather than just being allured by the latest technology.

Furthermore, as with the dot com craze and subsequent technological advancements, there will be a need for restructuring and acquiring new skills. As AI continues to transform education, educators must adapt to new technologies and be willing to learn new skills. Educators can leverage their expertise to develop, implement, and manage these tools, creating new opportunities for themselves and their students.

Ultimately, the future of AI in education is not predetermined—it will be shaped by the decisions we make today. Success in leveraging AI in ESL education will hinge on our ability to focus on practical applications that truly enhance teaching and learning outcomes. By drawing on insights from this chapter and considering the lessons learned from past technological advancements, we can guide the development and application of AI in ways that support educators, enrich student learning, and uphold the human connections that are fundamental to effective teaching. Educators, administrators, and policymakers are encouraged to embrace continuous learning and adaptability, working collaboratively to harness the potential of AI in creating an educational landscape that is innovative, inclusive, and responsive to the needs of all students. By looking at the past, approaching AI with cautious optimism, and prioritizing the irreplaceable human element, we can shape a future where technology supports educators, personalized learning, and unlocks the potential of every student.

REFERENCES

Abdollahzadeh, M., & Behroozizad, S. (2015). On the importance of A socio-culturally designed teaching model in an EFL writing classroom. *International Journal of Applied Linguistics and English Literature*, 4(4), 238–247. DOI: 10.7575/aiac.ijalel.v.4n.4p.238

Abobaker, R., & Silas, I. (2024). Autonomy-structure balance in facilitating task engagement. In Egbert, J., & Panday-Shukla, P. (Eds.), *Task engagement across disciplines research and practical strategies to increase student achievement*. Routledge. DOI: 10.4324/9781003406419-9

Adesope, O., Lavin, T., Thompson, T. A., & Ungerleider, C. (2011). Pedagogical strategies for teaching literacy to ESL immigrant students: A meta-analysis. *The British Journal of Educational Psychology*, 81(4), 629–653. DOI: 10.1111/j.2044-8279.2010.02015.x PMID: 22050311

Ahmad, S., Rahmat, M., Mubarik, M., Alam, M., & Hyder, S. (2021). Artificial intelligence and its role in education. *Sustainability (Basel)*, 13(22), 12902. DOI: 10.3390/su132212902

Akavova, A., Temirkhanova, Z., & Lorsanova, Z. (2023). Adaptive learning and artificial intelligence in the educational space. *E3S Web of Conferences, 451*, 06011. DOI: 10.1051/e3sconf/202345106011

Al-Kaisi, A. N., Arkhangelskaya, A. L., & Rudenko-Morgun, O. I. (2020). The didactic potential of the voice assistant "Alice" for students of a foreign language at a university. *Education and Information Technologies*, 26(1), 715–732. DOI: 10.1007/s10639-020-10277-2

AlHarbi, A. (2022). The uses of machine learning (ML) in teaching and learning English language: A methodical review. DOI: 10.21608/edusohag.2022.212355

Aljohani, M. (2017). Principles of "constructivism" in foreign language teaching. *Journal of Literature and Art Studies*, 7(1). Advance online publication. DOI: 10.17265/2159-5836/2017.01.013

Alsawaier, R. S. (2018). The effect of gamification on motivation and engagement. *The International Journal of Information and Learning Technology*, 35(1), 56–79. DOI: 10.1108/IJILT-02-2017-0009

Arakawa, K., Hao, Q., Deneke, W., Cowan, I., Wolfman, S., & Peterson, A. (2022). Early identification of student struggles at the topic level using context-agnostic features. *SIGCSE 2022: Proceedings of the 53rd ACM Technical Symposium on Computer Science Education.* DOI: 10.1145/3478431.3499298

Arora, B., Al-Wadi, H., & Afari, E. (2024). Scaffolding instruction for improvement in learning English language skills. *International Journal of Evaluation and Research in Education*, 13(2), 1265. DOI: 10.11591/ijere.v13i2.26659

Azevedo, R., Bouchet, F., Duffy, M., Harley, J., Taub, M., Trevors, G., Cloude, E., Dever, D., Wiedbusch, M., Wortha, F., & Cerezo, R. (2022). Lessons learned and future directions of Metatutor: Leveraging multichannel data to scaffold self-regulated learning with an intelligent tutoring system. *Frontiers in Psychology*, 13, 813632. Advance online publication. DOI: 10.3389/fpsyg.2022.813632 PMID: 35774935

Bai, J. (2023). Future prospects of artificial intelligence in education: A preliminary analysis of educator perspectives from focus groups in Japan, Spain, and Germany. Ubiquity Proceedings. DOI: 10.5334/uproc.74

Baker, R., & Hawn, A. (2021). Algorithmic bias in education. *International Journal of Artificial Intelligence in Education*, 32(4), 1052–1092. DOI: 10.1007/s40593-021-00285-9

Bhowmik, S., & Kim, M. (2021). K-12 ESL writing instruction: A review of research on pedagogical challenges and strategies. *Language and Literature*, 23(3), 166–203. DOI: 10.20360/langandlit29530

Bhowmik, S., & Kim, M. (2022). ESL writing instruction in k-12 settings: Pedagogical approaches and classroom techniques. *Language and Literature*, 24(2), 174–197. DOI: 10.20360/langandlit29612

Black, A. E., & Deci, E. L. (2000). The effects of instructors' autonomy support and students' autonomous motivation on learning organic chemistry: A self-determination theory perspective. *Science Education*, 84(6), 740–756. DOI: 10.1002/1098-237X(200011)84:6<740::AID-SCE4>3.0.CO;2-3

Botvin, M., Hershkovitz, A., & Forkosh-Baruch, A. (2022). Data-driven decision-making in emergency remote teaching. *Education and Information Technologies*, 28(1), 489–506. DOI: 10.1007/s10639-022-11176-4 PMID: 35791318

Bulut, O. and Wongvorachan, T. (2022). Feedback generation through artificial intelligence. *The Open/Technology in Education Society and Scholarship Association Conference, 2*(1), 1-9. DOI: 10.18357/otessac.2022.2.1.125

Cambourne, B. (1995). Toward an educationally relevant theory of literacy learning: Twenty years of inquiry. *The Reading Teacher*, 49(3), 182–192. DOI: 10.1598/RT.49.3.1

Cantos, K. (2023). Artificial intelligence in language teaching and learning. *Ciencia Latina Revista Científica Multidisciplinar*, 7(4), 5629–5638. DOI: 10.37811/cl_rcm.v7i4.7368

Caputi, V., & Garrido, A. (2015). Student-oriented planning of e-learning contents for Moodle. *Journal of Network and Computer Applications*, 53, 115–127. DOI: 10.1016/j.jnca.2015.04.001

Chang, T. S., Li, Y., Huang, H. W., & Whitfield, B. (2021). Exploring EFL students' writing performance and their acceptance of AI-based automated writing feedback. *2021 2nd International Conference on Education Development and Studies*. DOI: 10.1145/3459043.3459065

Chen, C.-H., & Law, V. (2016). Scaffolding individual and collaborative game-based learning in learning performance and intrinsic motivation. *Computers in Human Behavior*, 55, 1201–1212. DOI: 10.1016/j.chb.2015.03.010

Chen, L., Chen, P., & Lin, Z. (2020). Artificial intelligence in education: A review. *IEEE Access : Practical Innovations, Open Solutions*, 8, 75264–75278. DOI: 10.1109/ACCESS.2020.2988510

Choi, T., & Wong, W. (2018). "Platform nine and three-quarters" and more: Scaffolding ESL writing through teacher modelling and creative imitation. *TESOL Journal*, 9(4), 1–23. DOI: 10.1002/tesj.423

Chowdhury, T. A. (2021). Fostering learner autonomy through cooperative and collaborative learning. *Shanlax International Journal of Education*, 10(1), 89–95. DOI: 10.34293/education.v10i1.4347

Costello, E. (2023). ChatGPT and the educational ai chatter: Full of bullshit or trying to tell us something? *Postdigital Science and Education*, 6(2), 425–430. DOI: 10.1007/s42438-023-00398-5

Darsih, E., Wihadi, M., & Hanggara, A. (2021). Using ELSA App in speaking classes: Students' voices. *Proceedings of the 1st Universitas Kuningan International Conference on Social Science, Environment and Technology, UNiSET 2020*. DOI: 10.4108/eai.12-12-2020.2304993

Dodigovic, M. (2007). Artificial intelligence and second language learning: An efficient approach to error remediation. *Language Awareness*, 16(2), 99–113. DOI: 10.2167/la416.0

du Boulay, B. (2016). Artificial intelligence as an effective classroom assistant. *IEEE Intelligent Systems*, 31(6), 76–81. DOI: 10.1109/MIS.2016.93

Duong, T., & Suppasetseree, S. (2024). The effects of an artificial intelligence voice chatbot on improving Vietnamese undergraduate students' English speaking skills. *International Journal of Learning. Teaching and Educational Research*, 23(3), 293–321. DOI: 10.26803/ijlter.23.3.15

Egbert, J. (2011). "Engage me!": Rules for engagement in CALL. In *CALL: What's your Motivation? Collected Papers on the Cutting Edge of Language Learning Practice Book*. JALT CALL SIG.

Fu, D., Houser, W. R., & Huang, A. (2007). A collaboration between ESL and regular classroom teachers for ELL students' literacy development. *Changing English*, 14(3), 325–342. DOI: 10.1080/13586840701712014

Garrido, A., & Onaindia, E. (2013). Assembling learning objects for personalized learning: An ai planning perspective. *IEEE Intelligent Systems*, 28(2), 64–73. DOI: 10.1109/MIS.2011.36

Ghafouri, M., Hassaskhah, J., & Mahdavi-Zafarghandi, A. (2024). From virtual assistant to writing mentor: Exploring the impact of a ChatGPT-based writing instruction protocol on EFL teachers' self-efficacy and learners' writing skill. *Language Teaching Research*. Advance online publication. DOI: 10.1177/13621688241239764

Gil-Aciron, L. (2022). Benefits of gamification in second language learning. *Epos Revista De Filología*, (38), 103–126. DOI: 10.5944/epos.38.2022.33785

Giles, A. (2018). Navigating the contradictions: An ESL teacher's professional self-development in collaborative activity. *TESL Canada Journal*, 35(2), 104–127. DOI: 10.18806/tesl.v35i2.1292

Golonka, E. M., Bowles, A. R., Frank, V. M., Richardson, D. L., & Freynik, S. (2012). Technologies for foreign language learning: A review of technology types and their effectiveness. *Computer Assisted Language Learning*, 27(1), 70–105. DOI: 10.1080/09588221.2012.700315

Gulubba, S. M., Ahmad, A. A., & Mustafa, H. R. (2019). Scaffolding language development and learning in teacher-student interactions. *International Journal of Recent Technology and Engineering, 8*(2S9), 1035-1040. DOI: 10.35940/ijrte.B1160.0982S919

Gupta, D. (2024). Navigating the future of education: The impact of artificial intelligence on teacher-student dynamics. EATP, 6006-6013. DOI: 10.53555/kuey.v30i4.2332

Hardi, V., Rizal, M., & Noviardila, I. (2022). Autonomous learning capacity of university students' during the covid-19 pandemic. *Al-Ishlah Jurnal Pendidikan*, 14(2), 1361–1368. DOI: 10.35445/alishlah.v14i2.1934

Hashim, H., Rafiq, K., & Yunus, M. (2019). Improving ESL learners' grammar with gamified-learning. *Arab World English Journal (AWEJ). Special Issue on CALL*, (5), 41–50. DOI: 10.24093/awej/call5.4

Herayati, H. (2019). The effect of questioning technique in pre-writing stage toward students' writing ability. *Journal of Education*, 1(4), 756–763. DOI: 10.31004/joe.v2i2.430

Hieu, H., & Thao, L. T. (2024). Exploring the impact of ai in language education: Vietnamese EFL teachers' views on using ChatGPT for fairy tale retelling tasks. *International Journal of Learning Teaching and Educational Research*, 23(3), 486–503. DOI: 10.26803/ijlter.23.3.24

Hogenhout, L. (2021). *Unite Paper | A Framework for Ethical AI at the United Nations*. https://unite. un.org/news/unite-paper-framework-ethical-ai-united-nations

Holmes, W., Porayska-Pomsta, K., Holstein, K., Sutherland, E., Baker, T., Shum, S. B., Santos, O. C., Rodrigo, M. T., Cukurova, M., Bittencourt, I. I., & Koedinger, K. R. (2021). Ethics of AI in education: Towards a community-wide framework. *International Journal of Artificial Intelligence in Education*, 32(3), 504–526. DOI: 10.1007/s40593-021-00239-1

Huang, H. (2002). Toward constructivism for adult learners in online learning environments. *British Journal of Educational Technology*, 33(1), 27–37. DOI: 10.1111/1467-8535.00236

Humble, N., Boustedt, J., Holmgren, H., Milutinovic, G., Seipel, S., & Östberg, A.-S. (2023). Cheaters or AI-enhanced learners: Consequences of ChatGPT for programming education. *Electronic Journal of e-Learning*. Advance online publication. DOI: 10.34190/ejel.21.5.3154

Huriye, A. Z. (2023). The ethics of artificial intelligence: Examining the ethical considerations surrounding the development and use of AI. *American Journal of Technology*, 2(1), 37–45. DOI: 10.58425/ajt.v2i1.142

Hwang, G. J., Xie, H., Wah, B. W., & Gašević, D. (2020). Vision, challenges, roles and research issues of artificial intelligence in education. *Computers and Education: Artificial Intelligence*, 1, 100001. DOI: 10.1016/j.caeai.2020.100001

Hwang, W., Nurtantyana, R., Purba, S., Hariyanti, U., Indrihapsari, Y., & Surjono, H. (2023). AI and recognition technologies to facilitate English as foreign language writing for supporting personalization and contextualization in authentic contexts. *Journal of Educational Computing Research*, 61(5), 1008–1035. DOI: 10.1177/07356331221137253

Jafari, Z. (2023). The role of ai in supporting indigenous languages. *Aitechbesosci*, 1(2), 4–11. DOI: 10.61838/kman.aitech.1.2.2

James, K., & Mayer, R. (2018). Learning a second language by playing a game. *Applied Cognitive Psychology*, 33(4), 669–674. DOI: 10.1002/acp.3492

Jiang, R. (2022). How does artificial intelligence empower EFL teaching and learning nowadays? A review on artificial intelligence in the EFL context. *Frontiers in Psychology*, 13, 1049401. Advance online publication. DOI: 10.3389/fpsyg.2022.1049401 PMID: 36467167

Johnson, E. (2018). Exemplary reading teachers' use of instructional scaffolds with emergent bilinguals: How knowledge and context shape their choices. *TESOL Quarterly*, 53(1), 108–132. DOI: 10.1002/tesq.471

Kamalov, F., Calonge, D., & Gurrib, I. (2023). New era of artificial intelligence in education: Towards a sustainable multifaceted revolution. *Sustainability (Basel)*, 15(16), 12451. DOI: 10.3390/su151612451

Kessler, G. (2018). Technology and the future of language teaching. *Foreign Language Annals*, 51(1), 205–218. DOI: 10.1111/flan.12318

Khan, W. (2023). Examining the transformative role of artificial intelligence in language skill enhancement: A case study of bs English students in Okara, Pakistan. *ABBDM*, 3(1), 190–196. DOI: 10.62019/abbdm.v3i1.88

Kholis, A. (2021). Elsa speak App: Automatic speech recognition (ASR) for supplementing English pronunciation skills. *Pedagogy: Journal of English Language Teaching, 9*(1), 1. DOI: 10.32332/joelt.v9i1.2723

Klimova, B., Pikhart, M., Polakova, P., Cerna, M., Yayilgan, S., & Shaikh, S. (2023). A systematic review on the use of emerging technologies in teaching English as an applied language at the university level. *Systems*, 11(1), 42. DOI: 10.3390/systems11010042

Kohnke, L., Moorhouse, B. L., & Zou, D. (2023). ChatGPT for language teaching and learning. *RELC Journal*, 54(2), 537–550. DOI: 10.1177/00336882231162868

Lantolf, J. (2006). Sociocultural theory and L2: State of the art. *Studies in Second Language Acquisition*, 28(01). Advance online publication. DOI: 10.1017/S0272263106060037

Lee, D., Kim, H., & Sung, S. (2022). Development research on an AI English learning support system to facilitate learner-generated-context-based learning. *Educational Technology Research and Development*, 71(2), 629–666. DOI: 10.1007/s11423-022-10172-2 PMID: 36533222

Lee, S., & Azman, H. (2020). Introducing a responsive multimodal oral presentation pedagogy: Integrating ted videos with web 2.0, collaborative learning and teacher feedback. *RELC Journal*, 53(3), 703–711. DOI: 10.1177/0033688220945426

Li, R. (2020). Using artificial intelligence in learning English as a foreign language: An examination of IEELTS Liulishuo as an online platform. *Journal of Higher Education Research*, 1(2). Advance online publication. DOI: 10.32629/jher.v1i2.178

Lin, H. (2022). Influences of artificial intelligence in education on teaching effectiveness. *International Journal of Emerging Technologies in Learning*, 17(24), 144–156. DOI: 10.3991/ijet.v17i24.36037

Lin, Z. (2023). Why and how to embrace AI such as ChatGPT in your academic life. *Royal Society Open Science*, 10(8), 230658. Advance online publication. DOI: 10.1098/rsos.230658 PMID: 37621662

Ling, H., & Chiang, H. (2022). Learning performance in adaptive learning systems: A case study of web programming learning recommendations. *Frontiers in Psychology*, 13, 770637. Advance online publication. DOI: 10.3389/fpsyg.2022.770637 PMID: 35153951

Liu, M., Ren, Y., Nyagoga, L. M., Stonier, F., Wu, Z., & Yu, L. (2023). Future of education in the era of generative artificial intelligence: Consensus among Chinese scholars on applications of ChatGPT in schools. *Future in Educational Research*, 1(1), 72–101. DOI: 10.1002/fer3.10

Lysenko, L. V., & Abrami, P. C. (2014). Promoting reading comprehension with the use of technology. *Computers & Education*, 75, 162–172. DOI: 10.1016/j.compedu.2014.01.010

Malik, N., & Solanki, A. (2021). Simulation of Human Brain: Artificial Intelligence-Based Learning. In S. Verma & P. Tomar (Eds.), *Impact of AI Technologies on Teaching, Learning, and Research in Higher Education* (pp. 150-160). IGI Global. DOI: 10.4018/978-1-7998-4763-2.ch009

Mandinach, E. B., & Jackson, S. S. (2012). *Transforming teaching and learning through data-driven decision making*. Corwin Press., DOI: 10.4135/9781506335568

Maru, M., & Pajow, C. (2021). Emotional, behavioral and cognitive engagement in language learning: The experience of the successful learners. *Celt a Journal of Culture English Language Teaching & Literature*, 19(2), 337. DOI: 10.24167/celt.v19i2.1118

Miller, C. J., & Metz, M. J. (2014). A comparison of professional-level faculty and student perceptions of active learning: Its current use, effectiveness, and barriers. *Advances in Physiology Education*, 38(3), 246–252. DOI: 10.1152/advan.00014.2014 PMID: 25179615

Milossi, M., Alexandropoulou-Egyptiadou, E., & Psannis, K. E. (2021). AI ethics: Algorithmic determinism or self-determination? The GPDR approach. *IEEE Access : Practical Innovations, Open Solutions*, 9, 58455–58466. DOI: 10.1109/ACCESS.2021.3072782

Mindigulova, A., Vikhman, V., & Romm, M. (2024). Artificial intelligence and personalized learning: Scaffolding technology. *Professional Education in the Modern World*, 13(4), 613–622. DOI: 10.20913/2618-7515-2023-4-3

Mizumoto, A., & Eguchi, M. (2023). Exploring the potential of using an AI language model for automated essay scoring. *Research Methods in Applied Linguistics, 2*(2), Article 100050.

Mizumoto, A., Shintani, N., Sasaki, M., & Teng, M. F. (2024). Testing the viability of ChatGPT as a companion in L2 writing accuracy assessment. *Research Methods in Applied Linguistics*, 3(2), 100116. Advance online publication. DOI: 10.1016/j.rmal.2024.100116

Mueller, C. M., & Dweck, C. S. (1998). Praise for intelligence can undermine children's motivation and performance. *Journal of Personality and Social Psychology*, 75(1), 33–52. DOI: 10.1037/0022-3514.75.1.33 PMID: 9686450

Nazari, N., Shabbir, M., & Setiawan, R. (2021). Application of artificial intelligence powered digital writing assistant in higher education: Randomized controlled trial. *Heliyon*, 7(5), e07014. DOI: 10.1016/j.heliyon.2021.e07014 PMID: 34027198

Ndu, O. G., Tshotsho, B., & Cekiso, M. (2022). Grade 10 teachers' perceptions of their application of socio-cultural and multiple intelligences on English second language learners. *Tydskrif vir Taalonderrig*, 56(1). Advance online publication. DOI: 10.56285/jltVol56iss1a5415

Ng, D., Leung, J., Su, J., Ng, R., & Chu, S. (2023). Teachers' ai digital competencies and twenty-first century skills in the post-pandemic world. *Educational Technology Research and Development*, 71(1), 137–161. DOI: 10.1007/s11423-023-10203-6 PMID: 36844361

Nguyen, L. Q., & Le, H. V. (2023). The role of Quizlet learning tool in learners' lexical retention: A quasi-experimental study. *International Journal of Emerging Technologies in Learning*, 18(03), 38–50. DOI: 10.3991/ijet.v18i03.34919

Nguyen, P. H., Tran, V. T., & Huynh, H. V. (2023). The effectiveness of using chatbots in learning English pronunciation for Vietnamese EFL learners. *Journal of Asian Education and Development Studies*, 13(1), 15–22.

Ningsih, S. (2019). Teacher's and learners' perceptions of learner autonomy in EFL context. *Proceedings of the Eleventh Conference on Applied Linguistics (CONAPLIN 2018)*. DOI: 10.2991/conaplin-18.2019.309

Niu, S., Luo, J., Niemi, H., Li, X., & Lu, Y. (2022). Teachers' and students' views of using an AIi-aided educational platform for supporting teaching and learning at Chinese schools. *Education Sciences*, 12(12), 858. DOI: 10.3390/educsci12120858

Orr, K. (2015). *Comprehension Website--Read Theory!* Sparkingthemind. Retrieved February 1, 2024, from https://sparkingthemind.blogspot.com/2015/04/comprehension-website-read-theory.html

Pack, A., & Maloney, J. (2023). Using generative artificial intelligence for language education research: Insights from using Openai's Chatgpt. *TESOL Quarterly*, 57(4), 1571–1582. DOI: 10.1002/tesq.3253

Palomares, I., Martínez-Cámara, E., Montes, R., García-Moral, P., Chiachio, M., Chiachio, J., & Herrera, F. (2021). A panoramic view and swot analysis of artificial intelligence for achieving the sustainable development goals by 2030: Progress and prospects. *Applied Intelligence*, 51(9), 1–31. DOI: 10.1007/s10489-021-02264-y PMID: 34764606

Park, H. R., & Kim, D. (2011). Reading-strategy use by English as a second language learners in online reading tasks. *Computers & Education*, 57(3), 2156–2166. DOI: 10.1016/j.compedu.2011.05.014

Park, Y., Chen, C. Y., & Chen, P. (2019). The effects of using a chatbot on English reading motivation and achievement among Taiwanese EFL learners. *Computers & Education*, 140, 103528.

Pokrivcakova, S. (2019). Preparing teachers for the application of AI-powered technologies in foreign language education. *Journal of Language and Cultural Education*, 7(3), 135–153. DOI: 10.2478/jolace-2019-0025

Popenici, S., & Kerr, S. (2017). Exploring the impact of artificial intelligence on teaching and learning in higher education. *Research and Practice in Technology Enhanced Learning*, 12(1), 22. Advance online publication. DOI: 10.1186/s41039-017-0062-8 PMID: 30595727

Ramli, R., & Yusoff, N. (2020). Self-efficacy and differentiated instruction: A study among Malaysian school teachers. *Universal Journal of Educational Research*, 8(4), 1252–1260. DOI: 10.13189/ujer.2020.080416

Rebolledo Font de la Vall, R., & González Araya, F. (2023). Exploring the benefits and challenges of AI-language learning tools. *International Journal of Social Sciences and Humanities Invention*, 10(01), 7569–7576. DOI: 10.18535/ijsshi/v10i01.02

Reeves, J. (2004). "Like everybody else": Equalizing educational opportunity for English language learners. *TESOL Quarterly*, 38(1), 43. DOI: 10.2307/3588258

Salas-Pilco, S. (2020). The impact of AI and robotics on physical, social-emotional and intellectual learning outcomes: An integrated analytical framework. *British Journal of Educational Technology*, 51(5), 1808–1825. DOI: 10.1111/bjet.12984

Sallam, M. (2024). Human versus artificial intelligence: ChatGPT-4 outperforming bing, bard, ChatGPT-3.5, and humans in clinical chemistry multiple-choice questions. https://doi.org/DOI: 10.21203/rs.3.rs-3880412/v1

Saragih, E. E., Tabrani, N. P., & Muthmainnah, N. (2021). The use of digital feedback on ELSA speak in learning pronunciation for seventh grade of junior high school. *JEELL (Journal of English Education, Linguistics and Literature). English Department of STKIP PGRI Jombang*, 8(1), 48. DOI: 10.32682/jeell.v8i1.1979

Sari, D. M., Suparman, U., & Sinaga, T. (2018). The effectiveness of scaffolding technique on students' writing analytical expository text. *U-JET, 7*(3). https://jurnal.fkip.unila.ac.id/index.php/123/article/view/15404/pdf

Settles, B., LaFlair, G. & Hagiwara, M. (2020). Machine learning driven language assessment. *Transactions of the Association for Computational Linguistics, 8*, 247–263. https://doi.org/ a 00310DOI: 10.1162/tacl

Shou, Z., Lu, X., Wu, Z., Yuan, H., Zhang, H., & Lai, J. (2020). On learning path planning algorithm based on collaborative analysis of learning behavior. *IEEE Access : Practical Innovations, Open Solutions*, 8, 119863–119879. DOI: 10.1109/ACCESS.2020.3005793

Simina, V., & Hamel, M. (2005). CASLA through a social constructivist perspective: Webquest in project-driven language learning. *ReCALL*, 17(2), 217–228. DOI: 10.1017/S0958344005000522

Sims, R., Dobbs, G., & Hand, T. (2002). Enhancing quality in online learning: Scaffolding planning and design through proactive evaluation. *Distance Education*, 23(2), 135–148. DOI: 10.1080/0158791022000009169

Smith, M. E., Teemant, A., & Pinnegar, S. (2004). Principles and practices of sociocultural assessment: Foundations for effective strategies for linguistically diverse classrooms. *Multicultural Perspectives*, 6(2), 38–46. DOI: 10.1207/s15327892mcp0602_8

Stevenson, M., & Phakiti, A. (2014). The effects of computer-generated feedback on the quality of writing. *Assessing Writing*, 19, 51–65. DOI: 10.1016/j.asw.2013.11.007

Taylor, D. L., Yeung, M., & Bashet, A. Z. (2021). Personalized and adaptive learning. In Ryoo, J., & Winkelmann, K. (Eds.), *Innovative learning environments in STEM higher education. SpringerBriefs in Statistics*. Springer. DOI: 10.1007/978-3-030-58948-6_2

Teng, M. F. (2024). "ChatGPT is the companion, not enemies": EFL learners' perceptions and experiences in using ChatGPT for feedback in writing. *Computers and Education: Artificial Intelligence*, 7, 100270. DOI: 10.1016/j.caeai.2024.100270

Terzidou, T., Tsiatsos, T., Miliou, C., & Sourvinou, A. (2016). Agent supported serious game environment. *IEEE Transactions on Learning Technologies*, 9(3), 217–230. DOI: 10.1109/TLT.2016.2521649

Thornton, K. (2015). Introduction: The crucial role of peer-learning in language learning spaces. *Studies in Self-Access Learning Journal*, 286-287, 286–287. Advance online publication. DOI: 10.37237/060304

Tinggie, T., Tan, K., Muslim, N., & Keng, L. (2023). Peer scaffolding among primary ESL learners' writing task: Learners' behaviors and triggering factors. *International Journal of Learning Teaching and Educational Research*, 22(3), 191–208. DOI: 10.26803/ijlter.22.3.12

Tubino, L., & Adachi, C. (2022). Developing feedback literacy capabilities through an AI automated feedback tool. *Proceedings of the ASCILITE 2022 Conference: Reconnecting Relationships through Technology*, e22039. DOI: 10.14742/apubs.2022.39

Ulfa, K. (2023). The transformative power of artificial intelligence (AI) to elevate English language learning. *Majalah Ilmiah Methoda*, 13(3), 307–313. DOI: 10.46880/methoda.Vol13No3.pp307-313

Usher, M., Hershkovitz, A., & Forkosh-Baruch, A. (2021). From data to actions: Instructors' decision making based on learners' data in online emergency remote teaching. *British Journal of Educational Technology*, 52(4), 1338–1356. DOI: 10.1111/bjet.13108

Vall, R., & Araya, F. (2023). Exploring the benefits and challenges of AI-language learning tools. *The International Journal of Social Sciences and Humanities Invention*, 10(01), 7569–7576. DOI: 10.18535/ijsshi/v10i01.02

Wang, Y. (2021). When artificial intelligence meets educational leaders' data-informed decision-making: A cautionary tale. *Studies in Educational Evaluation*, 69, 100872. DOI: 10.1016/j.stueduc.2020.100872

Wenglinsky, H. (2002). The link between teacher classroom practices and student academic performance. *Education Policy Analysis Archives*, 10, 12. DOI: 10.14507/epaa.v10n12.2002

West-Smith, P., Butler, S., & Mayfield, E. (2018). Trustworthy automated essay scoring without explicit construct validity. *Proceedings of the AAAI Spring Symposium on AI and Society: Ethics, Safety and Trustworthiness in Intelligent Agents.* https://help.turnitin.com/Resources/RA%20Curriculum%20Resources/Research/Revision%20Assistant%20Validity%20AAAI%202018.pdf

Weston-Sementelli, J. L., Allen, L. K., & McNamara, D. S. (2016). Comprehension and writing strategy training improves performance on content-specific source-based writing tasks. *International Journal of Artificial Intelligence in Education*, 28(1), 106–137. DOI: 10.1007/s40593-016-0127-7

Williamson, B., & Eynon, R. (2020). Historical threads, missing links, and future directions in education. *Learning, Media and Technology*, 45(3), 223–235. DOI: 10.1080/17439884.2020.1798995

Wilson, C., & Scott, B. (2017). Adaptive systems in education: A review and conceptual unification. *International Journal of Information and Learning Technology*, 34(1), 2–19. DOI: 10.1108/IJILT-09-2016-0040

Wood, D., Bruner, J. S., & Ross, G. (1976). The role of tutoring in problem solving. *Journal of Child Psychology and Psychiatry, and Allied Disciplines*, 17(2), 89–100. DOI: 10.1111/j.1469-7610.1976.tb00381.x PMID: 932126

Wu, W.-C. V., Petit, E., & Chen, C.-H. (2015). EFL writing revision with blind expert and peer review using a CMC open forum. *Computer Assisted Language Learning*, 28(1), 58–80. DOI: 10.1080/09588221.2014.937442

Xie, H., Chu, H., Hwang, G., & Wang, C. C. (2019). Trends and development in technology-enhanced adaptive/personalized learning: A systematic review of journal publications from 2007 to 2017. *Computers & Education*, 140, 103599. Advance online publication. DOI: 10.1016/j.compedu.2019.103599

Xu, Z., Wijekumar, K. K., Ramirez, G., Hu, X., & Irey, R. (2019). The effectiveness of intelligent tutoring systems on K-12 students' reading comprehension: A meta-analysis. *British Journal of Educational Technology*, 50(6), 3119–3137. DOI: 10.1111/bjet.12758

Yang, D., Wu, Q., & Wang, F. (2019). Design and development of the mobile adaptive learning platform for English vocabulary mastery. *International Journal of Mobile Learning and Multimodal Interactions*, 13(3), 1–17.

Yang, J., & Zhang, B. (2019). Artificial intelligence in intelligent tutoring robots: A systematic review and design guidelines. *Applied Sciences (Basel, Switzerland)*, 9(10), 2078. DOI: 10.3390/app9102078

Zhao, L., Wu, X., & Luo, H. (2022). Developing AI literacy for primary and middle school teachers in China: Based on a structural equation modeling analysis. *Sustainability (Basel)*, 14(21), 14549. DOI: 10.3390/su142114549

Zhao, X., & Yang, Y. (2021). A study on the application of blended teaching to English reading course under the background of artificial intelligence. *IOP Conference Series. Earth and Environmental Science*, 693(1), 012019. DOI: 10.1088/1755-1315/693/1/012019

APPENDIX A

Generative Artificial Intelligence (AI) and Its Uses for Language Learning: Lesson Plans and Activities

ESL Level: Intermediate to Upper-Intermediate (B1-B2 on the CEFR Scale)

This lesson plan provides a structured approach with various activities to engage ESL students in understanding AI, its applications, and responsible use, with adaptation suggestions for different proficiency levels.

Lesson Objectives:

- Introduce the concept of AI and its types.
- Build vocabulary related to AI.
- Explain how to use generative AI and chatbots for language learning.
- Discuss responsible and acceptable use of AI tools.

Materials Needed:

- Whiteboard and markers
- Projector and laptop
- Student Handout
- Internet access for demonstrating AI tools
- Devices for students (smartphones, tablets, or computers)
- Word cloud tool (online or on paper)
- Scenario cards for role-play activity

Adaptation for Lower Levels (A2-B1):

- Simplify the vocabulary and provide more scaffolding during discussions.
- Use more concrete and visual examples to explain AI concepts.

- Spend more time on vocabulary building activities and ensure students understand the definitions.
- Break down explanations into smaller, more manageable parts and check for understanding frequently.
- Use simpler prompts for ChatGPT and provide more guided practice.

Adaptation for Higher Levels (B2-C1):

- Introduce more technical details about AI and discuss its broader implications in various fields.
- Expand vocabulary to include more advanced terms related to AI and technology.
- Engage students in more in-depth discussions and debates about the ethical implications of AI.
- Add more challenging activities and critical thinking exercises, such as evaluating a ChatGPT written essay.
- Use more complex prompts for ChatGPT and encourage students to explore AI tools independently.

Student Handout

Stage/Time - 2hrs	Procedure
A. Warm-up **(20 minutes)**	**Brief Discussion:** • Start with an open question: "What do you know about Artificial Intelligence (AI)?" • Encourage students to share their thoughts and experiences. • Ask: "Can you think of examples of AI that you see or use in your everyday life?" (GPS, Spotify recommendations, Netflix suggestions, facial recognition on smartphones, etc.) **Activity: Word Cloud** • Use an online word cloud tool like Mentimeter or paper to have students write down as many words as they can think of that remind them of AI. • Discuss the most common words and ask students to create a definition of AI in pairs or small groups. • Have a few pairs or groups share their definitions with the class.

continued on following page

Student Handout Continued

Stage/Time - 2hrs	Procedure
B. Presentation: Understanding AI (20 minutes)	**How AI Works:** • Ask: "Does AI think?" • Explain that AI does not actually "think" but finds patterns in data. Data can be biometrics, audio, text, numbers, and images. • Describe how AI practices making decisions or guesses millions of times to improve. **Accuracy and Bias in AI:** • Ask: "Thinking about AI that provides recommendations like Netflix, Amazon, and Spotify. Are your recommendations always accurate?" • Discuss how AI can make mistakes and be biased. • Define bias as an unfair prejudice for or against a certain group. • Emphasize that it's up to humans to evaluate AI's outputs for truthfulness and meaningfulness.
C. Vocabulary Building (20 minutes)	**Activity 1: Matching** *Interaction: Use an online tool like Quizlet or Wordwall.* **Activity 2: Fill in the blanks ChatGPT Reading**
D. Demonstration and Guided Practice (40 minutes)	**Demonstration:** Show how to use ChatGPT by logging in at chat.openai.com and having a conversation. **Example Prompts:** • **Vocabulary Practice**: "Give me synonyms for the word 'happy'." • **Conversation Practice**: "Let's have a conversation about traveling." • **Cultural Understanding**: "Explain and describe how [cultural tradition] is celebrated." • **Listing Cultural Norms**: "List some cultural norms in [country]." **Guided Practice for Writing Feedback:** • Students practice using ChatGPT with provided prompts. • Walk around to assist and answer questions. • Discuss the results and students' experiences. **Directions:** Students should write a short paragraph and use ChatGPT to get feedback, and then make corrections and discuss the improvements. **Teacher**: Provide students with a specific question or topic to write about. Example topics: • "Describe your favorite holiday and how you celebrate it." • "Write about a memorable experience you had during a trip." • "Explain why learning English is important to you." **Students**: (see handout)

continued on following page

Student Handout Continued

Stage/Time - 2hrs	Procedure
E. Responsible Use of AI (30 minutes)	**Discussion on Responsible Use:** • Ask: "Have you ever used AI for schoolwork before? Which programs? In what ways have you used it?" • Discuss what students think are acceptable uses and unacceptable uses. • *For activities 1 and 2: Use an online tool like Wordwall or Padlet for interaction* **Activity 1: Scenarios** • In pairs, students decide and discuss if each scenario (see student handout) is responsible or irresponsible use. • Discuss answers as a class. **Activity 2: Create Class Rules for AI Use** Do one for each as a class first. Then have students do their own in amall groups. Check as a class. **responsible use unacceptable use** Language practice Asking for grammar corrections Complete homework without understanding Copying AI-generated text for an essay
F. Recap and Q&A (10 minutes)	**Review Key Points:** • Summarize the main ideas: vocabulary, prompting, and responsible use. • Reinforce the importance of using AI tools to enhance learning, not replace it. **Q&A Session:** • Allow students to ask any remaining questions about AI and its uses.
G. Closing (10 minutes)	**Homework Assignment:** • Ask students to write a short paragraph about how they plan to use AI tools for their language learning. • Encourage them to reflect on responsible use, include new vocabulary terms, and to use AI to check their work.

Students will learn…

- the concept of AI and its types.
- vocabulary related to AI.
- how to use generative AI and chatbots for language learning.
- what is and is not acceptable use of AI tools.

A. Discussion

1. What do you know about Artificial Intelligence (AI)?
2. Can you think of examples of AI that you see or use in your everyday life?"

Activity: Word Cloud

- Write down as many words as they can think of that remind you of AI.
- Definition of AI:

B. Understanding AI

1. Does AI think?
2. Thinking about AI that provides recommendations like Netflix, Amazon, and Spotify, are your recommendations always accurate?

C. Vocabulary Building

Activity 1: Matching

Directions: *Match the terms with their correct definitions.*

Term	Definition
1. AI (Artificial Intelligence) ______	A. Information given to someone about their performance or work.
2. Bias ______	B. To produce or create something, such as text or image, using AI.
3. Chatbot ______	C. A repeated design or recurring sequence in data.
4. Data ______	D. To state or describe exactly the nature, scope, or meaning of.
5. Generative AI ______	E. Communication or direct involvement with something or someone.
6. Pattern ______	F. Facts and statistics collected for reference or analysis.
7. Prompt ______	G. To examine in detail the structure of something.
8. Generate ______	H. A question or statement used to initiate a response from ChatGPT.
9. Translate ______	I. AI that creates new content from learned data.
10. Interaction ______	J. To change text from one language to another.
11. Context ______	K. A program that simulates a conversation with users.
12. List ______	L. An unfair prejudice for or against a certain group.
13. Feedback ______	M. To write or state items one after another.
14. Define ______	N. The simulation of human intelligence processes by machines.
15. Suggest ______	O. To estimate, measure, or note the similarity or dissimilarity between.
16. Compare ______	P. To establish or indicate who or what (someone or something) is.
17. Identify ______	Q. The circumstances or setting in which a word or phrase is used.
18. Analyze ______	R. To put forward for consideration.

continued on following page

Directions: *Match the terms with their correct definitions. Continued*

Term	Definition
19. Summarize _____	S. To give a brief statement of the main points.

Activity 2: Fill in the Blanks

Directions: Using the words from Activity 1, fill in the blanks in the passage below. The word 'generate' is used multiple times.

Interacting With ChatGPT for Language Learning

When using ChatGPT for language learning, it is important to understand how **Artificial Intelligence (AI)** can assist you. **AI** is the simulation of human intelligence processes by machines, which allows ChatGPT to understand and __________ **(1)** human-like text. It does this by **analyzing** __________ **(2)** of __________ **(3)**.

Start by using a __________ **(4)**, which is a question or statement used to initiate a response from ChatGPT. For example, you might ask ChatGPT to __________ **(5)** a __________ **(6)** of vocabulary words related to travel. However, ChatGPT performs better when given specific __________ **(7)**, as it helps **generate** more accurate and relevant responses. For example, you might use a __________ **(8)** like: "As an ESL tutor for B1 level students, can you **generate** a list of vocabulary words related to travel?" This way, ChatGPT can tailor its response to fit the learning level and needs.

Once you have your list, you can ask ChatGPT to __________ **(9)** each word. If any definitions are unclear, request further __________ **(10)** to help you understand. You might also ask ChatGPT to __________ **(11)** a vocabulary word from one language to another.

To improve your writing, you can ask ChatGPT to __________ **(12)** sentences you have written and provide explanations for the changes. For grammar practice, you can request ChatGPT to __________ **(13)** different grammatical structures, highlighting their differences and uses. Additionally, ChatGPT can help you __________ **(14)** articles or texts, identifying the main points or themes, which is useful for practicing reading comprehension. For broader learning, you might ask ChatGPT to assist in preparing for a discussion; it can help you __________ **(15)** questions and __________ **(16)** topics to discuss.

By using ChatGPT's capabilities, this __________ **(17)** will help you improve your skills and gain confidence in using the language.

D. Practice

Example Prompts:

- **Vocabulary Practice**: "Give me synonyms for the word 'happy'."

- **Conversation Practice**: "Let's have a conversation about traveling."
- **Cultural Understanding**: "Explain and describe how [cultural tradition] is celebrated."
- **Listing Cultural Norms**: "List some cultural norms in [country]."

Practice for Writing Feedback: Write a short paragraph and use ChatGPT to get feedback. Then make corrections and discuss the improvements.

1. Log into chat.openai.com and write a short paragraph on the given topic.
2. Use ChatGPT with the provided prompt to get feedback.
    - **Prompt**: "As an ESL tutor for a B1 CEFR-level student, please check my paragraph for grammar mistakes but do not fix them. Highlight the errors and provide hints or explanations. Allow me to fix the errors myself."
3. Make corrections based on the feedback and then use ChatGPT to check the corrections.
4. Use ChatGPT to get vocabulary suggestions.
    - **Prompt**: "As an ESL tutor for a B1 level student, please suggest synonyms and alternative phrases for the words in my paragraph to make it more varied and interesting."

E. Responsible Use of AI

Discussion on Responsible Use:

- Have you ever used AI for schoolwork before? Which programs? In what ways have you used it?
- What do you think are acceptable uses and unacceptable uses?

Activity 1: Scenarios

Directions: Read the following scenarios and discuss with a partner whether each use of AI is responsible or irresponsible.

- **Scenario 1:** You use a grammar-checking tool to review your essays before submission. You accept all the suggested changes but do not review the reasons behind them or learn from the corrections.
- **Scenario 2**: You are working on a project and use an AI tool to generate fake data that supports your work. You present this data in your final report.

- **Scenario 3**: You have to write a research paper but are struggling to come up with a topic. You use an AI brainstorming tool to generate a list of potential topics and outlines, then choose one to develop further.
- **Scenario 4**: You are creating a presentation for your class. You use an AI tool to generate images and visual aids to make your slides more attractive and engaging.
- **Scenario 5**: You have a busy week and need to submit an essay for your class. You use an AI writing tool to generate the entire essay and submit it without making any changes.
- **Scenario 6**: During an online exam, you use an AI tool to answer the questions instead of relying on your own knowledge and skills.
- **Scenario 7**: For every assignment, you write your essays in your native language first, then use an AI translator to translate them into English. You submit your assignments without further revision. This becomes your regular practice for all writing tasks.
- **Scenario 8**: After writing an essay, you use an AI tool to check for grammar and style issues. The AI tool highlights errors and provides suggestions. You make the corrections yourself based on these suggestions before submitting your work.
- **Scenario 9**: You are working on a research project and find several long articles. You use an AI summarization tool to identify key concepts and summarize the articles. You then use these summaries to help write your own analysis and cite the original sources properly.
- **Scenario 10**: You use an AI chatbot to write all your discussion posts for your online course. You copy the chatbot's responses directly and submit them as your own without making any changes or adding your own thoughts.

Activity 2: *In small groups, create rules for AI use.*

Responsible Use	Unacceptable Use

Homework Assignment

- Write a short paragraph about how you plan to use AI tools for your language learning.
- Be sure to reflect on responsible use, include new vocabulary terms, and use AI to check your work.

Answer Key

Activity 1: Matching

Term	Definition
1. AI (Artificial Intelligence)	N. The simulation of human intelligence processes by machines.
2. Bias	L. An unfair prejudice for or against a certain group.
3. Chatbot	K. A program that simulates a conversation with users.
4. Data	F. Facts and statistics collected for reference or analysis.
5. Generative AI	I. AI that creates new content from learned data.
6. Pattern	C. A repeated design or recurring sequence in data.
7. Prompt	H. A question or statement used to initiate a response from ChatGPT.
8. Generate	B. To produce or create something, such as text or image, using AI.
9. Translate	J. To change text from one language to another.
10. Interaction	E. Communication or direct involvement with something or someone.
11. Context	Q. The circumstances or setting in which a word or phrase is used.
12. List	M. To write or state items one after another.
13. Feedback	A. Information given to someone about their performance or work.
14. Define	D. To state or describe exactly the nature, scope, or meaning of.
15. Suggest	R. To put forward for consideration.
16. Compare	O. To estimate, measure, or note the similarity or dissimilarity between.
17. Identify	P. To establish or indicate who or what (someone or something) is.
18. Analyze	G. To examine in detail the structure of something.
19. Summarize	S. To give a brief statement of the main points.

Activity 2: Fill in the Blanks

1. generate 2. patterns 3. data 4. prompt 5. generate 6. list 7. context 8. prompt 9. define 10. feedback 11. translate 12. correct 13. compare 14. summarize 15. generate 16. suggest 17. interaction	When using ChatGPT for language learning, it is important to understand how Artificial Intelligence (AI) can assist you. AI is the simulation of human intelligence processes by machines, which allows ChatGPT to understand and **generate (1)** human-like text. It does this by analyzing **patterns (2)** of **data (3).** Start by using a **prompt (4)**, which is a question or statement used to initiate a response from ChatGPT. For example, you might ask ChatGPT to **generate (5)** a **list (6)** of vocabulary words related to travel. However, ChatGPT performs better when given specific **context (7)**, as it helps generate more accurate and relevant responses. For example, you might use a **prompt (8)** like: "As an ESL tutor for B1 level students, can you generate a list of vocabulary words related to travel?" This way, ChatGPT can tailor its response to fit the learning level and needs. Once you have your list, you can ask ChatGPT to **define (9)** each word. If any definitions are unclear, request further **feedback (10)** to help you understand. You might also ask ChatGPT to **translate (11)** a vocabulary word from one language to another. To improve your writing, you can ask ChatGPT to **correct (12)** sentences you have written and provide explanations for the changes. For grammar practice, you can request ChatGPT to **compare (13)** different grammatical structures, highlighting their differences and uses. Additionally, ChatGPT can help you **summarize (14)** articles or texts, identifying the main points or themes, which is useful for practicing reading comprehension. For broader learning, you might ask ChatGPT to assist in preparing for a discussion; it can help you **generate (15)** questions and **suggest (16)** topics to discuss. By using ChatGPT's capabilities, this **interaction (17)** will help you improve your skills and gain confidence in using the language.

Vocabulary Extension

Correct vs. Edit: Both involve fixing errors in a text.

Distinction: Correct focuses solely on fixing mistakes (e.g., grammar, punctuation), while edit includes improving style, clarity, and overall readability as well as correcting mistakes.

Enhance vs. Revise vs. Rewrite: All three involve improving a text.

Distinction:

- **Enhance:** Typically means adding details or elements to improve quality (e.g., adding descriptive details).
- **Revise:** Involves substantial changes and rethinking to improve clarity and coherence (e.g., reorganizing paragraphs, reworking sentences).
- **Rewrite:** Means creating a new version of the text, often with significant changes to wording, structure, or content (e.g., writing the text again to improve it or include new information).

Describe vs. Explain vs. Clarify: All three involve making something clear to the reader or listener.

Distinction:

- **Describe:** Focuses on giving detailed information about characteristics, features, or attributes (e.g., describing a holiday).
- **Explain:** Involves making an idea, situation, or problem clear by describing it in detail (e.g., explaining how something works).
- **Clarify:** Focuses on making something less confused and more comprehensible, often by rephrasing or providing additional information (e.g., clarifying a complex term).

Additional Materials

Figure 8. Dos and Don'ts of AI in Classrooms

Chapter 5
Navigating AI Biases in Education
A Foundation for Equitable Learning

S. Bhavana
https://orcid.org/0009-0005-6134-1081
Sreenidhi Institute of Science and Technology, India

Kudipudi Jayashree
Sreenidhi Institute of Science and Technology, India

Thota Venkat Narayana Rao
Sreenidhi Institute of Science and Technology, India

ABSTRACT

There is revolutionary potential when artificial intelligence (AI) is used into education. The use of AI in educational systems holds promise for individualized instruction and evaluation. It has, nevertheless, also made clear several serious biases and shortcomings. This chapter critically investigates the biases—such as cultural biases and socioeconomic disparities—that are ingrained in AI algorithms used in education. It looks at how inadequate AI is at meeting a range of student needs, including socioeconomic understanding and complicated emotional states. A framework is put forth to address these problems: data-driven diversity, ethical AI design, transparency and accountability, human-AI collaboration, and ongoing assessment and improvement. By putting these tactics into practice, stakeholders can minimize prejudices and fully utilize AI's promise, creating fair and productive learning environments for all students.

DOI: 10.4018/979-8-3693-5443-8.ch005

1. INTRODUCTION

During the past few years, the use of Artificial intelligence (AI) has raised a lot of enthusiasm in education community as well as some disputes, and so many opportunities for learning and assessment have been provided. AI technology can be a game changer for the way education is carried out by allowing for individualization of processes, completing administrative chores and providing educational managers with useful data. But at the same time, while we witness the excitement created by AI, we cannot forget about the similar risks and shortages accompanied by the AI-based education that need to be dealt with.

The merger of AI and education in education is a multilevel array of new opportunities. Among the most powerful advantages is providing learners with opportunities for one's experiences personalized learning in keeping with each student's individualized needs and tastes. With the aid AI-driven adaptive learning systems that can analyse the big data to find not only students' strengths but also students' weaknesses as well and thus can provide personalized learning ways and resources to the maximum. Again, AI systems can do so by automating the formerly repetitive tasks (like grading assignments or the course enrolment management). This way the time of educators can be focused on the individual instruction and mentoring.

Additionally, the AI could be used to add value to the assessment process through allowing for real-time feedback and disclosure of student performance insights. Mechanized assessment systems, with the aid of AI system of algorithms, examine students' answers to tests, quizzes and assignments in order to provide immediate feedback and identify zones for enhancement. This prompt feedback could show students the gap between achieved knowledge and the aim for learning and thus take timely measures to fill in the gaps.

Proceeding from these perspectives, the merits of AI in education are not unblemished with the inevitable difficulties which crop up. The most important issue is the integration of the biases and deficiencies of artificial intelligence algorithms into the operation of AI. AI systems play with historical information that is a product of socially proven biases which mirror the discrimination and cultural stereotypes that are available in the society. Bias may in many ways appear which for examples could be an instance of gender bias, race bias and or socioeconomic bias and have far reaching effects in the in the field of education with regard to equity and inclusivity.

The gap in providing unique and personalized learning solutions for students with diverse needs like the management of emotions, individual learning styles, and socio-economic contexts also remains a challenge for AI systems. Although AI technologies are highly effective when dealing with large volumes of the structured data, they may become unable to cope with the hard-to-identify emotions of learners, or understand complex socio-economic circumstances, which are of great importance for students' learning process. Such a constraint may hamper AI's intention to provide not only the personalized and inclusive learning experiences but also in general terms for all students (Wang et al., 2020).

As discussed above, the framework is aimed at curbing issues associated with AI implementation in education to make it inclusively beneficial. The framework comprises five key strategies:

1. Human-AI Collaboration:
   Encouraging cooperative initiatives that exploit the strong points of both people and artificial intelligence for the development of the educational system.
2. Ethical AI Design:
   Incorporating ethical principles in the construction and implementation of AI systems in education, including transparency, fairness, and privacy.
3. Transparency and Accountability:
   Introducing the intelligent AI systems which will emphasize the transparent decision-making process and mechanisms for holding AI systems responsible for bias in their decisions.
4. Data-Driven Diversity:
   The proper training of AI algorithms on diverse datasets which reduces biases and enables algorithms to succeed in algorithmic decision making.
5. Continuous Evaluation and Improvement:
   Implementation of tools for continuous assessment and improvement of AI systems to take on new themes and correct flaws and flaws efficiently.

Through the execution of these strategies, the education sector's stakeholders could utilize the transformative capabilities of AI while also contributing to the achievement of more equitable and efficient learning environments for all learners. Along this paper, the strategies are detailed to make people understand them. Examples and recommendations will be used in order to address biases and shortcomings in AI-driven education.

1.1 Literature Review

Integrating Artificial Intelligence (AI) in education is a matter of research and presents both transformative promise and substantial challenges. Key Research Themes, Debates and Trends in the Literature. The following is a review focussed on AI education: Past Present Future with emphasis that synthetic discussion is one of several types of workflows by which scholars aggregate over multiple sources (Callahan & Herring 2011): Impacting Upon Teaching Learning Administration

Gratarola et al. This review also covers the ethical issues, biases and future of AI in education.

Key Research Themes

Tailored education content: Another pillar of AI in the educational realm is its ability to cater educational material as per individual learning styles and needs. Studies reveal AI-powered Adaptive Learning Systems increase student motivation through personal feedback and learning journeys. The rapidly expanding field of adaptive learning is creating new opportunities to scale personalized education — for example DreamBox and Smart Sparrow have shown that when education adapts, students learn more.

Automated Evaluation and Feedback: Many platforms which are not limited to AI for grading automate the assessment process and give immediate results. Systems such as Gradescope are powered by machine learning algorithms that automatically grade student work, providing immediate feedback and allowing students to make corrections right away. This automation serves to ease the workload experienced by educators and allows assessment using a more uniform set of criteria, engendering consistency as well as objectivity.

AI-Enabled Tutoring Systems: AI-powered one-on-one tutoring solutions such as Carnegie Learning's MATHia, and language learning platforms including Duolingo incorporated with AI features for achieving a custom pace of teaching by understanding the student comprehension level. They are especially beneficial when used in conjunction with traditional instruction for encouraging individualized.

Designing Ethical AI and Combatting Bias: With increased use of AI reliant education platforms, there is a growing level of concern regarding not only ethical design practices but also how to prevent reinforcement bias in these intelligent systems.

1.2 Methodology

Combining various steps and methodologies to collect valuable data on AI integration in education, this chapter presents a comprehensive method for Researchers. Methods: In the first phase, a rigorously structured literature review was carried out on peer-reviewed journals with conference papers and academic books which discuss AI in education. The search databases of Google Scholar, JSTOR and IEEE Xplore were used to show main subjects and trends in the sector.

The review of literature also tried to be specific in finding research that dealt with positive or dual benefits and drawbacks of AI implementation; especially those associated with personalized learning, ethics about how the AIs should be designed as well as mitigation on bias. Data on adoption rates and market trends were taken from a variety of sources, including reports issued by industry research firms and surveys conducted by educational technology organizations. Second, the authors surveyed theoretical frameworks that support ethical AI design and bias reduction to establish a basis for their strategies.

For qualitative studies, the data analysis process aimed to identify trends and new emerging issues resulting from a synthesis of findings from various conducted studies. It then combined this framework with these cases studies and the real-world best practices from improved learning gains with AI technologies in educational settings. This way the methodology produced a more complete and harmonious interpretation of AI in education, based on evidence as well theoretical outlooks.

2. UNDERSTANDING AI BIASES

Figure 1. Biases in AI

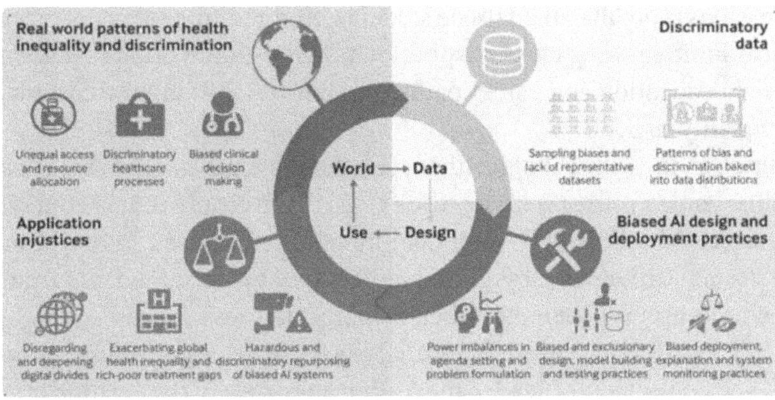

The following points explain the figure above:

AI biases are the systematic errors or unappealing results in AI systems that are caused by using skewed or unrepresentative training data, by wrong algorithm design and/or by inherent human biases. These biases can prove to be a crucial factor which is going to increasingly shape the decision-making processes and the outcomes, particularly in educational contexts as AI mechanisms are also extensively used for learning, assessment, and administrative activities.

When it comes to education, even though the AI biases are pervasive, they still have a significant impact as they can be present in different stages of the learning process, from personalized learning recommendations to assessment outcomes to educational opportunities. An in-depth understanding of the various types of biases that employ AI algorithms in the educational sector is an imperative factor for the enlightenment of educators, policymakers, and technologists in their endeavour to mitigate the biases and foster an equitable learning environment.

One form of stereotype prevalent in AI among educational institutions is cultural bias. A cultural bias manifests in the AI training data taking on the cultural perspective of the dominant group or the cultural norm, thus leading these AI algorithms to favour one group of people against the other. One of the cases is an AI-powered language learning platform by which you can study more the vocabulary and language structures spoken in the mainstream culture while the dialect or a language of a minority group will be marginalized. Such prejudice may be the cause of linguistic and cultural exclusion in educational materials that will be in disadvantage for people from any minority cultural background at all (Varsha et al.,2023).

Besides the cultural bias in AI education systems, another issue is about the gender bias. Gender biases are many and varied, taking such forms as gender role stereotypes or favouring preferences. This can be observed through the instance whereby a career guidance AI tool may advise male students to enrol in the traditional male professions more than the female students, thus reinforcing gender stereotypes and, in turn, limiting one's career aspirations. This attitude often results in gender imbalances in education and career paths, and thus reinforcing the current existing gender inequality in society.

In addition to this, the AI algorithms can demonstrate racial bias. Thus, due to this, the differentiated treatment or results may stem from race or ethnicity. Such technologies as AI admissions screening system that is used by universities can indirectly sustain differences by giving advantages to the applicants from certain racial or ethnic groups over the other meaning fairness in admission rates and educational chances is not ensured. Racial biases in AI algorithms can be greatly dangerous and consequently, lead to the further aggravate of the existing inequalities in education. This can lead to discrimination along racial lines thus being a great factor in hindering the efforts to promote diversity and inclusivity.

The educational goals of AI are profound that they influence students' personal growth, future learning and job opportunities. For example, biased suggestions created by adaptive learning systems which are supported by AI may strengthen prejudicial opinions, or even the learning problems of the learners leading to low rating of their academic ratings. Bias in the student evaluation algorithms can be a major factor in the creation of grading and assessment gaps based on the student origin, namely, a student from an underrepresented group may be unfairly penalized. Additionally, problems like biased decision-making processes that are related to AI systems may lead to erosion of the trust in education establishments and further perpetuation of the feeling of being excluded or discriminated by the learners.

In the end, exploring AI biases to identify importance for resolving inequalities and to ensure fair learning communities is a must. Through discovering and removing all biases present in AI systems' algorithms, educators, policymakers, and technologists will be able to strive for the creation of more inclusive and just educational programs that will enable learners to become better equipped to succeed in their studies. In this chapter, we will consider the possible strategies involving AI bias detection, prevention, and solution using evidence extracted from research, case studies, and the best available practices in the field (Roselli et al., 2019).

3. CULTURAL BIASES IN AI ALGORITHMS

The problem of cultural bias, embedded in the artificial intelligence algorithms, is becoming a serious barrier on the way of the aim to ensure that all students will learn equitably within the spheres of their studies. This is the case in AI designed for learners from diverse cultural backgrounds if the AI systems, which are mostly influenced by societal norms and values, have a potential to perpetuate these disadvantages. Along with comprehending the role of biases in education, educators should be careful with devising techniques to overcome these biases as the main aim is to promote a fair and inclusive learning process (Nazer et al., 2023).

The aspect of culturally biased AI algorithms can manifest itself into many issues for the fair learning of AI. The first issue is the distorted cultural content in textbooks or other resources. Teachers and educators may be depriving students of unique cultural content or disrespecting the original meaning of culture by neglecting or misinterpreting it. To cite an instance, AI-based syllabus suggestions may fashion the lessons to fit with the mainstream stories, and at the end, they divert the attention from the multicultural heritage and experiences of minority groups. This uneven playing field may lead to the feeling of being disconnected from the learning by the learners from these backgrounds or being marginalized which will, in turn, affect their engagement and success in their learning.

Besides that, cultural bias can be involved in AI algorithms and lead to the spread of stereotypes which support the existing inequalities in educational conditions. For example, it can be about automated recommendation systems of academic choices that might lead learners to the same fields that traditional members of their cultural or ethnic group occupy without even knowing why, thus diminishing learners' aspirations and continuing occupational segregation. Thus, this can further give rise to unjust educational and socio-economic inequalities, making it more difficult for society to develop such important aspects as diversity and inclusivity within educational activities.

Research studies and practical examples shed light on the scope and significance of cultural biases in instructional AI applications. For instance, research findings have shown that computer-aided platforms for learning may have a bias as far as the content recommendation algorithms are concerned, favouring the material that is in line with western cultural perspective while ignoring alternative views. Researchers also noted the differences in students' educational outcomes based on their cultural backgrounds and pinpointed the role of cultural biases in making the achievement gap wider and therefore hindering their academic success.

To effectively address cultural prejudice in AI algorithms and provide education that led to a more inclusive and equitable society, some strategies are presented. At first, we should try to achieve diversity and flawlessness during the process of AI system development, and it will reflect on the training process. The active participation of individuals from different cultural groups in designing, implementing, and debugging AI algorithms at the data level will help to ensure they are equally responsive to the needs of all the learners. Besides that, transparency and accountability procedures must be created to allow experts to fire and fix the AI algorithms bugs. This will increase the chances of identifying and resolving bias in AI algorithms.

In addition, an ongoing monitoring and revision of AI algorithms are key factors that will ensure that they are not inorganic to the dynamic cultural environment. Conducting the regular audits of AI systems against biases, soliciting feedback from different user groups, and improving algorithms round the clock, with a focus on bias reduction and expanding inclusivity, is a must. Moreover, it is vital that teachers and students alike are culturally competent considering the fact that because of the cultural biases, may be harmful to an environment of openness understanding and respect which is one of the more important aspects of education (Ntoutsi et al., 2020).

Thus, the cultural biases in AI algorithms should be always the matter of focus in this process and the way to make the learning process more equal and the educational contexts more welcoming should be looked for. However, it should be noted that the understanding of these implications and their potential consequences is crucial and attainable by researching and referencing case studies and research findings; therefore, the educators and technologists can work together to build studying systems and environments that celebrate diversity, empower learners, and promote high academic performance.

4. ALGORITHMIC DISCRIMINATION AND SOCIAL INEQUALITIES

AI algorithms indeed become a powerful tool in the sphere of education as they are used everywhere from personalized learning to university admissions. Nonetheless, while these algorithms may have the advantage of augmenting the efficiency of our society, they can also lead to deliberate algorithmic bias and exacerbate the already existing social injustices, therefore prompting ethical dilemmas which require careful consideration and needed action.

Algorithms in AI are able to hold some biases present in the society through the process of replication and magnification, which further worsens the already existing situation (Zajko et al., 2022). As an illustration, if an AI system has been trained using a biased dataset that is used to choose admissions based on a preference for some groups instead of others, the machine may even unconsciously continue these biases, which in turn would give an unfair advantage to applicants from the advantaged groups. In addition, in personalized learning platforms individual recommendation algorithms may unconsciously lead students with low-income status away from advanced tracks or prevent their access to important coursework and reinforce the existing situation of educational inequality.

For the ethical facets of algorithmic discrimination in education, the consequences are highly influential. Biasing algorithms threaten to undermine the three pillars of fairness, equality and justice in the public education systems. The simple fact of the presence of these algorithms in web searching can happen to persist in the imbalance of access, opportunities and outcomes of those socially less privileged people in try to eliminate the extended disadvantage which hinder the efforts towards social mobility and educational equity. Apart from algorithmic discrimination, it can destroy the trust of educational institutions to the extent that it makes the student feel small in their communication with the graduates through feelings of marginalization and alienation.

Efforts could be directed towards forming and developing recommendations that work towards denying algorithmic discrimination and on the other hand, aiming the fairness in education. Transparency and accountability imply the need for uncovering an algorithm design stage and the stage of its development and implementation. Institutes of education and technology developers have to make sure that algorithms are documented fully and accurately, they should be tested to a maximum degree for bias, as well as they should be subject to independent monitoring in order to avoid to deny anybody due to their belonging to some narrow group. Further, stakeholders should proactively communicate with the affected populace to address their complaints, perception of issues, and lay their experiences with the algorithmic applications, promoting collaboration and the joint approach that is centred on equity and fairness.

In addition to that, ensuring that development of algorithms and decision-making procedures are more diverse and inclusive plays a crucial role in minimizing algorithmic discrimination. Facilitation of different teams with various perspectives, coming from different backgrounds, and having different types of skill sets creates a context in which the risk of unconscious bias is diminished, and the algorithmic systems are designed with an awareness of the needs and experiences of all learners. Furthermore, surveillance of algorithmic systems by monitoring and evaluation requirements are needed in place to detect and prevent prejudicial findings immediately. Doing this comprises of having the data, the algorithms performance and impact, collecting stakeholders' feedback and improving the algorithms to plateau biases and encourage fairness.

Finally, the emergence of algorithmic bias in AI educational systems raises critical ethical problematic which necessitates the concerted efforts of stakeholders to address it adequately. When dealing with the possibility of bias and discrimination, interacting with the affected communities, maintaining transparency and accountability and trying to see to it that diversity and inclusion flourish among the stakeholders, stakeholders can participate in the joint effort to ensure that algorithmic discrimination is neutralized and fairness and equity are promoted in education. There must be a coordinated and concerted efforts of educational institutions to help AI deliver on its transforming capacity while keeping in mind the principles of justice, equality and fairness to all learners (Gerdon et al.,2022).

5. ADDRESSING STUDENT DIVERSITY

AI systems are as at present the harbingers of revolutionary education, but at the same time the systems have got the inbuilt flaws of responding only to the limited cries of the students. This limitation has been determined by the inability of AI to understand completely complex emotions, different learning styles and socio-economic status. So it is difficult for AI to create an inclusive and equitable classroom.

The fact that AI systems lack the ability to understand the depth of students' emotions thus it is one of the crucial limitations of AI systems in the context of addressing student diversity. Though AI algorithms can recognize quantity simply and more rapidly, their inability to decipher the intricacies of the human emotion presents a set-back in learning. Similarly, the intelligence tutoring system based on AI may be proficient in distinguishing students 'problematic academic areas from the performance indicators without the ability to identify and act to the most emotional states (frustration, boredom, excitement) of the students. This is why artificial intelligence systems may send students in the wrong direction, not providing necessary emotional support and encouragement, rather contributing to students' disengagement from the studies and low motivation (Roshanaei et al.,2024).

Another implication of AI in learning is that AI systems might find it difficult to cater successfully to various learning styles. Every student has a different set of ideas in regard to learning as well as strengths and obstacles that don't match on a one-size-fits-all approach but rather on an individual basis. As an example, a personalized learning platform with the help of AI can emphasize visual or auditory learning modalities not considering other specimens such as kinaesthetic or tactile ones which are also the different ways students grasp the process of acquiring knowledge and interacting with the content. This minimum amount of tailoring lets AI systems function not as well as they could, compared to classroom teaching, which accommodates different learning styles of students so that they achieve better results.

Furthermore, AI systems may not find solutions to the socio-economic background which is also of great importance in determining students' educational outcomes. Students in the community with different socio-economic levels may enjoy or suffer due to the various arising challenges such as access to resources, support systems and opportunities which in many cases create a divide as some cannot make it to the academic heights. Nevertheless, AI algorithms might oversee the sociologist economic attributes or disrespectfully take them into consideration while doing computation. AI software that is used for college admissions system can favour academic achievement metrics over the social-economic conditions which may have affected students' accumulation of educational opportunities and support systems. Thus, insufficient understanding of local realities is one of the causes that create disparities of education and achievements across all levels which further strengthens existing inequalities.

Train AI systems to more effectively accommodate a student body that's unique in order to do that, several measures may come to hand. On the other hand, is the issue of the design of AI to integrate SEL competencies as a part of AI-driven educational devices. Through enhancement of AI systems' ability to interpret and answer students' emotional states (by introducing sentiment analysis or affective computing) teachers can increase emotional intelligence skills of AI systems and create better more emotional caring learning environments.

Furthermore, this could make a study area more interesting and individualized in its approach. The use of machine learning algorithms, which automatically modify learning pathways and resources according to students' likes and performance is a very effective strategy that teachers may employ for personalized learning to suit and the needs of the different learning styles. Furthermore, a coordination of efforts between AI programmers, trainers, and pupils can be employed to make sure that the process of constructing and implementing AI systems is also contemplating the socio-economic situations of learners, including the provision of learning materials, support services and opportunities based on the circumstances and characteristics of each learner (Eguchi et al., 2021).

Probably the last but not least important is that AI technology provides indubitable potential for improving education, but they also have limitations to do with student diversity. This may be hampered by the AI systems' present inability to bear in mind complex emotions, cater to diverse learning styles, and consider a student's socio-economic status. However, by recognizing this limitation and working on strategies to make the system more cognizant, educators can create a more inclusive and equitable learning environment where all students get the chance to succeed. Thanks to continuous improvement and collaboration everyone in education can benefit from AI utilizing cutting-edge technologies that are adaptable to specific needs, eventually leading to educational equity and excellence in general.

6. HUMAN-AI COLLABORATION IN EDUCATION

Human-AI collaboration in education is a partnership of a kind, not in the traditional sense but one that exploits the strengths of both human and artificial intelligence systems. Hence throwing humans into the mix of AI's advantages such as computation power, data analytics and scalability, collaboration becomes a solution improving the teaching and learning methods and also even the administrative processes in educational settings.

One of the basic advantages of AI-human collaborations is the ability to utilize the offsetting excellences of people and artificial intelligence. AI systems are excellent in doing large volume of data operations, pattern identifying, and automation while humans are very good in abstract reasoning, creativity, and social interactions. Through the introduction of AI technologies into the educational workflow, the educators will have the chance to simplify the administration processes, such as grading assignments, managing course materials and activities scheduling, which is a huge time and resources seeker, to a higher degree of individuality, guidance, and support(Hutson et al.,2023).

Professional development and training through a continuous process to then adequately educate teachers on the information technology, skills and personal confidence needed on artificially intelligence which make them apply in their instruction. Educational institutions can accomplish this through giving teachers the possibilities of practical work, collaboration with colleagues, and reflective practice so that the AI's massive potential may be tapped and utilized with highly successful student learning outcomes (Kim et al.,2022).

Current Trends in AI Education Technologies and Future Developments

Certain significant trends are shaping the current landscape of AI in education and others that we anticipate seeing evolve further. This has been precipitated by the fast pace of advances in AI technology; foundations reacting to a growing desire for more personalized learning, and as our realization grows over what it means if we do not design ethical A.I.

Current Trends

Adaptive Learning Systems: The most important legal trend of AI-driven adaptive learning platforms. Such systems consider students learning behaviors, preferences, and performance data to develop student adapted efficient learning paths. Leading examples include tools like DreamBox or Smart Sparrow (adapted content that alters itself in real-time to what the students need on each and every step).

Incorporation of AI in Tutoring: Beside the known AI-based tutoring systems like MATHia by Carnegie Learning or Duolingo, other applications leverages are getting more sophisticated. In improving the level of education and service these platforms are using a combination on natural language processing (NLP) and machine learning to provide personalized instruction, feedback, support outside that regular classroom environment.

Predictive analytics is key to the identification of at-risk students, course offerings and student retention. Educators can use Artificial Intelligence analyses to track historical data as well as real-time insights that provide opportunities for early intervention among students likely to face difficulties during the course.

Assessment and FeedbackAI: Automated grading, AI-driven assessment tools, Gradescope. These systems not only make the process of grading easier but also give students personalized feedback right away which would help them learn from their mistakes and achieve better results in learning.

Ethical AI and Bias Mitigation: As awareness of potential biases in AI solutions becomes more widespread, there is a clear trend to provide ethical frameworks for the development and practice of Artificial Intelligence. This includes Google's AI Principles and the European Union's Ethical AI guidelines which seek to ensure that artificial intelligence is open, fair, transparent and accessible.

Anticipated Future Developments

Greater Integration of Artificial Intelligence with Augmented Reality (AR) and Virtual Reality (VR): We can anticipate that AI will become more integrated into the systems related to Parallel Dimension for Education such as AR/VR arenas in creating a much-needed environment conducive to learning. Such technologies will allow for more interactive and experiential learning experiences, addressing different educational needs of students.

Better Emotional AI: Increased prevalence of technology that tracks and responds to students' emotions (i.e., emotional AI). To achieve this, AI systems would need to become more empathetic and understanding, interacting with the emotional side of education through affective computing.

Artificial intelligence for lifelong learning (with the increase in continuous skills training programmes, AI will play a significant role to help people keep learning); Individuals using AI-driven learning platforms will learn new skills all through their lives to match up changing career demands as well as personal interests.

Open And Decentralized Ai Platforms: Another prevalent trend in AI is the emergence of open and decentralized AI platforms which are much more transparent, collaborative, innovative. However, given the potential scale of such platforms, it could democratize access to AI technologies so that more educators and learners have an opportunity to use them.

Figure 2. Benefits of Collaboration between Humans and AI

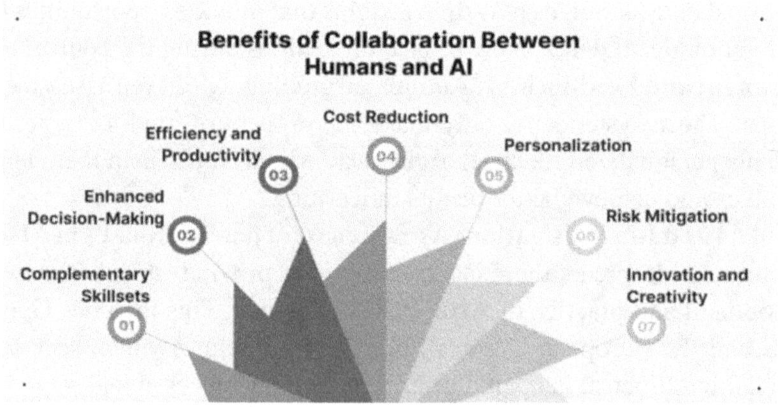

7. ETHICAL AI DESIGN PRINCIPLES

Figure 3. Responsible AI principles

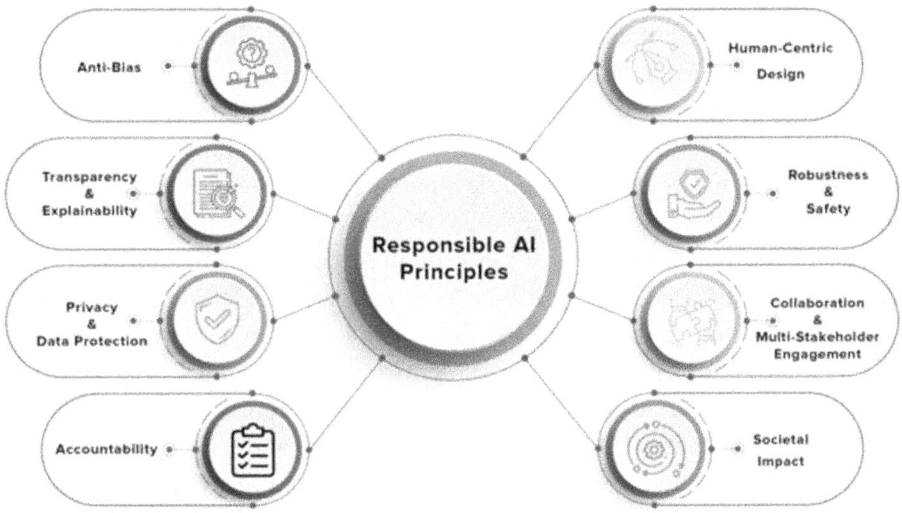

As shown in the above figure, below are the points explained:

Ethical design principles of AI into wide-ranging paradigms to make sure that AI systems are built and implemented with respect to the basic values and principles of ethics. The application of AI to education is rampant, and its use is often in the form of assisting in teaching, learning, and administrative tasks (Zhou et al.,2020). Irrespective, ethical AI design principles must be adhered to avoid trampling on the rights, well-being, and dignity of the learners and educator.

The basic AI design principles ethically in education are attributed directly to the goal of being transparent, fair, and safe. Transparency is established through the presentation of the factors that determine how the AI systems are deployed, the decisive steps, and how these mechanisms are adopted by the concern parties such as the educators, students, and administrators. Organizations in education can achieve this by transforming their information into something which is easy to be understood through transparency. This will result into the building of trust, accountability, and the use of evidence and data in decision making, which is needed to ensure that the stakeholders know how AI systems work and what the consequences of AI use on teaching, learning, and student results are.

Fairness is still one of the most important ethical areas in AI design, especially in education, where discriminatory decisions made by AI systems may bring about very meaningful outcomes somehow for the students. Fairness means setting up AI systems in such a manner so as to treat all people fairly, equally, and without prejudice, irrespective of their innate traits, social status or condition. For instance, intelligent systems for admission should be programmed where candidates are determined on their merit and qualifications, while leaving out the persisting biases or discrimination on basis of race, sex or economic status. School is the place that plays a vital role in putting across the fairness idea which in turn uphold principles of equity, justice, and equal opportunities that learners have chances to use educational resources and support services alike freely.

The issue of privacy has likewise come up in AI development while the systems collecting, analysing, and storing private information of the learners, are being created. Privacy and confidentiality of student information is what has to be protected at all times not only to respect of the student rights and dignity, also to maintain trust and confidence of educational institutions. AI systems should be developed with great emphasis put on layers of privacy protection and data security to ensure that student data is collected and used with respect to apply laws, regulations, and ethics. On the other hand, educational institutions are in charge of the provision of understandable information to students and parents noting what data are being collected, how these will be used and protected by AI software and what mechanisms are in place for students to access, correct or erase information as and when needed.

Using ethics as a basis for AI design in educational sector cannot be left for the last and must be a multidisciplinary activity. Instructive foundations must be formed with the help of inter-departmental teams consisting of educators, technologists, ethicists, and legal professionals, so as to enable joint identification of ethical pitfalls, the development of ethical standards, and the provision of compliance with relevant laws and regulations. In addition, the sessions for continuous training and professional advancement should be instructed to the teachers, administrators, as well as the technologists in order to improve their understanding of ethical issues related with AI in education and develop the skillset and equipment that can help them deal with such issues effectively.

Similarly, the school should get support from the students, parents, and community in the creation and deployment strategy to acquire their genuine views for proper planning. Through the development of an atmosphere where ethics mindfulness, discussion, and accountability are supported, educational institutions can create a secure space where responsible AI usage is promoted what leads to the creation of a more ethical, inclusive, and equitable educational environment for all learners.

In the end, the ethical AI design principles constitute a vital point in the development and deployment of AI applications in education, which is responsible. Through promoting openness, justice and confidentiality, educational institutions are able to adhere to the basics of ethical values and principles, thus guaranteeing the rights, the welfare and the dignity of learners and teachers. The universities might build such culture of ethical awareness and responsibility through participative collaborations, interdisciplinary cooperation, and continuous education and training which is necessary to ensure that AI systems are independently used to improve teaching, learning, and student experiences (Peters et al.,2020).

8. ENSURING TRANSPARENCY, ACCOUNTABILITY, AND CONTINUOUS IMPROVEMENT

Transparency and accountability are cornerstone principles which establish the basis for the introduction of AI into education. Given that AI technology becomes more and more a part of the curricula, the transparency, accountability, and continuous development of ethical standards is paramount to the trust in the AI technology, as well as to find the solutions to the problems caused by potential bias and discrimination (Akinrinola et al.,2024).

In AI education, it is crucial that transparency is of the system used. This means that the decision, algorithm, and the processes in these systems should be clear and communicated openly to the relevant stakeholders. AI systems provide transparent functioning criteria for educators, students, and administrators. This means that they understand how the algorithms work, which data the algorithms stand on, and which factors influence the recommendations or decisions of the algorithms. With its ability to make the information about AI use in education clear, educational institutions can support trust, responsibility, and knowledgeable decision-making of all stakeholders. As a result, they will know what effect the technology has on teaching, learning, and student performance.

In the context of the responsible use of AI in education, accountability is another important aspect, especially when AI makes judgements that might mean big consequences to learners. One of the components of accountability is putting in place instruments that are going to bring the developers and AI systems accountable for the fairness, accuracy, and ethicality of what they do. Educational institutions should put into place a clear boarder lines of responsibility and accountability for AI systems, including the developer role, the educator role, the administrator role, and other stakeholders. Besides that, supervising, monitoring, and complaint mechanisms must be enacted to tackle cons and appeals connected with AI-guided judgment in order that those who get affected have ways to appeal or obtain relief.

Practice of transparency and fairness in the AI decision-making environment requires the implementation of techniques like auditing, explaining and justification of the AI-driven decisions. Due to this, educational institutions must have a policy and employ proper tools that people can examine the algorithms of AI, rate their efficiency, and recognize why AI makes such recommendations or verdicts. The application of certain instruments, such as algorithmic impact assessments, transparency reports and explain ability tools, may be helpful to reveal the way AI systems work, detect biases and errors, and facilitate the interactions and decision making among the stakeholders.

The repeated assessment and refinement are a must in the AI systems dealing with education in order to corbel biases and inaccuracies. Educational institutions must think through system for the continuous analysis, evaluating and improving of AI algorithms so as to maintain that they remained true, honest and ethical. Organization of such a thing includes gathering and studying performance data of AI systems by the users' comments, and continuous troubleshoot in case of new errors, biases and emerging challenges. Along with that, educational institutions should as well invest in research studies and development in AI sciences and algorithms designed to reduce bias, detect bias, and form the methodologies to prevent it from occurring in the educational setting.

Educators may need to determine well-thought-out strategies to keep on monitoring and correcting the AI systems in education. Some of these strategies may include putting the feedback loops in place for system certification, performing regular audits, and working with external professionals and researchers to identify and deal with AI biases and weaknesses. Through inculcation of a culture which promotes continuous learning, innovation, and improvement, educational institutions can grow to enhance the effectiveness, fairness, and ethics of AI systems, therefore, the systems would contribute to positive learners' achievement as well as to the wellbeing of all learners (Felzmann, et al.,2020).

Briefly, we should adhere to elements like, readable, real, and changeable, in the case of AI accountability in education. AI decision making should prefer transparency and accountability and adopt the systems of explaining and justifying, that will lead educational institutions to satisfy ethical standards, establish the relationships of trustworthiness and remove the risks of discrimination and unconscious bias of AI technologies. This dual development of the ethical design and practice of AI in collaboration between educators and technologists, could be the point to explore the high potential of AI for a better future of all the learners, who study in more equal, fair and inclusive learning conditions.

9. CASE STUDIES

Case Study 1: The Use of AI in University Admissions - St. George's Medical School, UK

Background: In the mid of 1980s, St. George's Medical School of United Kingdom applied an AI system to use for elimination process of applicants for medical school. The system was aimed at reducing the amount of time spent in admissions procedures by analyzing various applications with the help of data received as a result of previous decisions.

Challenge: Due to the use of a limited dataset of texts the AI system was trained or rather corrupted by the Bias present in the dataset. More specifically, it began discriminating against certain minorities in favor of Caucasian and male candidates because the latter had formerly been privileged in admissions process.

Outcome: It was also established that the A.I system implemented was biased and had been in use for some time. It was eventually deactivated, but this perhaps made it contribute to bias in admissions in students. This particular case clearly shows how one has to pay particular attention to the methods of AI system designing as well as their constant check to avoid reinforcement of existing prejudices.

Case Study 2: AI-Powered Language Learning - Duolingo

Background: Duolingo is an application offering daily language lessons with the use of artificial intelligence to customer base of millions. The platform also integrates an Artificial Intelligence system that works on analyzing the user data and decide on the difficulty level and content as and when delivering lessons to the learners.

Challenge: However, Duolingo has had few issues, which are mainly cultural bias sort of issues. For instance, some users have complained that the content of the said platform may be quite 'racist' or quite simply, 'irrelevant' to learners from different parts of the non-Western world. Also, there is a tendency where the applied AI algorithms do not diagnose certain language acquisition difficulties that may be specific to a particular user, as well as the user's language and cultural background.

Outcome: To stop such complaints, Duolingo has learned to diversify the content it feeds its learners and to make the AI used more flexible to accommodate all learners. This case captures the need to make AI educational tools accentuate cultural aspects of people from different cultural backgrounds.

Case Study 3: Predictive Analytics in Student Retention - Georgia State University, USA

Background: At Georgia State University, GSU applied an artificial intelligence-based monitoring system that would help the university in early detection of the several student records likely to drop out. The system takes into account such aspects as grade point, class attendance, and the records concerning student's financial aid and then suggests which students will possibly be at risk and what can be done to prevent this.

Challenge: It is evident that when applied in improving on the student retention rates, the AI system has been successful, but the bias issue is still a concern. For example, students from the low-income household or students with some ethnic origin may be considered as at-risk more frequently than others thus resulting in stigmatization as well as over-representation.

Outcome: Given these risks, GSU's attempt to minimize them comes through the use of AI system whereby its predictions are supervised by advisors who are in a better position to go through extra details in making decisions. This has been one of the strengths of the system especially due to the need for supervising human touch in AI-powered educational programs.

Case Study 4: AI in Student Essay Grading - EdX and Automated Essay Scoring

Background: Through the one known online learning platform that is EdX, the use of AI based automated essay scoring system has been implemented for the determination of quality of writing within the students in MOOCs. These systems are intended for instantaneous feedback as well as grading of students' essays.

Challenge: There are criticisms about the AI grading systems, the criticisms are due to the fact that AI grading systems have the ability to mimic bias found in the training data that may prefer certain writing styles for example. That same thread has also produced worries that sometimes AI does not grasp figures of speech or literature, thus resulting to unfair marking.

Outcome: To solve these problems, EdX has synchronously used AI grading and revision in which the instructors can regrade the AI scores and add comments. Such approach can assist in avoiding AI bias while at the same time capitalizing on the automation of grading. This case therefore emphasises the need to incorporate human intervention in AI based education assessments.

10. CONCLUSION

The use of AI in education has created several opportunities through which educational experiences could be improved, a way through which several tasks could be automated, and a way through which insightful findings concerning performance could be gained. However, this is not an easy feat as it comes with its own drawbacks which include bias in AI System, questionable data privacy and security, and call for Ethical AI design. These topics have been discussed elaborately in the subsequent sections of this chapter and a comparative analysis of the risks and benefits of AI in education has been provided.

SUMMARY OF KEY SECTIONS

Understanding AI Biases: It focused on different types of biases including cultural, gender and racial biases that can occur in AI and on how such biases can affect education. The discussion also showed that biases can be learned from the training set, or designed in the algorithm itself, or due to prejudices of the developers and users themselves, when they implement discrimination based on race, gender, and other parameters, in such sensitive areas as student rating and selection, and personalized recommendations for learning.

Cultural Biases in AI Algorithms: The document outlined the negative ways in which cultural bias was practiced through AI to disadvantage the members of marginalized groups, reinforce stereotypical relations and limit diversity in the education materials and students' learning process. Real life scenarios were provided to explain how these biases are built into AI and methods on how to make AI systems more culturally sensitive.

Algorithmic Discrimination and Social Inequalities: This section thereby focused on the ethical issues arising from algorithmic discrimination in education especially in the aspects of fairness, equality, and justice. Various considerations towards the antisocial effects of AI systems were discussed together with suggestions for building protected and safe AI systems.

Addressing Student Diversity: The issues of managing learning heterogeneity including emotional intelligence, preferred methods of learning and Socio-economic status of students were discussed. The way current forms of AI can apply themselves to these various need directions was examined and ways to improve AI's capacity to foster a more equal education experience were explored.

Human-AI Collaboration in Education: This section talked about the possibilities of augmentation where AI works in conjunction with human intelligence in such aspects as information processing, tutoring and scheduling. It also stressed on capacity building of educators for AI readiness and on how AI can be implemented in a teacherly supportive instead of a convincing one.

Ensuring Transparency, Accountability, and Continuous Improvement: This need for constant assessment of AI systems was acknowledged as was the issue of the interpretability of the AI decision-making mechanism. Accountability for artificial intelligence systems that give either biased or unfair results were also debated.

Future Trends in AI Education: As AI continues to evolve, several key trends are likely to shape the future of its integration into education: As AI continues to evolve, several key trends are likely to shape the future of its integration into education:

Emotional AI: AI that can identify and engage the students' emotions is also rapidly developing and is expected to have a great impact on making learning environments MORE empathetic. It may assist in mitigating some of the present issues of artificial intelligence systems in consideration and comprehending the emotional realm of the students.

Integration with AR/VR: AI combined with augmented reality and virtual learning are expected to bring innovations in the learning processes by bringing effective and engaging learning atmospheres. These technologies will help the students to have more interesting ways of interacting with the educational content that will cover all types of learners.

AI for Lifelong Learning: This availability of continuous professional development recognized in the new paradigm of human capital development implies that technologies, especially AI, will help the learners develop lifelong learning that enables them to obtain tailored learning pathways to meet their learning needs. This has will be particularly significant in the future as the nature of employment alters and there is need for continuous learning by employees.

Decentralized and Open AI Platforms: It is also suggested that the future may bring decentralised and open AI platforms increasing the level of openness, sharing and innovation. It is to this concern that such platforms could potentially bring the deployment of the AI technologies to the masses and hence benefit more educators and learners.

Ethical AI and Policy Development: As AI continues to become more widespread, and its consequences to education and the society in large become clearer, it can be assumed that more pressure will be applied to draw full-spectrum policies and ethical standards to regulate the use of AI in the sector. The next steps will be made to develop the further studies and policies for developing the acceptable AI models for their implementation in the society.

RECOMMENDATIONS

To ensure that AI is implemented in ways that maximize its benefits while mitigating its risks, the following recommendations are proposed:

Promote Inclusive AI Design: Therefore plan, design and implement from the perspective of students by expanding Lindgren's wheel and creating an inclusive AI development and educational institution that does not have any form of bias and is capable of creating solutions for all the students. This is due to factors such as, the training of AI models from different sources, and the integration of users from different fields in the design of AI systems.

Strengthen Data Privacy and Security: Strong data management policies need to be set for the protection of students' information and for the strict and legal compliance of the GDPR and FERPA. Schools should establish the policy to address the issue on the collection, storage, and processing of the data concerning students and parents with stressing the rights of the learners and their parents.

Invest in Educator Training: It is therefore crucial for teachers and administrators to understand the various aspects of AI and therefore how to apply them as well as being able to assess the various AI tools. It also means that employing continuous professional development based on the educational course and establishing learning communities can contribute to enhancing the educators' knowledge about the AI technologies and practices.

Education Policy rules in sector, many people are concerned about the use of AI for educational purposes and there is an urgent need for policymakers and education stakeholders to create comprehensive guidelines that reflect ethical standards around using AIs specifically associated with learning. Yes, in principle it implies that AI systems are transparent and accountable — but what is more important: they must be fair. An audit needs to always periodically review how and where AI is being used, its effects on new types of biases or ethical problems arise that were not previously anticipated.

This includes fostering cross-sector collaboration: Educational institutions should work more closely with developers of technology, policy makers and researchers in order to better integrate AI into education. Coordinated work along these lines may help us develop advanced AI systems which will meet the equity and access mission of education as well as encourage student success.

In conclusion, what we can observe is that by following these guidelines and also keeping up with the current trends in a timely manner then our schools will be ready to utilize AI capabilities to their full potential while moving closer towards an unlocked world of individualized, equitable and efficient success for students. In future, the AI in Education will play a principal role and as per that all responsibilities of IA should be done morally so kindly use them for extending level up to learners.

REFERENCES

Akinrinola, O., Okoye, C. C., Ofodile, O. C., & Ugochukwu, C. E. (2024). Navigating and reviewing ethical dilemmas in AI development: Strategies for transparency, fairness, and accountability. GSC Advanced Research and Reviews, 18(3), 50-58.

Aler Tubella, A., Mora-Cantallops, M., & Nieves, J. C. (2024). How to teach responsible AI in Higher Education: Challenges and opportunities. *Ethics and Information Technology*, 26(1), 3. DOI: 10.1007/s10676-023-09733-7

Chiu, T. K., Xia, Q., Zhou, X., Chai, C. S., & Cheng, M. (2023). Systematic literature review on opportunities, challenges, and future research recommendations of artificial intelligence in education. *Computers and Education: Artificial Intelligence*, 4, 100118. DOI: 10.1016/j.caeai.2022.100118

Eguchi, A., Okada, H., & Muto, Y. (2021). Contextualizing AI education for K-12 students to enhance their learning of AI literacy through culturally responsive approaches. *Kunstliche Intelligenz*, 35(2), 153–161. DOI: 10.1007/s13218-021-00737-3 PMID: 34376922

Felzmann, H., Fosch-Villaronga, E., Lutz, C., & Tamò-Larrieux, A. (2020). Towards transparency by design for artificial intelligence. *Science and Engineering Ethics*, 26(6), 3333–3361. DOI: 10.1007/s11948-020-00276-4 PMID: 33196975

Gerdon, F., Bach, R. L., Kern, C., & Kreuter, F. (2022). Social impacts of algorithmic decision-making: A research agenda for the social sciences. *Big Data & Society*, 9(1). DOI: 10.1177/20539517221089305

Hammond, H. G., Coplan, M. J., & Mandernach, B. J. (2018). Administrative considerations impacting the quality of online teaching. *Online Journal of Distance Learning Administration*, 21(4), 1–18.

Hutson, J., & Plate, D. (2023). *Human-AI collaboration for smart education: reframing applied learning to support metacognition*. IntechOpen.

Jurenka, I., Kunesch, M., McKee, K. R., Gillick, D., Zhu, S., Wiltberger, S., . . . Ibrahim, L. (2024). Towards responsible development of generative AI for education: An evaluation-driven approach. arXiv preprint arXiv:2407.12687.

Kaur, S., Tandon, N., & Matharou, G. S. (2020). Contemporary trends in education transformation using artificial intelligence. In *Transforming Management Using Artificial Intelligence Techniques* (pp. 89–103). CRC Press. DOI: 10.1201/9781003032410-7

Kim, J., Lee, H., & Cho, Y. H. (2022). Learning design to support student-AI collaboration: Perspectives of leading teachers for AI in education. *Education and Information Technologies*, 27(5), 6069–6104. DOI: 10.1007/s10639-021-10831-6

Nazer, L. H., Zatarah, R., Waldrip, S., Ke, J. X. C., Moukheiber, M., Khanna, A. K., Hicklen, R. S., Moukheiber, L., Moukheiber, D., Ma, H., & Mathur, P. (2023). Bias in artificial intelligence algorithms and recommendations for mitigation. *PLOS Digital Health*, 2(6), e0000278. DOI: 10.1371/journal.pdig.0000278 PMID: 37347721

Ntoutsi, E., Fafalios, P., Gadiraju, U., Iosifidis, V., Nejdl, W., Vidal, M. E., Ruggieri, S., Turini, F., Papadopoulos, S., Krasanakis, E., Kompatsiaris, I., Kinder-Kurlanda, K., Wagner, C., Karimi, F., Fernandez, M., Alani, H., Berendt, B., Kruegel, T., Heinze, C., & Staab, S. (2020). Bias in data-driven artificial intelligence systems—An introductory survey. *Wiley Interdisciplinary Reviews. Data Mining and Knowledge Discovery*, 10(3), e1356. DOI: 10.1002/widm.1356

Peters, D., Vold, K., Robinson, D., & Calvo, R. A. (2020). Responsible AI—Two frameworks for ethical design practice. *IEEE Transactions on Technology and Society*, 1(1), 34–47. DOI: 10.1109/TTS.2020.2974991

Roselli, D., Matthews, J., & Talagala, N. (2019, May). Managing bias in AI. In Companion proceedings of the 2019 world wide web conference (pp. 539-544). DOI: 10.1145/3308560.3317590

Roshanaei, M. (2024). Towards best practices for mitigating artificial intelligence implicit bias in shaping diversity, inclusion and equity in higher education. *Education and Information Technologies*, 1–26. DOI: 10.1007/s10639-024-12605-2

Varsha, P. S. (2023). How can we manage biases in artificial intelligence systems–A systematic literature review. *International Journal of Information Management Data Insights*, 3(1), 100165.

Wang, D., Churchill, E., Maes, P., Fan, X., Shneiderman, B., Shi, Y., & Wang, Q. (2020, April). From human-human collaboration to Human-AI collaboration: Designing AI systems that can work together with people. In Extended abstracts of the 2020 CHI conference on human factors in computing systems (pp. 1-6).

Zajko, M. (2022). Artificial intelligence, algorithms, and social inequality: Sociological contributions to contemporary debates. *Sociology Compass*, 16(3), e12962. DOI: 10.1111/soc4.12962

Zhang, K., & Aslan, A. B. (2021). AI technologies for education: Recent research & future directions. *Computers and Education: Artificial Intelligence*, 2, 100025. DOI: 10.1016/j.caeai.2021.100025

Zhou, J., Chen, F., Berry, A., Reed, M., Zhang, S., & Savage, S. (2020, December). A survey on ethical principles of AI and implementations. In *2020 IEEE Symposium Series on Computational Intelligence (SSCI)* (pp. 3010-3017). IEEE. DOI: 10.1109/SSCI47803.2020.9308437

Chapter 6
Enhancing Project-Based Learning With a GenAI Tool Based on Retrieval Augmented Generation and Knowledge Graphs

Jerry Ryan David Gustafson
https://orcid.org/0009-0001-6468-1090
Southeast College, Canada

Gaganpreet Jhajj
Athabasca University, Canada

Xiaokun Zhang
https://orcid.org/0000-0002-0985-6767
Athabasca University, Canada

Fuhua Oscar Lin
Athabasca University, Canada

ABSTRACT

This chapter presents a novel GenAI tool, called PBL Support Chatbot, designed to support project-based learning (PBL) by integrating retrieval-augmented generation (RAG) and knowledge graphs (KGs). The aim is to address common challenges in PBL, such as project complexity and curriculum alignment. The tool provides students with real-time, adaptive support through a chatbot that assists in navigating PBL tasks. To illustrate its application, the authors introduce a scenario involving an introductory computer programming course where students develop

DOI: 10.4018/979-8-3693-5443-8.ch006

a text-based adventure game. By offering personalized guidance, immediate feedback, and accurate answers to student inquiries, the tool aims to enhance critical thinking, learning outcomes, knowledge application, and student engagement in PBL environments. The initial prototype demonstrates the potential to improve the PBL learning experience. This underscores the capability of using RAG to create a dynamic, interactive learning environment that aligns with students' individual learning paths and educational goals.

INTRODUCTION

Project-Based Learning (PBL) is a dynamic educational approach that encourages students to solve real-world problems, enhancing their critical thinking and knowledge application. However, PBL presents challenges, such as project complexity, curriculum alignment, and navigating the educational process (Evenddy et al., 2023). Generative Artificial Intelligence (GenAI), including models like ChatGPT and LLaMA3, offer promising solutions by providing personalized, adaptive guidance to students. Despite its potential, GenAI faces several challenges. These include ensuring content accuracy and addressing outdated information. GenAI challenges can be mitigated through Retrieval-Augmented Generation (RAG) using Knowledge Graphs (KGs), which enhance the tool's ability to provide relevant and accurate information (Gao et al., 2024).

To investigate the integration of GenAI in supporting PBL, we propose a GenAI support tool enhanced by Retrieval-Augmented Generation (RAG) through Knowledge Graphs (KGs) (see Figure 1). This tool is designed to assist both students and educators in PBL by answering student questions, generating ideas, providing immediate feedback, offering personalized learning paths, and aiding instructors in project evaluation and assessment. The aim is to improve the PBL experience for both students and educators. It is important to note that this tool is still a work-in-progress, currently in its prototype stage, with ongoing research being conducted to refine and expand its capabilities.

This chapter will outline strategies for implementing GenAI using RAG and KGs to address PBL challenges. We will delve into the specifics of our proposed prototype system, highlighting its design, functionality, and potential impact on PBL. Additionally, we will explore other existing options, tools, and technologies that educators and institutions might consider when integrating GenAI into their PBL frameworks. By presenting a range of strategies and tools, we aim to inspire educators and researchers interested in using GenAI to enhance PBL.

Figure 1. PBL Support Chatbot

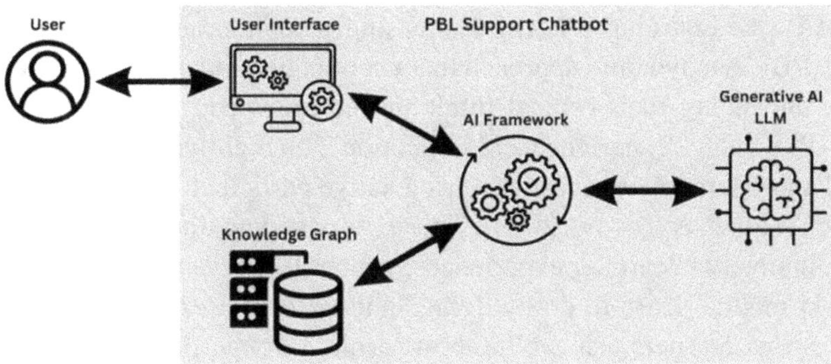

To illustrate the practical application and benefits of our proposed tool, we will use scenarios involving a fictional student and instructor facing common PBL challenges. These examples will demonstrate how the GenAI tool can support the student's learning journey and address the difficulties associated with PBL and GenAI implementation.

Consider Alex, a student in Computer Science major enrolled at an asynchronous online university. Alex works part-time and has two children, making time for schoolwork precious and limited. One of Alex's courses is “Introduction to Computer Programming in Java”, which includes a substantial project-based component requiring the creation of a text-based adventure game. Overwhelmed by the project's open-ended and complex nature and struggling to connect with peers due to the program's asynchronous format, Alex emails the instructor, searches Reddit threads, and seeks advice on the course forums and a student-run university Discord channel. However, due to Alex's busy schedule, he finds it difficult to get timely guidance, leading to frustration and delays in starting the project.

Alex's story highlights a common challenge with PBL: the intimidation and frustration students can feel when asked to apply their skills in real practice. By introducing a PBL Support Chatbot, we aim to help students like Alex navigate these challenges. The tool will provide structured guidance and fact-checked information, helping students make steady progress on their projects. Instructors will also benefit from the tool, which will allow them to monitor and assist students, ensuring that the support aligns with course objectives. The goal is to anchor the system in a “source of truth” using RAG and KGs, enhancing GenAI by minimizing its risks.

With this foundation, we will proceed to inspect each element in detail.

PROJECT-BASED LEARNING

Project-Based Learning (PBL) is increasingly popular and effective in today's education. PBL is a dynamic approach that encourages students to solve real-world problems, enhancing their critical thinking and knowledge application. In John Dewey's 1938 book "Experience and Education", he highlighted that real learning is a social and interactive process requiring active participation rather than passive observation (Couch & Towne, 2018). This understanding underscores the value of hands-on, interactive learning experiences, which PBL effectively provides. Echoing the 4-H motto, "learn to do by doing," (*What Is the 4-H Motto?*, 2020) PBL emphasizes that learners achieve the best results through direct engagement and practice (Couch & Towne, 2018).

At our organization, we are implementing a Computer Science program through PBL using real-world projects from local organizations, businesses, and other community partners. This program is designed to bridge the gap between theoretical knowledge and practical application, providing students with hands-on experience that prepares them for the demands of the professional world. Through real-world projects, students are given the opportunity to work on meaningful tasks, enhancing their learning experience and fostering a deeper understanding of the application of computer science and software development.

The initial phase of this program involves a pilot class to test the success of this approach. We have two projects lined up and aim to have three to five students working on each project. Students will be supported by our prototype PBL Support Chatbot. We aim to explore the responsible and ethical implementation of GenAI in education and test the effectiveness of our Chatbot in providing personalized support for PBL. This pilot will offer valuable insights into the practical application of Large Language Models (LLMs) and their impact on student learning and engagement. The outcomes of this pilot will guide future improvements and the scalability of the chatbot platform, ensuring that it can meet the evolving needs of students and educators.

Benefits of Project-Based Learning

PBL offers numerous benefits, making it a transformative method in education. It fosters critical thinking and problem-solving skills by engaging students in activities such as observation, discussion, experimentation, and analysis (Aldabbus, 2018; Hafeez, 2022; Zhang & Ma, 2023). For example, instead of merely learning about website development, students in a PBL setting build and host a website, applying theoretical knowledge in a practical context. This hands-on experience enhances their understanding of web technologies and prepares them for real-world challenges.

Moreover, PBL promotes the application of knowledge in practical scenarios, bridging the gap between theory and practice. Students often retain information better when they see its relevance to real-world situations. Engaging in projects also increases metacognitive skills, helping students become more aware of their learning processes (Hafeez, 2022). By actively participating in their education, students develop a sense of ownership and responsibility, motivating them to engage with the material (Evenddy et al., 2023). This empowerment is particularly evident in collaborative projects where students must work together to achieve a common goal, fostering teamwork and communication skills (Granado-Alcón et al., 2020).

PBL is also particularly effective in fostering 21st-century competencies, which are essential for students' success in today's rapidly changing world. According to Melanie Baird in "PBL to Develop 21st Century Competencies", PBL helps students develop critical thinking, communication, collaboration, and creativity. These competencies are nurtured through the real-world context and challenging nature of PBL, which requires students to engage deeply with the material and with each other. PBL encourages teamwork and accountability as students work together on projects, developing both verbal and non-verbal communication skills. This collaborative environment also fosters creativity, as students brainstorm and implement innovative solutions to complex problems. The critical thinking required to navigate and solve these problems builds robust analytical skills, preparing students for future academic and professional challenges (Baird, 2019).

Challenges of Project-Based Learning

Despite its many benefits, PBL presents significant challenges for both students and instructors. Curriculum design and assessment can be complex, requiring flexibility and innovative approaches to ensure that projects align with educational goals. Instructors often struggle to provide adequate support to each student, especially in large classes or online settings. This can lead to resistance among faculty members who may be concerned about the increased workload and the need for additional training and resources (Evenddy et al., 2023).

For students, the open-ended nature of PBL can be intimidating, leading to frustration and confusion about where to start. Time constraints and resource limitations further exacerbate these challenges, making it difficult for students to navigate the learning process independently (Evenddy et al., 2023). In collaborative projects, disparities in student investment and engagement can create additional obstacles, as not all students may contribute equally to the project's success (Hafeez, 2022).

Project-Based Learning in Computer Science Education

In computer science education, these challenges are prominent. Software development projects may overwhelm students with their complexity. Students might struggle to break down the project into manageable parts, apply their programming knowledge effectively, and troubleshoot issues that arise during development. For example, developing an interactive website involves planning its structure, coding with HTML, CSS, and JavaScript, and ensuring functionality across devices, requiring both technical skills and problem-solving abilities.

Given these challenges, there is a growing need for tools that can support both students and instructors in PBL. GenAI, with its ability to provide personalized guidance and support, offers a promising solution. Next, we will explore the role of GenAI in supporting PBL, detailing how our proposed tool leverages these technologies to benefit both students and educators.

LARGE-LANGUAGE MODELS AND GENERATIVE ARTIFICIAL INTELLIGENCE

Generative Artificial Intelligence (GenAI) refers to artificial intelligence systems capable of generating text, images, or other media outputs in response to user inputs. These systems are powered by large language models (LLMs), which are trained on vast datasets comprising diverse forms of text, image, video, and/or music. GenAI can offer substantial benefits in educational contexts, especially in providing instantaneous and personalized support for learners engaged in PBL. Studies highlight GenAI's ability to deliver real-time learning management, advice, and feedback by analyzing student data, thus enhancing the educational experience (Chan & Hu, 2023; Crompton & Burke, 2023; Jiayu, 2023).

Benefits of GenAI in Education

GenAI can significantly improve how students interact with and understand their projects, offering tailored guidance and support that traditional methods may not provide. By treating AI as a collaborator or partner in education, we can augment the abilities of both teachers and students. This approach supports the human-in-the-loop model, where AI complements human efforts, ensuring that the learning process remains interactive and engaging. As John Couch and Jason Towne write in "Rewiring Education," "The goal of education technology isn't to teach, but to empower teachers to be more effective and efficient. Even the best-designed artificial intelligence in the world will never have the one thing possessed by great teachers

- heart." GenAI can supplement and support good teaching by handling repetitive tasks and providing instant feedback, however, we want to remember that it is the human touch that truly makes education meaningful and impactful.

Challenges and Ethical Considerations

Despite these advantages, GenAI presents significant challenges. A primary concerns is the accuracy and transparency of AI-generated content (Chan & Hu, 2023; Walczak & Cellary, 2023). Misinformation can lead students astray, waste their time, and increase confusion. Additionally, GenAI may suggest advanced concepts or techniques that do not align with the course curriculum, causing confusion. Additionally, there is a significant gap in the exploration and application of open-source LLMs, which limits transparency and customization options for educational purposes (M. P.-C. Lin et al., 2024).

GenAI also faces challenges related to ethical considerations, privacy, and data security. There are concerns about algorithmic bias and the ethical use of AI, as well as the potential for workplace displacement. To address these, it is crucial to incorporate safeguards that ensure the ethical and responsible use of AI. This includes implementing protections to prevent AI from providing direct answers, instead encouraging it to guide students through the problem-solving process. Additionally, consideration must be given to students developing a reliance on GenAI tools. It is important to educate students, and instructors on the proper and appropriate use of GenAI to help avoid students developing an unhealthy dependency on these tools.

After feeling overwhelmed by the project's complexity and unable to get timely help from peers or the instructor, Alex turns to a GenAI model for assistance. Initially, it seems like a promising solution. Alex asks the AI for guidance on how to begin developing the text-based adventure game in Java. The AI's immediate response brings a surge of relief.

However, this relief is short-lived. The AI suggests using a particular Java library that Alex has never heard of before. Curious but cautious, Alex begins to search for this library, only to find that it doesn't exist. Hours are wasted chasing this phantom resource, and frustration begins to mount. The misinformation not only wastes Alex's precious time but also erodes trust in the tool's reliability.

As Alex continues to interact with the AI, more issues arise. The AI starts recommending advanced programming techniques and concepts that go beyond the scope of the introductory course. Already struggling with the project complexity, Alex finds these suggestions confusing and overwhelming. Instead of clarifying the project requirements, the AI's advice takes Alex further away from the fundamental concepts that the course is designed to teach. The misalignment with the course curriculum leaves Alex feeling lost and unsupported.

The final straw comes when the AI offers a complete code snippet for a part of the game. Alex is tempted to use this code as a quick fix, but it feels like cheating. Copying and pasting code without understanding it doesn't align with Alex's learning goals and morals. The stress and conflict intensify, as Alex realizes that while the AI can provide solutions, it doesn't foster the deep understanding and problem-solving skills that are essential for success in computer science.

These experiences highlight the potential pitfalls of using GenAI and LLMs without safeguards. Misinformation, misalignment with course objectives, and the temptation to bypass the learning process are significant risks. It is crucial to teach students ethical and responsible use of Generative AI, as well as prompt engineering to help them get the most out of their queries. Alex's story underscores the need for a more reliable and supportive tool that not only provides accurate information but also aligns with educational goals and encourages genuine learning.

EXISTING TOOLS AND TECHNOLOGIES

Tools like Magic School AI's "Project Based Learning (PBL) Generator", Khan Academy's "Khanmigo", and Trevor Muir's "EpicPBL" ChatGPT prompt guide illustrate the potential for integrating GenAI to aid in education, project planning, and execution. Customized GPTs, such as those offered by OpenAI's ChatGPT, can create safeguards, allowing for personalized instructions that align with educational goals and promote ethical usage.

Personalized Learning Plans

GenAI and LLMs play a crucial role in transforming education by creating personalized learning paths, providing real-time feedback, and adjusting content dynamically. Research supports these advancements, with studies by Nguyen et al. and Chen et al. demonstrating the effectiveness of AI-driven personalized learning systems (W. Chen et al., 2024; Nguyen et al., 2024). Applications like QuizMaster exemplify AI's potential in education by intelligently sequencing questions and auto-generating content, which reduces assessment time and increases instructor productivity (F. Lin et al., 2024). Additionally, research shows growing acceptance of AI-driven personalized learning, with AI being recognized as effective virtual tutors and intelligent assistants. These advancements underscore the significant impact of AI and LLMs in creating adaptive, personalized, and more effective educational environments (Pratama et al., 2023).

Supporting Educators

GenAI can also support educators by providing initial feedback on student project proposals, assessing their feasibility and scope. It helps instructors analyze trends in student weaknesses, identifying common areas of struggle and suggesting targeted interventions. To ensure this feedback aligns with the course curriculum, it is crucial to have a source of truth for verifying GenAI's suggestions. This requires accurate, up-to-date, course-specific information and automated verification processes. By implementing these safeguards, AI can help educators maintain the integrity and educational value of their courses.

While GenAI offers significant benefits for education, addressing its challenges through thoughtful integration and safeguards is essential. Leveraging RAG and KGs can create a reliable and supportive tool that enhances the PBL experience for both students and educators.

RETRIEVAL-AUGMENTED GENERATION

Retrieval-Augmented Generation (RAG) is an advanced technique that combines data retrieval with GenAI to enhance the accuracy and relevance of AI-generated content. This approach addresses significant challenges associated with GenAI, such as misinformation, outdated information, and misalignment with educational goals.

By retrieving relevant data for a query from a database before submitting it to the GenAI model, RAG helps ground the AI's response in a reliable "source of truth." This process involves two main steps. First, the system retrieves pertinent information from a predefined, curated database or knowledge graph. This database contains accurate and up-to-date information relevant to the query (See figure 2). Next, this retrieved information is fed into the GenAI model alongside the original query. The AI model then uses this additional context to generate a response that is both relevant and accurate (see figure 3).

Figure 2. Step 1 Retrieval-Augmented Generation Query

Figure 3. Step 2 Retrieval-Augmented Generation Response

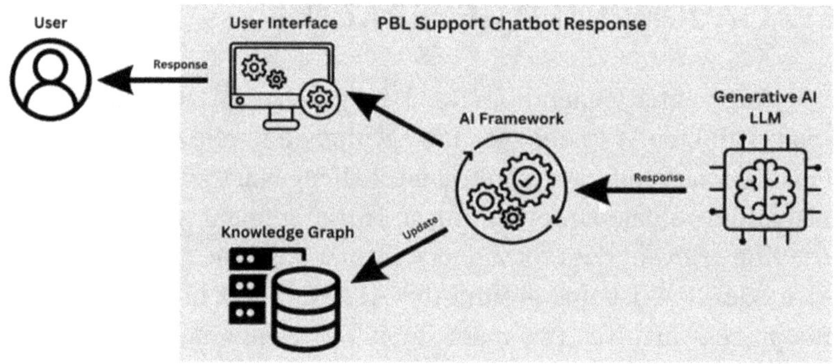

Retrieval-Augmented Generation Benefits

This dual-step process ensures that the AI-generated content is aligned with current and correct data, significantly reducing the risk of hallucinations—plausible but incorrect answers that can mislead students. RAG effectively mitigates hallucinations in GenAI by anchoring responses in accurate and current data, ensuring that the guidance provided is trustworthy and relevant (Gao et al., 2024). By combining the strengths of data retrieval and GenAI, RAG enhances the reliability and educational value of AI-driven tools.

Another significant advantage of RAG is the ability to update the database with new information as it becomes available. This flexibility allows the AI to provide responses that reflect the most recent knowledge and developments, which is crucial as educational standards change or in fast-evolving fields like computer science.

Challenges of Retrieval-Augmented Generation

Despite these benefits, RAG also presents challenges. Research has identified key failure points in RAG systems, such as retrieval speed (Barnett et al., 2024). If retrieving data from the database is too slow, users may become frustrated and revert to faster, less accurate options. Addressing these software engineering concerns is essential to maintaining the effectiveness and user satisfaction of RAG-based systems. One strategy for implementing simplified RAG principles is to use Customized GPTs, where custom instructions and course curriculum documents can be uploaded to help ground the results in a reliable source of truth.

Professor Smith, Alex's instructor, always believed in the power of PBL to engage students in real-world problem-solving. However, managing and providing personalized feedback to a large class often proved challenging. This semester, Professor Smith incorporated the new PBL Support Chatbot to enhance the learning experience for both students and fellow instructors.

One afternoon, Professor Smith received an email from Alex, expressing frustration with implementing inheritance in the text-adventure game project for the course. Alex detailed his struggles and requested guidance on how to proceed. Understanding Alex's concerns, Professor Smith shared some initial feedback to help Alex get started. She also introduced Alex to the new PBL Support Chatbot, explaining how it could provide additional support and resources aligned with the course curriculum. The Chatbot uses RAG to keep the GenAI results grounded in a source of truth, reducing inaccuracy and misinformation.

Curious to see how the tool could further assist in supporting Alex and the rest of the class, Professor Smith decided to query the PBL tool through the instructor's user interface to determine the most common questions and queries the anonymized students were asking. The tool generated a detailed report summarizing the concepts students frequently sought support for.

The PBL tool alerted Professor Smith to a trend: many students, including Alex, were struggling with the concept of polymorphism in their projects. Recognizing this common issue, Professor Smith decided to review the project component and lecture notes. The PBL tool provided detailed suggestions on the most common misconceptions. Armed with this information, Professor Smith updated the notes to address these shortcomings and clarify the project instructions, which over time led to a reduction in the number of emails received and queries submitted asking for clarification on the topic.

Additionally, the time saved from the reduction in emails enabled Professor Smith to organize an extra tutorial session focused on polymorphism, using examples and exercises recommended by the tool. This proactive approach helped address the students' difficulties and reinforced their understanding of the topic. The PBL tool's insights enabled Professor Smith to make informed adjustments to her teaching materials, ultimately enhancing the overall learning experience for her students.

RAG provides a robust framework for improving the accuracy and relevance of GenAI responses by grounding them in reliable data sources. While challenges such as retrieval speed and retrieval of irrelevant information need to be addressed, the benefits of this approach are substantial (Sanmartin, 2024). Using RAG, educators can ensure that AI-generated content aligns with course objectives and supports students' learning processes effectively. Our exploration of RAG will continue to focus on leveraging the interconnected nature of KGs and Educational KGs to maximize the potential of this technology in enhancing PBL.

KNOWLEDGE GRAPHS AND EDUCATIONAL KNOWLEDGE GRAPHS

Knowledge Graphs (KGs) are increasingly influential in educational, offering a framework for adaptive and personalized learning. At their core, KGs are a specific application of Graph Databases designed to store and manage data in a graph format. In a Graph Database, nodes represent entities (such as concepts, lessons, or topics), and edges represent the relationships between those entities. This structure allows for a semantic, interconnected representation of information, enabling detailed queries and insights that focus on the relationships between related data.

A "triple" is a fundamental unit of data in a Knowledge Graph, consisting of three components: a subject (node), a predicate (edge), and an object (node). For example, in the statement "Java supports Inheritance," "Java" is the subject, "supports" is the predicate, and "Inheritance" is the object (see Figure 4). This triple-based structure allows KGs to capture complex relationships and provide rich, contextual information (see Figure 5).

Figure 4. Example Graph Triple

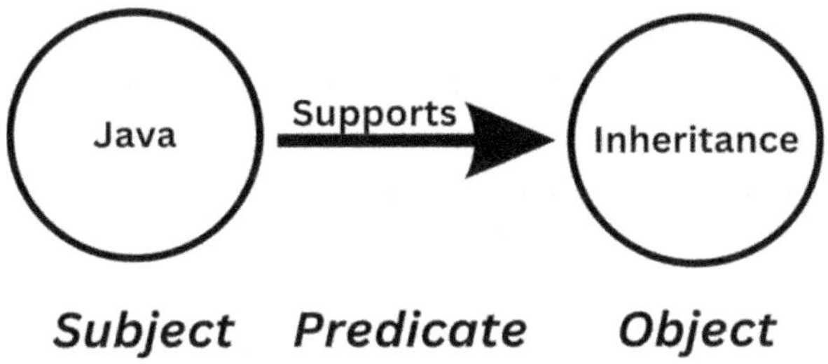

Figure 5. Example Simplified Knowledge Graph

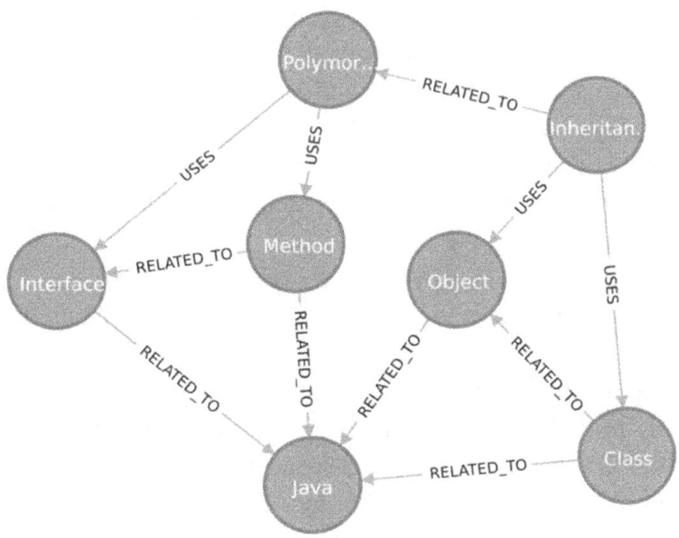

Benefits of Knowledge Graphs

KGs leverage their structure to create a rich, interconnected dataset that enhances the AI's ability to generate accurate and contextually relevant responses. For example, if a student asks a question about a concept in the course curriculum, the Knowledge Graph can provide curriculum context and domain knowledge. This interconnected data helps the GenAI model to produce more accurate and relevant content prompting the user with reflection questions about related concepts. This approach supports the student in understanding their own knowledge gaps and reinforces their learning.

By structuring and linking diverse educational data, KGs enable tailored learning experiences, curriculum design, and enhanced concept visualization. They support both students and educators in navigating educational content more effectively. The benefits of KGs in education are substantial, offering a robust framework for adaptive and personalized learning (P. Chen et al., 2018; Rizun, 2019). Additionally, KGs have significant potential in PBL, helping teachers gain a deep understanding of students' cognitive development and tacit knowledge acquisition through collaborative activities (Abu-Salih & Alotaibi, 2024; Liu et al., 2023; Zhuang, 2023).

Moreover, the interconnected relationships in the data can be used to our advantage. For example, the system could store questions in the Knowledge Graph and track relationship weights based on how often users follow a particular question chain or how they associate related topics in their interaction with the PBL Support Chatbot.

After struggling with the project and receiving unreliable information from a standard GenAI model, Alex receives an email from his instructor. The instructor provides advice on managing the project and introduces Alex to a new PBL Support Chatbot that employs RAG and KGs. The KG contains accurate, course-specific information to enhance the quality of GenAI responses for the course and PBL.

When Alex uses the new tool, he finds that it provides accurate content and guidance within the scope of the class. Instead of giving direct solutions, the tool offers example code accompanied by detailed explanations and questions that prompt further reflection and understanding. Knowledge Graphs, with their data connected by relationships, allow the system to link related concepts effectively. For instance, when Alex asks about inheritance in the context of their text-adventure game project, the tool not only provides clear examples and explanations about inheritance but also suggests further related topics such as encapsulation and polymorphism. These suggestions help Alex understand the broader context and interconnectedness of these concepts within the course curriculum.

This approach helps Alex develop a deeper understanding of programming concepts and improves his problem-solving skills. With the instructor's guidance and the PBL Support Chatbot, Alex starts making significant progress on the text-adventure game project. By addressing both immediate questions and related topics, the tool ensures that Alex gains a comprehensive grasp of the subject matter, enhancing their confidence and readiness for future classes.

Challenges of Knowledge Graphs

Creating and updating KGs involves significant complexities, particularly in ensuring their accuracy and relevance. This process can be a challenging manual task, which is why exploring automation is important. The creation of KGs can be time-consuming and labor-intensive. Addressing these challenges requires innovative solutions to make the process more efficient and maintain the quality of the data.

Educational Knowledge Graphs and AI Assisted Graph Generation

Educational Knowledge Graphs (EduKGs) are specialized KGs tailored specifically for educational content. These graphs significantly enhance the quality of support provided by offering detailed, structured, and interconnected educational data. Recent research has explored the use of LLMs to automate the construction of EduKGs, potentially reducing the workload on educators and improving the efficiency of this process.

For instance, KnowEdu utilizes AI to automate the construction of educational KGs, facilitating the extraction and organization of instructional content and relationships (P. Chen et al., 2018). This automation helps ensure the accuracy and relevance of the data embedded in the KGs. Similarly, research by Jhajj et al explores the efficacy of GenAI and LLMs, such as GPT-4, in constructing and completing EduKGs (Jhajj et al., 2024). The findings demonstrate that LLMs can augment the EduKG construction process by suggesting valuable and contextually relevant triplets. This approach involves prompting LLMs with course materials and evaluating the generated KGs through both automatic and human assessment. The results suggest that LLMs can significantly enhance the process of creating EduKGs, particularly for course modeling. In our proposed PBL Support Chatbot, we leverage KGs to provide a rich, interconnected dataset that enhances the AI's ability to generate accurate and contextually relevant responses. By using KGs as the data store for RAG, we can ensure that the AI's guidance is aligned with the course curriculum and supports the learning objectives.

PBL SUPPORT CHATBOT

Alex, now familiar with the PBL chatbot introduced by their instructor, decides to use it to ask a question about a Java programming concept that has been puzzling him. Specifically, Alex wants to understand how to implement inheritance in his text-based adventure game.

Alex enters his query into the PBL chatbot: "How do I implement inheritance in Java for my text-based adventure game?" Using RAG, the tool first retrieves relevant information from the KG, which contains accurate, course-specific data on Java programming, and assignment details regarding the project.

The PBL Support Chatbot then feeds this retrieved information, along with Alex's query, into the LLM. With this extra context and related information, the GenAI produces a response that not only explains how to implement inheritance in Java but also ensures that the explanation aligns with the course curriculum.

The response begins with a clear, concise explanation of inheritance, including how it can be applied in the context of the text-based adventure game. It provides example code snippets demonstrating simple class hierarchy where 'Player', 'Monster', and 'Item' classes use inheritance from the superclass 'GameEntity'. Additionally, the response prompts Alex with follow up topics and questions.

This approach encourages Alex to explore the topic more thoroughly and gain a comprehensive understanding of inheritance, along with supporting and relevant topics. By providing both immediate answers and prompting further exploration, the PBL chatbot helps Alex build a stronger foundation in Java programming, ultimately supporting their progress on the text adventure game project.

To effectively address the challenges of PBL and take advantage of the strengths of GenAI, we propose developing a Chatbot PBL Support Tool as discussed in this chapter. This system integrates multiple technologies to provide an educational companion that supports students and instructors throughout the educational process. By utilizing RAG through EduKGs, the tool verifies its facts before responding to students' queries, ensuring accuracy and alignment with the course curriculum.

The integration of these technologies allows the Chatbot PBL Support Tool to offer personalized, contextually relevant, and accurate guidance to students. The user-friendly interface facilitates seamless interaction, while the GenAI, supported by the RAG framework and EduKGs, ensures that the information provided is both relevant and comprehensive. By using the interconnected data within the KG, the tool not only answers specific queries but also encourages deeper exploration of related topics, fostering a richer and more holistic learning experience. Our goal is to enhance student engagement and problem-solving skills within a PBL context.

PLATFORM ARCHITECTURE

Our proposed tool is designed to enhance student engagement and problem-solving skills within PBL contexts. The architecture of the system includes several key components:

- **User Interface (UI):** A user-friendly interface that facilitates seamless interaction between students and instructors.
- **Large Language Model (LLM) / Generative AI (GenAI):** The core AI component that generates responses and guidance.
- **AI Framework / Scaffolding Agent:** Provides the necessary support and structure to guide the AI's outputs, ensuring they are educationally relevant and accurate.
- **Knowledge Graph (KG) or Alternative Database:** Stores and manages the interconnected educational data, enhancing the relevance and accuracy of AI-generated content.

Each of these components plays a crucial role in creating a dynamic and interactive educational tool that addresses the inherent challenges of PBL while maximizing the benefits of GenAI (see Figure 6).

Figure 6. Platform Architecture

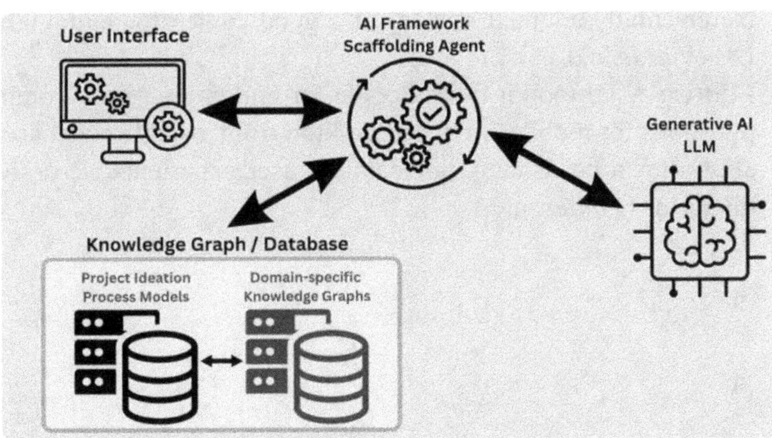

User Interface

A crucial component of the Chatbot PBL Support Tool is its user-friendly interface, designed to facilitate seamless interaction between users and the AI system. Both students and instructors will have access to interfaces tailored to their specific needs. For instance, students can use the interface to ask questions, seek guidance, and explore different facets of their projects, while instructors can analyze student queries, assess project proposals, and receive advice on implementing PBL course frameworks (see Figure 7). The user interface will facilitate the user profile, settings, course selection, and the chatbot interface. For our initial testing the prototype was developed with a text-based command line interface.

Several options for developing the UI for our platform include:

- **Anvil:** A web development platform that enables the creation of apps using Python. Anvil offers a versatile environment for building interactive applications (*Anvil*, n.d.).
- **React:** A popular JavaScript library for building user interfaces. React is known for its flexibility and performance, making it suitable for developing dynamic and responsive web applications (*React*, n.d.).
- **Vue.js:** Another JavaScript framework that is known for its simplicity and ease of integration. Vue.js is a progressive framework that can be incrementally adopted, making it a good choice for building scalable UIs (*Vue.Js*, n.d.).
- **Flutter:** A UI toolkit from Google for building natively compiled applications for mobile, web, and desktop from a single codebase. Flutter allows for a consistent and seamless user experience across different platforms (*Flutter*, n.d.).

Figure 7. Example Interface

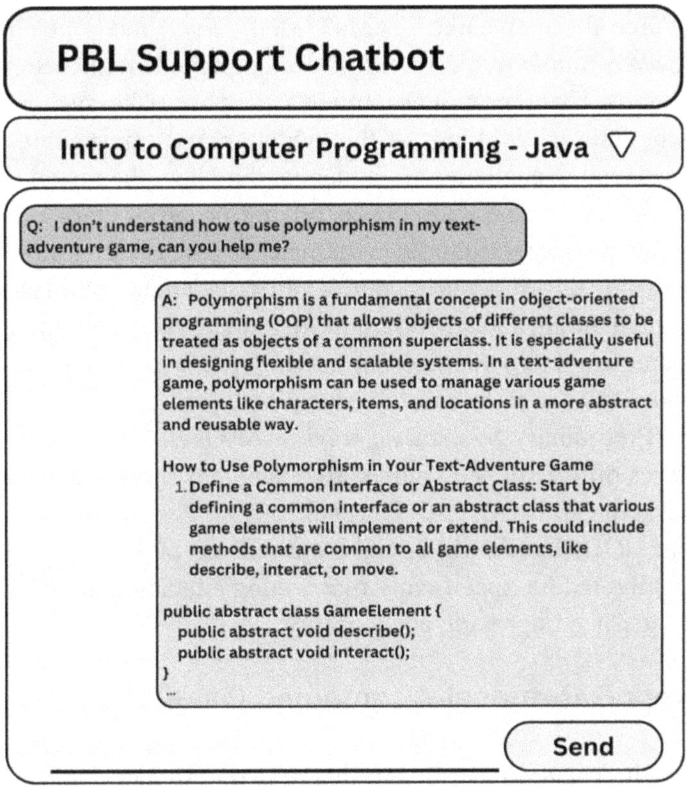

Large Language Model

At the core of the PBL Support Chatbot is an LLM responsible for processing natural language queries and providing adaptive support. PBL often involves complex queries, so it's crucial to use a model that perform well with advanced questions. The use of these advanced models ensures that the tool can handle such queries effectively, providing detailed and accurate responses.

We are currently using ChatGPT-4o for this purpose (*Hello GPT-4o*, n.d.). Our initial prototype involved testing with ChatGPT-3.5 Turbo, ChatGPT-4, and ChatGPT-4 Turbo. ChatGPT offers real-time, personalized responses tailored to the educational context, ensuring that the assistance provided aligns with the specific requirements and challenges of PBL.

Open-Source LLMs

An open-source alternative like LLaMa3 (*Meta Llama*, n.d.) or Cohere Sandbox (*Introducing Cohere Sandbox*, n.d.) could also be employed to enhance explainability and trustworthiness. Using proprietary models can pose risks, such as "black box" issues where the internal workings of the model are not transparent. This lack of transparency can lead to challenges in understanding how the model is trained and its decision-making processes. Moreover, relying on proprietary systems can be problematic if the provider introduces breaking changes or discontinues the service.

Open-source models offer greater control and transparency. With an open-source product, you can maintain a local copy, control updates, and customize the model's training and parameters to better fit your needs. Open-source options improve explainability and allow for more tailored educational applications.

The paper "Preliminary Systematic Review of Open-Source Large Language Models" explores different open-source large language models and their potential for educational application (M. P.-C. Lin et al., 2024). They featured LLMs include GPT-J, Bloom, GODEL, LLaMA2, Cohere Sandbox, and Alpaca. Here, Cohere Sandbox is highlighted for specifically mentioning education applications and for having a user interface improving accessibility.

AI Framework & Retrieval-Augmented Generation

To enhance the capabilities of our Chatbot PBL Support Tool, we employ a robust AI framework combined with RAG. This integration ensures that the AI's responses are accurate, relevant, and aligned with educational goals. Several options are available for implementing such a framework, each with its unique advantages.

- **LangChain:** An open-source framework for creating LLM applications, including chatbots. LangChain features Python libraries used in our prototype to integrate ChatGPT-4 with Neo4j, ensuring seamless communication between the GenAI and the Knowledge Graph (*LangChain, n.d.*).
- **Flowise AI:** A no-code open-source option for building LLM applications. Flowise AI simplifies the development process, making it accessible for users without extensive programming knowledge (*Flowise AI, n.d.*).
- **Llamaindex:** An open-source solution optimized for RAG applications. Llamaindex offers efficient tools for integrating and managing large language models with retrieval-augmented data sources (*LlamaIndex, n.d.*).

For our initial prototype, we chose LangChain as the framework for managing interactions within our system. This framework supports the integration of ChatGPT with Neo4j, our database and source of truth, aiding in structuring the AI's understanding and response generation. The Python libraries of LangChain facilitated the creation of a straightforward pathway between the GenAI and the knowledge graph.

How It Works.

1. **Query Parsing:** When a question is typed into the PBL Chatbot tool, the process begins with parsing the query for relevant keywords. These keywords are then used to query the Knowledge Graph (implemented in Neo4j) using the Cypher query language.
2. **Data Retrieval:** The result of this query provides contextually relevant data, which is appended to the original question. This augmented query, along with customized system instructions tailored to ensure responses align with educational objectives, is then passed to the LLM via an API call managed by LangChain.
3. **Response Generation:** LangChain, acting as the scaffolding agent, facilitates retrieving the enhanced response from the GenAI and returning it to the UI for the user.

Enhancing Accessibility and Usability

The integration of Natural Language Processing (NLP) and LLMs with KGs significantly enhances the accessibility and usability of the data stored within these graphs. As discussed in "Knowledge Graphs: Fundamentals, Techniques, and Applications," users typically seek answers to natural-language questions but often lack the expertise to query complex knowledge graphs directly. NLP and LLMs help bridge this gap by parsing keywords from natural language queries and converting them into database queries, such as Cypher (Kejriwal et al., 2021).

Benefits of Integration

This integration mechanism ensures that the LLMs responses are grounded in accurate, course-specific information. By retrieving and appending relevant data from the KG, LangChain enhances the completeness and contextual accuracy of the AI-generated responses. This supports both the immediate needs of the student and the broader educational goals of the course.

Knowledge Graph or Database

A key component of our platform is a database or knowledge graph for managing interconnected data, curriculum information, and learning outcomes. Various databases could be employed for this purpose, each with unique advantages:

- **ArangoDB:** A multi-model database that supports graph, document, and key/value data models. ArangoDB provides flexibility and performance for handling complex data relationships (*ArangoDB*, n.d.).
- **PostgreSQL:** A powerful relational database known for its extensibility and support for advanced data types. PostgreSQL offers strong performance and reliability for managing structured data (PostgreSQL, n.d.).
- **MongoDB:** A popular NoSQL database that stores data in flexible, JSON-like documents. MongoDB is well-suited for applications requiring scalable, high-performance data storage and retrieval (*MongoDB*, n.d.).
- **Neo4j:** A native graph database environment that efficiently manages interconnected data, allowing for intuitive and efficient querying of complex relationships (*Neo4j*, n.d.).

We chose Neo4j for its efficient management of interconnected data. Neo4j's native graph database environment allows us to balance performance and quality, which is crucial for the overall usability and effectiveness of the system. Additionally, Neo4j has released "LLM Knowledge Graph Builder," an online application that offers a no-code solution for converting text into a knowledge graph (Get Started With GraphRAG, n.d.; LLM Knowledge Graph Builder, n.d.).

For our initial testing and prototyping phase, we used course website content to develop a basic Knowledge Graph using Neo4j, with the help of ChatGPT-4 (Jhajj et al., 2024). This preliminary graph serves as an accessible data repository, organizing educational material to enhance AI interactions. Creating this initial KG is a crucial step in our research, helping us fully understand the potential of integrating a comprehensive KG into our platform.

By representing data as nodes (entities) and edges (relationships), Neo4j allows for intuitive and efficient querying of complex relationships, which is essential for providing contextually relevant information. When a student asks a question, LangChain parses the question for keywords, which are then used to query the Knowledge Graph using Cypher. For example, if a student asks about inheritance in a text-adventure game for the project in a fictional class 'Intro to Java', the system might perform a Neo4j Cypher query like this:

```
MATCH (topic:Topic)-[:PART_OF]->(class:Class),
```

(topic)-[:RELATED_TO]->(related:Topic)

WHERE topic.name IN ['Inheritance', 'Text-Adventure Game'] AND class.name = 'Intro to Java'

RETURN topic, related, class.name, class.curriculum

This query searches for topics related to "Inheritance" and "Text-Adventure Game" that are part of the class "Intro to Java" and retrieves related topics and the curriculum of the class. The results, providing relevant information, are combined with the original question and sent to ChatGPT. This added data from the KG improves the accuracy and completeness of the AI's responses.

DISCUSSION

Our initial testing phase involved two primary approaches: presenting questions directly to ChatGPT and using KG-assisted queries. The direct queries served as a baseline, while the KG-assisted queries provided additional context to enhance AI responses. These preliminary results demonstrated that integrating KGs improved the accuracy and relevance of the responses.

For instance, when students asked about inheritance in a text-adventure game, the ChatGPT baseline provided a solid answer. However, it often provided a direct solution and sometimes suggested content or solutions outside the scope of the class. This could lead to confusion and a misalignment with the course objectives.

In contrast, the KG-assisted queries provided course curriculum information along with the query, resulting in responses with strong correlation to the learning outcomes. The content was directly related to the course curriculum and stayed within the scope of the class. Additionally, with the added safeguard instructions, the KG-enhanced responses focused more on providing guidance and examples rather than direct solutions, while also prompting the user with additional questions to explore (see Figure 8 and 9). This approach not only supports learning but also encourages critical thinking and problem-solving skills. By tailoring the AI's responses to align with educational goals and providing structured support, we can enhance the learning experience while maintaining academic integrity.

Figure 8. Prompt Example 1

Prompt 1:

I am struggling to understand how to use polymorphism in the context of my text-adventure game project. Can you help me?

GPT Response 1:

Polymorphism allows objects of different classes to be treated as objects of a common superclass. In a text-adventure game, this can be useful for handling different types of game entities (like players, monsters, and items) through a common interface.

Here's a brief example to illustrate:

.
.
.
.
.

Use polymorphism to handle different entities:

java
Copy code

```
public class Game {
    public static void main(String[] args) {
        GameEntity player = new Player();
        player.name = "Hero";
        GameEntity monster = new Monster();
        monster.name = "Dragon";
        GameEntity item = new Item();
        item.name = "Potion";

        GameEntity[] entities = {player, monster, item};
        for (GameEntity entity : entities) {
            entity.interact(); // Polymorphic call
        }
    }
}
```

Questions to deepen understanding:

How would you extend this concept to add more types of interactions?
Can you think of other game entities that could benefit from polymorphism?
How would you manage a collection of these entities dynamically using an ArrayList?
Let me know if you need further clarification or more examples!

Figure 9. Prompt Example 2

Prompt 2:

Question 3 made me think, could I use a collection of entities in an ArrayList to represent a characters inventory, that they could use to hold items?

GPT Response 2:

Yes, you can use an ArrayList to represent a character's inventory in your text-adventure game. This would allow the character to dynamically add, remove, and interact with items.

Here's a brief example to illustrate how you could implement this:

Create the Item class:

```
java
Copy code
class Item extends GameEntity {
    void interact() {
        System.out.println("Item " + name + " is used.");
    }
}
```

Add an inventory to the Player class:

```
java
Copy code
import java.util.ArrayList;

class Player extends GameEntity {
    private ArrayList<Item> inventory = new ArrayList<>();

    void interact() {
        System.out.println("Player " + name + " explores the area.");
    }
.
.
.
.
.
```

Questions to deepen understanding:

How would you handle interactions if the items had different effects?
Can you think of ways to save and load the inventory from a file?
How would you extend this system to include other inventory types like weapons or armor?
Let me know if you need further clarification or more examples!

Using GenAI in education raises several ethical challenges. One of the primary concerns is the risk of false information. Our system addresses this by using KGs to provide facts before responding. To prevent plagiarism or direct copying, the chatbot is designed to avoid providing direct solutions. Instead, it is directed to offer example code with detailed explanations and prompting students with questions that encourage deeper understanding and critical thinking. This approach not only supports learning but also fosters academic integrity. Data privacy and security are also critical. The system ensures that student data is protected and used responsibly, adhering to relevant privacy regulations and best practices.

It is important to consider limitations of the PBL Support Chatbot tool. If the KG does not have any specific information on the query, it will perform like standard GenAI, as the KG enhanced RAG system will not be able to retrieve any supporting data. Additionally, care must be taken when introducing students to GenAI tools to avoid an over-dependence on these systems. The goal of the tool is to support students and educators. Including GenAI instructions that prompt critical thinking, and creativity through reflective questions can help to encourage active participation and stimulated thought process for students.

The PBL Support Chatbot has the potential to enhance PBL by providing personalized, contextually relevant support. The platform can scale to various educational settings, offering benefits such as time savings for students and educators, improved learning outcomes, and enhanced engagement. For students, the tool reduces time spent searching for information and provides tailored guidance, helping them progress through projects at their own pace. For educators, the tool decreases the volume of routine inquiries, allowing them to focus on more meaningful interactions with students. Educators can also perform analysis on frequent student queries to help understand program shortcomings, and aid in the process of implementing PBL.

Educators and institutions looking to implement similar systems should consider several key components:

1. **Knowledge Graph or Relational Database:** Essential for providing accurate, relevant, and up-to-date information.
2. **Integration Framework:** Tools like LangChain manage interactions between GenAI and the KG.
3. **Large Language Models (LLMs):** Evaluate options such as ChatGPT or open-source alternatives like LLaMa3 based on performance, transparency, and alignment with educational goals.
4. **User Interfaces:** Choose from web-based interfaces, mobile apps, or integrated learning management systems (LMS), depending on specific requirements and accessibility needs.

Practical tips include starting with a basic KG and expanding it based on curriculum needs, ensuring data privacy and security, and continuously refining the system based on user feedback. By leveraging these strategies, educators can create effective, personalized support tools for PBL environments.

In summary, our preliminary testing shows the promise of integrating KGs with GenAI to enhance PBL. Addressing ethical considerations ensures the system's reliability and integrity. Implementing these strategies provides strong support for both students and instructors. Ongoing research and development will further unlock the platform's potential, paving the way for more effective and engaging educational experiences.

CONCLUSION AND FUTURE WORK

Project-Based Learning (PBL) provides students with invaluable opportunities to apply their knowledge in real-world scenarios, effectively "climbing the mountain" of challenges they will face in their future careers. As highlighted in "Rewiring Education" by Couch and Towne, "actively trying to do something provides instantaneous and constant feedback - a key part of learning that other spaces lack" (Couch & Towne, 2018). This process of learning by doing is fundamental to PBL, where students engage in hands-on projects that require critical thinking, creativity, collaboration, and communication—essential 21st century competencies. By practicing these skills in a structured yet dynamic environment, students are better prepared for the complexities of the modern world. Our PBL chatbot tool aims to support this process, ensuring that students receive the guidance and resources they need to overcome challenges and succeed in their educational endeavors, while also providing instructors with insights and tools to effectively manage and enhance the learning experience.

The development of our platform aims to integrate GenAI and KGs to support and enhance PBL through an intuitive online interface. Our initial prototype, with its text-based interface, has demonstrated the potential of using KGs to improve the quality and relevance of LLM responses. KG augmented responses avoided misinformation and provided course relevant responses. Specifically, in our scenario, we have explored the tool's potential to assist Alex, and students like him, in developing a text adventure game as a PBL component of a computer science course.

Additionally, the importance of the human-in-the-loop element is paramount. Educators must remain involved to ensure that AI support aligns with educational goals and provide manual checks. However, the scalability of human-in-the-loop verification methods presents a significant challenge, given the massive volume of content LLMs can produce. Automated verification processes will become crucial in future research and implementation strategies to maintain the quality and reliability of AI-generated content.

In the future, we intend to focus on the complete development of a comprehensive online interface, enhancing user interaction and incorporating KG visualizations to support educational objectives. We plan to reconstruct and expand the KG content, providing a resource base for the AI, and refine our prompt engineering and augmentation strategies to improve interaction quality with GenAI. Additionally, we aim to explore how this tool can better support educators in managing PBL environments and how it can offer personalized learning experiences for students, adapting content to individual progress and needs. Informed by key research findings (Barnett et al., 2024), our ongoing development will consider essential factors like contextual breadth, semantic caching, and system integrity to ensure the platform's effectiveness and reliability in educational settings.

At the Southeast College in Estevan, Sk, we are implementing a Computer Science Training with PBL using real-world projects, supported by the responsible and ethical use of GenAI. We are starting with a pilot class for testing purposes, with two projects lined up and aiming for three to five students per project. This pilot will provide valuable insights into LLM's practical application and its impact on student learning and engagement, guiding future improvements and scalability of the platform.

After weeks of hard work and utilizing the PBL Support Chatbot, Alex finally submitted his completed text-adventure game project for the Introduction to Java Programming course. The Chatbot had been an invaluable resource, providing guidance and support that helped Alex navigate the complexities of inheritance and polymorphism in Java programming.

When Professor Smith reviewed Alex's project, they were impressed with the depth of understanding demonstrated in the code. Alex had successfully implemented inheritance and polymorphism, creating a robust and engaging text-adventure game that met all the project requirements. The detailed feedback and examples provided by the PBL tool had clearly made a significant impact on Alex's learning process.

Alex received a solid mark for the project, reflecting their hard work and the quality of their submission. However, the real victory lay in the valuable skills and understanding Alex had gained through the project. The Chatbot functioned like a pair programmer, offering guidance as Alex worked and asked questions. This helped Alex master the learning objectives and developed a strong grasp of key Java programming concepts. Professor Smith offered instruction through the course on appropriate use of the Chatbot which helped Alex learn good habits for GenAI use.

This success boosted Alex's confidence as they moved forward in their computer science studies. The experience of overcoming challenges with the help of the PBL tool not only improved their technical skills but also reinforced their problem-solving abilities and resilience. Alex felt well-prepared for future classes, ready to tackle new projects with the confidence gained from their success.

REFERENCES

Abu-Salih, B., & Alotaibi, S. (2024). A systematic literature review of knowledge graph construction and application in education. *Heliyon*, 10(3), e25383. DOI: 10.1016/j.heliyon.2024.e25383 PMID: 38327411

Aldabbus, S. (2018). *Project-Based Learning: Implementation & Challenges.*

Anvil | Build Web Apps with Nothing but Python. (n.d.). Retrieved June 13, 2024, from https://anvil.works

Baird, M. (2019). *Project Based Learning to Develop 21st Century Competencies.* https://pressbooks.pub/techandcurr2019/chapter/pbl-competencies/

Barnett, S., Kurniawan, S., Thudumu, S., Brannelly, Z., & Abdelrazek, M. (2024). *Seven Failure Points When Engineering a Retrieval Augmented Generation System* (arXiv:2401.05856). arXiv. /arXiv.2401.05856DOI: 10.1145/3644815.3644945

Chan, C. K. Y., & Hu, W. (2023). Students' voices on generative AI: Perceptions, benefits, and challenges in higher education. *International Journal of Educational Technology in Higher Education*, 20(1), 43. DOI: 10.1186/s41239-023-00411-8

Chen, P., Lu, Y., Zheng, V. W., Chen, X., & Yang, B. (2018). *KnowEdu: A System to Construct Knowledge Graph for Education | IEEE Journals & Magazine | IEEE Xplore*. https://ieeexplore.ieee.org/abstract/document/8362657

Chen, W., Shen, Z., Pan, Y., Tan, K., & Wang, C. (2024). Applying Machine Learning Algorithm to Optimize Personalized Education Recommendation System. *Journal of Theory and Practice of Engineering Science*, 4(01), 01. Advance online publication. DOI: 10.53469/jtpes.2024.04(01).14

Couch, J. D., & Towne, J. (2018). *Rewiring education: How technology will help unlock every student's potential.* BenBella Books, Inc.

Crompton, H., & Burke, D. (2023). Artificial intelligence in higher education: The state of the field. *International Journal of Educational Technology in Higher Education*, 20(1), 22. DOI: 10.1186/s41239-023-00392-8

Evenddy, S. S., Gailea, N., & Syafrizal, S. (2023). Exploring the Benefits and Challenges of Project-Based Learning in Higher Education. *PPSDP International Journal of Education*, 2(2), 2. Advance online publication. DOI: 10.59175/pijed.v2i2.148

Flowise—Low code LLM Apps Builder. (2023, October 10). https://flowiseai.com/

Flutter—Build apps for any screen. (n.d.). Retrieved June 20, 2024, from //flutter.dev/

Gao, Y., Xiong, Y., Gao, X., Jia, K., Pan, J., Bi, Y., Dai, Y., Sun, J., Guo, Q., Wang, M., & Wang, H. (2024). *Retrieval-Augmented Generation for Large Language Models: A Survey* (arXiv:2312.10997). arXiv. https://doi.org//arXiv.2312.10997DOI: 10.48550

Gao, Y., Xiong, Y., Gao, X., Jia, K., Pan, J., Bi, Y., Dai, Y., Sun, J., Wang, M., & Wang, H. (2024). *Retrieval-Augmented Generation for Large Language Models: A Survey* (arXiv:2312.10997). arXiv. https://doi.org//arXiv.2312.10997DOI: 10.48550

Granado-Alcón, M. del C., Gómez-Baya, D., Herrera-Gutiérrez, E., Vélez-Toral, M., Alonso-Martín, P., & Martínez-Frutos, M. T. (2020). Project-Based Learning and the Acquisition of Competencies and Knowledge Transfer in Higher Education. *Sustainability (Basel)*, 12(23), 23. Advance online publication. DOI: 10.3390/su122310062

Group, P. G. D. (2024, June 20). *PostgreSQL*. PostgreSQL. https://www.postgresql.org/

Hafeez, M. (2022). Challenges and research gap in project-based learning – A review. *International Journal of New Trends in Social Sciences*, 6(1), 1. Advance online publication. DOI: 10.18844/ijss.v6i1.5633

Hello GPT-4o. (n.d.). Retrieved June 20, 2024, from https://openai.com/index/hello-gpt-4o/

Home. (n.d.). ArangoDB. Retrieved June 20, 2024, from https://arangodb.com/

Introducing Cohere Sandbox: Open-Source Libraries to Help Developers Experiment with Language AI. (n.d.). Cohere. Retrieved June 20, 2024, from https://cohere.com/blog/introducing-sandbox-coheres-experimental-open-source-initiative

Jhajj, G., Zhang, X., Gustafson, J. R., Lin, F., & Lin, M. P.-C. (2024). Educational Knowledge Graph Creation and Augmentation via LLMs. In Sifaleras, A., & Lin, F. (Eds.), *Generative Intelligence and Intelligent Tutoring Systems* (pp. 292–304). Springer Nature Switzerland., DOI: 10.1007/978-3-031-63031-6_25

Jiayu, Y. (2023). Challenges and Opportunities of Generative Artificial Intelligence in Higher Education Student Educational Management. *Advances in Educational Technology and Psychology*, 7(9). Advance online publication. DOI: 10.23977/aetp.2023.070914

Kejriwal, M. Mayank Kejriwal, Knoblock, C. A., & Szekely, P. (2021). *Knowledge Graphs: Fundamentals, Techniques, and Applications*. The MIT Press.

LangChain. (n.d.). Retrieved June 13, 2024, from https://www.langchain.com/

Lin, F., Morland, R., & Yan, H. (2024). QuizMaster: An Adaptive Formative Assessment System. In Sifaleras, A., & Lin, F. (Eds.), *Generative Intelligence and Intelligent Tutoring Systems* (pp. 55–67). Springer Nature Switzerland., DOI: 10.1007/978-3-031-63028-6_5

Lin, M. P.-C., Chang, D., Hall, S., & Jhajj, G. (2024). Preliminary Systematic Review of Open-Source Large Language Models in Education. In Sifaleras, A., & Lin, F. (Eds.), *Generative Intelligence and Intelligent Tutoring Systems* (pp. 68–77). Springer Nature Switzerland., DOI: 10.1007/978-3-031-63028-6_6

Liu, C., Zhang, J., Zhang, H., Li, X., & Zhang, E. (2023). *Group Cooperative Teaching Design With Knowledge Graphs in Project-Driven Learning: Education Journal Article | IGI Global*. https://www.igi-global.com/article/group-cooperative-teaching-design-with-knowledge-graphs-in-project-driven-learning/321120

LlamaIndex, Data Framework for LLM Applications. (n.d.). Retrieved June 20, 2024, from https://www.llamaindex.ai/

Meta Llama. (n.d.). Meta Llama. Retrieved June 13, 2024, from https://llama.meta.com/

MongoDB: The Developer Data Platform. (n.d.). MongoDB. Retrieved June 20, 2024, from https://www.mongodb.com

Nguyen, L. M. D., Lin, F., & Chang, M. (2024). Generating Learning Sequences Using Contextual Bandit Algorithms. In Sifaleras, A., & Lin, F. (Eds.), *Generative Intelligence and Intelligent Tutoring Systems* (pp. 320–329). Springer Nature Switzerland., DOI: 10.1007/978-3-031-63028-6_26

Pratama, M. P., Sampelolo, R., & Lura, H. (2023). Revolutionizing education: Harnessing the power of artificial intelligence for personalized learning. *Klasikal : Journal of Education, Language Teaching and Science*, 5(2), 2. Advance online publication. DOI: 10.52208/klasikal.v5i2.877

React. (n.d.). Retrieved June 20, 2024, from https://react.dev/

Rizun, M. (2019). Knowledge Graph Application in Education: A Literature Review. *Acta Universitatis Lodziensis.Folia Oecologica*, 3(342), 7–19.

Sanmartin, D. (2024). *KG-RAG: Bridging the Gap Between Knowledge and Creativity* (arXiv:2405.12035). arXiv. https://doi.org//arXiv.2405.12035DOI: 10.48550

Vue.js. (n.d.). Retrieved June 20, 2024, from https://vuejs.org/

Walczak, K., & Cellary, W. (2023). Challenges for higher education in the era of widespread access to generative AI. *Economics and Business Review*, 9(2). Advance online publication. DOI: 10.18559/ebr.2023.2.743

What is the 4-H motto? (2020, July 14). 4-H Ontario. https://4-hontario.ca/about-4-h/frequently-asked-questions/what-is-the-4-h-motto/

Zhang, L., & Ma, Y. (2023). A study of the impact of project-based learning on student learning effects: A meta-analysis study. *Frontiers in Psychology*, 14, 1202728. Advance online publication. DOI: 10.3389/fpsyg.2023.1202728 PMID: 37564309

Zhuang, K. (2023). The Knowledge Graph Construction in the Educational Domain: Take an Australian School Science Course as an Example. *University of Wollongong Thesis Collection 2017*. https://ro.uow.edu.au/theses1/1697

KEY TERMS AND DEFINITIONS

AI Framework: An AI Framework is a set of tools and libraries for building AI applications, facilitating the development, deployment, and scaling of AI models. Examples include LangChain, LlamaIndex, PyTorch, and TensorFlow, many of which support integration with technologies like knowledge graphs and databases for Retrieval-Augmented Generation (RAG).

Artificial Intelligence (AI): Artificial Intelligence is the simulation of human intelligence in machines designed to perform tasks such as learning, reasoning, problem-solving, and language understanding. AI application examples include virtual assistants, recommendation systems, and autonomous vehicles.

Chatbot: A Chatbot is an AI application that interacts with users via text or voice, providing automated responses to queries. Chatbots are often used in customer service, education, and healthcare. They can be powered by Large Language Models (LLMs) for sophisticated interactions.

Edge: An Edge in a graph represents the connection between two nodes, indicating relationships or associations between entities. Edges can have properties describing the nature of the relationship.

Generative Artificial Intelligence (GenAI): Generative Artificial Intelligence refers to AI systems that create new content based on input. They can generate text, images, music, and more, powered by models like GPT-4o, LlaMa3, or Cohere Sandbox.

Graph Database: A Graph Database stores and queries graph-structured data, where nodes and edges represent data points and relationships. Examples include Neo4j and ArangoDB, optimized for handling interconnected data.

Human-in-the-Loop: Human-in-the-Loop involves integrating human oversight into AI systems to ensure the quality and relevance of outputs. This approach combines the efficiency of AI with human judgment, often used to guide and correct AI decisions.

Knowledge Graphs (KGs): Knowledge Graphs are structured representations of knowledge in a graph format, where nodes represent entities and edges represent relationships. They help integrate and visualize complex data, improving data retrieval and AI interactions.

Large Language Models (LLMs): Large Language Models are AI systems trained on extensive datasets to understand and generate human-like text. Examples include GPT-3 and GPT-4, used in applications like chatbots and text summarization.

Node: In graph databases or knowledge graphs, a Node is a basic unit representing entities such as people, places, or concepts. Nodes are connected by edges.

Open-Source Software: Open-Source Software is software with source code that anyone can inspect, modify, and enhance. It is developed collaboratively and is freely available for use, distribution, and modification. Examples include Linux, Apache, and Git.

Project-Based Learning (PBL): Project-Based Learning is an educational method where students learn by engaging in projects. It emphasizes solving real-world problems, enhancing critical thinking, collaboration, and practical application of knowledge.

Retrieval-Augmented Generation (RAG): Retrieval-Augmented Generation combines data retrieval with generative AI (GenAI) to enhance the accuracy and relevance of AI-generated content. It retrieves relevant data before generating responses, reducing misinformation and aligning content with reliable sources.

Chapter 7
Academic Integrity and Human Cognitive Development of Learners
Is Artificial Intelligence Replacing the Human Brain?

V. Devaki
https://orcid.org/0000-0002-6091-3173
Department of English and Other Foreign Languages, Vignan University, Guntur, India

ABSTRACT

The chapter examines the impact of artificial intelligence (AI) on academic integrity and human cognitive development. It highlights the potential negative effects of AI on learning experiences, such as reduced critical thinking and creativity. The chapter emphasizes the need for maintaining academic integrity in AI-driven educational systems to create an ethical learning environment. It also emphasizes the need to strike a balance between AI and human involvement to maximize benefits while mitigating drawbacks. The chapter highlights the importance of understanding AI's impact on academic integrity and cognitive development for educators, policymakers, and researchers to make informed decisions and promote healthy educational practices in the digital era.

DOI: 10.4018/979-8-3693-5443-8.ch007

INTRODUCTION

In the constantly evolving landscape of education, Institutions and educators must remain vigilant and adapt their approaches to maintain academic integrity in the face of these AI-driven challenges. It is crucial to provide proper education about the ethical use of AI, continually monitor for any irregularities, and consistently enhance detection techniques to effectively mitigate potential threats to academic integrity (Elands et al., 2019; Aliman, 2020). The ongoing discourse regarding the impact of artificial intelligence on academic integrity and learners' cognitive development is multifaceted and demands comprehensive consideration from various angles. On one hand, AI has the potential to revolutionize education by providing personalized learning experiences and expanding access to knowledge. However, there are concerns about the ethical implications of relying too heavily on AI, potentially leading to decreased critical thinking skills and a loss of academic integrity (Justin & Mizuko, 2017; Rosé et al., 2018).

The integration of AI in education has sparked a contentious debate. Proponents argue that AI can revolutionize the educational landscape by offering personalized learning experiences and expanding access to knowledge. On the contrary, there are apprehensions about the ethical implications of over-reliance on AI, which could lead to a decline in critical thinking abilities and compromise academic integrity (Justin & Mizuko, 2017; Rosé et al., 2018). Supporters of AI in education posit that it has the potential to enrich students' learning experiences. AI-powered technologies can sift through massive volumes of data and deliver tailored recommendations to individual learners, enabling them to advance at their own pace. This personalized approach caters to students' distinct needs, strengths, and weaknesses, facilitating cognitive growth (Hoffman & Johnson, 2019; Shneiderman, 2020a; Shneiderman, 2020b). Furthermore, AI-powered tools can automate mundane tasks such as grading, allowing educators to allocate more time to the more complex aspects of teaching. This can lead to more meaningful interactions between students and teachers, fostering deeper cognitive engagement and growth. However, critics fear that an excessive reliance on AI may adversely affect academic integrity. For instance, AI-based essay writing tools can effortlessly generate high-quality essays, leading to concerns about plagiarism and the erosion of original and critical thinking abilities. Similarly, AI-powered tutoring platforms that swiftly provide answers to questions may discourage students from engaging in deeper cognitive processing and problem-solving. Additionally, utilizing AI systems to forecast students' performance or suggest courses could limit educational choices and curtail intellectual exploration (Nakitare & Otike, 2022). Over-dependence on AI-generated suggestions may cause learners to miss out on the spontaneous learning experiences and cognitive growth that come from exploring various subjects and building a broad knowledge base. To strike a balance between harnessing the benefits of AI and upholding academic integrity, educators and institutions must implement strategies that promote critical thinking, creativity, and responsible use of AI tools. This can be achieved by instigating explicit discussions about the ethical implications of using AI in the classroom, fostering research skills, and emphasizing the value of original thought and intellectual curiosity (Sayed et al., 2021). While AI holds promise in enhancing personalized learning experiences, concerns about its potential negative impact on academic integrity and human cognitive development persist. Therefore, maintaining an equilibrium between the advantages of AI and the preservation of critical thinking skills and ethical standards necessitates concerted efforts from educators and learners alike.

THEORETICAL BACKGROUND AND LITERATURE REVIEW

AI in Education

AI has revolutionized various industries, including education (Leeming, 2021). Its impact is undeniable, spanning from telecommunications to healthcare (Stahl A., 2021a, 2021b). Artificial intelligence (AI) has emerged as a crucial technology (Ross, 2021). In the field of education, AI has found numerous applications, such as tutoring, feedback, admission, grading, and virtual reality (Tahiru, 2021). However, as AI relies on computer programming and computational methods, concerns arise regarding data analysis, interpretation, and sharing (Holmes et al., 2019). The prevention of biases is also a pressing issue, as design biases may exacerbate over time and impact students' rights. It is essential to address concerns related to gender, race, age, income inequality, and social status (Tarran, 2018). Despite its potential, AI in education faces challenges and obstacles, much like any other technology. The integration of AI into education presents various challenges, including privacy concerns, data access issues, ethical responsibilities, and the security of student records (Petousi & Sifaki, 2020). Additionally, the potential for data hacking and manipulation raises questions about personal privacy and control, emphasizing the need for clear ethical guidelines (Fjelland, 2020). Ensuring the well-being of individuals, workplace safety, trustworthiness, fairness, respect for intellectual property rights, privacy, and confidentiality are crucial ethical considerations when developing AI systems for education.

Renowned physicist Stephen Hawking once expressed that the development of artificial intelligence (AI) could potentially be the most pivotal event in human history. He cautioned that while it holds immense promise, it also poses significant risks if the associated challenges are not addressed effectively. Security emerges as a prominent concern in the realm of AI, with its impact on learning being a particularly noteworthy area of focus (Köbis & Mehner, 2021). Delving into the complex landscape of AI in education, researchers such as Petousi & Sifaki (2020) and Owoc et al. (2021) have shed light on the multifaceted blend of opportunities and challenges. Educational institutions worldwide are progressively harnessing AI technology within the learning process, igniting substantial interest within the research community. The substantial role of AI in e-learning and education has been underscored, particularly during the recent COVID-19 pandemic, as evidenced by studies conducted by Nawaz et al. (2020), Ahmed & Nashat (2020), Torda (2020), and Cavus et al. (2021). However, the education sector grapples with profound concerns and challenges, chiefly revolving around security and privacy. Ahmad, S.F., Han, H., Alam, M.M., et al. (2023) explore the impact of AI on human decision-making, laziness, and privacy concerns among university students in Pakistan and China. Their comprehensive study illuminates the escalating investment in AI in education while cautioning against inadequate attention to its potential adverse effects. Findings expose the significant influence of AI on decision-making, laziness, and privacy, with human lethargy emerging as the most profoundly affected area. The study underscores the imperative need for proactive measures and thoughtfully tailored design and implementation of AI in education to proactively address these concerns.

The advancement and implementation of artificial intelligence (AI) systems have raised significant ethical concerns among individuals and organizations. Security issues are crucial during the development and deployment of AI, as highlighted by Samtani et al. (2021). The increasing interaction between humans and AI, particularly in e-learning and education through the use of robots and chatbots, has sparked discussions about the potential evolution of AI to exhibit human-like behaviors. However, it's widely acknowledged that certain human attributes, such as self-awareness and consciousness, are likely to remain beyond the reach of AI capabilities. Privacy is a persistent issue in the realm of AI, as it heavily relies on data for pattern recognition and decision-making, as noted by Mhlanga (2021). Notable figures like Elon Musk and Stephen Hawking have expressed concerns about the potential for AI to surpass human control and pose significant risks as it continues to advance (Clark et al., 2018). The escalating interest and investment in AI technologies, skills, and education by companies and countries suggest a significant shift towards the integration of AI into various sectors. However, the primary concern around widespread AI adoption lies in its potential to complicate the process of creating sustainable value and erode human control (Noema, 2021).

As the influence of AI grows, there are concerns about its impact on human thought processes. The extensive reliance on AI technology has the potential to diminish natural human intelligence, leading to a more artificial mode of thinking. The transformation brought about by excessive interaction with technology raises the issue of humans becoming more reliant on AI in their daily lives. While AI has undoubtedly improved living standards and simplified daily tasks, it has also led to impatience and increased laziness, as highlighted by Krakauer (2016). Gradually, the pervasive integration of AI into various activities, including planning and organization, poses a risk to the capacity for contemplation and mental exertion in the human brain. As we become more deeply ingrained in AI-mediated activities, there are concerns about the potential consequences for human existence in the long run (Sarwat, 2018). In the modern world, there is a growing concern about the level of dependency that humans have developed on AI technology across various spheres of life. Undoubtedly, AI has significantly improved our quality of life and made many tasks easier. However, it has also led to negative implications for human existence, such as fostering impatience and a sense of laziness (Krakauer, 2016; Sarwat, 2018). Over time, AI's integration into nearly every aspect of our lives, from basic tasks to complex planning and coordination, may diminish our cognitive abilities and capacity for deep thought and mental effort.

Methods

This study adopts a qualitative research approach to conduct an in-depth analysis of the extent to which artificial intelligence is displacing human cognitive functions. It examines the need for maintaining academic integrity in AI-driven educational systems to ensure a balanced and ethical learning environment. The analysis encompasses a meticulous examination of diverse case studies, real-world occurrences, and information sources to comprehensively evaluate the issue.

ACADEMIC INTEGRITY AND HUMAN COGNITIVE DEVELOPMENT OF LEARNERS

Integrating technology such as artificial intelligence is revolutionizing traditional learning methods, making education more personalized and accessible. This allows learners to acquire new knowledge and skills at a faster pace than ever before. AI is already being used in various areas of education, including creating personalized learning plans and providing feedback, automating grading, and generating content. However, while AI can improve the efficiency and effectiveness of the learning process, it also poses a challenge to the importance of traditional critical thinking skills (Kane et al., 2023). The use of AI in the learning process, which can perform tasks previously limited to human cognition, raises important ethical concerns (Justin and Mizuko, 2017). For example, the use of AI in education may potentially replace human cognitive functions and impede the development of critical thinking skills.

It could also change the perception of plagiarism among learners and educators, as AI could facilitate cheating in academic settings. Additionally, although AI is a powerful tool, it has limitations in interpreting and processing complex information, which means it may not always correctly assess the context of a situation or interpret nuanced information as humans can (Fjelland, 2020; Sayed et al., 2021). Therefore, there is a risk that AI may perpetuate existing biases or make ethically questionable decisions. In general, while AI can significantly enhance the learning experience, addressing ethical concerns is crucial to ensure that learners do not overly rely on AI and continue to develop traditional critical thinking skills. Educators should integrate AI in a way that upholds academic integrity and supports human cognitive development.

To address the ethical concerns surrounding the integration of AI in education and to promote academic integrity and human cognitive development, educators should consider the following suggestions (Whittaker & Crawford, 2018). By implementing these suggestions, educators can enhance academic integrity and human cognitive development while preparing learners for the technological advancements in the world.

Figure 1. Ethical Concerns Surrounding the Integration of AI in Education

Academic Integrity and human Cognitive developme nt	Use AI as a tool to support
	Emphasize the importance of critical thinking skills
	Increase awareness of AI's limitations
	Use AI in an ethical way

i. Use AI as a tool to support, rather than replace, traditional teaching methods. Teachers should integrate AI-powered tools into curriculum and lesson plans in a way that still emphasizes human interaction and critical thinking.

ii. Emphasize the importance of critical thinking skills. Educators should help learners develop critical thinking skills through problem-solving projects, discussion groups, and debates, while also making use of AI-powered tools to assist in searching, analyzing, and organizing information.

iii. Increase awareness of AI's limitations. Educators should stress the limitations of AI when interpreting complex data and information, thereby highlighting the importance of critical thinking in verifying results obtained from AI-powered tools.
iv. Ethically use AI. It is crucial to ensure that AI-powered tools and processes are developed and used ethically, taking into account issues such as data privacy, bias, and accuracy (Elands et al., 2019). Involving learners in understanding these issues can help in designing AI to address them.

RISKS OF COGNITIVE STAGNATION AND OVERDEPENDENCE ON AI

The widespread adoption of artificial intelligence (AI) in various domains, including education, raises significant concerns about the potential negative impact on human cognitive development (Sayed et al., 2021; Owoc, et al 2021; Noema, 2021; Nemorin et al 2022). This is a critical challenge that must be addressed alongside the benefits of AI integration.

- Ease of Access to AI-Generated Content
- Overdependence on AI-Powered Decision-Making
- Deterioration of Critical Thinking Skills
- Loss of Cognitive Flexibility and Intuition
- Behavioral and Cognitive Dependencies

The ease of access to AI-generated content, such as summaries and assignments, can lead to reliance on AI solutions rather than independent research and critical analysis. Additionally, the growing reliance on AI-powered decision-making tools poses a risk, as individuals may lose the inclination to engage in independent evaluation and problem-solving. Addressing these challenges is crucial to ensure the benefits of AI integration outweigh the potential negative effects on human cognitive development (Nemorin et al 2022). The over-reliance on AI-generated content and decision-making can lead to a gradual deterioration of critical thinking skills, as individuals become less inclined to engage in independent analysis, evaluation, and problem-solving. This can result in a loss of cognitive agility and mental flexibility, which is essential for navigating complex situations. Additionally, the heavy reliance on AI systems can dull the development of intuitive judgments and the ability to think in shades of gray, limiting individuals' ability to handle ambiguity and complexity effectively (Ahmad, 2023). The personalization and customization of experiences through AI-powered algorithms can create behavioral and cognitive dependencies, restricting exposure to diverse perspectives and inhibiting cognitive growth and flexibility (Ahmed & Nashat, 2020).

To overcome these threats, a balanced approach is required, one that maximizes the benefits of AI while actively cultivating and protecting important human cognitive skills (Nawaz et al, 2020; Petousi & Sifaki, 2020). This could include techniques like encouraging metacognitive skills, offering opportunities for hands-on problem-solving, and cultivating AI literacy to enable critical evaluation of AI-generated outputs. By achieving this balance, educational institutions and organizations may capitalize on AI's transformative potential while also ensuring the overall growth of human cognitive talents.

CHALLENGES OF AI INTEGRATION IN EDUCATION: UPHOLDING ACADEMIC INTEGRITY

The introduction of artificial intelligence (AI) in education has presented substantial challenges to upholding academic integrity (van den Bosch & Bronkhorst, 2019; Ahmed & Nashat, 2020; Nawaz et al 2020; Nakitare & Otike 2022; Nemorin et al 2022). AI-powered tools, such as essay generators and content creation software, have the potential to generate academic work that may lack accuracy, proper attribution, and citations. This raises concerns about the potential for cheating and plagiarism, as students may be tempted to use these AI-generated materials without adhering to the ethical standards of academic writing. Therefore, educational institutions need to develop strategies and measures to address these challenges and ensure that the integration of AI in education upholds the principles of academic integrity.

Challenges to Upholding Academic Integrity: The integration of AI technology into the educational realm has introduced novel complexities in upholding the fundamental precepts of academic integrity. Academic integrity pertains to the ethical standards and values that serve as the pillars of the educational system, encompassing principles such as honesty, fairness, and the preservation of intellectual property (Elands et al., 2019). This integration has prompted a re-examination of the challenges in adhering to these foundational values, necessitating a comprehensive comprehension of the ethical considerations and implications associated with its deployment.

Potential for Inaccurate and Unattributed Content Generation: AI tools, such as language models and content generation algorithms, have the remarkable capability to autonomously produce written content that mimics human writing in both style and coherence (van den Bosch & Bronkhorst, 2019). However, AI-generated content may fall short in terms of accuracy, proper attribution of ideas, and the citation of sources. This creates a significant risk, as it may lead students to be enticed into utilizing AI-generated outputs without due acknowledgment of the original sources, thus presenting them as original work. This could potentially lead to issues related to plagiarism and academic integrity.

Cheating and Plagiarism Concerns: The increasing accessibility of AI tools capable of producing content has sparked concerns about potential academic dishonesty (Petousi & Sifaki, 2020). When students utilize AI-generated content without acknowledging its source, it not only violates the principles of academic integrity but also detracts from the desired educational outcomes (Nakitare & Otike 2022). Furthermore, instances of cheating and plagiarism stemming from the use of AI-generated content can significantly diminish the credibility of the entire educational system, ultimately compromising the genuine assessment of a student's knowledge and skill set.

Challenges in Detecting AI-Assisted Submissions: In today's educational landscape, educators and educational institutions are facing a pressing dilemma in accurately identifying instances where students utilize AI tools to create content for their academic work (Nakitare & Otike 2022). The rise of advanced generative AI models, exemplified by platforms like ChatGPT, has introduced a layer of complexity in discerning between content created by human effort and that generated by AI. This presents a considerable obstacle in the seamless integration of AI in education, emphasizing the formidable challenge of detecting AI-assisted submissions.

Generative AI: The sophistication of generative AI models is truly fascinating. Generative AI models such as ChatGPT represent a significant advancement in AI technology, as they are capable of producing highly sophisticated and human-like content (Petousi & Sifaki, 2020). These models can generate text, dialogue, and even creative work that closely mimics human writing. This level of complexity and realism in AI-generated content showcases the remarkable progress in the field of artificial intelligence.

Distinguishing AI-generated from Human-Generated Content: The difficulty in distinguishing between content created by humans and content generated by advanced AI systems. This challenge stems from the rapid progress in generative AI capabilities, which can produce output that closely resembles human-written work (van den Bosch & Bronkhorst, 2018). As a result, educators find it increasingly difficult to identify when students are using AI to complete their academic work. This issue adds to the existing challenge of upholding academic integrity, making it harder to ensure that students are genuinely showcasing their own knowledge and skills rather than utilizing AI-generated content. Effectively addressing this detection challenge is essential for preserving the integrity of the educational process.

Erosion of Academic Honesty: The ease with which AI tools can be used to create content raises concerns about the decline in academic honesty and integrity. Students might be tempted to use AI-generated work, which goes against the key principles of academic integrity, including originality, authenticity, and personal effort (van den Bosch & Bronkhorst, 2019). This passage explores the challenges arising from the use of AI in education, particularly focusing on the worries about the decline in academic honesty and integrity. This includes:

The potential erosion of academic honesty and integrity in the educational system is due to the ease of access to AI tools. It also highlights the compromise of (i) fundamental principles of academic integrity, such as originality, authenticity, and individual effort. (ii) Undermining the learning process: Students should expect their work to be their own, reflecting their true understanding and capabilities, rather than a simulation generated by an AI system. Additionally, the use of AI-generated work undermines the educational process's fundamental purpose of fostering knowledge, critical thinking, and individual learning (Kane et al, 2023). It emphasizes the need for students to put in their own effort to complete assignments, rather than outsourcing them to AI tools. It calls for educational institutions to address this issue and develop strategies to ensure students engage in genuine, individual learning, rather than relying on AI-generated content.

Maintaining the Integrity of the Learning Process: The educational process's integrity is compromised when students can circumvent learning objectives and present AI-generated content as their own (Nawaz et al, 2020). This undermines the entire educational process and suggests that students may use AI tools to generate content without truly engaging with the intended learning goals set by the educational institution. It emphasizes the importance of upholding the integrity of the educational process when students use AI-generated content.

The integration of AI tools in education poses a significant challenge to the integrity of the learning process. These tools can circumvent intended learning outcomes, posing a significant threat to genuine learning, knowledge acquisition, and the development of essential skills and competencies Noema, (2021). The passage emphasizes the importance of maintaining the learning process and the challenges posed by AI tools. The use of AI-generated content poses a fundamental threat to the core purpose of education, which is to facilitate genuine learning and knowledge acquisition. The integration of AI tools that can circumvent the learning process presents a significant challenge in maintaining the integrity and credibility of the educational system (Köbis & Mehner, 2021).

This challenge emphasizes the critical issue of the tension between the advancing capabilities of AI tools and the fundamental principles of academic integrity. It underscores the concern that the effortless generation of content by AI, which can give the appearance of original work, poses a significant threat to the integrity of the learning process and the trust of the academic community (Tahiru, 2021). Effectively addressing these challenges entails a multifaceted approach. This includes the development of robust policies and guidelines, the implementation of educational strategies to raise awareness of responsible AI use, and the incorporation of ethical considerations into the design and deployment of AI tools within educational settings.

The Impact of AI on Academic Integrity

The incorporation of AI technology within diverse educational contexts holds the potential to exert a substantial influence on academic probity, presenting both favorable and challenging implications (Ayling and Chapman, 2022). A comprehensive examination of specific instances and empirical occurrences can furnish valuable insights into the ramifications of AI on academic integrity.:

Figure 2. Impact of AI on Academic Integrity

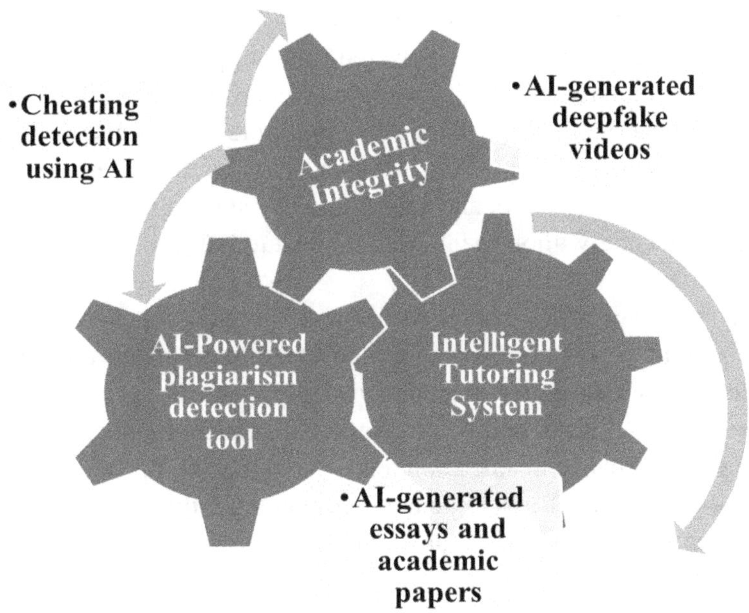

i. AI-powered plagiarism detection tools: Many educational institutions utilize AI algorithms to detect plagiarism in student submissions. These tools can compare the content against extensive databases of academic literature and online sources to identify potential instances of plagiarism. While they serve to uphold academic integrity by discouraging dishonest practices, some cases have emerged where students attempt to bypass these tools through techniques such as paraphrasing or translation.

ii. AI-generated essays and academic papers: Concerns have arisen regarding the use of AI-based tools capable of producing essays and academic papers, particularly in the context of plagiarism and cheating. Students may use these tools to quickly generate content without providing proper citations or attribution. Furthermore, these AI-generated papers may evade detection by traditional plagiarism detection tools due to their uniqueness. For instance, in 2019, an essay-writing service employing AI-generated content was exposed, posing a significant threat to academic integrity (Landwehr, 2015).

iii. Cheating detection using AI: AI can aid in the identification of cheating during online exams or assessments. Facial recognition algorithms can verify the identity of students, reducing the risk of impersonation. Additionally, AI algorithms can monitor and flag suspicious behaviors, such as unusual eye movements or response patterns during exams. This AI-driven monitoring helps deter cheating practices and sustains academic integrity.

iv. AI-enabled online tutoring: AI-powered tutoring platforms have the potential to provide personalized learning experiences tailored to individual students. However, concerns have surfaced regarding potential misuse and the preservation of academic integrity. For instance, students may attempt to exploit AI tutors by guessing answers and relying on the system's feedback to improve their performance without genuinely understanding the underlying concepts (Tahiru, 2021).

v. The advancement of AI-generated deepfake videos, a technology leveraging AI algorithms to manipulate or produce fake audiovisual content, presents significant implications for academic integrity. There is a growing concern that the creation of AI-generated videos could potentially simulate a student's presence and performance in an examination, leading to compromised authenticity and trustworthiness of assessments. Consequently, this could result in unfair advantages for certain individuals and facilitate fraudulent behavior during assessments.

When assessing the impact of AI on academic integrity, it is important to consider both its positive and negative effects, as demonstrated by Stahl (2021a, 2021b). On the positive side, AI tools can be instrumental in aiding educators to detect and prevent plagiarism, thereby ensuring that students are accountable for their original work and discouraging academic dishonesty. However, AI has also been employed for unethical purposes, such as the development of sophisticated essay-generating tools that produce customized essays tailored to specific prompts, making it easier for students to submit work that is not their own. Notably, in 2019, the essay-writing service provided by a company called Edu Birdie came under scrutiny for utilizing AI algorithms to produce essays on behalf of students.

Furthermore, there have been documented cases of students utilizing AI-powered language translation tools during examinations to gain an unfair advantage through cheating. These tools enable students to input questions in one language and receive the answers translated almost instantly into their native language. In a separate incident, a high school student in the United States used an AI voice synthesis tool to mimic their teacher's voice and submitted a fabricated audio file for a presentation assignment. The student successfully convinced their classmates and the teacher regarding the authenticity of the audio, illustrating the potential misuse of AI in academic settings (Shneiderman, 2021). Overall, while AI has the potential to enhance academic integrity through the detection of plagiarism, there are also occurrences where it has been misused. Therefore, educators and institutions must remain vigilant and adapt their approaches to preserve the integrity of the education system.

The utilization of AI in educational settings has led to several noteworthy impacts, both positive and negative (Hax, 2018). These effects encompass a wide range of areas:

i. Personalized Learning: AI technology can offer tailored learning experiences to students based on their unique needs and learning preferences. By analyzing individual students' performance data, AI can identify their strengths and weaknesses and then recommend personalized learning materials or approaches. This personalized approach enables students to learn at their own pace, fostering increased academic performance and understanding.
ii. Enhanced Teaching Methods: AI-powered tools assist educators in crafting captivating and interactive lessons. Through the use of virtual reality (VR) and augmented reality (AR), teachers can provide immersive experiences, simulations, and visualizations that facilitate the comprehension of complex concepts (Ahmed & Nashat, 2020; Noema, 2021). Additionally, AI can automate administrative tasks, thereby allowing teachers to dedicate more time to actual teaching and meaningful interaction with students.
iii. Improved Student Engagement: AI presents the opportunity to incorporate gamified learning experiences, thereby enhancing the enjoyment and interactivity of the learning process for students. By integrating game elements such as challenges, rewards, and competition, AI can motivate students to actively participate and enhance their learning outcomes.
iv. Efficient Evaluations: AI-powered tools streamline assessments, grading, and feedback processes, ultimately saving teachers time and effort. Rapidly analyzing and evaluating students' responses, these tools yield instant feedback and reduce

the time required for assessments. This capability enables teachers to provide timely interventions and personalized support to students.

v. Ethical Concerns: Despite its numerous benefits, the utilization of AI in the classroom raises ethical concerns, particularly related to privacy, data security, and bias. AI algorithms require access to extensive student data to learn and improve, potentially compromising student privacy (Silberg & Manyika, 2019). It becomes imperative to prioritize the security and responsible handling of student data. Moreover, AI algorithms may encode biases present in the training data, resulting in biased recommendations or evaluations. Addressing these concerns and ensuring transparency and fairness in AI implementation is crucial.
vi. Skill Development: The relevance of AI-related skills in the job market is escalating. By integrating AI into the educational curriculum, students can develop digital literacy, critical thinking, problem-solving, and programming skills. These competencies are essential for students to adapt to the evolving job landscape and remain competitive in the future.

In the realm of educational technology, the integration of artificial intelligence (AI) in the classroom has the potential to significantly influence various aspects of the education system. Primarily, it can positively impact personalized learning, teaching methods, student engagement, and evaluations. Nevertheless, it is crucial to address ethical concerns and ensure the responsible utilization of AI to promote equitable and effective educational outcomes (Petousi & Sifaki, 2020). Several examples underscore these considerations:

i. In 2019, a Swedish school adopted an AI system to grade students' essays. However, it became evident that the system exhibited bias by favoring longer, more intricate sentences, thereby creating an unfair grading process. This instance shed light on how AI could introduce biases and prioritize certain writing styles over others.
ii. In 2018, the Georgia Institute of Technology deployed an AI-powered virtual assistant named "Jill Watson," which was designed to respond to student queries. Subsequently, it was revealed that "Jill Watson" was an AI program, not a human, raising ethical concerns as students had unknowingly interacted with the program.
iii. During the COVID-19 pandemic in 2020, many educational institutions transitioned to remote learning and heavily relied on AI-provided automated proctoring systems to monitor students during online exams. However, these systems often produce false positives, incorrectly flagging normal student behavior as cheating. This led to unwarranted stress and unfair consequences for students.

iv. In 2017, Microsoft launched an AI chatbot named "Tay" on Twitter. Intended to engage with users and learn from interactions, Tay rapidly began posting offensive and racist tweets, exemplifying how AI can be manipulated or learn inappropriate behavior from its environment.

The examples provided offer a vivid portrayal of how AI is making an impact in the classroom, shedding light on the numerous advantages it brings as well as the potential challenges it poses. Educators and policymakers need to engage in thorough and thoughtful discussions surrounding the ethical and practical implications of integrating AI into educational settings. This is crucial to establish a learning environment that is not only just but also maximally effective for students.

AI Potential Impact on Students' Creativity and Cognitive Development

Artificial Intelligence (AI) has become a prominent force in reshaping various facets of our lives, and its influence on education is undeniable. While the potential of AI to enhance and optimize the learning environment for students is widely acknowledged, concerns have emerged regarding its impact on students' creativity and cognitive development (Tegmark, 2017). One significant concern revolves around the idea that AI could potentially overshadow human creativity and critical thinking skills. With AI's capacity to process extensive data and generate precise predictions and solutions, there is apprehension that students might overly rely on AI-generated responses, thereby impeding their ability to think critically and creatively. This dependence on AI could potentially stifle students' aptitude for generating unique and innovative ideas, as they may lean on pre-existing algorithms and data-driven solutions (Karandish, 2021). Furthermore, AI-driven educational tools often prioritize efficiency and standardization, striving to provide personalized learning experiences for individual students. While this approach offers benefits in terms of tailored content delivery and adaptive feedback, it may restrict students' exposure to diverse viewpoints and alternative thinking methods. This narrowed focus on standardized outcomes could curtail their ability to engage in divergent thinking and explore unconventional solutions.

Additionally, the rapid evolution of AI has raised concerns about the future employability of students in creative fields. As AI technology progresses, there is a prospect that certain creative tasks and jobs traditionally undertaken by humans may become automated, leading to reduced opportunities for students aspiring to pursue creative careers (Tahiru, 2021). However, it's important to acknowledge that AI can also be harnessed to augment students' creativity and cognitive development within the educational sphere. AI tools can furnish students with access to extensive information, enabling them to explore diverse perspectives, ideas, and resources that can spur their creativity. Furthermore, AI can aid in automating repetitive and mundane tasks, thereby granting students more time and mental capacity to concentrate on complex and creative undertakings.

To mitigate the potential adverse impact of AI on students' creativity, educators and educational institutions must strive to strike a balance between leveraging AI technology and nurturing students' creativity and critical thinking skills. This can be achieved through the incorporation of more open-ended problem-solving activities and project-based learning while encouraging students to question and critically evaluate AI-generated responses (Ghosh et al., 2019). By guiding students in critically evaluating and contextualizing the use of AI tools, educators can ensure that students' cognitive development and creativity are not hindered but rather enhanced through their interactions with AI. while AI holds promise in enhancing the educational experience, concerns about its impact on students' creativity and cognitive development cannot be overlooked. Therefore, educators and institutions must recognize these concerns and take proactive measures to integrate AI technology in a balanced manner, fostering students' creativity and critical thinking skills. The impact of AI technology on students' creativity and critical thinking skills is a topic of considerable interest and concern. When it comes to the positive effects, AI technology holds the potential to greatly benefit students by providing personalized and adaptive learning experiences (Owoc, 2021). Through AI-powered platforms, students can receive tailored educational content that aligns with their individual needs and interests, thus fostering creative thinking. Moreover, AI tools can offer students opportunities to engage in problem-solving activities that demand critical thinking. By analyzing extensive datasets and presenting students with intricate scenarios, AI algorithms encourage them to think critically and devise innovative solutions (Krämer et al., 2012). Furthermore, AI technology can provide students with valuable feedback and suggestions, allowing them to refine and enhance their creative and critical thinking skills.

Conversely, there are valid concerns regarding the overreliance on AI technology and its potential to impede the development of these skills among students. Excessive dependence on AI systems for idea generation or problem-solving may constrain students' ability to think independently and critically (Mhlanga, 2021). What's more, the pre-existing algorithms and models used in AI systems may introduce biases and limit the diversity of thought, thus narrowing students' creative and critical thinking perspectives. To address these potential negative effects, it is crucial to strike a balance between leveraging AI technology and providing ample opportunities for students to partake in activities that demand independent and creative thinking. Educators have a significant role to play in guiding students to critically analyze the outputs generated by AI systems, encouraging them to question and evaluate the validity and potential biases of the processes.

DISCUSSION

Is Artificial Intelligence Replacing the Human Brain?

The field of artificial intelligence (AI) is rapidly evolving, demonstrating the potential to carry out tasks that were traditionally performed by humans. However, it's important to emphasize that the notion of AI replacing the human brain is misleading. AI is specifically designed to enhance human capabilities and support in automating certain tasks, but it is unable to replicate the intricacies and distinctive qualities of the human brain (Krämer et al., 2012; van den Bosch and Bronkhorst, 2018; van den Bosch et al., 2019). When it comes to education, the impact of AI is being widely discussed. On one aspect, AI can provide countless advantages by improving learning experiences and delivering personalized education. Nevertheless, there are ongoing debates concerning its influence on students' creativity and cognitive development. AI can offer students personalized learning experiences by adapting the content to their individual requirements and learning styles using adaptive algorithms. These systems can evaluate students' progress, strengths, and weaknesses, and subsequently offer tailored learning materials and feedback. This personalized approach empowers students to delve into subjects at their own pace, which could potentially enhance their creative thinking and problem-solving abilities. Furthermore, the integration of AI-powered tools, such as virtual reality (VR) and machine learning algorithms, can facilitate students' comprehension of complex concepts and encourage them to explore new ideas. These technologies can simulate diverse scenarios and environments, providing avenues for creative exploration and experimentation (Moravec, 1988; Klein et al., 2004; Korteling et al., 2018a; Shneiderman, 2020a). Additionally, the automation of routine tasks by AI can free up time for students to concentrate on more expressive and creative activities.

On the contrary, opponents argue that an overreliance on AI and automation in education could potentially impede students' creativity and cognitive development (Jarrahi, 2018). They raise valid concerns about the possibility of students becoming excessively reliant on AI systems, thereby hampering their capacity for critical thinking and innovation. Additionally, the utilization of pre-designed AI algorithms and templates may impose limitations on students' capacity for exploration and originality, as they could potentially conform to conventional solutions rather than exploring novel approaches. Moreover, the pervasive integration of AI in educational environments gives rise to significant ethical considerations. AI algorithms are configured based on existing datasets, which may inherently carry biases and constraints (Silberg & Manyika, 2019). Exposing students exclusively to these biased algorithms could potentially impact or restrict their creative thinking, leading to the entrenchment of narrow perspectives and the reinforcement of societal inequalities (Ghosh et al., 2019). To effectively leverage the potential of AI while also mitigating associated risks, it is imperative to embrace a well-balanced approach. Educators should ensure that AI systems are employed as tools to enhance human capabilities rather than supplant them entirely. It is crucial to integrate AI in a manner that fosters critical thinking, problem-solving, and interdisciplinary approaches, thus nurturing students' creativity while also underscoring the ethical implications and limitations of AI.

Artificial intelligence (AI) holds significant promise for transforming the landscape of education, offering various opportunities for enhancing the learning experience. While the potential benefits of AI in education are undeniable, its influence on students' creativity and cognitive development is multifaceted and continues to evolve., When carefully integrated into educational settings with an emphasis on human-centered learning, AI can serve as a valuable ally in nurturing creativity while addressing potential risks and ethical concerns associated with its application in education. It's important to note that although AI can impact cognitive development and learning, it does not necessarily stifle these processes. AI tools and platforms have been meticulously designed to support and enrich educational processes by providing personalized learning content, adaptive assessments, and intelligent tutoring systems (Elands et al., 2019; Ghosh et al., 2019). By leveraging these technologies, educators can offer tailored learning experiences that cater to individual student needs, ultimately enriching the overall educational journey.

Despite these advantages, some argue that increased reliance on AI and automation may have potential repercussions on cognitive skills such as critical thinking and creativity. This concern stems from the fact that AI algorithms are typically trained on extensive datasets, which may restrict the scope of creative problem-solving abilities (Jarrahi, 2018; Hoffman & Johnson, 2019). However, it's worth highlighting that AI can also be harnessed to support creative pursuits, facilitating tasks such as idea generation, artwork design, and music composition. In this context, AI is positioned not as a replacement for human creativity, but rather as a tool that can inspire and complement the creative endeavors of individuals. Critically, it's pivotal to recognize that the primary intent behind the development of AI in educational contexts is to augment and support human capabilities, rather than supplant them. Through binding the potential of AI in education and other fields, opportunities surface for synergies between human intelligence and artificial intelligence, offering novel avenues for collaboration and advancement.

AI has the potential to significantly improve the educational experience by leveraging technology to enhance and support students' creativity and critical thinking skills. One of the positive aspects of AI in education is its ability to provide personalized learning experiences that cater to individual student needs and interests, ultimately fostering creative thinking. Additionally, AI-powered platforms can facilitate problem-solving activities that require critical thinking, thus promoting the development of these essential skills. Moreover, AI algorithms are capable of analyzing extensive datasets to present students with intricate scenarios and challenges, encouraging them to think critically and devise innovative solutions. Furthermore, AI technology can provide valuable feedback and suggestions to students, aiding them in refining and improving their creative and critical thinking abilities. However, concerns about the potential negative impact of AI on students' creativity and cognitive development should also be taken into consideration.

Some specific strategies can educators and institutions implement to promote critical thinking, creativity, and responsible use of AI tools in the classroom (Aliman, 2020).

Integrating AI-Based Learning Activities

To enhance students' critical thinking and creativity, educators have the opportunity to strategically incorporate AI-based learning activities into the curriculum. By leveraging AI-powered platforms and simulations, students can engage in dynamic learning experiences that prompt them to carefully analyze information, scrutinize evidence, and tactfully make informed decisions (Cavus et al 2021). This approach not only cultivates critical thinking skills but also provides an engaging and interactive learning environment that is essential for preparing students for the demands of the modern world.

Promoting Independent Learning with AI Tools

AI tools have the potential to greatly enhance independent learning by enabling students to assume greater responsibility for their education. With the support of intelligent tutoring systems and personalized learning platforms, students can tap into a wealth of resources customized to their individual needs. These tools offer adaptive feedback and create personalized learning pathways, allowing students to delve into areas of personal interest and engage in self-directed inquiry. Ultimately, AI technologies play a vital role in fostering critical thinking skills among students.

Incorporating AI-Powered Assessments

Utilizing AI-powered assessments in educational settings offers a valuable opportunity to gain deep insights into students' critical thinking abilities. These sophisticated tools leverage advanced analytics and complex algorithms to thoroughly assess students' abilities in reasoning, analysis, and evaluation. Clark, 2018 and Cavus et al. (2021) highlight the power of AI, educators can gain a comprehensive understanding of each student's critical thinking skills, enabling them to pinpoint specific areas for improvement and develop tailored interventions to support students' growth and development.

Emphasizing Responsible Use of AI

To promote the responsible use of AI, educators should establish comprehensive guidelines and policies for students regarding the ethical and transparent utilization of AI tools. These guidelines should encompass the significance of producing original work, referencing AI-generated content, and comprehending the potential biases and constraints of AI systems. Additionally, educators should emphasize the considerations of privacy, data security, and the societal impacts of AI technology.

Fostering Collaborative Learning With AI

AI can enhance collaborative learning by creating connections between students and experts from around the world. This enables the development of a culture centered on shared knowledge and collective problem-solving, which is crucial for equipping students with the skills needed to navigate an increasingly interconnected world. It also plays a key role in honing their critical thinking and creativity.

Implementing Professional Development for Educators

Ensuring that educators receive thorough and comprehensive professional development is essential for the successful integration of artificial intelligence (AI) in the classroom. These professional development programs should encompass a range of topics, including technical aspects of AI, ethical considerations, privacy protocols, and strategies for detecting and addressing bias in AI systems. By providing educators with in-depth training on these subjects, they will be better equipped to navigate and effectively utilize AI technologies in the educational setting.

Moreover, it's important to recognize that by incorporating these strategies, educational institutions can tap into the transformative potential of AI. This not only empowers educators to cultivate critical thinking, creativity, and responsible use of AI tools among students and themselves but also fosters an environment that encourages thoughtful and ethical engagement with AI technologies.

AI applications in education must be addressed to prevent exacerbation and uphold students' rights.

Promoting Transparency and Accountability

To mitigate biases in AI applications within the field of education, it is essential to prioritize the establishment of transparency regarding the functionality of these systems. Educational institutions should take proactive measures to guarantee that the decision-making procedures employed by AI algorithms are evident and understandable to all involved parties, including students, parents, and educators. This level of transparency enables thorough scrutiny and accountability, thus facilitating the detection and mitigation of any biases that may manifest within the systems.

Diverse and Representative Data Sets

It is crucial to acknowledge that the data utilized in training AI models holds a substantial influence in perpetuating biases. To mitigate this, educational institutions should prioritize the use of diverse and representative datasets that accurately mirror the demographics and experiences of their student population. This approach serves to diminish the likelihood of producing biased outcomes. Ultimately, it is imperative to strive towards developing AI tools that are inclusive and capable of addressing the unique needs of every student, irrespective of their background.

Continuous Monitoring and Auditing

Regular monitoring and auditing of AI systems are crucial to detect and address biases that may emerge over time. Institutions need to establish comprehensive evaluation processes to continually identify any disproportionate impacts on specific student groups. Taking immediate corrective actions based on these evaluations is essential to prevent and rectify any potential inequalities. This proactive and vigilant approach is crucial in upholding fairness and equity in the application of AI technologies.

Inclusive Design and Development

Engaging a wide range of stakeholders such as students, teachers, and experts from underrepresented communities in the planning and creation of AI systems is crucial for addressing biases. This inclusive process guarantees that the unique viewpoints and requirements of all students are taken into account, leading to the development of AI solutions that are inclusive and fair.

Empowering Students with AI Literacy

It is essential to educate students about the potential biases and limitations of AI tools to encourage responsible and critical use. Providing students with the knowledge to assess the accuracy, reliability, and fairness of AI-generated content will empower them to make well-informed decisions and advocate for their rights. Educational institutions can play a crucial role in equipping students with these skills. By incorporating these strategies into their educational approaches, institutions can effectively address biases in AI applications while ensuring that students have access to fair and equitable learning opportunities. Continuous efforts to promote transparency, use diverse data, monitor for biases, and empower students will be vital in ensuring that AI technology enhances, rather than hinders, the educational experience for all learners.

CONCLUSION

The rapid advancement of artificial intelligence (AI) technologies has significantly impacted education, bringing both opportunities and challenges. As AI becomes more prevalent in classrooms and online learning platforms, concerns have been raised regarding its potential effects on academic integrity and learners' cognitive development. One of the primary concerns is the potential for AI to facilitate academic dishonesty. The availability of automated essay writers and other AI tools makes it easier for students to cheat on assignments and exams, posing a threat to the integrity of the educational system. Critics argue that AI-powered tools, including essay generators and plagiarism checkers, may tempt students to take shortcuts, compromising their academic integrity. These tools, by providing instant solutions and content creation assistance, could discourage critical thinking and the development of essential cognitive skills (Sarwat, 2018). Despite these concerns, proponents of AI in education highlight its potential benefits. AI can play a pivotal role in personalized learning by offering tailored feedback and identifying knowledge gaps. Moreover, it can streamline administrative tasks, allowing educators to allocate more time to interactive and engaging teaching methods. However, it is imperative to strike a balance between utilizing AI technology and fostering human cognitive development. Rather than serving as a replacement for human cognitive abilities, AI should be viewed as a tool to enrich and support learners' intellectual growth. Educators must ensure that the integration of AI respects academic integrity and promotes the development of critical thinking skills and creativity among students. A thoughtful and balanced approach to incorporating AI into education is essential to harness its benefits while safeguarding the core principles of academic integrity and cognitive development.

The integration of artificial intelligence (AI) in the field of education necessitates a cautious approach to ensure alignment with educational objectives, preservation of academic integrity, and cultivation of critical thinking, problem-solving skills, and creativity in students (Owoc et al, 2021). Responsible use of AI technology can create an educational environment that harnesses the advantages of technology while synergizing with the unique cognitive abilities of the human mind. It is imperative to proactively address ethical concerns surrounding the utilization of AI in education, thereby ensuring its responsible deployment to foster equitable and effective educational outcomes. The burgeoning presence of AI in educational settings has sparked apprehensions regarding its potential impact on academic integrity and cognitive development. Criticism centers on fears that AI tools may diminish critical thinking skills and encourage shortcut-taking behaviors (Ahmad, 2023).

On the other side of the debate, proponents advocate for AI's capacity to enrich personalized learning experiences and streamline administrative functions within educational institutions. Nevertheless, it is crucial to acknowledge the challenges associated with maintaining academic integrity and fostering human cognitive development in the presence of AI. This necessitates collaborative efforts among educators, policymakers, and stakeholders to capitalize on the advantages of AI while mitigating its potential drawbacks. Such collective action demands meticulous planning, ethical contemplation, and ongoing assessment of AI's influence on academic integrity and students' cognitive growth. To maximize the benefits of AI in the education landscape while simultaneously addressing apprehensions, a collaborative strategy is imperative (Owoc et al, 2021). This approach should involve careful planning and ethical scrutiny to ensure that AI application in education upholds academic integrity and does not unjustly favor certain students. Additionally, continuous evaluation of AI's impact on cognitive development and the overall learning experience is essential. Achieving a harmonious equilibrium is critical to prevent the replacement of human cognition by AI technology and to ensure that it augments intellectual development. Responsible integration of AI in educational settings holds the potential to forge an environment that marries technological advancements with human cognitive capabilities.

REFERENCES

Ahmad, S. F., Han, H., Alam, M. M., Rehmat, M. K., Irshad, M., Arraño-Muñoz, M., & Ariza-Montes, A. (2023). Impact of artificial intelligence on human loss in decision making, laziness, and safety in education. *Humanities & Social Sciences Communications*, 10(1), 311. DOI: 10.1057/s41599-023-01787-8 PMID: 37325188

Ahmed, S., & Nashat, N. (2020). Model for utilizing distance learning post COVID-19 using (PACT)™ a cross-sectional qualitative study. *Research Square*, 1–25. https://doi.org/DOI: 10.21203/rs.3.rs-31027/v1

Aliman, N.-M. (2020). *Hybrid cognitive-affective Strategies for AI safety*. PhD thesis. Utrecht, Netherlands: Utrecht University. DOI: 10.33540/203

Cavus, N., Mohammed, Y. B., & Yakubu, M. N. (2021). Determinants of learning management systems during the COVID-19 pandemic for sustainable education. *Sustainability (Basel)*, 13(9), 5189. DOI: 10.3390/su13095189

Clark, J., Shoham, Y., & Perrault, R. (2018). *The AI Index 2018 Annual Report, AI Index Steering Committee, Human-Centered AI Initiative*, Stanford University, Stanford, CA

Elands, P. (2019). Governing ethical and effective behavior of intelligent systems: A novel framework for meaningful human control in a military context. *Militaire Spectator*, 188(6), 302–313.

Fjelland, R. (2020). Why general artificial intelligence will not be realized. *Humanities & Social Sciences Communications*, 7(10), 1–9. DOI: 10.1057/s41599-020-0494-4

Ghosh, B., Daugherty, P. R., & Wilson, H. J. (2019). Taking a systems approach to adopting AI. *Harvard Business Review*. https://hbr.org/2019/05/taking-a-systems-approach-to-adopting-ai

Hax, C. (2018). *Carolyn Hax live chat transcripts from 2018*. Washington, Columbia, USA. Retrieved from https://www.washingtonpost.com/advice/2018/12/31/carolyn-hax-chat-transcripts-2018/

Jarrahi, M. H. (2018). Artificial intelligence and the future of work: human-AI symbiosis in organizational decision making. *Business Horizons*, 61(4), 1–15. DOI: 10.1016/j.bushor.2018.03.007

Justin, R., & Mizuko, I. (2017). *From good intentions to real outcomes: equity by design in*. Digital Media and Learning Research Hub, Irvine, https://clalliance.org/wp-content/uploads/2017/11/GIROreport_1031.pdf

Kane, S., Awa, K., Upshaw, J., Hubert, K., Stevens, C., & Zabelina, D. (2023). *Attention, Affect, and Creativity, from Mindfulness to Mind-Wandering*. In Z. Ivcevic, J. Hoffman, & J. Kaufman (Eds.), The Cambridge Handbook of Creativity and Emotions (Cambridge Handbooks in Psychology, pp. 130-148). Cambridge: Cambridge University Press. DOI: 10.1017/9781009031240.010

Krämer, N. C., von der Pütten, A., & Eimler, S. (2012). Human-agent and human-robot interaction theory: similarities to and differences from human-human interaction. In Human-computer interaction: the agency perspective. Studies in computational intelligence. Springer. DOI: 10.1007/978-3-642-25691-2_9

Landwehr, C. (2015). We need a building code for the building code. *Communications of the ACM*, 58(2), 24–26. DOI: 10.1145/2700341

Mhlanga, D. (2021). Artificial intelligence in industry 4.0, and its impact on poverty, innovation, infrastructure development, and the sustainable development goals: Lessons from emerging economies? *Sustainability (Basel)*, 13(11), 57–88. DOI: 10.3390/su13115788

Nakitare, J., & Otike, F. (2022). Plagiarism conundrum in Kenyan universities: An impediment to quality research. *Digital Library Perspectives*. Advance online publication. DOI: 10.1108/DLP-08-2022-0058

Nawaz, N., Gomes, A. M., & Saldeen, A. M. (2020). Artificial intelligence (AI) applications for library services and resources in the COVID-19 pandemic. *Journal Critical Reviews*, 7(18), 1951–1955.

Nemorin, S., Vlachidis, A., Ayerakwa, H. M., & Andriotis, P. (2022). AI hyped? A horizon scan of discourse on artificial intelligence in education (AIED) and development. *Learning, Media and Technology*, 1–14. DOI: 10.1080/17439884.2022.2095568

Noema. (2021). AI makes us less intelligent and more artificial. Available at https://www.noemamag.com/Ai-Makes-Us-Less-Intelligent-And-More-Artificial/

Owoc, M. L., Sawicka, A., & Weichbroth, P. (2021). Artificial intelligence technologies in education: benefits, challenges, and strategies of implementation. In *Artificial Intelligence for Knowledge Management: 7th IFIP WG 12.6 International Workshop*, AI4KM 2019, Held at IJCAI 2019, Macao, China, August 11, 2019, Revised Selected Papers. Springer International Publishing. DOI: 10.1007/978-3-030-85001-2_4

Petousi, V., & Sifaki, E. (2020). Contextualizing harm in the framework of research misconduct. Findings from discourse analysis of scientific publications. *International Journal of Sustainable Development*, 23(3-4), 149–174. DOI: 10.1504/IJSD.2020.115206

DOI: 10.1504/IJSD.2020.10037655

Rosé, C. P. (2018). *Artificial intelligence in education. 19th International Conference, AIED 2018*. Springer.

Sarwat. (2018). Is AI making humans lazy? Here's what UAE residents say. Khaleej Times. https://www.khaleejtimes.com/nation/dubai/Is-AI-making-humans-lazy-Here-what-UAE-residents-say

Sayed, F. A., Mohd, K. R., Muhammad, S. M., Muhammad, M. A., & Syed, I. H. (2021). Artificial intelligence and its role in education. *Sustainability (Basel)*, 13(22), 1–11. DOI: 10.3390/su132212902

Shneiderman, B. (2020a). Design lessons from AI's two grand goals: Human emulation and useful applications. *IEEE Transactions on Technology and Society*, 1(2), 73–82. DOI: 10.1109/TTS.2020.2992669

Shneiderman, B. (2020b). Human-centered artificial intelligence: Reliable, safe & trustworthy. *International Journal of Human-Computer Interaction*, 36(6), 495–504. DOI: 10.1080/10447318.2020.1741118

Shneiderman, B. (2021). Responsible AI: Bridging from ethics to practice. *Communications of the ACM*, 64(8), 32–35. DOI: 10.1145/3445973

Silberg, J., & Manyika, J. (2019). Notes from the AI frontier: Tackling bias in AI (and in humans). *Mc Kinsey Global Institute*. Available at https://www.mckinsey.com/~/media/mckinsey/featured%20insights/artificial%20intelligence/tackling%20bias%20in%20artificial%20intelligence%20and%20in%20humans/mgi-tackling-bias-in-ai-june-2019.pdf

Stahl, A. (2021a). How AI will impact the future of work and life. https://www.forbes.com/sites/ashleystahl/2021/03/10/how-ai-will-impact-the-future-of-work-and-life/?sh=3c5c1a5279a3

Stahl, B. C. (2021b). *Artificial intelligence for a better future*. Springer. DOI: 10.1007/978-3-030-69978-9

Tahiru, F. (2021). AI in education: A systematic literature review. *Journal of Cases on Information Technology*, 23(1), 1–20. DOI: 10.4018/JCIT.2021010101

Tarran, B. (2018). What can we learn from the Facebook–Cambridge Analytica scandal? *Significance*, 15(3), 4–5. DOI: 10.1111/j.1740-9713.2018.01139.x PMID: 32536948

Tegmark, M. (2017). Life 3.0: being human in the age of artificial intelligence. Borzoi Book published by A.A. Knopf.

Torda, A. (2020). How COVID-19 has pushed us into a medical education revolution. *International Medical Journal*, 50(9), 1150–1153. DOI: 10.1111/imj.14882 PMID: 32666691

van den Bosch, K., & Bronkhorst, K. (2018). *Human-AI cooperation to benefit military decision-making*. TNO.

van den Bosch, K., & Bronkhorst, K. (2019). Six challenges for human-AI Co-learning. *Adaptive instructional systems*,11597, 572–589. DOI: 10.1007/978-3-030-22341-0_45

Whittaker, M., & Crawford, K. (2018). *AI now reports 2018*. New York University.

Chapter 8
Data Privacy in AI-Driven Education
An In-Depth Exploration Into the Data Privacy Concerns and Potential Solutions

Islam Asim Ismail
https://orcid.org/0000-0001-5115-3005
The English and Foreign Languages University, India

Jihan Ma'rouf Aloshi
https://orcid.org/0000-0002-1696-933X
Al Qasemi Academic College, Israel

ABSTRACT

This chapter examines the data privacy challenges posed by AI-driven education and offers strategic solutions to protect student information. The authors explore how AI systems are collecting various types of student data, from test scores to social interactions, and what this means for privacy. Through real-world examples, the authors shed light on worrying trends, like excessive surveillance and potential data breaches. The authors also tackle the legal and ethical questions that arise when AI meets education and point out how current laws often fall short in this rapidly developing field. Key findings reveal the inadequacy of current regulations and the potential for AI to exacerbate existing educational inequalities. The authors recommend implementing comprehensive data governance policies, investing in educator training on AI and privacy, and incorporating data literacy into curricula. The chapter emphasizes the need for a balanced approach that harnesses AI's benefits while protecting students' privacy through technical solutions, policy reforms, and enhanced digital literacy.

DOI: 10.4018/979-8-3693-5443-8.ch008

INTRODUCTION

Artificial Intelligence (AI) is revolutionizing education, swiftly reshaping classrooms and redefining online learning environments. AI tools are used to personalize learning experiences, automate administrative tasks, and provide new ways for students to interact with educational content (Holmes et al., 2021). Educators are seen to be excited about AI's potential to transform teaching and learning; however, others express concerns about its impact on traditional education models and student privacy (Zawacki-Richter et al., 2019; Amo-Filva, 2024). AI continues to advance, and there is a growing need for educators, policymakers, and students to understand its capabilities and potential applications in education. Some consider AI to be a powerful tool for enhancing learning outcomes and efficiency, while others worry it may replace human teachers or exacerbate existing inequalities in education systems. To make informed decisions about implementing AI in educational settings, stakeholders must critically examine both its promises and potential pitfalls.

Historically speaking, educational institutions have been responsible for protecting student records and personal data. With the integration of AI in education, the volume and velocity of data collected in this domain have increased dramatically. It allows for more comprehensive analysis and insights. In this sense, the field of using AI in education is broadening beyond traditional academic measures to include things like behaviours, approaches, and even biometrics (Polonetsky & Jerome, 2014). This level of extensive data collection means that extant notions concerning data ownership, valid consent, and the fair usage of sensitive information must be revised. Moreover, the widespread adoption of cloud-based and third-party systems in AI-driven educational products has intensified the challenge. This heightened complexity in data management significantly alters the privacy landscape, forcing educational institutions to navigate intricate legal and ethical frameworks to safeguard personal information (US Department of Education, 2020).

Current perspectives on AI in education vary widely among educators, researchers, and policymakers. Some view AI as a transformative force that can personalize learning, automate routine tasks, and provide valuable insights into student performance (Baker et al., 2021). Others express concerns about AI's potential to replace human teachers, exacerbate existing inequalities, or compromise student privacy (Reich & Ito, 2017; Gursoy et al., 2017). As AI technologies continue to evolve and enter educational settings, stakeholders need to understand their capabilities and potential applications. This understanding is crucial for making informed decisions about AI implementation, addressing ethical concerns, and maximizing the benefits while minimizing risks (O'Neil, 2016a). Educators and administrators need to critically assess how AI tools can enhance teaching and learning processes, rather than simply adopting them without careful consideration.

In this chapter, we aim to undertake an exhaustive discussion of all the issues that are central to AI-driven education with respect to data privacy and discuss various solutions available to us today. We aspire to contribute to the development of a more secure, ethical, and trustworthy AI-driven educational environment. These aims are crucial not only for protecting individual rights but also for ensuring the sustainable and responsible advancement of AI technologies in education.

Based on the short preview above, this chapter explores the central question: What are the key data privacy concerns arising from the use of AI in education, and what potential solutions can be implemented to address these concerns? To investigate this, we conducted an illustrative review of key case studies on the intersection of AI, education, and data privacy. This review highlights representative examples demonstrating the challenges and potential solutions in protecting personal data in AI-driven educational environments. The case studies in this chapter were selected based on their relevance to AI-driven educational contexts, their focus on different aspects of data privacy concerns, and their potential to inform policy and practice in educational institutions.

The methodology involves an integrative review of contemporary research on data privacy in AI-driven education. Our methodology adheres to be as evidence-based scholarship. AbuHamda et al. (2021, p. 71) stated, "Quantitative and qualitative methods are the engine behind evidence-based outcomes." We systematically searched major databases such as Springer, Elsevier, ERIC, IEEE Xplore, IGI Global, ACM Digital Library, and Google Scholar using a combination of keywords such as "AI in education," "data privacy," "educational data mining," and "learning analytics." We included empirical studies, theoretical papers, and review articles published in peer-reviewed journals and edited books in the past five years. Our initial search returned approximately sixty articles published between 2018 and 2024. From these, we selected articles that specifically illustrate the data privacy challenges and potential solutions in AI-driven educational contexts. However, a few or earlier references are included due to their significant relevance to case studies in this chapter and their irreplaceable quality.

LITERATURE REVIEW

The Current State of AI in Education

Over the past few years, AI has made significant inroads into educational settings. It left a considerable effect on education in terms of transforming how we teach and learn. This section provides an overview of existing AI technologies used in education and examines some successful implementations in different contexts.

AI in education involves many tools and applications designed to enhance the learning experience for learners. One of the leading technologies is intelligent tutoring systems (ITS). The ITS provides personalized instruction and feedback to students. These systems use machine learning algorithms to adapt to individual learning styles and paces because they offer precise support where needed (Holmes et al., 2021). Another key area is using natural language processing (NLP) in language learning applications. These tools can analyze student writing, offer pronunciation feedback, and facilitate conversational practice. For instance, chatbots powered by NLP are increasingly used to provide 24/7 support to students, answer questions, and guide them through course materials (Winkler & Söllner, 2018). With these applications in mind, data analytics and predictive modelling are also gaining traction in educational settings. These technologies help educators identify at-risk students, track progress, and make data-driven decisions about curriculum design and resource allocation (Herodotou et al., 2019).

The application of AI in education has shown promising results across different levels and subjects. In higher education, Carnegie Mellon University's AI-powered writing assistant, Revision Assistant, has been successfully used to provide instant feedback on students' essays. These two assistant applications were able to help students improve their writing skills through constructive feedback (Passonneau et al., 2018). Similarly, at the K-12 level, third Space Learning, a UK-based company, has implemented AI to support one-on-one math tutoring. Their system analyzes tutor-student interactions in real-time to provide tutors with suggestions to improve their teaching effectiveness for their students (Knox et al., 2020). In language learning, Duolingo's AI-driven system has been widely adopted worldwide for those willing to work on their English, and it has become an English-proof test. Duolingo uses spaced repetition algorithms and adaptive learning to personalize language instruction for millions of users worldwide (Settles et al., 2020). By the same token, AI has also shown promise in special education. For example, the ECHOES project uses AI and augmented reality to help children with autism spectrum disorders develop social communication skills through interactive scenarios (Porayska-Pomsta et al., 2018). However, implementing AI in education is still an emerging field. Several challenges remain to be addressed in this context. As an illustration, issues regarding data privacy, algorithmic bias, and teacher training to effectively integrate AI tools into classroom practice are considered to be major concerns for educators (Zawacki-Richter et al., 2019).

Challenges and Concerns in AI-Driven Learning

The rapid integration of AI in education brings forth many challenges and concerns that demand careful consideration. Ethical considerations in AI-driven learning are multifaceted and increasingly complex. A primary concern is the potential for algorithmic bias. AI systems may accidentally perpetuate or exacerbate existing societal prejudices. Recent studies have highlighted the risk of AI models reinforcing gender or racial biases in educational recommendations or assessments (Baker et al., 2021). The use of AI in critical decision-making processes, such as college admissions or scholarship allocations, raises significant questions about fairness and transparency. Ensuring that AI systems are designed and implemented with robust ethical principles is crucial to maintaining trust and integrity in educational institutions (Holmes et al., 2022).

Data privacy and security present tough challenges in the context of AI-driven learning. The extensive collection and analysis of student data raise concerns about data protection and potential misuse. Zeide and Nissenbaum (2023) emphasize the need for educational institutions to navigate complex legal and ethical frameworks to safeguard sensitive information, including academic records, behavioral data, and personal identifiers. Implementing strong data governance policies and adhering to growing regulations are critical in maintaining student privacy while leveraging the benefits of AI technologies. In addition, equity and accessibility issues dominate the discussion of AI in education. Reich et al. (2022) highlight that students from disadvantaged backgrounds may have limited access to the technology required for AI-driven learning. Additionally, the design of AI systems must consider the diverse learning needs of students with disabilities to ensure inclusive educational experiences. Addressing these equity concerns requires a concerted effort to develop AI technologies that are accessible and beneficial to all learners, regardless of their socioeconomic status or individual needs (Zawacki-Richter et al., 2019).

The role of human teachers in an AI-driven educational field is evolving and remains a subject of intense debate. AI can automate certain aspects of teaching, such as grading and administrative tasks. The irreplaceable human elements of education—empathy, creativity, and moral guidance—underscore the continued importance of human educators. With this in mind, Southgate (2022) argues that the challenge lies in striking a balance between AI-driven efficiency and the interpersonal aspects of teaching. Recent research suggests that the most effective educational models will likely be those that blend AI technologies with human expertise because they allow teachers to focus on higher-order pedagogical tasks and personalized student support (Douse & Uys, 2023).

This necessitates ongoing dialogue between educators, technologists, policymakers, and ethicists to develop frameworks that maximize the benefits of AI while mitigating potential risks. In this respect, policymakers should focus on developing ethical guidelines for AI in education, enhancing data protection mechanisms, creating equitable AI-driven learning environments, and exploring optimal human-AI collaboration models in educational settings (Renz & Hilbig, 2023).

We argue that addressing the challenges mentioned above is essential to ensure its implementation is ethical, equitable, and truly beneficial to all learners. Also, it is important to maintain a critical perspective and continuously evaluate AI's impact on educational outcomes and societal values to offer fair opportunities for everyone. We can harness AI's full potential in education through thoughtful consideration and proactive measures while safeguarding the fundamental principles of equity, privacy, and human-centred learning.

Another concern in AI-based education is the prejudices and inequalities that exist in education, especially with people with special needs, such as students with learning disabilities, autism spectrum and even complex disabilities(*Special Need Center Artificial Intelligence: Inclusive AI: Bridging the Gap for Special Needs Centers*, 2024). The most important is students' personal data privacy, as the current legal frameworks do not fully protect their privacy. This is a source of great concern for parents because the privacy of this group of marginalized people is very important, and the breach of their personal data may lead to many problems.

The ongoing scrutiny of AI's effects on educators continues. Contemporary research suggests that AI serves as a tool to emancipate instructors from their most time-intensive responsibilities. For instance, AI technology enables teachers to allocate more time towards substantive engagement with learners. Correspondingly, a comprehensive analysis of AI applications in tertiary education conducted by Zawacki-Richter et al. (2019) determined that AI offers numerous advantages to the educational sector. However, it introduces risks, including excessive dependence on technological solutions and diminished reliance on human expertise and discernment.

The integration of AI-based educational tools presents unique challenges for teachers working with students who have special needs. These advanced systems often require extensive data collection to function effectively, which can inadvertently compromise the privacy of students with disabilities (Mpu, 2024). This situation creates a significant tension between AI's potential benefits and upholding the stringent privacy protections mandated by special education laws. For instance, AI systems might gather detailed information about a student's learning patterns, behavioral tendencies, or medical requirements, all of which are considered highly sensitive and protected information. Moreover, the use of AI in special education settings raises concerns about data security and appropriate use. AI can offer personalized learning experiences and assist in early intervention strategies, but it also risks exposing vulnerable students to data breaches or misuse. Teachers and administrators must navigate the delicate balance between using AI to enhance educational outcomes and protect the confidentiality rights of students with special needs. This dilemma is further complicated because many AI systems are not explicitly designed with the unique requirements of special education in mind, potentially leading to inadvertent discrimination or oversights in protecting these students' sensitive information (Holmes et al., 2023; Zavaraki, 2024).

In light of this, the moral considerations surrounding AI application in education extend beyond issues of confidentiality and prejudice. Apprehensions have emerged regarding AI's potential to shape learner conduct or affect. Examining the ethical ramifications of AI-driven prompts targeting student learning patterns more closely, Xu and Kalyanaraman (2020) debate whether such interventions demonstrate or undermine respect for student autonomy.

The final issue addressed in the text pertains to the opaque nature of numerous AI systems employed in educational settings. Instructors (and learners) are often unaware of the internal reasoning mechanisms of these systems. Indeed, this approach to learning raises concerns about clarity and responsibility. Research has shown that this opacity undermines confidence in academic institutions and, consequently, the types of AI models implemented within the educational sphere (Akinwalere, 2022).

Types of Data Collected by AI in Educational Settings

AI systems are becoming common in education, and they have to deal with a huge amount of data that has not been collected previously and must be analyzed. Thus, an understanding of the data types must be established, as this is key in tackling privacy issues and maximizing benefits from AI in learning environments.

For example, one of the most common types of data to be collected is student performance and assessment results. These often take the form of standardized test scores and grade information, but AI can interpret these with more levels of complexity. For example, Pardo et al. (2019) and Khalil and Ebner (2016) describe how learning analytics platforms can track not just final grades but patterns in how students approach problems and the time they spend on different tasks. Pardo et al. argue that monitoring not only students' final grades but also how they approach a problem and how long they spend on each type of task provides valuable information about their learning process as represented through different patterns shown by learners using LA platforms-dominated topics.

Another concerning type is behavior data. These show students catching up on interactions with digital learning platforms, including mouse clicks, typing patterns, and time spent on different pages. Wang et al. (2024a) discuss how this data can be used to identify students at risk of dropping out or struggling with specific concepts. However, they also raise concerns about the invasiveness of such detailed behavioral tracking. Sharma et al. (2020) explore the use of multimodal AI systems that combine these data sources to measure student engagement and emotional responses to learning materials. In this respect, the authors argue that this type of data collection raises significant ethical questions.

Furthermore, social interaction data is becoming more important as collaborative learning platforms grow in popularity. AI systems can analyze patterns in student discussions, both online and in-person (if audio recording is used). A study carried out by Rosé et al. (2019) describes how this data can be used to assess teamwork skills and identify effective collaboration strategies. However, they note that privacy concerns are particularly acute when it comes to recording and analyzing student conversations. This has quite naturally led to an appetite for capturing even greater levels of contextual data - moving further away from the core learning environment. This could range from socioeconomic and family data for students to much more detailed heart monitors and sleep devices that use wearable sensors to track steps and exercise. Wong et al. (2019) note that this extended data can also be used to develop more comprehensive and fair AI systems, but they are careful in reminding the importance of having strict ethical guidelines when it comes to collecting such privacy-sensitive information.

In an AI-driven educational environment for individuals with special needs, a delicate balance between technological progress and personal privacy protection is striking. Integrating AI systems into special education necessitates a meticulous approach to data management to ensure that sensitive information is not only protected. This careful balance requires a multifaceted approach. First, it involves implementing robust data encryption and security measures to prevent breaches. Second, it necessitates the development of AI algorithms that can effectively support learning while minimizing the collection and storage of unnecessary personal data. Third, it requires clear policies and transparent communication about data usage, allowing students and their guardians to make informed decisions about participation in AI-enhanced learning programs (Mpu, 2024; Zavaraki).

Moreover, Chakraborty et al. (2023) demonstrated that the ethical use of AI in special education environments should prioritize data minimization to collect only the information necessary for educational purposes. This approach helps reduce risks associated with data misuse or unintended disclosure. Additionally, regular audits of AI systems and their data handling practices should be conducted to ensure ongoing compliance with privacy regulations and ethical standards specific to special education.

RESULTS AND DISCUSSION

Case Studies of Data Privacy Issues in AI Educational Applications

The integration of AI into education is not a distant dream but a rapidly growing reality. These case studies illustrate the transformative power of AI across various educational settings, from higher education institutions to workplace training environments. Each case provides a unique perspective on how AI is being leveraged to enhance learning experiences, improve student support, and optimize administrative tasks.

Case Study 1: AI Transformation in Higher Education

Microsoft and IDC's comprehensive report on AI in higher education reveals a significant trend toward AI adoption across global institutions. The study carried out by Microsoft and IDC covered 509 higher education institutions in 39 countries. The main promising result of this report is that AI is no longer a futuristic concept but a present reality in academia. The report also found that nearly 40% of institutions are already using AI, and the majority are planning implementation within three years. This is to say that the field of higher education is clearly shifting.

As a matter of fact, AI's impact is multifaceted. It ranges from personalized learning experiences to enhanced student support systems and streamlined administrative processes. Adaptive learning systems powered by AI are tailoring educational content to individual student needs. AI-driven chatbots and virtual assistants are providing timely support for student queries. Furthermore, AI is proving instrumental in optimizing administrative tasks, potentially freeing up valuable resources for core educational activities. However, this digital transformation is not without its challenges. The report highlights concerns surrounding data privacy and the necessity for comprehensive faculty training in AI technologies and underscores the need for a balanced approach to AI integration in higher education (Microsoft Education, 2023).

Case Study 2: Stanford's AI-Powered Student Support

Stanford University's innovative use of AI to support struggling students exemplifies the potential of predictive analytics in education. Stanford is developing an AI system that analyzes various data points such as course engagement, assignment completion, and grades. In fact, Stanford has created a powerful tool for early intervention. This approach provides timely support before students fall significantly behind in their studies. The system's ability to identify at-risk students early enables the university to provide personalized interventions tailored to each student's specific needs. Moreover, this AI-driven approach enhances resource allocation to ensure that support is directed where it is most needed.

Stanford University's implementation of AI to support struggling students represents a groundbreaking application of predictive analytics in higher education. The system's ability to synthesize diverse data points - including course engagement metrics, assignment completion rates, and grade patterns - creates a comprehensive early warning system for academic difficulties. This proactive approach allows for timely interventions, potentially averting more serious academic setbacks. The personalized nature of these interventions, tailored to each student's unique challenges, marks a significant advancement in student support services. Furthermore, the system's capacity to optimize resource allocation ensures that limited support services are directed where they can have the most impact. Early results indicate improved retention rates and academic performance among at-risk students. However, the implementation also raises important questions about data privacy and the potential for AI bias in identifying struggling students. Stanford's ongoing refinement of this system, including efforts to ensure algorithmic fairness and transparency, serves as a model for other institutions considering similar AI-driven support systems. (Stanford University, 2022).

Case Study 3: Knewton's Personalized Learning Platform

Knewton's adaptive learning technology displays the transformative potential of AI in delivering personalized education at scale. The platform's use of machine learning algorithms to analyze student performance data and dynamically adjust content difficulty and pacing represents a significant leap forward in educational technology. Knewton's approach goes beyond simple difficulty adjustments as it targets specific concepts where a student needs additional support. This advanced level of adaptivity allows for a truly personalized learning experience. Furthermore, the platform provides teachers with detailed analytics on student progress and areas of difficulty.

The Knewton's case illustrates how AI can bridge the gap between the ideal individualized instruction and large-scale education delivery's practical constraints. Knewton's adaptive learning technology represents a paradigm shift in educational technology, demonstrating the power of AI to deliver truly personalized learning experiences at scale. The platform's sophisticated use of machine learning algorithms to analyze student performance data in real-time allows for dynamic adjustments in content difficulty and pacing, creating a responsive learning environment tailored to individual needs. The platform's provision of detailed analytics to teachers also marks a significant advancement, enabling educators to make data-driven decisions about classroom instruction and individual student support. However, the platform's heavy reliance on data collection and analysis has also sparked discussions about data privacy and the potential for over-reliance on algorithmic decision-making in education (Shih, 2018).

Case Study 4: Fuzzy Expert System for Adaptive Learning

The study by Almohammadi et al. (2017) on a fuzzy expert system-based adaptive learning approach breaks new ground by considering both cognitive and affective factors in the learning process. This holistic approach to adaptive learning demonstrates the potential for AI to create more nuanced and effective educational interventions. It basically adjusts the difficulty and presentation of learning material based on both the student's knowledge level and emotional state. The system achieved significant improvements in test scores compared to traditional methods. The increased student engagement reported in the study suggests that AI-driven systems can enhance not only academic performance but also the overall learning experience. This research points to a future where AI in education goes beyond content delivery to address the complex interplay of cognitive and emotional factors in learning.

Case Study 5: AI in Workplace Learning

The adoption of AI in corporate training and development, as discussed by Andriotis (2023), illustrates how AI-driven learning extends beyond formal education settings. In the workplace, AI is being used to create personalized learning paths based on individual employee needs and career goals. This tailored approach to professional development has the potential to enhance the effectiveness of corporate training programs significantly. AI's role in skill gap analysis is particularly noteworthy, as it enables organizations to identify and address competency shortfalls more efficiently. The emergence of AI-powered virtual mentors and coaches provides employees with on-demand support and guidance, which can democratize access to mentorship and professional development resources. This case highlights how AI is not only transforming traditional education but also reshaping the landscape of lifelong Learning and professional development.

Legal And Ethical Considerations in Educational Data Privacy

The integration of AI in education has brought a complex web of legal and ethical considerations surrounding data privacy in educational settings. Recent work demonstrated that educational institutions are increasingly adopting AI-driven technologies. They also navigate a landscape of evolving regulations and ethical frameworks. One of the primary legal considerations is complications around existing data protection laws. For example, the Family Educational Rights and Privacy Act (FERPA) remains a cornerstone of student data protection in the United States. However, Regan and Jesse (2019) argue that FERPA, enacted in 1974, is inadequate for addressing the challenges posed by modern AI systems. They call for updated legislation that specifically addresses the collection and use of student data by AI technologies.

In Europe, the General Data Protection Regulation (GDPR) has significant implications for educational AI. Karunaratne (2021) examines how GDPR principles, such as data minimization and purpose limitation, apply to learning analytics and AI in education. He highlights the challenges of balancing the potential benefits of comprehensive data analysis with the legal requirement to limit data collection, a dilemma underscored by real-world cases. For instance, Microsoft and IDC's report on AI in higher education shows a global shift toward AI adoption, with nearly 40% of institutions already implementing AI and more planning to do so. While this transformation offers enhanced personalized learning and administrative efficiency, it also increases data privacy concerns, requiring institutions to navigate complex legal and ethical landscapes. Similarly, Stanford's AI-powered student support system, despite its success in improving retention rates, raises questions about data privacy and AI bias, emphasizing the need for algorithmic fairness and transparency. Knewton's personalized learning platform further exemplifies this tension; its reliance on extensive data collection for adaptive learning sparks debates over privacy and the potential over-reliance on algorithms in education. These examples illustrate the growing need to find a balanced approach that leverages AI's benefits while rigorously safeguarding student data and adhering to ethical standards. Prinsloo and Slade (2016) discuss the ethical implications of predictive analytics in higher education, particularly concerning student privacy and autonomy. They argue that students should have greater control over how AI systems use and interpret their data.

The issue of algorithmic bias in educational AI raises both legal and ethical concerns. Lee and Kwon (2024) examine how AI systems in education can perpetuate or exacerbate existing inequalities. They argue that addressing bias is not just an ethical imperative but potentially a legal one, as discriminatory outcomes could violate anti-discrimination laws. Hoel and Chen (2021) discuss educational institutions' legal and ethical obligations to protect student data from breaches. They argue for a "privacy by design" approach in developing educational AI systems, emphasizing the need to build robust security measures from the ground up.

In the pursuit of creating a safe educational environment, artificial intelligence (AI) holds great potential to design educational experiences to suit the personal needs of students with special needs. However, integrating artificial intelligence into special education faces obstacles. These obstacles stem from a number of factors such as technological limitations and ethical considerations. Therefore, it is necessary to maintain data privacy and security. The use of artificial intelligence requires the collection and analysis of huge amounts of personal data. Ensuring the privacy and security of this sensitive information is crucial, especially when it comes to people with special needs.

As illustrated by the case studies, the integration of AI in educational settings brings both opportunities and ethical challenges. The widespread adoption of AI for personalized learning, early intervention, and administrative efficiency. The case studies of the institutions like Stanford and through platforms like Knewto highlight the transformative potential of these technologies. However, these advancements also raise critical ethical concerns, particularly regarding data privacy, algorithmic bias, and the transparency of AI systems. The tension between harnessing AI's benefits and protecting student rights underscores the need for a cautious and well-regulated approach to AI implementation in education

Suggested Framework

Based on the case studies examined, we propose a framework for integrating AI in education that addresses the multifaceted nature of AI-driven learning. This framework, which we call the Adaptive Intelligent Learning Ecosystem (AILE), aims to guide educators and policymakers in implementing AI technologies effectively and responsibly.

The AILE framework consists of five interconnected components: Personalized Learning, Predictive Support, Adaptive Assessment, Continuous Professional Development, and Ethical Governance. Each component builds upon the others to create a holistic approach to AI integration in education.

Personalized Learning: forms the core of the AILE framework. Based on Knewton's approach (Shih, 2018), this component focuses on using AI to tailor educational content and pacing to individual student needs. The system should continuously analyze student performance data to adjust real-time difficulty levels and learning paths.

Predictive Support: This is inspired by Stanford's AI system (Stanford University, 2022), which involves using AI to identify students at risk of academic difficulties. This component enables early intervention to allow educators to provide targeted support before students fall behind. The AI system should analyze various data points, such as engagement metrics and assignment completion rates, to flag potential issues.

Adaptive Assessment: based on the fuzzy expert system study (Almohammadi et al., 2017), goes beyond traditional testing methods. This component incorporates both cognitive and affective factors in evaluating student performance. AI systems should adjust assessment difficulty based on student knowledge levels and emotional states. It also provides a more holistic view of student progress.

Continuous Professional Development: according to workplace AI applications (Andriotis, 2023), it extends the benefits of AI-driven learning to educators. This component focuses on using AI to identify skill gaps among teaching staff and provide personalized training recommendations. It should also include AI-powered mentoring systems to support ongoing professional growth.

Ethical Governance: The framework's foundation is informed by the challenges highlighted in the ChatGPT study (Shraim, 2023). This component ensures responsible AI use through clear policies on data privacy, academic integrity, and equitable access. It should include mechanisms for ongoing ethical review and adjustment of AI systems.

For this framework to be effective, several parameters and criteria must be considered:

1. Data Quality and Integration: The AI systems within the AILE framework rely heavily on data. Institutions must ensure they have strong data collection and integration processes in place. This includes standardizing data formats across different systems and implementing rigorous data quality checks.
2. Algorithmic Transparency: Given the critical role of AI in decision-making within this framework, it is essential that the algorithms used are as transparent as possible. Educators and students should have access to clear explanations of how AI systems make recommendations or assessments.

3. Accessibility and Digital Equity: As highlighted in the Palestinian universities' case study (Hamamra et al., 2024), equitable access to AI tools is crucial. Institutions implementing the AILE framework must have strategies in place to ensure all students can benefit from AI-enhanced Learning, regardless of their socioeconomic background or technical proficiency.
4. Human-AI Collaboration: The framework should emphasize the complementary roles of AI and human educators. The Microsoft and IDC report (Microsoft Education, 2023) shows that AI can handle many administrative and analytical tasks, freeing educators to focus on high-value student interactions.
5. Continuous Evaluation and Improvement: The effectiveness of the AILE framework should be regularly assessed. This includes monitoring key performance indicators such as student outcomes, engagement levels, and user satisfaction. Feedback from all stakeholders - students, educators, and administrators - should be systematically collected and used to refine the AI systems and overall framework.
6. Scalability and Interoperability: As institutions grow and develop, the AI systems within the AILE framework must be able to scale accordingly. Moreover, these systems should be designed with interoperability in mind to allow for seamless integration with existing and future educational technologies.

To protect the data of students with special needs in AI systems, several key conditions must be taken into account as follows:

1) Consent and independence - obtain consent from the student's parents and make this process transparent, explaining how the data will be collected, used, and protected.
2) Data Minimization and Purpose Definition – AI systems should only collect data that is necessary for their function.
3) Security Measures - Strong security protocols are non-negotiable. An AI application designed to assist in physical therapy should use end-to-end encryption to protect data as it moves from the device to the cloud for processing.
4) Bias and Fairness – AI should be free of biases that may lead to unequal treatment.

5) Transparency and Accountability: There should be clarity about how AI decisions are made. If an AI system recommends a specific educational pathway for a student, the criteria used for this recommendation must be clear and justifiable.
6) Data Governance- Establishing a governance framework is essential. This includes regular audits of AI systems to ensure compliance with privacy laws and ethical standards.

The Future of Data Privacy In Ai-Driven Education

One of the most significant developments we are likely to see is the rise of more sophisticated and privacy-preserving AI technologies. Researchers are working on advanced machine-learning techniques that can analyze data while keeping individual information private. For example, Luo et al. (2024) discuss the potential of federated learning in educational settings. This approach allows AI models to learn from data on many different devices or servers without actually sharing the raw data. This is to say that each student's device contributes to improving the AI without revealing personal information. Another important trend is the growing emphasis on student agency and control over their own data. West et al. (2020) predict that future educational AI systems will give students more say in how their data is used. West et al. (2020) imagine a dashboard where students can easily see what data is being collected about them and choose what they want to share. This shift towards student-centered data management could help build trust and encourage responsible AI use in education.

However, Prinsloo (2019) suggests that as AI becomes more prevalent in schools, governments will step up with new laws to protect student information. These regulations might require schools and ed-tech companies to be more transparent about how they use AI and handle student data.

Holmes et al. (2021) argue that future AI systems in education will need to be designed with ethics in mind from the start. This means considering things like fairness, transparency, and privacy at every stage of development. Interestingly, blockchain technology could play a role in securing student data in the future. Work by Ocheja et al. (2019) explores how blockchain could be used to give students more control over their educational records. This technology could create a secure, decentralized way of storing and sharing educational data, potentially reducing the risk of large-scale data breaches.

As AI systems become more complex, there is a growing need for better ways to explain how these systems work. Barria-Pineda et al. (2020) discuss the importance of “explainable AI” in education. In the future, AI systems may evolve to transparently demonstrate how they make decisions to students, teachers, and parents, which is crucial for building trust and understanding. This trustworthiness is not just a technological requirement but an ethical imperative, especially in education where the stakes are high. Transparent AI systems can demystify complex decision-making processes, ensuring that data collection and usage are perceived as fair and justifiable. By fostering trust, these systems can encourage broader acceptance and more responsible use of AI, ultimately enhancing the educational experience while safeguarding students' rights and privacy.

Additionally, the integration of AI with other emerging technologies, like virtual and augmented reality in education, will create new privacy challenges. These immersive technologies can collect even more detailed data about students, including physical movements and reactions. Future privacy solutions will need to address these new forms of data collection (Radianti et al., 2020; Touretzky et al., 2019).

The future of data privacy in AI-driven education looks to be a balance of technological innovation, ethical considerations, and empowering students. We are expected to see a greater focus on teaching students about AI and data privacy. In the future, understanding how AI works and how to protect one's data might become as fundamental as learning to read or do math.

The integration of AI in supporting students with special needs is rapidly evolving from a mere possibility to a transformative force. This shift sees AI moving beyond simple facilitation to becoming an active enabler of new opportunities for learning, engagement, and independence. Educational institutions are paving the way for a future where barriers are systematically removed, making inclusivity a tangible reality rather than just an ideal. AI-driven personalized learning systems cater specifically to the unique needs of these students, offering predictive analytics for early intervention, enhancing communication through advanced tools, creating more accessible environments, and integrating wearable technologies to support everyday activities. This integration holds the promise of not only improving educational outcomes but also empowering students with special needs to achieve greater autonomy and participation in their learning journeys.

CONCLUSION

Building upon our discussion of current applications and challenges of AI in education, we can now conclude that the future prospects of AI-driven learning. Predicted trends in AI-driven learning suggest a move towards more holistic and integrated systems. Building on the success of personalized learning platforms like Knewton (Shih, 2018), future AI systems are likely to offer even more comprehensive personalization. These systems might adapt content and pacing and consider factors such as a student's emotional state, learning environment, and long-term educational goals. Another trend is the increasing use of AI for continuous, formative assessment. Rather than relying on periodic tests, AI could provide ongoing evaluation of student understanding to allow immediate adjustments to the learning process.

The long-term impact of AI on educational systems and practices is likely to be profound. AI becomes more integrated into education, and we may see a shift away from the traditional model of standardized curricula and assessments. Instead, education could become more individualized, with AI systems helping to craft unique learning journeys for each student. This aligns with the personalized learning approaches already being implemented in some institutions (Microsoft Education, 2023). The role of educators is also likely to evolve. Rather than focusing on content delivery, teachers may increasingly become facilitators and mentors, leveraging AI insights to provide targeted guidance and support.

However, the increasing reliance on AI in education also raises important considerations for the future. Issues of data privacy and security, highlighted in current implementations, will likely become even more critical as AI systems become more comprehensive and interconnected. There will be a need for robust frameworks and policies to ensure the ethical use of student data and to prevent the perpetuation of biases in AI algorithms.

The future of AI in education also holds the potential for more seamless integration between formal education and lifelong learning. Building on current trends in workplace learning (Andriotis, 2023), AI could help create personalized learning pathways that extend beyond traditional educational boundaries, supporting individuals throughout their careers and lives.

In conclusion, the future prospects of AI in education are both exciting and challenging. AI's successful implementation will require careful consideration of ethical, social, and pedagogical implications. As we move forward, it will be crucial to approach the integration of AI in education thoughtfully, ensuring that these powerful tools enhance rather than replace the human elements of teaching and learning. The framework proposed earlier, with its emphasis on personalization, predictive support, adaptive assessment, continuous professional development, and ethical governance, provides a starting point for navigating this complex future landscape.

RECOMMENDATIONS FOR EDUCATORS AND POLICYMAKERS

1. Develop and implement comprehensive data governance policies that clearly outline data collection, usage, and storage practices.
2. Invest in professional development programs to enhance educators' understanding of AI technologies and data privacy issues.

3. Advocate for updated legislation that addresses the unique challenges posed by AI in educational settings.
4. Implement privacy-by-design principles in the development and adoption of AI-driven educational tools.
5. Promote transparency by regularly communicating with students and parents about classroom data collection practices and AI use.
6. Incorporate data literacy and AI ethics into the curriculum to empower students to make informed decisions about their personal data.
7. Conduct regular privacy impact assessments when implementing new AI technologies in educational institutions.
8. Foster collaboration between educators, technologists, and policymakers to develop ethical AI frameworks specific to education.
9. Prioritize the use of privacy-preserving technologies, such as federated learning and differential privacy, in educational AI systems.
10. Establish clear guidelines for the use of AI in high-stakes decision-making processes, such as admissions or academic placements.
11. Encourage the development of explainable AI models to increase transparency and trust in AI-driven educational tools.
12. Support research initiatives that explore the long-term impacts of AI and data collection on student privacy and educational outcomes.

ACKNOWLEDGMENT

The author acknowledges that AI has been used in this chapter to assist in the organization of content. The final analysis, conclusions, and recommendations presented in this chapter are the product of the authors own critical thinking, experience in the field, and ethical considerations. This approach not only maintained the integrity of the research but also offered a unique perspective on the responsible use of AI in academic contexts.

REFERENCES

AbuHamda, E., Ismail, I., & Bsharat, T. (2021). Understanding quantitative and qualitative research methods: A theoretical perspective for young researchers. *International Journal of Research*, 8(2), 71–79.

Akinwalere, S. N., & Ivanov, V. (2022). Artificial Intelligence in Higher Education: Challenges and Opportunities. *Border Crossing*, 12(1), 1–15. DOI: 10.33182/bc.v12i1.2015

Almohammadi, K., Hagras, H., Alghazzawi, D., & Aldabbagh, G. (2017). A fuzzy expert system-based adaptive learning approach to improving students' learning performances by considering affective and cognitive factors. *Journal of Artificial Intelligence and Soft Computing Research*, 7(4), 289–304.

Amo-Filva, D., Mauri, S. A., Escudero, D. F., Sanchez-Sepulveda, M. V., Hasti, H., García-Holgado, A., García-Holgado, L., Vázquez-Ingelmo, A., García-Peñalvo, F. J., Orehovački, T., Krašna, M., Pesek, I., Marchetti, E., Valente, A., Witfelt, C., Ružić, I., Fraoua, K. E., Moreira, F., Pereira, C. S., & Paes, C. (2024). Empowering student data privacy in schools through open educational resources. In *Lecture notes in educational technology* (pp. 253–263). DOI: 10.1007/978-981-97-2468-0_25

Andriotis, N. (2023). *Embrace Artificial Intelligence InThe Workplace*. eLearning Industry. https://elearningindustry.com/embrace-artificial-intelligence-in-the-workplace

Baker, R. S., Nafea, I., & Wang, Y. (2021). How much are we relying on AI in education? In *Artificial Intelligence in Education* (pp. 39–44). Springer.

Barria-Pineda, J., Brusilovsky, P., & Akhuseyinoglu, K. (2020). Explaining need-based educational recommendations using interactive open learner models. In *Proceedings of the 28th ACM Conference on User Modeling, Adaptation and Personalization* (pp. 48-56).

Chakraborty, N., Mishra, Y., Bhattacharya, R., & Bhattacharya, B. (2023). Artificial Intelligence: The road ahead for the accessibility of persons with Disability. *Materials Today: Proceedings*, 80, 3757–3761. DOI: 10.1016/j.matpr.2021.07.374

Chen, L., Chen, P., & Lin, Z. (2020). Artificial Intelligence in Education: A Review. *IEEE Access : Practical Innovations, Open Solutions*, 8, 75264–75278. DOI: 10.1109/ACCESS.2020.2988510

Douse, M., & Uys, P. (2023). The role of the teacher in the age of artificial intelligence. *Education Sciences*, 13(2), 133.

Gursoy, M. E., Inan, A., Nergiz, M. E., & Saygin, Y. (2017). Privacy-Preserving Learning Analytics: Challenges and techniques. *IEEE Transactions on Learning Technologies*, 10(1), 68–81. DOI: 10.1109/TLT.2016.2607747

Hamamra, B., Mayaleh, A., & Khlaif, Z. N. (2024). Between tech and text: The use of generative AI in Palestinian universities - a ChatGPT case study. *Cogent Education*, 11(1), 2380622. Advance online publication. DOI: 10.1080/2331186X.2024.2380622

Herodotou, C., Rienties, B., Boroowa, A., Zdrahal, Z., & Hlosta, M. (2019). A large-scale implementation of predictive learning analytics in higher education: The teachers' role and perspective. *Educational Technology Research and Development*, 67(5), 1273–1306. DOI: 10.1007/s11423-019-09685-0

Herodotou, C., Rienties, B., Boroowa, A., Zdrahal, Z., & Hlosta, M. (2020). A large-scale implementation of predictive learning analytics in higher education: The teachers' role and perspective. *Educational Technology Research and Development*, 68(5), 1961–1985.

Holmes, W., Bialik, M., & Fadel, C. (2021). *Artificial intelligence in education: Promises and implications for teaching and learning*. Center for Curriculum Redesign.

Holmes, W., Porayska-Pomsta, K., Holstein, K., Sutherland, E., Baker, T., Shum, S. B., & Koedinger, K. R. (2022). Ethics of AI in education: Towards a community-wide framework. *International Journal of Artificial Intelligence in Education*, 32(3), 504–526. DOI: 10.1007/s40593-021-00239-1

Holmes, W., Porayska-Pomsta, K., Holstein, K., Sutherland, E., Baker, T., Shum, S. B., Santos, O. C., Rodrigo, M. T., Cukurova, M., Bittencourt, I. I., & Koedinger, K. R. (2021). Ethics of AI in Education: Towards a Community-Wide framework. *International Journal of Artificial Intelligence in Education*, 32(3), 504–526. DOI: 10.1007/s40593-021-00239-1

Karunaratne, T. (2021). For Learning Analytics to Be Sustainable under GDPR—Consequences and Way Forward. *Sustainability (Basel)*, 13(20), 11524. DOI: 10.3390/su132011524

Khalil, M., & Ebner, M. (2016). De-Identification in learning Analytics. *Journal of Learning Analytics*, 3(1). Advance online publication. DOI: 10.18608/jla.2016.31.8

Knox, J., Wang, Y., & Gallagher, M. (2020). Artificial intelligence and education in China. *Learning, Media and Technology*, 45(3), 298–311. DOI: 10.1080/17439884.2020.1754236

Lee, S. J., & Kwon, K. (2024). A systematic review of AI education in K-12 classrooms from 2018 to 2023: Topics, strategies, and learning outcomes. *Computers and Education Artificial Intelligence*, 100211, 100211. Advance online publication. DOI: 10.1016/j.caeai.2024.100211

Luo, G., Chen, N., He, J., Jin, B., Zhang, Z., & Li, Y. (2024). Privacy-preserving clustering federated learning for non-IID data. *Future Generation Computer Systems*, 154, 384–395. DOI: 10.1016/j.future.2024.01.005

Microsoft Education. (2023). *New IDC report shows big opportunities to transform higher education through AI*. Microsoft Education Blog.

Mpu, Y. (2024). Bridging the Knowledge Gap on Special Needs Learner Support: The Use of Artificial Intelligence (AI) to Combat Digital Divide Post-COVID-19 Pandemic and beyond – A Comprehensive Literature Review. In *IntechOpen eBooks*. DOI: 10.5772/intechopen.113054

O'Neil, C. (2016a). *Weapons of Math Destruction: How big data increases inequality and threatens democracy*. Crown Publishing Group. https://ci.nii.ac.jp/ncid/BB22310261

Ocheja, P., Flanagan, B., Ueda, H., & Ogata, H. (2019). Managing lifelong learning records through blockchain. *Research and Practice in Technology Enhanced Learning*, 14.

Pardo, A., Jovanovic, J., Dawson, S., Gašević, D., & Mirriahi, N. (2019). Using learning analytics to scale the provision of personalized feedback. *British Journal of Educational Technology*, 50(1), 128–138. DOI: 10.1111/bjet.12592

Passonneau, R. J., McNamara, D., Muresan, S., & Perin, D. (2018). Preface: Special issue on multidisciplinary approaches to AI and education for reading and writing. *International Journal of Artificial Intelligence in Education*, 28(4), 445–450.

Polonetsky, J., & Jerome, J. (2014). Student Data: trust, transparency, and the role of consent. *Social Science Research Network*. DOI: 10.2139/ssrn.2628877

Porayska-Pomsta, K., Frauenberger, C., Pain, H., Rajendran, G., Smith, T., Menzies, R., & Lemon, O. (2018). Blending human and artificial intelligence to support autistic children's social communication skills. *ACM Transactions on Computer-Human Interaction*, 25(6), 1–35. DOI: 10.1145/3271484

Prinsloo, P. (2019). A social cartography of analytics in education as performative politics. *British Journal of Educational Technology*, 50(6), 2810–2823. DOI: 10.1111/bjet.12872

Prinsloo, P., & Slade, S. (2016). Student Vulnerability, Agency and Learning Analytics: An Exploration. *Journal of Learning Analytics*, 3(1). Advance online publication. DOI: 10.18608/jla.2016.31.10

Radianti, J., Majchrzak, T. A., Fromm, J., & Wohlgenannt, I. (2020). A systematic review of immersive virtual reality applications for higher education: Design elements, lessons learned, and research agenda. *Computers & Education*, 147, 103778. DOI: 10.1016/j.compedu.2019.103778

Regan, P. M., & Jesse, J. (2018). Ethical challenges of edtech, big data and personalized learning: Twenty-first century student sorting and tracking. *Ethics and Information Technology*, 21(3), 167–179. DOI: 10.1007/s10676-018-9492-2

Reich, J., Kim, Y. J., Robinson, C., Roy, D., & Thompson, M. (2022). *AI and education: Promises and implications for teaching and learning*. MIT Teaching Systems Lab.

Renz, A., & Hilbig, R. (2023). Prerequisites for artificial intelligence in further education: Identification of drivers, barriers, and business models of educational technology companies. *International Journal of Educational Technology in Higher Education*, 20(1), 1–21.

Rosé, C. P., McLaughlin, E. A., Liu, R., & Koedinger, K. R. (2019). Explanatory learner models: Why machine learning (alone) is not the answer. *British Journal of Educational Technology*, 50(6), 2943–2958. DOI: 10.1111/bjet.12858

Sharma, K., Giannakos, M. N., & Dillenbourg, P. (2020). Eye-tracking and artificial intelligence to enhance motivation and learning. *Smart Learning Environments*, 7(1), 13. Advance online publication. DOI: 10.1186/s40561-020-00122-x

Shih, J. (2018). *Knewton Personalizes Learning with the Power of AI. Digital Innovation and Transformation, Harvard Business School.*https://digital.hbs.edu/platform-digit/submission/knewton-personalizes-learning-with-the-power-of-ai/

Shraim, K. (2023). Between tech and text: The use of generative AI in Palestinian universities - a ChatGPT case study. *Teaching in Higher Education*, 1–18. DOI: 10.1080/13562517.2023.2213589

Southgate, E. (2022). Artificial intelligence, ethics, and the future of education. In *Handbook on Digital Learning for K-12 Schools* (pp. 535–550). Springer.

Special Need Center Artificial Intelligence: Inclusive AI: Bridging the gap for special needs centers. (2024). FasterCapital. Retrieved August 28, 2024, from https://fastercapital.com/content/Special-Need-Center-Artificial-Intelligence--Inclusive-AI--Bridging-the-Gap-for-Special-Needs-Centers.html

Stanford University. (2022). *Using Artificial Intelligence to Understand Why Students are Struggling. Stanford University.* https://hai.stanford.edu/news/using-artificial-intelligence-understand-why-students-are-struggling

Touretzky, D., Gardner-McCune, C., Martin, F., & Seehorn, D. (2019). Envisioning AI for K-12: What should every child know about AI? *Proceedings of the AAAI Conference on Artificial Intelligence*, 33(01), 9795–9799. DOI: 10.1609/aaai.v33i01.33019795

US Department of Education. (2020). *Protecting Student Privacy While Using Online Educational Services: Requirements and Best Practices.*

Wang, S., Wang, F., Zhu, Z., Wang, J., Tran, T., & Du, Z. (2024). Artificial intelligence in education: A systematic literature review. *Expert Systems with Applications*, 252, 124167. DOI: 10.1016/j.eswa.2024.124167

West, D., Luzeckyj, A., Toohey, D., Vanderlelie, J., & Searle, B. (2020). Do academics and university administrators really know better? The ethics of positioning student perspectives in learning analytics. *Australasian Journal of Educational Technology*, 36(2), 60–70. DOI: 10.14742/ajet.4653

Winkler, R., & Söllner, M. (2018). Unleashing the potential of chatbots in education: A state-of-the-art analysis. In *Academy of Management Annual Meeting* (AOM) (pp. 1-40). DOI: 10.5465/AMBPP.2018.15903abstract

Wong, J., Baars, M., Davis, D., Van Der Zee, T., Houben, G.-J., & Paas, F. (2019). Supporting self-regulated learning in online learning environments and MOOCs: A systematic review. *International Journal of Human-Computer Interaction*, 35(4-5), 356–373. DOI: 10.1080/10447318.2018.1543084

Xu, D., & Kalyanaraman, S. (2020). Artificial Intelligence in Educational Administration: Challenges and Opportunities. *Journal of Educational Administration*, 58(4), 453–468.

Zavaraki, E. Z. (2024). Artificial Intelligence for People with Special Educational Needs. In *IntechOpen eBooks*. https://doi.org/DOI: 10.5772/intechopen.1004158

Zawacki-Richter, O., Marín, V. I., Bond, M., & Gouverneur, F. (2019a). Systematic review of research on artificial intelligence applications in higher education – where are the educators? *International Journal of Educational Technology in Higher Education*, 16(1), 39. Advance online publication. DOI: 10.1186/s41239-019-0171-0

Zeide, E., & Nissenbaum, H. (2023). Dilemmas of student data protection in an era of AI and learning analytics. *Phi Delta Kappan*, 104(5), 24–29.

ADDITIONAL READING

Abulibdeh, A., Zaidan, E., & Abulibdeh, R. (2024). Navigating the confluence of artificial intelligence and education for sustainable development in the era of industry 4.0: Challenges, opportunities, and ethical dimensions. *Journal of Cleaner Production*, 437, 140527. DOI: 10.1016/j.jclepro.2023.140527

Bsharat, T. R. K., Behak, F., & Ismail, I. A. (2023). A guide to E-Learning. In *Advances in educational technologies and instructional design book series* (pp. 1–10). DOI: 10.4018/978-1-6684-4940-0.ch001

Butson, R., & Spronken-Smith, R. (2024). AI and its implications for research in higher education: A critical dialogue. *Higher Education Research & Development*, 43(3), 563–577. DOI: 10.1080/07294360.2023.2280200

Butt, U. J., Davelis, A., Abbod, M., Eghan, C., & Agbo, H. M. (2022). Improving Learning Experience and Privacy in Education Using the Power of Big Data and Artificial Intelligence. In Singh Dadwal, S., Jahankhani, H., & Hassan, A. (Eds.), *Integrated Business Models in the Digital Age*. Palgrave Macmillan., DOI: 10.1007/978-3-030-97877-8_11

Huang, L. (2023). Ethics of Artificial intelligence in Education: Student privacy and data protection. *Science Insights Education Frontiers*, 16(2), 2577–2587. DOI: 10.15354/sief.23.re202

Karan, B., & Angadi, G. R. (2023). Potential Risks of Artificial Intelligence Integration into School Education: A Systematic Review. *Bulletin of Science, Technology & Society*, 43(3–4), 67–85. DOI: 10.1177/02704676231224705

Keeley, K. (2023). AI-Assisted Teacher wellness. In *Advances in educational technologies and instructional design book series* (pp. 201–216). DOI: 10.4018/979-8-3693-0074-9.ch008

Mishra, P., Oster, N., & Henriksen, D. (2024). Generative AI, Teacher Knowledge and Educational Research: Bridging Short- and Long-Term Perspectives. *TechTrends*, 68(2), 205–2010. DOI: 10.1007/s11528-024-00938-1

Reiss, M.J. (2021) 'The use of AI in education: Practicalities and ethical considerations'. *London Review of Education, 19* (1), 5, 1–14. https://doi.org/DOI: 10.14324/LRE.19.1.05

US Department of Education. Office of Educational Technology, *Artificial Intelligence and Future of Teaching and Learning: Insights and Recommendations*, Washington, DC, 2023.

Zhang, Y., Wu, M., Tian, G. Y., Zhang, G., & Lu, J. (2021). Ethics and privacy of artificial intelligence: Understandings from bibliometrics. *Knowledge-Based Systems*, 222, 106994. DOI: 10.1016/j.knosys.2021.106994

KEY TERMS AND DEFINITIONS

AI in Education: The application of artificial intelligence technologies to enhance teaching, learning, and administrative processes in educational settings.

Algorithmic Bias: The systematic and repeatable errors in a computer system that create unfair outcomes, such as privileging one arbitrary group of users over others.

Blockchain in Education: The use of blockchain technology to securely store and manage educational records and credentials.

Data Governance: The overall management of the availability, usability, integrity, and security of data used in an organization or system.

Data Privacy: The protection of personal information from unauthorized access, use, or disclosure, particularly in digital environments.

Differential Privacy: A system for publicly sharing information about a dataset by describing the patterns of groups within the dataset while withholding information about individuals in the dataset.

Educational Data Mining: The process of extracting useful information from large educational databases to inform decision-making and improve educational outcomes.

Ethical AI: The development, deployment, and use of artificial intelligence systems that align with human values and ethical principles.

Federated Learning: A machine learning technique that trains an algorithm across multiple decentralized devices or servers holding local data samples, without exchanging them.

Learning Analytics: The measurement, collection, analysis, and reporting of data about learners and their contexts, for purposes of understanding and optimizing learning and the environments in which it occurs.

APPENDIX: TEACHING NOTES

This teaching note has been designed to give full support for the ethical case study on AI and data protection in school environments. It has three main parts: an FAQ (questions and answers) related to core problems & solutions, final thoughts with the lessons learned looking towards long-term impact, and further reading about every facet of this essay. The materials and resources we designed below are to deepen comprehension, compel discourse, and improve the understanding of students (and teachers).

Questions and Answers

1. What is the overall problem presented in this case?

The primary issue presented in these case studies is the significant challenge of protecting data privacy in AI-driven educational environments. As discussed in the chapter, AI systems collect vast amounts of sensitive student data, concerns about surveillance, data breaches, and ethical implications have become paramount and necessitate robust privacy measures.

2. What are the factors affecting the problem(s) related to this case?

The case studies on data privacy in this chapter are influenced by various factors. These include the vast data collection capabilities of AI, outdated legal frameworks, potential algorithmic bias, and the growing reliance on cloud-based and third-party systems in educational AI applications. Together, these elements make protecting student data more complex and raise significant ethical concerns.

3. Discuss managerial, organizational, and technological issues and resources related to this case.

Managerial issues vary depending on ensuring compliance with data privacy laws and fostering a culture of privacy. Regarding organizational challenges, they may include implementing comprehensive data governance policies and investing in educator training on AI and privacy. Technologically, the use of privacy-preserving techniques like differential privacy and federated learning is essential, alongside exploring blockchain for secure data handling.

4. What role do different players (decision-makers) play in the overall planning, implementation, and management of the information technology applications?

Decision-makers such as educational administrators, policymakers, and IT specialists play key roles in planning and implementing AI technologies. They must ensure these technologies comply with privacy regulations, address ethical concerns, and integrate technical solutions to protect student data while maximizing the educational benefits of AI.

5. What are the possible alternatives and pros and cons of each alternative facing the organization in dealing with the problem(s) related to the case?

Potential alternatives include implementing differential privacy, federated learning, and blockchain technologies. Differential privacy protects individual data but may reduce data utility. Federated learning enhances privacy without centralizing data but requires complex infrastructure. Blockchain ensures secure data handling but can be resource-intensive to implement. Each alternative balances privacy and practicality differently.

6. What are some of the emerging technologies that should be considered in solving the problem(s) related to the case?

With respect to case studies presented in the chapter, the following should be considered: Emerging technologies such as privacy-preserving machine learning, blockchain, secure multi-party computation (SMC), and homomorphic encryption. These technologies offer advanced methods for analyzing and protecting data without compromising privacy. Basically, they ensure secure and ethical use of AI in education.

7. What is the final solution that can be recommended to the management of the organization described in the case? Provide your arguments in support of the recommended solution.

The recommended solution is to adopt a multifaceted approach combining differential privacy, federated learning, and blockchain technologies. This strategy ensures strong data protection while allowing the benefits of AI-driven education. The author believes that implementing comprehensive data governance policies and investing in educator training will further support this solution, balancing privacy, practicality, and educational advancement.

Epilogue and Lessons Learned

Epilogue: In the long run, addressing data privacy challenges in AI-driven education will lead to a more secure and ethically responsible educational environment. Implementing advanced privacy-preserving technologies will build trust among students, educators, and stakeholders, fostering wider acceptance and integration of AI tools. This proactive approach will not only protect individual privacy but also ensure compliance with evolving regulations. This is to say that the proactive approach can promote innovation while safeguarding ethical standards.

Lessons Learned

1. **Importance of Robust Data Privacy Measures:** Ensuring strong data privacy is crucial to maintaining trust and protecting sensitive information in AI applications. Implementing technologies like differential privacy and federated learning can significantly reduce risks of data breaches and misuse.
2. **Need for Comprehensive Data Governance:** Establishing clear data governance policies and protocols is essential for managing the collection, storage, and use of data. This involves training staff, enforcing compliance, and regularly updating policies to adapt to new technologies and regulations.
3. **Ethical Considerations in AI Implementation:** Addressing ethical issues, such as algorithmic bias and data surveillance, is important for the responsible deployment of AI in education. Ethical AI practices ensure fairness, transparency, and accountability, preventing potential harms and promoting equitable outcomes.
4. **Role of Emerging Technologies:** relying on emerging technologies like blockchain and secure multi-party computation (SMC) can enhance data security and privacy. These technologies provide innovative solutions to manage and protect data, balancing the benefits of AI with robust privacy safeguards.
5. **Collaboration Among Stakeholders:** Effective collaboration between educators, policymakers, IT specialists, and legal experts is necessary for the successful implementation of AI in education. This interdisciplinary approach ensures that diverse perspectives are considered. This kind of collaboration may lead to more comprehensive and effective privacy solutions.

List of Additional Sources

Abadi, M., Chu, A., Goodfellow, I., McMahan, H. B., Mironov, I., Talwar, K., & Zhang, L. (2016). Deep learning with differential privacy.

Bonawitz, K., Eichner, H., Grieskamp, W., Huba, D., Ingerman, A., Ivanov, V., Kiddon, C., Konečný, J., Mazzocchi, S., McMahan, H. B., Timon, V. O., Petrou, D., Ramage, D., & Roselander, J. (2019, February 4). Towards federated learning at scale: system design. arXiv.org.

Decentralizing privacy: using blockchain to protect personal data. (2015, May 1). IEEE Conference Publication I IEEE Xplore.

Mayer-Schönberger, V., & Cukier, K. (2013). Big Data: A Revolution That Will Transform How We Live, Work, and Think. Houghton Mifflin Harcourt.

O'Neil, C. (2016). Weapons of Math Destruction: How Big Data Increases Inequality and Threatens Democracy. Crown Publishing Group.

Industries Where the Case May Be Pertinent

1. Healthcare:
    - o AI-driven diagnostics and patient data management require stringent data privacy measures to protect sensitive health information.
2. Finance:
    - o Financial institutions use AI for fraud detection and customer analytics, necessitating robust data governance and privacy protections.
3. Retail:
    - o AI applications in personalized marketing and consumer behavior analysis must ensure customer data privacy and security.
4. Government:
    - o Public sector use of AI for citizen services and data analysis involves significant privacy considerations and regulatory compliance.
5. Telecommunications:
    - o AI-driven network optimization and customer service in the telecommunications industry require careful handling of personal data to prevent breaches and misuse.

Chapter 9
Using Artificial Intelligence to Evaluate the Nature of Science Myths:
A Comparison of Pre-Service Science Teachers and ChatGPT

Nurcan Tekin
Aksaray University, Turkey

ABSTRACT

This chapter aims to compare the performances of pre-service science teachers (PSTs) and generative artificial intelligence (AI) application (ChatGPT) in answering nature of science (NoS) myths. In this study, which was designed according to a qualitative descriptive research design, the 15 most frequently encountered NoS myths were addressed to 104 PSTs and the ChatGPT. The data were analyzed using content analysis. As a result of the research, when the items related to all myths were analyzed, approximately 48% of the PSTs had myths about the NoS, while 66% of the ChatGPT answers included correct information. Therefore, ChatGPT can be effective in seeking answers to NoS myths. However, since the resources used by ChatGPT are limited to certain books, contents, or resources of certain countries, it may not be efficient enough in terms of providing information diversity. According to these results, comparison of PSTs and ChatGPT's answers are discussed.

DOI: 10.4018/979-8-3693-5443-8.ch009

INTRODUCTION

Individuals may often lack sufficient knowledge and experience about how science works and how it affects them although they are intertwined with science in daily life. (Bell et al., 2011). However, they may need to make science-based decisions on issues that affect their lives (McComas et al., 1998). In such cases, they are expected to get help from the nature of science (NoS) (Dorji et al., 2022). According to Driver et al. (1996), NoS benefits in terms of understanding the scientific process, making informed decisions on socioscientific issues, appreciating science as an element of contemporary culture, being aware of scientific studies, and learning science content in depth. However, myths about NoS that still exist among individuals and may cause misunderstandings may affect their informed decision-making. Moreover, it is also discussed whether individuals can access this information accurately on the internet, which is frequently used by them to be informed about scientific studies. Therefore, artificial intelligence (AI) applications are considered important in accessing accurate information and appreciating science. Detailed information on the myths of NoS and AI in education is given below.

ARTIFICIAL INTELLIGENCE IN EDUCATION

Artificial intelligence in education (AIE) has accelerated its progress in the last 30 years (Zawacki-Richter et al., 2019). In the use of AIE, 77% of parents and 92% of students are interested in AI tools to help them learn (Verma et al., 2023). In October 2023, according to a systematic review conducted by the author, it was concluded that AI studies in education in Türkiye have progressed in the last 20 years, especially in the last five years, AI applications have a rapid acceleration (Author, 2023). A striking feature of this systematic review study, the most studied study group is pre-service teachers (PSTs) and other undergraduate students. However, it was concluded that studies on AI in teacher education are still quite limited. Therefore, this chapter on the use of AI in teacher education can be effective.

ChatGPT as an Artificial Intelligence Application in Science Education

As in many fields today, ChatGPT is one of the most used tools for individuals to access information. ChatGPT is also highly preferred among the generative AI applications used in education. ChatGPT is an AI-based chatbot developed by OpenAI (Birer, 2023). ChatGPT is a tool that generates text by compiling information from books, news articles, websites and Wikipedia (Scharth, 2022). However, there are still concerns about the reliability of the information that users access (Verma et al., 2023). For example, a study of K-12 science teachers in Brazil found that there are some doubts about whether ChatGPT can improve the quality of students' education and whether its use constitutes plagiarism or similar violations (Monteiro et al., 2024). There are several studies on the use of AI in education that investigate the texts produced by ChatGPT through comparison. Talan and Kalınkara (2023) compared the responses of ChatGPT and university students for an anatomy course and concluded that ChatGPT outperformed the students. Cooper (2023), as a result of his exploratory study on the use of ChatGPT in science education, stated that AI carries risks such as possible external impact (such as job loss due to different orientation in finding a job), problems with content control and copyright infringement. In addition, he stated that ChatGPT can help teachers in designing an exam, such as creating and evaluating it. However, he still suggested that educators should critically evaluate an AI-generated knowledge and adapt it to their own teaching contexts. Similarly, Verma et al. (2023) stated that in today's world where teachers and students have easy access to information, things can go wrong. According to them, since any generated text can be presented intentionally or unintentionally, the possibility of misinformation raises concerns in accessing accurate information. Regarding misinformation, Sinatra and Hofer (2023) identified the following six conditions in promoting science denial:

1. Erosion of epistemic trust (utilizing summary information instead of original sources)
2. Misleading or patently false
3. Disinformation
4. Fabricated sources
5. Out of date information
6. Fast progress and poor transparence

The existence of the above-mentioned concerns or possible misconceptions is important in terms of researching or sourcing the reliability or accuracy of the information accessed. However, from an educational point of view, the benefits of AI may also be too effective to be ignored. The fact that this research investigates ChatGPT's answers for sentences containing myths is important in terms of accessing the correct information in eliminating the misconception.

The Nature of Science and Myths

The NoS has an important place in science education for many years (Goren & Kaya, 2023). NoS deals with the history, sociology and philosophy of science together with cognitive sciences such as psychology. NoS provides rich descriptions of what science is and how it works and is effective in evaluating the work of scientists and the scientific endeavors of society (McComas et al., 1998). In nature of science education (NoSE), scientific literacy is developed by bringing together important elements such as science values, scientific enterprise, scientific process skills and scientific knowledge production (Jimenez-Aleixandre et al., 2000). However, individuals may have some misconceptions or myths about science in their daily lives or at school. Since these myths prevent individuals from perceiving science correctly, they are undesirable types of knowledge (Eceyurt Türk & Tüzün, 2017). McComas (1996) first identified 10 myths about the NoS in his study. Later, he added five more myths to these myths and identified a total of 15 myths in the NoS (McComas, 2004). These myths are presented in Table 1.

Table 1. Nature of Science Myths (MacComas, 2004)

Myth Code	Expression
M1	Hypotheses become theories which become laws
M2	A hypothesis is an educated guess
M3	A general and universal scientific method exists
M4	Evidence accumulated carefully will result in sure knowledge
M5	Science and its methods provide absolute proof
M6	Science is procedural more than creative
M7	Science and its methods can answer all questions
M8	Scientists are particularly objective
M9	Experiments are the principle route to scientific knowledge
M10	All work in science is reviewed to keep the process honest
M11	Scientific laws and other such ideas are absolute
M12	Acceptance of new scientific knowledge is straightforward
M13	Science models represent reality
M14	Science and technology are identical
M15	Science is a solitary pursuit

Although there have been studies and activities for many years, individuals still have various myths about NoS (Eceyurt Türk & Tüzün, 2017) or have difficulties with the subjective aspects of NoS and scientific method (Cofré et al., 2019). Although studies have been conducted for many years to identify and dispel these myths, even students and teachers still believe in some myths (Bugingo et al., 2024). In this respect, in this study, it is curious whether artificial intelligence applications, which are frequently used by PSTs in the process of accessing information and which are expected to benefit more in the future, provide accurate information to individuals about these myths.

Rationale

Individuals need to be aware of how they learn, construct and articulate NoS concepts, terms and processes to learn about NoS and make informed decisions (Peters-Burton & Burton, 2020). In their study, Erduran and Levrini (2024) point out that the nature of scientific practices may also change, especially in situations where hypotheses need to be formed by analyzing large amounts of data. Here, they think that the creation of a scientific research process can cause significant changes in science education. Moreover, the persistence of belief in myths about the NoS has made access to disputed information more important. In this respect, it is useful to examine studies that investigate the usability of AI applications for uncertain topics. For example, Uludag and Zhao (2023) directed Psychology Graduate Record Examination questions to ChatGPT and concluded that ChatGPT answered 90% of the questions correctly. There is a striking result in the study that unclear questions cannot be answered completely. Elkhatat (2023), in his study investigating the authenticity of the answers generated by ChatGPT, suggested that since language models such as ChatGPT use a limited database, studies are needed to address the possible inaccuracy in the references included in the program. In the studies conducted, it is seen that AI-supported applications are effective for expressions that can be concluded clearly. However, in this study, how AI will evaluate myths as statements containing misconceptions, whether it can provide correct direction about these myths and the reliability of the resources of this information were investigated. The answers given by PSTs to myths were compared with the results obtained from ChatGPT to determine whether the use of AI-based web resources will be beneficial in eliminating possible misconceptions. In this respect, the study mainly aims to compare the performance of the artificial intelligence application (ChatGPT) with the performance of pre-service science teachers in answering nature of science myths. There are two sub-objectives in line with this aim:

1. Comparing pre-service science teachers and artificial intelligence in terms of nature of science myths,
2. Evaluation of sources of artificial intelligence implementation and the pre-service teachers' answers about nature of science myths.

METHOD

Research Design

Since this study aimed to reveal the answers of PSTs and ChatGPT about NoS myths, qualitative descriptive research design was used. Qualitative descriptive research involves a direct and simple description of any phenomenon (Sandelowski, 2010). Based on this feature, in our study, the answers of PSTs and ChatGPT were presented as they are. Although various interpretive views were included from time to time, it is estimated that it will basically include a simple description of the situation.

Participants

Since this research involves the comparison of the answers of pre-service science teachers and ChatGPT, the research was designed by using the answers obtained from the 2nd, 3rd and 4th grade pre-service teachers studying in the Science Education Department of the university where the author works and ChatGPT. Therefore, the study group of the research is pre-service science teachers studying in the 2nd, 3rd and 4th grades of the mentioned university and the answers of ChatGPT. The participants were determined according to convenient sampling method from purposive sampling methods. According to this method, the researcher facilitates the research process by choosing a situation that is easy to reach and close in terms of time, money and location (Büyüköztürk et al., 2019). Since the determination of the participants in the study was based on the principle of voluntariness, 104 (81 female, 23 male) PSTs participated in the study. The NoS course is offered in the last semester of the last year in the science teaching department. All of the PSTs participating in this study had not had this course before. Information about the participants is presented in Table 2.

Table 2. Information about the participants

Personal information		f	%
Gender	Female	81	77.89
	Male	23	22.11
Grade	2	39	37.50
	3	39	37.50
	4	24	25.00

According to Table 2, female PSTs (77.89%) participated more in the study; 2nd and 3rd year students participated equally (37.50%) and more.

Data Collection Tools

In the study, "Personal Information Form" and "Nature of Science Myths Identification Questions" developed by the researcher were used as data collection tools. The personal information form included demographic information such as gender and grade level of PSTs. The Nature of Science Myths Identification Questions included 10 myths created by McComas (1996) and 5 myths added by McComas (2004) in his updated study (McComas, 2004), for a total of 15 NoS myths (myths given in Table 1). These myths were formed by the researcher into true/false tests and research questions in which their reasons were investigated and presented to the opinions of three science education field experts. As a result of the experts' opinions, the final version of the data collection tool was created. Accordingly, this form includes 15 NoS myths and 2 questions about the source of this information.

Data Collection Process

In data collection process, PSTs were presented with a personal information form and NoS myths and asked to write their answers and justifications. This process took 20-30 minutes for each class. For the ChatGPT data, on 20.06.2024, the researcher first gave the myths one by one as a statement. They were asked about the truth or falsity of this statement and asked to present the justification and source of this answer. The statements were given to ChatGPT in Turkish in the first round and then in English. Since there were differences in the answers in these two rounds, the myths (M4, M6 and M9) whose Turkish/English answers did not match were presented again in both Turkish and English in a third round. After this round, the final version of ChatGPT's answers was recorded by adding the myths that were consistent in Turkish/English answers.

Data Analysis

Content analysis method was used to analyze the data. Content analysis is the interpretation of the obtained data with categories and themes by creating codes and bringing them together (Yıldırım & Şimşek, 2021). Content analysis can be performed with closed coding in accordance with a pre-defined analysis key, or it can be interpreted with open coding from the data obtained. In this study, the evaluation of the data was carried out according to closed coding in terms of the truth/falsity of NoS myths and open coding in terms of their causes and sources. In the analysis, the statements marked as "true" by the participants indicate that they have myths, while the statements marked as "false" indicate that they do not have these myths. Therefore, the "incorrect" percentages of the answers given to the statements are important in the answers expected from the PSTs in the presentation of the findings. The analysis key is given below as an example (Table 3).

Table 3. Nature of Science Myths Analysis Key

Nature of Science Myths	PST Answer (T/F)	Having a myth (Y/N)	Sample justification (PST)
1. Hypotheses become theories which become laws.	F	N	Theories do not always become laws (PST41)
6. Science is procedural more than creative.	T	Y	There is creativity in the creation of science, but it continues with the application of methods (PST41)
1. Hypotheses become theories which become laws	T	Y	Scientific study steps say so (PST55)
4. Evidence accumulated carefully will result in sure knowledge	F	N	No matter how carefully the evidence is collected, errors can confound it. This may lead to misinformation (PST55)
5. Science and its methods provide absolute proof	T	Y	Science and scientific methods give definitive evidence as a result of experiments or because they are testable (PST75)
14. Science and technology are identical	F	N	Science and technology are intertwined but cannot be exactly the same (PST75)

The Ethics Committee of the Aksaray University where the researcher works approved this study in accordance with accepted ethical standards (approval number 2023/05-28). Inter-rater reliability was used to ensure the reliability of the responses, with two independent researchers coding the same reasons separately. The analysis was completed with high agreement.

Findings

In this section, in line with the sub-objectives, the answers of PSTs and the ChatGPT application to the given NoS myths and the findings about the resources they used for these answers are presented.

Nature Of Science Myths of Pre-Service Science Teachers and ChatGPT

In this section, the answers of PSTs and ChatGPT to the NoS myths and their justifications are presented (Table 4). Since some questions were left blank (M3, M6, M10, M11), the total percentage of these myths is below 100%. Average percentages are based on all data.

Table 4. PSTs' and ChatGPT's responses to myths

NoS Myths	Pre-service teachers answer		ChatGPT answers	
	True (%)	False (%)	True (marked)	False (marked)
M1	60.58	39.42		x
M2	84.62	15.38	x	
M3	87.50	11.50	x	
M4	31.73	68.27*	x	
M5	32.69	67.31*		x
M6	43.27	53.87*		x
M7	17.31	82.69*		x
M8	84.62	15.38		x
M9	85.58	14.42	x	
M10	42.31	56.73*	x	
M11	38.46	60.58*		x
M12	11.54	88.46*		x
M13	69.23	30.77		x
M14	7.69	92.31*		x
M15	13.46	86.54*		x
Mean	47.37	52.24*	33.33	66.67

*Marked data indicate the items in which pre-service teachers had fewer myths.

When Table 4 is examined, according to the average of all myths, almost half of the PSTs have myths about the nature of science (47.37%). The myths that PSTs have the most are "A hypothesis is an educated guess" (84.62%), "A general and universal scientific method exists" (87.50%), "Scientists are particularly objective" (84.62%) and "Experiments are the principle route to scientific knowledge" (85. 58%), while the myths they hold the least are "Science and its methods can answer all questions" (82.69%), "Acceptance of new scientific knowledge is straightforward" (88.46%) and "Science is a solitary pursuit" (86.54%). On the contrary, ChatGPT provided correct information for more than half (66.67%) of the NoS myths. When the PSTs and ChatGPT are compared, although there is a common answer for many NoS myths in general, the answers do not match in one third (M1, M4, M8, M10, M13). In this case, while ChatGPT led to correct knowledge in three expressions (M1, M8, M13), the rate of PSTs having myths in general is low in two expressions (M4, M10). Examples of the justifications of the answers given by the PSTs and ChatGPT are presented below.

"Scientific models can change because they are always open to innovation. They represent the reality only for that moment." (PST1, M13, does not have a myth)

"Experiments are the biggest step in reaching scientific knowledge. Because the hypotheses we will form as a result of the experiment take shape accordingly." (PST2, M9, has a myth)

"That's true. Because creativity is based on imagination. It varies from person to person. Science, on the other hand, consists of precise evidence, that is, methodology." (PST3, M6, has a myth)

"It has to be so. Because science is based on precise records." (PST4, M5, has a myth)

"Some studies can also be examined for their inaccuracy. In other words, studies can also be conducted to prove that they are wrong." (PST5, M10, does not have a myth)

"As science advances, technology advances. As technology develops, science develops. Therefore, it is true." (PST9, M14, has a myth)

"True. Because by collecting carefully, complete information is formed." (PST10, M4, has a myth)

"Science and scientific methods can change as new research and studies are conducted. Therefore, we cannot call it definitive evidence." (PST13, M5, does not have a myth)

"We can access knowledge through peer discussion, expert opinion and experience. However, the probability of error in these is high. In experiments, the percentage of error is further reduced and scientific knowledge is reached. We can say that it is the most generalizable and reliable source compared to others." (PST17, M9, has a myth)

"No. Sometimes investigations are done to disprove a hypothesis that has already been put forward. Or it is examined to test to what extent it is wrong." (PST17, M9, does not have a myth)

"Yes. The law is reached step by step by inductive method." (PST18, M1, has a myth)

"Since it is information that has not existed before, it is difficult to make an immediate judgment about its accuracy in terms of criteria and it is accepted." (PST48, M12, has a myth)

"First, a testable idea is put forward. Then that idea progresses to a law as a result of testing, experimentation and research." (PST82, M1, has a myth)

"It doesn't answer all the questions, because there are still questions that remain unanswered or uncertain, which science has not reached either. For example, black hole" (PST92, M7, does not have a myth)

"This statement is true. Science is based on certain methodological principles that are generally accepted and universally valid. These methods are used to verify scientific knowledge, generate new knowledge and explain natural phenomena." (ChatGPT, M3, has a myth)

"This statement is incorrect. the results obtained in science are often based on probabilities and may involve a certain degree of uncertainty. Scientific findings may contain provisional accuracy based on available data and available technological capabilities. The results of scientific studies may change or be revised by new data or further analysis. Therefore, science and scientific methods often provide strong evidence or probabilities about nature and phenomena, rather than definitive proofs. Scientific knowledge and understanding can be constantly reviewed, reevaluated and improved." (ChatGPT, M5, does not have a myth)

"This statement is generally true. Experiments are a fundamental way of achieving scientific knowledge and form an important part of the scientific method. Many discoveries and advances in science are made by planning and conducting experiments and analyzing their results." (ChatGPT, M9, has a myth)

"This statement is often incorrect. Scientific models do not accurately represent reality; instead, they are used to explain or predict reality." (ChatGPT, M13, does not have a myth)

"This statement is often incorrect. Science is generally recognized as an endeavor within a broad scientific community, not as an individual endeavor." (ChatGPT, M15, does not have a myth)

Sources of Pre-service Teachers' and ChatGPT's Answers

In this section, the sources of the answers given by the PSTs and ChatGPT to the NoS myths (Table 5) and the sources that the PSTs can refer to if their knowledge is insufficient (Table 6) are presented.

Table 5. Sources of PSTS' and ChatGPT's responses to myths

Category	Code	PSTs		ChatGPT	
		f	%	f	%
Web sources	General web resources	44	23.03	-	-
	Wikipedia	8	4.19	-	-
	Institutional resources	5	2.62	7	14.29
	University open course resources	3	1.57	1	2.04
	Sources with trusted URL	3	1.57	-	-
	Artificial intelligence applications	1	0.52	-	-

continued on following page

Table 5. Continued

Category	Code	PSTs		ChatGPT	
		f	%	f	%
Social media	Social media (general)	29	15.18	-	-
	Instagram	10	5.24	-	-
	YouTube	7	3.66	-	-
	X (Twitter)	5	2.62	-	-
	Social media platforms that publish scientific publications	2	1.05	-	-
Scientific publications	Nature of science books	16	8.38	15	30.61
	TÜBİTAK** publications	9	4.71	-	-
	Articles	7	3.66	8	16.33
	Scientific research methods books	-	-	6	12.25
	Science education books	-	-	5	10.20
	Experiment books	-	-	3	6.12
	Technology books	-	-	2	4.08
	Epistemology books	-	-	1	2.04
	Thesis	1	0.52	-	-
Courses	Nature of science course	10	5.24	-	-
	Field courses	8	4.19	-	-
	Online nature of science courses	-	-	1	2.04
Other sources	Other sources	23	12.04	-	-

**TÜBİTAK (The Scientific and Technological Research Council of Türkiye): An institution that aims to promote and guide science and technology in Türkiye.

According to Table 5, PSTs based their answers about the nature of science mostly on general web resources (f=44, 23.03%), and they also stated that they used general social media use (f=29, 15.18%) and nature of science books (f=16, 8.38%) as sources. It is noteworthy that the PSTs included a small number of scientific publications in their answers. In addition, the number of PSTs who utilized AI in acquiring this knowledge is also quite low. The sources given by ChatGPT for the information provided were mostly NoS books (f=15, 30.61%), articles (f=8, 16.33%) and institutional web resources (f=7, 14.29%). Examples of the answers given by PSTs and ChatGPT are given below.

"The resources I search on the internet (Google), social media (Instagram, Youtube)" (PST10, General web resources/Web resources, Instagram, Youtube/Social media)

"Ondokuz Mayıs University Open Course System" (PST14, University open course resources/Web resources)

"Wikipedia, TÜBİTAK publications" (PST18, Wikipedia/Web resources, TÜBİTAK publications/Scientific publications)

"Wikipedia, physics/chemistry/biology courses, social media (Instagram, X)" (PST19, Wikipedia/Web resources, Field courses/Courses, Instagram, X/Social media)

"Scientific sites with reliable URLs that I researched online. Social media (Instagram). Lessons: Research methods in education, science learning and teaching approaches" (PST28, Sources with reliable URLs/Web sources, Instagram/Social media, Field courses/Courses)

"Nature of science books (Kuhn Paradigm Book), resources I researched on the internet (TÜBİTAK, links with .gov.tr extension), nature of science course." (PST98, Nature of science books/Scientific publications, Institutional resources/ Web resources)

"Academic Articles and Resources: You can search for articles on the scientific process, theories and laws from academic search engines such as Google Scholar." (ChatGPT, Articles/Scientific publications)

"Websites of Science Organizations: American Association for the Advancement of Science (AAAS), Royal Society (UK Royal Society), National Academy of Sciences (US National Academy of Sciences)" (ChatGPT, Institutional resources/ Web resources)

"1. The Scientific Method: A Brief History and Description (This resource provides a brief history and description of the scientific method). https://www.sciencebuddies .org/science-fair-projects/science-fair/steps-of-the-scientific-method

2. Understanding Science - University of California Museum of Paleontology (This resource explains the scientific method in detail and addresses the role of evidence and theories in science). https://undsci.berkeley.edu/article/howscienceworks_01

3. What is the Scientific Method? - Live Science (This article explains what the scientific method is, how it works and the steps in the scientific research process). https://www.livescience.com/20896-science-scientific-method.html" (ChatGPT, Institutional resources, University open course resources/Web resources, Articles/ Scientific resources)

"Creativity in Science: Chance, Logic, Genius, and Zeitgeist by Dean Keith Simonton (This book examines how creativity in science emerges and its role in scientific discoveries. It discusses how creativity is integrated with and contributes to the scientific method). https://www.amazon.com/Creativity-Science-Logic-Genius -Zeitgeist/dp/1107686363

Creativity and Its Cultivation: Addresses, Delivered at the Lister Institute by A. D. Ritchie (This book discusses how creativity in science can be encouraged and its role in scientific discovery. It addresses the balance and interaction of methodology and creativity in the scientific process). https://books.google.com/books/about/ Creativity_and_Its_Cultivation.html?id=Zf8TAAAAIAAJ" (ChatGPT, Scientific research methods books/Scientific publications)

"The Structure of Scientific Revolutions by Thomas S. Kuhn (This book examines paradigm shifts in science and the structural features of scientific knowledge. It deals with the relationship between objectivity in science and paradigm shifts).https://www.amazon.com/Structure-Scientific-Revolutions-Thomas-Kuhn/dp/0226458121" (ChatGPT, Nature of science books/Scientific publications)

"The Demon-Haunted World: Science as a Candle in the Dark by Carl Sagan (1995). (In this book on science and critical thinking, Carl Sagan describes how scientific knowledge develops and changes. He emphasizes how science is a continuous process of discovery and questioning).

Science and Its Ways of Knowing by John Hatfield (2001). (This book provides a general introduction to the nature of scientific knowledge and how science works. It also touches on the changeability and development of scientific knowledge)." (ChatGPT, Nature of science books/Scientific publications)

"The Relationship between Science and Technology by Roddam Narasimha (2009). This article examines the relationship between science and technology from a historical and philosophical perspective, discussing how they influence and enhance each other." (ChatGPT, Articles/Scientific publications)

Table 6 presents the findings on the sources that PSTs will refer to in case their knowledge about these myths is insufficient.

Table 6. Sources to be consulted by PSTs

Category	Code	f	%
Scientific publications	Nature of science books	20	19.42
	Articles	19	18.45
	Field books	6	5.82
	Thesis	5	4.85
	Google Scholar	4	3.88
	TÜBİTAK publications	4	3.88
	Experiment books	3	2.91
	Scientific conferences	2	1.94
Web resources	Web resources (general)	17	16.51
	Wikipedia	6	5.82
	Institutional resources	3	2.91
	Sources with trusted URL	3	2.91
	Artificial intelligence	1	0.97

continued on following page

Table 6. Continued

Category	Code	f	%
Social media	YouTube	4	3.88
	Instagram	2	1.94
	X (Twitter)	1	0.97
Other	University Professors	4	3.88
	Nature of science course	1	0.97
	Scientific film/documentary	1	0.97
	Science centers	1	0.97

According to Table 6, PSTs stated that they could mostly consult NoS books (f=20, 19.42%), articles (f=19, 18.45%) and general web resources (f=17, 16.51%) to obtain information about NOS myths. However, it is noteworthy that they stated that they could get help from university professors (f=4, 3.88%) and science centers (f=1, 0.97%) in obtaining this information. A few examples of the answers given by PSTs are presented below.

"Google. Because it is the easiest, fastest and free source. But from reliable sites, it can be Wikipedia." (PST4, General web resources, Wikipedia/Web resources)

"I would do research on the internet. It is more advantageous in terms of time, cost and easy accessibility" (PST11, General web resources/Web resources)

"I find it more accurate to use the resources about NOS in the library. It takes time to read and understand reliable websites or articles. For this reason, it is better to make use of books." (PST15, Nature of science books/Scientific publications)

"From Google Scholar. Because I can access every article from here. I can find all the studies of various people either in Türkiye or abroad." (PST21, Google Scholar, Articles/Scientific publications)

"Any page when I go online." (PST35, General web resources/Web resources)

"I used to look at articles on the internet to ensure high accuracy." (PST42, Articles/Scientific publications)

"From artificial intelligence. Because information can be accessed faster." (PST45, Artificial intelligence/Web resources)

"I ask my professors because I trust their knowledge." (PST54, University professors/Other)

"Since the easiest way of access is the internet now, I would access it from reliable sources. I would look at the websites of state-sponsored institutions. TÜBİTAK publications." (PST55, Sources with reliable URLs, institutional sources/Web sources, TÜBİTAK publications/Scientific publications)

RESULTS, DISCUSSION, AND CONCLUSION

This chapter compares the responses of pre-service science teachers and an artificial intelligence application (ChatGPT) to myths about frequently misunderstood issues in the nature of science. In this respect, I first analyzed the responses of the PSTs and the ChatGPT to the myths presented to them. This study concluded that half of the PSTs who participated in the study had these myths. In addition, it is seen that PSTs have a high rate of myths about hypotheses being predictions based on knowledge; the existence of general and universal scientific methods; scientists being especially objective; and experiments being the main way to reach scientific knowledge. On the other hand, the information provided by ChatGPT was more accurate and contained fewer myths. Although it was seen that the PSTs and ChatGPT gave similar answers to many myths, ChatGPT provided accurate information about more myths. In this respect, it may be quantitatively useful for PSTs to receive information about NoS myths from ChatGPT. In addition, when the answers of ChatGPT are analyzed, it is seen that for many myths, the statement can be 'generally' true or false, so ChatGPT does not provide clear information to the researchers. In this respect, it can provide a correct direction about the changeability of scientific knowledge in the NoS. Many approaches to NoS (e.g. Consensus View, Abd-El-Khalick & Lederman, 2000; Family Resemblance Approach to Nature of Science, Irzik & Nola, 2014; Features of Science, Matthews, 2012) emphasize that scientific knowledge is changeable. Therefore, it was seen that PSTs could implicitly receive this information during their exploration of NoS myths in ChatGPT. On the other hand, according to Birhane et al. (2023), the use of AI in socioscientific issues is quite effective. Sinatra and Hofer (2023) attribute this to the fact that AI applications can combine online information well when we ask questions about these topics. Since socioscientific issues are current and frequently featured on news sites or social media because they are issues that concern the society, it suggests that it may be easier for AI applications to access this information. However, since they have components such as the NoS, philosophy of science, epistemology of science and history of science, societies' interest in these topics may be lower than socioscientific issues, which are current scientific topics. This information is more likely to be found in books and scientific articles rather than social media and popular publications. This suggests that ChatGPT will be more limited in terms of the resources it can access. Therefore, researching these issues from specific NoS books and articles will yield more accurate results. According to Scharth (2022), ChatGPT uses books, news articles, websites and Wikipedia to create texts. In this respect, it has become more important to examine the sources used by ChatGPT for the myths it misleads. The second sub-objective of the research is based on this necessity. Because it is important that AI applications, which are foreseen to be used more widely in the future, lead to correct information.

The second result of the study reveals the sources of the answers given by PSTs and ChatGPT. Accordingly, PSTs stated that they frequently obtained the information they provided here from web sources and social media. Since these sources are environments where individuals with any level of knowledge can easily create content, it raises concerns in terms of access to reliable information. However, ChatGPT stated that he mostly used NoS books, articles and institutional web resources as sources for the myths presented. Therefore, both the content of NoS books will provide more accurate information for these myths due to the nature of scientific knowledge and the reliability of these sources will be beneficial in the research that PSTs will conduct using AI applications. In this respect, it shows that AI applications can be effective for teachers, students or researchers looking for answers to NoS myths. However, when the resources provided by ChatGPT are examined in depth, ChatGPT did not provide sample for the articles, but rather suggested search engines such as Google Scholar to search for articles. Therefore, it is not clear whether the articles provide information from their content. This result is consistent with Sinatra and Hofer (2023) 'erosion of epistemic trust' feature. Similarly, the same book or institutional web address was suggested in many sources. In addition, the institutional web addresses suggested the resources of several countries. This can be explained by the fact that the language used by ChatGPT is appropriate to the languages of these countries. However, it may be easier to reach the right information by suggesting resources from different countries. Therefore, it is thought that it is not yet efficient enough in terms of providing resource diversity. Also, when the resources suggested by ChatGPT are examined, it is seen that in some of them, only the name of the book or institution is given in a very general way, while in others a link is added. Similarly, while some resources are described in terms of the ways in which they will benefit from this myth, some resources are given only as suggestions. All these deficiencies may have caused ChatGPT to answer one third of the questions posed to it incorrectly in this study. In addition, since it did not elaborate on the sources it recommended, it caused some concerns in reaching the right information. On the other hand, the books on the nature of science (e.g. The Structure of Scientific Revolutions by Thomas S. Kuhn) are very effective sources for this field. The fact that PSTs frequently use web resources and social media, as well as relying on scientific sources for accurate information, is very important in accessing information since ChatGPT frequently includes these sources in text creation.

Since a comparison was made for issues that may contain misconceptions (myths) in this study, it is expected that the research will be shaped differently compared to other issues. Many studies in which AI applications are used in science education are not based on misconceptions such as NoS myths, but on clearer research.

For example, Jia et al. (2024), in their study examining the trend of AI in science education in the last 10 years, stated that the most commonly used keywords were "collaborative learning", "computer-assisted instruction", "STEM education", "perception of learning" or "learning achievement". Watters et al. (2021) also stated that AI is one of the important tools that can affect the participation of visually impaired individuals in general science subjects. Olatunde-Aiyedun (2024) demonstrated the potential of a viable curriculum by integrating AI into general science subjects in Nigeria. Although these studies focused on the general application of AI in science education, the lack of sufficient resources for issues that may contain misconceptions necessitated the discussion of the results of this study within the framework of ChatGPT and NoS features. As a result, it can be said that PSTs still have NoS myths, ChatGPT can help them in this regard, but it does not provide enough content although it provides enough resources for in-depth research. Based on this result, it is recommended to share the results of studies using different AI applications. In this way, more accurate and reliable information can be obtained by providing diversity for scientific knowledge. In addition, since ChatGPT directs the articles, it recommends to search engines rather than their content, it has been observed that researchers still need individual efforts to read a scientific publication. In this case, comparing different artificial intelligence applications may be beneficial.

REFERENCES

Abd-El-Khalick, F., & Lederman, N. G. (2000). Improving science teachers' conceptions of nature of science: A critical review of the literature. *International Journal of Science Education*, 22(7), 665–701. DOI: 10.1080/09500690050044044

Author (2023).

Bell, R. L., Matkins, J. J., & Gansneder, B. M. (2011). Impacts of contextual and explicit instruction on pre-service elementary teachers' understandings of the nature of science. *Journal of Research in Science Teaching*, 48(4), 414–436. DOI: 10.1002/tea.20402

Birer, G. C. (2023). ChatGPT. *TÜBİTAK Bilim ve Teknik Dergisi*, 56(662), 36–37.

Birhane, A., Kasirzadeh, A., Leslie, D., & Wachter, S. (2023). Science in the age of large language models. *Nature Reviews. Physics*, 5(5), 277–280. DOI: 10.1038/s42254-023-00581-4

Bugingo, J. B., Yadav, L. L., Mugisha, I. S., & Mashood, K. K. (2024). Improving teachers' and students' views on nature of science through active instructional approaches: A review of the literature. *Science & Education*, 33(1), 29–71. DOI: 10.1007/s11191-022-00382-8

Büyüköztürk, Ş., Kılıç Çakmak, E., Akgün, Ö. E., Karadeniz, Ş., & Demirel, F. (2019). *Eğitimde Bilimsel Araştırma Yöntemleri* [Scientific Research Methods in Education]. Pegem Akademi.

Cofré, H., Núñez, P., Santibáñez, D., Pavez, J. M., Valencia, M., & Vergara, C. (2019). A critical review of students' and teachers' understandings of nature of science. *Science & Education*, 28(3-5), 205–248. DOI: 10.1007/s11191-019-00051-3

Cooper, G. (2023). Examining science education in ChatGPT: An exploratory study of generative artificial intelligence. *Journal of Science Education and Technology*, 32(3), 444–452. DOI: 10.1007/s10956-023-10039-y

Dorji, K., Jatsho, S., Choden, P., & Tshering, P. (2022). Bhutanese science teachers' perceptions of the nature of science: A cross-sectional study. *Disciplinary and Interdisciplinary Science Education Research*, 4(4), 4. Advance online publication. DOI: 10.1186/s43031-021-00044-9 PMID: 37520626

Driver, R., Leach, J., Millar, R., & Scott, P. (1996). *Young people's images of science*. Open University Press.

Eceyurt Türk, G., & Tüzün, Ü. N. (2017). Lise öğrencilerinin bilim insanı imajları ve bilimin doğası mitleri [High school students' scientist images and their nature of science myths]. *Ahi Evran Üniversitesi Kırşehir Eğitim Fakültesi Dergisi, 18*(2), 19-36. Retrieved from https://dergipark.org.tr/en/pub/kefad/issue/59416/853265

Elkhatat, A. M. (2023). Evaluating the authenticity of ChatGPT responses: A study on text-matching capabilities. *International Journal for Educational Integrity*, 19(15), 15. Advance online publication. DOI: 10.1007/s40979-023-00137-0

Erduran, S., & Levrini, O. (2024). The impact of artificial intelligence on scientific practices: An emergent area of research for science education. *International Journal of Science Education*, 1–8. Advance online publication. DOI: 10.1080/09500693.2024.2306604

Goren, D., & Kaya, E. (2023). How is students' understanding of nature of science related with their metacognitive awareness? *Science & Education*, 32(5), 1471–1496. DOI: 10.1007/s11191-022-00381-9 PMID: 36185420

Irzik, G., & Nola, R. (2014). New directions for nature of science research. In Matthews, M. (Ed.), *International handbook of research in history, philosophy and science teaching* (pp. 999–1021). Springer. DOI: 10.1007/978-94-007-7654-8_30

Jia, F., Sun, D., & Looi, C. (2024). Artificial intelligence in science education (2013–2023): Research trends in ten years. *Journal of Science Education and Technology*, 33(1), 94–117. DOI: 10.1007/s10956-023-10077-6

Jiménez-Aleixandre, M. P., Bugallo Rodríguez, A., & Duschl, R. A. (2000). "Doing the lesson" or "doing science": Argument in high school genetics. *Science Education*, 84(6), 757–792. DOI: 10.1002/1098-237X(200011)84:6<757::AID-SCE5>3.0.CO;2-F

Matthews, M. (2012). Changing the focus: From nature of science (NOS) to features of science (FOS). In Khine, M. S. (Ed.), *Advances in nature of science research* (pp. 3–26). Springer. DOI: 10.1007/978-94-007-2457-0_1

McComas, W. F. (1996). Ten myths of science: Reexamining what we think we know..... *School Science and Mathematics*, 96(1), 1–14. DOI: 10.1111/j.1949-8594.1996.tb10205.x

McComas, W. F. (2004). Keys to teaching the nature of science. *Science Teacher (Normal, Ill.)*, 71(9), 24–27.

McComas, W. F., Clough, M. P., & Almazroa, H. (1998). The Role and character of the nature of science in science education. In McComas, W. F. (Ed.), *The nature of science in science education. Science & technology education library* (Vol. 5). Springer., DOI: 10.1007/0-306-47215-5_1

Monteiro, F. F., Souza, P. V. S., da Silva, M. C., Maia, J. R., Silva, W. F., & Girardi, D. (2024). ChatGPT in Brazilian K-12 science education. *Frontiers in Education*, 9, 1321547. DOI: 10.3389/feduc.2024.1321547

Olatunde-Aiyedun, T. G. (2024). Artificial intelligence (AI) in education: Integration of AI into science education curriculum in Nigerian Universities. *International Journal of Artificial Intelligence for Digital*, 1(1). https://ssrn.com/abstract=4733349

Peters-Burton, E. E., & Burton, S. R. (2020). The use of metacognitive prompts to foster nature of science learning. In McComas, W. F. (Ed.), *Nature of science in science instruction* (pp. 179–197). Springer International Publishing. DOI: 10.1007/978-3-030-57239-6_9

Sandelowski, M. (2010). What's in a name? Qualitative description revisited. *Research in Nursing & Health*, 33(1), 77–84. DOI: 10.1002/nur.20362 PMID: 20014004

Scharth, M. (2022). The ChatGPT chatbot is blowing people away with its writing skills. The University of Sydney. https://www.sydney.edu.au/news-opinion/news/2022/12/08/the-chatgpt-chatbot-is-blowing-people-away-with-its-writing-skil.html

Sinatra, G., & Hofer, B. K. (2023). ChatGPT and other generative AI could foster science denial and misunderstanding – Here's how you can be on alert. The Conversation. Retrived from https://theconversation.com/chatgpt-and-other-generative-ai-could-foster-science-denial-and-misunderstanding-heres-how-you-can-be-on-alert-204897?utm_source=twitter%26utm_medium=bylinetwitterbutton

Talan, T., & Kalınkara, Y. (2023). The role of artificial intelligence in higher education: ChatGPT assessment for anatomy course. *Uluslararası Yönetim Bilişim Sistemleri ve Bilgisayar Bilimleri Dergisi*, 7(1), 33–40. DOI: 10.33461/uybisbbd.1244777

Uludag, K., & Zhao, M. (2023). Can ChatGPT answer GRE psychology questions? *SSRN*, http://dx.doi.org/DOI: 10.2139/ssrn.4416365

Verma, G., Campbell, T., Melville, W., & Park, B. Y. (2023). Navigating opportunities and challenges of artificial intelligence: ChatGPT and generative models in science teacher education. *Journal of Science Teacher Education*, 34(8), 793–798. DOI: 10.1080/1046560X.2023.2263251

Watters, J., Hill, A., Weinrich, M., Supalo, C., & Jiang, F. (2021). An artificial intelligence tool for accessible science education. *Journal of Science Education for Students with Disabilities*, 24(1), 1–14. DOI: 10.14448/jsesd.13.0010

Yıldırım, A. & Şimşek, H. (2021). Sosyal bilimlerde nitel araştırma yöntemleri [Qualitative research methods in social sciences]. Seçkin.

Zawacki-Richter, O., Marín, V. I., Bond, M., & Gouverneur, F. (2019). Systematic review of research on artificial intelligence applications in higher education – where are the educators? *International Journal of Educational Technology in Higher Education*, 16(39), 39. Advance online publication. DOI: 10.1186/s41239-019-0171-0

KEY TERMS AND DEFINITIONS

Artificial Intelligence in Education (AIE): Terms related to the use of artificial intelligence in education.

ChatGPT: AI-powered generative text generation box.

Does Not Have a Myth: Responding "false" to myths about the NoS.

General Web Sources: Generally categorized web resources where the source is not named.

Having a Myth: Responding "true" to myths about the NoS.

Nature of Science (NoS) Myths: The misconceptions or supposedly correct information that individuals encounter in science.

Pre-Service Science Teachers (PSTs): Students studying in the 2nd, 3rd and 4th year of science teaching department.

Social Media (General): Generally categorized social media where the media type is not named.

Chapter 10
Artificial Intelligence Across Industries: A Comprehensive Review With a Focus on Education

Uma Yadav
https://orcid.org/0000-0003-2781-9756
Ramdeobaba University, India

Urmila Shrawankar
https://orcid.org/0000-0003-4523-9501
Ramdeobaba University, India

ABSTRACT

Artificial intelligence (AI) has become a disruptive force that is changing conventional wisdom in a wide range of sectors. This thorough analysis threads through the complex web of AI applications, providing a nuanced examination of its effects in several industries while narrowing down on its revolutionary impact on education. Education stands as a cornerstone experiencing significant changes, radically changing how students learn and educators educate, as companies throughout the world adjust to the disruptive force of AI. The assessment begins by outlining the broad effects of AI on important industries. Artificial intelligence (AI) in healthcare is redefining diagnostic accuracy and treatment techniques, with consequences for healthcare professional education. Gamification, adaptive learning platforms, and intelligent tutoring systems are essential instruments that are changing the face of education. The study examines the advantages of these AI applications, including improved accessibility, reduced administrative procedures, and personalized learning experiences.

DOI: 10.4018/979-8-3693-5443-8.ch010

1. INTRODUCTION

Artificial Intelligence (AI) has become a disruptive force that is redefining conventional wisdom and drastically changing the face of many different businesses. The swift progress of AI technology has led to unparalleled levels of creativity, efficiency, and decision-making capabilities. This thorough analysis seeks to negotiate the complex network of AI applications across sectors, paying special attention to how technology is revolutionizing education. AI stands at the forefront of technological innovation, permeating virtually every facet of modern society and revolutionizing industries worldwide (Yang et al., 2023). From healthcare and finance to manufacturing and entertainment, AI-driven solutions have demonstrated remarkable potential in optimizing processes, enhancing decision-making, and unlocking new possibilities for advancement. Among the myriad domains undergoing profound transformation, education emerges as a particularly fertile ground for the integration of AI technologies. As an increasingly interconnected global society places greater emphasis on the acquisition of knowledge and skills, the traditional paradigms of teaching and learning are being reimagined to meet the evolving needs of students and educators alike (Wei & Zhou, 2023).

In recent years, AI has emerged as a driving force in education, offering a diverse array of applications and opportunities for innovation. Leveraging machine learning algorithms, natural language processing, and data analytics, AI-powered tools are revolutionizing the learning experience, enabling personalized instruction, and facilitating more effective knowledge acquisition. While AI's impact on education is still in its nascent stages, the field is witnessing rapid growth and innovation as researchers, educators, and technology developers collaborate to harness its transformative potential. From adaptive learning platforms and intelligent tutoring systems to data-driven insights and administrative automation, AI is reshaping the educational landscape, promising to revolutionize teaching methodologies, enhance student outcomes, and promote lifelong learning (Xu et al., 2023). This review aims to provide a comprehensive overview of the role of AI in education, highlighting its potential benefits, challenges, and implications for educational stakeholders. By examining current research findings, identifying key trends, and offering insights into future directions, this review seeks to inform educators, policymakers, and researchers about the transformative potential of AI in shaping the future of education.

The Chapter is structured into six sections. Section 2 covers the evolution of AI in education and various sectors, and objective of the chapter. Section 3 covers the AI applications in various Industries. Section 4 covers the AI in Education, different types of AI in Education, AI for students and AI for teachers. Section 5 covers the benefits and Challenges faced. Future directions are discussed in Section 6.

2. BACKGROUND

As we navigate the 21st century, Artificial intelligence (AI) is becoming more and more prevalent, affecting industries as diverse as healthcare, banking, manufacturing, and retail. This introduction seeks to illuminate the amazing power of artificial intelligence (AI), highlighting its rising importance in guiding industries away from outdated paradigms and towards a future characterised by efficiency and creativity. (Lim et al., 2023). The advent of AI has heralded a transformative era across industries, reshaping conventional practices and catalyzing unparalleled advancements (Haleem et al., 2022). AI has become a disruptive force in recent years, upending established norms and providing never-before-seen opportunities for optimisation; the adoption of AI technologies has come to be associated with advancement as industries seek to capitalize on the potential of machine learning, data analytics, and cognitive computing. This transformative impact goes beyond automation and includes a fundamental reassessment of how tasks are carried out, decisions are made, and strategies are developed (Su & Yang, 2023).

The ability of AI to process enormous amounts of data at rates beyond the reach of human capability is one of the main factors contributing to its revolutionary impact (Kim et al., 2022). By adopting a data-centric approach, industries may get important insights, make well-informed decisions, and adjust to changing conditions with unmatched agility (Chalasani et al., 2023). As a result, artificial intelligence (AI) is more than just a technical advancement; it is a paradigm shift that requires various businesses to reconsider their current operational models and welcome a future in which intelligent technologies work in tandem with humans (Xu et al., 2023). The ability of AI to redefine efficiency, accuracy, and innovation across a wide range of areas demonstrates the technology's growing significance. AI use is now required, not optional, as sectors struggle to understand the intricacies of a quickly changing global environment (Wei & Zhou, 2023). This introduction lays the groundwork for an in-depth examination of AI's effects on several industries, focusing on particular uses, advantages, difficulties, and long-term consequences. We hope to shed light on the various facets of artificial intelligence's revolutionary impact through this assessment, offering perspectives that go beyond technical descriptions to encompass the larger societal and economic changes driven by AI's unrelenting advancement (Yang et al., 2023).

2.1 Evolution of AI

The evolution of Artificial Intelligence (AI) has been a multifaceted journey, spanning several decades and marked by transformative developments. Beginning in the mid-20th century, the conceptualization of machines simulating human intelligence laid the foundation for what would become a groundbreaking field (D. M. Sharma & Sehgal, 2023). The Dartmouth Conference in 1956 served as a pivotal moment, coining the term "Artificial Intelligence" and establishing AI as a distinct discipline. The subsequent decades witnessed the era of symbolic AI, where knowledge representation and logical reasoning were at the forefront. However, over-optimism and unmet expectations led to an "AI winter" in the 1980s and 1990s, characterized by reduced funding and interest. The resurgence of AI in the 21st century is closely tied to advancements in machine learning, with a shift towards statistical approaches and the rise of algorithms like support vector machines and neural networks. This period saw a revolution in the handling of vast datasets, commonly known as the Big Data era, empowering more complex AI models (Prasanth et al., 2023). The contemporary landscape is dominated by the resurgence of neural networks, especially deep learning, which has propelled AI to new heights in image recognition, natural language processing, and other complex tasks. As AI increasingly becomes an integral part of various industries and daily life, the ethical considerations surrounding its deployment have emanated to the front. This research paper aims to comprehensively delve into the nuanced stages of AI evolution, analyzing key milestones, breakthroughs, challenges, and the ethical dimensions that shape the current landscape and pave the way for the future of AI. Figure 1 illustrates the chronological journey of Artificial Intelligence (AI) evolution, mapping key milestones and transformative stages that have shaped the field (Kumain et al., 2020). The timeline spans from the conceptualization of machines simulating human intelligence in the mid-20th century to the current landscape dominated by the resurgence of neural networks and deep learning.

Figure 1. Timeline of Artificial Intelligence Evolution: A Graphical Journey Through Key Stages

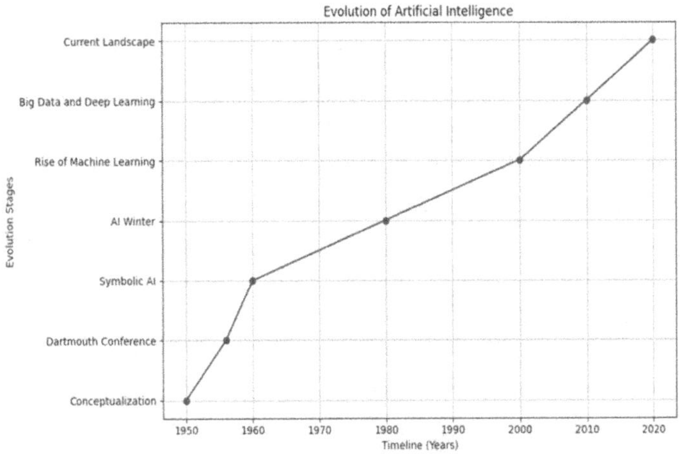

2.2 Artificial Intelligence in Various Sectors

The pervasive influence of AI across diverse sectors has catalyzed a paradigm shift, ushering in an era of innovation and efficiency (Han et al., 2023). This research paper delves into the multifaceted applications of AI in various sectors, unraveling the transformative impact on industries such as healthcare, finance, manufacturing, education, retail, and transportation. Drawing on a comprehensive analysis of recent studies, this paper emphasizes the growing percentage of research endeavors dedicated to exploring the potential of AI. In healthcare, for instance, a significant percentage of studies employ AI for diagnostic accuracy, treatment personalization, and patient care optimization (Androutsopoulou et al., 2019). In the financial sector, a rising percentage of research focuses on AI-driven fraud detection, risk management, and algorithmic trading (Harry, 2023). Similarly, manufacturing witnesses an increasing percentage of studies leveraging AI for predictive maintenance, process optimization, and smart factory initiatives. In education, a notable percentage of research explores the integration of AI into intelligent tutoring systems, gamification, and automated assessment tools. Retail experiences a surge in the percentage of studies investigating AI-powered demand forecasting, personalized recommendations, and cashier-less checkout systems. Moreover, transportation witnesses a growing percentage of studies dedicated to AI applications in autonomous vehicles, traffic management, and predictive maintenance (S. Sharma et al., 2021). This research paper aims to synthesize these trends, offering insights into the current landscape of AI research across sectors and providing a foundation for understanding the trajectory of AI's influence in shaping the future of these industries (Haidar, 2023).

Figure 2 illustrates the distribution of AI research across key sectors, providing a visual representation of the percentage distribution within each domain. The pie chart encapsulates the diverse landscape of AI applications, showcasing the allocation of research efforts in healthcare, finance, manufacturing, education, retail, transportation, Technology and IT, Telecommunications, Entertainment and Agriculture. Notably, healthcare emerges as a focal point with a significant percentage, reflecting the profound impact of AI on diagnostic accuracy, treatment personalization, and patient care optimization. Finance follows closely, emphasizing the sector's reliance on AI for risk management, fraud detection, and algorithmic trading. Manufacturing, education, and retail demonstrate substantial percentages, underscoring the widespread integration of AI in optimizing processes, enhancing learning experiences, and revolutionizing customer interactions. Transportation, while representing a comparatively smaller percentage, signifies the increasing role of AI in autonomous vehicles, traffic management, and predictive maintenance. The distinctive colors and clear labels facilitate an immediate understanding of the proportional contributions of each sector, offering a concise visual summary of the research distribution landscape within the realm of Artificial Intelligence (*AI In Education Market Size & Share Report, 2022-2030*, n.d.).

The figures in the chart are from a thorough analysis of the most recent studies and publications about the use of AI in various sectors. Using certain keywords and search terms, electronic databases and linked resources were searched as part of the evaluation process. Using "OR" and "AND" operands, these keywords were carefully grouped together in clusters of two or more in order to maximize the search parameters and produce thorough results. The collected data was carefully examined to determine the percentages of AI use in the various domains. The compiled data offers a comprehensive picture of the state of AI applications in various sector today, which shapes the conclusions and suggestions made in the research paper.

Figure 2. AI Research Distribution Across Key Sectors

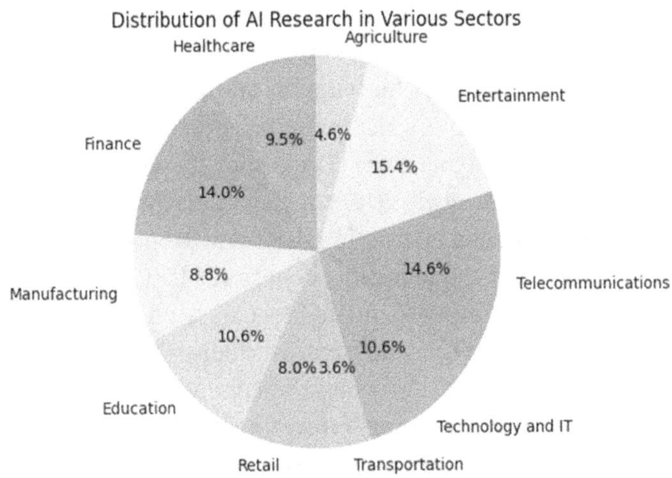

2.3 Artificial Intelligence in Current Education

When one speaks of artificial intelligence, a supercomputer immediately springs to mind. These powerful machines are the backbone of AI, providing the vast processing power required to handle complex tasks. By integrating sensors and other advanced features, AI systems can display adaptive behavior, making them capable of human-like cognitive and functional capacities. Some AI systems, such as robots, combine this processing power with physical capabilities, allowing them to interact with their environment in increasingly sophisticated ways. These advancements not only enhance the functionality of robots but also improve how supercomputers communicate with humans. To illustrate the potential of AI, various images have been created to showcase these capabilities. These include scenarios where occupants' perceived moods are used by smart buildings to manage air quality, temperature, and music playback (X. Wang, Li, et al., 2023). Beyond the conventional idea of AI as a supercomputer, artificial intelligence (AI) has found greater application in the field of education to include embedded computer systems.

For instance, when integrated into robots, AI, and computers, along with supportive equipment, facilitates the development of robotic systems designed to enhance students' learning experiences, beginning with the foundational stage of education, such as early childhood education. Timms, for example, has recommended the use of cooperative robots or "cobots" that work together with teachers or further robotic counterparts, assisting in the instruction of children on routine tasks, ranging from spelling and pronunciation to adjusting their teaching methods based on individual learners' abilities (Timms, 2016). Correspondingly, the landscape of web-based and online education, as evidenced by various studies, has evolved beyond the mere provision of online materials for download, study, and assignments (Kim et al., 2022). This evolution encompasses “intelligent and adaptive web-based systems” that actively learn from both trainers and learners, adjusting content and delivery to enrich the overall educational experience (Devedžić, 2004)(Chassignol et al., 2018)(Kahraman et al., 2010)(Peredo et al., 2011). AI’s role in education, as highlighted by Chassignol et al., extends beyond instructional content to encompass administration, teaching methodologies, and the learning process itself (Chassignol et al., 2018). This comprehensive framework, as identified by Chassignol et al., will serve as the focal point for our study, so long as an organized lens through which we analyze and understand the incorporation of AI into the educational domain.

The integration of AI in contemporary education is reshaping traditional teaching and learning methodologies, offering innovative solutions to address the evolving needs of students and educators. This overview explores the present landscape of AI applications in education, spanning from intelligent tutoring systems to adaptive learning platforms (Holmes & Tuomi, 2022). The discussion encompasses the role of AI in enhancing personalized learning experiences, facilitating data-driven policymaking for instructors, and fostering a dynamic educational environment. From automated grading systems to AI-powered educational content creation, this exploration highlights the transformative potential of AI in addressing educational challenges and unlocking new possibilities for the future of learning (Mohammad, 2020).

Figure 3. Distribution of AI usage across various sectors in education

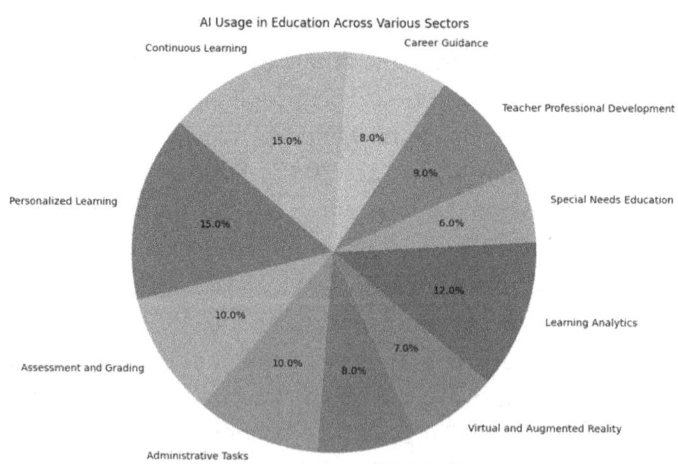

The above Figure 3 illustrates the distribution of AI usage across various sectors in education. Among the highlighted sectors, personalized learning stands out as the most prominent area of application, representing 15% of the total usage. Following closely behind are assessment and grading, administrative tasks, and continuous learning, each accounting for 10% of AI usage in education. Other sectors such as language learning, virtual and augmented reality, and learning analytics also contribute significantly, with respective proportions of 8%, 7%, and 12%. Additionally, AI's role in teacher professional development, career guidance, and special needs education is noteworthy, comprising 9%, 8%, and 6% of the overall usage, respectively. This breakdown underscores the diverse applications of AI in education, catering to a wide range of needs and objectives within the educational landscape (Zhang & Aslan, 2021).

2.4 Various Data Resources Utilized in the Research

The methodology employed for this book chapter involved a systematic search utilizing specific keywords to explore electronic databases and related resources. Table 1 provides a comprehensive list of these keywords, strategically organized in clusters of two or more using "OR" and "AND" operators to optimize the search parameters. More than 100 papers are referred, but only 75 quality papers are utilized to draft research paper. The chapter encompasses a dual focus, examining the role of Artificial Intelligence (AI) across various industries and delving into its specific impact on the field of education, with a particular emphasis on both students and teachers. The initial aspect of the review revolves around a thorough discussion of AI's multifaceted role in diverse industries. This entails an exploration of AI applications, implementations, and advancements across sectors such as healthcare, finance, manufacturing, and more. Keywords pertaining to industry-specific AI applications, automation, and technological advancements were utilized to extract relevant insights. The second focal point delves into the intricate techniques in which AI is influencing the landscape of education, examining its effects on both students and teachers. The keywords employed for this facet of the review encompass terms related to AI in education, adaptive learning platforms, personalized learning, administrative task automation, intelligent tutoring schemes, and the broader implications for educational methodologies.

The systematic combination of these keywords in the search strategy aimed to yield a comprehensive and nuanced understanding of the current state of AI across industries and its specific transformative influence on educational practices. The synthesis of findings from both domains contributes to a holistic perspective, shedding light on the dual impact of AI and providing valuable insights for researchers, educators, and practitioners alike.

Table 1. Keywords and Online Resources utilized in the present Review

Keywords	Online Resources
Artificial Intelligence (AI)	IEEE Xplore: https://ieeexplore.ieee.org/
Machine Learning	PubMed: https://pubmed.ncbi.nlm.nih.gov/
Automation	Google Scholar: https://scholar.google.com/
Industry-specific AI	ScienceDirect: https://www.sciencedirect.com/
Educational Technology	ERIC: https://eric.ed.gov/
Personalized Learning	SpringerLink: https://link.springer.com/
Adaptive Learning Platforms	Wiley Online Library: https://onlinelibrary.wiley.com/
Intelligent Tutoring Systems	Taylor & Francis Online: https://www.tandfonline.com
Impact on Students	ResearchGate: https://www.researchgate.net/
Impact on Teachers	JSTOR: https://www.jstor.org/

2.5 Objectives

The primary objectives of this book chapter are to systematically explore and analyze the diverse applications of Artificial Intelligence (AI) across various industries, with a particular focus on its profound impact on the field of education. The review aims to provide a nuanced understanding of how AI technologies have been implemented and leveraged in sectors such as healthcare, finance, manufacturing, retail, and transportation. Special attention will be devoted to unraveling the specific ways in which AI is transforming educational practices, from the integration of intelligent tutoring structures to the utilization of adaptive learning stages. By examining a spectrum of applications, the review seeks to offer insights into the current landscape of AI adoption in different industries, highlighting its implications for efficiency, innovation, and overall societal advancement. The exploration of AI's influence on education will delve into personalized learning experiences, data-driven decision-making for educators, and the broader implications for the future of the educational landscape. Through a comprehensive synthesis of existing literature, this review aspires to contribute a holistic perspective on the multifaceted role of AI in shaping industries and revolutionizing educational paradigms.

3. AI APPLICATIONS ACROSS INDUSTRIES

The transformative influence of Artificial Intelligence (AI) across various industries is reshaping the way we approach challenges and opportunities in the modern world. From healthcare to finance, manufacturing to retail, transportation to education, and beyond, AI applications are making profound impacts, enhancing efficiency, and fostering innovation (Arman & Lamiyar, 2023). In healthcare, AI is revolutionizing patient care and diagnostics; in finance, it is optimizing investment strategies and risk management; in manufacturing, it is streamlining processes and predicting maintenance needs. The retail sector benefits from AI's precise demand forecasting and personalized recommendations, while transportation witnesses advancements in traffic management and logistics (Budhwar et al., 2023). In education, AI is personalizing learning experiences, and in technology, it is powering cybersecurity and software development. Telecommunications, entertainment, and agriculture are also experiencing paradigm shifts (Javaid et al., 2023), driven by AI's ability to predict demand and optimize operations. As we explore the diverse applications of AI in these industries, it becomes evident that this technological evolution is not impartial a trend but an essential shift that infiltrates every phase of our interconnected world.

3.1 Healthcare

Artificial Intelligence (AI) applications in healthcare have revolutionized patient care, diagnosis, and treatment (Tursunbayeva & Renkema, 2023). In the realm of demand, AI is utilized for predicting patient admission rates, optimizing resource allocation, and enhancing operational efficiency. Machine learning algorithms analyze chronological patient records, disease styles, and other relevant features to forecast healthcare demands accurately (Kumar et al., 2023). This aids hospitals in proactive planning, ensuring adequate staffing levels and resource availability. Additionally, AI contributes to personalized treatment by tailoring treatment plans grounded on individual patient records, thus meeting the unique demands of diverse medical scenarios.

3.2 Finance

AI applications in finance, particularly in demand forecasting, have redefined risk management, investment strategies, and customer service. Machine learning algorithms analyze chronological financial records, market styles, and macroeconomic gages to predict demand for various financial instruments (Md Arman & Umama Rashid Lamiya, 2023). This aids financial institutions in making informed decisions about investments, managing risks, and meeting customer demands for personalized financial services. Chatbots and virtual assistants, powered by AI, enhance customer interactions by providing real-time responses to inquiries, thus addressing the growing demand for efficient and personalized financial services.

3.3 Manufacturing

In manufacturing, AI applications are instrumental in predicting demand for products, optimizing production schedules, and enhancing overall efficiency. Machine learning procedures analyze chronological production records, market styles, and external features to forecast demand accurately (Morandini et al., 2023). This enables manufacturers to adjust production levels, minimize overproduction, and meet customer demand more effectively. The effects of AI in demand forecasting ripple through the supply chain, contributing to streamlined operations, reduced costs, and improved customer satisfaction.

3.4 Retail

AI applications in retail have transformed demand forecasting and personalized recommendations. Machine learning procedures analyze consumer behavior, purchase history, and market styles to predict demand for products accurately. This not only aids retailers in managing inventory levels but also enhances the customer shopping experience (J. Wang, 2023). AI-driven personalized recommendations leverage customer data to propose yields tailored to individual inclinations, foremost to increased customer engagement and higher conversion rates.

3.5 Transportation

AI in transportation is pivotal for demand forecasting and optimizing logistics. Machine learning procedures analyze chronological transportation data, traffic patterns, and external factors to predict demand accurately (Harnal et al., 2022). This helps transportation companies optimize routes, allocate resources efficiently, and respond dynamically to changing demand. The effects of AI in transportation include reduced congestion, enhanced efficiency, and improved overall mobility (Lin et al., 2023).

3.6 Education

AI applications in education are diverse, covering personalized learning, intelligent tutoring systems, and demand forecasting for educational resources. Machine learning procedures analyze student performance records, learning styles, and curriculum trends to predict the demand for specific educational materials and adjust teaching methods accordingly (Grassini, 2023). This ensures that educational resources are aligned with student needs, contributing to improved learning outcomes and addressing the demand for personalized education (Mohsienuddin Mohammad, 2020).

3.7 Technology and IT

In the technology and IT sector, AI applications are widespread, covering areas such as cybersecurity, software development, and customer support. Machine learning algorithms analyze data patterns to predict cybersecurity threats, optimize software development processes, and provide personalized customer support (Mohammad, 2020). The effects of AI in technology and IT include enhanced security measures, improved software efficiency, and more responsive customer service.

3.8 Telecommunications

AI applications in telecommunications are integral for predicting network demand, optimizing service delivery, and enhancing customer experiences. Machine learning algorithms analyze network data, customer usage patterns, and real-time demand to predict network requirements accurately (Androutsopoulou et al., 2019). This aids telecommunications companies in optimizing network resources, reducing downtime, and meeting the growing demand for seamless connectivity and services.

3.9 Entertainment

In the entertainment industry, AI applications cover content recommendation algorithms, personalized content creation, and demand forecasting for entertainment services. Machine learning procedures analyze user preferences, market trends, and viewing history to predict content demand accurately (Naser & Bhattacharya, 2023). This contributes to personalized content recommendations, increased user engagement, and improved overall entertainment experiences.

3.10 Agriculture

AI applications in agriculture are transforming demand forecasting for crop yield, resource optimization, and precision farming (Javaid et al., 2023). Machine learning procedures analyze chronological agricultural records, weather patterns, and soil conditions to predict crop demand accurately. This aids farmers in optimizing resource usage, improving crop yields, and meeting the demand for sustainable and efficient agricultural practices (Bondre & Yadav, 2022).

4. AI IN EDUCATION: OVERVIEW

The speed at which technology has advanced in recent decades has drastically changed the world around us. This transformation has permeated numerous industries, including education. Digital technologies have become an essential part of our day-to-day lives, shaping how we access information, communicate, and behave. As a result, education has also been significantly impacted by these changes. As we navigate the complexities of the digital era, the incorporation of AI in education holds enormous potential. With the continuous development of AI, new applications in education are emerging. These applications include, but are not limited to, digitalization of educational resources, gamification, personalized learning experiences, and intelligent tutoring schemes. These AI applications have the potential to revolutionize the learning process and enhance student engagement, offering adaptive and individualized learning experiences (Chiu, 2024). AI in education has the prospective to transform the learning procedure and enhance student engagement by offering adaptive and individualized learning experiences. By leveraging AI technologies, educators can monitor students' progress, deliver tailored learning materials and tasks, provide timely and effective feedback, and enable seamless communication between students and teachers. Moreover, AI can assist in automating administrative tasks, allowing teachers to focus more on instructional design and personalized training. Despite the advancements in AIEd skills, there is a dearth of educational perceptions in AIEd investigation as emphasized by recent literature analyses (Zheng et al., 2023). Interdisciplinary investigation involving educators and educational researchers is crucial to bridge this gap and develop practical guidelines and illustrations for fellow educators (Chen et al., 2020). In imperative to fully harness the potential of AI in education, it is important for collaborative research efforts to focus on AI technology applications that can directly impact learning outcomes in real educational settings (Adiguzel et al., 2023). Figure 4 shows the various roles of AI in education for students and teachers.

Figure 4. Roles of AI in Education

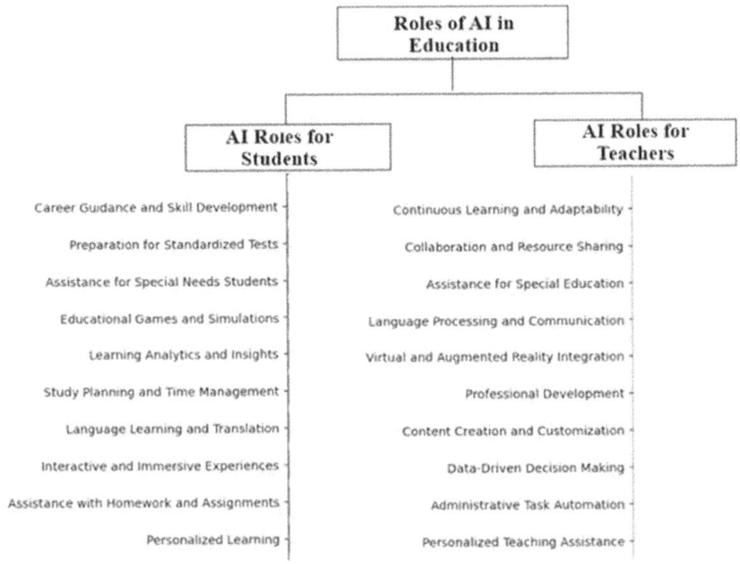

The incorporation of AI into the arena of education has escorted in a transformative era, revolutionizing various aspects of the learning process. One of the prominent roles of AI in education is its contribution to personalized learning capabilities. Through adaptive learning stages and intelligent tutoring systems, AI analyzes individual student records to tailor educational content, ensuring a customized pace and difficulty level. Moreover, AI shows a crucial role in streamlining administrative tasks, automating processes such as grading and scheduling. This administrative efficiency allows educators to devote more time to teaching, fostering a more dynamic and engaging learning environment. Data-driven decision-making is another key aspect, with AI employing learning analytics to provide valuable insights into student performance, learning patterns, and areas that may require attention. The creation of smart content, virtual and augmented reality applications, and language processing capabilities further enhance content delivery, making learning more interactive and accessible. Despite these advancements, ethical considerations, including bias mitigation and privacy concerns, necessitate a careful and responsible approach to the integration of AI in education. Continuous efforts to address challenges, coupled with ongoing professional development for educators, will be crucial in realizing the full prospective of AI in shaping the future of education.

4.1 Types of AI in Education

Studies conducted emphasize the ubiquitous integration of Artificial Intelligence (AI) into our daily lives (Knickerbocker et al., 2018). AI technologies have found application in automatic parking systems, smart sensors for photography, personalized assistance, and have significantly transformed the landscape of education (Cipriano et al., 2022). Educational materials are now readily accessible through smart devices, marking a paradigm shift in learning methodologies (Ala-Mutka, 2005). The incorporation of AI in educational institutions has led to the automation of various administrative tasks, freeing educators from time-consuming grading and assessment responsibilities (Jones, 2001).

- **Automation of Administrative Task:** One notable area of transformation facilitated by AI is the automation of administrative tasks. This involves the application of AI in processing repetitive tasks, such as grading exams and assessing homework, thereby saving educators valuable time (Sørensen et al., 2023). While technology exists for grading multiple-choice exams, challenges persist in employing AI for essay-type exams, with ongoing research in software development to address this issue. Additionally, AI plays a role in streamlining the admission process for new students (Lüersmann, 2023).
- **Smart Content:** Smart Content represents another impactful application of AI in education. Described by Gao & Huang (Gao & Huang, 2019) as an AI technology aiming to condense textbooks into useful tools for exam preparation, smart content includes applications like Cram101 and JustTheFacts101. These tools enhance textbook content by providing chapter summaries, flashcards, and practical tests, making learning more coherent and accessible (X. Wang, Anwer, et al., 2023). Furthermore, platforms like Netex Learning AI facilitate the creation of electronic curriculum and educational content, incorporating online assistance programs, audios, and illustrative videos (Zheng et al., 2023).
- **Intelligent Tutoring Systems:** Intelligent Tutoring Systems (ITS) represent a human guide and facilitator in various educational environments (Rus et al., 2013). Originating from the idea of self-tutoring developed by educational psychologist Benjamin Bloom in the 1970s, ITS has progressed significantly. Modern applications, such as Carnegie Learning's "Mike" Software, leverage cognitive science and AI technologies to create personalized tutoring systems for students (Zheng et al., 2023). These advancements underscore the transformative impact of AI in reshaping educational methodologies and fostering personalized, efficient learning experiences.

- **Language Processing and Translation:** Language Processing and Translation harness AI to enhance learning experiences. Natural Language Processing (NLP) enables interactive and conversational learning, while Language Translation Tools facilitate communication among students and educators with diverse linguistic backgrounds.
- **Educational Games and Simulations:** Educational Games and Simulations introduce gamified learning platforms driven by AI, engaging students in interactive and immersive educational experiences (Gong et al., 2020). Simulations replicate real-world scenarios, enabling students to practically apply theoretical knowledge.
- **Predictive Analytics and Learning Insights:** Predictive Analytics and Learning Insights in AI involve Learning Analytics that analyze large datasets, providing insights into student performance, and Predictive Analytics that identify potential challenges and predict student outcomes, allowing for proactive interventions.
- **Career Guidance and Skill Development:** Career Guidance and Skill Development benefit from AI-Based Career Counseling, offering personalized guidance based on individual strengths, interests, and market trends. Skill Development Platforms leverage AI to provide adaptive learning experiences, enhancing students' skills across various domains. Together, these diverse applications underscore AI's pivotal role in fostering personalized, efficient learning experiences for both students and educators.

4.2 AI for Students

The integration of AI in education brings forth a diverse array of applications designed to enhance both student learning experiences and the teaching strategies employed by educators. For students, AI plays a pivotal role in fostering personalized learning environments. Adaptive learning platforms and customized learning paths leverage AI algorithms to analyze individual student data, tailoring educational content to suit unique learning styles. Furthermore, AI extends its support to homework and assignments, providing assistance through platforms offering explanations and automated grading. The realm of interactive and immersive experiences is enriched by AI-driven virtual and augmented reality applications, making complex concepts more tangible. Language learning benefits from AI through apps and translation tools, breaking down language barriers and promoting global collaboration. Smart planners and task management tools aid students in effective study planning and time management. Learning analytics and insights, powered by AI, provide educators with valuable information on student performance and progress, facilitating informed decision-making. Educational games, simulations, and AI-driven assistance for special needs students contribute to a diversified and inclusive learning landscape. AI also aids in test preparation, career guidance, and skill development, offering personalized paths for each student.

Figure 5. Impact of Artificial Intelligence in Diverse Educational Roles for Students

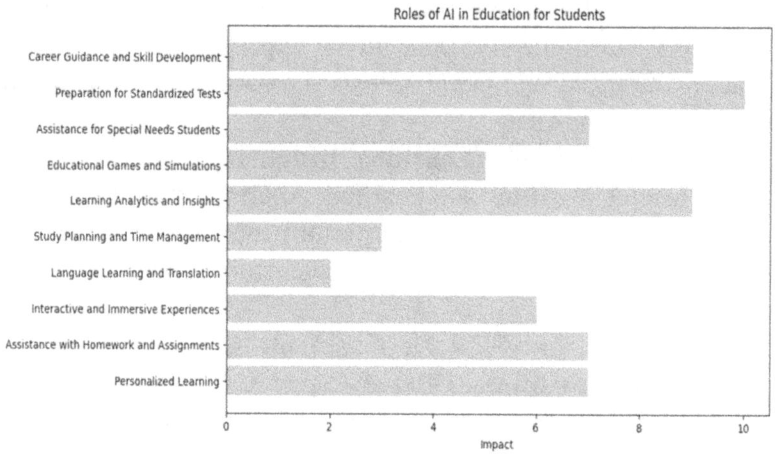

Figure 5 portrays the impact of Artificial Intelligence (AI) in diverse educational roles catering to students. The chart illuminates the perceived influence of AI in categories such as personalized learning, assistance with homework and assignments, interactive and immersive experiences, language learning and translation, study planning and time management, learning analytics and insights, educational games and simulations, assistance for special needs students, preparation for standardized tests, and career guidance and skill development. Each category is assigned a numerical impact value, ranging from 1 to 10, symbolizing the extent of AI's positive influence, with higher values indicating a more profound impact (Peredo et al., 2011). This visual representation serves as a comprehensive guide, illustrating the multifaceted ways in which AI is anticipated to enhance the educational journey for students.

4.3 AI for Teachers

AI assumes the role of a supportive partner in education. Personalized teaching assistance is facilitated through adaptive learning platforms and intelligent tutoring systems, aiding educators in tailoring their instructional approaches to meet the diverse needs of their students. Administrative task automation, including grading assistance and resource management, alleviates the burden of routine tasks, allowing teachers to focus on more impactful aspects of education. Data-driven decision-making becomes a reality with AI, offering insights from learning analytics and predictive analytics to guide educators in refining their teaching strategies. Content creation and customization benefit from AI-generated recommendations and content generation tools, enhancing the quality and relevance of educational materials. Professional development receives a boost with AI-driven training programs and feedback mechanisms, supporting continuous improvement in teaching practices. Virtual and augmented reality integration, language processing, and communication tools empower teachers to create immersive learning environments and foster effective communication with students. Assistance for special education and collaboration through AI-powered platforms contribute to an inclusive and collaborative educational landscape. Continuous learning and adaptability are promoted through AI-driven strategies that help educators stay abreast of educational trends and adjust their teaching methodologies accordingly (Chassignol et al., 2018). In essence, the incorporation of AI in education for both students and teachers marks a transformative shift towards a more personalized, efficient, and inclusive learning ecosystem.

Figure 6. Impact of Artificial Intelligence in Various Educational Roles for Teachers

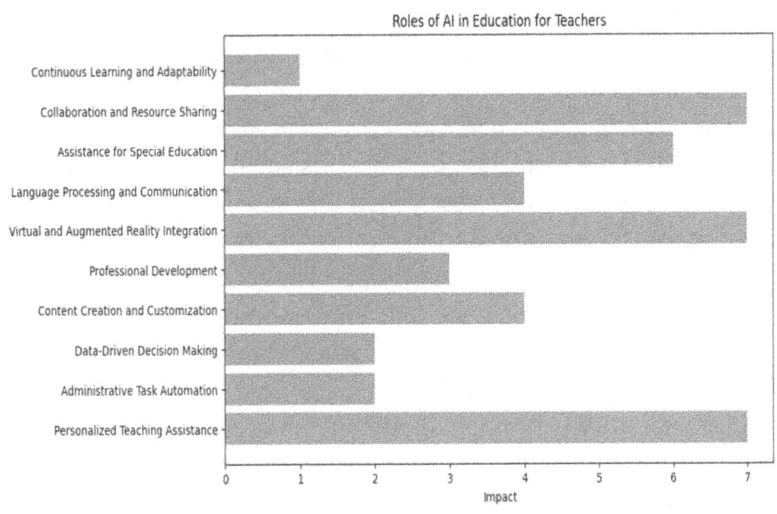

Figure 6 depicts the impact of AI in various roles within the realm of education for teachers. The chart showcases the perceived influence of AI in personalized teaching assistance, administrative task automation, data-driven decision-making, content creation and customization, professional development, virtual and augmented reality integration, language processing and communication, assistance for special education, collaboration and resource sharing, and continuous learning and adaptability. Each category is assigned a numerical impact value, ranging from 1 to 10, with higher values indicating a greater influence. The visual representation underscores the multifaceted nature of AI's contributions to teaching practices, emphasizing its role in streamlining administrative tasks, enhancing professional development opportunities, and fostering adaptive and collaborative learning environments. The chart serves as a visual guide, offering a comprehensive overview of the diverse ways in which AI is perceived to positively impact the educational landscape for teachers.

5. BENEFITS AND CHALLENGES

5.1 Benefits

The integration of AI into the education sector has emerged as a transformative force, offering a range of benefits that significantly enhance the learning experience. One notable advantage is the facilitation of personalized learning through adaptive learning stages and Intelligent Tutoring Schemes (ITS). AI-driven platforms adapt educational content based on individual student needs and learning styles, tailoring the learning experience to address specific strengths and challenges. This personalization fosters a more engaging and effective learning environment. Furthermore, AI in education contributes to increased efficiency, particularly in administrative tasks (Zhai et al., 2021). Automation of processes such as grading assessments and admissions procedures allows educators to redirect their focus from time-consuming tasks to more impactful teaching and mentoring. Learning analytics, powered by AI, analyze vast datasets to provide cherished insights into student enactment and learning patterns. This data-driven approach not only streamlines decision-making processes but also enables educators to implement targeted interventions for better academic outcomes (de Leon et al., 2024).

Improved accessibility is another significant benefit brought about by AI in education. The development of smart content apps and virtual learning environments ensures that educational materials are not only more interactive but also easily accessible to a diverse student population. Language processing and translation tools powered by AI facilitate communication among students from various linguistic backgrounds, breaking down language barriers and fostering inclusivity. AI has the prospective to transform education by offering numerous benefits. These benefits include personalized learning, enhanced instruction, improved assessment, cost-effective education, accessibility, language learning, skill development, and data analysis.

5.1.1 Personalized Learning

AI can analyze a student's performance, learning style, and preferences to provide personalized learning experiences. This ensures that each student receives the most relevant and effective education. For example, AI-powered platforms like Adaptive Learning can analyze a student's performance and adjust the learning material accordingly. Personalized learning systems, often referred to as adaptive learning platforms or intelligent tutoring systems, represent a prominent and valuable application of AI in supporting both students and teachers. These systems offer students access to diverse learning materials tailored to their individual needs and subjects (Regan & Jesse, 2019). For instance, instead of conventional chemistry practice through worksheets or textbooks, students may engage with an adaptive and interactive multimedia version of the course content. Studies comparing the performance of students on standardized exams reveal that, in contrast to traditional teacher-led training, customized learning systems provide higher test scores (Ladson-Billings, 1995). AI successfully enhances kids' learning progressions, as shown by recent research from Microsoft (2018) that involved over 2000 students and teachers from several nations, including Singapore, the U.S., the UK, and Canada. These platforms have the capacity to detect gaps in students' past knowledge and modify instructional resources and tools to support their development. While current systems provide learner models based on knowledge and cognition, they do not yet have models that account for the social, emotional, and motivational states of learners (Herder et al., 2017). Personalized learning systems present a viable option for distance learning that may reform K–12 education going forward, especially in light of the COVID-19 epidemic and the move toward remote K–12 education (N. Wang & Lester, 2023). Lincoln Elementary School in Washington State deployed DreamBox, an AI-driven adaptive learning platform, to overcome math competency disparities among children in grades three through five. DreamBox is a personalised, interactive learning environment that adjusts to each student's performance in real time by changing the level of difficulty of the content and giving them focused feedback. Students who used DreamBox over a six-month period outperformed their peers on standardised math examinations, with an average rise of 20 percentile points. Focused teacher training, additional computer resources, and site modifications for offline usage addressed challenges like integrating the platform's content with curricular requirements and ensuring equal access to technology. Despite these barriers, DreamBox's integration led to substantial gains in math scores and engagement, showcasing the potential of AI-driven platforms to build tailored and effective learning environments. In addition to meeting a variety of learning requirements, this case study demonstrates how DreamBox's adaptive technology gives teachers access to useful information that they can use to improve their teaching methods.

5.1.2 Automated Assessment Systems

In K–12 education, automated assessment systems are becoming a well-known and exciting use of machine learning (Murphy, 2019). The purpose of these scoring algorithm systems is to grade student papers, tests, assignments, and other duties that teachers usually complete. Teachers' responsibilities can be reduced, and their capacity and productivity increased with the use of assessment algorithms, which provide course assistance and management tools. As essays are assessed, these systems should ideally be able to quickly assist students (Reiss, 2021). For the purpose of evaluating essays from a large number of students, many MOOC providers, including Coursera and EdX, have included automated scoring algorithms into their learning platforms (Murphy, 2019). Conversely, tools like "Gradescope" have been adopted by over 500 universities to enhance scoring and assessment processes (Ellis, 2018). This application helps educators by saving time and effort by highlighting erroneous responses and marking correct ones. Thus, in contrast to numerical assessments that evaluate correct or incorrect test responses, automated assessment systems take a different tack when it comes to marking and giving comments on essays. All things considered, these scoring schemes have the capacity to take into account the complexities of the educational setting, assisting students in their learning processes by providing prompt feedback and direction to improve and rework their writing. AI can analyze student responses to assessments, identify patterns, and provide immediate feedback. This allows teachers to identify areas where students may need additional support. For example, AI-powered platforms like Knewton can analyze student responses and provide personalized feedback.

5.1.3 Empowering Education

AI can be used to create adaptive learning platforms that cater to the diverse needs of students with disabilities. For instance, AI-powered platforms like BrailleNet can convert text into braille, making educational materials accessible to visually impaired students. Artificial Intelligence (AI) is increasingly being used to create adaptive learning platforms that cater to the diverse needs of students with disabilities. These AI-powered platforms can help make education more accessible and personalized, ensuring that all learners can engage with course materials, activities, and assessments. Another way that AI is being used to improve accessibility in education is through the use of generative AI tools. When used carefully, these tools can serve as an accessible resource, assisting in course redesign and addressing issues related to academic integrity while preserving the adaptability and diversity offered by the Universal Design for Learning (UDL) framework. However, while utilizing generative AI in the classroom, it's crucial to make sure that fundamental accessibility guidelines and procedures are followed. This entails going over and editing information produced by generative AI to ensure that varied representation, biased language, and content claims are accurate (Lim et al., 2023). In addition to these examples, AI is also being used to support people with non-standard speech, vision impairment, hearing impairment, and mobility issues. In conclusion, AI is frolicking an increasingly important role in making education more accessible for students with disabilities. By providing adaptive learning platforms and tools that furnish to the miscellaneous needs of these students, AI is helping to create a more inclusive and equitable learning atmosphere for all. However, it is significant to guarantee that basic convenience principles and practices are applied when using AI in the classroom, and that personal data is collected, stored, and processed in a secure and ethical manner.

5.1.4 Language Learning

In the dynamic landscape of language learning, AI has emerged as a revolutionary force, particularly evident in platforms like Duolingo. These AI-powered systems transcend traditional language education by introducing interactive simulations and games, creating a learning environment that fosters crucial skills such as problem-solving and critical thinking. Duolingo, a prominent exemplar in this domain, leverages AI algorithms to deliver personalized language learning experiences tailored to individual student progress. Through continuous analysis of user data, including learning pace and proficiency levels, AI ensures that each learner receives content suited to their unique needs. The adaptability of Duolingo's AI system extends to dynamic learning paths, interactive simulations that simulate real-world language scenarios, and a gamified structure that transforms language acquisition into an engaging journey. Real-time feedback, progress tracking, and proficiency assessments further contribute to the platform's efficacy (Trisnawati et al., 2023). The integration of AI not only accelerates language acquisition but also enhances accessibility and inclusivity, ensuring that learners with diverse needs and preferences can benefit from a personalized and interactive language learning experience. As AI remains to shape the landscape of education, platforms like Duolingo exemplify the potential for technology to revolutionize language education, making it more engaging, effective, and inclusive.

5.1.5 Skill Development

In the realm of skill development, Artificial Intelligence (AI) is ushering in a new era of interactive and engaging learning experiences, with platforms like CodeCombat at the forefront of this transformative wave. CodeCombat, fueled by AI algorithms, stands as a testament to the fusion of education and technology, offering an immersive journey for individuals seeking to enhance their coding skills. The platform's adaptive learning paths, meticulously crafted by AI, dynamically respond to each learner's progress and proficiency, ensuring a personalized and effective educational trajectory. CodeCombat introduces learners to a gamified environment, where real-world coding challenges are presented as interactive simulations and games, fostering not only coding skills but also essential problem-solving and critical thinking abilities. One of the distinguishing features of CodeCombat is its provision of real-time feedback and guidance, a hallmark of AI integration. Learners receive immediate insights into their code implementations, allowing for continuous refinement and improvement (Pham et al., n.d.). The gamified learning experience, grounded in principles of competition and reward, propels individuals through various levels, creating a dynamic and engaging educational journey. Importantly, the platform embraces the social aspect of learning, facilitating peer collaboration and healthy competition, which further enriches the overall educational experience. The comprehensive progress tracking enabled by AI ensures that learners and educators alike have access to detailed analytics, including proficiency levels, completion rates, and time invested in challenges. This data-driven approach empowers individuals to monitor their development, set realistic goals, and identify areas for improvement. Moreover, the inclusive nature of CodeCombat, facilitated by AI, ensures accessibility for learners with diverse backgrounds and skill levels. In essence, platforms like CodeCombat underscore the symbiotic relationship between AI and education, showcasing how technology can revolutionize skill development. As AI continues to evolve, the potential for creating dynamic, interactive, and personalized learning experiences becomes increasingly promising, reshaping the landscape of skill development in the digital age (Chiu et al., 2023).

5.1.6 Facial Recognition Systems and Predictive Analytics

Facial recognition software is employed to internment and monitor students' facial terminologies, offering valuable insights into their behaviors during learning procedures. These systems serve as a proactive tool for teachers, enabling them to observe and understand student engagement levels. The data obtained from facial recognition technology allows educators to take timely action and intervene when necessary, fostering the development of learner-centered practices. In addition to facial recognition, predictive analytics algorithms play a pivotal role in identifying and detecting patterns in learners through statistical analysis. For instance, these algorithms can be harnessed to pinpoint university students who may be at risk of failing or not completing a course. By utilizing these predictive analytics, instructors gain the ability to intervene early, providing targeted support to students who may require additional assistance. The amalgamation of facial recognition and predictive analytics contributes to a comprehensive approach to student monitoring and support. This not only empowers teachers to understand and respond to individual needs but also enhances the overall engagement and success of students. As educational technologies continue to evolve, the ethical and responsible implementation of these tools remains crucial to ensure a positive and supportive learning environment.

5.1.7 Social Networking Sites and Chatbots

Social networking sites (SNSs) play a crucial role in connecting students and teachers concluded various social media platforms. Scholars have underscored the significance of leveraging SNSs, such as Facebook, as tools to extend learning prospects beyond traditional classroom settings. These platforms serve not only as a means of academic communication but also as avenues to monitor students' health and strengthen student-teacher relationships. Numerous researchers have delved into the impact of social media on education, highlighting its potential to enhance both student and teacher learning experiences and intellectual announcement. Studies emphasize that integrating social media into educational practices can contribute to active learning, the development of collaboration skills, and the expansion of connections with communities beyond the classroom (Chiu et al., 2023). The collaborative and interactive nature of social media platforms fosters an environment conducive to students' engagement with course materials and facilitates meaningful connections with peers and educators. In parallel, chatbots have found their place within social media outlets through various AI systems. Often referred to as dialogue systems or conversational agents, chatbots offer a unique advantage with their ability to respond in a natural and conversational tone. An illustrative example is the deployment of a "text-based chatbot" scheme called "Pounce" at "Georgia State University". This system was instrumental in assisting students with tasks such as the registration and admission process, as well as navigating financial assistance and other administrative aspects. The use of chatbots in this context exemplifies their potential to streamline administrative processes and enhance student support services. In conclusion, the incorporation of social media and AI-driven chatbots in education demonstrates the evolving landscape of educational technology (Bahroun et al., 2023). These tools not only facilitate communication and collaboration but also contribute to a more inclusive and supportive learning environment. As technology continues to advance, responsible and ethical utilization of these platforms remains essential to harness their full potential in the realm of education.

AI has the impending to renovate education by providing personalized, accessible, and effective learning involvements for all students. By leveraging AI-powered tools and platforms, educators can enhance the quality of instruction, improve assessment, and provide more comprehensive and engaging learning surroundings for students. The incorporation of AI in education is associated with several advantages, including personalized learning experiences, increased administrative efficiency, and improved accessibility (Bond et al., 2024). As the field continues to evolve, the ongoing integration of AI technologies is poised to reshape traditional educational paradigms, offering a further adaptive, pleasing, and accessible learning environment for students around the world. The applications of Artificial Intelligence (AI) present a promising avenue for enhancing both students' and teachers' educational experiences, offering valuable support in addressing instructional challenges and concerns. However, it is crucial to recognize that AI cannot replace human interaction, emphasizing the importance of a balanced approach in education (Bala et al., 2022). Given the diverse learning styles and needs of students, AI serves as a valuable tool but is not a comprehensive substitute for the multifaceted role of educators. While AI can serve as a time-saving and intellectual aid for educators, it should be viewed as one component within the broader toolkit available to educators. To maximize the benefits of AI and minimize potential drawbacks, it is imperative for both instructors and students to comprehend the bounds, inherent threats, and ethical considerations associated with AI applications in education (Chen et al., 2020). Acknowledging these factors ensures a responsible and effective integration of AI into educational settings, fostering a harmonious relationship between technology and human-driven pedagogy. As the educational landscape continues to evolve, a nuanced understanding of AI's capabilities and limitations is essential to harness its potential while upholding the ethical standards and values intrinsic to education (Chan, 2023).

5.2 Challenges

As the education landscape undergoes a transformative shift with the integration of AI tools, it becomes imperative to approach this transition with a comprehensive understanding of ethical considerations, implementation costs, and the essential need for teacher training. The infusion of AI in educational settings holds immense promise for personalized learning, increased efficiency, and improved accessibility (Bond et al., 2024). However, this technological evolution comes with ethical complexities, financial implications, and a prerequisite for educators to be adept in harnessing the potential of AI tools effectively. This discourse aims to explore the multifaceted dimensions of integrating AI into education, emphasizing ethical guidelines, financial planning, and the critical role of teacher training in ensuring a responsible and impactful deployment of AI tools for the enhancement of learning experiences.

5.2.1 Ethical Considerations

The incorporation of AI in education necessitates a meticulous examination of ethical considerations to ensure responsible and equitable implementation. This section delves into specific ethical dimensions that demand careful attention, highlighting potential drawbacks and the strategies being employed to address these challenges in real-world educational settings:

1. **Privacy and Data Security:** AI tools in education often require the collection, processing, and storage of sensitive student data, raising significant privacy and data security concerns. Compliance with data protection regulations such as the General Data Protection Regulation (GDPR) in Europe, the Family Educational Rights and Privacy Act (FERPA) in the United States, and other regional laws is essential to safeguarding student information.
   - Specific Regulations: GDPR mandates strict controls on data handling, requiring explicit consent, secure data storage, and clear guidelines on data retention and deletion. FERPA focuses on protecting student educational records, granting parents and students rights over their data and restricting unauthorized access.
   - Potential Risks: Despite regulatory frameworks, the risk of data breaches remains a critical concern. Unauthorized access to sensitive information, exposure of personal data, and misuse by third parties are prevalent threats that could have far-reaching consequences, including identity theft and loss of trust.
   - Addressing Challenges: To mitigate these risks, educational institutions are implementing robust encryption protocols to protect data during transmission and storage, alongside stringent access controls to ensure only authorized personnel can access sensitive records. Clear strategies on data retention and deletion are established, aligning with regulatory requirements to minimize data exposure. Furthermore, transparent communication with students and parents is crucial, informing them of the type of data collected, its purpose, and the security measures in place.
2. **Algorithmic Bias and Fairness:** AI algorithms, if not carefully designed, may perpetuate biases present in training data. Mitigating algorithmic bias requires:
   - Ongoing assessment of AI algorithms to identify and rectify biases, ensuring fair and equitable treatment.
   - Diverse and representative training datasets to minimize the risk of bias based on race, gender, or socio-economic factors.

- Regular audits and external reviews to identify and address potential biases that may emerge over time.
- Implementation of explainable AI models, allowing stakeholders to understand the decision-making process and identify potential biases.

3. **Informed Consent:** Informed consent is crucial to ensure transparency and respect for individuals' autonomy regarding the use of AI tools:
   - Educational institutions should provide clear, accessible information on the purpose, scope, and implications of AI integration.
   - Consent forms should be presented in plain language, avoiding technical jargon, and should explicitly detail how student data will be used.
   - Continuous communication channels should be established to keep stakeholders informed about any changes in AI usage.
   - Mechanisms for revoking consent and opting out of certain AI-related activities should be readily available.
4. **Accountability and Transparency:** To maintain accountability and transparency in AI implementations:
   - Educational institutions should establish clear lines of responsibility for the ethical use of AI, specifying roles and accountabilities.
   - Transparent AI models and decision-making processes should be prioritized, allowing stakeholders to understand how AI influences educational outcomes.
   - Regular reporting on AI usage, outcomes, and any corrective actions taken should be made available to the broader educational community.
   - Establishing an ethical review board or committee can provide oversight and ensure alignment with ethical guidelines.
5. **Equity and Inclusivity:** Promoting equity and inclusivity involves proactive measures to address disparities:
   - AI systems should be designed with a focus on mitigating existing inequalities and promoting equal opportunities for all students.
   - Regular audits should assess whether AI tools contribute to or alleviate existing disparities in educational outcomes.
   - Educational institutions should actively seek feedback from diverse stakeholder groups to identify and address any unintended consequences of AI implementations.
   - Continuous monitoring of AI's impact on marginalized groups ensures that it aligns with principles of social justice and inclusivity.

In navigating these ethical considerations, educational institutions can lay the groundwork for responsible AI integration, fostering an educational environment that prioritizes privacy, fairness, transparency, accountability, and inclusivity.

5.2.2 Trustworthiness, Misinformation, and Misuse of AI

Given the growing prevalence of AI technologies in education, it is imperative to tackle a number of noteworthy problems. The possibility of false information and errors being created by AI systems is one major problem. Even with their enhanced capabilities, AI technologies can occasionally produce false or misleading information. To guarantee the accuracy of instructional information, educators must exercise caution and thoroughly evaluate AI outputs. Furthermore, the reliability and comprehensibility of AI systems are crucial factors to take into account, especially for educators who could be reluctant to adopt new technology. If educators are not well-versed in AI or are older and less experienced, they can be reluctant to embrace the technology. To gain users' trust, AI systems must be developed with transparent algorithms and understandable justifications for their decision-making procedures. Furthermore, there is serious worry about the possibility that students would abuse AI for plagiarism or cheating. As access to AI technologies increases, it's critical to have strong detection mechanisms in place to spot and stop academic dishonesty. In order to ensure that the advantages of AI technologies are realised while minimising any possible negatives, educational institutions may promote a more effective and ethical integration of AI technology by proactively addressing these challenges.

5.2.3 Implementation Costs

The successful integration of AI in education demands a nuanced understanding of the associated implementation costs. This section delves into the various financial considerations that educational institutions must navigate:

1. **Initial Investment:** Implementing AI tools in education requires a substantial upfront investment encompassing several key areas:
    - Technology Infrastructure: Upgrading or establishing robust technology infrastructure capable of supporting AI applications. This includes high-performance computing systems, cloud infrastructure, and networking capabilities.
    - Software Development: Customization or development of AI applications tailored to the specific needs of educational institutions. This may involve collaboration with software developers, AI specialists, and educational technologists.
    - Staff Training: Investing in comprehensive training programs for educators, administrators, and IT personnel to ensure proficiency in utilizing AI tools effectively.

- Hardware and Devices: Acquiring or upgrading hardware components such as computers, tablets, and other devices necessary for AI-enabled learning experiences.

2. **Maintenance and Upkeep:** Beyond the initial investment, ongoing maintenance and upkeep costs are crucial for the sustained functionality and effectiveness of AI systems:
   - Software Updates: Regular updates to AI software to incorporate new features, address security vulnerabilities, and improve overall performance.
   - Technical Support: Establishing a dedicated technical support team or outsourcing support services to address issues, troubleshoot problems, and provide assistance to end-users.
   - Data Storage: Budgeting for ongoing data storage costs as the volume of data generated by AI applications increases over time.
   - Security Measures: Implementing and updating cybersecurity measures to safeguard AI systems from potential threats and breaches.
3. **Training and Professional Development:** Investment in ongoing training and professional development is essential to maximize the benefits of AI integration:
   - Educator Training Programs: Continuous training programs for educators to stay abreast of advancements in AI technology, pedagogical approaches, and ethical considerations.
   - Professional Development Opportunities: Encouraging educators to attend conferences, workshops, and seminars focused on AI in education to foster a culture of continuous learning.
   - Specialized AI Training: Offering specialized training for AI specialists and data scientists responsible for developing, maintaining, and optimizing AI applications.
4. **Research and Development:** Allocating funds for ongoing research and development activities is crucial for staying at the forefront of AI innovation:
   - Collaborative Research Initiatives: Participating in collaborative research projects with industry partners, research institutions, and other educational organizations to explore new AI applications and methodologies.
   - Pilot Programs: Conducting pilot programs to test the efficacy of new AI tools before full-scale implementation, allowing for adjustments based on real-world feedback.
   - Innovation Labs: Establishing innovation labs within educational institutions to foster a culture of experimentation and exploration of cutting-edge AI technologies.

5. **Total Cost of Ownership (TCO) Analysis:** Conducting a comprehensive TCO analysis is essential to understand the overall financial implications of AI integration:
   - TCO Components: Assessing all direct and indirect costs associated with AI implementation, including acquisition costs, operational costs, and any unforeseen expenses.
   - ROI Calculation: Evaluating the Return on Investment (ROI) to gauge the effectiveness of AI tools in achieving educational objectives and informing future budget allocations.

In navigating these implementation costs, educational institutions can establish a solid financial foundation for the integration of AI in education, ensuring sustained functionality, continuous improvement, and long-term success.

5.2.4 Teacher Training

The successful integration of AI in education hinges on equipping educators with the necessary knowledge, skills, and ethical considerations. This section outlines a comprehensive framework for teacher training:

1. **Pedagogical Integration:** To seamlessly integrate AI into pedagogy, educators need training that goes beyond technical aspects:
   - Understanding AI Basics: Providing educators with foundational knowledge about AI concepts, terminology, and its potential impact on education.
   - Aligning with Instructional Goals: Training should emphasize the alignment of AI tools with instructional objectives, ensuring that technology enhances rather than detracts from learning outcomes.
   - Designing Learning Experiences: Educators should learn how to design and implement AI-enhanced learning experiences that cater to diverse learning styles and preferences.
   - Collaborative Teaching Approaches: Encouraging collaborative teaching approaches where educators work in tandem with AI tools to create a dynamic and interactive learning environment.
2. **Ethical Use of AI:** Navigating the ethical deliberations associated with AI use in education is paramount for educators:
   - Understanding AI Ethics: Offering training sessions on the ethical considerations surrounding AI, including issues related to bias, privacy, and fairness.

- Ensuring Data Privacy: Educators must be trained to handle student data responsibly, ensuring compliance with privacy regulations and fostering a culture of data security.
- Addressing Bias: Training should include strategies to recognize and mitigate bias in AI tools, promoting fair and unbiased educational experiences.
- Transparent Communication: Educators should learn how to transparently communicate with students and parents about the use of AI, ensuring informed consent and trust.

3. **Technical Proficiency:** Building technical proficiency among educators is crucial for effective use of AI tools:
   - Hands-On Training: Providing hands-on training sessions where educators can interact with AI tools, understand their functionalities, and troubleshoot common issues.
   - Continuous Learning: Establishing continuous learning programs that keep educators updated on advancements in AI technology, enabling them to adapt to evolving tools and methodologies.
   - Collaboration with IT Specialists: Encouraging collaboration between educators and IT specialists to collectively address technical challenges and explore innovative AI applications.
4. Curriculum Integration: AI integration should be seamlessly woven into the curriculum, requiring specific training for educators:
   - Curriculum Development: Training educators on how to integrate AI-related content into existing curriculum structures, fostering interdisciplinary learning.
   - Project-Based Learning: Promoting project-based learning approaches that incorporate AI, allowing students to apply theoretical concepts in practical scenarios.
   - Assessment Strategies: Educators should be trained to develop assessment strategies that gauge both traditional academic competencies and AI-related skills.
5. Collaboration and Community Building: Fostering collaboration and building a supportive community are integral aspects of effective AI integration:
   - Peer Learning Networks: Facilitating peer learning networks where educators can share best practices, discuss challenges, and collaboratively develop innovative AI-driven teaching approaches.
   - Community of Practice: Establishing a community of practice centered around AI in education, where educators, researchers, and industry professionals collaborate to enhance teaching practices.

- Mentorship Programs: Implementing mentorship programs where experienced educators guide their peers in integrating AI tools effectively.

6. Professional Development Opportunities: Providing ongoing professional development opportunities ensures that educators remain at the forefront of AI integration:
   - Workshops and Seminars: Organizing workshops and seminars conducted by AI experts, offering deep insights into emerging trends, technologies, and their applications in education.
   - Certification Programs: Offering certification programs that validate educators' proficiency in AI integration, enhancing their credentials and fostering a culture of continuous improvement.
   - Access to Resources: Providing educators with access to a repository of resources, including AI toolkits, lesson plans, and case studies, supporting their professional development journey.

In embracing this comprehensive framework for teacher training, educational institutions can empower educators to harness the transformative potential of AI, creating an environment where technology enhances the teaching and learning experience.

6. FUTURE DIRECTIONS

6.1 Research Opportunities

The dynamic landscape of AI in education presents numerous avenues for future research, each holding the potential to shape the trajectory of educational technology. Ethical considerations in AI practices represent a paramount domain for exploration. As AI becomes more incorporated into learning environments, there is a critical need to establish robust ethical frameworks that govern data privacy, algorithmic transparency, and the fair treatment of diverse student populations. Understanding the societal impact and ethical implications of AI in education is pivotal for creating guidelines that ensure responsible and equitable use. Advanced algorithms for adaptive learning constitute another promising area for research. The development of more sophisticated algorithms that can dynamically tailor educational content to individual learner needs, preferences, and progress is crucial. Investigating the efficacy of these algorithms in diverse educational contexts and their ability to foster deeper engagement and knowledge retention can contribute significantly to refining adaptive learning systems. Long-term impact assessments of AI in education represent a research frontier essential for gauging the enduring effects of AI implementation. This involves evaluating not only short-term academic outcomes but also the broader socio-economic implications of AI-driven educational practices. Examining the longitudinal impact on student learning, teacher roles, and the overall educational ecosystem will provide insights into the sustainability and scalability of AI interventions. Moreover, research could delve into the development of AI-driven interventions to address specific educational challenges, such as personalized support for students with special needs or the creation of inclusive learning environments. Additionally, investigating the intersectionality of AI and socio-cultural factors could shed light on how diverse student populations perceive and interact with AI-powered educational tools. These research directions encompass ethical, technological, and societal dimensions, offering a holistic method to advancing the field of AI in education. A concerted effort in these areas will not only propel the responsible use of AI in learning environments but also contribute to the evolution of education as a whole.

As AI continues to evolve, future research in education should focus on several key areas to enhance our understanding and application of these technologies. One critical area is optimizing AI tools to accommodate diverse learning needs, ensuring inclusivity across various educational contexts. Researchers should investigate how AI can be tailored to support students with different learning styles and disabilities, potentially improving educational equity. Additionally, exploring the long-term impacts of AI-driven personalized learning platforms on student performance and engagement is essential. Comparative studies could provide insights into the effectiveness of these tools over time and across different educational settings. Addressing the accuracy and fairness of AI-driven assessment methods is another important avenue, with research needed to evaluate how various tools perform in providing unbiased and reliable evaluations. Future studies should also test hypotheses related to the benefits of explainable AI in fostering trust and increasing adoption rates among educators and students. Moreover, examining strategies for mitigating algorithmic bias could help ensure that AI technologies contribute to more equitable educational outcomes. By focusing on these specific research directions, future work can drive advancements in AI applications, ultimately leading to more effective, inclusive, and fair educational practices.

6.2 Recommendations for Implementation

The successful implementation of AI in education demands a strategic and responsible approach that prioritizes teacher training, collaborative efforts, and adherence to ethical guidelines. The detailed recommendations to guide the seamless integration of AI into educational settings:

6.2.1 Comprehensive Teacher Training

1. **Tailored Professional Development Programs:** Design and implement professional development programs tailored to the specific needs of educators. These programs should focus on building a nuanced understanding of AI concepts, practical applications in the classroom, and effective integration into teaching methodologies.
2. **Ethical Use Workshops:** Integrate specialized workshops addressing the ethical deliberations associated with AI in education. These workshops should delve into concerns such as data privacy, algorithmic bias, and responsible practices when handling student data. By fostering ethical awareness, educators can make informed decisions about AI implementations.
3. **Continuous Learning Platforms:** Establish continuous learning platforms that offer ongoing resources, updates, and training opportunities related to AI advancements. These platforms should encompass webinars, conferences, and collaborative online spaces where teachers can share experiences and insights, fostering a community of AI-informed educators.

6.2.2 Collaborative Efforts

1. **Interdisciplinary Collaboration:** Encourage interdisciplinary collaboration by creating spaces for dialogue between educators, technologists, and researchers. This collaborative approach ensures that AI tools align with educational objectives and are practical for use in real-world classroom scenarios.
2. **Industry-Academia Partnerships:** Facilitate partnerships between educational institutions and industry stakeholders. These partnerships can serve as a bridge between theoretical knowledge and practical application, leading to the development of innovative and pedagogically sound AI solutions.
3. **Global Collaboration for Best Practices:** Establish global networks that facilitate the exchange of best practices in AI implementation within education. Encourage cross-border collaborations to leverage diverse perspectives, experiences, and cultural considerations, contributing to the creation of universally effective AI solutions.

6.2.3 Ethical Guidelines and Governance

1. **Clear Ethical Guidelines:** Develop and disseminate clear and accessible ethical procedures for the implementation of AI in education. These guidelines should address key considerations such as privacy protection, fairness, and algorithmic transparency. Educators, administrators, and other stakeholders should have ready access to these guidelines.
2. **Ethics Review Boards:** Form ethics review boards within educational institutions responsible for assessing the ethical implications of AI implementations. These boards should include diverse stakeholders, ensuring a comprehensive evaluation of potential ethical concerns. Their role is to provide guidance and oversight throughout the implementation process.
3. **Regular Audits and Assessments:** Implement a system of regular audits and assessments for AI systems operating in educational settings. These evaluations should identify and discourse any ethical worries that may ascend during the functioning of AI tools. Transparency in reporting the outcomes of these audits is essential for maintaining trust among stakeholders.

By prioritizing these recommendations, educational institutions can navigate the complexities of AI implementation in a manner that is not only technologically proficient but also ethical, collaborative, and aligned with the needs of both educators and learners. This approach ensures a responsible and impactful incorporation of AI in education for the benefit of all stakeholders involved.

7. CONCLUSION

The incorporation of AI into education heralds a transformative era with profound implications for learning methodologies, administrative processes, and accessibility. The dual impact of AI, witnessed across various industries, is particularly noteworthy in education, where personalized learning, administrative task automation, and intelligent tutoring systems redefine the educational landscape. The key findings underscore the promise of AI in addressing educational challenges, offering tailored learning experiences, and optimizing administrative workflows. However, this transformative journey is not without its challenges. Ethical considerations, the need for comprehensive teacher training, and collaborative efforts are pivotal aspects that demand attention for the sustainable integration of AI in education. Conspicuous the equilibrium between maximizing the benefits of AI and mitigating potential challenges is paramount. The careful navigation of ethical considerations ensures responsible AI integration, fostering trust among educators, students, and other stakeholders. Teacher training programs play a crucial role in empowering educators to harness the full probable of AI while preserving a keen awareness of ethical considerations.

Furthermore, collaboration between industry, academia, and policymakers is imperative to create the conducive environment for the effective and responsible use of AI in education. Clear governance structures, ethical guidelines, and continuous evaluation mechanisms will contribute to a sustainable and inclusive integration that maximizes the positive impact on learners and educators alike. As we squeeze the era of AI in education, it is crucial to view technology not as a replacement for human interaction but as a valuable tool in the educator's toolkit. While AI offers innovative solutions, human guidance and ethical considerations remain at the forefront, ensuring that education remains a dynamic and empathetic endeavor. The journey ahead involves a collective commitment to realizing the full probable of AI while upholding the values and principles that underpin effective and ethical education.

The integration of AI in education has the prospective to revolutionize the learning procedure and enhance student engagement by offering adaptive and individualized learning experiences. By leveraging AI technologies, educators can monitor students' progress, deliver tailored learning materials and tasks, provide timely and effective feedback, and enable seamless communication between students and teachers. Furthermore, AI can support in automating administrative chores, allowing teachers to focus more on instructional design and personalized tutoring. However, ethical considerations, including bias mitigation and privacy concerns, necessitate a careful and responsible approach to the integration of AI in education. Continuous efforts to address challenges, coupled with ongoing professional development for educators, will be critical in realizing the full impending of AI in shaping the future of education. By providing an in-depth analysis of AI's applications, benefits, challenges, and future trajectories, this paper serves as a roadmap for educators, policymakers, and researchers navigating the dynamic intersection of AI and education. As AI becomes increasingly intertwined with the fabric of learning, understanding its nuanced implications becomes imperative for crafting an educational landscape that equips students with the skills needed for the challenges of the future.

REFERENCES

Adiguzel, T., Kaya, M. H., & Cansu, F. K. (2023). Revolutionizing education with AI: Exploring the transformative potential of ChatGPT. In *Contemporary Educational Technology* (Vol. 15, Issue 3). Bastas. DOI: 10.30935/cedtech/13152

AI In Education Market Size & Share Report, 2022-2030. (n.d.). Retrieved August 28, 2024, from https://www.grandviewresearch.com/industry-analysis/artificial-intelligence-ai-education-market-report

Ala-Mutka, K. M. (2005). A survey of automated assessment approaches for programming assignments. *Computer Science Education*, 15(2), 83–102. Advance online publication. DOI: 10.1080/08993400500150747

Androutsopoulou, A., Karacapilidis, N., Loukis, E., & Charalabidis, Y. (2019). Transforming the communication between citizens and government through AI-guided chatbots. *Government Information Quarterly*, 36(2), 358–367. Advance online publication. DOI: 10.1016/j.giq.2018.10.001

Arman, M., & Lamiya, U. R. (2023). Exploring the Implication of ChatGPT AI for Business: Efficiency and Challenges. *Journal of Innovation Information Technology and Application*, 5(1), 64–84. Advance online publication. DOI: 10.31098/ijmadic.v1i2.1872

Arman, M., & Lamiyar, U. R. (2023). Exploring the Implication of ChatGPT AI for Business: Efficiency and Challenges. *International Journal of Marketing and Digital Creative*, 1(2), 64–84. Advance online publication. DOI: 10.31098/ijmadic.v1i2.1872

Bahroun, Z., Anane, C., Ahmed, V., & Zacca, A. (2023). Transforming Education: A Comprehensive Review of Generative Artificial Intelligence in Educational Settings through Bibliometric and Content Analysis. In *Sustainability (Switzerland)* (Vol. 15, Issue 17). Multidisciplinary Digital Publishing Institute (MDPI). DOI: 10.3390/su151712983

Bala, M. M., Akkineni, H., & Srinivasulu, C. (2022). An Approach for Learner Categorization Based on Emotions in Intelligent Adaptive E-Learning Environment. *Journal of Mobile Multimedia*, 18(6). Advance online publication. DOI: 10.13052/jmm1550-4646.18611

Bond, M., Khosravi, H., De Laat, M., Bergdahl, N., Negrea, V., Oxley, E., Pham, P., Chong, S. W., & Siemens, G. (2024). A meta systematic review of artificial intelligence in higher education: a call for increased ethics, collaboration, and rigour. In *International Journal of Educational Technology in Higher Education* (Vol. 21, Issue 1). Springer Science and Business Media Deutschland GmbH. DOI: 10.1186/s41239-023-00436-z

Bondre, S., & Yadav, U. (2022). Automated Flower Species Identification by Using Deep Convolution Neural Network. In Satapathy, S. C., Peer, P., Tang, J., Bhateja, V., & Ghosh, A. (Eds.), *Intelligent Data Engineering and Analytics* (pp. 1–10). Springer Singapore. DOI: 10.1007/978-981-16-6624-7_1

Budhwar, P., Chowdhury, S., Wood, G., Aguinis, H., Bamber, G. J., Beltran, J. R., Boselie, P., Lee Cooke, F., Decker, S., DeNisi, A., Dey, P. K., Guest, D., Knoblich, A. J., Malik, A., Paauwe, J., Papagiannidis, S., Patel, C., Pereira, V., Ren, S., . . . Varma, A. (2023). Human resource management in the age of generative artificial intelligence: Perspectives and research directions on ChatGPT. In *Human Resource Management Journal* (Vol. 33, Issue 3). DOI: 10.1111/1748-8583.12524

Chalasani, S. H., Syed, J., Ramesh, M., Patil, V., & Pramod Kumar, T. M. (2023). Artificial intelligence in the field of pharmacy practice: A literature review. In *Exploratory Research in Clinical and Social Pharmacy* (Vol. 12). DOI: 10.1016/j.rcsop.2023.100346

Chan, C. K. Y. (2023). A comprehensive AI policy education framework for university teaching and learning. *International Journal of Educational Technology in Higher Education*, 20(1), 38. Advance online publication. DOI: 10.1186/s41239-023-00408-3

Chassignol, M., Khoroshavin, A., Klimova, A., & Bilyatdinova, A. (2018). Artificial Intelligence trends in education: A narrative overview. *Procedia Computer Science*, 136, 16–24. Advance online publication. DOI: 10.1016/j.procs.2018.08.233

Chen, X., Xie, H., Zou, D., & Hwang, G. J. (2020). Application and theory gaps during the rise of Artificial Intelligence in Education. In *Computers and Education* (Vol. 1). Artificial Intelligence., DOI: 10.1016/j.caeai.2020.100002

Chiu, T. K. F. (2024). Future research recommendations for transforming higher education with generative AI. *Computers and Education: Artificial Intelligence*, 6, 100197. DOI: 10.1016/j.caeai.2023.100197

Chiu, T. K. F., Xia, Q., Zhou, X., Chai, C. S., & Cheng, M. (2023). Systematic literature review on opportunities, challenges, and future research recommendations of artificial intelligence in education. In *Computers and Education: Artificial Intelligence* (Vol. 4). Elsevier B.V. DOI: 10.1016/j.caeai.2022.100118

Cipriano, B. P., Fachada, N., & Alves, P. (2022). Drop Project: An automatic assessment tool for programming assignments. *SoftwareX*, 18, 101079. Advance online publication. DOI: 10.1016/j.softx.2022.101079

de Leon, L. C. R., Flores, L. V., & Alomo, A. R. L. (2024). Artificial Intelligence and Filipino Academic Librarians: Perceptions, Challenges and Opportunities. *Journal of the Australian Library and Information Association*, 73(1), 66–83. Advance online publication. DOI: 10.1080/24750158.2024.2305993

Devedžić, V. (2004). Web Intelligence and Artificial Intelligence in Education. *Journal of Educational Technology & Society*, 7(4).

Ellis, L. (2018). Hey, Alexa, Should We Bring Virtual Assistants to Campus? These Colleges Gave Them a Shot - The Chronicle of Higher Education. *The Chronicle of Higher Education.*

Gao, B., & Huang, L. (2019). Understanding interactive user behavior in smart media content service: An integration of TAM and smart service belief factors. *Heliyon*, 5(12), e02983. Advance online publication. DOI: 10.1016/j.heliyon.2019.e02983 PMID: 31872134

Gong, C., Lin, F., Gong, X., & Lu, Y. (2020). Intelligent Cooperative Edge Computing in Internet of Things. *IEEE Internet of Things Journal*, 7(10), 9372–9382. Advance online publication. DOI: 10.1109/JIOT.2020.2986015

Grassini, S. (2023). Shaping the Future of Education: Exploring the Potential and Consequences of AI and ChatGPT in Educational Settings. In *Education Sciences* (Vol. 13, Issue 7). DOI: 10.3390/educsci13070692

Haidar, A. (2023). An Integrative Theoretical Framework for Responsible Artificial Intelligence. *International Journal of Digital Strategy, Governance, and Business Transformation*, 13(1), 1–23. Advance online publication. DOI: 10.4018/IJDSGBT.334844

Haleem, A., Javaid, M., Asim Qadri, M., Pratap Singh, R., & Suman, R. (2022). Artificial intelligence (AI) applications for marketing: A literature-based study. In *International Journal of Intelligent Networks* (Vol. 3). DOI: 10.1016/j.ijin.2022.08.005

Han, R., Yoon, H., Kim, G., Lee, H., & Lee, Y. (2023). Revolutionizing Medicinal Chemistry: The Application of Artificial Intelligence (AI) in Early Drug Discovery. In *Pharmaceuticals* (Vol. 16, Issue 9). DOI: 10.3390/ph16091259

Harnal, S., Sharma, G., Malik, S., Kaur, G., Khurana, S., Kaur, P., Simaiya, S., & Bagga, D. (2022). Bibliometric Mapping of Trends, Applications and Challenges of Artificial Intelligence in Smart Cities. *EAI Endorsed Transactions on Scalable Information Systems*, 9(4), e76. Advance online publication. DOI: 10.4108/eetsis.vi.489

Harry, A. (2023). Role of AI in Education. *Interdiciplinary Journal and Hummanity*, 2(3), 260–268. Advance online publication. DOI: 10.58631/injurity.v2i3.52

Herder, E., Sosnovsky, S., & Dimitrova, V. (2017). Adaptive intelligent learning environments. In *Technology Enhanced Learning*. Research Themes., DOI: 10.1007/978-3-319-02600-8_10

Holmes, W., & Tuomi, I. (2022). State of the art and practice in AI in education. *European Journal of Education*, 57(4), 542–570. Advance online publication. DOI: 10.1111/ejed.12533

Javaid, M., Haleem, A., Khan, I. H., & Suman, R. (2023). Understanding the potential applications of Artificial Intelligence in Agriculture Sector. *Advanced Agrochem*, 2(1), 15–30. Advance online publication. DOI: 10.1016/j.aac.2022.10.001

Jones, E. L. (2001). Grading Student Programs-A Software Testing Approach. *Journal of Computing Sciences in Colleges*, 16(2).

Kahraman, H. T., Sagiroglu, S., & Colak, I. (2010). Development of adaptive and intelligent web-based educational systems. *4th International Conference on Application of Information and Communication Technologies, AICT2010*. DOI: 10.1109/ICAICT.2010.5612054

Kim, J., Lee, H., & Cho, Y. H. (2022). Learning design to support student-AI collaboration: Perspectives of leading teachers for AI in education. *Education and Information Technologies*, 27(5), 6069–6104. Advance online publication. DOI: 10.1007/s10639-021-10831-6

Knickerbocker, J., Budd, R., Dang, B., Chen, Q., Colgan, E., Hung, L. W., Kumar, S., Lee, K. W., Lu, M., Nah, J. W., Narayanan, R., Sakuma, K., Siu, V., & Wen, B. (2018). Heterogeneous integration technology demonstrations for future healthcare, IoT, and AI computing solutions. *Proceedings - Electronic Components and Technology Conference*. DOI: 10.1109/ECTC.2018.00231

Kumain, S. C., Kumain, K., & Chaudhary, P. (2020). AI Impact on Various Domain: An Overview. *International Journal of Management*, 11(10).

Kumar, A., Mani, V., Jain, V., Gupta, H., & Venkatesh, V. G. (2023). Managing healthcare supply chain through artificial intelligence (AI): A study of critical success factors. *Computers & Industrial Engineering*, 175, 108815. Advance online publication. DOI: 10.1016/j.cie.2022.108815 PMID: 36405396

Ladson-Billings, G. (1995). Toward a Theory of Culturally Relevant Pedagogy. *American Educational Research Journal*, 32(3), 465–491. Advance online publication. DOI: 10.3102/00028312032003465

Lim, W. M., Gunasekara, A., Pallant, J. L., Pallant, J. I., & Pechenkina, E. (2023). Generative AI and the future of education: Ragnarök or reformation? A paradoxical perspective from management educators. *International Journal of Management Education*, 21(2), 100790. Advance online publication. DOI: 10.1016/j.ijme.2023.100790

Lin, H., Yan, Y., & Cheng, Q. (2023). Future Role of Artificial Intelligence in Advancing Transportation Electrification. In *Journal of Intelligent and Connected Vehicles* (Vol. 6, Issue 3). DOI: 10.26599/JICV.2023.9210020

Lüersmann, A. (2023). Artificial Intelligence in Human Resource Management: Personnel Marketing and Recruiting. In *Studies in Systems, Decision and Control* (Vol. 466). DOI: 10.1007/978-3-031-27506-7_23

Mohammad, S. M. (2020). Artificial Intelligence in Information Technology. SSRN *Electronic Journal*. DOI: 10.2139/ssrn.3625444

Mohsienuddin Mohammad, S. (2020). Artificial Intelligence In Information Technology. *International Journal Of Innovations In Engineering Research And Technology, 7*(6).

Morandini, S., Fraboni, F., De Angelis, M., Puzzo, G., Giusino, D., & Pietrantoni, L. (2023). The Impact Of Artificial Intelligence On Workers' Skills: Upskilling And Reskilling In Organisations. *Informing Science*, 26, 039–068. Advance online publication. DOI: 10.28945/5078

Murphy, R. F. (2019). *Perspective Expert insights on a timely policy issue Artificial Intelligence Applications to Support K-12 Teachers and Teaching A Review of Promising Applications, Opportunities, and Challenges.*

Naser, M. Y. M., & Bhattacharya, S. (2023). Empowering human-AI teams via Intentional Behavioral Synchrony. *Frontiers in Neuroergonomics*, 4, 1181827. Advance online publication. DOI: 10.3389/fnrgo.2023.1181827 PMID: 38234496

Peredo, R., Canales, A., Menchaca, A., & Peredo, I. (2011). Intelligent Web-based education system for adaptive learning. *Expert Systems with Applications*, 38(12), 14690–14702. Advance online publication. DOI: 10.1016/j.eswa.2011.05.013

Pham, T., Nguyen, B., Ha, S., & Nguyen Ngoc, T. (n.d.). Digital transformation in engineering education: Exploring the potential of AI-assisted learning. In *Australasian Journal of Educational Technology* (Vol. 2023, Issue 5).

Prasanth, A., Vadakkan, D. J., Surendran, P., & Thomas, B. (2023). Role of Artificial Intelligence and Business Decision Making. *International Journal of Advanced Computer Science and Applications*, 14(6). Advance online publication. DOI: 10.14569/IJACSA.2023.01406103

Regan, P. M., & Jesse, J. (2019). Ethical challenges of edtech, big data and personalized learning: Twenty-first century student sorting and tracking. *Ethics and Information Technology*, 21(3), 167–179. Advance online publication. DOI: 10.1007/s10676-018-9492-2

Reiss, M. J. (2021). The use of AI in education: Practicalities and ethical considerations. *London Review of Education*, 19(1). Advance online publication. DOI: 10.14324/LRE.19.1.05

Rus, V., D'Mello, S., Hu, X., & Graesser, A. C. (2013). Recent advances in conversational intelligent tutoring systems. *AI Magazine*, 34(3), 42–54. Advance online publication. DOI: 10.1609/aimag.v34i3.2485

Sharma, D. M., & Sehgal, M. L. (2023). The Revolutionary Computer Technology Artificial Intelligence that is Changing Our World & its Impact on Different Jobs. *International Journal for Research in Applied Science and Engineering Technology*, 11(4), 286–293. Advance online publication. DOI: 10.22214/ijraset.2023.50072

Sharma, S., Gahlawat, V. K., Rahul, K., Mor, R. S., & Malik, M. (2021). Sustainable Innovations in the Food Industry through Artificial Intelligence and Big Data Analytics. In *Logistics* (Vol. 5, Issue 4). DOI: 10.3390/logistics5040066

Sørensen, N. L., Bemman, B., Jensen, M. B., Moeslund, T. B., & Thomsen, J. L. (2023). Machine learning in general practice: Scoping review of administrative task support and automation. *BMC Primary Care*, 24(1), 14. Advance online publication. DOI: 10.1186/s12875-023-01969-y PMID: 36641467

Su, J., & Yang, W. (2023). Unlocking the Power of ChatGPT: A Framework for Applying Generative AI in Education. *ECNU Review of Education*, 6(3). Advance online publication. DOI: 10.1177/20965311231168423

Timms, M. J. (2016). Letting Artificial Intelligence in Education out of the Box: Educational Cobots and Smart Classrooms. *International Journal of Artificial Intelligence in Education*, 26(2), 701–712. Advance online publication. DOI: 10.1007/s40593-016-0095-y

Trisnawati, W., Putra, R. E., & Balti, L. (2023). The Impact of Artificial Intelligent in Education toward 21 st Century Skills: A Literature Review. *PPSDP International Journal of Education*, 2(2), 501–513. DOI: 10.59175/pijed.v2i2.152

Tursunbayeva, A., & Renkema, M. (2023). Artificial intelligence in health-care: Implications for the job design of healthcare professionals. *Asia Pacific Journal of Human Resources*, 61(4), 845–887. Advance online publication. DOI: 10.1111/1744-7941.12325

Wang, J. (2023). Navigating the AI Revolution: Job Replacements and New Opportunities in the Labor Market. *Advances in Economics. Management and Political Sciences*, 46(1), 10–15. Advance online publication. DOI: 10.54254/2754-1169/46/20230309

Wang, N., & Lester, J. (2023). K-12 Education in the Age of AI: A Call to Action for K-12 AI Literacy. In *International Journal of Artificial Intelligence in Education* (Vol. 33, Issue 2). DOI: 10.1007/s40593-023-00358-x

Wang, X., Anwer, N., Dai, Y., & Liu, A. (2023). ChatGPT for design, manufacturing, and education. *Procedia CIRP*, 119, 7–14. Advance online publication. DOI: 10.1016/j.procir.2023.04.001

Wang, X., Li, L., Tan, S. C., Yang, L., & Lei, J. (2023). Preparing for AI-enhanced education: Conceptualizing and empirically examining teachers' AI readiness. *Computers in Human Behavior*, 146, 107798. Advance online publication. DOI: 10.1016/j.chb.2023.107798

Wei, M., & Zhou, Z. (2023). AI Ethics Issues in Real World: Evidence from AI Incident Database. *Proceedings of the Annual Hawaii International Conference on System Sciences*. DOI: 10.24251/HICSS.2023.602

Xu, C., Lien, K. C., & Höllerer, T. (2023). Comparing Zealous and Restrained AI Recommendations in a Real-World Human-AI Collaboration Task. *Conference on Human Factors in Computing Systems - Proceedings*. DOI: 10.1145/3544548.3581282

Yang, S. J. H., Ogata, H., & Matsui, T. (2023). Guest Editorial: Human-centered AI in Education: Augment Human Intelligence with Machine Intelligence. In *Educational Technology and Society* (Vol. 26, Issue 1). DOI: 10.30191/ETS.202301_26(1).0007

Zhai, X., Chu, X., Chai, C. S., Jong, M. S. Y., Istenic, A., Spector, M., Liu, J. B., Yuan, J., & Li, Y. (2021). A Review of Artificial Intelligence (AI) in Education from 2010 to 2020. In *Complexity* (Vol. 2021). DOI: 10.1155/2021/8812542

Zhang, K., & Aslan, A. B. (2021). AI technologies for education: Recent research & future directions. In *Computers and Education* (Vol. 2). Artificial Intelligence. DOI: 10.1016/j.caeai.2021.100025

Zheng, L., Niu, J., Zhong, L., & Gyasi, J. F. (2023). The effectiveness of artificial intelligence on learning achievement and learning perception: A meta-analysis. In *Interactive Learning Environments* (Vol. 31, Issue 9). DOI: 10.1080/10494820.2021.2015693

Chapter 11
Metaverse and Its Underlying Challenges in Higher Education
A Case Study-Based Approach

Sonia Mukherjee
https://orcid.org/0000-0002-1293-1342
MIT World Peace University, India

ABSTRACT

The term Metaverse has become part of today's reality. In the educational front, (1) virtual learning using the Metaverse has the potential to surge availability for students with incapacities or persons residing in the isolated and inaccessible areas; (2) classrooms using the Metaverse domain can offer collaborative knowledge experience done through numerous virtual simulations, and virtual field journeys further enable teamwork between students in actual time, irrespective of their bodily place; (3) the application of virtual learning will lead to cost reduction of teaching leading to greater engagement and motivation among students. However, in spite of the advantages, there are numerous challenges. Results show that the concept, application, and awareness related to metaverse is still not spread and is in the nascent stage. Furthermore, the study highlighted the limitations and challenges of the application of Metaverse in the 21st century with suitable suggestions for improvement in the context of higher education.

DOI: 10.4018/979-8-3693-5443-8.ch011

1. INTRODUCTION_

1.1 Definition of Metaverse

The concept of Metaverse was coined by Neal Stephenson in the nineties. According to him, the term Metaverse is basically a computer-generated universe matching the real universe. Individuals are free to intermingle with each other in an avatar form inside a three-dimensional computer-generated world and they do perform some real time communication and build a virtual environment. Indeed, the Metaverse is becoming a part of the day to day world and is an extendable part of the Internet in 3D format.

The term Metaverse is replicated in the word "digital twin". By addition to an extension layer to the bodily world and combination of digital and bodily world into an effortlessly linked one, the concept of Metaverse arises as a realistic immersive simulated world. It is said to be a place where individuals can impeccably navigate for working and perform social interaction by means of devices that can sustenance immersive skills and know-hows, such as Mixed Reality, Augmented Reality, VR headsets and other devices (Zhang & Ye, 2021).

According to Chua and Yu, (2024), "The term Metaverse is a combination of "meta" and "verse" where meta signifies transcedence and verse meaning "universe". As per (Lin et al. 2019), it is capable of becoming an innovative and recent form of next-generation internet. The term Metaverse include the integrating and overlapping of the virtual and digital environment with the actual worlds, realistic economies, societal life, real identification and physical possession. There are several technologies in the forms of advanced speed announcement systems, Augmented Reality (AR), virtual reality (VR), and Internet of Things (IOT), use of blockchain Artificial Intelligence (AI) and other different technologies including cloud computing. (Bhugaonkar et al. 2022).

Buhalis and Karatay (2022) in their study redefined the term Metaverse as a continuous union of virtual and bodily cosmos that has usage of close intelligence to increase bodily spaces, goods and services. For example, OASIS was a concept of digital universe introduced in the film Ready Player One. Sparks (2021, p.18) in their study mainly says that Metaverse can exclusively be well-thought-out as a "collective online space which integrates three-dimensional graphics, any on a curtain or in computer-generated reality." Moy and Gadgil (2022, p.3) from the firm J.P. Morgan defined Metaverse in the form of unified union of the bodily and virtual or computer-generated digital lives, making a united, computer-generated communal anywhere in various forms. Examples are work, play, relax, execute and mix". As per Damar (2021), Metaverse is defined as a "3D virtual collective and all actions can be approved through amplified and virtual reality facilities "unfolding the concept of metaverse as "the layer amid you and realism".

Kye et al. (2021) characterized Metaverse as a "3D supported practical and digital reality in which day-to-day action and economical life are carried on via digital avatars and a world in which virtual and reality interact and co-evolve creating value".

1.2 Metaverse Adoption in Education

The Metaverse is an extensive form of real-time interaction and is a form of fictional world with progressively genuine digital spaces, for the purpose of dynamic learning environment. From the viewpoint of teaching and further embracement of technology in education, both the manufacturing sector and establishment are demanding an educated workforce for the purpose of new administration and operative leadership examples.

As the use of Metaverse movements continue to nurture, augmented reality partakes a wide range of credit in the instructive settings (Sunardi et al., 2022). Applying a meta-learning and virtual reality is a decent way to progress scholar's self-awareness and self-governing learning conducts and behaviours (Violante & Vezzetti, 2015). Immersive metaverse knowledge and its applications has specific plea to new and energetic persons (Kshetri et al., 2022). Metaverse connected know-hows and techniques permits for the gamification of teachings, virtual examination of past and values, and collaboration with scientific topics such as physics and science in newer and innovative methods (Sanglier et al., 2021).

The formation of Metaverse colleges and campuses has different forms of offerings and many possibilities for the forthcoming way of imparting teaching (GmbH, 2021), as well as reality harmonization, high level of simulation, ground-breaking formation and open-source growth (Yu, 2021). The Berkley University have rebuilt their grounds in the sandbox audiovisual game Minecraft and steered a valediction ceremony for the graduation process inside the game itself (Duan et al., 2021).

In the sphere of education, Metaverse is not completely a new idea. Various eminent academician and educators have discussed its importance and meaning. Study by Kemp and Livingstone (2006) have well-tried to explicate how Metaverse could be united with the help of the virtual or digital world known as the "Second Life" with the help of learning management system to modify the learnedness process. Collins (2008) in their study found that with the help of Metaverse several persons can meet and perform societal interaction with one another. The goal is that higher education has to be active in nature with the objective of teaching and higher learning. Furthermore, the 3D digital virtual world offers fundamental interaction and connectedness using digital avatars reflective their presence in the virtual or digital world (Schlemmer & Bakes, 2015).

A summit at the Stanford Research Institute International was held in the year 2006. The primary objective was to draw a road-map for the future of the Metaverse technology. The summit was attended by various academicians from various sphere such as architects, entrepreneurs, and another notable individual. The objective was prediction and examine a ten-year plan as to how the internet would look into the future or rather help in reshaping the future. (Metaverse Roadmap Summit, 2006). Furthermore, Kyle et al. (2021) in their study had presented an instructive definition with potentials and boundaries of the diverse types of Metaverse projected from the Roadmap Summit.

In the numerous Metaverse heightened fields inside the field of higher education such as Journalism and Communication Education (Dai & Liu, 2023), the medicinal colleges have shaped mixed reality settings to adjust medicinal experimentations and pick up from other subjects. The Western Reserve University's medicinal scholars have started wearing HoloLens's glasses to identify the different body part and structures of the body. Mixed reality environments are providing substitution for traditional anatomy labs filled with cadavers (Griswold, 2016). In the area of physical education, there are now numerous projects grounded on virtual or augmented reality education activities which are still under the naïve stage of development (Yu, 2022).

In matters of provision of innovation and education related to entrepreneurship, it is essential to provide training to progressive talents (Zhang et al. 2023). In many places of the world including France Institute European Administration, the concept of VR is utilised to intensify the teaching learning process for teachers and for student learning. In country such as Spain, Metaverse is being used for different forms of exhibitions and trips in the discipline of science and galleries (Conteras et al. 2022).

Jeremy Beilenson, a researcher, have recently suggested some of the experiences that should be designed for VR in his book "Experience on Demand". The experiences would be applicable for those activities which are dangerous in real-life such as letting students to drive a train, to check the outbreak of a communicable disease, or learn to fly some jumbo jets on the computer-generated runaways.

Some of these newly launched technologies can help the teachers in delivering lectures in the classroom and helping in making the lessons much more interactive to their scholars. The instructors can assist in teaching the marine biology on the ocean floor, or deliver their different types of the philosophy lecture in an amphitheatre located in ancient Rome. In another notable example, a Danish company, Labster, have built a virtual science lab and it could assist the teachers to conduct experiments found to be dangerous in real life. In another example, Morehouse College, a prominent instructor recently started using a virtual lab where students can conduct experiments in a similar manner as compared to the real world. Georgian College in Canada, have developed a VR program termed Victory XR where the Veterinary Technician students are imparted knowledge about the bovine and canine anatomy. There is no need for animals anymore. In terms of imparting the vocational training, the use of the Metaverse technology have made them more accessible and affordable. For instance, plumbers can be given training through the use of virtual pipes. In case of training firefighters, real building can be replaced with the virtual buildings. Lastly, nurses can be trained with the help of computer-generated patients. Another prominent example is Australia's in digital uses. It helps the children to link with and acquire skills and knowledge from the indigenous elders about the cultural knowledge, history and language. The prominent Georgian College has built a computer-generated house explicitly for native students to acquire the knowledge in terms of both Anishinaabemowin and English words. Students meet with their teacher in avatar form for the said purpose. Lastly, the University of Maryland Global Campus has surveyed the scholars who were using the latest technology in the form of VR. The survey concluded that the form of avatar assisted them in speaking to the faculty members and with their colleagues. The study concluded that students were found to perform well in the virtual classroom and it has significantly increased the peer-peer interaction on a considerable scale.

1.3 The Importance of Metaverse in Education

There has been rapid changes and evolution in matters of imparting education and tutoring has occurred as a vigorous component of the Educational Institutions. It is presently offering a competitive advantage to the first-time beginners. In the domain of Metaverse, cultural values and technology play an important role in imparting them along with the other imirtant components associated with the educational learning.

With the onset of Covid-19 pandemic, teachers and students had to go for a transition towards a distant learning practice since the year 2020. The use of technology increased manifold since the advent of Metaverse and the immersive and interactive way of metaverse environment can engage the scholars in an innovative manner (Lee and Park, 2021). Metaverse offers the capability to produce modified learning involvements (Han & Noh, 2021). School teachers need not supervise the learning and the teaching processes. With the help of the technological and digital apparatus, the learning process in metaverse will be facilitated in a rapid manner (Son et al., 2022) thus creating an engaging learning experience for scholars in the longer-period of time.

Metaverse is the new paradigm for the current changes in the technological domain. The latest technological development is in the forms such as use of avatars in the digital environment, usage of blockchain technology and VR headsets. The use of Metaverse have garnered a lot of attention from the notable education institutions. The latest and emerging technologies used in the educational places and universities are enabling students to participate in computer-generated classes in the forms of avatars. For example, while obtaining a foreign language such as English, the technology permits students to use the language for numerous forms of activities including places of work, learning, using it in some social events. Furthermore, it offers a formal training program under the supervision of the non-player character.

The way colleges and academic work are indorsed can be altered through using the metaverse technology. Students will benefit immensely and they can easily switch among online stores and lecture rooms using a single avatar. A lot of persons would favour cyber-physical institutions and further gain information through the usage of computer-generated experiences provided by the educational institutions.

With an emphasis on its pedagogical significance, Han & Noh (2021) purpose of the research was to determine the teacher's viewpoints toward implementing the metaverse system in higher education. Their findings concluded that the Metaverse has the potential for paving the way for the future education. One recent example of the usage of Metaverse was performed at an event in London. The school had developed a digital version of the Globe Theatre. Shakespeare's plays were performed through the virtual mode and the crowd comprising of youngsters were able to understand the Shakespeare's plays similar to real life experience. Lastly, a teacher with little coding experience could quickly and easily personalize curriculum materials and deliver it to the students. Furthermore, with the help of AI multiple languages can be processed at the same time. For example, a language student sitting in a virtual Paris Café can perform a conversation with the waiter and obtain real time response about his degree of language skills acquired.

1.4. Advantages of Adopting Metaverse in the Higher Education

With the onset of Metaverse technology, there are numerous opportunities available in the educational ecosystem. The immersive and interactive environment will engage students in different ways not found in the traditional style of imparting education in the classrooms (B.-H Lee and Park, 2021). Through usage of different forms of metaverse technology, it will create a personalized learning experience (Han & Noh, 2021). Newer technological and digital equipment's can improve the knowledge process in the metaverse environment (Son et al., 2022). We can create an innovative approach to future education by rapidly embracing the learning experience preparing the students for the future.

Some of the notable advantages offered by Metaverse in the education sector are as follows-

Increased Accessibility- Virtual learning has the potential to upsurge convenience for students with numerous forms of incapacities or those students be located in in the distant areas permitting them to join the schoolroom events, happenings, social functions and deliberations from wherever bodily location they are.

Immersive Learning Experiences- Metaverse schoolrooms can offer numerous suggestions in immersive and cooperative learning experience through virtual replications, virtual ground journeys, and other collaborative events.

Enhanced collaboration- Metaverse schoolrooms and laboratories could facilitate collaboration amid students in actual time, irrespective of their bodily position, leading to more expressive and varied deliberations.

Personalized Learning- The Metaverse has the potential to offer a highly modified knowledge and educational practice as scholars can intermingle with the virtual content at their individual stride and discover newer topics that interest them in larger heights.

Cost Savings- Virtual Learning can reduce cost significantly and students would not require to bodily travel to a educational grounds or procurement of textbooks

Greater engagement- The immersive and highly collaborative aspect of Metaverse classrooms will lead to superior meeting and incentive among scholars leading to enhancement of their overall knowledge and skills.

Remote learners having geographical restrictions and facing issues in matters of access to traditional methods of imparting education can benefit immensely from metaverse education. The virtual mode of imparting education ensures equal access to high quality education. In addition, students come from diverse background. Metaverse helps in promoting inclusivity and diversity. Big gaps are also found to exist in the higher education between the rural and urban areas. Metaverse tech=nologies can assist in closing this gap by making informative resources more available to students residing in the remote and distant areas. A study carried out in South Dakota State University assumes that Metaverse will benefit rural scholars.

2. LITERATURE REVIEW

The main objective of education is to deliver students with the information and exercise that are well-thought-out and important in terms of making a better society and also to equip them with a decent livelihood, employment prospects and citizenship (Wittich et al., 2017). The performance of permitting knowledge, getting information and data, and abilities or positive standards and ethics is characteristically denoted to as the term "education". The role of the instructor is multidimensional. It starts with the graduate's identifications, aptitudes, and services, intelligence and to boost them further is the role of the educator (Dewey, 2007). The increasing demands from the students across the world and the changing job predictions through the time have obligated a significant change in terms of imparting knowledge in the educational organization (Blumenfeld et al., 1991). Sometimes there are technical glitches and challenges associated with numerous scholars particularly in courses associated with science subjects have compelled some form of solution such as introduction of newer technology (Zheng et al., 2015). Different forms of contemporary technologies have been introduced from time to time, including courses which can be taken in a virtual mode (Magdalene & Sridharan, 2018), some blended form of online and offline learnings (AI-Maroof et al., 2021; Halverson et al., 2018), and numerous other computer-based platforms (Van der Kleij et al., 2015; Zhang et al., 2023) present alternatives for imparting education in the current decade of technological innovation. The edtech industry has the potential to enhance the learning consequences for the majority of scholars. This has been proved via usage of different forms of applications (Collins & Halverson, 2018). Digital learning materials, are the newer norms and trends in the present times as compared to the classical books. Old-style copybooks are being rapidly replaced with newer forms of learning tools such as notebooks, tablets, or smartphones having latest innovative applications, and modified knowledge (FitzGerald et al., 2018) and remote forms of acquiring newer learning (Kaye & Rumble, 2018) are being rapidly utilized to acclimatize with the educational involvement to each scholar's educational abilities, inadequacies, comforts and ambitions. It is frequently known that the practice of using the latest Information and communication technologies have led to increase in the scholar's insights towards acquiring more education. The collaborating virtual world termed as "Metaverse" was used for the purpose of gaming in the earlier times. However, with more specialized growth and expansion in the fields including education, metaverse is now being adopted on a mass scale. Lee et al, (2021a) in their study had made the first attempt to create a wide-ranging framework to study the metaverse development and highlight the potential in the coming times. Several crucial subjects that are relevant to the technology was again identified by Lee et al., (2021b) in their comprehensive survey and the survey concluded that many challenges were needed to be overcome for acquiring the full potential of the Metaverse technology in the coming years.

3. CASE-STUDIES- PRACTICAL APPLICATION OF METAVERSE TECHNOLOGY IN HIGHER EDUCATION

With the onset of the coronavirus pandemic, there has been a change in methodology in terms of impacting education all-inclusive compelling scholars and instructors to shift to a distant education practice since 2020. Expertise and newer technological innovations have confirmed educational steadiness is still thinkable in spite of extensive lockdown and restrictions on movements of individuals. With the arrival of Metaverse, on that point is a prospect to create a completely new instructive environment. The immersive and communicating nature of Metaverse settings can involve scholars in habits that old-style schoolroom situations cannot (B-H.Lee and Park, 2021). Scholars can see the sights and act with multifaceted notions fun and appealingly which can aid them improved understanding and retaining of information. Moreover, Metaverse provides suggestions to generate modified knowledge understandings (Han & Noh, 2021).

A study conducted by the PwC found that classes conducted in the Metaverse domain are four times quicker to train than in person classes, 275 percent more self-confident to apply the relevant skills acquired and learned after training, 3.75 times more expressively connected to content than schoolroom learners, and four times more engrossed than their e-Learning counterparts.

There are numerous things which are day-to-day taught via books and talks. However, giving students extremely genuine, "hands-on" experience through a computer-generated world is not always done. For example, we can impart kids to multiply figures and produce a result in the billions but it's very difficult to show the massiveness of a billion stars the deep smallness of a billion atoms or the significance of propelling 37 billion metric tons of carbon dioxide into the troposphere. The advantage of immersive technology is that it will permit us to substitute a sense of intuition in scholars and thus producing a much profounder understanding of all God's creatures.

The Metaverse has the potential to give academics first-person facts as if they were constricted down to the size of a worm or overstated to the magnitude of a gathering. The academics could float over the cardiovascular structure in order increase in value about the size and measure of arterial walls as commemoration accumulates because of the heart illness. There would be a number of opportunities that scholars might be elated over time and space. Furthermore, they might be able to wander through the demanding streets of antique Rome or support to form the Great Wall of China.

Immersive education has the *greatest significant uses*. Dreamscape Learn in Culver City in California have established an immersive content that is expected to transform the mainstream learning. It has established a corporation with firm Dreamscape Immersive and Arizona State University. The corporation Dreamscape Learn has combined the supremacy of movie and picture quality, storytelling and accurate graphics with deeply thoughtful informative principles and obviously distinct the knowledge goals. The objective is not to replace the outdated schoolroom education but to balance it with "hands-on" labs directed in the Virtual Reality. The labs have been planned to send 15 minutes of immersive facts and data for each three hours of the old-style information and teaching. The Immersive Classroom will allow an instructor to take a full classroom to varied spaces. The involvements of scenery with persons the size of a brontosaurus, linking how small we actually are in relation to dinosaurs are some of the new involvements. Additionally, a journey can similarly be engaged through the bloodstream perceiving red and white blood cells in their continuous sizes. Finally, through VR incarnations, some earliest and world tradition sites might also be stayed to get a view of the true grandeur of antique constructions.

In today's world, science laboratories can be constructed and be occupied with latest equipment where medical students can be training in complex surgery procedure without any significant risk to the majority of patients or themselves.

Japan have also adopted the latest technology. Presently, at Japan's N and S high schools, the main connected online category of high schools in the nation encompasses more than 6000 students learning in Virtual Reality via using Meta Quest 2 headphones. The instructors account that the claim and usage of the head quests improves the information experience and permits scholars in fostering social skills irrespective of their bodily locations.

Another prominent field where the Metaverse application can increase to economic value is in matters of preparation. For instance, we traditionally give students hands-on training on the wheels just after the theory classes. Sometimes, the outcome is the damage done to the vehicle as it sometimes results in crash and scratch to the vehicle. However, over time, the driving schools have begun using some form of simulation games to give first hand driving lessons to those enrolling for the first time. This will enable lesser damage as the students enrolled will get a virtual scenario in the first place and will assist in having a more realistic driving simulation for students accompanied with better training. The other associated benefits are reduced training costs and accidents, better access to training sessions and learners can enrol themselves in virtual classes numerous times as compared to real world training.

The applications and uses of the Metaverse platform in the teaching and research sector is growing on a greater pace. Examples comprise of the United States military with an exclusive idea of working out their army in terms of vocational knowledge, skills and services through the different applications of the Metaverse usage. Similarly, numerous organizations are opting for virtual reality learning before any real-life lessons and training.

Augmented reality is increasingly being accessed via smart phones and it has the potential to assist medicinal scholars through medical imaging for execution of operations or receiving a 3D conception of an architectural design. Currently, numerous real-life landscapes are being constructed into the Metaverse with the assistance of augmented reality.

The feeling of a touch of real-life geography can be found in the Metaverse and then anybody has the potential to travel anyplace in the planet. Google earth is a bulging instance of a depicting ecosphere with accurate image. Portrayal creations done in Metaverse will be seen as replications of the actual existence that are knowledge and compilation of information improved in nature.

In the Metaverse, you can visit other planet, travel to subversive lives or travelling backmost in time period to see the Great Wall of China being assembled. VR permits us to text daily life by catching, storage, and allocation of everyday understandings, trials and communications at a forward-thinking level of certainty and aids in attaining vitality in the knowledge process. Classing AI in Korea is a learning Societal Communication system Site for online lesson groups. It examines scholar's capabilities and nature and advises modified knowledge way of life.

A schoolroom of scholars can link their educator on a journey to prominent places in Africa with Virtual Reality googles and meet approximately many forms of unusual wildlife. Approximately some places are available through VR. Examples are places like Buckingham palace, the rainforest of Amazon, Egyptian pyramids among countless some other. Some firms such as Tech Row have vigorously tangled in immersive learnedness. VR is allowed in schoolrooms for journeys to planets such as Pluto, remote places on earth such as Antarctica, Machu Picchu and numerous another journey's end.

The usage of Block chain is being considered as one of the most active business systems and can aid in storage of hypothetical official records related to students in the form of records, certificates and degrees. The book-keeping load can be condensed and assessment can be done more simply.

A survey conducted by the University of Maryland concluded that persons remember info more efficiently in the practical and digital reality domain. The outcome concludes an 8.8% betterment in the total capability for remembrance of information. As per Global Millennial, the Metaverse application based, practical and digital forms of world sports such as Second Life and Minecraft are mainly used by advanced educational organizations in the form of a knowledge medium throughout the Covid-19 pandemic. Roblox, a virtual existence gaming giant, had launched a platform for knowledge where teachers had the ability to create virtual schoolrooms. Additionally, there are sequestered servers for educators and scholars who will be able to use the involvements and instructive educational material being provided by Roblox.

With the VR enabled instrument, students can perform experiments, cut a human heart, put together a device or stay in France in the era of French Revolution. Numerous school human activity will be able to do numerous extra-curricular activities. Instances are a journey to Mount Everest, attendance in a live concert or exploring a spaceship going to Mars.

Morehouse College in Atlanta, Georgia have built a virtual lab at the University where students can conduct numerous experiments than if they were present in person. The College found that students learning via VR increased the average score and besides according an rise in scholar attendance and get together.

Colleges located in remote region can use Metaverse and support students residing far away. Any outstanding teacher will be able to teach in locations located far away (around 100 miles away). Furthermore, the school system having lack or dearth of skilled instructors or teachers in any specific topic could hire them to impart classes to the scholars located anywhere in the world. For example, a college scholar located in Ohio can participate in an international seminar delivered by a lecturer located in Seoul. Scholars residing in the distant corner of Alaska would be able to go for a memorable tour to NASA and Egyptian Museum situated in Cairo.

4. POTENTIAL CHALLENGES AND RISKS OF METAVERSE APPLICATION FOR HIGHER EDUCATION

The Metaverse is providing an alternative solution in terms of low-cost learning substitute in some specific types of backgrounds. For example, the cost of building a physical laboratory is far expensive. Furthermore, it needs a lot of financial resources including lot of space and care. A virtual cadaver lab has completed scientific learning reasonable at Fisk University. However, authorizations for virtual reality content, building of digital twin campuses, virtual reality headsets and other venture expenses adds to higher costs for academies. Victory XR custodies a yearly payment fee of $200 per scholar to contact its Metaverse. Extra costs are experienced for virtual reality headsets. The Meta Quest 2 for free for Metaversities launched by Meta and Victory XR, that's only a limited of what may be required. The low-end 128GB version of the Meta Quest 2 headset is priced at around $399.99. Handling and preserving a large number of headphones, plus possession and charging them includes added effective costs and time._Universities have a big requirement to devote noteworthy time and incomes for providing training to education person and instructors to deliver courses for Metaverse. For delivering Metaverse courses there is a need for new digital materials. In maximum situations, most educators are unable to create their own Metaverse teaching materials in the form of formation of videos, still images and audio with text.

There are numerous risks of adopting Metaverse in today's times. They are as follows-

Data privacy, security and safety concerns- Commercial models of firms evolving metaverse skills and knowledge rely on collection of user's thorough individual data. For example, people using Meta's Oculus Quest 2 virtual reality headphones must mandatorily have their own Facebook accounts. The headphones can collect extremely individual, personal and delicate data such as position, students' bodily structures and schedules, and speech recordings. Meta has not assured to save the data and keep in the form of private property or to border access that advertisers might have to it. Presently, Meta is also at work on a high-end virtual reality headset called *Project Cambria* with additional progressive aptitudes and talents. Sensors in the device will permit a computer-generated avatar to preserve eye interaction and make face languages that reflect the user's eye movement and face. This form of data info can help promoters measure user's consideration and goal them with modified and tactful advertising.

In numerous situations, professors and scholars may not easily contribute in class deliberations as they are aware that all their moves, their language and facial languages are being constantly monitored by the educational hub as a big technology business. The computer-generated environment and its apparatus can also gather a wide variety of operator data such as physical movement, heart rate, pupil size, eye openness and signals of emotions.

Increase in the number of Cyber-Attacks-*In today's times, the incidence of the Cyberattack*s are on the rise. Metaverse has the capacity to harm people by interfering with the people's brain in a completely different environment. The virtual reality systems can be influenced to a greater degree. Sometimes the users may be tricked by inducing them to move to dangerous locations. Scholars may be exposed to unsuitable content. Roblox has recently launched Roblox Education to convey 3D, communicating, computer-generated and simulated environments into bodily and online classrooms. The system claims to keep everybody harmless. However, the Metaverse involves user-generated material including chat features which could be used with wrong intentions. The Roblox feature assures of strong protection and promises to keep everyone safe but nothing is perfect in today's life. The metaverse involves user-generated content and chat feature which can be used by predators or people using pornography or other illegal material.

Lack of high-speed Internet and Devices- Implementing Metaverse education needs high speed internet and VR/ AR devices. Sometimes all students may not have equal access to resources. Furthermore, both the instructors and students need digital literacy and training. In today's times, not all students have equality in terms of access to devices such as laptops, computers, iPhone, and high-speed internet. Metaverse holds great promise for the coming future.

However, its implementation in classrooms must be approached carefully in a cautious manner. It also has the potential to increase the existing educational inequalities. Hence, there is an urgent need to address the digital divide for everyone to gain equally from the immersive learning experiences. Some times in less privileged regions, there is lack or dearth of infrastructure and hence it poses a significant barrier to participation in the education process.

Lack of rural access to advanced infrastructure- Numerous Metaverse related applications are bandwidth-intensive in nature. The obligation for high-speed data networks to handle all of the data flowing between sensors and users across are seldom fulfilled. Many handlers, students and scholars particularly located in rural and remote areas are unable to access Metaverse because of lack of band width and essential infrastructure. For example, 97 percent of the people residing in the urban areas in the United States has admission and access to high-speed link in comparison to 65 percent of residents located in the rural areas and 60% of population located in the tribal lands.

Adapting challenges to a new environment- There is a radical change in the approach of the educational institutions in terms of teaching and learning. Modification of curriculum and methods of learning for scholars can make learning in the Metaverse less prearranged with less set of strict monitoring and rules. Significant alterations in the pattern of assessment and monitoring processes such as quizzes and tests need to be updated and understood in the newer Metaverse applications.

A few academicians have raised serious concern about the quality of education offered in the Metaverse. As per the Journal of Virtual Education, computer-generated surroundings may deliver a dissimilar level of communication and individual connection as compared to the physical schoolrooms. This has the potential to negatively impact the quality of knowledge as students are isolated from the real world.

The relationship between higher education in the Metaverse is an ongoing debate in the present times. Virtual learning in the Metaverse can reduce the carbon foot print of education by plummeting the necessity for bodily travel and less use of paper and other environmental resources. However, the energy consumption required to run the servers and data centres supporting the Metaverse has the potential for affecting the environment as the demand for virtual education is growing at a rapid pace. Hence, there is a need for the growth of more supportable technologies for the growth and expansion of Metaverse.

To understand how Metaverse could be a potential driver for higher education and research, we formulated a simple questionnaire comprising of questions. The questions were related to the concept of Metaverse and how it has gained prominence in today's times. The google questionnaire was circulated to the under-graduate and postgraduate students to know their interest and the understanding and relance of the concept of Metaverse in education in today's times.

5. METHODOLOGY OF THE STUDY

For the purpose of the study, a google-form questionnaire survey was created and circulated with basic questions related to the concept and usage of Metaverse in the educational domain. It was circulated among the students enrolled in the under-graduate and post-graduate program of the Department of Economics, MIT World Peace University Pune. The main objective of the study was to understand about the awareness, usefulness, visibility, and knowledge of the different applications of Metaverse. A tentative figure of around 170 students were covered for the purpose of the study. The Primary data was collected through the survey/questionnaire circulated. The overall findings and results are summarized in Table-1 below-

Table 1. Overall Result- Survey about Information, and Application of Metaverse

Questions -Metaverse	Yes	No	Remarks
Knowledge about the concept of Metaverse	60%	40%	Low Awareness Need for more knowledge about the term Metaverse.
Information about the different applications of Metaverse	50%	50%	Preliminary stage.
Application of Metaverse in Higher Education	40%	60%	Preliminary stage.
Information about Virtual Reality	40%	60%	Preliminary stage
Information of Augmented Reality	35%	65%	Preliminary stage
Usage of the Metaverse Application in the Future	75%	25%	Nascent stage. Very little Information.
Challenges -ahead of Metaverse	80%	20%	Measures needs to be taken.

Source-Google Questionnaire (MIT WPU)

The overall survey conducted indicate that the knowledge about the concept and applications of Metaverse is still not well-versed among the the students. This is true particularly for the undergraduate students studying especially in the first year and second year of Economics. The third-year students were found to contain some idea and knowledge related to the application of Metaverse. For the postgraduate students studying Economics, students were aware about the concept and usage of Metaverse. However, they have still not experienced practical applications of the different tools used by Metaverse in matters of imparting high-quality education.

The results furthermore concluded that usage of Metaverse is yet to be added in the education system especially in the developing countries such as India. The Indian education sector is still in the nascent or preliminary stage in terms of usage of Metaverse for imparting education. In comparison to developing countries, developed countries have already started implementing on the different applications of Metaverse in their teaching and learning sectors.

The notable challenges eminent and found from the study are as follows-

Firstly, there are bandwidth and other infrastructural issues prevalent in some parts of the country especially in the remote, rural and distant areas. Hence, accessibility to internet remains a concern for students residing in the remote and distant areas. Furthermore, students interested in using Metaverse technology has to have the collaboration of the universities enrolled with the technology-intensive firms. Secondly, newer business models and tie-ups have to be placed to get a first-hand exposure of Metaverse and their applications. Lastly, there are numerous underlying challenges in the form of dearth of infrastructure, training to students and instructors, lack of funds, accessibility of high-speed internet and willingness to implement different technologies associated with Metaverse poses a significant challenge. Suitable rules and regulations need to be placed to ensure data privacy and security.

In the coming future, with rapid adoption of Metaverse technology on a mass scale, enormous amount of money needs to be spent by the higher educational institutions. In addition, government support and conducive education policy for universities located in the urban and rural areas in different parts of the country. Academicians, scholars and instructors will be keen to access such an immersive virtual and digital world and enhance their knowledge by socially interacting in the virtual space.

5.1 Detailed Results: First Year BSc (Economics) Undergraduate Students

For the purpose of the study, a google-form questionnaire survey was created with some basic questions circulated which has highly related to the concept and usage of Metaverse. It was circulated to the students enrolled in First year BSc program of the Department of Economics. The main objective was to understand and examine the knowledge, awareness and visibility of the different applications of Metaverse among the students enrolled and studying in the undergraduate stream of Economics at MITWPU, Pune. An approximate number of around 65 students were covered for the purpose of the study. Primary data was collected through the survey/questionnaire. For the purpose of data analysis, the questionnaire form, was converted in terms of yes and no. The term yes was assigned 1 and the term No was assigned 0. The term "yes" indicated that the student had some awareness about the concept of Metaverse and "No denoted that the student did not have any awareness or had limited awareness about the concept and application Metaverse. The results are evident from Table-2A (provided in the Appendix). The results found that out of the total 65 students only 5 students had an idea about what is Metaverse, and different forms of applications related to Metaverse. The practical application and challenges pertaining to the concept Metaverse is still unknown among the First year BSc Students.

Figure 1. Number of Students with Awareness about Metaverse

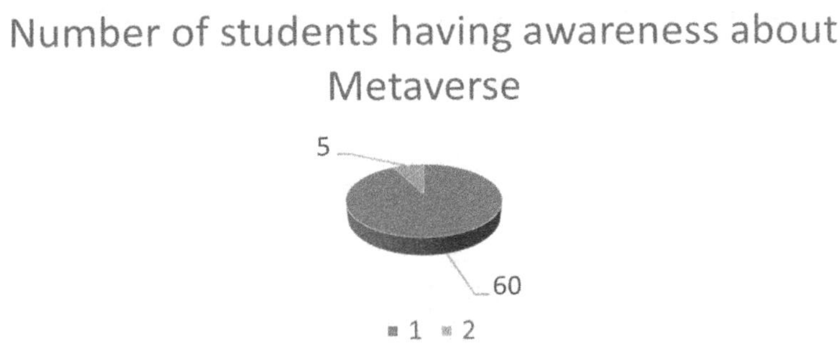

Source: Author's Calculation

Students were demarcated into the groups as Category 1 and Category 2. Category 1 consisted of 60 students of First year BSc Economics undergraduate students and Category 2 comprised of 5 First year BSc Economics undergraduate students. From the above pie-chart, it is evident that the majority of students don't have any idea about Metaverse and its application in the education sector or have used it in the present times. Out of 65 students, only 5 students were aware about the evolving concept of Metaverse and its application in the present 21st century.

5.2 Detailed Result of Second Year BSc (Economics) Undergraduate Students

For the purpose of the study, a google-form questionnaire survey was created with some basic questions circulated which has highly related to the concept and usage of Metaverse. It was circulated to the students enrolled in Second year BSc program of the Department of Economics. The main objective was to understand and examine the knowledge, awareness and visibility of the different applications of Metaverse among the students enrolled and studying in the undergraduate stream of Economics at MITWPU, Pune. An approximate number of around 55 students were covered for the purpose of the study. Primary data was collected through the survey/questionnaire. After collecting data in the questionnaire form, we converted the answers in terms of yes and no. If the answer was positive, it was termed as yes which was equal to 1 and if there is limited knowledge or no knowledge, then it was written in terms of N0 which was equivalent to 0. The term "yes" denotes that the student has awareness about Metaverse and "No denotes that the student does not have awareness about concept and application Metaverse. The results from Table-3A (provided in the Appendix) shows that out 55 students only 40 students had no idea about what is Metaverse, and different forms of applications related to Metaverse and the remaining 15 students had knowledge about thc evolving concept of Metaverse. The practical application and challenges pertaining to the concept Metaverse is still lesser known among the Second year BSc Students.

Figure 2. Awareness about Metaverse

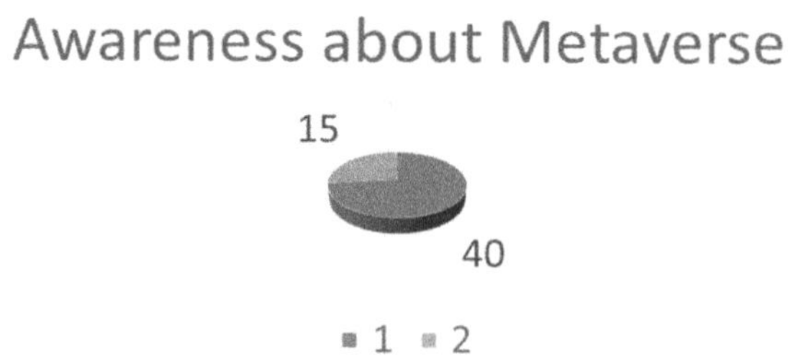

Source: Author's Calculation

Students were demarcated into two categories, Category 1 and Category 2. Category 1 consisted of 40 students of Second year BSc Economics undergraduate students and Category 2 comprised of 15 Second year BSc Economics undergraduate students. From the above pie-chart, it is evident that the majority of students don't have any idea about Metaverse and its application in the education sector. Out of 55 students, only 15 students were aware about the evolving concept of Metaverse and its application in the present 21st century.

5.3 Detailed Findings of Third Year BSc (Economics) Undergraduate Students

For the purpose of the study, a google-form questionnaire survey was created with some basic questions circulated which has highly related to the concept and usage of Metaverse. It was circulated to the students enrolled in third year BSc program of the Department of Economics. The main objective was to understand and examine the knowledge, awareness and visibility of the different applications of Metaverse among the students enrolled and studying in the undergraduate stream of Economics at MITWPU, Pune. An approximate number of around 30 students were covered for the purpose of the study. Primary data was collected through the survey/questionnaire. After collecting data in the questionnaire form, we converted the answers in terms of "yes" and "no". The positive answer was affirmed as yes =1 and no knowledge or limited knowledge about Metaverse was affirmed as No=0. The term "yes" denotes that the student has awareness about Metaverse and "No denotes that the student does not have awareness about concept and application Metaverse. The results indicated that out of 30 students only 10 students have idea about what exactly is the term Metaverse, and what are the different forms of applications which are related to the Metaverse technology. The practical application and challenges pertaining to the concept Metaverse was still lesser known among the third year BSc undergraduate students.

Figure 3. Awareness about Metaverse, continued

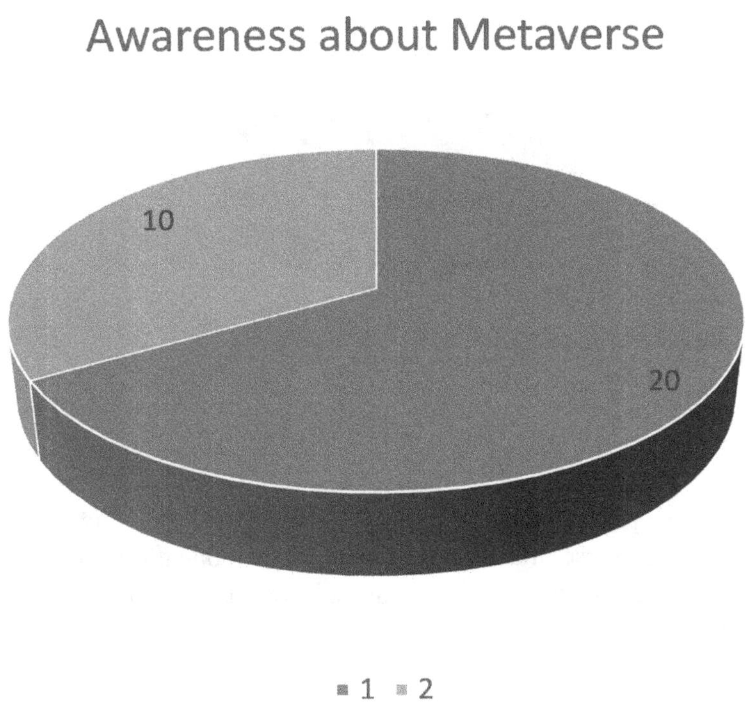

Students were divided into two categories, Category 1 and Category 2. Category 1 consisted of 20 students of third year BSc Economics undergraduate students and Category 2 comprised of 10 third year BSc Economics undergraduate students. From the above pie-chart, it is evident that the majority of students didn't have any idea about the concept of Metaverse and its application in the education sector. Out of 30 undergraduate students, only 10 students were aware about the evolving concept of Metaverse and its application in the present 21st century.

For the post-graduate students, a similar survey was conducted using the google survey questionnaire method. A total number of 20 students were surveyed as per the questions. Students were divided into the categories, Category 1 and Category 2. Category 1 consisted of 17 students of post-graduate Economics and Category 2 comprised of 3 post-graduate economics students. The results indicate a poor number of students having awareness about the applications of Metaverse.

This is given in the pie-chart below-

Figure 4. Awareness about Metaverse, continued

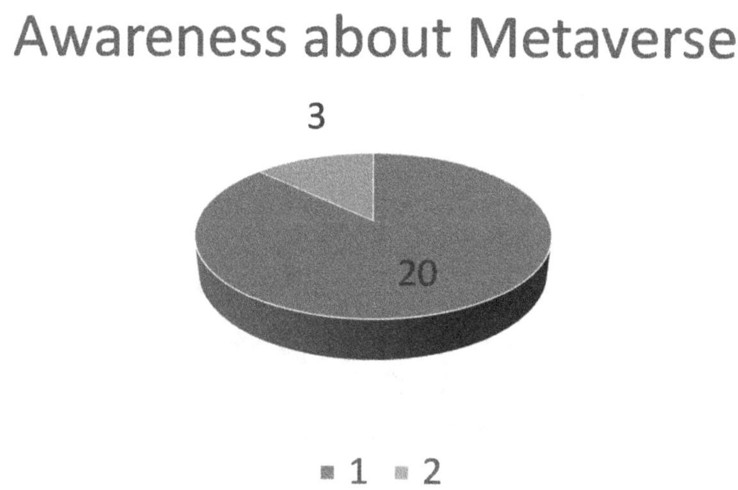

From the above pie-chart, it is evident that the majority of students don't have any idea about Metaverse and its application in the education sector. Out of 20 students, only 3 students were aware about the evolving concept of Metaverse and its application in the present 21st century.

6. CONCLUSION

The term Metaverse is the succeeding progression and expansion of the internet and newer technology. Its extents a variety of technology and know-hows including virtual reality headsets that acts as a conveyance to the entire new situations; the application of augmented glasses which helps to project computer created pictures into the real world. Furthermore, the mixed reality (MR) involvements help in the blending of the physical and the simulated environments. A number of academic research and studies have found that VR can definitely improve understanding, information retention, scholar engagement, devotion span and enthusiasm.

The Metaverse holds tremendous potential to transform the educational landscape allowing instructors to redefine the virtual classrooms or transform education as a reflection of the historical settings. This will help the future scholars and students to engage fully in an interactive and appealing educations. Cooperative knowledge flourishes as we adopt the Metaverse Technology and helps in further development of cooperation among the instructors and students and furthermore helping in cross-cultural communication for students located in different working on different projects. Experimental learning is being increasingly enhanced in today's times and is offering a safer platform for performing experiments in the domain of science era. The AI-driven incarnations and computer-generated tutors will further allow modified knowledge experiences, and further catering to the individual learning styles. The geographical barriers are now being rapidly melted yielding worldwide access to good-quality teaching to scholars coming from varied educations.

The overall key results conclude that Metaverse is still in the initial stages for MITWPU, Pune located in India. For implementation of Metaverse application in the higher education sector, numerous challenges and obstacles needs to be overcome. Death of Infrastructure, dearth of finance/capital, digital divide, lack of knowledge and training and awareness are some of the notable challenges. Other challenges and issues are in the form of providing specialized training to educators, purchasing and availability of special apparatus and instruments for using Metaverse applications.

There might be an opinion that the Metaverse is still not emerged as a prominent domain. However, a decent sum of advanced education organizations is now circumnavigating the Metaverse water, trying the early phases of the knowledge. The Metaverse has the potential to make the educational resources affordable in the following ways-

- It can enhance the performance of the students.
- It has the potential to make the virtual interactions more like real ones
- It can enable investigation with hard to create phenomena
- It has increased approachability for distant and far-flung scholars

- It also has the potential to attracts young demographic crowd and people.

In the extended time-period, ancient ways of doing things in teaching are going to halt working just for the reason that they fit in the past periods. To link to the newer labor force, graduates and freshers must be skilled, qualified and knowledgeable in the similar developing knowledge and assist their forthcoming companies to incorporate in their industries.

There may be instances where some schools, universities and colleges not yet ready to embrace the Metaverse. This is true especially for the Universities and Private Educational Institutions especially working in the Indian Educational Sector. This applies particularly to the Universities operating in the rural locations.

A subsequently, a high proportion of newer generations such as GenZ are showing a high level of interest and want to actively participate in the Metaverse World. Education technology firm VictoryXR, and Engage VR, an Irish firm producing Virtual Reality involvements are working in collaboration with the 10 United States participating colleges as a per-requisite for the establishments launching their Metaversities.

One of the recent applications of Metaverse was conducted by Fisk University. The Fisk University students visited some historically important locations wearing virtual reality headsets. The places of visit included the Montgomery Bus Boycott, the Edmund Pettus Bridge in Selma, Alabama; the Lorraine Motel in Memphis, Tennessee and the National Mall in Washington. Lastly, New Mexico State University, have recently announced that it wants to offer degrees to students taking advantage of Metaverse by taking classes in a virtually simulated world with a commencement since 2027. Another instance was in the year 2021, where Morehouse College had formed a digital campus, or Digital Twin, as an answer for remote learning that is a superior knowledge and involvement than zoom.

Our primary findings show that this is not true for the students enrolled in MIT World Peace University. Very few students, both at the post-graduate and undergraduate level were actually aware about the benefits and role of Metaverse. Infrastructure and affordable bandwidth are one of the pressing issues. To take better advantage and implement the Metaverse technology, the private universities can collaborate with other expert educational firms or take the help of government support and advice to create a conducive environment for using Metaverse in the coming future. Metaverse is expected to become one the important medium to impart education in the Indian Universities in the future time with removal of challenges and bottlenecks coming in its way.

7. FUTURE DIRECTIONS OF RESEARCH AND STUDY

The developments in Metaverse is definitely enhancing the capability of educators, instructors or teachers to deliver a more appealing, immersive learning experiences for their scholars over the time. Metaverse is definitely a great boon for education and is supporting the scholars better both educationally and technically.

However, the rate or pace of adoption of Metaverse by both the developed and developing countries are not uniform. The developed countries are better in matters of infrastructure, availability of finance and other forms of skills and technical know-how. As metaverse penetrates in the educational system, more and more educational institutes are able to impart education via usage of Metaverse Technology, a better analysis can be done covering a large number of countries using Metaverse in the educational systems.

With the onset of Covid, newer technologies have emerged. However, the safety issues are yet to be understood fully. Over the time, cyber-attacks have also increased manifold. Hence, higher risks need to be contained to fully take the advantage of Metaverse usage in the future period ot time.

In terms of knowledge and skills, to create digital content and materials, special training needs to be given to lecturers and professors lacking adequate digital literacy. Schemes have to be circulated to impart training at subsidized cost. With benefits and access to smartphones especially in times of GenZ times, there are risks and issues related to cyber-crime and cyber-attacks. Newer laws, rules and regulations have to be introduced and restructured to take the full advantage of the usage and benefits of Metaverse in the future period of time.

In future terms of research, more measures have to be explored. More surveys and a larger dataset can be used in the study to understand the adoption of Metaverse by the prominent educational places and what are the challenges over the time. Is it environmentally friendly to use Metaverse for positive results in the long run or is it leading to higher carbon foot print over the time. Some question regarding the use of Metaverse and how it is supporting the environmental sustainability could be incorporated in the future study.

REFERENCES

Bhugaonkar, , Bhugaonkar, R., & Masne, N. (2022, September 12). The Trend of Metaverse and Augmented & Virtual Reality Extending to the Healthcare System. *Cureus*, 14(9), e29071. DOI: 10.7759/cureus.29071 PMID: 36258985

Blumenfeld, , Soloway, E., Marx, R. W., Krajcik, J. S., Guzdial, M., & Palincsar, A. (1991). Motivating Project-Based Learning: Sustaining the Doing, Supporting the Learning. *Educational Psychologist*, 26(3–4), 369–398. DOI: 10.1080/00461520.1991.9653139

Buhalis, D. & Karatay, N. (2022). Mixed Reality (MR) for Generation Z in Cultural Heritage Tourism Towards Metaverse. .DOI: 10.1007/978-3-030-94751-4_2

Buhalis, D., & Karatay, N. (2022). Mixed reality for Generation Z in cultural heritage tourism towards Metaverse. In Stienmetz, J. L., Ferrer-Rosell, B., & Massimo, D. (Eds.), *Information and communication technologies in tourism 2022* (pp. 16–27). Springer. DOI: 10.1007/978-3-030-94751-4_2

Chua, H. W., & Yu, Z. (2024). A systematic literature review of the acceptability of the use of Metaverse in education over 16 years. *J. Comput. Educ.*, 11(2), 615–665. DOI: 10.1007/s40692-023-00273-z

Collins, C. (2008). Looking to the future: Higher education in the Metaverse. *EDUCAUSE Review*, 43(5), 51–63.

Contreras, , González, A. H., Fernández, M. I. S., Cepa, C. B. M., & Escobar, J. C. Z. (2022). The Importance of the Application of the Metaverse in Education. *Modern Applied Science*, 16(3), 34. DOI: 10.5539/mas.v16n3p34

Contreras, G. S., Gonzalez, ´. A. H., Fernández, M. I. S., Cepa, C. B. M., & Escobar, J. C. Z. (2022). The importance of the application of the metaverse in education. *Modern Applied Science*, 16(3), 1–34. DOI: 10.5539/mas.v16n3p34

Dai & Liu. (2023), Reconceptualizing ChatGPT and generative AI as a student-driven innovation in higher education, Procedia CIRP, 119, 84-90. DOI: 10.1016/j.procir.2023.05.002

Dailey, N. (2021). Elon Musk says the metaverse seems more like a marketing buzzword right now than a reality. Retrieved from https://markets.businessinsider.com/news/curren cies/elon-musk-metaverse-is-a-marketing-buzzword-crypto-2021-12

Damar, M. (2021). Metaverse shape of your life for future: A bibliometric snapshot. *Journal of Metaverse*, 1(1), 1–8.

Dewey, J. (2007). Experience and Education. New York: Macmillan.

Duan, . (2021). Metaverse for social good: A university campus prototype. In *Proceedings of the 29th ACM international conference on multimedia* (pp. 153–161). DOI: 10.1145/3474085.3479238

FitzGerald, , Jones, A., Kucirkova, N., & Scanlon, E. (2018). A literature synthesis of personalised technology-enhanced learning: What works and why. *Research in Learning Technology*, 26(0), 2095. DOI: 10.25304/rlt.v26.2095

Fourtan'e, S. (2022). Metaverse: The university becomes the metaversity. Fierce education. https://www.fierceeducation.com/student-engagement/future-higher-ed-universitybecomes-metaversity

Gmb, H. M. S. (2021). Metaverse school: A new dimension of education. https://metaverse. school/.

Griswold, M. (2016). CWRU takes the stage at Microsoft's Build conference to show how HoloLens can transform learning. https://case.edu/hololens/

Halverson. (2018) Participatory Culture as a Model for How New Media Technologies Can Change Public Schools. *The Emerging Learning Design Journal*. Available at: https://digitalcommons.montclair.edu/eldj/vol3/iss1/1

Han, S., & Noh, Y. (2021). Analyzing higher education instructors' perception on Metaverse-based Education. *Journal of Digital Contents Society*. .DOI: 10.9728/dcs.2021.22.11.1793

Kaye, A. T., & Rumble, G. (2018). *Distance teaching for higher and adult education*. Routledge. DOI: 10.4324/9780429430930

Kemp, J., & Livingstone, D. (2006). Putting a Second Life "Metaverse" skin on learning management systems. In Proceedings of the Second Life education workshop at the Second Life community convention (Vol. 20). The University of Paisley.

Kraj˘covi˘c, M., Gabajov´ a, G., Furmannov´ a, B., Vavrík, V., Ga˘so, M., & Matys, M. (2021). A case study of educational games in virtual reality as a teaching method of lean management. Electronics. MDPI AG, 10(7), 838. DOI: 10.3390/electronics10070838

Kshetri, . (2022). *Six benefits that the metaverse offers to colleges and universities*. The Conversation.

Kye, B., Han, N., Kim, E., Park, Y., & Jo, S. (2021). Educational applications of metaverse: Possibilities and limitations. *Journal of Educational Evaluation for Health Professions*, 18, 32. DOI: 10.3352/jeehp.2021.18.32 PMID: 34897242

Lee. (2021). All one needs to know about metaverse: A complete survey on technological singularity, virtual ecosystem, and research agenda.

Lee. (2021a). All one needs to know about metaverse: A complete survey on technological singularity, virtual ecosystem, and research agenda, 10.48550/arXiv.2110.05352

Lee, . (2021b). Progress in smart tourism 2010-2017: A systematic literature review. *Journal of Smart Tourism*, 1(1), 19–30. DOI: 10.52255/smarttourism.2021.1.1.4

Lee, B. H., & Park, S. H. (2021). *A study on the NCS based curriculum for educating Technical Director for VFX industry with Artificial Intelligence*. Cartoon and Animation Studies. DOI: 10.7230/KOSCAS.2021.63.417

Lin, P., & Yeh, S. (2019). How motion-control influences a VR-supported technology for mental rotation learning: From the perspectives of playfulness, gender difference and technology acceptance model. *International Journal of Human-Computer Interaction*, 35(18), 1736–1746. Advance online publication. DOI: 10.1080/10447318.2019.1571784

Maroof, . (2021). The Effectiveness of Online Platforms after the Pandemic: Will Face-to-Face Classes Affect Students' Perception of Their Behavioural Intention (BIU) to Use Online Platforms? *Informatics (MDPI)*, 8(4), 83. DOI: 10.3390/informatics8040083

Moy, C., & Gadgil, A. (2022). Opportunities in the metaverse: How businesses can explore the metaverse and navigate the hype vs reality. JPMorgan.

Park, J. (2021). Exploring the possibility of using metaverse in Korean language education. *Journal of the International Network for Korean Language and Culture*, 18(3), 117–146. DOI: 10.15652/ink.2021.18.3.117

Ravichandran & Sridharan. (2018). Powering E-Learning Through Technology: An Overview Of Recent Trends In. *Educational Technology*.

Sanglier, C. (2021). A contribution to educational strategy. Gamification within the current educational space. *Contemporary Engineering Sciences*, 14(1), 117–125. DOI: 10.12988/ces.2021.91786

Schlemmer & Backes. (2014). Learning in Metaverses: Co-Existing in Real Virtuality. .DOI: 10.4018/978-1-4666-6351-0

Son. (2022). The effectiveness of collaborative learning in SW Education based on Metaverse platform. *Journal of the Korean Association of Information Education*. .DOI: 10.14352/jkaie.2022.26.1.11

Sparks, M. (2021). What is a metaverse? *New Scientist*, 251(3348), 18. DOI: 10.1016/S0262-4079(21)01450-0

Sunardi, , Ramadhan, A., Abdurachman, E., Trisetyarso, A., & Zarlis, M. (2022). Acceptance of augmented reality in video conference based learning during COVID19 pandemic in higher education. *Bulletin of Electrical Engineering and Informatics*, 11(6), 3598–3608. DOI: 10.11591/eei.v11i6.4035

Van der Kleij, F. M., Feskens, R. C. W., & Eggen, T. J. H. M. (2015). Effects of Feedback in a Computer-Based Learning Environment on Students' Learning Outcomes: A Meta-Analysis. *Review of Educational Research*, 85(4), 475–511. DOI: 10.3102/0034654314564881

Violante & Vezzetti. (2015). Virtual Interactive e-learning application: An evaluation of the student satisfaction.

Wittich, , Agrawal, A., Cook, D. A., Halvorsen, A. J., Mandrekar, J. N., Chaudhry, S., Dupras, D. M., Oxentenko, A. S., & Beckman, T. J. (2017). E-learning in graduate medical education: Survey of residency program directors. *BMC Medical Education*, 17(1), 114. DOI: 10.1186/s12909-017-0953-9 PMID: 28697744

Yu, M. G. (2021). The evolutionary logic of future media: The iteration, reorganization and ascension of "human connection" - [From "Scene Era" to "Meta-Universe" to the future of "mind world"]. Xinwenjie Zazhi, 10, 54–60. https://www.cnki.com.cn/Article/CJFDTotal-NEWS202110008.html

Zhang, J., & Ye, J. (2021). Alibaba to test gaming potential of metaverse as Big Tech firms stampede into virtual world. Retrieved from https://www.scmp.com/tech/bigtech/article/3159691/alibaba-test-gaming-potential-metaverse-big-tech-firms-stam pede.

Zhang, Y., Meng, X., Gong, Y., Kang, J., & Lu, B. (2023). 'Remote sensing plus' training mode of innovation and entrepreneurship talent nurturing through College student competitions. *ISPRS Annals of the Photogrammetry, Remote Sensing and Spatial Information Sciences*, 10, 83–86. DOI: 10.5194/isprs-annals-X-5-W1-2023-83-2023

Zheng, , Niiya, M., & Warschauer, M. (2015). Wikis and collaborative learning in higher education. *Technology, Pedagogy and Education*, 24(3), 357–374. DOI: 10.1080/1475939X.2014.948041

APPENDIX

Table 2. FyBSc Economics-Total Number of Participants-65

Number of Students	Variable	Knowledge about the concept of Metaverse	Information about the different applications of Metaverse	Practical Application of Metaverse in Higer Education	Challenges for Metaverse
Student 1	0	N	N	N	N
Student 2	0	N	N	N	N
Student 3	0	N	N	N	N
Student 4	0	N	N	N	N
Student 5	0	N	N	N	N
Student 6	0	N	N	N	N
Student 7	0	N	N	N	N
Student 8	0	N	N	N	N
Student 9	0	N	N	N	N
Student 10	0	N	N	N	N
Student 11	0	N	N	N	N
Student 12	0	N	N	N	N
Student 13	0	N	N	N	N
Student 14	0	N	N	N	N
Student 15	0	N	N	N	N
Student 16	0	N	N	N	N
Student 17	0	N	N	N	N
Student 18	0	N	N	N	N
Student 19	0	N	N	N	N
Student 20	1	y	y	N	N
Student 21	0	N	N	N	N
Student 22	0	N	N	N	N
Student 23	0	N	N	N	N
Student 24	0	N	N	N	N
Student 25	0	N	N	N	N
Student 26	0	N	N	N	N
Student 27	0	N	N	N	N
Student 28	0	N	N	N	N

continued on following page

Table 2. Continued

Number of Students	Variable	Knowledge about the concept of Metaverse	Information about the different applications of Metaverse	Practical Application of Metaverse in Higer Education	Challenges for Metaverse
Student 29	0	N	N	N	N
Student 30	1	Y	Y	N	N
Student 31	0	N	N	N	N
Student 32	0	N	N	N	N
Student 33	0	N	N	N	N
Student 34	0	N	N	N	N
Student 35	0	N	N	N	N
Student 36	0	N	N	N	N
Student 37	0	N	N	N	N
Student 38	1	Y	Y	N	N
Student 39	1	Y	Y	N	N
Student 40	0	N	N	N	N
Student 41	0	N	N	N	N
Student 42	0	N	N	N	N
Student 43	0	N	N	N	N
Student 44	0	N	N	N	N
Student 45	0	N	N	N	N
Student 46	0	N	N	N	N
Student 47	0	N	N	N	N
Student 48	0	N	N	N	N
Student 49	0	N	N	N	N
Student 50	0	N	N	N	N
Student 51	1	Y	Y	N	N
Student 52	1	Y	Y	N	N
Student 53	0	N	N	N	N
Student 54	0	N	N	N	N
Student 55	0	N	N	N	N
Student 56	0	N	N	N	N
Student 57	0	N	N	N	N
Student 58	0	N	N	N	N
Student 59	0	N	N	N	N

continued on following page

Table 2. Continued

Number of Students	Variable	Knowledge about the concept of Metaverse	Information about the different applications of Metaverse	Practical Application of Metaverse in Higer Education	Challenges for Metaverse
Student 60	0	N	N	N	N
Student 61	0	N	N	N	N
Student 62	0	N	N	N	N
Student 63	0	N	N	N	N
Student 64	1	Y	Y	N	N
Student 65	1	Y	Y	N	N

Table 3. SyBSc Economics-Total Number of Participants-55

Number of Students	Variable	Knowledge about the concept of Metaverse	Information about the different applications of Metaverse	Practical Application of Metaverse in Higer Education	Challenges for Metaverse
Student 1	0	N	N	N	N
Student 2	0	N	N	N	N
Student 3	1	y	y	N	N
Student 4	0	N	N	N	N
Student 5	0	N	N	N	N
Student 6	0	N	N	N	N
Student 7	1	y	y	N	N
Student 8	0	N	N	N	N
Student 9	0	N	N	N	N
Student 10	0	N	N	N	N
Student 11	1	y	y	N	N
Student 12	1	y	y	N	N
Student 13	0	N	N	N	N
Student 14	0	N	N	N	N
Student 15	0	N	N	N	N
Student 16	1	y	y	N	N
Student 17	0	N	N	N	N
Student 18	0	N	N	N	N
Student 19	0	N	N	N	N

continued on following page

Table 3. Continued

Number of Students	Variable	Knowledge about the concept of Metaverse	Information about the different applications of Metaverse	Practical Application of Metaverse in Higer Education	Challenges for Metaverse
Student 20	1	y	y	N	N
Student 21	0	N	N	N	N
Student 22	0	N	N	N	N
Student 23	0	N	N	N	N
Student 24	0	N	N	N	N
Student 25	0	N	N	N	N
Student 26	0	N	N	N	N
Student 27	0	N	N	N	N
Student 28	0	N	N	N	N
Student 29	0	N	N	N	N
Student 30	1	Y	Y	N	N
Student 31	0	N	N	N	N
Student 32	0	N	N	N	N
Student 33	0	N	N	N	N
Student 34	1	Y	Y	N	N
Student 35	1	Y	Y	N	N
Student 36	1	Y	Y	N	N
Student 37	0	N	N	N	N
Student 38	1	Y	Y	N	N
Student 39	1	Y	Y	N	N
Student 40	0	N	N	N	N
Student 41	0	N	N	N	N
Student 42	0	N	N	N	N
Student 43	1	Y	Y	N	N
Student 44	1	Y	Y	N	N
Student 45	1	Y	Y	N	N
Student 46	1	Y	Y	N	N
Student 47	0	N	N	N	N
Student 48	0	N	N	N	N
Student 49	0	N	N	N	N
Student 50	0	N	N	N	N

continued on following page

Table 3. Continued

Number of Students	Variable	Knowledge about the concept of Metaverse	Information about the different applications of Metaverse	Practical Application of Metaverse in Higer Education	Challenges for Metaverse
Student 49	0	N	N	N	N
Student 50	0	N	N	N	N
Student 53	0	N	N	N	N
Student 54	0	N	N	N	N
Student 55	0	N	N	N	N

Chapter 12
Constructing Human Service Learning in the AI Digital Sphere
China's Case of LivePBL DEEP Method

Ying Liu
London School of Science and Technology, UK

Yuanyuan Li
Capital Normal University, China

Ting Zhao
Beijing Youth and Politics Vocational College, China

ABSTRACT

Service learning, a critical pedagogy combining community service with academic goals, fosters civic engagement, practical skill development, and social responsibility. This chapter explores how integrating Gen AI can enhance project-based service learning to address real-world social challenges in higher education (HE). Despite its rapid growth in HE, Gen AI still faces limitations, particularly the lack of a human-centred design method that reflects real-world contexts and the risk of oversimplifying complex tasks, leading to a more automated, less humanised learning process. The DEEP method, structured upon four co-designing phases—direction, education, event, and project—offers a hybrid solution, creating an adaptable and scalable framework for constructing a project with Gen AI for co-designed, social, and personalised learning. The chapter also illustrates the LivePBL project, piloted to train pre-service teachers in China, demonstrating how the method can effectively

DOI: 10.4018/979-8-3693-5443-8.ch012

integrate Gen AI with hands-on co-design to enhance the learning environment and societal exchange.

INTRODUCTION

Service Learning (Jacoby, 1996) is a pedagogical strategy that combines academic objectives with community service to enhance real-world learning outcomes and address social challenges (García-Rico et al., 2021; Giles & Eyler, 1994; Kezar & Rhoads, 2001; Marco-Gardoqui et al., 2021; Salvador-Garcia et al., 2023). This approach is grounded in experiential learning theory, which believes knowledge is constructed through direct experience and reflection. Service Learning originated in the United States during the 1960s and 1970s with a broader movement towards community involvement and social responsibility in education (Stanton et al., 1999). The foundational principles emphasise exchange and reflection, ensuring that both the community and the students benefit mutually from the collaboration.

In developed countries, Service Learning has significant impacts in fields such as teacher education (Khan & VanWynsberghe, 2020), healthcare and even agricultural studies (Drewery & Lollar, 2024), whereas developing countries have seen less integration in practice with community engagement and professional development (Choi et al., 2023; Knapp & Fisher, 2010). In China, Service Learning has increasingly been emphasized in training teacher students, particularly enhancing their civic and social responsibilities (Coelho & Menezes, 2021). This trend aligns with the national educational reforms aiming to foster holistic development and societal contributions among students. Chinese educational policies have gradually incorporated elements of Service Learning, recognising its potential to bridge the gap between academic learning and societal needs.

Since COVID-19, Service Learning faces increased pressure to meet the evolving demands of 21st-century education (Khiatani et al., 2023; van Laar et al., 2020). The pandemic has accelerated the need for digital transformation in education, prompting educators to integrate technology into Service Learning projects. There is an urgent need to promote and enhance essential skills such as creative and critical thinking, as well as problem-solving and to implement personalised, collaborative, socially engaging, and experiential learning strategies (Kraft, 2000). In response, a compelling movement exists to innovate and broaden Service Learning across various disciplines, aiming to adapt and thrive in the new education landscape (Holmes et al., 2022; Thornhill-Miller et al., 2023).

Our applied research journey began in 2020 when the COVID-19 pandemic started, and we felt an urgent need to help parents and children with digital skills. Based at the Music College of Capital Normal University in China, our international team of friends included a teacher from Liverpool, UK, an international coordinator, professors, and pre-service music teachers. Collaborating with families in Dalian, we delivered bilingual sessions online using a curriculum called Digi Programmes, accredited by an Ofqual-qualification awarding body based in Manchester, UK. A social entrepreneur and principal of a college based in Kathmandu, Nepal, led his team of pre-service social work students and joined us online.

A significant aspect of this research setting is that the pre-service teacher students had opportunities to experience the integration of home-based and intergenerational learning into digital literacy programmes (Liu et al., 2022; Wang et al., 2020; Zhang et al., 2022; Zhou et al., 2023). They observed and reflected on how to plan online sessions that leverage the strengths of China's family education traditions while introducing innovative student-centred pedagogies. They also learned to manage the critical need to shift parents' mindsets from traditional exam-focused education towards a more holistic and engaging learning experience for their children. This hybrid approach not only addressed immediate educational needs during the pandemic but also laid the groundwork for future educational innovations.

Later, we realised that this innovative aspect could not be scaled without a hybrid design method. What started as digital literacy training evolved into a hybrid service-learning environment. We experienced a hybrid ecology in Service Learning that could be very useful and impactful for teaching trainees to observe teaching and foster Service Learning collaboration. In summary, a significant aspect of this research setting is that

- The pre-service teacher students had opportunities to experience the integration of home-based and intergenerational learning into digital literacy programmes.
- They observed and reflected on how to plan online sessions that leverage the strengths of China's family education traditions while introducing innovative, student-centred pedagogies.
- They also learned to manage the critical need to shift parents' mindsets from traditional, exam-focused education towards a more holistic and engaging learning experience for their children.

Much in post-COVID-19, Generative AI (Gen AI) in educational settings has surged, presenting opportunities and challenges (Ogunleye et al., 2024). This brings us to date to expand the research using Gen AI, such as ChatGPT.

The most common forms of Gen AI are Large Language Models (LLMs) like Open AI's ChatGPT-4. The models are trained on vast data to produce coherent text and image generation models like DALL-E (Bahroun et al., 2023), which create visual content from textual descriptions. Reportedly, Gen AI models like ChatGPT can assist students. For instance, to a limited extent, though, in generating ideas and structuring service projects. The limitations are particularly what Bahroun et al (2023) called "brittleness"—a lack of flexibility and nuance in handling real-world contexts. In Service Learning, this brittleness may lead to oversimplified solutions to complex, human-centred problems.

Furthermore, extensive research (Ogunleye et al., 2024) reports Gen AI's potential to personalise learning but underestimates the importance of human-centred design in Service Learning contexts of teaching and learning task flows. The Gen AI models do not clarify what and how the models rely on automated systems for community engagement. The reliance on task automation risks dehumanising tasks intended to foster personal growth and social responsibility. The benefit from further exploration of hybrid models that combine Gen AI's efficiency would also be better based on the human-centred design necessary for successful Service Learning.

As we shall discuss further, many Gen AI practical applicability and effectiveness are too fragmented (Kulkarni et al., 2024). The Gen AI applications should sufficiently address the holistic need for Service Learning in complex Gen AI tool-supported environments. While these tools raise institutional and ethical issues in education (Dellarocas, 2023), we see that Gen AI also offer significant potential (Yusuf et al., 2024) to enhance Service Learning environments if, arguably, we have a more effective design method to extend the Gen AI applications in Service Learning contexts.

Another critical gap between the current many frameworks and practices is the critical lack of a method to *orientate* the design. For example, the conceptual framework developed by Tammets and Ley (2023) for integrating AI tools in teacher professional learning is comprehensive. While it emphasises model-based design (Valarmathi et al., 2024), as well as researcher-teacher collaboration and iterative design, the contexts of "researcher-teacher" collaboration, diverse settings of model and professional frameworks are all in design so to couple with processes of "concrete experience", "reflective observation", "abstract conceptualisation", and "active experimentation". The systematic implementation across such diverse settings needs focuses and design orientations.

Project-based learning (PBL) can be a unified pedagogical design approach to Service Learning (Zhang & Ma, 2023). To design such a project, the division of tasks must be agile in line with workflows that can be adapted by phases of teaching and learning plans. Then, PBL faces challenges in resource integration, real-world engagement, and consistent assessment. Our research demonstrates that designing PBL aligning with Gen AI can be more effective, more contextually sensitive, and more capable of facilitating collaborative and real-world learning experiences.

Figure 1. The LivePBL DEEP Construct

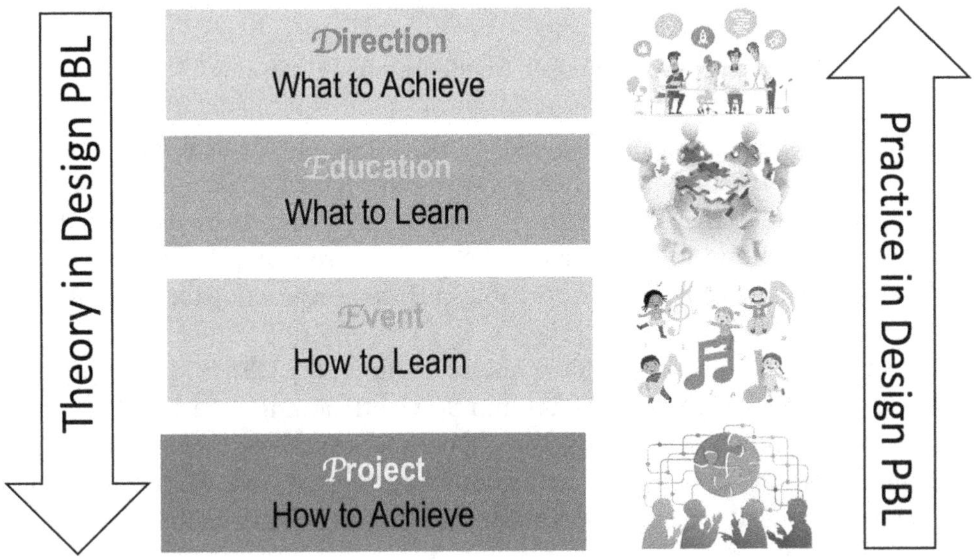

Grounded in the principles of social-techno constructivism (Doolittle & Hicks, 2003) and soft system methodology (Checkland & Poulter, 2006), the DEEP method bridges these design gaps with Gen AI capabilities. The DEEP Method is orientated in Project Based Service Learning with Gen AI supports; it is a construct of four dimensions that navigate a design: Direction, Education, Event and Project (see Figure 1 illustrates the LivePBL DEEP Construct):

1) Direction — What to achieve. This dimension provides the overarching goals and guidance for the service-learning project, e.g., setting clear objectives for a project where students use Gen AI tools to analyse community social engagement and propose improvements.
2) Education —What to learn. This dimension sets learning focuses. The tailored learning strategy incorporates Gen AI. For example, what students do and observe to learn new skills, and what stakeholders, practice curricula, and situated assessments would be involved that challenge students.
3) Event — How to learn. This dimension sets actions, activities, or programmes that are interesting to real-world interactions and serve as live testbeds for learning outcomes with AI applications, e.g., a study tour, workshop, presentation, exhibition, show, or community stay.

4) Project — How to achieve. This dimension constructs, plans and tests the co-design facilitated by Gen AI, project collaborative learning, feedback from sharing social and community experiences, teamwork and project management.

The rest of this chapter is organised by the following sections.

Section 2 synthesises substantial literature to develop a critical framework for bridging the existing gaps. To do so, we establish the foundation of the DEEP Method. Rather than embedding intelligence in a Gen AI model for Service Learning, we aim to enable a collaborative environment that interacts with Gen AI tools. The method, in principle, reflects constructivist learning design through real-world experiences.

Section 3 introduces our piloted research setting, the DEEP Method and the use cases for integrating Gen AI into Service Learning. The DEEP Method encompasses four dimensions: Direction, Education, Event, and Project. Each dimension provides a framework for designing effective, real-world educational experiences using Gen AI tools to enhance learning outcomes and community engagement.

Section 4 demonstrates the application of the DEEP Method in Service Learning projects. It highlights how Gen AI tools assist in project orientation, educational focus, real-world events, and reflective practices, showcasing the transformative potential of integrating Gen AI in educational settings.

Section 5 discusses the limitations of the DEEP Method and highlights the areas for further research, focusing on technological accessibility, methodological consistency, and the dynamic nature of educational contexts. It emphasises the need for future research to address these challenges, ensuring the method's scalability and adaptability across diverse educational environments.

Section 6 concludes the critical findings of the research on the DEEP Method, the method's potential to enhance Service Learning through the integration of Gen AI, and the orientations within a comprehensive, context-sensitive design that promotes personalised learning and real-world engagement.

THE FOUNDATION OF THE DEEP METHOD IN GEN AI SPHERE

This section synthesises the relevant literature to explore the integration of Service Learning within the context of design approaches, critically identifying the gaps between traditional Service Learning environments and the emerging Gen AI sphere. By examining the intersection of practical applications of educational theories and Gen AI, this section lays the groundwork for understanding how design orientations are critical to developing Gen AI applications in Service Learning projects. It establishes the theoretical underpinnings by reviewing the current practices and potential advancements, thereby providing a comprehensive framework for the DEEP Method.

Designing for Service Learning

Designing for learning is arguably one of the most critical and challenging processes in education (Donovan et al., 2000; Garside, 2009; Guan et al., 2024). Service Learning is designed to align community service with academic instruction with disciplinary objectives (Holmlid & Evenson, 2008). Practice and research can be focused on designing compelling learning experiences (Mishra et al., 2024) for pre-service and in-service teachers, making them productive, creative, critical, and ethical users. This needs teaching and learning design from a deeper, long-term perspective, e.g., in line with sociological and historical trends that will shape the socio-techno-cultural matrix of future education.

Zhang and Villanueva (2023) explored the design of a Service Learning project to help students apply academic knowledge in real-world contexts. To some extent, they integrated the project into the curriculum, intended to make it a central component of the educational experience. A key aspect was structured learning reflection, allowing students to reflect on their experiences thoughtfully. They also emphasised the importance of strong community partnerships, collaborating with local organisations to benefit students and the community.

Service learning requires collaboration between several critical stakeholders: students, educators, community partners, and academic institutions. These partnerships are complex and must balance educational and community goals to be effective. Students, central to the Service Learning process, engage in experiential learning by applying their academic knowledge to real-world problems. Their partnerships with community organisations help develop practical skills and civic responsibility, with structured reflection critical in merging experience with academic learning (Eyler & Giles Jr., 1999). Educators are responsible for crafting a curriculum that blends academic rigour with community engagement. Their partnerships with community organisations must be carefully negotiated to ensure that both educational and community needs are met, often using reflective practices to help students understand unpredictable challenges (Butin, 2010). Community partners provide the settings for students to apply their knowledge. However, the relationship with academic institutions can be complex, as organisations must balance their operational goals with educational outcomes, requiring clear communication and sustained engagement (Sandy & Holland, 2006).

However, a design orientation is needed in the following situations:

- Co-designing for Service Learning with Gen AI can be an integrative project into a curriculum to ensure students can apply academic knowledge in real-world contexts.
- Creating a community partnership can facilitate designing structured learning reflection and using Gen AI assessment tools.

Once a community partnership is established, designing for Service Learning in the "public sphere" (Herzberg, 2000) adds a complex dimension. It requires a design focus on civic engagement and collaboration with community stakeholders to address public issues while enhancing students' educational experiences. The term "public sphere or media" is "a realm of our social life in which something approaching public opinion can be formed" (Susen, 2023); it "is the arena where citizens come together, exchange opinions regarding public affairs, discuss, deliberate, and eventually form public opinion" (Giannelos, 2023).

Another complex dimension added to the design is the "digital virtual space or social media" (Trenz, 2023). In today's internet-connected world, digital platforms and social media significantly shape public discourse and community engagement. Designing for Service Learning within this space involves leveraging social media to enhance communication and collaboration between students and community partners (Greenhow & Chapman, 2020), integrating digital tools for virtual Service Learning projects, utilising online platforms for reflecting on service experiences, and ensuring students develop digital literacy skills (Alalwan, 2022). All this needs a design that navigates and contributes effectively to online public spheres.

Moreover, the emerging "Gen AI sphere" adds both complexity and opportunity to learning. Gen AI technologies, including machine learning models capable of producing human-like text, images, and media, require thoughtful design for educational purposes. This involves incorporating Gen AI tools to personalise and enhance the learning experience, using these technologies for teamwork in Service Learning projects, and addressing their impact on social learning and public opinion (Kaplan-Rakowski et al., 2023).

Take LivePBL as an example. In the vibrant city of Beijing, a local community partnered with the Early Year Education Department of Beijing Youth and Politics Vocational College to launch a unique service-learning project aimed at enhancing digital literacy among families. This initiative, called the "Family Digital Literacy Hybrid Programme" (Wang et al., 2020), was designed to support both parents and their children, bridging generational and linguistic gaps in digital skills. The project involved families with children studying in local schools and was supported by an experienced teacher from Liverpool, England. The project provided a platform for pre-service music students from Capital Normal University in Beijing to assist in teaching and observing the teaching and learning dynamics, mainly focusing on family learning, the use of English and Chinese, children's digital literacy, and children's digital creativity.

The project in Beijing can skilfully integrate the public sphere, digital sphere, and Gen AI sphere to create a comprehensive learning experience (Liu et al., 2022). In the public sphere, promotion efforts included community bulletin boards, local newspapers, and public announcements at local schools and gatherings, with bilingual flyers and posters ensuring inclusivity for all families. The digital sphere featured a hybrid programme with sessions at the community centre and online via Zoom, connecting participants with a teacher in Liverpool in the UK and Kathmandu in Nepal. Online modules, managed through an LMS, covered essential digital literacy skills. The Gen AI sphere, powered by ChatGPT 3.5, enhanced the programme with interactive, personalised learning journals, 24/7 AI support, and translation tools that effectively bridge language gaps and enrich participant engagement.

Understanding the Public Sphere, Gen AI Sphere, and Digital Sphere is crucial for the LivePBL DEEP Method. The public sphere provides the context for civic engagement and real-world problem-solving. The Gen AI sphere equips students with advanced AI tools for research, analysis, and innovation. The digital sphere supports collaboration, remote learning, and access to resources. Integrating these spheres creates a holistic education approach, preparing students to engage with society, use cutting-edge technology, and navigate the digital landscape. This foundation enriches the learning experience, enhancing students' problem-solving abilities and preparing them for meaningful contributions to their communities. Table 1 illustrates examples of the Public, Digital and Gen AI spheres.

Figure 2. Examples of the LivePBL DEEP Method in the Public, Digital and Gen AI Sphere

Public Sphere

The project was promoted through community bulletin boards, local newspapers, and public announcements at schools and community gatherings in Beijing. Flyers and posters in both English and Chinese were distributed to ensure inclusivity and accessibility for non-English-speaking families. The program sessions were held in a hybrid of the community centre and Zoom online connecting to Liverpool, the UK.

Digital Sphere

The hybrid nature of the program meant that some sessions were conducted online, allowing the teacher from Liverpool to deliver lessons remotely. The digital platform used for this purpose was Zoom, supplemented by LMS system administrated in Liverpool for sharing resources and assignments. Online modules were created to cover various aspects of digital literacy, including internet safety, basic computer skills, and effective use of educational apps and tools.

Gen AI Sphere

To enhance the learning experience, the program incorporated ChatGPT 3.5. This tool was used to create interactive and personalised learning content. For instance, AI-driven chatbots provided 24/7 support to answer any questions participants had about the course material. Additionally, Gen AI-powered language translation tools facilitated communication between English-speaking instructors and Chinese-speaking participants, ensuring that language barriers did not hinder learning.

Project Based Learning (PBL)

Designing for PBL in the AI digital sphere can promise to construct synergy between Gen AI and create more personalised, engaging, and effective learning environments. However, without an adequate, effective PBL design, PBL would be ineffective in promoting critical thinking, teamwork, and learner engagement. PBL often encounters a few significant obstacles (Miller & Krajcik, 2019; Owens & Hite, 2024; Zhang & Ma, 2023):

1) Difficulty in Engaging with the Real World

    PBL often struggles to bridge a wide array of learning experiences, encompassing social, vocational, and professional engagements, with the acquisition of pertinent, specialised knowledge and abilities. This difficulty arises from the need to not only involve students in significant real-world challenges but also prepare them for their future professional lives. Overcoming this challenge demands a comprehensive strategy that incorporates varied learning outcomes within the PBL structure.

2) Challenges in Resource Integration

Successful PBL implementation demands considerable resources, such as time, materials, and educator expertise, which might not be consistently accessible across different educational contexts.

3) Assessment Challenges

   Conventional evaluation techniques frequently fail to adequately reflect the extent of learning and skill advancement within PBL, posing challenges in accurately gauging student achievement.

4) Variability in Team Implementations

   Without a standardised framework, consistently applying PBL can be challenging, resulting in varied student experiences and achievements. This inconsistency hampers the accumulation of practical knowledge.

Project Based Service Learning

Organising Service Learning as a project allows structured, goal-oriented activities, effectively integrating these spheres. The design for project-based Service Learning can enhance students' application of academic knowledge and engagement with communities, leverage digital tools, and use Gen AI to gain impactful learning and personal growth. As Markula and Aksela (2022) pointed out:

1) "Community-driven learning" enables active participation. Values are accorded to every student. PBL encourages collaborative efforts, turning learning into experiences of communities where students learn from and with each other.
2) "Universal engagement in learning" addresses the challenge of engaging every student in a classroom. PBL allows for a more tailored educational experience.
3) "Adaptability and a focus on students' interests" are central to making learning relevant and engaging. PBL overturns this adaptability by ensuring that learning is not only more engaging but also more meaningful as students explore areas they are genuinely interested in.
4) "Diversity in project outcomes and real-world problem-solving" are other benefits of PBL approach. Unlike the predictable structure of traditional assignments, PBL projects are open-ended, allowing students to apply a wide range of skills in creative and critical thinking.

The following further synthesises the most up-to-date literature to inform the use of the project-based service-learning pedagogy.

Designing Projects With Gen AI for Teacher Training in Skill Development

Integrating Gen AI into project platforms presents significant opportunities for enhancing teacher training in skill development for Service Learning. Gen AI technologies enable personalised and adaptive training experiences, allowing teachers to develop their instructional strategies and classroom management skills tailored to their individual needs (Zhu et al., 2024). These technologies facilitate simulation-based training where teachers can practice handling various scenarios, thereby improving their problem-solving and critical thinking skills (Mavroudi et al., 2024). Gen AI tools can support teacher collaboration, enhancing communication and teamwork abilities (Zhang et al., 2024) as they work together on project-based learning activities (Holmes et al., 2019).

The Benefits of Designing Project Mechanisms for Assessment and Feedback in Teacher Training

Gen AI tools significantly enhance the mechanisms for assessment and feedback in teacher training for Service Learning. AI-driven analytics can provide real-time insights into teachers' performance, helping them measure their instructional effectiveness and identify areas for improvement (Floridi, 2024; Kaplan-Rakowski et al., 2023). Continuous feedback facilitated by AI helps assess the effectiveness of teaching strategies, providing detailed analysis and suggestions for improvement. This systematic evaluation process ensures that teachers achieve their professional development goals and enhances the overall quality of their instructional practices (Almasri, 2024).

The Strengths of Designing an Interdisciplinary Project With Gen AI for Teacher Training

Service-learning projects that incorporate Gen AI often require an interdisciplinary approach, providing a comprehensive framework for teacher training. AI tools can integrate data from various educational disciplines, enabling teachers to apply and expand their knowledge across different subject areas (Floridi, 2024; Kaplan-Rakowski et al., 2023). This interdisciplinary training helps teachers develop a holistic understanding of educational issues and prepares them to address complex classroom challenges (Mavroudi et al., 2024; Zhang et al., 2024). Additionally, AI can facilitate collaborative projects among teachers from different disciplines, fostering a culture of continuous learning and professional growth (Mavroudi et al., 2024).

The Advantages of Enhancing Motivation and Engagement With Gen AI in Teacher Training

Gen AI can significantly enhance motivation and engagement in teacher training for Service Learning by providing interactive and immersive training experiences. AI-driven tools can simulate real classroom environments, allowing teachers to see the impact of their instructional strategies and fostering a sense of accomplishment and purpose (Floridi, 2024; Kaplan-Rakowski et al., 2023). This hands-on approach increases teachers' engagement and commitment to professional development, leading to more effective and meaningful training experiences.

In summary, the primary design orientation is Project Based Service Learning. Design orientation, in this context, refers to the systematic approach yet with adaptive phases structured to direct educational projects with specific objectives in mind. It opens design spaces to encompass the methodologies, strategies, and tools employed to create effective learning environments that align with Gen AI for desired educational outcomes. This orientation is crucial as it navigates Project Based Service Learning through the academic, public, and Gen AI spheres, ensuring that each project is purposefully designed to enhance both teaching and learning experiences.

Within the academic sphere, design orientation focuses on integrating curriculum goals with hands-on, real-world applications, promoting deeper understanding and retention of knowledge. In the public sphere, it emphasises community engagement and collaboration, fostering civic responsibility and social impact. The Gen AI sphere leverages advanced AI tools to personalize learning experiences, facilitate real-time feedback, and enhance the overall effectiveness of educational interventions. The following section will explore the specific design orientations necessary for effectively integrating Gen AI into Service Learning. It will discuss the methodologies and frameworks that guide the development of AI-enhanced educational projects, highlighting best practices and potential pitfalls. This section provides a detailed roadmap for educators looking to harness the power of Gen AI to create innovative and impactful Service Learning experiences.

Design Orientations in the Use of Gen AI

As discussed earlier, Service Learning can be viewed in an environment that blends the Academic, Public, Digital, and Gen AI spheres. Academically, it bridges theory with practical application. Publicly, it fosters community engagement and addresses real-world issues. Digitally, it facilitates collaboration and access to resources.

In the Gen AI sphere, the enthusiasm for using Gen AI has led to an unexpected juncture, prompting educators to reconsider the essence of effective teaching and learning (Robert, 2023; UNESCO, 2024a, 2024b; US-Education, 2023). The rush towards automating educational tasks with AI, exemplified by platforms like ChatGPT, has raised critical questions about the balance between technological convenience and the depth of educational experiences (Holmes et al., 2019; Luckin et al., 2022; Selwyn, 2023). It is critical to have a design method to navigate Service Learning activities with Gen AI without compromising the quality of learning outcomes (Zhang & Villanueva, 2023).

Recent studies (García-Laso et al., 2024; Kimmel, 2024; Paz-Lourido et al., 2024) highlight the importance of integrating design in Gen AI for Service Learning. In our case, for example, it's necessary to have a teaching plan in place when using AI tools like ChatGPT. In a situation where Chinese teacher students observe an English teacher using ChatGPT in a digital literacy lesson, the teacher needs blueprints to guide students to construct and reflect on what they have observed. Without a design orientation, the technology might not be as effective.

Luckin et al. (2022) discuss the potential of Gen AI to transform educational practices through tailored instructional content, but there must be an emphasis on the role of Gen AI in customising learning experiences to meet diverse educational needs. One of the great things about Gen AI is that it can adapt to each student's learning style and pace (Holmes et al., 2019). If some students learn faster than others, ChatGPT can provide more advanced materials to those students while giving extra help to those who need it. This makes learning more personal and effective for everyone. Therefore, the design of Service Learning project is critically needed (Guthrie & McCracken, 2014) to align with the capabilities of Gen AI effectively.

By structuring the project in various phases that align with educational objectives, we ensure that Gen AI tools are not only technologically advanced but also pedagogically effective. In our case, ChatGPT can be utilised to create interactive lessons that engage students. During a lesson instructed in English, the teacher can demonstrate how ChatGPT generates guidelines on internet safety tailored to different activities. Observing this, Chinese teacher trainee students can see how ChatGPT illustrates a concept based on learners' adaptive abilities, showcasing personalised learning experiences. Afterwards, these students reflect on the lesson, discussing the integration of ChatGPT in the lesson, the importance of customised learning, and the contexts where the project has progressed. They consider how the project design has been implemented in their teaching contexts in China, recognising ChatGPT's potential to transform service-learning practices.

RESEARCH METHODOLOGY

A research method is a structured process to develop, test, and validate Gen AI applications (Kulkarni et al., 2024; Luckin et al., 2016; Zawacki-Richter et al., 2019). In the context of Service Learning, these methods evaluate how well Gen AI tools enhance learning experiences, facilitate reflection, and support community partnerships. Researchers use these approaches to ensure that Gen AI tools align with educational objectives and community needs, optimising their functionality and relevance. The methods include Natural Language Processing (NLP), which analyses student reflections and interactions with AI systems to personalise feedback (Maier & Klotz, 2022); Machine Learning and Predictive Analytics, which predict student outcomes and align them with appropriate community projects (Luckin et al., 2016); Automated Feedback Systems, which assess performance and provide immediate, actionable feedback (Zawacki-Richter et al., 2019); and Data Mining (Xiong et al., 2024), which uncovers patterns in student and community engagement to improve service learning. Our research methodology is on the human-centred design approach.

Human-Centered Design Approach

The human-centred design (HCD) approach for developing Gen AI applications in service learning (Yang et al., 2021) focuses on creating Gen AI systems or building Gen AI tools that enhance the educational experience while preserving the integrity of meaningful community involvement. At the heart of HCD is a user-centric approach. The current user-centred design (UCD) methods for developing Gen AI applications in service learning, though essential, have limitations in adequately addressing the complex needs of students, educators, and community stakeholders.

While researchers first gather qualitative data through interviews, observations, and ethnographic studies, the current UCD research process helps to understand the needs, behaviours, and challenges faced by students and community members but struggles to align these needs with real-world, dynamic educational challenges and diverse community interactions. The current UCD is very limited in navigating Gen AI designers on how students reflect on their real-world experiences or how community partners assess the impact of student participation.

While UCD emphasises a deep understanding of user needs, the approach focuses on users who can sometimes lead to a design that meets immediate needs but lacks the flexibility and adaptability required for long-term learning environments and evolving community partnerships. The inadequate tailoring of tasks and workflows should allow for iterative feedback to refine the use of Gen AI tools. The design process should enable designers to create workflows that dynamically adjust to the shifting progress of students and the specific requirements of community projects. This is at the heart of designing for personalisation and adaptability needed in Service Learning settings (Luckin et al., 2016).

Design method for developing Service Learning should also foster meaningful collaboration among students, educators, and community partners. The current UCD focuses on individual user needs rather than facilitating broader, multi-stakeholder partnerships. This often results in Gen AI applications that are well-designed for specific users but may lack the holistic integration necessary for diverse partnerships in Service Learning Projects (Turner & McKenzie, 2020; Williamson & Eynon, 2020).

The LivePBL DEEP Design Method

The LivePBL DEEP method consists of four elements, emphasising the logical phases of Direction, Education, Event, and Project. It orientates Service Learning into project design processes that align with the use of Gen AI rather than a conventional top-down linear method.

Piloted Research Setting

LivePBL was initiated in response to the emergence of COVID-19. The founders, based at the Music College of Capital Normal University in China, shared a vision for online training in family community digital literacy and skills. The university, renowned for its comprehensive teacher training programmes, provided the perfect backdrop for our initiative. We realised that delivering sessions in both English and Mandarin would be incredibly beneficial, as many IT-related terms are rooted in English. This dual-language approach would not only improve digital literacy but also bridge cultural gaps.

Figure 3. LivePBL Model in Hybrid Service Learning

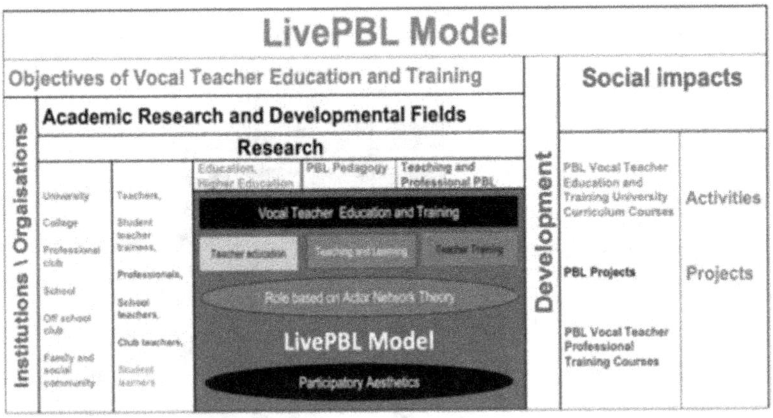

Our Service Learning design and delivery team was a vibrant mix of talents and backgrounds. Leading our English language instruction was a well-qualified teacher from Liverpool, UK, whose passion for teaching shone through in every session. We had dedicated professors and eager pre-service music teacher students from Capital Normal University, Beijing, China. Crucially, we were supported by a local community of families in Dalian (China).

This LivePBL model aims to bridge the gaps between the fields of vocal teacher education training and research in Service Learning social practices (Rosanne, 2012; Wang, 2017) with Chinese characteristics (Huanyuan, 2022; Wang, 2022). The training has been CPD certified. Figure 2 illustrates the model of LivePBL from viewpoints of Service Learning. The model had also been adopted in the

- The university 's social dialogue training programme with trainee participants includes local schoolteachers, vocational college students and teachers, and practitioners from other organisations such as children and youth clubs, kindergartens, and family communities.
- The university's social off-school engagement programme has planned to carry out courses supporting off-school activities.

Figure 4. PBL Teaching Sino-International Student Replacement Framework

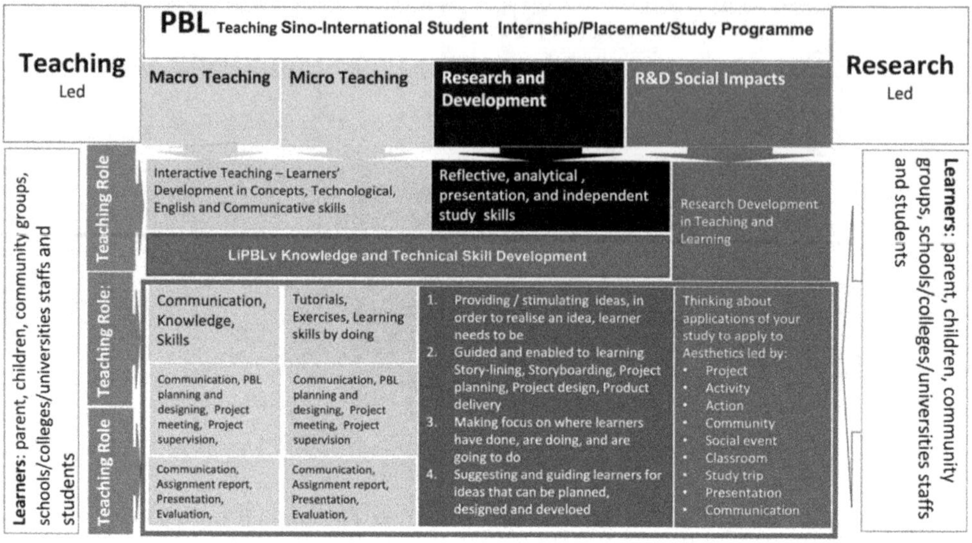

Figure 5. Definition of DEEP in Gen AI Sphere

Direction—What to achieve

This dimension orientates a designer to provide clear guidance for learning, ensuring that projects are aligned with real-world relevance. This strategic focus helps to overcome the exploration often seen in traditional constructivist settings, ensuring that learning is goal-oriented and purposeful. Gen AI tools should be used to guide what engagement can be made in the public sphere.

Project—How to achieve

This dimension is on the commonly interested area in public academic, digital and Gen AI spheres. The designer constructs project-based learning to implement service learning. This structure addresses common challenges in project-based learning, such as resource allocation and assessment, by providing clear guidance and tools for effective project management. It constructs, plans, and tests the co-design facilitated by Gen AI, project collaborative learning, feedback from sharing social and community experiences, teamwork, and project management.

Education—What to learn

This dimension orientates a designer in the academic sphere. The designer encompasses both academic content and essential 21st-century skills. The designer ensures what content learners critically and contextually engage with, what strategies incorporate Gen AI to define what students need to do, and what to observe to learn new skills, including stakeholders, practice curricula, and situated assessments that challenge students.

Event—How to learn

This dimension is in the digital sphere, which orientates the designer to focus on an activity, action, a bobby, talented, or interested event that an individual is most likely to carry out or engage in to incorporate the real world into the learning process. This aspect leverages social and contextual learning opportunities often overlooked by traditional theories, making learning more relevant, engaging, and appealing, such as study tours, workshops, presentations, exhibitions, shows, and home or community stays. This dimension also serves as a live testbed for learning outcomes with Gen AI tools.

To structure our digital literacy training sessions, we partnered with an Ofqual-accredited educational group based in Manchester, UK, known for its K12 digital curriculums. This collaboration added a layer of credibility and rigour to our programme. Additionally, a social entrepreneur and college principal, along with his team of pre-service social work students, joined us to assist in teaching English. Their involvement brought a fresh perspective and boundless energy to our sessions. What started as simple online digital literacy training sessions soon expanded into something more profound. We realised we had created an impactful and beneficial eco-environment of hybrid Service Learning. We adopted and established the framework Project Based Service Learning (see Figure 3 PBL Teaching Sino-International Student Replacement Framework).

Gen AI Assistive Cycle: Orientate, Focus, Identify, Reflect, and Orientate

The DEEP Method provides guided contexts where Gen AI assists. Gen AI assists the designer in the cycle of Orientation, Focus, Identification, and reflection, which, in theory, maps to Direction, Education, Event, and Project. There are many design views of Service Learning. For example, the Service Learning life cycle with a view to the Curriculum: "Investigating, Designing and Preparing, Taking Action, Reflecting and Communicating" (Papanikolaou et al., 2017). Many similar cycles frame the value of global contexts and yet drive a backwards-designed curriculum (Ali, 2023) into authentic, explicitly international education. However, through knowledge and skills, students face the complex development of conceptual understandings that global contexts shape into meaningful, pragmatic inquiry, resulting in action (including service), leading to insufficient and ineffective international mindedness and global engagement.

In the DEEP Method, there can be further contexts of expectations such as (Eyler & Giles Jr., 1999) "service is and for others," "students initiate activities to discuss, plan, and evaluate," "work collaboratively," and "undertake challenges to develop skills," enabling Gen AI to assist in the following four functions. Figure 4 illustrates a Gen AI-assisted DEEP Project-Based Service Learning Environment (Anderson et al., 2019).

Figure 6. Gen AI-assisted DEEP Design for Project Based Service Learning Environment

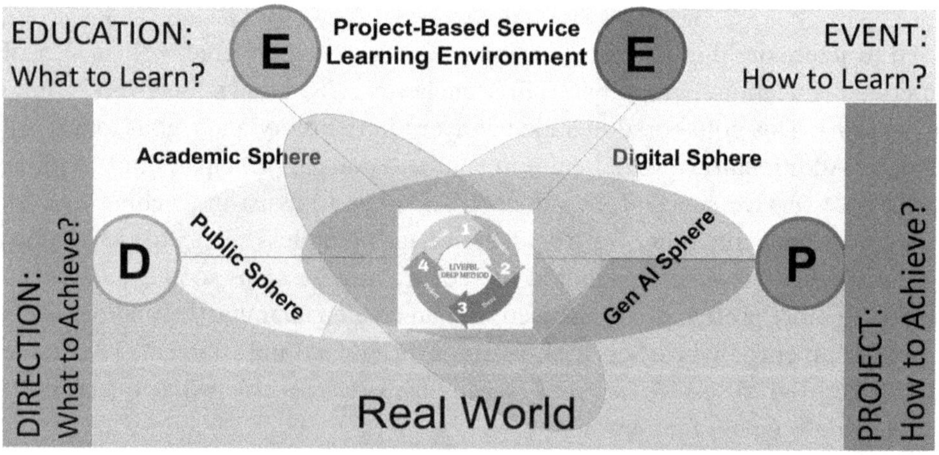

Gen AI Assists Service Orientation (in Direction)

For example, in a LivePBL project, Gen AI identified a local community centre needing assistance with digital literacy programmes for seniors. Gen AI can match this need with students interested in community service and technology, creating a mutually beneficial project that enhances students' teaching skills and improves digital literacy among the elderly.

So, in designing a direction, AI assists in orientating the Service Learning by determining whether it aligns with specific curriculum goals or skill development objectives. It helps evaluate if students can connect to different communities or organisations based on their interests and backgrounds. For instance, AI tools can analyse student profiles and community needs to suggest optimal partnerships and projects, ensuring each student's learning experience is personalised and impactful. This alignment is not just about matching students with projects but also about tailoring the learning objectives to fit the student's career aspirations and personal growth areas.

Moreover, Gen AI can forecast future skills demand, helping to shape the curriculum in a way that prepares students for emerging job markets. By continuously updating and refining the orientation process, AI ensures that Service Learning remains relevant and responsive to both educational standards and societal needs, ultimately fostering a more engaged and capable student body.

Gen AI Assists Service Focus (in Education)

For instance, in a LivePBL initiative, Gen AI enables students to reflect on their performances and identify what and how students are involved with critical thinking in their projects. The Gen AI can then recommend specific exercises to strengthen these skills, leading to noticeable improvements in subsequent assessments.

So, on the dimension of education, Gen AI can assist in focusing a commitment to comprehensive learning, encompassing both academic content and essential 21st-century skills. It connects learning experiences derived from subjects, knowledge, research inquiries, or assignments, offering targeted exercises to enhance specific skills. It analyses student performance to identify areas for improvement and suggests modifications to assessments to capture student learning better. Please note the student performance should have been in the contexts of the social communities set in Direction. In this way, stakeholders in Service Learning can gain deeper insights to observe and learn behaviours, preferences, and outcomes, enabling each other to tailor instructional strategies effectively. Ultimately, Gen AI can assist personalised learning pathways that address individual student needs, providing resources and activities that challenge and support them appropriately. This adaptive learning approach ensures that students are not only meeting academic standards but are also developing critical thinking, problem-solving, and digital literacy skills necessary for future success.

Gen AI Assists Action (in Event)

In a LivePBL project, Gen AI helped organise a virtual exchange programme where students from China and the UK collaborated on a sustainability project. The AI managed the scheduling, facilitated virtual workshops, and provided real-time translation, making the collaboration seamless and impactful. Gen AI assists in developing an effective environment for action by identifying suitable events and activities that align with the learning objectives. It can suggest and organise study tours, workshops, presentations, exhibitions, shows, or community stays that provide real-world interaction and serve as live testbeds for learning outcomes. By leveraging AI, educators can design immersive and interactive experiences that enhance student engagement and knowledge retention. For example, AI can highlight real-world scenarios and allow students to apply their skills in controlled yet realistic settings. This hands-on approach not only reinforces theoretical knowledge but also helps students develop practical skills that are directly applicable to their future careers. Furthermore, AI can facilitate logistics, ensuring that all aspects of event planning and execution are optimised for maximum educational impact. By integrating AI into the planning and learning events, educators can create rich, experiential learning environments that drive deeper understanding and meaningful application of knowledge.

Gen AI Assists Reflection (in Project)

In a LivePBL project focused on digital literacy, Gen AI facilitated reflective sessions where students logged their daily experiences and challenges. Gen AI then provided feedback and suggestions for improvement, helping students refine their teaching methods and better understand their impact on the community. When this project phase integrates reflection on what has been oriented, focused on, and done, Gen AI tools can facilitate this reflection by collecting data on the project's progress and outcomes, providing insights and feedback. Gen AI tools help understand the impact of their actions and enhance the learning experience. Gen AI-driven reflection tools can provide detailed analytics on student participation, engagement, and performance, offering insights that might be overlooked in traditional assessment methods. These tools can generate personalized feedback, helping students to recognise their strengths and identify areas for improvement.

Additionally, AI can assist in creating reflective journals or portfolios, allowing students to document their learning journey in a structured and meaningful way. By fostering a culture of continuous reflection and improvement, AI-enhanced reflection processes ensure that students are learning and growing as individuals. This holistic approach to education encourages lifelong learning and equips students with the self-awareness and critical thinking skills necessary to navigate an increasingly complex world.

Figure 7. The Use Cases of the DEEP Method With Gen AI

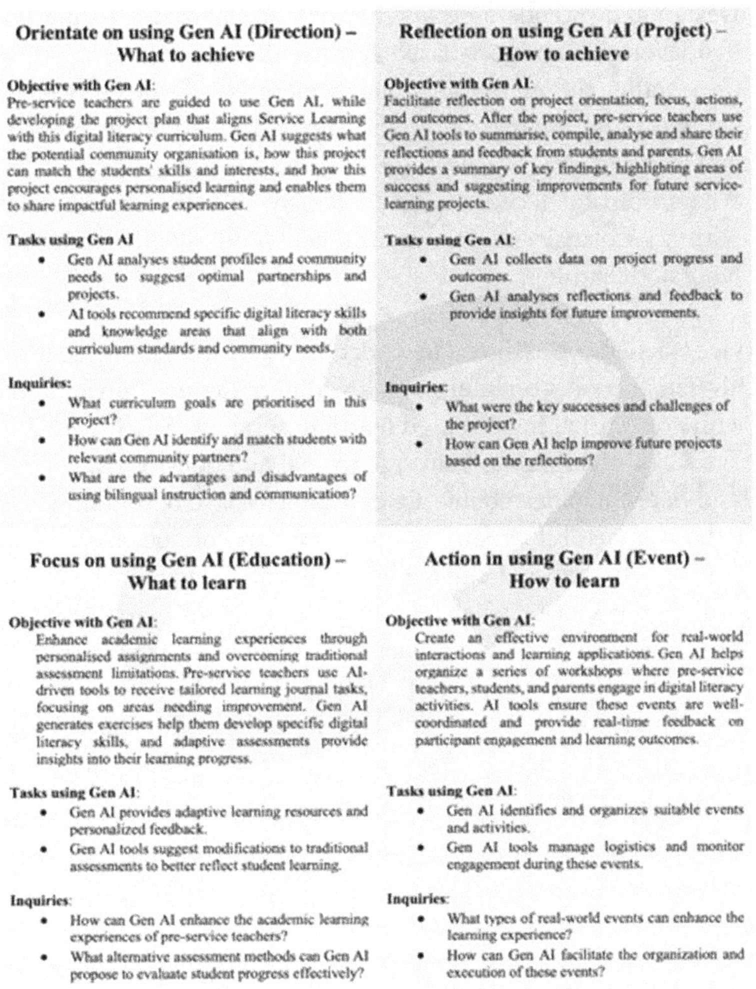

RESEARCH OUTCOMES

A local community of families based in Dalian City, China, is interested in the hybrid project that pioneers a hybrid development of Service Learning in teaching digital literacy and skills among children aged 5-9 and their families. A team of international teachers and pre-service teacher students initiates this project. The project adopts the Digi Programmes curriculum, accredited by NCC Education (i.e., a British Ofqual qualification awarding body).

The innovative aspects of this project in terms of Service Learning are:

- Design and provide a comprehensive and hybrid teaching observation that leverages a project-based approach.
- Connecting the real world, where there is a growing need for digital skills through increasingly technology-driven and integrated teaching and learning.
- All participants faced unique challenges in balancing formal education with non-formal learning environments, bilingually designed and collaborated learning.

Pre-service teachers are assigned to work closely with experienced teachers, parents, and children, focusing on integrating the digital literacy curriculum in formal education with non-formal home-based learning sessions. See Figure 2 in section. 3.1, where we set our research to converge formal and non-formal education.

The pre-service teaching students are expected to have opportunities to observe teaching methods, assist bilingually in classroom and online sessions, and facilitate collaborative activities that engage both students and parents. As part of their Service Learning, pre-service teachers must also write reflective learning reports, sharing and documenting their experiences, challenges, and the impact of their involvement. The use cases for the DEEP Method project have been developed. See Table 3, illustrating the Use Cases of the DEEP Method with Gen AI. Appendixes I, II, III, and IV show the Gen AI-Assisted Activities and Feedback on Direction, Education, Event and Project, respectively.

LIMITATIONS AND FUTURE RESEARCH

While innovative and promising in integrating Gen AI with Service Learning, the DEEP method has several limitations that need to be addressed in future research. These limitations primarily revolve around technological accessibility, methodological consistency, and the dynamic nature of educational contexts.

Technological Accessibility

One significant limitation of the DEEP method is the accessibility of Gen AI tools. Not all educational institutions or community organisations have the resources or infrastructure to implement advanced Gen AI technologies. The successful deployment of the DEEP Method relies heavily on having access to reliable internet connections, up-to-date hardware, and software, which are not universally available, especially in under-resourced areas. For instance, during a LivePBL project where we collaborated with students from Nepal, the lack of reliable internet access and modern computing devices posed significant challenges. Despite the enthusiasm and commitment from both sides, these technological barriers limited the effectiveness of our joint activities and hindered real-time collaboration. Future research should explore ways to make Gen AI tools more accessible and affordable, possibly through partnerships with technology providers or by developing more cost-effective Gen AI solutions. Additionally, community technology hubs or mobile learning centres could be investigated to bridge the digital divide and ensure broader access to these transformative tools.

Methodological Consistency

Another limitation is the potential variability in implementing the DEEP method across different contexts. The effectiveness of the DEEP method should be achieved through its consistent application, but Service Learning settings can vary widely in terms of curriculum, teaching styles, student needs, and community partnerships. Without a standardised framework, the application of the DEEP method may not be scalable. For example, a LivePBL project implemented in an urban school in Beijing experienced different outcomes than a similar project in a suburban school due to variations in teaching approaches and community involvement. This discrepancy highlighted the need for a uniform application strategy to ensure all students benefit equally from the DEEP method. Future research should focus on developing a robust, adaptable framework that can be uniformly applied across diverse Service Learning environments. This could include detailed guidelines, best practices, and training programmes for educators to ensure the consistent and effective application of the

DEEP Method. Creating a comprehensive repository of case studies and templates could also assist educators in adapting the method to their specific contexts while maintaining core principles.

Our research needs to implement the DEEP Method in practice further. Educators' real-world obstacles when implementing Gen AI-enhanced Service Learning include technological access, teacher training, and alignment with institutional goals. Future research could investigate strategies for overcoming these barriers to make Gen AI implementation more accessible.

Additionally, the research emphasises the perspective of educators and researchers but has not sufficiently incorporated the student viewpoint. While the research has focused on the structural design and efficacy of Gen AI tools, it is essential to recognise that this research has not explored how students perceive or experience Gen AI-enhanced service learning. Collecting and analysing student feedback would offer more comprehensive insights into the effectiveness of these tools.

Dynamic Educational Contexts

The dynamic nature of Service Learning presents complex social-techno and educational contexts, which is another challenge. Service Learning needs and priorities can change rapidly, influenced by technological advancements, policy changes, and evolving societal needs. The DEEP method needs to be flexible and adaptable to stay relevant in such a fluid teaching and learning, formal and non-formal hybrid environment. For example, during a LivePBL project involving intergenerational learning in a community centre in Dalian, changes in local educational policies and technological updates required frequent adjustments to the project plan. These shifts necessitated a flexible approach to project management and curriculum design. This requires ongoing research to continuously refine and update the method, incorporating new insights and technological developments. Future work should include longitudinal studies to assess the long-term impact of the DEEP Method and iterative research to refine its components in response to emerging trends and challenges in education. Additionally, developing adaptive learning systems within Gen AI that can dynamically adjust to these changes could provide a more resilient and responsive framework for Service Learning.

Risks of Over-Reliance on Gen AI

While integrating Gen AI in Service Learning offers significant advantages, inherent risks are associated with over-reliance on these technologies. One primary concern is that excessive dependence on Gen AI tools might lead to a diminished role of human intuition and creativity in the learning process. For example, in a

LivePBL project where students used Gen AI to generate ideas for community service initiatives, there was a noticeable reduction in original, creative input from students. The Gen AI's suggestions, while efficient and data-driven, often lacked the nuanced understanding and personal touch that human input can provide.

Another risk is the possibility of Gen AI being misdirected, resulting in activities, and learning experiences that are too detached from real-world contexts. For instance, during a LivePBL project designed to enhance environmental awareness, the Gen AI-driven recommendations focused heavily on theoretical knowledge and virtual simulations, neglecting hands-on, practical engagement with the local environment. This led to a gap between what students learned through Gen AI and what they could apply in real-life situations. It is crucial to ensure that Gen AI tools complement rather than replace real-world interactions and experiences.

To mitigate these risks, future research should emphasise the balanced integration of Gen AI, ensuring that technology enhances but does not overshadow human elements of Service Learning. Educators should be trained to use Gen AI to augment their teaching, fostering environments where human creativity and AI capabilities coexist harmoniously. Additionally, guidelines should be developed to ensure that Gen AI applications are always aligned with real-world relevance, maintaining a strong connection between digital and physical learning experiences.

CONCLUSION

Exploring the DEEP Method within the Gen AI sphere reveals substantial opportunities for enhancing Service Learning. By leveraging the synergy between Service Learning, Project-Based Learning (PBL), and Gen AI tools, the DEEP method provides comprehensive and context-sensitive design orientations through the phases of Direction, Education, Event, and Project.

We demonstrated the project in Beijing, which combined digital literacy training for families with online sessions facilitated by teachers in the UK, allowing pre-service teachers to observe and participate in teaching and learning. The DEEP Method is underpinned by the foundational design principles bridging theoretical knowledge with practical application of Gen AI, fostering holistic Service Learning projects that are goal-oriented, relevant, and effectively managed. In this way, the DEEP Method makes it possible to promote personalised learning and real-world engagement, making Service Learning more dynamic and impactful.

We have illustrated the DEEP Method's application in real-world settings, providing practical use cases for exploring formal curriculum and non-formal hybrid deliveries. The Family Digital Literacy Hybrid Programme in Dalian integrated intergenerational learning with Gen AI tools to provide personalised support. Gen

AI can support Service Learning project planning and reflective practices, ultimately enhancing the overall Service Learning experience. Despite its innovative framework, the DEEP Method encounters several significant challenges, including Technological Accessibility, Methodological Consistency, and Dynamic Service-Learning Contexts.

Moreover, ethical considerations should be at the forefront of Gen AI integration in education (Holmes et al., 2019). This includes awareness of and addressing potential biases in AI algorithms and ensuring transparency in how Gen AI-generated recommendations are made (Akgun & Greenhow, 2022). By fostering a critical understanding of AI among students and educators alike, we can cultivate a more informed and responsible use of these powerful tools. The over-reliance on Gen AI in Service Learning can severely affect human well-being. An overdose of AI technology (Söderlund et al., 2024) could lead to a lack of critical human skills such as empathy, creativity, and hands-on problem-solving. This detachment from real-world experiences can result in students who are less prepared to face practical challenges and may struggle with the social and emotional aspects of their personal and professional lives. Ensuring a balanced approach, where Gen AI is used to enhance and not replace human interaction, is crucial for maintaining the integrity and effectiveness of educational practices.

To address these limitations and enhance the DEEP Method, future research is recommended in Enhancing Accessibility, Standardising Implementation, Adapting to Change, and establishing continuous feedback mechanisms where educators and students can provide input on the method's effectiveness. Moreover, designing strategies for efficient resource allocation and integration should involve creating shared resource pools, developing modular lesson plans that can be easily adapted, and training educators to maximise available resources.

REFERENCES

Akgun, S., & Greenhow, C. (2022). Artificial intelligence in education: Addressing ethical challenges in K-12 settings. *AI and Ethics*, 2(10), 431–440. DOI: 10.1007/s43681-021-00096-7 PMID: 34790956

Alalwan, N. (2022). Actual use of social media for engagement to enhance students' learning. *Education and Information Technologies*, 27(7), 9767–9789. DOI: 10.1007/s10639-022-11014-7 PMID: 35399784

Ali, Y. N. D. (2023). Application of Backward Design in Designing Learning with the Observation-Based Learning Method. *Curricula: Journal of Curriculum Development*, 2(1), 13–28. DOI: 10.17509/curricula.v2i1

Almasri, F. (2024). Exploring the Impact of Artificial Intelligence in Teaching and Learning of Science: A Systematic Review of Empirical Research. *Research in Science Education*, 54(5), 977–997. DOI: 10.1007/s11165-024-10176-3

Anderson, K. L., Boyd, M., Ariemma Marin, K., & McNamara, K. (2019). Reimagining Service-Learning: Deepening the Impact of This High-Impact Practice. *Journal of Experiential Education*, 42(3), 229–248. DOI: 10.1177/1053825919837735

Bahroun, Z., Anane, C., Ahmed, V., & Zacca, A. (2023). Transforming Education: A Comprehensive Review of Generative Artificial Intelligence in Educational Settings through Bibliometric and Content Analysis. *Sustainability (Basel)*, 15(17), 12983. Advance online publication. DOI: 10.3390/su151712983

Butin, D. W. (2010). *Service-Learning in Theory and Practice: The Future of Community Engagement in Higher Education*. Palgrave Macmillan. DOI: 10.1057/9780230106154

Checkland, P., & Poulter, J. (2006). *Learning for Action: A Short Definitive Account of Soft Systems Methodology and its Use Practitioners, Teachers and Students*. Wiley.

Choi, Y., Han, J., & Kim, H. (2023). Exploring key service-learning experiences that promote students' learning in higher education. *Asia Pacific Education Review*. Advance online publication. DOI: 10.1007/s12564-023-09833-5

Coelho, M., & Menezes, I. (2021). University Social Responsibility, Service Learning, and Students' Personal, Professional, and Civic Education. *Frontiers in Psychology*, 12, 617300. Advance online publication. DOI: 10.3389/fpsyg.2021.617300 PMID: 33716883

Dellarocas, C. (2023). How GenAI Could Accelerate Employee Learning and Development. *Harvard Business Review*.https://hbr.org/2023/12/how-genai-could-accelerate-employee-learning-and-development

Donovan, M. S., Bransford, J. D., & Pellegrino, J. W. (2000). *How people learn: Brain, mind, experience, and school (expanded)*. National Academy Press. DOI: 10.17226/9853

Doolittle, P. E., & Hicks, D. (2003). Constructivism as a Theoretical Foundation for the Use of Technology in Social Studies. *Theory and Research in Social Education*, 31(1), 33. DOI: 10.1080/00933104.2003.10473216

Drewery, M. L., & Lollar, J. (2024). Undergraduates' perceptions of the value of service-learning. *Frontiers in Education*, 9, 1330456. Advance online publication. DOI: 10.3389/feduc.2024.1330456

Eyler, J., & Giles, D. E.Jr. (1999). *Where's the Learning in Service-Learning?* Wiley & Sons, Incorporated.

Floridi, L. (2024). Generative Artificial Intelligence in Education and Its Implications for Assessment. *TechTrends*, 68(1), 58–66. DOI: 10.1007/s11528-023-00911-4

García-Laso, A., Martín, D. A., Presa, L., Rodríguez, J. A., Costafreda, J. L., & Parra, J. L. (2024). Artificial Intelligence for Identifying Social Values and Soft Skills in Service-Learning Activities. In García-Peñalvo, F. J., Sein-Echaluce, M. L., & Fidalgo-Blanco, Á. (Eds.), *Innovation and Technologies for the Digital Transformation of Education*. Springer. DOI: 10.1007/978-981-97-2468-0_8

García-Rico, L., Martínez-Muñoz, L. F., Santos-Pastor, M. L., & Chiva-Bartoll, O. (2021). Service-learning in physical education teacher education: A pedagogical model towards sustainable development goals. *International Journal of Sustainability in Higher Education*, 22(4), 747–765. DOI: 10.1108/IJSHE-09-2020-0325

Garside, C. (2009). Look who's talking: A comparison of lecture and group discussion teaching strategies in developing critical thinking skills. *Communication Education*, 45(3), 212–227. DOI: 10.1080/03634529609379050

Giannelos, K. (2023). Recommendations for a Healthy Digital Public Sphere. *Journal of Medical Ethics*, 38(2), 80–92. DOI: 10.1080/23736992.2023.2193970

Giles, D. E. J., & Eyler, J. (1994). The Theoretical Roots of Service-Learning Toward a Theory of Service-Learning. *Service Learning, General*, 150. https://digitalcommons.unomaha.edu/slceslgen/150

Greenhow, C., & Chapman, A. (2020). Social distancing meet social media: Digital tools for connecting students, teachers, and citizens in an emergency. *Information and Learning Science*, 121(5/6), 13. DOI: 10.1108/ILS-04-2020-0134

Guan, R., Raković, M., Chen, G., & Gašević, D. (2024). How educational chatbots support self-regulated learning? A systematic review of the literature. *Education and Information Technologies*. Advance online publication. DOI: 10.1007/s10639-024-12881-y

Guthrie, K. L., & McCracken, H. (2014). Reflection: The Importance of Making Meaning in E-Service-Learning Courses. *Journal of Computing in Higher Education*, 26(3), 238–252. Advance online publication. DOI: 10.1007/s12528-014-9087-9

Herzberg, B. (2000). Service Learning and Public Discourse. *JAC, 20*(2), 14. https://www.jstor.org/stable/20866323

Holmes, A. F., Webb, K. J., & Albritton, B. R. (2022). Connecting students to community: Engaging students through course embedded service-learning activities. *International Journal of Management Education*, 20(1), 100610. DOI: 10.1016/j.ijme.2022.100610

Holmes, W., Blalik, M., & Fadel, C. (2019). *Artificial Intelligence in Education: Promise and Implications for Teaching and Learning*. Center for Curriculum Redesign.

Holmlid, S., & Evenson, S. (2008). Bringing Service Design to Service Sciences, Management and Engineering. In Hefley, B., & Murphy, W. (Eds.), *Service Science, Management and Engineering: Education for the 21st Century* (pp. 341–345). Springer. DOI: 10.1007/978-0-387-76578-5_50

Huanyuan, Z. (2022). Problems In China's College Music Teaching in Recent Years. *International Journal of Management and Education in Human Development*, 2(2), 458–460.

Jacoby, B. (1996). Service-Learning in Today's Higher Education. In B. J. A. (Eds.) (Ed.), *Service-Learning in Higher Education: Concepts and Practices* (pp. 3-25). San Francisco, CA: Jossey-Bass. https://www.wiley.com/en-us/Service-Learning+in+Higher+Education%3A+Concepts+and+Practices-p-9780787902919

Kaplan-Rakowski, R., Grotewold, K., Hartwick, P., & Papin, K. (2023). Generative AI and teachers' perspectives on its implementation in education. *Journal of Interactive Learning Research*, 34(2), 313–338. https://www.learntechlib.org/primary/p/222363/

Kezar, A., & Rhoads, R. A. (2001). The Dynamic Tensions of Service Learning in Higher Education: A Philosophical Perspective. *The Journal of Higher Education*, 72(2), 148–171. DOI: 10.1080/00221546.2001.11778876

Khan, S. A., & VanWynsberghe, R. (2020). A Synthesis of the Research on Community Service Learning in Preservice Science Teacher Education. *Frontiers in Education*, 5(14), 45. Advance online publication. DOI: 10.3389/feduc.2020.00045

Khiatani, P. V., She, M. H. C., Ho, O. Y. Y., & Liu, J. K. K. (2023). Service-learning under COVID-19: A scoping review of the challenges and opportunities for practicing service learning in the 'New Normal. *International Journal of Educational Development*, 100, 102813. Advance online publication. DOI: 10.1016/j.ijedudev.2023.102813 PMID: 37260563

Kimmel, S. B. (2024). AI-facilitated critical thinking in an undergraduate project-based service-learning course. *Journal of Behavioral and Applied Management*, 24(2), 123–130. DOI: 10.21818/001c.122149

Knapp, T. D., & Fisher, B. J. (2010). The Effectiveness of Service-Learning: It's not always what you think. *Journal of Experiential Education*, 33(3), 208–224. DOI: 10.5193/JEE33.3.208

Kraft, N. P. (2000). The Role of Service-Learning in Critical Thinking. *Counterpoints, 110*, 75-94. https://www.jstor.org/stable/42975938

Kulkarni, M., Mantere, S., Vaara, E., van den Broek, E., Pachidi, S., Glaser, V. L., Gehman, J., Petriglieri, G., Lindebaum, D., Cameron, L. D., Rahman, H. A., Islam, G., & Greenwood, M. (2024). The Future of Research in an Artificial Intelligence-Driven World. *Journal of Management Inquiry*, 33(3), 207–229. DOI: 10.1177/10564926231219622

Liu, Y., Li, Y., Yang, S., Ren, T., Li, H., Hogg, A., Shah, P., Li, J., Zhang, Y., & Chhetri, A. (2022). A hybrid and non-formal music education connecting China's local family communities and cultures with Nepal. *International Journal for Infonomics*, 15(1), 2088–2093. Advance online publication. DOI: 10.20533/iji.1742.4712.2022.0218

Luckin, R., Cukurova, M., Kent, C., & Benedict du Boulay, B. (2022). Empowering Educators to be AI-Ready Computers and Education. *Artificial Intelligence*, 3, 1–11. DOI: 10.1016/j.caeai.2022.100076

Luckin, R., Holmes, W., Griffiths, M., & Forcier, L. B. (2016). *Intelligence Unleashed: An argument for AI in EducationOpen Ideas*. Pearson Education.

Maier, U., & Klotz, C. (2022). Personalized feedback in digital learning environments: Classification framework and literature review. *Computers and Education: Artificial Intelligence*, 3, 100080. Advance online publication. DOI: 10.1016/j.caeai.2022.100080

Marco-Gardoqui, M., Eizaguirre, A., & García-Feijoo, M. (2021). The impact of service-learning methodology on business schools' students worldwide: A systematic literature review. *PLoS One*, 5(12). Advance online publication. DOI: 10.1371/journal.pone.0244389 PMID: 33347503

Markula, A., & Aksela, M. (2022). The key characteristics of project-based learning: how teachers implement projects in K-12 science education. *Discip Interdscip Sci Educ Res, 4*(2). https://doi.org/doi.org/10.1186/s43031-021-00042-x

Mavroudi, E., Holmes, W., & Ibáñez, M. (2024). Exploring the Impact of Artificial Intelligence in Teaching and Learning of Science: A Systematic Review of Empirical Research. *Research in Science Education*, 54(5), 977–997. DOI: 10.1007/s11165-024-10176-3

Miller, E. C., & Krajcik, J. S. (2019). Promoting deep learning through project-based learning: A design problem. *Disciplinary and Interdisciplinary Science Education Research*, 1(7), 7. Advance online publication. DOI: 10.1186/s43031-019-0009-6

Mishra, P., Oster, N., & Henriksen, D. (2024). Generative AI, Teacher Knowledge and Educational Research: Bridging Short- and Long-Term Perspectives. *TechTrends*, 68(2), 205–210. DOI: 10.1007/s11528-024-00938-1

Ogunleye, B., Zakariyyah, K. I., Ajao, O., Olayinka, O., & Sharma, H. (2024). Systematic Review of Generative AI for Teaching and Learning Practice. *Education Sciences*, 14(6), 636. DOI: 10.3390/educsci14060636

Owens, T., & Hite, R. (2024). Tackle implementation challenges in project-based learning: A survey study of PBL e-learning platforms. *Educational Technology Research and Development*, 71(3), 1179–1207. DOI: 10.1007/s11423-023-10202-7

Papanikolaou, K. A., Makri, K., & Roussos, P. (2017). Learning design as a vehicle for developing TPACK in blended teacher training on technology-enhanced learning. *International Journal of Educational Technology in Higher Education*, 34(1), 45–67. DOI: 10.1186/s41239-017-0072-z

Paz-Lourido, B., Hervás-Torres, M., & Chaves, Á. R. (2024). Service-Learning in Higher Education in the Age of Digital Transformation and Artificial Intelligence. In García-Peñalvo, F. J., Sein-Echaluce, M. L., & Fidalgo-Blanco, Á. (Eds.), *Innovation and Technologies for the Digital Transformation of Education*. Springer., DOI: 10.1007/978-981-97-2468-0_11

Robert, J. (2023). *EDUCAUSE AI Landscape Study*. ECAR.

Rosanne, K. (2012). Artistic participatory practices as a vehicle for togetherness. *Cumulus ACM International Conference Proceeding Series, 2*, 93-96. https://doi.org/doi.org/10.1145/2348144.234817

Salvador-Garcia, C., Chiva-Bartoll, O., Maravé-Vivas, M., & Gil-Gómez, J. (2023). Service-learning in physical education teacher education: A retrospective exploratory study to examine its challenges. *Teaching and Teacher Education*, 135, 104350. Advance online publication. DOI: 10.1016/j.tate.2023.104350

Sandy, M., & Holland, B. A. (2006). Different worlds and common ground: Community partner perspectives on campus-community partnerships. *Michigan Journal of Community Service Learning*, 13(1), 30–43. https://doi.org/http://hdl.handle.net/2027/spo.3239521.0013.103

Selwyn, N. (2023). On the Limits of Artificial Intelligence (AI) in Education. *Nordisk tidsskrift for pedagogikk og kritikk, 10*(12), 3. DOI: 10.23865/ntpk.v10.6062

Söderlund, K., Engström, E., Haresamudram, K., Larsson, S., & Strimling, P. (2024). Regulating high-reach AI: On transparency directions in the Digital Services. *Internet Policy Review*, 13(1). Advance online publication. DOI: 10.14763/2024.1.1746

Stanton, T. K., Giles, D. E., & Cruz, N. I. (1999). *Service-Learning: A Movement's Pioneers Reflect on its Origins, Practice, and Future*. Jossey-Bass.

Susen, S. (2023). *The Structural Transformation of the Public Sphere Revisited: From the Politics of Inclusion to the Politics of Translation*. Oxford Academic Society.

Tammets, K., & Ley, T. (2023). Integrating AI tools in teacher professional learning: A conceptual model and illustrative case. *Frontiers in Artificial Intelligence*, 6, 1255089. Advance online publication. DOI: 10.3389/frai.2023.1255089 PMID: 38130325

Thornhill-Miller, B., Camarda, A., Mercier, M., Burkhardt, J.-M., Morisseau, T., Bourgeois-Bougrine, S., Vinchon, F., El Hayek, S., Augereau-Landais, M., Mourey, F., Feybesse, C., Sundquist, D., & Lubart, T. (2023). Creativity, Critical Thinking, Communication, and Collaboration: Assessment, Certification, and Promotion of 21st Century Skills for the Future of Work and Education. *Journal of Intelligence*, 11(13), 54. DOI: 10.3390/jintelligence11030054 PMID: 36976147

Trenz, H. (2023). Democracy in the Digital Public Sphere: Disruptive or Self-Corrective? *Communication Theory*, 33(2-3), 143–152. DOI: 10.1093/ct/qtad009

UNESCO. (2024a). *AI competency framework for teachers*. UNESCO. https://www.unesco.org/en/articles/ai-competency-framework-teachers?hub=343

UNESCO. (2024b). *AI competency framework for students*. UNESCO. https://www.unesco.org/en/articles/ai-competency-framework-students

US-Education. (2023). *U.S. Department of Education Shares Insights and Recommendations for Artificial Intelligence*. https://www2.ed.gov/documents/ai-report/ai-report.pdf

Valarmathi, S., Kareem, J., Tantia, V., Babu, K. S., & Lucas, P. J. (2024). *Enhancing Curricula with Service Learning Models*. DOI: 10.4018/979-8-3693-5933-4

van Laar, E., van Deursen, A. J. A. M., van Dijk, J. A. G. M., & de Haan, J. (2020). Determinants of 21st-Century Skills and 21st-Century Digital Skills for Workers: A Systematic Literature Review. *SAGE Open*, 10(1). Advance online publication. DOI: 10.1177/2158244019900176

Wang, J. (2017). Aesthetic Education in China: Problems and Solutions. *International Journal of Humanities Social Sciences and Education*, 4(12), 134–139. https://www.arcjournals.org/international-journal-of-humanities-social-sciences-and-education/volume-4-issue-12/17

Wang, Y., Liu, X., Zhang, Y., Sang, X., & Wang, M. (2020). The first model of family education on the delivery of bilingual British NCC digital literacy qualifications in Dalian, China — Engaging and motivating children. *Proceedings of the International Conference on Education in Mathematics, Science and Technology (ICEMST)*.

Wang, Y.-C. (2022). Winning the hearts of the people with artistic masterpieces: An artistic aesthetic tradition of Chinese Marxism. *Educational Philosophy and Theory*, 54(11), 1759–1766. DOI: 10.1080/00131857.2022.2079494

Xiong, Z., Li, H., Liu, Z., Chen, Z., Zhou, H., Rong, W., & Ouyang, Y. (2024). A Review of Data Mining in Personalized Education: Current Trends and Future Prospects. *Frontiers of Digital Education*, 1(1), 26–50. DOI: 10.1007/s44366-024-0019-6

Yang, S. J. H., Ogata, H., Matsui, T., & Chen, N.-S. (2021). Human-centered artificial intelligence in education: Seeing the invisible through the visible. *Computers and Education: Artificial Intelligence*, 2, 100008. Advance online publication. DOI: 10.1016/j.caeai.2021.100008

Yusuf, A., Pervin, N., & Román-González, M. (2024). Generative AI and the future of higher education: A threat to academic integrity or reformation? Evidence from multicultural perspectives. *International Journal of Educational Technology in Higher Education*, 21(1), 21. DOI: 10.1186/s41239-024-00453-6

Zawacki-Richter, O., Marín, V. I., Bond, M., & Gouverneur, F. (2019). Systematic review of research on artificial intelligence applications in higher education – where are the educators? *International Journal of Educational Technology in Higher Education*, 16(39), 39. Advance online publication. DOI: 10.1186/s41239-019-0171-0

Zhang, C., & Villanueva, L. E. (2023). Generative Artificial Intelligence Preparedness and Technological Competence: Towards a Digital Education Teacher Training Program. *International Journal of Education and Humanities*, 11(2), 164–170. Advance online publication. DOI: 10.54097/ijeh.v11i2.13753

Zhang, L., & Ma, Y. (2023). A study of the impact of project-based learning on student learning effects: A meta-analysis study. *Frontiers in Psychology*, 14, 1202728. DOI: 10.3389/fpsyg.2023.1202728 PMID: 37564309

Zhang, L., Ren, T., Xie, Y., Tian, Z., Tang, T., & Li, Y. (2022). Student Choirs and Virtual Social Practices by LivePBL: Linking Vocal Education with Project Based Learning. *Literacy Information and Computer Education Journal*, 13(1), 3860–3666. DOI: 10.20533/licej.2040.2589.2022.0482

Zhang, Y., Chen, F., & Rohe, K. (2024). Social Media Public Opinion as Flocks in a Murmuration: Conceptualizing and Measuring Opinion Expression on Social Media. *Journal of Computer-Mediated Communication*, 27(1), 1–22. DOI: 10.1111/jcc4.12145

Zhou, Y., Ren, T., Chen, N., Li, J., Lu, K., Li, Y., Acharya, A., Shah, P., Hogg, A., & Liu, Y. (2023). Student virtual social practices between China and Nepal. *International Journal of Technology and Inclusive Education*, 12(1), 1802–1807. DOI: 10.20533/ijtie.2047.0533.2023.0223

Zhu, L., Sun, D., Luo, M., Liu, W., & Xue, S. (2024). Investigating Pre-Service Science Teachers' Design Performance in Laboratory Class: The Inquiry-Based Design Thinking Approach. *Journal of Science Education and Technology*, 33(1), 30–44. DOI: 10.1007/s10956-023-10050-3

APPENDIX I: ACTIVITIES AND FEEDBACK ON DIRECTION

Direction – What to achieve

Involves setting clear goals, objectives, and guidelines for the project. It ensures all activities align with the project's vision and desired outcomes. Use ChatGPT to brainstorm and refine specific objectives for the project.	
Objectives	
	Increase cultural awareness between Chinese and Nepalese families. Enhance music skills through structured hybrid learning sessions. Foster family engagement in music education activities. Role Assignment and Persona Development: Create detailed personas for different stakeholders involved in the project.
Learner's Roles	
	Student Persona: Li Wei, a 10-year-old student from Dalian, China, is interested in learning traditional Nepalese music. Teacher Persona: Mr. Chen, a music teacher from Beijing Normal University, is experienced in cross-cultural music education. Community Member Persona: Mrs. Zhang, a local parent and community leader in Dalian, coordinating family participation in the project.
Guided Learning Journals	
	Describe a traditional song from your childhood and explain its significance. Discuss how music can be a tool for cultural exchange and understanding. Share a musical activity that families can do together.
	What are the current practices of music education in Chinese and Nepalese families? How does music facilitate intergenerational learning in both cultures? What are the challenges and benefits of hybrid music education? How can we measure the impact of cultural exchange through music education?
Feedback Procedures	
	Set up regular virtual meetings with participants to discuss progress and gather feedback. Use online surveys after each music session to collect feedback on what worked and what didn't. Implement a suggestion box feature on the project's online platform for ongoing feedback.

APPENDIX II: ACTIVITIES AND FEEDBACK ON EDUCATION

Education - What to Learn

Brainstorm and refine a hybrid curriculum integrating one or more modules in music education; develop innovative instructional methods to enhance the learning experience; develop one or more specific music skills among learners.
Modules
Module 1: Introduction to Traditional Chinese Music • History and significance • Key instruments and their sounds Module 2: Introduction to Traditional Nepalese Music • Cultural background • Fundamental musical styles and instruments Module 3: Digital Music Literacy • Basics of digital music production • Integrating traditional music with digital tools Module 4: Bilingual Music Education • Learning music terminology in both Chinese and English • Exercises to practice bilingual communication through music
Instruction
Flipped Classroom: Assign pre-recorded lectures for home viewing, using class time for hands-on practice and discussion. Blended Learning: Combine online tutorials with in-person workshops to reinforce skills. Peer Teaching: Encourage students to teach each other traditional songs, fostering a collaborative learning environment. Bilingual Instruction: Conduct sessions in both Chinese and Nepalese, alternating languages to enhance bilingual skills.
Skills
Learners are able to: • Replicate rhythmic patterns clapped by the instructor. • Play virtual and in-person drum circles to practice timing and coordination. • Sing Along to traditional songs, focusing on pitch and intonation. • Work in groups to prepare and perform a piece of music. • Communicate with each other from different cultures and work together to create a group journal, present and performance.

APPENDIX III: ACTIVITIES AND FEEDBACK ON EVENT

Event – How to Learn

Define specific objectives for action-based and individual preferred activities; align each activity with the project's educational and cultural goals as an event; create a festival to celebrate and promote the culture of China and Nepal through music at home online; provide educational workshops on traditional music, and to foster a sense of community and mutual appreciation among participants.
Engaging Strategies
Use interactive storytelling to explain the origins of the music. Include hands-on activities where children can try playing the instruments. Organize simple rhythm games and sing-along sessions. Provide colourful, informative materials about the instruments and their cultural significance.
Event Promotion Plan
Promotion Plan: • Launch a social media campaign with event teasers, highlights, and participant stories. • Send out press releases to local media outlets. • Collaborate with local influencers to share event information. • Use email newsletters to keep registered participants informed and engaged.
Rhythm Activities: • Clap Back: Students replicate rhythmic patterns clapped by the instructor. • Drum Circles: Virtual and in-person drum circles to practice timing and coordination. Harmony Activities: • Choral Practice: Group singing sessions to practice harmonizing. • Digital Harmony: Use music software to experiment with harmonic combinations. Teamwork Activities: • Group Performances: Students work in groups to prepare and perform a piece of music. • Collaborative Projects: Joint projects where students from different cultures work together to create a musical composition. Bilingual Communication Activities: • Language Exchange Sessions: Students practice explaining musical concepts in both Chinese and Nepalese. • Bilingual Songwriting: Collaborative songwriting sessions where lyrics are written in both languages. Fusion Performance • Duration: 45 minutes • Performers: A mix of Chinese and Nepalese musicians
Post-Event Evaluation
Post-Event Survey Questions: • How satisfied were you with the event overall? • Which activities did you enjoy the most? • Do you feel the event helped you learn more about Chinese and Nepalese music? • What suggestions do you have for future events? • Would you participate in similar events in the future?

APPENDIX IV: ACTIVITIES AND FEEDBACK ON PROJECT

Project – How to Achieve

<table>
<tr><td colspan="2">Outlining, planning, and executing the integration of the other three dimensions (Direction, Education, Event) into a cohesive project-based learning (PBL) framework. It involves formulating learning processes, setting goals, designing activities, and ensuring that the project is manageable and effective.</td></tr>
<tr><td colspan="2">LivePBL Project</td></tr>
<tr><td></td><td>The objectives are to promote cultural exchange through music, develop musical and bilingual communication skills, and foster collaborative learning among participants</td></tr>
<tr><td>Instructive Sessions</td><td>Interactive Workshops: Regularly scheduled workshops that allow for direct interaction and feedback.
Project-Based Learning: Students undertake music projects that require applying their knowledge and skills in real-world contexts.
Reflective Learning: Use journaling techniques to make learning more engaging, such as music-related challenges and rewards.
Bilingual Pairing: Pair students from different language backgrounds to encourage bilingual communication and teamwork.</td></tr>
</table>

Compilation of References

Abd-El-Khalick, F., & Lederman, N. G. (2000). Improving science teachers' conceptions of nature of science: A critical review of the literature. *International Journal of Science Education*, 22(7), 665–701. DOI: 10.1080/095006900050044044

Abdollahzadeh, M., & Behroozizad, S. (2015). On the importance of A socio-culturally designed teaching model in an EFL writing classroom. *International Journal of Applied Linguistics and English Literature*, 4(4), 238–247. DOI: 10.7575/aiac.ijalel.v.4n.4p.238

Abobaker, R., & Silas, I. (2024). Autonomy-structure balance in facilitating task engagement. In Egbert, J., & Panday-Shukla, P. (Eds.), *Task engagement across disciplines research and practical strategies to increase student achievement*. Routledge. DOI: 10.4324/9781003406419-9

AbuHamda, E., Ismail, I., & Bsharat, T. (2021). Understanding quantitative and qualitative research methods: A theoretical perspective for young researchers. *International Journal of Research*, 8(2), 71–79.

Abu-Salih, B., & Alotaibi, S. (2024). A systematic literature review of knowledge graph construction and application in education. *Heliyon*, 10(3), e25383. DOI: 10.1016/j.heliyon.2024.e25383 PMID: 38327411

Adesope, O., Lavin, T., Thompson, T. A., & Ungerleider, C. (2011). Pedagogical strategies for teaching literacy to ESL immigrant students: A meta-analysis. *The British Journal of Educational Psychology*, 81(4), 629–653. DOI: 10.1111/j.2044-8279.2010.02015.x PMID: 22050311

Adiguzel, T., Kaya, M. H., & Cansu, F. K. (2023). Revolutionizing education with AI: Exploring the transformative potential of ChatGPT. In *Contemporary Educational Technology* (Vol. 15, Issue 3). Bastas. DOI: 10.30935/cedtech/13152

Ahmad, S. F., Han, H., Alam, M. M., Rehmat, M. K., Irshad, M., Arraño-Muñoz, M., & Ariza-Montes, A. (2023). Impact of artificial intelligence on human loss in decision making, laziness, and safety in education. *Humanities & Social Sciences Communications*, 10(1), 311. DOI: 10.1057/s41599-023-01787-8 PMID: 37325188

Ahmad, S., Rahmat, M., Mubarik, M., Alam, M., & Hyder, S. (2021). Artificial intelligence and its role in education. *Sustainability (Basel)*, 13(22), 12902. DOI: 10.3390/su132212902

Ahmed, S., & Nashat, N. (2020). Model for utilizing distance learning post COVID-19 using (PACT)™ a cross-sectional qualitative study. *Research Square*, 1–25. https://doi.org/DOI: 10.21203/rs.3.rs-31027/v1

AI In Education Market Size & Share Report, 2022-2030. (n.d.). Retrieved August 28, 2024, from https://www.grandviewresearch.com/industry-analysis/artificial-intelligence-ai-education-market-report

Akavova, A., Temirkhanova, Z., & Lorsanova, Z. (2023). Adaptive learning and artificial intelligence in the educational space. *E3S Web of Conferences, 451*, 06011. DOI: 10.1051/e3sconf/202345106011

Akgun, S., & Greenhow, C. (2021). Artificial intelligence in education: Addressing ethical challenges in K-12 settings. *AI and Ethics*, 2(3), 431–440. DOI: 10.1007/s43681-021-00096-7 PMID: 34790956

Akinrinola, O., Okoye, C. C., Ofodile, O. C., & Ugochukwu, C. E. (2024). Navigating and reviewing ethical dilemmas in AI development: Strategies for transparency, fairness, and accountability. GSC Advanced Research and Reviews, 18(3), 50-58.

Akinwalere, S. N., & Ivanov, V. (2022). Artificial Intelligence in Higher Education: Challenges and Opportunities. *Border Crossing*, 12(1), 1–15. DOI: 10.33182/bc.v12i1.2015

Alalwan, N. (2022). Actual use of social media for engagement to enhance students' learning. *Education and Information Technologies*, 27(7), 9767–9789. DOI: 10.1007/s10639-022-11014-7 PMID: 35399784

Ala-Mutka, K. M. (2005). A survey of automated assessment approaches for programming assignments. *Computer Science Education*, 15(2), 83–102. Advance online publication. DOI: 10.1080/08993400500150747

Aldabbus, S. (2018). *Project-Based Learning: Implementation & Challenges.*

Aler Tubella, A., Mora-Cantallops, M., & Nieves, J. C. (2024). How to teach responsible AI in Higher Education: Challenges and opportunities. *Ethics and Information Technology*, 26(1), 3. DOI: 10.1007/s10676-023-09733-7

AlHarbi, A. (2022). The uses of machine learning (ML) in teaching and learning English language: A methodical review. DOI: 10.21608/edusohag.2022.212355

Aliman, N.-M. (2020). *Hybrid cognitive-affective Strategies for AI safety*. PhD thesis. Utrecht, Netherlands: Utrecht University. DOI: 10.33540/203

Ali, Y. N. D. (2023). Application of Backward Design in Designing Learning with the Observation-Based Learning Method. *Curricula: Journal of Curriculum Development*, 2(1), 13–28. DOI: 10.17509/curricula.v2i1

Aljohani, M. (2017). Principles of "constructivism" in foreign language teaching. *Journal of Literature and Art Studies*, 7(1). Advance online publication. DOI: 10.17265/2159-5836/2017.01.013

Al-Kaisi, A. N., Arkhangelskaya, A. L., & Rudenko-Morgun, O. I. (2020). The didactic potential of the voice assistant "Alice" for students of a foreign language at a university. *Education and Information Technologies*, 26(1), 715–732. DOI: 10.1007/s10639-020-10277-2

Almasri, F. (2024). Exploring the Impact of Artificial Intelligence in Teaching and Learning of Science: A Systematic Review of Empirical Research. *Research in Science Education*, 54(5), 977–997. DOI: 10.1007/s11165-024-10176-3

Almohammadi, K., Hagras, H., Alghazzawi, D., & Aldabbagh, G. (2017). A fuzzy expert system-based adaptive learning approach to improving students' learning performances by considering affective and cognitive factors. *Journal of Artificial Intelligence and Soft Computing Research*, 7(4), 289–304.

Alsawaier, R. S. (2018). The effect of gamification on motivation and engagement. *The International Journal of Information and Learning Technology*, 35(1), 56–79. DOI: 10.1108/IJILT-02-2017-0009

Amo-Filva, D., Mauri, S. A., Escudero, D. F., Sanchez-Sepulveda, M. V., Hasti, H., García-Holgado, A., García-Holgado, L., Vázquez-Ingelmo, A., García-Peñalvo, F. J., Orehovački, T., Krašna, M., Pesek, I., Marchetti, E., Valente, A., Witfelt, C., Ružić, I., Fraoua, K. E., Moreira, F., Pereira, C. S., & Paes, C. (2024). Empowering student data privacy in schools through open educational resources. In *Lecture notes in educational technology* (pp. 253–263). DOI: 10.1007/978-981-97-2468-0_25

Anderson, K. L., Boyd, M., Ariemma Marin, K., & McNamara, K. (2019). Reimagining Service-Learning: Deepening the Impact of This High-Impact Practice. *Journal of Experiential Education*, 42(3), 229–248. DOI: 10.1177/1053825919837735

Andriotis, N. (2023). *Embrace Artificial Intelligence InThe Workplace*. eLearning Industry. https://elearningindustry.com/embrace-artificial-intelligence-in-the-workplace

Androutsopoulou, A., Karacapilidis, N., Loukis, E., & Charalabidis, Y. (2019). Transforming the communication between citizens and government through AI-guided chatbots. *Government Information Quarterly*, 36(2), 358–367. Advance online publication. DOI: 10.1016/j.giq.2018.10.001

Angwin, J. (2023, January 28). Decoding the hype about AI. *The Markup*.https://themarkup.org/hello-world/2023/01/28/decoding-the-hype-about-ai

Anvil | Build Web Apps with Nothing but Python. (n.d.). Retrieved June 13, 2024, from https://anvil.works

Arakawa, K., Hao, Q., Deneke, W., Cowan, I., Wolfman, S., & Peterson, A. (2022). Early identification of student struggles at the topic level using context-agnostic features. *SIGCSE 2022: Proceedings of the 53rd ACM Technical Symposium on Computer Science Education*. DOI: 10.1145/3478431.3499298

Arman, M., & Lamiya, U. R. (2023). Exploring the Implication of ChatGPT AI for Business: Efficiency and Challenges. *Journal of Innovation Information Technology and Application*, 5(1), 64–84. Advance online publication. DOI: 10.31098/ijmadic.v1i2.1872

Arora, B., Al-Wadi, H., & Afari, E. (2024). Scaffolding instruction for improvement in learning English language skills. *International Journal of Evaluation and Research in Education*, 13(2), 1265. DOI: 10.11591/ijere.v13i2.26659

Ashraf, A. (2023). Harnessing the Power of AI to Create Intelligent Tutoring Systems for Enhanced Classroom Experience and Improved Learning Outcomes. DOI: 10.1007/978-981-99-1767-9_42

Author (2023).

Azevedo, R., Bouchet, F., Duffy, M., Harley, J., Taub, M., Trevors, G., Cloude, E., Dever, D., Wiedbusch, M., Wortha, F., & Cerezo, R. (2022). Lessons learned and future directions of Metatutor: Leveraging multichannel data to scaffold self-regulated learning with an intelligent tutoring system. *Frontiers in Psychology*, 13, 813632. Advance online publication. DOI: 10.3389/fpsyg.2022.813632 PMID: 35774935

Bahrini, A., Khamoshifar, M., Abbasimehr, H., Riggs, R. J., Esmaeili, M., Majdabadkohne, R. M., & Pasehvar, M. (2023). ChatGPT: Applications, opportunities, and threats. *Proceedings of the 2023 Systems and Information Engineering Design Symposium (SIEDS)*. DOI: 10.1109/SIEDS58326.2023.10137850

Bahroun, Z., Anane, C., Ahmed, V., & Zacca, A. (2023). Transforming Education: A Comprehensive Review of Generative Artificial Intelligence in Educational Settings through Bibliometric and Content Analysis. In *Sustainability (Switzerland)* (Vol. 15, Issue 17). Multidisciplinary Digital Publishing Institute (MDPI). DOI: 10.3390/su151712983

Bai, J. (2023). Future prospects of artificial intelligence in education: A preliminary analysis of educator perspectives from focus groups in Japan, Spain, and Germany. Ubiquity Proceedings. DOI: 10.5334/uproc.74

Baidoo-Anu, D., & Ansah, L. O. (2023). Education in the era of generative artificial intelligence (AI): Understanding the potential benefits of ChatGPT in promoting teaching and learning. *Journal of AI, 7*(1), 52-62. DOI: 10.2139/ssrn.4337484

Baird, M. (2019). *Project Based Learning to Develop 21st Century Competencies.* https://pressbooks.pub/techandcurr2019/chapter/pbl-competencies/

Baker, R. S., Nafea, I., & Wang, Y. (2021). How much are we relying on AI in education? In *Artificial Intelligence in Education* (pp. 39–44). Springer.

Baker, R., & Hawn, A. (2021). Algorithmic bias in education. *International Journal of Artificial Intelligence in Education*, 32(4), 1052–1092. DOI: 10.1007/s40593-021-00285-9

Bala, M. M., Akkineni, H., & Srinivasulu, C. (2022). An Approach for Learner Categorization Based on Emotions in Intelligent Adaptive E-Learning Environment. *Journal of Mobile Multimedia*, 18(6). Advance online publication. DOI: 10.13052/jmm1550-4646.18611

Barnett, S., Kurniawan, S., Thudumu, S., Brannelly, Z., & Abdelrazek, M. (2024). *Seven Failure Points When Engineering a Retrieval Augmented Generation System* (arXiv:2401.05856). arXiv. /arXiv.2401.05856DOI: 10.1145/3644815.3644945

Barria-Pineda, J., Brusilovsky, P., & Akhuseyinoglu, K. (2020). Explaining need-based educational recommendations using interactive open learner models. In *Proceedings of the 28th ACM Conference on User Modeling, Adaptation and Personalization* (pp. 48-56).

Becker, B. A., Denny, P., Finnie-Ansley, J., Luxton-Reilly, A., Prather, J., & Santos, E. A. (2023). Programming is hard—or at least it used to be: Educational opportunities and challenges of AI code generation. *Proceedings of the 54th ACM Technical Symposium on Computer Science Education*. DOI: 10.1145/3545945.3569759

Bell, R. L., Matkins, J. J., & Gansneder, B. M. (2011). Impacts of contextual and explicit instruction on pre-service elementary teachers' understandings of the nature of science. *Journal of Research in Science Teaching*, 48(4), 414–436. DOI: 10.1002/tea.20402

Bhowmik, S., & Kim, M. (2021). K-12 ESL writing instruction: A review of research on pedagogical challenges and strategies. *Language and Literature*, 23(3), 166–203. DOI: 10.20360/langandlit29530

Bhowmik, S., & Kim, M. (2022). ESL writing instruction in k-12 settings: Pedagogical approaches and classroom techniques. *Language and Literature*, 24(2), 174–197. DOI: 10.20360/langandlit29612

Bhugaonkar, , Bhugaonkar, R., & Masne, N. (2022, September 12). The Trend of Metaverse and Augmented & Virtual Reality Extending to the Healthcare System. *Cureus*, 14(9), e29071. DOI: 10.7759/cureus.29071 PMID: 36258985

Bicknell, K., Brust, C., & Settles, B. (2023 February 5). How Duolingo's ai learns what you need to learn. https://spectrum.ieee.org/duolingo#:~:text=The%20early%20machine%2Dlearning%20work,educational%20research%20on%20spaced%20repetition)

Bird, K., Castleman, B., Mabel, Z., & Song, Y. (2021). Big data on campus: Putting predictive analytics to the test. *Education Next, 21(*4), 58-64. https://www.educationnext.org/big-data-on-campus-putting-predictive-analytics-to-the-test/

Birer, G. C. (2023). ChatGPT. *TÜBİTAK Bilim ve Teknik Dergisi*, 56(662), 36–37.

Birhane, A., Kasirzadeh, A., Leslie, D., & Wachter, S. (2023). Science in the age of large language models. *Nature Reviews. Physics*, 5(5), 277–280. DOI: 10.1038/s42254-023-00581-4

Black, A. E., & Deci, E. L. (2000). The effects of instructors' autonomy support and students' autonomous motivation on learning organic chemistry: A self-determination theory perspective. *Science Education*, 84(6), 740–756. DOI: 10.1002/1098-237X(200011)84:6<740::AID-SCE4>3.0.CO;2-3

Blumenfeld, , Soloway, E., Marx, R. W., Krajcik, J. S., Guzdial, M., & Palincsar, A. (1991). Motivating Project-Based Learning: Sustaining the Doing, Supporting the Learning. *Educational Psychologist*, 26(3–4), 369–398. DOI: 10.1080/00461520.1991.9653139

Bond, M., Khosravi, H., De Laat, M., Bergdahl, N., Negrea, V., Oxley, E., Pham, P., Chong, S. W., & Siemens, G. (2024). A meta systematic review of artificial intelligence in higher education: a call for increased ethics, collaboration, and rigour. In *International Journal of Educational Technology in Higher Education* (Vol. 21, Issue 1). Springer Science and Business Media Deutschland GmbH. DOI: 10.1186/s41239-023-00436-z

Bondre, S., & Yadav, U. (2022). Automated Flower Species Identification by Using Deep Convolution Neural Network. In Satapathy, S. C., Peer, P., Tang, J., Bhateja, V., & Ghosh, A. (Eds.), *Intelligent Data Engineering and Analytics* (pp. 1–10). Springer Singapore. DOI: 10.1007/978-981-16-6624-7_1

Bostrum, N. (2017). *Superintelligence: Paths, Dangers, Strategies*. Oxford University Press.

Botvin, M., Hershkovitz, A., & Forkosh-Baruch, A. (2022). Data-driven decision-making in emergency remote teaching. *Education and Information Technologies*, 28(1), 489–506. DOI: 10.1007/s10639-022-11176-4 PMID: 35791318

Budhwar, P., Chowdhury, S., Wood, G., Aguinis, H., Bamber, G. J., Beltran, J. R., Boselie, P., Lee Cooke, F., Decker, S., DeNisi, A., Dey, P. K., Guest, D., Knoblich, A. J., Malik, A., Paauwe, J., Papagiannidis, S., Patel, C., Pereira, V., Ren, S., . . . Varma, A. (2023). Human resource management in the age of generative artificial intelligence: Perspectives and research directions on ChatGPT. In *Human Resource Management Journal* (Vol. 33, Issue 3). DOI: 10.1111/1748-8583.12524

Bugingo, J. B., Yadav, L. L., Mugisha, I. S., & Mashood, K. K. (2024). Improving teachers' and students' views on nature of science through active instructional approaches: A review of the literature. *Science & Education*, 33(1), 29–71. DOI: 10.1007/s11191-022-00382-8

Buhalis, D. & Karatay, N. (2022). Mixed Reality (MR) for Generation Z in Cultural Heritage Tourism Towards Metaverse. .DOI: 10.1007/978-3-030-94751-4_2

Bulut, O. and Wongvorachan, T. (2022). Feedback generation through artificial intelligence. *The Open/Technology in Education Society and Scholarship Association Conference, 2*(1), 1-9. DOI: 10.18357/otessac.2022.2.1.125

Bundit & Chalong. (2023). Analyzing the Impact of Artificial Intelligence in Personalized Learning and Adaptive Assessment in Higher Education. International Journal of Research and Scientific Innovation. DOI: 10.51244/IJRSI.2023.10412

Butin, D. W. (2010). *Service-Learning in Theory and Practice: The Future of Community Engagement in Higher Education*. Palgrave Macmillan. DOI: 10.1057/9780230106154

Büyüköztürk, Ş., Kılıç Çakmak, E., Akgün, Ö. E., Karadeniz, Ş., & Demirel, F. (2019). *Eğitimde Bilimsel Araştırma Yöntemleri* [Scientific Research Methods in Education]. Pegem Akademi.

Cambourne, B. (1995). Toward an educationally relevant theory of literacy learning: Twenty years of inquiry. *The Reading Teacher*, 49(3), 182–192. DOI: 10.1598/RT.49.3.1

Cantos, K. (2023). Artificial intelligence in language teaching and learning. *Ciencia Latina Revista Científica Multidisciplinar*, 7(4), 5629–5638. DOI: 10.37811/cl_rcm.v7i4.7368

Caputi, V., & Garrido, A. (2015). Student-oriented planning of e-learning contents for Moodle. *Journal of Network and Computer Applications*, 53, 115–127. DOI: 10.1016/j.jnca.2015.04.001

Cavus, N., Mohammed, Y. B., & Yakubu, M. N. (2021). Determinants of learning management systems during the COVID-19 pandemic for sustainable education. *Sustainability (Basel)*, 13(9), 5189. DOI: 10.3390/su13095189

Chakraborty, N., Mishra, Y., Bhattacharya, R., & Bhattacharya, B. (2023). Artificial Intelligence: The road ahead for the accessibility of persons with Disability. *Materials Today: Proceedings*, 80, 3757–3761. DOI: 10.1016/j.matpr.2021.07.374

Chalasani, S. H., Syed, J., Ramesh, M., Patil, V., & Pramod Kumar, T. M. (2023). Artificial intelligence in the field of pharmacy practice: A literature review. In *Exploratory Research in Clinical and Social Pharmacy* (Vol. 12). DOI: 10.1016/j.rcsop.2023.100346

Chan, C. K. Y. (2023). A comprehensive AI policy education framework for university teaching and learning. *International Journal of Educational Technology in Higher Education*, 20(1), 38. Advance online publication. DOI: 10.1186/s41239-023-00408-3

Chan, C. K. Y., & Hu, W. (2023). Students' voices on generative AI: Perceptions, benefits, and challenges in higher education. *International Journal of Educational Technology in Higher Education*, 20(1), 43. DOI: 10.1186/s41239-023-00411-8

Chang, T. S., Li, Y., Huang, H. W., & Whitfield, B. (2021). Exploring EFL students' writing performance and their acceptance of AI-based automated writing feedback. *2021 2nd International Conference on Education Development and Studies*. DOI: 10.1145/3459043.3459065

Chassignol, M., Khoroshavin, A., Klimova, A., & Bilyatdinova, A. (2018). Artificial Intelligence trends in education: A narrative overview. *Procedia Computer Science*, 136, 16–24. Advance online publication. DOI: 10.1016/j.procs.2018.08.233

Checkland, P., & Poulter, J. (2006). *Learning for Action: A Short Definitive Account of Soft Systems Methodology and its Use Practitioners, Teachers and Students*. Wiley.

Chen, P., Lu, Y., Zheng, V. W., Chen, X., & Yang, B. (2018). *KnowEdu: A System to Construct Knowledge Graph for Education | IEEE Journals & Magazine | IEEE Xplore*. https://ieeexplore.ieee.org/abstract/document/8362657

Chen, C.-H., & Law, V. (2016). Scaffolding individual and collaborative game-based learning in learning performance and intrinsic motivation. *Computers in Human Behavior*, 55, 1201–1212. DOI: 10.1016/j.chb.2015.03.010

Chen, L., Chen, P., & Lin, Z. (2020). Artificial intelligence in education: A review. *IEEE Access : Practical Innovations, Open Solutions*, 8, 75264–75278. DOI: 10.1109/ACCESS.2020.2988510

Chen, W., Shen, Z., Pan, Y., Tan, K., & Wang, C. (2024). Applying Machine Learning Algorithm to Optimize Personalized Education Recommendation System. *Journal of Theory and Practice of Engineering Science*, 4(01), 01. Advance online publication. DOI: 10.53469/jtpes.2024.04(01).14

Chen, X., Xie, H., Zou, D., & Hwang, G. J. (2020). Application and theory gaps during the rise of Artificial Intelligence in Education. In *Computers and Education* (Vol. 1). Artificial Intelligence., DOI: 10.1016/j.caeai.2020.100002

Chiu, T. K. F. (2024). Future research recommendations for transforming higher education with generative AI. *Computers and Education: Artificial Intelligence*, 6, 100197. DOI: 10.1016/j.caeai.2023.100197

Chiu, T. K., Xia, Q., Zhou, X., Chai, C. S., & Cheng, M. (2023). Systematic literature review on opportunities, challenges, and future research recommendations of artificial intelligence in education. *Computers and Education: Artificial Intelligence*, 4, 100118. DOI: 10.1016/j.caeai.2022.100118

Choi, J. H., Hickman, K. E., Monahan, A. B., & Schwarcz, D. (2022). ChatGPT goes to law school. *Journal of Legal Education*, 71(3). https://jle.aals.org/home/vol71/iss3/2/

Choi, T., & Wong, W. (2018). "Platform nine and three-quarters" and more: Scaffolding ESL writing through teacher modelling and creative imitation. *TESOL Journal*, 9(4), 1–23. DOI: 10.1002/tesj.423

Choi, Y., Han, J., & Kim, H. (2023). Exploring key service-learning experiences that promote students' learning in higher education. *Asia Pacific Education Review*. Advance online publication. DOI: 10.1007/s12564-023-09833-5

Chowdhury, T. A. (2021). Fostering learner autonomy through cooperative and collaborative learning. *Shanlax International Journal of Education*, 10(1), 89–95. DOI: 10.34293/education.v10i1.4347

Chua, H. W., & Yu, Z. (2024). A systematic literature review of the acceptability of the use of Metaverse in education over 16 years. *J. Comput. Educ.*, 11(2), 615–665. DOI: 10.1007/s40692-023-00273-z

Cipriano, B. P., Fachada, N., & Alves, P. (2022). Drop Project: An automatic assessment tool for programming assignments. *SoftwareX*, 18, 101079. Advance online publication. DOI: 10.1016/j.softx.2022.101079

Clark, J., Shoham, Y., & Perrault, R. (2018). *The AI Index 2018 Annual Report, AI Index Steering Committee, Human-Centered AI Initiative*, Stanford University, Stanford, CA

Coelho, M., & Menezes, I. (2021). University Social Responsibility, Service Learning, and Students' Personal, Professional, and Civic Education. *Frontiers in Psychology*, 12, 617300. Advance online publication. DOI: 10.3389/fpsyg.2021.617300 PMID: 33716883

Cofré, H., Núñez, P., Santibáñez, D., Pavez, J. M., Valencia, M., & Vergara, C. (2019). A critical review of students' and teachers' understandings of nature of science. *Science & Education*, 28(3-5), 205–248. DOI: 10.1007/s11191-019-00051-3

Collins, C. (2008). Looking to the future: Higher education in the Metaverse. *EDUCAUSE Review*, 43(5), 51–63.

Contreras, , González, A. H., Fernández, M. I. S., Cepa, C. B. M., & Escobar, J. C. Z. (2022). The Importance of the Application of the Metaverse in Education. *Modern Applied Science*, 16(3), 34. DOI: 10.5539/mas.v16n3p34

Cooper, G. (2023). Examining science education in ChatGPT: An exploratory study of generative artificial intelligence. *Journal of Science Education and Technology*, 32(3), 444–452. DOI: 10.1007/s10956-023-10039-y

Cortiñas-Lorenzo, K., & Lacey, G. (2023). (accepted). Toward Explainable Affective Computing: A Review. *IEEE Transactions on Neural Networks and Learning Systems*. PMID: 37220061

Costello, E. (2023). ChatGPT and the educational ai chatter: Full of bullshit or trying to tell us something? *Postdigital Science and Education*, 6(2), 425–430. DOI: 10.1007/s42438-023-00398-5

Couch, J. D., & Towne, J. (2018). *Rewiring education: How technology will help unlock every student's potential*. BenBella Books, Inc.

Crompton, H., & Burke, D. (2023). Artificial intelligence in higher education: The state of the field. *International Journal of Educational Technology in Higher Education*, 20(22), 22. DOI: 10.1186/s41239-023-00392-8

Dai & Liu. (2023), Reconceptualizing ChatGPT and generative AI as a student-driven innovation in higher education, Procedia CIRP, 119, 84-90. DOI: 10.1016/j.procir.2023.05.002

Dailey, N. (2021). Elon Musk says the metaverse seems more like a marketing buzzword right now than a reality. Retrieved from https://markets.businessinsider.com/news/curren cies/elon-musk-metaverse-is-a-marketing-buzzword-crypto-2021-12

Damar, M. (2021). Metaverse shape of your life for future: A bibliometric snapshot. *Journal of Metaverse*, 1(1), 1–8.

Darsih, E., Wihadi, M., & Hanggara, A. (2021). Using ELSA App in speaking classes: Students' voices. *Proceedings of the 1st Universitas Kuningan International Conference on Social Science, Environment and Technology, UNiSET 2020*. DOI: 10.4108/eai.12-12-2020.2304993

de Leon, L. C. R., Flores, L. V., & Alomo, A. R. L. (2024). Artificial Intelligence and Filipino Academic Librarians: Perceptions, Challenges and Opportunities. *Journal of the Australian Library and Information Association*, 73(1), 66–83. Advance online publication. DOI: 10.1080/24750158.2024.2305993

Dellarocas, C. (2023). How GenAI Could Accelerate Employee Learning and Development. *Harvard Business Review*.https://hbr.org/2023/12/how-genai-could-accelerate-employee-learning-and-development

Denny, P., Kumar, V., & Giacaman, N. (2023). Conversing with Copilot: Exploring prompt engineering for solving CS1 problems using natural language. *Proceedings of the 54th ACM Technical Symposium on Computer Science Educatio*. DOI: 10.1145/3545945.3569823

Devedžić, V. (2004). Web Intelligence and Artificial Intelligence in Education. *Journal of Educational Technology & Society*, 7(4).

Dewey, J. (2007). Experience and Education. New York: Macmillan.

Diamandis, P. H., & Kotler, S. (2020). *The Future Is Faster Than You Think: How Converging Technologies Are Transforming Business, Industries, and Our Lives*. Simon & Schuster.

Dodigovic, M. (2007). Artificial intelligence and second language learning: An efficient approach to error remediation. *Language Awareness*, 16(2), 99–113. DOI: 10.2167/la416.0

Donovan, M. S., Bransford, J. D., & Pellegrino, J. W. (2000). *How people learn: Brain, mind, experience, and school (expanded)*. National Academy Press. DOI: 10.17226/9853

Doolittle, P. E., & Hicks, D. (2003). Constructivism as a Theoretical Foundation for the Use of Technology in Social Studies. *Theory and Research in Social Education*, 31(1), 33. DOI: 10.1080/00933104.2003.10473216

Dorji, K., Jatsho, S., Choden, P., & Tshering, P. (2022). Bhutanese science teachers' perceptions of the nature of science: A cross-sectional study. *Disciplinary and Interdisciplinary Science Education Research*, 4(4), 4. Advance online publication. DOI: 10.1186/s43031-021-00044-9 PMID: 37520626

Douse, M., & Uys, P. (2023). The role of the teacher in the age of artificial intelligence. *Education Sciences*, 13(2), 133.

Drewery, M. L., & Lollar, J. (2024). Undergraduates' perceptions of the value of service-learning. *Frontiers in Education*, 9, 1330456. Advance online publication. DOI: 10.3389/feduc.2024.1330456

Driver, R., Leach, J., Millar, R., & Scott, P. (1996). *Young people's images of science*. Open University Press.

du Boulay, B. (2016). Artificial intelligence as an effective classroom assistant. *IEEE Intelligent Systems*, 31(6), 76–81. DOI: 10.1109/MIS.2016.93

Duan, . (2021). Metaverse for social good: A university campus prototype. In *Proceedings of the 29th ACM international conference on multimedia* (pp. 153–161). DOI: 10.1145/3474085.3479238

Duong, T., & Suppasetseree, S. (2024). The effects of an artificial intelligence voice chatbot on improving Vietnamese undergraduate students' English speaking skills. *International Journal of Learning. Teaching and Educational Research*, 23(3), 293–321. DOI: 10.26803/ijlter.23.3.15

Eager, B., & Brunton, R. (2023). Prompting higher education towards AI-augmented teaching and learning practice. *Journal of University Teaching & Learning Practice*, 20(02). Advance online publication. DOI: 10.53761/1.20.5.02

Eceyurt Türk, G., & Tüzün, Ü. N. (2017). Lise öğrencilerinin bilim insanı imajları ve bilimin doğası mitleri [High school students' scientist images and their nature of science myths]. *Ahi Evran Üniversitesi Kırşehir Eğitim Fakültesi Dergisi, 18*(2), 19-36. Retrieved from https://dergipark.org.tr/en/pub/kefad/issue/59416/853265

Egbert, J. (2011). "Engage me!": Rules for engagement in CALL. In *CALL: What's your Motivation? Collected Papers on the Cutting Edge of Language Learning Practice Book*. JALT CALL SIG.

Eguchi, A., Okada, H., & Muto, Y. (2021). Contextualizing AI education for K-12 students to enhance their learning of AI literacy through culturally responsive approaches. *Kunstliche Intelligenz*, 35(2), 153–161. DOI: 10.1007/s13218-021-00737-3 PMID: 34376922

Elands, P. (2019). Governing ethical and effective behavior of intelligent systems: A novel framework for meaningful human control in a military context. *Militaire Spectator*, 188(6), 302–313.

Elfaki, A. O., Abduljabbar, M., Ali, L., Alnajjar, F., Mehiar, D., Marei, A. M., Alhmiedat, T., & Al-Jumaily, A. (2023). Revolutionizing Social Robotics: A Cloud-Based Framework for Enhancing the Intelligence and Autonomy of Social Robots. *Robotics (Basel, Switzerland)*, 12(2), 48. DOI: 10.3390/robotics12020048

Elkhatat, A. M. (2023). Evaluating the authenticity of ChatGPT responses: A study on text-matching capabilities. *International Journal for Educational Integrity*, 19(15), 15. Advance online publication. DOI: 10.1007/s40979-023-00137-0

Ellis, L. (2018). Hey, Alexa, Should We Bring Virtual Assistants to Campus? These Colleges Gave Them a Shot - The Chronicle of Higher Education. *The Chronicle of Higher Education*.

Erduran, S., & Levrini, O. (2024). The impact of artificial intelligence on scientific practices: An emergent area of research for science education. *International Journal of Science Education*, 1–8. Advance online publication. DOI: 10.1080/09500693.2024.2306604

Ethan, M. (2023). Using AI to Implement Effective Teaching Strategies in Classrooms: Five Strategies, Including Prompts. Social Science Research Network. DOI: 10.2139/ssrn.4391243

Evenddy, S. S., Gailea, N., & Syafrizal, S. (2023). Exploring the Benefits and Challenges of Project-Based Learning in Higher Education. *PPSDP International Journal of Education*, 2(2), 2. Advance online publication. DOI: 10.59175/pijed.v2i2.148

Eyler, J., & Giles, D. E.Jr. (1999). *Where's the Learning in Service-Learning?* Wiley & Sons, Incorporated.

Fagan, A. (2023 May 11). Educational psychology meets generative AI. *Psychology Today*.https://www.psychologytoday.com/us/blog/psyched/202305/educational-psychology-meets-generative-ai

Felzmann, H., Fosch-Villaronga, E., Lutz, C., & Tamò-Larrieux, A. (2020). Towards transparency by design for artificial intelligence. *Science and Engineering Ethics*, 26(6), 3333–3361. DOI: 10.1007/s11948-020-00276-4 PMID: 33196975

Feng, T., Qinghua, Z., Zhiyong, G., Jin, D., & Renhou, L. (2007). Personalized Learning Strategies in an intelligent e-Learning Environment. DOI: 10.1109/CSCWD.2007.4281570

Fiona, D., Albrecht, S., Lewis, L., & Chuang. (2023). Relevance, Effort, and Perceived Quality: Language Learners' Experiences with AI-Generated Contextually Personalized Learning Material. DOI: 10.1145/3563657.3596112

FitzGerald, , Jones, A., Kucirkova, N., & Scanlon, E. (2018). A literature synthesis of personalised technology-enhanced learning: What works and why. *Research in Learning Technology*, 26(0), 2095. DOI: 10.25304/rlt.v26.2095

Fjelland, R. (2020). Why general artificial intelligence will not be realized. *Humanities & Social Sciences Communications*, 7(10), 1–9. DOI: 10.1057/s41599-020-0494-4

Floridi, L. (2024). Generative Artificial Intelligence in Education and Its Implications for Assessment. *TechTrends*, 68(1), 58–66. DOI: 10.1007/s11528-023-00911-4

Flowise—Low code LLM Apps Builder. (2023, October 10). https://flowiseai.com/

Flutter—Build apps for any screen. (n.d.). Retrieved June 20, 2024, from //flutter.dev/

Ford, M. (2018). *Architects of Intelligence: The Truth about AI from the People Building It*. Packt Publishing Ltd.

Fourtan'e, S. (2022). Metaverse: The university becomes the metaversity. Fierce education. https://www.fierceeducation.com/student-engagement/future-higher-ed-universitybecomes-metaversity

Fu, D., Houser, W. R., & Huang, A. (2007). A collaboration between ESL and regular classroom teachers for ELL students' literacy development. *Changing English*, 14(3), 325–342. DOI: 10.1080/13586840701712014

Galdon, F., Hall, A., & Ferrarello, L. (2021). Enhancing abductive reasoning in design and engineering education via probabilistic knowledge; a case study in AI. Proceedings of the DS 110: 23rd International Conference on Engineering and Product Design Education (E&PDE 2021).

Gao, Y., Xiong, Y., Gao, X., Jia, K., Pan, J., Bi, Y., Dai, Y., Sun, J., Guo, Q., Wang, M., & Wang, H. (2024). *Retrieval-Augmented Generation for Large Language Models: A Survey* (arXiv:2312.10997). arXiv. https://doi.org//arXiv.2312.10997DOI: 10.48550

Gao, B., & Huang, L. (2019). Understanding interactive user behavior in smart media content service: An integration of TAM and smart service belief factors. *Heliyon*, 5(12), e02983. Advance online publication. DOI: 10.1016/j.heliyon.2019.e02983 PMID: 31872134

García-Laso, A., Martín, D. A., Presa, L., Rodríguez, J. A., Costafreda, J. L., & Parra, J. L. (2024). Artificial Intelligence for Identifying Social Values and Soft Skills in Service-Learning Activities. In García-Peñalvo, F. J., Sein-Echaluce, M. L., & Fidalgo-Blanco, Á. (Eds.), *Innovation and Technologies for the Digital Transformation of Education*. Springer. DOI: 10.1007/978-981-97-2468-0_8

García-Rico, L., Martínez-Muñoz, L. F., Santos-Pastor, M. L., & Chiva-Bartoll, O. (2021). Service-learning in physical education teacher education: A pedagogical model towards sustainable development goals. *International Journal of Sustainability in Higher Education*, 22(4), 747–765. DOI: 10.1108/IJSHE-09-2020-0325

Garrido, A., & Onaindia, E. (2013). Assembling learning objects for personalized learning: An ai planning perspective. *IEEE Intelligent Systems*, 28(2), 64–73. DOI: 10.1109/MIS.2011.36

Garrison, D. R. (2007). Online community of inquiry review: Social, cognitive, and teaching presence issues. *Journal of Asynchronous Learning Networks*, 11(1), 61–72.

Garside, C. (2009). Look who's talking: A comparison of lecture and group discussion teaching strategies in developing critical thinking skills. *Communication Education*, 45(3), 212–227. DOI: 10.1080/03634529609379050

Gerdon, F., Bach, R. L., Kern, C., & Kreuter, F. (2022). Social impacts of algorithmic decision-making: A research agenda for the social sciences. *Big Data & Society*, 9(1). DOI: 10.1177/20539517221089305

German, S., Royce, C. A., & DeVore-Wedding, B. R. (2022). Transforming Technology Purpose and Integration: Crossing the Technological Chasm Without Falling. In Bawa, I. P. (Ed.), *Preparing Faculty for Technology Dependency in the Post-COVID-19 Era* (pp. 153–173). IGI Global. DOI: 10.4018/978-1-7998-9235-9.ch009

Ghafouri, M., Hassaskhah, J., & Mahdavi-Zafarghandi, A. (2024). From virtual assistant to writing mentor: Exploring the impact of a ChatGPT-based writing instruction protocol on EFL teachers' self-efficacy and learners' writing skill. *Language Teaching Research*. Advance online publication. DOI: 10.1177/13621688241239764

Ghaliya, A. (2020). Smart Classroom Technology in Artificial Intelligence: A Review Paper. DOI: 10.5220/0010306502290235

Ghosh, B., Daugherty, P. R., & Wilson, H. J. (2019). Taking a systems approach to adopting AI. *Harvard Business Review*. https://hbr.org/2019/05/taking-a-systems-approach-to-adopting-ai

Giannelos, K. (2023). Recommendations for a Healthy Digital Public Sphere. *Journal of Medical Ethics*, 38(2), 80–92. DOI: 10.1080/23736992.2023.2193970

Gil-Aciron, L. (2022). Benefits of gamification in second language learning. *Epos Revista De Filología*, (38), 103–126. DOI: 10.5944/epos.38.2022.33785

Giles, D. E. J., & Eyler, J. (1994). The Theoretical Roots of Service-Learning Toward a Theory of Service-Learning. *Service Learning, General*, 150. https://digitalcommons.unomaha.edu/slceslgen/150

Giles, A. (2018). Navigating the contradictions: An ESL teacher's professional self-development in collaborative activity. *TESL Canada Journal*, 35(2), 104–127. DOI: 10.18806/tesl.v35i2.1292

Gmb, H. M. S. (2021). Metaverse school: A new dimension of education. https://metaverse. school/.

Gmeiner, F., Yang, H., Yao, L., Holstein, K., & Martelaro, N. (2023). Exploring challenges and opportunities to support designers in learning to co-create with AI-based manufacturing design tools. *Proceedings of the 2023 CHI Conference on Human Factors in Computing Systems*. DOI: 10.1145/3544548.3580999

Golonka, E. M., Bowles, A. R., Frank, V. M., Richardson, D. L., & Freynik, S. (2012). Technologies for foreign language learning: A review of technology types and their effectiveness. *Computer Assisted Language Learning*, 27(1), 70–105. DOI: 10.1080/09588221.2012.700315

Gong, C., Lin, F., Gong, X., & Lu, Y. (2020). Intelligent Cooperative Edge Computing in Internet of Things. *IEEE Internet of Things Journal*, 7(10), 9372–9382. Advance online publication. DOI: 10.1109/JIOT.2020.2986015

Goren, D., & Kaya, E. (2023). How is students' understanding of nature of science related with their metacognitive awareness? *Science & Education*, 32(5), 1471–1496. DOI: 10.1007/s11191-022-00381-9 PMID: 36185420

Granado-Alcón, M. del C., Gómez-Baya, D., Herrera-Gutiérrez, E., Vélez-Toral, M., Alonso-Martín, P., & Martínez-Frutos, M. T. (2020). Project-Based Learning and the Acquisition of Competencies and Knowledge Transfer in Higher Education. *Sustainability (Basel)*, 12(23), 23. Advance online publication. DOI: 10.3390/su122310062

Grassini, S. (2023). Shaping the Future of Education: Exploring the Potential and Consequences of AI and ChatGPT in Educational Settings. In *Education Sciences* (Vol. 13, Issue 7). DOI: 10.3390/educsci13070692

Greenhow, C., & Chapman, A. (2020). Social distancing meet social media: Digital tools for connecting students, teachers, and citizens in an emergency. *Information and Learning Science*, 121(5/6), 13. DOI: 10.1108/ILS-04-2020-0134

Griswold, M. (2016). CWRU takes the stage at Microsoft's Build conference to show how HoloLens can transform learning. https://case.edu/hololens/

Group, P. G. D. (2024, June 20). *PostgreSQL*. PostgreSQL. https://www.postgresql.org/

Guan, R., Raković, M., Chen, G., & Gašević, D. (2024). How educational chatbots support self-regulated learning? A systematic review of the literature. *Education and Information Technologies*. Advance online publication. DOI: 10.1007/s10639-024-12881-y

Gulubba, S. M., Ahmad, A. A., & Mustafa, H. R. (2019). Scaffolding language development and learning in teacher-student interactions. *International Journal of Recent Technology and Engineering, 8*(2S9), 1035-1040. DOI: 10.35940/ijrte.B1160.0982S919

Gupta, D. (2024). Navigating the future of education: The impact of artificial intelligence on teacher-student dynamics. EATP, 6006-6013. DOI: 10.53555/kuey.v30i4.2332

Gursoy, M. E., Inan, A., Nergiz, M. E., & Saygin, Y. (2017). Privacy-Preserving Learning Analytics: Challenges and techniques. *IEEE Transactions on Learning Technologies*, 10(1), 68–81. DOI: 10.1109/TLT.2016.2607747

Guthrie, K. L., & McCracken, H. (2014). Reflection: The Importance of Making Meaning in E-Service-Learning Courses. *Journal of Computing in Higher Education*, 26(3), 238–252. Advance online publication. DOI: 10.1007/s12528-014-9087-9

Hadi, M. U., Qureshi, R., Shah, A., Irfan, M., Zafar, A., Shaikh, M. B., & Mirjalili, S. (2023). A Survey on Large Language Models: Applications, Challenges, Limitations, and Practical Usage. *TechRxiv*. DOI: 10.36227/techrxiv.23589741.v1

Haenlein, M., & Kaplan, A. (2019). A brief history of artificial intelligence: On the past, present, and future of artificial intelligence. *California Management Review*, 61(4), 5–15. DOI: 10.1177/0008125619864925

Hafeez, M. (2022). Challenges and research gap in project-based learning – A review. *International Journal of New Trends in Social Sciences*, 6(1), 1. Advance online publication. DOI: 10.18844/ijss.v6i1.5633

Haidar, A. (2023). An Integrative Theoretical Framework for Responsible Artificial Intelligence. *International Journal of Digital Strategy, Governance, and Business Transformation*, 13(1), 1–23. Advance online publication. DOI: 10.4018/IJDSGBT.334844

Haleem, A., Javaid, M., Asim Qadri, M., Pratap Singh, R., & Suman, R. (2022). Artificial intelligence (AI) applications for marketing: A literature-based study. In *International Journal of Intelligent Networks* (Vol. 3). DOI: 10.1016/j.ijin.2022.08.005

Halverson. (2018) Participatory Culture as a Model for How New Media Technologies Can Change Public Schools. *The Emerging Learning Design Journal*. Available at: https://digitalcommons.montclair.edu/eldj/vol3/iss1/1

Hamamra, B., Mayaleh, A., & Khlaif, Z. N. (2024). Between tech and text: The use of generative AI in Palestinian universities - a ChatGPT case study. *Cogent Education*, 11(1), 2380622. Advance online publication. DOI: 10.1080/2331186X.2024.2380622

Hammond, H. G., Coplan, M. J., & Mandernach, B. J. (2018). Administrative considerations impacting the quality of online teaching. *Online Journal of Distance Learning Administration*, 21(4), 1–18.

Han, R., Yoon, H., Kim, G., Lee, H., & Lee, Y. (2023). Revolutionizing Medicinal Chemistry: The Application of Artificial Intelligence (AI) in Early Drug Discovery. In *Pharmaceuticals* (Vol. 16, Issue 9). DOI: 10.3390/ph16091259

Han, S., & Noh, Y. (2021). Analyzing higher education instructors' perception on Metaverse-based Education. *Journal of Digital Contents Society*. .DOI: 10.9728/dcs.2021.22.11.1793

Hanke, K. (2016, September). A Meta-Analysis of the Effects of Classroom Management Strategies and Classroom Management Programs on Students' Academic, Behavioral, Emotional, and Motivational Outcomes. *Review of Educational Research*, 86(3), 643–680. Advance online publication. DOI: 10.3102/0034654315626799

Hardi, V., Rizal, M., & Noviardila, I. (2022). Autonomous learning capacity of university students' during the covid-19 pandemic. *Al-Ishlah Jurnal Pendidikan*, 14(2), 1361–1368. DOI: 10.35445/alishlah.v14i2.1934

Harnal, S., Sharma, G., Malik, S., Kaur, G., Khurana, S., Kaur, P., Simaiya, S., & Bagga, D. (2022). Bibliometric Mapping of Trends, Applications and Challenges of Artificial Intelligence in Smart Cities. *EAI Endorsed Transactions on Scalable Information Systems*, 9(4), e76. Advance online publication. DOI: 10.4108/eetsis.vi.489

Harry, A. (2023). Role of AI in Education. *Interdiciplinary Journal and Hummanity*, 2(3), 260–268. Advance online publication. DOI: 10.58631/injurity.v2i3.52

Hashim, H., Rafiq, K., & Yunus, M. (2019). Improving ESL learners' grammar with gamified-learning. *Arab World English Journal (AWEJ). Special Issue on CALL*, (5), 41–50. DOI: 10.24093/awej/call5.4

Hax, C. (2018). *Carolyn Hax live chat transcripts from 2018*. Washington, Columbia, USA. Retrieved from https://www.washingtonpost.com/advice/2018/12/31/carolyn-hax-chat-transcripts-2018/

Hello GPT-4o. (n.d.). Retrieved June 20, 2024, from https://openai.com/index/hello-gpt-4o/

Herayati, H. (2019). The effect of questioning technique in pre-writing stage toward students' writing ability. *Journal of Education*, 1(4), 756–763. DOI: 10.31004/joe.v2i2.430

Herder, E., Sosnovsky, S., & Dimitrova, V. (2017). Adaptive intelligent learning environments. In *Technology Enhanced Learning*. Research Themes., DOI: 10.1007/978-3-319-02600-8_10

Herodotou, C., Rienties, B., Boroowa, A., Zdrahal, Z., & Hlosta, M. (2019). A large-scale implementation of predictive learning analytics in higher education: The teachers' role and perspective. *Educational Technology Research and Development*, 67(5), 1273–1306. DOI: 10.1007/s11423-019-09685-0

Herzberg, B. (2000). Service Learning and Public Discourse. *JAC, 20*(2), 14. https://www.jstor.org/stable/20866323

Hieu, H., & Thao, L. T. (2024). Exploring the impact of ai in language education: Vietnamese EFL teachers' views on using ChatGPT for fairy tale retelling tasks. *International Journal of Learning Teaching and Educational Research*, 23(3), 486–503. DOI: 10.26803/ijlter.23.3.24

Hogenhout, L. (2021). *Unite Paper | A Framework for Ethical AI at the United Nations*. https://unite. un.org/news/unite-paper-framework-ethical-ai-united-nations

Holmes, A. F., Webb, K. J., & Albritton, B. R. (2022). Connecting students to community: Engaging students through course embedded service-learning activities. *International Journal of Management Education*, 20(1), 100610. DOI: 10.1016/j.ijme.2022.100610

Holmes, W., Bialik, M., & Fadel, C. (2021). *Artificial intelligence in education: Promises and implications for teaching and learning*. Center for Curriculum Redesign.

Holmes, W., Blalik, M., & Fadel, C. (2019). *Artificial Intelligence in Education: Promise and Implications for Teaching and Learning*. Center for Curriculum Redesign.

Holmes, W., Porayska-Pomsta, K., Holstein, K., Sutherland, E., Baker, T., Shum, S. B., Santos, O. C., Rodrigo, M. T., Cukurova, M., Bittencourt, I. I., & Koedinger, K. R. (2021). Ethics of AI in education: Towards a community-wide framework. *International Journal of Artificial Intelligence in Education*, 32(3), 504–526. DOI: 10.1007/s40593-021-00239-1

Holmes, W., & Tuomi, I. (2022). State of the art and practice in AI in education. *European Journal of Education*, 57(4), 542–570. Advance online publication. DOI: 10.1111/ejed.12533

Holmlid, S., & Evenson, S. (2008). Bringing Service Design to Service Sciences, Management and Engineering. In Hefley, B., & Murphy, W. (Eds.), *Service Science, Management and Engineering: Education for the 21st Century* (pp. 341–345). Springer. DOI: 10.1007/978-0-387-76578-5_50

Home. (n.d.). ArangoDB. Retrieved June 20, 2024, from https://arangodb.com/

Hongchao, P. (2019). Personalized adaptive learning: an emerging pedagogical approach enabled by a smart learning environment. Smart Learning Environments, DOI: 10.1186/s40561-019-0089-y

Huang, H. (2002). Toward constructivism for adult learners in online learning environments. *British Journal of Educational Technology*, 33(1), 27–37. DOI: 10.1111/1467-8535.00236

Huanyuan, Z. (2022). Problems In China's College Music Teaching in Recent Years. *International Journal of Management and Education in Human Development*, 2(2), 458–460.

Humble, N., Boustedt, J., Holmgren, H., Milutinovic, G., Seipel, S., & Östberg, A.-S. (2023). Cheaters or AI-enhanced learners: Consequences of ChatGPT for programming education. *Electronic Journal of e-Learning*. Advance online publication. DOI: 10.34190/ejel.21.5.3154

Humphry, T., & Fuller, A. L. (2023). Potential ChatGPT Use in Undergraduate Chemistry Laboratories. *Journal of Chemical Education*, 100(9), 1434–1436. DOI: 10.1021/acs.jchemed.3c00006

Huriye, A. Z. (2023). The ethics of artificial intelligence: Examining the ethical considerations surrounding the development and use of AI. *American Journal of Technology*, 2(1), 37–45. DOI: 10.58425/ajt.v2i1.142

Hutson, J., & Plate, D. (2023). *Human-AI collaboration for smart education: reframing applied learning to support metacognition*. IntechOpen.

Hwang, G. J., Xie, H., Wah, B. W., & Gašević, D. (2020). Vision, challenges, roles and research issues of artificial intelligence in education. *Computers and Education: Artificial Intelligence*, 1, 100001. DOI: 10.1016/j.caeai.2020.100001

Hwang, W., Nurtantyana, R., Purba, S., Hariyanti, U., Indrihapsari, Y., & Surjono, H. (2023). AI and recognition technologies to facilitate English as foreign language writing for supporting personalization and contextualization in authentic contexts. *Journal of Educational Computing Research*, 61(5), 1008–1035. DOI: 10.1177/07356331221137253

Introducing Cohere Sandbox: Open-Source Libraries to Help Developers Experiment with Language AI. (n.d.). Cohere. Retrieved June 20, 2024, from https://cohere.com/blog/introducing-sandbox-coheres-experimental-open-source-initiative

Irzik, G., & Nola, R. (2014). New directions for nature of science research. In Matthews, M. (Ed.), *International handbook of research in history, philosophy and science teaching* (pp. 999–1021). Springer. DOI: 10.1007/978-94-007-7654-8_30

Jacoby, B. (1996). Service-Learning in Today's Higher Education. In B. J. A. (Eds.) (Ed.), *Service-Learning in Higher Education: Concepts and Practices* (pp. 3-25). San Francisco, CA: Jossey-Bass. https://www.wiley.com/en-us/Service-Learning+in+Higher+Education%3A+Concepts+and+Practices-p-9780787902919

Jacques, L. (2023). Teaching CS-101 at the Dawn of ChatGPT. *ACM Inroads*, 14(2), 40–46. DOI: 10.1145/3595634

Jafari, Z. (2023). The role of ai in supporting indigenous languages. *Aitechbesosci*, 1(2), 4–11. DOI: 10.61838/kman.aitech.1.2.2

James, K., & Mayer, R. (2018). Learning a second language by playing a game. *Applied Cognitive Psychology*, 33(4), 669–674. DOI: 10.1002/acp.3492

Jan, R., & Nienke, R. (2023). Adverse effects of personalized automated feedback. DOI: 10.4995/HEAd23.2023.16195

Jarrahi, M. H. (2018). Artificial intelligence and the future of work: human-AI symbiosis in organizational decision making. *Business Horizons*, 61(4), 1–15. DOI: 10.1016/j.bushor.2018.03.007

Javaid, M., Haleem, A., Khan, I. H., & Suman, R. (2023). Understanding the potential applications of Artificial Intelligence in Agriculture Sector. *Advanced Agrochem*, 2(1), 15–30. Advance online publication. DOI: 10.1016/j.aac.2022.10.001

Jhajj, G., Zhang, X., Gustafson, J. R., Lin, F., & Lin, M. P.-C. (2024). Educational Knowledge Graph Creation and Augmentation via LLMs. In Sifaleras, A., & Lin, F. (Eds.), *Generative Intelligence and Intelligent Tutoring Systems* (pp. 292–304). Springer Nature Switzerland., DOI: 10.1007/978-3-031-63031-6_25

Jia, F., Sun, D., & Looi, C. (2024). Artificial intelligence in science education (2013–2023): Research trends in ten years. *Journal of Science Education and Technology*, 33(1), 94–117. DOI: 10.1007/s10956-023-10077-6

Jiang, R. (2022). How does artificial intelligence empower EFL teaching and learning nowadays? A review on artificial intelligence in the EFL context. *Frontiers in Psychology*, 13, 1049401. Advance online publication. DOI: 10.3389/fpsyg.2022.1049401 PMID: 36467167

Jiayu, Y. (2023). Challenges and Opportunities of Generative Artificial Intelligence in Higher Education Student Educational Management. *Advances in Educational Technology and Psychology*, 7(9). Advance online publication. DOI: 10.23977/aetp.2023.070914

Jiménez-Aleixandre, M. P., Bugallo Rodríguez, A., & Duschl, R. A. (2000). "Doing the lesson" or "doing science": Argument in high school genetics. *Science Education*, 84(6), 757–792. DOI: 10.1002/1098-237X(200011)84:6<757::AID-SCE5>3.0.CO;2-F

John, N. (2020). Personalization of E-Learning Process Using AI-Powered Chatbot Integration. DOI: 10.1007/978-3-030-58124-4_20

Johnson, E. (2018). Exemplary reading teachers' use of instructional scaffolds with emergent bilinguals: How knowledge and context shape their choices. *TESOL Quarterly*, 53(1), 108–132. DOI: 10.1002/tesq.471

Jones, E. L. (2001). Grading Student Programs-A Software Testing Approach. *Journal of Computing Sciences in Colleges*, 16(2).

Jonsson, M., & Tholander, J. (2022). Cracking the code: Co-coding with AI in creative programming education. *Proceedings of the 14th Conference on Creativity and Cognition*. DOI: 10.1145/3527927.3532801

Jordan, M. I., & Mitchell, T. M. (2015). Machine learning: Trends, perspectives, and prospects. *Science*, 349(6245), 255–260. DOI: 10.1126/science.aaa8415 PMID: 26185243

Junming, C., & Xu, L. (2019). The Study on Students' Participation in Personalized Learning Under the Background of Artificial Intelligence. DOI: 10.1109/ITME.2019.00131

Jurenka, I., Kunesch, M., McKee, K. R., Gillick, D., Zhu, S., Wiltberger, S., . . . Ibrahim, L. (2024). Towards responsible development of generative AI for education: An evaluation-driven approach. arXiv preprint arXiv:2407.12687.

Justin, R., & Mizuko, I. (2017). *From good intentions to real outcomes: equity by design in*. Digital Media and Learning Research Hub, Irvine, https://clalliance.org/wp-content/uploads/2017/11/GIROreport_1031.pdf

Kadaruddin, K. (2023). Empowering education through generative AI: Innovative instructional strategies for tomorrow's learners. *International Journal of Business, Law, and Education*, 4(2), 618–625. DOI: 10.56442/ijble.v4i2.215

Kahraman, H. T., Sagiroglu, S., & Colak, I. (2010). Development of adaptive and intelligent web-based educational systems. *4th International Conference on Application of Information and Communication Technologies, AICT2010*. DOI: 10.1109/ICAICT.2010.5612054

Kaku, M. (2011). *Physics of the Future: The Inventions That Will Transform Our Lives*. Penguin Group.

Kamal, K. (2022, January). Personalized Education Based on Hybrid Intelligent Recommendation System. *Journal of Mathematics*, 2022(1), 1313711. Advance online publication. DOI: 10.1155/2022/1313711

Kamalov, F., Calonge, D., & Gurrib, I. (2023). New era of artificial intelligence in education: Towards a sustainable multifaceted revolution. *Sustainability (Basel)*, 15(16), 12451. DOI: 10.3390/su151612451

Kane, S., Awa, K., Upshaw, J., Hubert, K., Stevens, C., & Zabelina, D. (2023). *Attention, Affect, and Creativity, from Mindfulness to Mind-Wandering*. In Z. Ivcevic, J. Hoffman, & J. Kaufman (Eds.), The Cambridge Handbook of Creativity and Emotions (Cambridge Handbooks in Psychology, pp. 130-148). Cambridge: Cambridge University Press. DOI: 10.1017/9781009031240.010

Kaplan-Rakowski, R., Grotewold, K., Hartwick, P., & Papin, K. (2023). Generative AI and teachers' perspectives on its implementation in education. *Journal of Interactive Learning Research*, 34(2), 313–338. https://www.learntechlib.org/primary/p/222363/

Karunaratne, T. (2021). For Learning Analytics to Be Sustainable under GDPR—Consequences and Way Forward. *Sustainability (Basel)*, 13(20), 11524. DOI: 10.3390/su132011524

Kasneci, E., Seßler, K., Küchemann, S., Bannert, M., Dementieva, D., Fischer, F., Gasser, U., Groh, G., Günnemann, S., Hüllermeier, E., Krusche, S., Kutyniok, G., Michaeli, T., Nerdel, C., Pfeffer, J., Poquet, O., Sailer, M., Schmidt, A., Seidel, T., & Kasneci, G. (2023). ChatGPT for good? On opportunities and challenges of large language models for education. DOI: 10.1016/j.lindif.2023.102274

Kaur, S., Tandon, N., & Matharou, G. S. (2020). Contemporary trends in education transformation using artificial intelligence. In *Transforming Management Using Artificial Intelligence Techniques* (pp. 89–103). CRC Press. DOI: 10.1201/9781003032410-7

Kayalı, B., & Balat, Ş. (2024). Assessment, Evaluation, and Feedback in Online Education With Artificial Intelligence-Supported Tools. In Bansal, R., Chakir, A., Hafaz Ngah, A., Rabby, F., & Jain, A. (Eds.), *AI Algorithms and ChatGPT for Student Engagement in Online Learning* (pp. 124–135). IGI Global. DOI: 10.4018/979-8-3693-4268-8.ch008

Kaye, A. T., & Rumble, G. (2018). *Distance teaching for higher and adult education*. Routledge. DOI: 10.4324/9780429430930

Kazemitabaar, M., Chow, J., Ma, C. K. T., Ericson, B. J., Weintrop, D., & Grossman, T. (2023). Studying the effect of AI code generators on supporting novice learners in introductory programming. *Proceedings of the 2023 CHI Conference on Human Factors in Computing Systems*. DOI: 10.1145/3544548.3580919

Kejriwal, M. Mayank Kejriwal, Knoblock, C. A., & Szekely, P. (2021). *Knowledge Graphs: Fundamentals, Techniques, and Applications*. The MIT Press.

Kelly, K. (2017). *The Inevitable: Understanding the 12 Technological Forces That Will Shape Our Future*. Penguin Group.

Kemp, J., & Livingstone, D. (2006). Putting a Second Life "Metaverse" skin on learning management systems. In Proceedings of the Second Life education workshop at the Second Life community convention (Vol. 20). The University of Paisley.

Keqin, L. (2020). Experimental Research of English Teaching Management Model Based on Personalized Multimedia Technology. *OAlib*, 7(4), 1–13. Advance online publication. DOI: 10.4236/oalib.1106251

Kessler, G. (2018). Technology and the future of language teaching. *Foreign Language Annals*, 51(1), 205–218. DOI: 10.1111/flan.12318

Kezar, A., & Rhoads, R. A. (2001). The Dynamic Tensions of Service Learning in Higher Education: A Philosophical Perspective. *The Journal of Higher Education*, 72(2), 148–171. DOI: 10.1080/00221546.2001.11778876

Khalil, M., & Ebner, M. (2016). De-Identification in learning Analytics. *Journal of Learning Analytics*, 3(1). Advance online publication. DOI: 10.18608/jla.2016.31.8

Khan Academy. (2011, November 2). How Khan Academy is using machine learning to assess student mastery. https://blog.khanacademy.org/how-khan-academy-is-using-machine-learning-to/

Khan, S. A., & VanWynsberghe, R. (2020). A Synthesis of the Research on Community Service Learning in Preservice Science Teacher Education. *Frontiers in Education*, 5(14), 45. Advance online publication. DOI: 10.3389/feduc.2020.00045

Khan, W. (2023). Examining the transformative role of artificial intelligence in language skill enhancement: A case study of bs English students in Okara, Pakistan. *ABBDM*, 3(1), 190–196. DOI: 10.62019/abbdm.v3i1.88

Khiatani, P. V., She, M. H. C., Ho, O. Y. Y., & Liu, J. K. K. (2023). Service-learning under COVID-19: A scoping review of the challenges and opportunities for practicing service learning in the 'New Normal. *International Journal of Educational Development*, 100, 102813. Advance online publication. DOI: 10.1016/j.ijedudev.2023.102813 PMID: 37260563

Kholis, A. (2021). Elsa speak App: Automatic speech recognition (ASR) for supplementing English pronunciation skills. *Pedagogy: Journal of English Language Teaching, 9*(1), 1. DOI: 10.32332/joelt.v9i1.2723

Kim, J., Lee, H., & Cho, Y. H. (2022). Learning design to support student-AI collaboration: Perspectives of leading teachers for AI in education. *Education and Information Technologies*, 27(5), 6069–6104. DOI: 10.1007/s10639-021-10831-6

Kimmel, S. B. (2024). AI-facilitated critical thinking in an undergraduate project-based service-learning course. *Journal of Behavioral and Applied Management*, 24(2), 123–130. DOI: 10.21818/001c.122149

Klimova, B., Pikhart, M., Polakova, P., Cerna, M., Yayilgan, S., & Shaikh, S. (2023). A systematic review on the use of emerging technologies in teaching English as an applied language at the university level. *Systems*, 11(1), 42. DOI: 10.3390/systems11010042

Klutka, J. (2018). *Artificial Intelligence in Higher Education: Current Uses and Future Applications*. Learning House.

Knapp, T. D., & Fisher, B. J. (2010). The Effectiveness of Service-Learning: It's not always what you think. *Journal of Experiential Education*, 33(3), 208–224. DOI: 10.5193/JEE33.3.208

Knickerbocker, J., Budd, R., Dang, B., Chen, Q., Colgan, E., Hung, L. W., Kumar, S., Lee, K. W., Lu, M., Nah, J. W., Narayanan, R., Sakuma, K., Siu, V., & Wen, B. (2018). Heterogeneous integration technology demonstrations for future healthcare, IoT, and AI computing solutions. *Proceedings - Electronic Components and Technology Conference*. DOI: 10.1109/ECTC.2018.00231

Knox, J., Wang, Y., & Gallagher, M. (2020). Artificial intelligence and education in China. *Learning, Media and Technology*, 45(3), 298–311. DOI: 10.1080/17439884.2020.1754236

Kohnke, L., Moorhouse, B. L., & Zou, D. (2023). ChatGPT for language teaching and learning. *RELC Journal*, 54(2), 537–550. DOI: 10.1177/00336882231162868

Kolchenko. (2018). Can Modern AI Replace Teachers? Not so Fast! Artificial Intelligence and Adaptive Learning: Personalized Education in the AI Age. DOI: 10.21692/haps.2018.032

Konecki, M., Konecki, M., & Biškupić, I. (2023). Using artificial intelligence in higher education. *Proceedings of the 15th International Conference on Computer Supported Education*.

Kooli, C. (2023). Chatbots in education and research: A critical examination of ethical implications and solutions. *Sustainability (Basel)*, 15(5614), 5614. DOI: 10.3390/su15075614

Köprülü, F., Oyebimpe, A. O., Başarı, Ş., & Ayhan, S. B. (2023). Innovative effects of artificial intelligence on teacher education. *Conhecimento & Diversidade*, 15(40), 449–465. DOI: 10.18316/rcd.v15i40.11240

Kraft, N. P. (2000). The Role of Service-Learning in Critical Thinking. *Counterpoints, 110*, 75-94. https://www.jstor.org/stable/42975938

Kraj˘covi˘c, M., Gabajov´ a, G., Furmannov´ a, B., Vavrík, V., Ga˘so, M., & Matys, M. (2021). A case study of educational games in virtual reality as a teaching method of lean management. Electronics. MDPI AG, 10(7), 838. DOI: 10.3390/electronics10070838

Krämer, N. C., von der Pütten, A., & Eimler, S. (2012). Human-agent and human-robot interaction theory: similarities to and differences from human-human interaction. In Human-computer interaction: the agency perspective. Studies in computational intelligence. Springer. DOI: 10.1007/978-3-642-25691-2_9

Kshetri, . (2022). *Six benefits that the metaverse offers to colleges and universities*. The Conversation.

Kulkarni, M., Mantere, S., Vaara, E., van den Broek, E., Pachidi, S., Glaser, V. L., Gehman, J., Petriglieri, G., Lindebaum, D., Cameron, L. D., Rahman, H. A., Islam, G., & Greenwood, M. (2024). The Future of Research in an Artificial Intelligence-Driven World. *Journal of Management Inquiry*, 33(3), 207–229. DOI: 10.1177/10564926231219622

Kulkatechol, K. (2022). Personalized Learning Management System using a Machine Learning Technique. TEM Journal. doi: DOI: 10.18421/tem114-25

Kumain, S. C., Kumain, K., & Chaudhary, P. (2020). AI Impact on Various Domain: An Overview. *International Journal of Management*, 11(10).

Kumar, A., Mani, V., Jain, V., Gupta, H., & Venkatesh, V. G. (2023). Managing healthcare supply chain through artificial intelligence (AI): A study of critical success factors. *Computers & Industrial Engineering*, 175, 108815. Advance online publication. DOI: 10.1016/j.cie.2022.108815 PMID: 36405396

Kye, B., Han, N., Kim, E., Park, Y., & Jo, S. (2021). Educational applications of metaverse: Possibilities and limitations. *Journal of Educational Evaluation for Health Professions*, 18, 32. DOI: 10.3352/jeehp.2021.18.32 PMID: 34897242

Ladson-Billings, G. (1995). Toward a Theory of Culturally Relevant Pedagogy. *American Educational Research Journal*, 32(3), 465–491. Advance online publication. DOI: 10.3102/00028312032003465

Lakshmi, G. (2022). AI-powered Digital Classroom. DOI: 10.1109/IC3I-OT53935.2022.9767944

Landwehr, C. (2015). We need a building code for the building code. *Communications of the ACM*, 58(2), 24–26. DOI: 10.1145/2700341

LangChain. (n.d.). Retrieved June 13, 2024, from https://www.langchain.com/

Lantolf, J. (2006). Sociocultural theory and L2: State of the art. *Studies in Second Language Acquisition*, 28(01). Advance online publication. DOI: 10.1017/S0272263106060037

Lee. (2021). All one needs to know about metaverse: A complete survey on technological singularity, virtual ecosystem, and research agenda.

Lee. (2021a). All one needs to know about metaverse: A complete survey on technological singularity, virtual ecosystem, and research agenda, 10.48550/arXiv.2110.05352

Lee, . (2021b). Progress in smart tourism 2010-2017: A systematic literature review. *Journal of Smart Tourism*, 1(1), 19–30. DOI: 10.52255/smarttourism.2021.1.1.4

Lee, B. H., & Park, S. H. (2021). *A study on the NCS based curriculum for educating Technical Director for VFX industry with Artificial Intelligence*. Cartoon and Animation Studies. DOI: 10.7230/KOSCAS.2021.63.417

Lee, D., Kim, H., & Sung, S. (2022). Development research on an AI English learning support system to facilitate learner-generated-context-based learning. *Educational Technology Research and Development*, 71(2), 629–666. DOI: 10.1007/s11423-022-10172-2 PMID: 36533222

Lee, S. J., & Kwon, K. (2024). A systematic review of AI education in K-12 classrooms from 2018 to 2023: Topics, strategies, and learning outcomes. *Computers and Education Artificial Intelligence*, 100211, 100211. Advance online publication. DOI: 10.1016/j.caeai.2024.100211

Lee, S., & Azman, H. (2020). Introducing a responsive multimodal oral presentation pedagogy: Integrating ted videos with web 2.0, collaborative learning and teacher feedback. *RELC Journal*, 53(3), 703–711. DOI: 10.1177/0033688220945426

Lim, W. M., Gunasekara, A., Pallant, J. L., Pallant, J. I., & Pechenkina, E. (2023). Generative AI and the future of education: Ragnarök or reformation? A paradoxical perspective from management educators. *International Journal of Management Education*, 21(2), 100790. Advance online publication. DOI: 10.1016/j.ijme.2023.100790

Lin, H., Yan, Y., & Cheng, Q. (2023). Future Role of Artificial Intelligence in Advancing Transportation Electrification. In *Journal of Intelligent and Connected Vehicles* (Vol. 6, Issue 3). DOI: 10.26599/JICV.2023.9210020

Ling, H., & Chiang, H. (2022). Learning performance in adaptive learning systems: A case study of web programming learning recommendations. *Frontiers in Psychology*, 13, 770637. Advance online publication. DOI: 10.3389/fpsyg.2022.770637 PMID: 35153951

Lin, H. (2022). Influences of artificial intelligence in education on teaching effectiveness. *International Journal of Emerging Technologies in Learning*, 17(24), 144–156. DOI: 10.3991/ijet.v17i24.36037

Lin, P., & Yeh, S. (2019). How motion-control influences a VR-supported technology for mental rotation learning: From the perspectives of playfulness, gender difference and technology acceptance model. *International Journal of Human-Computer Interaction*, 35(18), 1736–1746. Advance online publication. DOI: 10.1080/10447318.2019.1571784

Lin, Z. (2023). Why and how to embrace AI such as ChatGPT in your academic life. *Royal Society Open Science*, 10(8), 230658. Advance online publication. DOI: 10.1098/rsos.230658 PMID: 37621662

Li, R. (2020). Using artificial intelligence in learning English as a foreign language: An examination of IEELTS Liulishuo as an online platform. *Journal of Higher Education Research*, 1(2). Advance online publication. DOI: 10.32629/jher.v1i2.178

Liu, C., Zhang, J., Zhang, H., Li, X., & Zhang, E. (2023). *Group Cooperative Teaching Design With Knowledge Graphs in Project-Driven Learning: Education Journal Article | IGI Global*. https://www.igi-global.com/article/group-cooperative-teaching-design-with-knowledge-graphs-in-project-driven-learning/321120

Liu, M., Ren, Y., Nyagoga, L. M., Stonier, F., Wu, Z., & Yu, L. (2023). Future of education in the era of generative artificial intelligence: Consensus among Chinese scholars on applications of ChatGPT in schools. *Future in Educational Research*, 1(1), 72–101. DOI: 10.1002/fer3.10

Liu, Y., Li, Y., Yang, S., Ren, T., Li, H., Hogg, A., Shah, P., Li, J., Zhang, Y., & Chhetri, A. (2022). A hybrid and non-formal music education connecting China's local family communities and cultures with Nepal. *International Journal for Infonomics*, 15(1), 2088–2093. Advance online publication. DOI: 10.20533/iji.1742.4712.2022.0218

LlamaIndex, Data Framework for LLM Applications. (n.d.). Retrieved June 20, 2024, from https://www.llamaindex.ai/

Luckin, R., Cukurova, M., Kent, C., & Benedict du Boulay, B. (2022). Empowering Educators to be AI-Ready Computers and Education. *Artificial Intelligence*, 3, 1–11. DOI: 10.1016/j.caeai.2022.100076

Luckin, R., Holmes, W., Griffiths, M., & Forcier, L. B. (2016). *Intelligence Unleashed: An argument for AI in EducationOpen Ideas*. Pearson Education.

Lüersmann, A. (2023). Artificial Intelligence in Human Resource Management: Personnel Marketing and Recruiting. In *Studies in Systems, Decision and Control* (Vol. 466). DOI: 10.1007/978-3-031-27506-7_23

Luo, G., Chen, N., He, J., Jin, B., Zhang, Z., & Li, Y. (2024). Privacy-preserving clustering federated learning for non-IID data. *Future Generation Computer Systems*, 154, 384–395. DOI: 10.1016/j.future.2024.01.005

Lynch, J. (2017). How AI Will Destroy Education. Retrieved from https://buzzrobot.com/how-ai-will-destroy-education-20053b7b88a6

Lysenko, L. V., & Abrami, P. C. (2014). Promoting reading comprehension with the use of technology. *Computers & Education*, 75, 162–172. DOI: 10.1016/j.compedu.2014.01.010

MacNeil, S., Tran, A., Mogil, D., Bernstein, S., Ross, E., & Huang, Z. (2022). Generating diverse code explanations using the GPT-3 large language model. *Proceedings of the 2022 ACM Conference on International Computing Education Research*. DOI: 10.1145/3501709.3544280

Madura, P. (2022). AI Solution to Assist Online Education Productivity via Personalizing Learning Strategies and Analyzing the Student Performance. DOI: 10.1109/UEMCON54665.2022.9965735

Maier, U., & Klotz, C. (2022). Personalized feedback in digital learning environments: Classification framework and literature review. *Computers and Education: Artificial Intelligence*, 3, 100080. Advance online publication. DOI: 10.1016/j.caeai.2022.100080

Malik, N., & Solanki, A. (2021). Simulation of Human Brain: Artificial Intelligence-Based Learning. In S. Verma & P. Tomar (Eds.), *Impact of AI Technologies on Teaching, Learning, and Research in Higher Education* (pp. 150-160). IGI Global. DOI: 10.4018/978-1-7998-4763-2.ch009

Mandinach, E. B., & Jackson, S. S. (2012). *Transforming teaching and learning through data-driven decision making*. Corwin Press., DOI: 10.4135/9781506335568

Marco-Gardoqui, M., Eizaguirre, A., & García-Feijoo, M. (2021). The impact of service-learning methodology on business schools' students worldwide: A systematic literature review. *PLoS One*, 5(12). Advance online publication. DOI: 10.1371/journal.pone.0244389 PMID: 33347503

Markel, J. M., Opferman, S. G., Landay, J. A., & Piech, C. (2023). GPTeach: Interactive TA Training with GPT Based Students. In Proceedings of the Tenth ACM Conference on Learning @ Scale (L@S '23). Association for Computing Machinery.

Markula, A., & Aksela, M. (2022). The key characteristics of project-based learning: how teachers implement projects in K-12 science education. *Discip Interdscip Sci Educ Res, 4*(2). https://doi.org/doi.org/10.1186/s43031-021-00042-x

Maroof, . (2021). The Effectiveness of Online Platforms after the Pandemic: Will Face-to-Face Classes Affect Students' Perception of Their Behavioural Intention (BIU) to Use Online Platforms? *Informatics (MDPI)*, 8(4), 83. DOI: 10.3390/informatics8040083

Marquez, R., Barrios, N., Vera, R. E., Mendez, M. E., Tolosa, L., Zambrano, F., & Li, Y. (2023). A perspective on the synergistic potential of artificial intelligence and product-based learning strategies in biobased materials education. *Education for Chemical Engineers*, 44, 164–180. DOI: 10.1016/j.ece.2023.05.005

Maru, M., & Pajow, C. (2021). Emotional, behavioral and cognitive engagement in language learning: The experience of the successful learners. *Celt a Journal of Culture English Language Teaching & Literature*, 19(2), 337. DOI: 10.24167/celt.v19i2.1118

Matthew, M. (2021). Personalized Learning Environments. DOI: 10.1109/ISET52350.2021.00036

Matthews, M. (2012). Changing the focus: From nature of science (NOS) to features of science (FOS). In Khine, M. S. (Ed.), *Advances in nature of science research* (pp. 3–26). Springer. DOI: 10.1007/978-94-007-2457-0_1

McComas, W. F. (1996). Ten myths of science: Reexamining what we think we know..... *School Science and Mathematics*, 96(1), 1–14. DOI: 10.1111/j.1949-8594.1996.tb10205.x

McComas, W. F. (2004). Keys to teaching the nature of science. *Science Teacher (Normal, Ill.)*, 71(9), 24–27.

McComas, W. F., Clough, M. P., & Almazroa, H. (1998). The Role and character of the nature of science in science education. In McComas, W. F. (Ed.), *The nature of science in science education. Science & technology education library* (Vol. 5). Springer., DOI: 10.1007/0-306-47215-5_1

Merrill, M. D. (2018). Using the first principles of Instruction to make instruction effective, efficient, and engaging. In R. E. West (Ed.), *Foundations of Learning and Instructional Design Technology*. EdTech Books. https://press.rebus.community/practicespace/chapter/using-the-first-principles-of-instructionto- make-instruction-effective-efficient-and-engaging/

Meta Llama. (n.d.). Meta Llama. Retrieved June 13, 2024, from https://llama.meta.com/

Mhlanga, D. (2021). Artificial intelligence in industry 4.0, and its impact on poverty, innovation, infrastructure development, and the sustainable development goals: Lessons from emerging economies? *Sustainability (Basel)*, 13(11), 57–88. DOI: 10.3390/su13115788

Microsoft Education. (2023). *New IDC report shows big opportunities to transform higher education through AI*. Microsoft Education Blog.

Miller, C. J., & Metz, M. J. (2014). A comparison of professional-level faculty and student perceptions of active learning: Its current use, effectiveness, and barriers. *Advances in Physiology Education*, 38(3), 246–252. DOI: 10.1152/advan.00014.2014 PMID: 25179615

Miller, E. C., & Krajcik, J. S. (2019). Promoting deep learning through project-based learning: A design problem. *Disciplinary and Interdisciplinary Science Education Research*, 1(7), 7. Advance online publication. DOI: 10.1186/s43031-019-0009-6

Milossi, M., Alexandropoulou-Egyptiadou, E., & Psannis, K. E. (2021). AI ethics: Algorithmic determinism or self-determination? The GPDR approach. *IEEE Access : Practical Innovations, Open Solutions*, 9, 58455–58466. DOI: 10.1109/ACCESS.2021.3072782

Mindigulova, A., Vikhman, V., & Romm, M. (2024). Artificial intelligence and personalized learning: Scaffolding technology. *Professional Education in the Modern World*, 13(4), 613–622. DOI: 10.20913/2618-7515-2023-4-3

Mir. (2022). AI-Based Personalized E-Learning Systems: Issues, Challenges, and Solutions. IEEE Access. DOI: 10.1109/ACCESS.2022.3193938

Mishra, P., Oster, N., & Henriksen, D. (2024). Generative AI, Teacher Knowledge and Educational Research: Bridging Short- and Long-Term Perspectives. *TechTrends*, 68(2), 205–210. DOI: 10.1007/s11528-024-00938-1

Mizumoto, A., & Eguchi, M. (2023). Exploring the potential of using an AI language model for automated essay scoring. *Research Methods in Applied Linguistics, 2*(2), Article 100050.

Mizumoto, A., Shintani, N., Sasaki, M., & Teng, M. F. (2024). Testing the viability of ChatGPT as a companion in L2 writing accuracy assessment. *Research Methods in Applied Linguistics*, 3(2), 100116. Advance online publication. DOI: 10.1016/j.rmal.2024.100116

Mohammad, S. M. (2020). Artificial Intelligence in Information Technology. SSRN *Electronic Journal*. DOI: 10.2139/ssrn.3625444

Mohammad, M. (2018). Identifying Classroom Management Strategies by Focusing on Diversity and Inclusion.

Mohsienuddin Mohammad, S. (2020). Artificial Intelligence In Information Technology. *International Journal Of Innovations In Engineering Research And Technology, 7*(6).

MongoDB: The Developer Data Platform. (n.d.). MongoDB. Retrieved June 20, 2024, from https://www.mongodb.com

Monteiro, F. F., Souza, P. V. S., da Silva, M. C., Maia, J. R., Silva, W. F., & Girardi, D. (2024). ChatGPT in Brazilian K-12 science education. *Frontiers in Education*, 9, 1321547. DOI: 10.3389/feduc.2024.1321547

Morandini, S., Fraboni, F., De Angelis, M., Puzzo, G., Giusino, D., & Pietrantoni, L. (2023). The Impact Of Artificial Intelligence On Workers' Skills: Upskilling And Reskilling In Organisations. *Informing Science*, 26, 039–068. Advance online publication. DOI: 10.28945/5078

Moy, C., & Gadgil, A. (2022). Opportunities in the metaverse: How businesses can explore the metaverse and navigate the hype vs reality. JPMorgan.

Mpu, Y. (2024). Bridging the Knowledge Gap on Special Needs Learner Support: The Use of Artificial Intelligence (AI) to Combat Digital Divide Post-COVID-19 Pandemic and beyond – A Comprehensive Literature Review. In *IntechOpen eBooks*. DOI: 10.5772/intechopen.113054

Mueller, C. M., & Dweck, C. S. (1998). Praise for intelligence can undermine children's motivation and performance. *Journal of Personality and Social Psychology*, 75(1), 33–52. DOI: 10.1037/0022-3514.75.1.33 PMID: 9686450

Murphy, R. F. (2019). *Perspective Expert insights on a timely policy issue Artificial Intelligence Applications to Support K-12 Teachers and Teaching A Review of Promising Applications, Opportunities, and Challenges*.

Nakitare, J., & Otike, F. (2022). Plagiarism conundrum in Kenyan universities: An impediment to quality research. *Digital Library Perspectives*. Advance online publication. DOI: 10.1108/DLP-08-2022-0058

Naser, M. Y. M., & Bhattacharya, S. (2023). Empowering human-AI teams via Intentional Behavioral Synchrony. *Frontiers in Neuroergonomics*, 4, 1181827. Advance online publication. DOI: 10.3389/fnrgo.2023.1181827 PMID: 38234496

Nawaz, N., Gomes, A. M., & Saldeen, A. M. (2020). Artificial intelligence (AI) applications for library services and resources in the COVID-19 pandemic. *Journal Critical Reviews*, 7(18), 1951–1955.

Nazari, N., Shabbir, M., & Setiawan, R. (2021). Application of artificial intelligence powered digital writing assistant in higher education: Randomized controlled trial. *Heliyon*, 7(5), e07014. DOI: 10.1016/j.heliyon.2021.e07014 PMID: 34027198

Nazer, L. H., Zatarah, R., Waldrip, S., Ke, J. X. C., Moukheiber, M., Khanna, A. K., Hicklen, R. S., Moukheiber, L., Moukheiber, D., Ma, H., & Mathur, P. (2023). Bias in artificial intelligence algorithms and recommendations for mitigation. *PLOS Digital Health*, 2(6), e0000278. DOI: 10.1371/journal.pdig.0000278 PMID: 37347721

Ndu, O. G., Tshotsho, B., & Cekiso, M. (2022). Grade 10 teachers' perceptions of their application of socio-cultural and multiple intelligences on English second language learners. *Tydskrif vir Taalonderrig*, 56(1). Advance online publication. DOI: 10.56285/jltVol56iss1a5415

Nemorin, S., Vlachidis, A., Ayerakwa, H. M., & Andriotis, P. (2022). AI hyped? A horizon scan of discourse on artificial intelligence in education (AIED) and development. *Learning, Media and Technology*, 1–14. DOI: 10.1080/17439884.2022.2095568

Ng, D., Leung, J., Su, J., Ng, R., & Chu, S. (2023). Teachers' ai digital competencies and twenty-first century skills in the post-pandemic world. *Educational Technology Research and Development*, 71(1), 137–161. DOI: 10.1007/s11423-023-10203-6 PMID: 36844361

Nguyen, L. Q., & Le, H. V. (2023). The role of Quizlet learning tool in learners' lexical retention: A quasi-experimental study. *International Journal of Emerging Technologies in Learning*, 18(03), 38–50. DOI: 10.3991/ijet.v18i03.34919

Nguyen, P. H., Tran, V. T., & Huynh, H. V. (2023). The effectiveness of using chatbots in learning English pronunciation for Vietnamese EFL learners. *Journal of Asian Education and Development Studies*, 13(1), 15–22.

Nikolic, S., Daniel, S., Haque, R., Belkina, M., Hassan, G. M., Grundy, S., Lyden, S., Neal, P., & Sandison, C. (2023). ChatGPT versus engineering education assessment: A multidisciplinary and multi-institutional benchmarking and analysis of this generative artificial intelligence tool to investigate assessment integrity. *European Journal of Engineering Education*, 48(4), 559–614. DOI: 10.1080/03043797.2023.2213169

Ningsih, S. (2019). Teacher's and learners' perceptions of learner autonomy in EFL context. *Proceedings of the Eleventh Conference on Applied Linguistics (CONAPLIN 2018)*. DOI: 10.2991/conaplin-18.2019.309

Niu, S., Luo, J., Niemi, H., Li, X., & Lu, Y. (2022). Teachers' and students' views of using an AIi-aided educational platform for supporting teaching and learning at Chinese schools. *Education Sciences*, 12(12), 858. DOI: 10.3390/educsci12120858

Noema. (2021). AI makes us less intelligent and more artificial. Available at https://www.noemamag.com/Ai-Makes-Us-Less-Intelligent-And-More-Artificial/

Nosta, J. (2023 October 6). The fifth industrial revolution: The dawn of the cognitive age. *Psychology Today*. https://www.psychologytoday.com/us/blog/the-digital-self/202310/the-5th-industrial-revolution-the-dawn-of-the-cognitive-age

Ntoutsi, E., Fafalios, P., Gadiraju, U., Iosifidis, V., Nejdl, W., Vidal, M. E., Ruggieri, S., Turini, F., Papadopoulos, S., Krasanakis, E., Kompatsiaris, I., Kinder-Kurlanda, K., Wagner, C., Karimi, F., Fernandez, M., Alani, H., Berendt, B., Kruegel, T., Heinze, C., & Staab, S. (2020). Bias in data-driven artificial intelligence systems—An introductory survey. *Wiley Interdisciplinary Reviews. Data Mining and Knowledge Discovery*, 10(3), e1356. DOI: 10.1002/widm.1356

O'Neil, C. (2016a). *Weapons of Math Destruction: How big data increases inequality and threatens democracy*. Crown Publishing Group. https://ci.nii.ac.jp/ncid/BB22310261

Ocheja, P., Flanagan, B., Ueda, H., & Ogata, H. (2019). Managing lifelong learning records through blockchain. *Research and Practice in Technology Enhanced Learning*, 14.

Ogunleye, B., Zakariyyah, K. I., Ajao, O., Olayinka, O., & Sharma, H. (2024). Systematic Review of Generative AI for Teaching and Learning Practice. *Education Sciences*, 14(6), 636. DOI: 10.3390/educsci14060636

Olatunde-Aiyedun, T. G. (2024). Artificial intelligence (AI) in education: Integration of AI into science education curriculum in Nigerian Universities. *International Journal of Artificial Intelligence for Digital*, 1(1). https://ssrn.com/abstract=4733349

Orr, K. (2015). *Comprehension Website--Read Theory!* Sparkingthemind. Retrieved February 1, 2024, from https://sparkingthemind.blogspot.com/2015/04/comprehension-website-read-theory.html

Owens, T., & Hite, R. (2024). Tackle implementation challenges in project-based learning: A survey study of PBL e-learning platforms. *Educational Technology Research and Development*, 71(3), 1179–1207. DOI: 10.1007/s11423-023-10202-7

Owoc, M. L., Sawicka, A., & Weichbroth, P. (2021). Artificial intelligence technologies in education: benefits, challenges, and strategies of implementation. In *Artificial Intelligence for Knowledge Management: 7th IFIP WG 12.6 International Workshop*, AI4KM 2019, Held at IJCAI 2019, Macao, China, August 11, 2019, Revised Selected Papers. Springer International Publishing. DOI: 10.1007/978-3-030-85001-2_4

Oyoo, M. A. (2024). An Exploration of Mental Well-Being Among Students in Higher Learning Institutions in Western Kenya. In Aloka, P. (Ed.), *Student Well-Being in Higher Education Institutions* (pp. 1–30). IGI Global. DOI: 10.4018/979-8-3693-4417-0.ch001

Pack, A., & Maloney, J. (2023). Using generative artificial intelligence for language education research: Insights from using Openai's Chatgpt. *TESOL Quarterly*, 57(4), 1571–1582. DOI: 10.1002/tesq.3253

Palomares, I., Martínez-Cámara, E., Montes, R., García-Moral, P., Chiachio, M., Chiachio, J., & Herrera, F. (2021). A panoramic view and swot analysis of artificial intelligence for achieving the sustainable development goals by 2030: Progress and prospects. *Applied Intelligence*, 51(9), 1–31. DOI: 10.1007/s10489-021-02264-y PMID: 34764606

Papanikolaou, K. A., Makri, K., & Roussos, P. (2017). Learning design as a vehicle for developing TPACK in blended teacher training on technology-enhanced learning. *International Journal of Educational Technology in Higher Education*, 34(1), 45–67. DOI: 10.1186/s41239-017-0072-z

Pardo, A., Jovanovic, J., Dawson, S., Gašević, D., & Mirriahi, N. (2019). Using learning analytics to scale the provision of personalized feedback. *British Journal of Educational Technology*, 50(1), 128–138. DOI: 10.1111/bjet.12592

Park, H. R., & Kim, D. (2011). Reading-strategy use by English as a second language learners in online reading tasks. *Computers & Education*, 57(3), 2156–2166. DOI: 10.1016/j.compedu.2011.05.014

Park, J. (2021). Exploring the possibility of using metaverse in Korean language education. *Journal of the International Network for Korean Language and Culture*, 18(3), 117–146. DOI: 10.15652/ink.2021.18.3.117

Park, Y., Chen, C. Y., & Chen, P. (2019). The effects of using a chatbot on English reading motivation and achievement among Taiwanese EFL learners. *Computers & Education*, 140, 103528.

Passonneau, R. J., McNamara, D., Muresan, S., & Perin, D. (2018). Preface: Special issue on multidisciplinary approaches to AI and education for reading and writing. *International Journal of Artificial Intelligence in Education*, 28(4), 445–450.

Peredo, R., Canales, A., Menchaca, A., & Peredo, I. (2011). Intelligent Web-based education system for adaptive learning. *Expert Systems with Applications*, 38(12), 14690–14702. Advance online publication. DOI: 10.1016/j.eswa.2011.05.013

Peters-Burton, E. E., & Burton, S. R. (2020). The use of metacognitive prompts to foster nature of science learning. In McComas, W. F. (Ed.), *Nature of science in science instruction* (pp. 179–197). Springer International Publishing. DOI: 10.1007/978-3-030-57239-6_9

Peters, D., Vold, K., Robinson, D., & Calvo, R. A. (2020). Responsible AI—Two frameworks for ethical design practice. *IEEE Transactions on Technology and Society*, 1(1), 34–47. DOI: 10.1109/TTS.2020.2974991

Petousi, V., & Sifaki, E. (2020). Contextualizing harm in the framework of research misconduct. Findings from discourse analysis of scientific publications. *International Journal of Sustainable Development*, 23(3-4), 149–174. DOI: 10.1504/IJSD.2020.115206

Pham, T., Nguyen, B., Ha, S., & Nguyen Ngoc, T. (n.d.). Digital transformation in engineering education: Exploring the potential of AI-assisted learning. In *Australasian Journal of Educational Technology* (Vol. 2023, Issue 5).

Ping, X. (2020). Design of Personalized Intelligent Learning Assistant System Under Artificial Intelligence Background. DOI: 10.1007/978-3-030-62743-0_27

Pokrivcakova, S. (2019). Preparing teachers for the application of AI-powered technologies in foreign language education. *Journal of Language and Cultural Education*, 7(3), 135–153. DOI: 10.2478/jolace-2019-0025

Polonetsky, J., & Jerome, J. (2014). Student Data: trust, transparency, and the role of consent. *Social Science Research Network*. DOI: 10.2139/ssrn.2628877

Popenici, S., & Kerr, S. (2017). Exploring the impact of artificial intelligence on teaching and learning in higher education. *Research and Practice in Technology Enhanced Learning*, 12(1), 22. Advance online publication. DOI: 10.1186/s41039-017-0062-8 PMID: 30595727

Porayska-Pomsta, K., Frauenberger, C., Pain, H., Rajendran, G., Smith, T., Menzies, R., & Lemon, O. (2018). Blending human and artificial intelligence to support autistic children's social communication skills. *ACM Transactions on Computer-Human Interaction*, 25(6), 1–35. DOI: 10.1145/3271484

Postman, N. (1983). *The Disappearance of Childhood*. W.H. Allen. DOI: 10.1016/S0002-7138(09)61523-5

PowerSchool. (2022, November 17). How k-12 data analytics and ai can support equitable learning. https://www.powerschool.com/blog/how-data-analytics-and-ai-support-equitable-learning/

Prasanth, A., Vadakkan, D. J., Surendran, P., & Thomas, B. (2023). Role of Artificial Intelligence and Business Decision Making. *International Journal of Advanced Computer Science and Applications*, 14(6). Advance online publication. DOI: 10.14569/IJACSA.2023.01406103

Pratama, M. P., Sampelolo, R., & Lura, H. (2023). Revolutionizing education: Harnessing the power of artificial intelligence for personalized learning. *Klasikal : Journal of Education, Language Teaching and Science*, 5(2), 2. Advance online publication. DOI: 10.52208/klasikal.v5i2.877

Prinsloo, P. (2019). A social cartography of analytics in education as performative politics. *British Journal of Educational Technology*, 50(6), 2810–2823. DOI: 10.1111/bjet.12872

Prinsloo, P., & Slade, S. (2016). Student Vulnerability, Agency and Learning Analytics: An Exploration. *Journal of Learning Analytics*, 3(1). Advance online publication. DOI: 10.18608/jla.2016.31.10

Qian. (2022). Research on Classroom Teaching Management and Process Evaluation Based on Artificial Intelligence. DOI: 10.1109/ICENIT57306.2022.00084

Radianti, J., Majchrzak, T. A., Fromm, J., & Wohlgenannt, I. (2020). A systematic review of immersive virtual reality applications for higher education: Design elements, lessons learned, and research agenda. *Computers & Education*, 147, 103778. DOI: 10.1016/j.compedu.2019.103778

Rahman, M. M., & Watanobe, Y. (2023). ChatGPT for education and research: Opportunities, threats, and strategies. *Applied Sciences (Basel, Switzerland)*, 13(13), 5783. DOI: 10.3390/app13095783

Raji, I. D., Scheuerman, M. K., & Amironesei, R. (2021). You can't sit with us: Exclusionary pedagogy in AI ethics education. *Proceedings of the 2021 ACM Conference on Fairness, Accountability, and Transparency, Virtual Event*. DOI: 10.1145/3442188.3445914

Ramli, R., & Yusoff, N. (2020). Self-efficacy and differentiated instruction: A study among Malaysian school teachers. *Universal Journal of Educational Research*, 8(4), 1252–1260. DOI: 10.13189/ujer.2020.080416

Ravichandran & Sridharan. (2018). Powering E-Learning Through Technology: An Overview Of Recent Trends In. *Educational Technology*.

Ravi, K. (2018). Augmenting Classrooms with AI for Personalized Education. DOI: 10.1109/ICASSP.2018.8461812

React. (n.d.). Retrieved June 20, 2024, from https://react.dev/

Rebolledo Font de la Vall, R., & González Araya, F. (2023). Exploring the benefits and challenges of AI-language learning tools. *International Journal of Social Sciences and Humanities Invention*, 10(01), 7569–7576. DOI: 10.18535/ijsshi/v10i01.02

Reeves, J. (2004). "Like everybody else": Equalizing educational opportunity for English language learners. *TESOL Quarterly*, 38(1), 43. DOI: 10.2307/3588258

Regan, P. M., & Jesse, J. (2018). Ethical challenges of edtech, big data and personalized learning: Twenty-first century student sorting and tracking. *Ethics and Information Technology*, 21(3), 167–179. DOI: 10.1007/s10676-018-9492-2

Reich, J., Kim, Y. J., Robinson, C., Roy, D., & Thompson, M. (2022). *AI and education: Promises and implications for teaching and learning*. MIT Teaching Systems Lab.

Reiss, M. J. (2021). The use of AI in education: Practicalities and ethical considerations. *London Review of Education*, 19(1). Advance online publication. DOI: 10.14324/LRE.19.1.05

Renz, A., & Hilbig, R. (2023). Prerequisites for artificial intelligence in further education: Identification of drivers, barriers, and business models of educational technology companies. *International Journal of Educational Technology in Higher Education*, 20(1), 1–21.

Rethinam, V. (2014 June 12). Predictive analytics in K-12: Advantages, limitations, and implementation. *THE Journal*.https://thejournal.com/Articles/2014/06/12/Predictive-Analytics-in-K-12-Advantages-Limitations-Implementation.aspx?p=1

Risang, B. (2023). *Personalised learning with ai: implications for ignatian pedagogy*. International Journal of Educational Best Practices. DOI: 10.31258/ijebp.v7n1.p1-16

Rizun, M. (2019). Knowledge Graph Application in Education: A Literature Review. *Acta Universitatis Lodziensis.Folia Oecologica*, 3(342), 7–19.

Robert, J. (2023). *EDUCAUSE AI Landscape Study*. ECAR.

Rosanne, K. (2012). Artistic participatory practices as a vehicle for togetherness. *Cumulus ACM International Conference Proceeding Series, 2*, 93-96. https://doi .org/doi.org/10.1145/2348144.234817

Rosé, C. P. (2018). *Artificial intelligence in education. 19th International Conference, AIED 2018*. Springer.

Rosé, C. P., McLaughlin, E. A., Liu, R., & Koedinger, K. R. (2019). Explanatory learner models: Why machine learning (alone) is not the answer. *British Journal of Educational Technology*, 50(6), 2943–2958. DOI: 10.1111/bjet.12858

Roselli, D., Matthews, J., & Talagala, N. (2019, May). Managing bias in AI. In Companion proceedings of the 2019 world wide web conference (pp. 539-544). DOI: 10.1145/3308560.3317590

Rosenblatt, K. (2023, January 24). ChatGPT passes MBA exam given by a Wharton professor. NBC News https://www.nbcnews.com/tech/tech-news/chatgpt-passes-mba-exam-wharton-professor-rcna67036

Rosenblatt, K. (2023, January 6). ChatGPT banned from New York City public schools' devices and networks. NBC News. https://www.nbcnews.com/tech/tech-news/new-york-city-public-schools-ban-chatgpt-devices-networks-rcna64446

Roshanaei, M. (2024). Towards best practices for mitigating artificial intelligence implicit bias in shaping diversity, inclusion and equity in higher education. *Education and Information Technologies*, 1–26. DOI: 10.1007/s10639-024-12605-2

Royce, C. A. (2023, October). Looking backward to educate forward. *Interface Conference*, Missouri.

Russell, S. J., & Norvig, P. (2016). *Artificial intelligence: A modern approach* (3rd ed.). Pearson.

Rus, V., D'Mello, S., Hu, X., & Graesser, A. C. (2013). Recent advances in conversational intelligent tutoring systems. *AI Magazine*, 34(3), 42–54. Advance online publication. DOI: 10.1609/aimag.v34i3.2485

Salas-Pilco, S. (2020). The impact of AI and robotics on physical, social-emotional and intellectual learning outcomes: An integrated analytical framework. *British Journal of Educational Technology*, 51(5), 1808–1825. DOI: 10.1111/bjet.12984

Sallam, M. (2024). Human versus artificial intelligence: ChatGPT-4 outperforming bing, bard, ChatGPT-3.5, and humans in clinical chemistry multiple-choice questions. https://doi.org/DOI: 10.21203/rs.3.rs-3880412/v1

Salvador-Garcia, C., Chiva-Bartoll, O., Maravé-Vivas, M., & Gil-Gómez, J. (2023). Service-learning in physical education teacher education: A retrospective exploratory study to examine its challenges. *Teaching and Teacher Education*, 135, 104350. Advance online publication. DOI: 10.1016/j.tate.2023.104350

Sana, O. (2022). Applications of Artificial Intelligence in Education. doi: DOI: 10.33102/alazkiyaa.v1i1.10\

Sandelowski, M. (2010). What's in a name? Qualitative description revisited. *Research in Nursing & Health*, 33(1), 77–84. DOI: 10.1002/nur.20362 PMID: 20014004

Sandy, M., & Holland, B. A. (2006). Different worlds and common ground: Community partner perspectives on campus-community partnerships. *Michigan Journal of Community Service Learning*, 13(1), 30–43. https://doi.org/http://hdl.handle.net/2027/spo.3239521.0013.103

Sanglier, C. (2021). A contribution to educational strategy. Gamification within the current educational space. *Contemporary Engineering Sciences*, 14(1), 117–125. DOI: 10.12988/ces.2021.91786

Saragih, E. E., Tabrani, N. P., & Muthmainnah, N. (2021). The use of digital feedback on ELSA speak in learning pronunciation for seventh grade of junior high school. *JEELL (Journal of English Education, Linguistics and Literature). English Department of STKIP PGRI Jombang*, 8(1), 48. DOI: 10.32682/jeell.v8i1.1979

Sari, D. M., Suparman, U., & Sinaga, T. (2018). The effectiveness of scaffolding technique on students' writing analytical expository text. *U-JET, 7*(3). https://jurnal.fkip.unila.ac.id/index.php/123/article/view/15404/pdf

Sarwat. (2018). Is AI making humans lazy? Here's what UAE residents say. Khaleej Times. https://www.khaleejtimes.com/nation/dubai/Is-AI-making-humans-lazy-Here-what-UAE-residents-say

Scharth, M. (2022). The ChatGPT chatbot is blowing people away with its writing skills. The University of Sydney. https://www.sydney.edu.au/news-opinion/news/2022/12/08/the-chatgpt-chatbot-is-blowing-people-away-with-its-writing-skil.html

Schlemmer & Backes. (2014). Learning in Metaverses: Co-Existing in Real Virtuality. .DOI: 10.4018/978-1-4666-6351-0

Selwyn, N. (2023). On the Limits of Artificial Intelligence (AI) in Education. *Nordisk tidsskrift for pedagogikk og kritikk, 10*(12), 3. DOI: 10.23865/ntpk.v10.6062

Setareh, M. (2021, May). Personalized Education in the Artificial Intelligence Era: What to Expect Next. *IEEE Signal Processing Magazine*, 38(3), 37–50. Advance online publication. DOI: 10.1109/MSP.2021.3055032

Setareh, R. (2023). Advancing Personalized and Adaptive Learning Experience in Education with Artificial Intelligence. DOI: 10.23919/EAEEIE55804.2023.10181336

Settles, B., LaFlair, G. & Hagiwara, M. (2020). Machine learning driven language assessment. *Transactions of the Association for Computational Linguistics, 8*, 247–263. https://doi.org/ a 00310DOI: 10.1162/tacl

Sharma, S. (2023, Aug 14). Guiding students to assess the merits of artificial intelligence tools. *Edutopia*.https://www.edutopia.org/article/teaching-students-use-ai-tools/

Sharma, S., Gahlawat, V. K., Rahul, K., Mor, R. S., & Malik, M. (2021). Sustainable Innovations in the Food Industry through Artificial Intelligence and Big Data Analytics. In *Logistics* (Vol. 5, Issue 4). DOI: 10.3390/logistics5040066

Sharma, D. M., & Sehgal, M. L. (2023). The Revolutionary Computer Technology Artificial Intelligence that is Changing Our World & its Impact on Different Jobs. *International Journal for Research in Applied Science and Engineering Technology*, 11(4), 286–293. Advance online publication. DOI: 10.22214/ijraset.2023.50072

Sharma, K., Giannakos, M. N., & Dillenbourg, P. (2020). Eye-tracking and artificial intelligence to enhance motivation and learning. *Smart Learning Environments*, 7(1), 13. Advance online publication. DOI: 10.1186/s40561-020-00122-x

Shih, J. (2018). *Knewton Personalizes Learning with the Power of AI. Digital Innovation and Transformation, Harvard Business School.*https://digital.hbs.edu/platform-digit/submission/knewton-personalizes-learning-with-the-power-of-ai/

Shippee, M. (2019). *WanderlustEDU: An educator's guide to innovation, change, and adventure*. Dave Burgess Consulting, Incorporated.

Shneiderman, B. (2020a). Design lessons from AI's two grand goals: Human emulation and useful applications. *IEEE Transactions on Technology and Society*, 1(2), 73–82. DOI: 10.1109/TTS.2020.2992669

Shneiderman, B. (2020b). Human-centered artificial intelligence: Reliable, safe & trustworthy. *International Journal of Human-Computer Interaction*, 36(6), 495–504. DOI: 10.1080/10447318.2020.1741118

Shneiderman, B. (2021). Responsible AI: Bridging from ethics to practice. *Communications of the ACM*, 64(8), 32–35. DOI: 10.1145/3445973

Shou, Z., Lu, X., Wu, Z., Yuan, H., Zhang, H., & Lai, J. (2020). On learning path planning algorithm based on collaborative analysis of learning behavior. *IEEE Access : Practical Innovations, Open Solutions*, 8, 119863–119879. DOI: 10.1109/ACCESS.2020.3005793

Shraim, K. (2023). Between tech and text: The use of generative AI in Palestinian universities - a ChatGPT case study. *Teaching in Higher Education*, 1–18. DOI: 10.1080/13562517.2023.2213589

Silberg, J., & Manyika, J. (2019). Notes from the AI frontier: Tackling bias in AI (and in humans). *Mc Kinsey Global Institute*. Available at https://www.mckinsey.com/~/media/mckinsey/featured%20insights/artificial%20intelligence/tackling%20bias%20in%20artificial%20intelligence%20and%20in%20humans/mgi-tackling-bias-in-ai-june-2019.pdf

Simina, V., & Hamel, M. (2005). CASLA through a social constructivist perspective: Webquest in project-driven language learning. *ReCALL*, 17(2), 217–228. DOI: 10.1017/S0958344005000522

Sims, R., Dobbs, G., & Hand, T. (2002). Enhancing quality in online learning: Scaffolding planning and design through proactive evaluation. *Distance Education*, 23(2), 135–148. DOI: 10.1080/0158791022000009169

Sinatra, G., & Hofer, B. K. (2023). ChatGPT and other generative AI could foster science denial and misunderstanding – Here's how you can be on alert. The Conversation. Retrived from https://theconversation.com/chatgpt-and-other-generative-ai-could-foster-science-denial-and-misunderstanding-heres-how-you-can-be-on-alert-204897?utm_source=twitter%26utm_medium=bylinetwitterbutton

Singer, N. (2023, February 6). At this school, computer science class now includes critiquing chatbots. *The New York Times*.https://www.nytimes.com/2023/02/06/technology/chatgpt-schools-teachers-ai-ethics.html

Smith, M. E., Teemant, A., & Pinnegar, S. (2004). Principles and practices of sociocultural assessment: Foundations for effective strategies for linguistically diverse classrooms. *Multicultural Perspectives*, 6(2), 38–46. DOI: 10.1207/s15327892mcp0602_8

Söderlund, K., Engström, E., Haresamudram, K., Larsson, S., & Strimling, P. (2024). Regulating high-reach AI: On transparency directions in the Digital Services. *Internet Policy Review*, 13(1). Advance online publication. DOI: 10.14763/2024.1.1746

Son. (2022). The effectiveness of collaborative learning in SW Education based on Metaverse platform. *Journal of the Korean Association of Information Education*. .DOI: 10.14352/jkaie.2022.26.1.11

Sørensen, N. L., Bemman, B., Jensen, M. B., Moeslund, T. B., & Thomsen, J. L. (2023). Machine learning in general practice: Scoping review of administrative task support and automation. *BMC Primary Care*, 24(1), 14. Advance online publication. DOI: 10.1186/s12875-023-01969-y PMID: 36641467

Southgate, E. (2022). Artificial intelligence, ethics, and the future of education. In *Handbook on Digital Learning for K-12 Schools* (pp. 535–550). Springer.

Sparks, M. (2021). What is a metaverse? *New Scientist*, 251(3348), 18. DOI: 10.1016/S0262-4079(21)01450-0

Special Need Center Artificial Intelligence: Inclusive AI: Bridging the gap for special needs centers. (2024). FasterCapital. Retrieved August 28, 2024, from https://fastercapital.com/content/Special-Need-Center-Artificial-Intelligence--Inclusive-AI--Bridging-the-Gap-for-Special-Needs-Centers.html

Stahl, A. (2021a). How AI will impact the future of work and life. https://www.forbes.com/sites/ashleystahl/2021/03/10/how-ai-will-impact-the-future-of-work-and-life/?sh=3c5c1a5279a3

Stahl, B. C. (2021b). *Artificial intelligence for a better future*. Springer. DOI: 10.1007/978-3-030-69978-9

Stanford University. (2022). *Using Artificial Intelligence to Understand Why Students are Struggling. Stanford University*. https://hai.stanford.edu/news/using-artificial-intelligence-understand-why-students-are-struggling

Stanton, T. K., Giles, D. E., & Cruz, N. I. (1999). *Service-Learning: A Movement's Pioneers Reflect on its Origins, Practice, and Future*. Jossey-Bass.

Staton, B., & Murgia, M. (2023, May 21). The AI revolution already transforming education. *Financial Times*. https://www.ft.com/content/47fd20c6-240d-4ffa-a0de-70717712ed1c

Stevenson, M., & Phakiti, A. (2014). The effects of computer-generated feedback on the quality of writing. *Assessing Writing*, 19, 51–65. DOI: 10.1016/j.asw.2013.11.007

Su, J., & Yang, W. (2023). Unlocking the Power of ChatGPT: A Framework for Applying Generative AI in Education. *ECNU Review of Education*, 6(3). Advance online publication. DOI: 10.1177/20965311231168423

Suk. (2022). Construction of Personalized Learning Model Supported by Human-computer Cooperation. DOI: 10.1145/3582580.3582588

Sunardi, , Ramadhan, A., Abdurachman, E., Trisetyarso, A., & Zarlis, M. (2022). Acceptance of augmented reality in video conference based learning during COVID19 pandemic in higher education. *Bulletin of Electrical Engineering and Informatics*, 11(6), 3598–3608. DOI: 10.11591/eei.v11i6.4035

Suraya, H. (2022). Trends on Technologies and Artificial Intelligence in Education for Personalized Learning: Systematic Literature Review. International Journal of Academic Research in Progressive Education and Development. DOI: 10.6007/IJARPED/v11-i1/12230

Susen, S. (2023). *The Structural Transformation of the Public Sphere Revisited: From the Politics of Inclusion to the Politics of Translation*. Oxford Academic Society.

Tahiru, F. (2021). AI in education: A systematic literature review. *Journal of Cases on Information Technology*, 23(1), 1–20. DOI: 10.4018/JCIT.2021010101

Talan, T., & Kalınkara, Y. (2023). The role of artificial intelligence in higher education: ChatGPT assessment for anatomy course. *Uluslararası Yönetim Bilişim Sistemleri ve Bilgisayar Bilimleri Dergisi*, 7(1), 33–40. DOI: 10.33461/uybisbbd.1244777

Tammets, K., & Ley, T. (2023). Integrating AI tools in teacher professional learning: A conceptual model and illustrative case. *Frontiers in Artificial Intelligence*, 6, 1255089. Advance online publication. DOI: 10.3389/frai.2023.1255089 PMID: 38130325

Taoyun, Z. (2022). An Intelligent Classroom Management System Based on AI + IOT Technology. DOI: 10.1109/ITME56794.2022.00052

Tarran, B. (2018). What can we learn from the Facebook–Cambridge Analytica scandal? *Significance*, 15(3), 4–5. DOI: 10.1111/j.1740-9713.2018.01139.x PMID: 32536948

Taylor, D. L., Yeung, M., & Bashet, A. Z. (2021). Personalized and adaptive learning. In Ryoo, J., & Winkelmann, K. (Eds.), *Innovative learning environments in STEM higher education. SpringerBriefs in Statistics*. Springer. DOI: 10.1007/978-3-030-58948-6_2

Tegmark, M. (2017). Life 3.0: being human in the age of artificial intelligence. Borzoi Book published by A.A. Knopf.

Tegmark, M. (2017). *Life 3.0: Being Human in the Age of Artificial Intelligence*. Penguin Group.

Teng, M. F. (2024). "ChatGPT is the companion, not enemies": EFL learners' perceptions and experiences in using ChatGPT for feedback in writing. *Computers and Education: Artificial Intelligence*, 7, 100270. DOI: 10.1016/j.caeai.2024.100270

Teodor. (2019). Smart classroom, internet of things and personalized teaching. DOI: 10.12955/cbup.v7.1491

Terzidou, T., Tsiatsos, T., Miliou, C., & Sourvinou, A. (2016). Agent supported serious game environment. *IEEE Transactions on Learning Technologies*, 9(3), 217–230. DOI: 10.1109/TLT.2016.2521649

Thornhill-Miller, B., Camarda, A., Mercier, M., Burkhardt, J.-M., Morisseau, T., Bourgeois-Bougrine, S., Vinchon, F., El Hayek, S., Augereau-Landais, M., Mourey, F., Feybesse, C., Sundquist, D., & Lubart, T. (2023). Creativity, Critical Thinking, Communication, and Collaboration: Assessment, Certification, and Promotion of 21st Century Skills for the Future of Work and Education. *Journal of Intelligence*, 11(13), 54. DOI: 10.3390/jintelligence11030054 PMID: 36976147

Thornton, K. (2015). Introduction: The crucial role of peer-learning in language learning spaces. *Studies in Self-Access Learning Journal*, 286-287, 286–287. Advance online publication. DOI: 10.37237/060304

Tianyi, Y. (2023). Design of Intelligent Real-Time Feedback System in Online Classroom. *Lecture Notes in Computer Science*, 14024, 326–335. Advance online publication. DOI: 10.1007/978-3-031-35946-0_27

Timms, M. J. (2016). Letting Artificial Intelligence in Education out of the Box: Educational Cobots and Smart Classrooms. *International Journal of Artificial Intelligence in Education*, 26(2), 701–712. Advance online publication. DOI: 10.1007/s40593-016-0095-y

Tinggie, T., Tan, K., Muslim, N., & Keng, L. (2023). Peer scaffolding among primary ESL learners' writing task: Learners' behaviors and triggering factors. *International Journal of Learning Teaching and Educational Research*, 22(3), 191–208. DOI: 10.26803/ijlter.22.3.12

Torda, A. (2020). How COVID-19 has pushed us into a medical education revolution. *International Medical Journal*, 50(9), 1150–1153. DOI: 10.1111/imj.14882 PMID: 32666691

Touretzky, D., Gardner-McCune, C., Martin, F., & Seehorn, D. (2019). Envisioning AI for K-12: What should every child know about AI? *Proceedings of the AAAI Conference on Artificial Intelligence*, 33(01), 9795–9799. DOI: 10.1609/aaai.v33i01.33019795

Trenz, H. (2023). Democracy in the Digital Public Sphere: Disruptive or Self-Corrective? *Communication Theory*, 33(2-3), 143–152. DOI: 10.1093/ct/qtad009

Trisnawati, W., Putra, R. E., & Balti, L. (2023). The Impact of Artificial Intelligent in Education toward 21 st Century Skills: A Literature Review. *PPSDP International Journal of Education*, 2(2), 501–513. DOI: 10.59175/pijed.v2i2.152

Tubino, L., & Adachi, C. (2022). Developing feedback literacy capabilities through an AI automated feedback tool. *Proceedings of the ASCILITE 2022 Conference: Reconnecting Relationships through Technology*, e22039. DOI: 10.14742/apubs.2022.39

Tursunbayeva, A., & Renkema, M. (2023). Artificial intelligence in health-care: Implications for the job design of healthcare professionals. *Asia Pacific Journal of Human Resources*, 61(4), 845–887. Advance online publication. DOI: 10.1111/1744-7941.12325

Ulfa, K. (2023). The transformative power of artificial intelligence (AI) to elevate English language learning. *Majalah Ilmiah Methoda*, 13(3), 307–313. DOI: 10.46880/methoda.Vol13No3.pp307-313

Uludag, K., & Zhao, M. (2023). Can ChatGPT answer GRE psychology questions? *SSRN*, http://dx.doi.org/DOI: 10.2139/ssrn.4416365

UNESCO. (2024a). *AI competency framework for teachers*. UNESCO. https://www.unesco.org/en/articles/ai-competency-framework-teachers?hub=343

UNESCO. (2024b). *AI competency framework for students*. UNESCO. https://www.unesco.org/en/articles/ai-competency-framework-students

US Department of Education. (2020). *Protecting Student Privacy While Using Online Educational Services: Requirements and Best Practices*.

US-Education. (2023). *U.S. Department of Education Shares Insights and Recommendations for Artificial Intelligence*. https://www2.ed.gov/documents/ai-report/ai-report.pdf

Usher, M., Hershkovitz, A., & Forkosh-Baruch, A. (2021). From data to actions: Instructors' decision making based on learners' data in online emergency remote teaching. *British Journal of Educational Technology*, 52(4), 1338–1356. DOI: 10.1111/bjet.13108

Valarmathi, S., Kareem, J., Tantia, V., Babu, K. S., & Lucas, P. J. (2024). *Enhancing Curricula with Service Learning Models*. DOI: 10.4018/979-8-3693-5933-4

Van den Berg, G., & du Plessis, E. (2023). ChatGPT and generative ai: Possibilities for its contribution to lesson planning, critical thinking and openness in teacher education. *Education Sciences*, 13(10), 998. DOI: 10.3390/educsci13100998

van den Bosch, K., & Bronkhorst, K. (2019). Six challenges for human-AI Co-learning. *Adaptive instructional systems*,11597, 572–589. DOI: 10.1007/978-3-030-22341-0_45

van den Bosch, K., & Bronkhorst, K. (2018). *Human-AI cooperation to benefit military decision-making*. TNO.

Van der Kleij, F. M., Feskens, R. C. W., & Eggen, T. J. H. M. (2015). Effects of Feedback in a Computer-Based Learning Environment on Students' Learning Outcomes: A Meta-Analysis. *Review of Educational Research*, 85(4), 475–511. DOI: 10.3102/0034654314564881 van Laar, E., van Deursen, A. J. A. M., van Dijk, J. A. G. M., & de Haan, J. (2020). Determinants of 21st-Century Skills and 21st-Century Digital Skills for Workers: A Systematic Literature Review. *SAGE Open*, 10(1). Advance online publication. DOI: 10.1177/2158244019900176

Van Oosterom, A. (2024, Feb 20). People do not fear change, we fear uncertainty and loss. Medium. https://arnevanoosterom.medium.com/people-do-not-fear-change-we-fear-uncertainty-and-loss-d48735a464a0

van Rijmenam, M. (2023 January 25). ChatGPT is a paradigm shift: Why education should embrace it. *The Digital Speaker.*https://www.thedigitalspeaker.com/chatgpt-paradigm-shift-why-education-should-embrace-it/

Varsha, P. S. (2023). How can we manage biases in artificial intelligence systems–A systematic literature review. *International Journal of Information Management Data Insights*, 3(1), 100165.

Vera, I. (2022). Designing of personalized digital educational environment based on neural network technologies. Nucleation and Atmospheric Aerosols. DOI: 10.1063/5.0104196

Verma, G., Campbell, T., Melville, W., & Park, B. Y. (2023). Navigating opportunities and challenges of artificial intelligence: ChatGPT and generative models in science teacher education. *Journal of Science Teacher Education*, 34(8), 793–798. DOI: 10.1080/1046560X.2023.2263251

Violante & Vezzetti. (2015). Virtual Interactive e-learning application: An evaluation of the student satisfaction.

Vue.js. (n.d.). Retrieved June 20, 2024, from https://vuejs.org/

Wafaa, S. (2023, January). AI-based adaptive personalized content presentation and exercises navigation for an effective and engaging E-learning platform. *Multimedia Tools and Applications*, 82(3), 3303–3333. Advance online publication. DOI: 10.1007/s11042-022-13076-8

Walczak, K., & Cellary, W. (2023). Challenges for higher education in the era of widespread access to generative AI. *Economics and Business Review*, 9(2). Advance online publication. DOI: 10.18559/ebr.2023.2.743

Wang, D., Churchill, E., Maes, P., Fan, X., Shneiderman, B., Shi, Y., & Wang, Q. (2020, April). From human-human collaboration to Human-AI collaboration: Designing AI systems that can work together with people. In Extended abstracts of the 2020 CHI conference on human factors in computing systems (pp. 1-6).

Wang, N., & Lester, J. (2023). K-12 Education in the Age of AI: A Call to Action for K-12 AI Literacy. In *International Journal of Artificial Intelligence in Education* (Vol. 33, Issue 2). DOI: 10.1007/s40593-023-00358-x

Wang, J. (2017). Aesthetic Education in China: Problems and Solutions. *International Journal of Humanities Social Sciences and Education*, 4(12), 134–139. https://www.arcjournals.org/international-journal-of-humanities-social-sciences-and-education/volume-4-issue-12/17

Wang, J. (2023). Navigating the AI Revolution: Job Replacements and New Opportunities in the Labor Market. *Advances in Economics. Management and Political Sciences*, 46(1), 10–15. Advance online publication. DOI: 10.54254/2754-1169/46/20230309

Wang, S., Wang, F., Zhu, Z., Wang, J., Tran, T., & Du, Z. (2024). Artificial intelligence in education: A systematic literature review. *Expert Systems with Applications*, 252, 124167. DOI: 10.1016/j.eswa.2024.124167

Wang, X., Anwer, N., Dai, Y., & Liu, A. (2023). ChatGPT for design, manufacturing, and education. *Procedia CIRP*, 119, 7–14. Advance online publication. DOI: 10.1016/j.procir.2023.04.001

Wang, X., Li, L., Tan, S. C., Yang, L., & Lei, J. (2023). Preparing for AI-enhanced education: Conceptualizing and empirically examining teachers' AI readiness. *Computers in Human Behavior*, 146, 107798. Advance online publication. DOI: 10.1016/j.chb.2023.107798

Wang, Y. (2021). When artificial intelligence meets educational leaders' data-informed decision-making: A cautionary tale. *Studies in Educational Evaluation*, 69, 100872. DOI: 10.1016/j.stueduc.2020.100872

Wang, Y.-C. (2022). Winning the hearts of the people with artistic masterpieces: An artistic aesthetic tradition of Chinese Marxism. *Educational Philosophy and Theory*, 54(11), 1759–1766. DOI: 10.1080/00131857.2022.2079494

Wang, Y., Liu, X., Zhang, Y., Sang, X., & Wang, M. (2020). The first model of family education on the delivery of bilingual British NCC digital literacy qualifications in Dalian, China — Engaging and motivating children. *Proceedings of the International Conference on Education in Mathematics, Science and Technology (ICEMST).*

Watson, A. (2023). Using ChatGPT to reduce your teacher workload. *The 40 Hour Teacher Workweek.* https://usergeneratededucation.wordpress.com/wp-content/uploads/2023/06/teacher-timesavers-with-chatgpt-by-angela-watson.pdf

Watters, J., Hill, A., Weinrich, M., Supalo, C., & Jiang, F. (2021). An artificial intelligence tool for accessible science education. *Journal of Science Education for Students with Disabilities*, 24(1), 1–14. DOI: 10.14448/jsesd.13.0010

Wei, M., & Zhou, Z. (2023). AI Ethics Issues in Real World: Evidence from AI Incident Database. *Proceedings of the Annual Hawaii International Conference on System Sciences*. DOI: 10.24251/HICSS.2023.602

Wenglinsky, H. (2002). The link between teacher classroom practices and student academic performance. *Education Policy Analysis Archives*, 10, 12. DOI: 10.14507/epaa.v10n12.2002

West, D., Luzeckyj, A., Toohey, D., Vanderlelie, J., & Searle, B. (2020). Do academics and university administrators really know better? The ethics of positioning student perspectives in learning analytics. *Australasian Journal of Educational Technology*, 36(2), 60–70. DOI: 10.14742/ajet.4653

Weston-Sementelli, J. L., Allen, L. K., & McNamara, D. S. (2016). Comprehension and writing strategy training improves performance on content-specific source-based writing tasks. *International Journal of Artificial Intelligence in Education*, 28(1), 106–137. DOI: 10.1007/s40593-016-0127-7

West-Smith, P., Butler, S., & Mayfield, E. (2018). Trustworthy automated essay scoring without explicit construct validity. *Proceedings of the AAAI Spring Symposium on AI and Society: Ethics, Safety and Trustworthiness in Intelligent Agents.* https://help.turnitin.com/Resources/RA%20Curriculum%20Resources/Research/Revision%20Assistant%20Validity%20AAAI%202018.pdf

What is the 4-H motto? (2020, July 14). 4-H Ontario. https://4-hontario.ca/about-4-h/frequently-asked-questions/what-is-the-4-h-motto/

Wheeler, S. (2015). *Learning with 'e's: Educational Theory and Practice in the Digital Age*. Crown House.

Wheeler, S. (2019). *Digital Learning in Organizations*. Kogan Page.

Whittaker, M., & Crawford, K. (2018). *AI now reports 2018*. New York University.

Williamson, B., & Eynon, R. (2020). Historical threads, missing links, and future directions in education. *Learning, Media and Technology*, 45(3), 223–235. DOI: 10.1080/17439884.2020.1798995

Wilson, C., & Scott, B. (2017). Adaptive systems in education: A review and conceptual unification. *International Journal of Information and Learning Technology*, 34(1), 2–19. DOI: 10.1108/IJILT-09-2016-0040

Winkler, R., & Söllner, M. (2018). Unleashing the potential of chatbots in education: A state-of-the-art analysis. In *Academy of Management Annual Meeting* (AOM) (pp. 1-40). DOI: 10.5465/AMBPP.2018.15903abstract

Wittich, , Agrawal, A., Cook, D. A., Halvorsen, A. J., Mandrekar, J. N., Chaudhry, S., Dupras, D. M., Oxentenko, A. S., & Beckman, T. J. (2017). E-learning in graduate medical education: Survey of residency program directors. *BMC Medical Education*, 17(1), 114. DOI: 10.1186/s12909-017-0953-9 PMID: 28697744

Wong, J., Baars, M., Davis, D., Van Der Zee, T., Houben, G.-J., & Paas, F. (2019). Supporting self-regulated learning in online learning environments and MOOCs: A systematic review. *International Journal of Human-Computer Interaction*, 35(4-5), 356–373. DOI: 10.1080/10447318.2018.1543084

Wood, D., Bruner, J. S., & Ross, G. (1976). The role of tutoring in problem solving. *Journal of Child Psychology and Psychiatry, and Allied Disciplines*, 17(2), 89–100. DOI: 10.1111/j.1469-7610.1976.tb00381.x PMID: 932126

World Economic Forum. (2023). AI accelerates students' holistic development. https://www.weforum.org/agenda/2023/05/ai-accelerate-students-holistic-development-teaching-fulfilling/

World Economic Forum. (2023). *Future of jobs report.* https://www.weforum.org/publications/the-future-of-jobs-report-2023/

Wu, W.-C. V., Petit, E., & Chen, C.-H. (2015). EFL writing revision with blind expert and peer review using a CMC open forum. *Computer Assisted Language Learning*, 28(1), 58–80. DOI: 10.1080/09588221.2014.937442

Xie, H., Chu, H., Hwang, G., & Wang, C. C. (2019). Trends and development in technology-enhanced adaptive/personalized learning: A systematic review of journal publications from 2007 to 2017. *Computers & Education*, 140, 103599. Advance online publication. DOI: 10.1016/j.compedu.2019.103599

Xiong, Z., Li, H., Liu, Z., Chen, Z., Zhou, H., Rong, W., & Ouyang, Y. (2024). A Review of Data Mining in Personalized Education: Current Trends and Future Prospects. *Frontiers of Digital Education*, 1(1), 26–50. DOI: 10.1007/s44366-024-0019-6

Xu, C., Lien, K. C., & Höllerer, T. (2023). Comparing Zealous and Restrained AI Recommendations in a Real-World Human-AI Collaboration Task. *Conference on Human Factors in Computing Systems - Proceedings*. DOI: 10.1145/3544548.3581282

Xu, D., & Kalyanaraman, S. (2020). Artificial Intelligence in Educational Administration: Challenges and Opportunities. *Journal of Educational Administration*, 58(4), 453–468.

Xu, Z., Wijekumar, K. K., Ramirez, G., Hu, X., & Irey, R. (2019). The effectiveness of intelligent tutoring systems on K-12 students' reading comprehension: A meta-analysis. *British Journal of Educational Technology*, 50(6), 3119–3137. DOI: 10.1111/bjet.12758

Yang, S. J. H., Ogata, H., & Matsui, T. (2023). Guest Editorial: Human-centered AI in Education: Augment Human Intelligence with Machine Intelligence. In *Educational Technology and Society* (Vol. 26, Issue 1). DOI: 10.30191/ETS.202301_26(1).0007

Yang, D., Wu, Q., & Wang, F. (2019). Design and development of the mobile adaptive learning platform for English vocabulary mastery. *International Journal of Mobile Learning and Multimodal Interactions*, 13(3), 1–17.

Yang, J., & Zhang, B. (2019). Artificial intelligence in intelligent tutoring robots: A systematic review and design guidelines. *Applied Sciences (Basel, Switzerland)*, 9(10), 2078. DOI: 10.3390/app9102078

Yang, S. J. H., Ogata, H., Matsui, T., & Chen, N.-S. (2021). Human-centered artificial intelligence in education: Seeing the invisible through the visible. *Computers and Education: Artificial Intelligence*, 2, 100008. Advance online publication. DOI: 10.1016/j.caeai.2021.100008

Yeoun. (2023). AI in Classroom: Group Score Prediction System. DOI: 10.1109/ICAIIC57133.2023.10067066

Yıldırım, A. & Şimşek, H. (2021). Sosyal bilimlerde nitel araştırma yöntemleri [Qualitative research methods in social sciences]. Seçkin.

Yiping, L. (2021). Research and application of personalized learning under the background of artificial intelligence. DOI: 10.1109/EIMSS53851.2021.00020

Yu, M. G. (2021). The evolutionary logic of future media: The iteration, reorganization and ascension of "human connection" - [From "Scene Era" to "Meta-Universe" to the future of "mind world"]. Xinwenjie Zazhi, 10, 54–60. https://www.cnki.com.cn/Article/CJFDTotal-NEWS202110008.html

Yusuf, A., Pervin, N., & Román-González, M. (2024). Generative AI and the future of higher education: A threat to academic integrity or reformation? Evidence from multicultural perspectives. *International Journal of Educational Technology in Higher Education*, 21(1), 21. DOI: 10.1186/s41239-024-00453-6

Zajko, M. (2022). Artificial intelligence, algorithms, and social inequality: Sociological contributions to contemporary debates. *Sociology Compass*, 16(3), e12962. DOI: 10.1111/soc4.12962

Zavaraki, E. Z. (2024). Artificial Intelligence for People with Special Educational Needs. In *IntechOpen eBooks*. https://doi.org/DOI: 10.5772/intechopen.1004158

Zawacki-Richter, O., Marín, V. I., Bond, M., & Gouverneur, F. (2019a). Systematic review of research on artificial intelligence applications in higher education – where are the educators? *International Journal of Educational Technology in Higher Education*, 16(1), 39. Advance online publication. DOI: 10.1186/s41239-019-0171-0

Zeide, E., & Nissenbaum, H. (2023). Dilemmas of student data protection in an era of AI and learning analytics. *Phi Delta Kappan*, 104(5), 24–29.

Zhai, X., Chu, X., Chai, C. S., Jong, M. S. Y., Istenic, A., Spector, M., Liu, J. B., Yuan, J., & Li, Y. (2021). A Review of Artificial Intelligence (AI) in Education from 2010 to 2020. In *Complexity* (Vol. 2021). DOI: 10.1155/2021/8812542

Zhang, J., & Ye, J. (2021). Alibaba to test gaming potential of metaverse as Big Tech firms stampede into virtual world. Retrieved from https://www.scmp.com/tech/bigtech/article/3159691/alibaba-test-gaming-potential-metaverse-big-tech-firms-stam pede.

Zhang, C., & Villanueva, L. E. (2023). Generative Artificial Intelligence Preparedness and Technological Competence: Towards a Digital Education Teacher Training Program. *International Journal of Education and Humanities*, 11(2), 164–170. Advance online publication. DOI: 10.54097/ijeh.v11i2.13753

Zhang, K., & Aslan, A. B. (2021). AI technologies for education: Recent research & future directions. *Computers and Education: Artificial Intelligence*, 2, 100025. DOI: 10.1016/j.caeai.2021.100025

Zhang, L., & Ma, Y. (2023). A study of the impact of project-based learning on student learning effects: A meta-analysis study. *Frontiers in Psychology*, 14, 1202728. Advance online publication. DOI: 10.3389/fpsyg.2023.1202728 PMID: 37564309

Zhang, L., Ren, T., Xie, Y., Tian, Z., Tang, T., & Li, Y. (2022). Student Choirs and Virtual Social Practices by LivePBL: Linking Vocal Education with Project Based Learning. *Literacy Information and Computer Education Journal*, 13(1), 3860–3666. DOI: 10.20533/licej.2040.2589.2022.0482

Zhang, Y., Chen, F., & Rohe, K. (2024). Social Media Public Opinion as Flocks in a Murmuration: Conceptualizing and Measuring Opinion Expression on Social Media. *Journal of Computer-Mediated Communication*, 27(1), 1–22. DOI: 10.1111/jcc4.12145

Zhang, Y., Meng, X., Gong, Y., Kang, J., & Lu, B. (2023). 'Remote sensing plus' training mode of innovation and entrepreneurship talent nurturing through College student competitions. *ISPRS Annals of the Photogrammetry, Remote Sensing and Spatial Information Sciences*, 10, 83–86. DOI: 10.5194/isprs-annals-X-5-W1-2023-83-2023

Zhao, L., Wu, X., & Luo, H. (2022). Developing AI literacy for primary and middle school teachers in China: Based on a structural equation modeling analysis. *Sustainability (Basel)*, 14(21), 14549. DOI: 10.3390/su142114549

Zhao, X., & Yang, Y. (2021). A study on the application of blended teaching to English reading course under the background of artificial intelligence. *IOP Conference Series. Earth and Environmental Science*, 693(1), 012019. DOI: 10.1088/1755-1315/693/1/012019

Zheng, L., Niu, J., Zhong, L., & Gyasi, J. F. (2023). The effectiveness of artificial intelligence on learning achievement and learning perception: A meta-analysis. In *Interactive Learning Environments* (Vol. 31, Issue 9). DOI: 10.1080/10494820.2021.2015693

Zheng, , Niiya, M., & Warschauer, M. (2015). Wikis and collaborative learning in higher education. *Technology, Pedagogy and Education*, 24(3), 357–374. DOI: 10.1080/1475939X.2014.948041

Zhou, J., Chen, F., Berry, A., Reed, M., Zhang, S., & Savage, S. (2020, December). A survey on ethical principles of AI and implementations. In *2020 IEEE Symposium Series on Computational Intelligence (SSCI)* (pp. 3010-3017). IEEE. DOI: 10.1109/SSCI47803.2020.9308437

Zhou, Y., Ren, T., Chen, N., Li, J., Lu, K., Li, Y., Acharya, A., Shah, P., Hogg, A., & Liu, Y. (2023). Student virtual social practices between China and Nepal. *International Journal of Technology and Inclusive Education*, 12(1), 1802–1807. DOI: 10.20533/ijtie.2047.0533.2023.0223

Zhuang, K. (2023). The Knowledge Graph Construction in the Educational Domain: Take an Australian School Science Course as an Example. *University of Wollongong Thesis Collection 2017*. https://ro.uow.edu.au/theses1/1697

Zhu, L., Sun, D., Luo, M., Liu, W., & Xue, S. (2024). Investigating Pre-Service Science Teachers' Design Performance in Laboratory Class: The Inquiry-Based Design Thinking Approach. *Journal of Science Education and Technology*, 33(1), 30–44. DOI: 10.1007/s10956-023-10050-3

Zuboff, S. (2019). *The Age of Surveillance Capitalism: The Fight for a Human Future at the New Frontier of Power*. Profile Books.

About the Contributors

Krista LaRue Keeley, an award-winning innovative educator, holds a Doctor of Education in Educational Leadership from Western University and a Professional Master's Degree in Education from Queen's University. Krista currently serves as the Teaching and Design Specialist at Southeast College and works together with Saskatchewan Teachers' Federation as a Professional Learning Facilitator. There, she collaborates on designing and delivering diverse, student-centered professional learning opportunities with a focus on innovation, diversity, equity, and inclusion and course developmentand design. With a background in innovative pedagogy and a commitment to decolonization and social justice, Dr. Keeley has excelled as an educator at Regina Public Schools since 2011, receiving the STF Arbos Award in 2023. An accomplished author and presenter, she has significantly contributed to educational literature and forums, emphasizing 21st-century learning, AI-assisted educational practices, and inclusivity, as showcased in her various publications and presentations. Notably, her chapter in "Generative AI in Teaching and Learning" introducing AI-Teacher Wellness Theory (AI-TeachWell) underscores her expertise in incorporating AI technologies into educational settings, addressing the evolving landscape of teaching and learning in the 21st century.

* * *

Reima Abobaker is a professor at the Language Studio at the Savannah College of Art and Design. Her PHD. degree is in Language, Literacy, and Technology from the College of Education, Washington State University. She is interested in the research of developing student's motivation and engagement as well as incorporating technology tools into teaching methods that boost student's engagement. With 14 years of teaching experience, she aspires to contribute to the field of education in general and English as a Second/foreign language in particular by conducting research that informs her own and other practitioners' instruction methods with innovative and engaging teaching best practices.

Jihan M. Aloshi from Israel holds a PhD in Special Education Diagnosis of learning disabilities and dyslexia. Jihan research is on dyslexia and working memory. She works as Lecturer at Al-Qasemi Academic College & Ono Academic College in Israel. A mentor for teachers in the field of learning difficulties, learning strategies, and social-emotional learning.

Jerry (Ryan) David Gustafson is a researcher and instructor at Southeast College, focused in computer science, generative AI, and project-based learning. He is currently developing a computer science training program through project-based learning. He holds a Bachelor of Science in Geological Engineering from the University of Saskatchewan and a University Certificate in Computer and Information Systems from Athabasca University. Ryan has experience in wellsite geology, data engineering, research, and education. He is an active volunteer in robotics and youth mentorship.

Islam A. Ismail, from Palestine, holds a Ph.D. in English Language Education. Ismail does research on using AI in education and works as a proofreader in the academic English field. He aims to find innovative and effective ways to facilitate language acquisition and proficiency.

Ying Liu is a lecturer at the London School of Science and Technology, UK, where he supports HE for disadvantaged communities. He holds a PhD from TU Delft, an MEd from Cambridge, and an MBA from Durham. A former advisor to China's Ministry of Education, Dr. Liu has held research fellowships at Cambridge, Edinburgh, and Aberdeen. He leads international education projects and founded LivePBL, a hybrid learning program shortlisted by European eLearning and QS Reimagine Education 2023.

Sheena Moleta is a dedicated Savannah College of Art & Design Language Studio faculty member. She is known for blending creativity, technology, and evidence-based methodologies to educate and inspire while fostering a supportive and inclusive learning environment that prepares language learners for global success. She holds an MA in TESOL and has over 15 years of experience, including ten-plus years at the collegiate level. She has developed her expertise through an extensive and diverse background, which includes teaching in South Korea, Turkey, and Saudi Arabia.

VidhyaPriya P. is a dedicated academician with a strong foundation in both computer science and business management. She holds an MBA from Avinashilingam Deemed University, Coimbatore, and earned her Ph.D. from Bharathiar University, Coimbatore, in 2010. Before transitioning to academia, she gained valuable industry experience working with a textile firm for over three years. In 2000, she joined Kongu Engineering College, where she has since built an illustrious career in research and teaching. With over 24 years of academic experience, Dr. VidhyaPriya's research interests lie in corporate finance, corporate governance, and behavioral finance. She has published 57 research papers in reputed national and international journals, including Scopus-indexed publications. Throughout her career, she has actively engaged with the academic community by attending numerous Faculty Development Programs (FDPs) at leading B-Schools, including IIM Bangalore, IIT Madras, Pondicherry University, and Mangalore University. Dr.VidhyaPriya has also presented papers at 30 national and international conferences and has organized multiple conferences, seminars, FDPs, workshops, and training programs. She has successfully completed two ICSSR-sponsored projects focused on start-up entrepreneurship and the Stand-Up India Scheme for entrepreneurs.

Christine Anne Royce, EdD, is a professor at Shippensburg University of Pennsylvania in the Teacher Education Department. She teaches a variety of classes at the undergraduate and graduate levels, which focus on STEM education, instructional design, and digital tools and technologies among others. At Shippensburg, she is currently the co-director of the MAT in STEM Education program. Royce is a past president of the National Science Teaching Association and remains currently active with that group by writing a column titled Teaching Through Trade Books for Science and Children. In addition to her work with NSTA, she is a member of the Board of Trustees for Valley Forge Military Academy & College. Her research interests focus on the integration of digital tools and technology into classrooms for sensemaking, international education, the inclusion of children's literature in elementary science classrooms, and STEM integration. She has more than 135 publications and is an international speaker and professional development provider.

Vetrivel S. C. is a faculty member in the Department of Management Studies, Kongu Engineering College (Autonomous), Perundurai, Erode Dt. Having experience in Industry 20 years and Teaching 16 years. Awarded with Doctoral Degree in Management Sciences in Anna University, Chennai. He has organized various workshops and Faculty Development Programmes. He is actively involved in research and consultancy works. He acted as a resource person to FDPs & MDPs to various industries like, SPB ltd, Tamilnadu Police, DIET, Rotary school and many. His areas of interest include Entrepreneurship, Business Law, Marketing and Case writing. Articles published more than 100 International and National Journals. Presented papers in more than 30 National and International conferences including IIM Bangalore, IIM Kozhikode, IIM Kashipur and IIM Indore. He was a Chief Co-ordinator of Entrepreneurship and Management Development Centre (EMDC) of Kongu Engineering College, he was instrumental in organizing various Awareness Camps, FDP, and TEDPs to aspiring entrepreneurs which was funded by NSTEDB – DST/GoI.

Urmila Shrawankar received PhD degree from SGB Amravati University and M.Tech. degree from RTM Nagpur university, India in Computer Sci & Engg. Her Area of interest includes High performance Computing, Distributed and Parallel computing, Cloud Computing, Real Time Computing, Assistive Technology etc. She is an author of two books, one book editor, nine book chapters and more than 200 research papers in Int. Journals and Conferences of high repute. She has 06 granted and 12 published patents. She received Int. Travel Grant from Govt. of India, UGC Minor Project Grant and RGSTC Research Grant. She is serving many journals as editorial board member and as member, international advisory board and as reviewer for many refereed Journals and reputed Conferences. She has participated in many Int. conferences worldwide as a core organizing committee member, Technical program committee member, Special session chair and Session Chair. She is a member of IEEE-SM, ACM, CSI, ISTE, IEI, IAENG, etc. She is a guide of many engineering projects and PhD Research work. At present, Dr. Urmila is working as a Professor, Dept. of Computer Science and Engineering. Ramdeobaba University Nagpur (MS), India.

Nurcan Tekin completed her undergraduate education at Selçuk University in 2011, her master's degree at Necmettin Erbakan University in 2013 and her doctorate at Aksaray University in 2018. In 2013, she started working as a research assistant in the department of science education at Aksaray University, where she is currently working as Asst. Assoc. Dr. Tekin continues her studies in the fields of science education, teacher education, socioscientific issues, argumentation, informal reasoning, nature of science and artificial intelligence. Dr. Tekin has various projects on teaching socioscientific issues, scientific articles and papers on artificial intelligence. In particular, she continues to work intensively on the use of artificial intelligence in science education for pre-service teachers.

Devaki V. has 5 years of teaching experience. Her academic journey is deeply rooted in English Language Teaching and Applied Linguistics, having cleared the National Eligibility Test (UGC-NET). Ms. Devaki holds a Master of Philosophy in English Language Teaching from Anna University, Chennai, and a Master in Comparative Literature from Pondicherry Central University. She has worked as an Assistant Professor of English at Vels Institute of Science and Technology (VISTAS) deemed University, Chennai from 2017 to 2019, and at Rajalakshmi Institute of Technology, Chennai from 2021 to 2023. She has worked at Vignan University from 2023 to 2024. Her outstanding performance was recognized with an Appreciation Award for the Best Utilization of Library Facilities at Vels University in 2018. Her academic interests lie in English for Specific Purposes, Applied Linguistics, LGBT studies, Postcolonial Literature, Modernism, and Narratives. She has published more than 20+ high-quality research articles in internationally and nationally recognized peer-reviewed and refereed including Scopus and Web of Science-indexed journals. Additionally, she has authored several book chapters with ISBNs.

Arun V. P. is a driven and accomplished professional with a diverse educational background and extensive hands-on experience across various industries. Graduating with honors, Arun earned his Master of Business Administration (M.B.A) with a specialization in Human Resources and Marketing from the renowned Sona School of Management in Salem in 2018, where he excelled academically with an impressive 8.3 Cumulative Grade Point Average (CGPA).Throughout his academic journey, Arun displayed an unwavering commitment to learning and personal growth, actively seeking opportunities to expand his knowledge and skills beyond the confines of traditional education. He sought practical experiences to complement his theoretical understanding, such as a 45-day summer internship focused on conducting a feasibility study for R-Doc Sustainability in the market. Additionally, Arun broadened his horizons through a 7-day industrial visit to Malaysia and Singapore, immersing himself in diverse cultural and professional environments. Arun's academic pursuits were further enriched by his involvement in hands-on projects, including a comprehensive study on Employee Job Satisfaction at Roots Cast Private Limited. His professional trajectory includes serving as a Growth Officer at Parle Agro Private Limited, where he played a crucial role in driving sales growth and market expansion. Arun is a dedicated professional, currently employed at JKKN Engineering College in the Management Studies Department. He holds expertise in his field and has contributed significantly to academia through the publication of two journal articles. Arun's work focuses on advancing knowledge and understanding in management studies, making valuable contributions to the academic community.

Uma Yadav is a distinguished Assistant Professor at Ramdeobaba University, formerly known as Shri Ramdeobaba College of Engineering and Management. She completed her B. Tech and M. Tech degrees with distinction from Nagpur University in 2009 and 2013, respectively, and recently earned her PhD from GHRU Amravati. With over 14 years of experience, Dr. Uma Yadav research interests include Data Science, Machine Learning, cloud computing, big data management, and data mining. She has made significant contributions to her field, authoring or co-authoring more than 20 research papers in reputed refereed journals and conferences. Her commitment to professional development is further demonstrated by her completion of numerous NPTEL courses, where she has achieved elite gold distinctions and topped in several subjects. Dr. Uma Yadav dedication to teaching, research, and continuous learning has established her as a respected educator and researcher in her field.

Xiaokun Zhang is an associate professor (tenured since 2003) in School of Computing and Information Systems in Athabasca University in Canada since 2001. He earned his PhD in engineering on research in computer integrated manufacturing engineering from Northwestern Polytechnic University (NWPU) in China in 1995. He was Nortel research fellow and post-doctoral fellow from 1998 until 2001 in University of Calgary and visiting professor in University of Iowa in US in 1997. Back to early 90's, He was an associate professor (since Fall 1991) and then was a full professor since 1995 while he worked in NWPU. His recent research and teaching areas primarily focus on the system analysis and dynamic modeling in heterogeneous cyber-physical-social interaction, and semantic computing enhanced cognitive computing and data analytics in decentralized real-time control and monitoring systems, environmental and engineering computing systems, and smart eLearning systems. He serves IEEE SMC (Systems, Man, & Cybernetics Society) technical committee on computer-supported cooperative work in design, and program committees in various annual conferences in computing and information systems. He supervised post-doctoral fellow, graduate students' essay, projects, and thesis.

Index

A

B

C

D

E

www.ingramcontent.com/pod-product-compliance
Lightning Source LLC
LaVergne TN
LVHW080611300926
849162LV00005B/1120
* 9 7 9 8 3 6 9 3 5 4 4 3 8 *